THE THEORY OF
GENERAL ECONOMIC EQUILIBRIUM

. . . no philosophical objector would maintain that the love of the soul for the universal is then only legitimate, when it has been blessed with the production of the useful. The love of the soul for the universal is undoubtedly capable of extravagance, as in the devotion of Plato to the idea. *Amor ipse ordinate amandus est.* But the limits are to be traced by a loving hand, and not to be narrowed by a too severe construction of utility.

F. Y. Edgeworth, *Mathematical Psychics*, p. 94.

THE THEORY OF GENERAL ECONOMIC EQUILIBRIUM

BY ROBERT E. KUENNE

PRINCETON UNIVERSITY PRESS
PRINCETON, NEW JERSEY

L. C. Card No. 62-21105
ISBN 0-691-04184-9

Second Printing, with corrections, 1967
Third Printing, with additional corrections, 1974

PRINTED IN THE UNITED STATES OF AMERICA

FOR JANET B. KUENNE

CONTENTS

PART III. EXTENSIONS OF THE NEOCLASSICAL CONSTRUCTS

Chapter 6. Static Linear Systems

PART I

INTRODUCTION

CHAPTER 1

GENERAL EQUILIBRIUM ANALYSIS: ITS MEANING, PURPOSES, AND LIMITATIONS

1. The Phenomenon of Variation

The need for scientific analysis springs from a fundamental bias of our natural and social environment against sameness and constancy. Physical objects that are similar in specified attributes will vary among themselves in the exact degree to which they possess such attributes. Static variation of this type is compounded with dynamic variation—or *change*—in the same object's attributes over time. The ubiquity of variation, manifest in the very triviality of its assertion, forces upon man, individually and collectively, a concern for its patterns. Upon his ability to accept and shape them to his ends in a nonintuitive fashion are based his sanity and his survival.

For the limited purposes of this book, we may define a "vision of variation," or, more simply, a "vision,"[1] as a mechanism or model whose structural components are patterns of association among variates, and whose purpose is the prediction of variation. That is to say, by postulating significant covariation relationships among sky conditions and rain; temperature, volume, and pressure of gases; Wall Street and the occurrence of war; time elapsed and the velocity of falling bodies; the amount of money in existence and the price level; drawing to inside straights and the loss of money, and so forth, models can be constructed for the prediction (or back-casting) of the value or attribute of a variate in the model.

In our wholly general definition of "vision," the witch-doctor's magic mechanism to explain illness, the supernatural constructions of religion, the intuitive explanatory mechanisms of a child's fantasy, as well as the sophisticated hypotheses of the nuclear physicist, are equally well covered. The touchstone of the definition is the existence of some predictive mechanism to cope with a field of variation, whether that mechanism proves to be a useful device or not, whether its construction is purposive or intuitive, sophisticated or naïve.

"Science" or "the scientific method" may be defined as a body of

[1] The importance of the "vision" with which an investigator approaches a set of phenomena, and its essentially prescientific character, has been stressed by J. A. Schumpeter in his later writings. His concept of the vision is a different one than the one used above in that his includes only the phenomena chosen for study and the *initial* view of their interrelationships. See J. Schumpeter, (4), pp. 345–59, especially pp. 350–1, and J. Schumpeter, (5), pp. 41–3, 561–3.

techniques designed to yield criteria of choice for certain classes of these causal visions. It provides objective procedures and standards with which to judge the usefulness of the models against their explanatory pretensions. Science brings analytically uncontrolled ideas under control.[2] It provides the means of filtering out the distortions introduced by idealogical commitment, personality structure, and the imperfect perception of the holder of the vision. For that subset of visions (a) whose concepts may be defined by a set of mental or physical operations, (b) whose subject variation is capable of being reproduced or is recurrent under acceptably stable generating conditions, and (c) whose variation is observable in a manner relevant to the predictions of the vision, this body of methods can be used to gauge the usefulness of visions by testing against reality their responses to questions for which operations may be defined to obtain answers.[3]

This task of deriving operationally meaningful theorems from visions or models implies the need to deduce in a valid manner a set of predictions for which a set of operations may be specified which, actually or ideally, can test the correspondence of the predictions to empirical fact. If such operations are actually capable of performance, current scientific methods are applicable; if it is believed they are only potentially capable of use, current scientific methods are inapplicable, but future methods may be useful; if they are currently thought to be neither actually nor potentially capable of performance, the vision falls outside of that subset amenable to scientific method. According to this view, "The function of a scientific hypothesis is to enable us to 'predict' phenomena not yet observed, that is, to make statements about phenomena not yet observed that are (a) capable of being contradicted and (b) will not in fact be contradicted. . . ."[4]

[2] Cf. J. Schumpeter, (4), p. 356.

[3] Operationalism, as enunciated by P. W. Bridgman, stresses (a) the identity of the scientific concept and the set of physical or mental operations which must be specified to determine it, and (b) the exclusive concern of science (social as well as physical) with questions which are operationally meaningful in the sense that a set of operations may be specified to obtain an answer. See P. W. Bridgman, (1), pp. 1–32.

We do not presume to judge the issues in the debate on operationalism, but merely assert that the outlook, as presented to some extent in P. Samuelson, (4), pp. 3–20, is a valuable guide in framing the vision, interpreting such concepts as "utility," and testing the usefulness of a model's theorems.

Our use of the terms "operationally meaningful," "meaningful," and "operational theorem," in the final analysis, is less a blind adoption of Bridgman's outlook and more the purely practical desire to avoid the term "testable" theorem, since this implies a *current* ability to verify hypotheses and does not connote our acceptance of methods which yield theorems only potentially testable. We seek, that is, to avoid such propositions as Cotton Mather's hypothesis: "That there is a Devil is a thing Doubted by none but such as are under the influence of the Devil"—which may be true but is not subject to validation by scientific techniques. The operational outlook seems a convenient way to avoid dealing with such questions.

[4] M. Friedman, (2), p. 465.

It is possible to agree with the assertion of the operationalist that only those visions which yield such hypotheses are in an ultimate sense useful. Yet visions which are not themselves capable of rendering such services may perform an important, if prescientific, role in shaping other models which are able to do so. This book will be concerned largely with the efforts of economists to evolve models of economic variation as prescientific steps toward other visions which can yield meaningful theorems about reality. The most important factor militating against the analytical usefulness of these models is their "generality" or ambition: indeed, it will be shown that the ability of a model to yield operational theorems declines rapidly to zero as the number of variables to be determined is increased, even when huge expenditures of ingenuity are invested in the manipulation of the model.

Some of these general models have been framed, it is true, to yield operational theorems, and these, too, will be analyzed. But for the most part the models that we shall study will contain the intuitive, largely untested hypotheses of the economist's domain, many of which are actually or potentially untestable for one reason or another. These models are cumbersome, nonmanipulable, nonoperational, analytically valueless in the direct senses defined above. Why, then, should economists dwell upon the gargantuan visions at all? Why not allow the glacial age of operationalism to kill off these impressive but ill-adapted dinosaurs to the advantage of simpler and analytically more viable organisms? Of what value are general economic models which have never left the stage of prescientific vision and never will, at least in unaltered form?

2. The General Model and Interdependence

Before attempting answers to these questions, we must discuss at greater length the more distinctive features of the "general" model. Any formal model requires a fundamental distinction between those phenomena whose variation is assumed to be frozen by analytical controls and those phenomena whose values or attributes are predicted by the model. The former—termed the *data* of the model—lie beyond the analytical ambition of the model, in the sense that they are determining rather than determined. The latter—the *variables* of the model—are determined in value by the constraining interaction of the data and the interrelationships that exist among the data and variables by virtue of the natural or behavioral assumptions of the model, or both. A set of data, relationships, and variables, therefore, constitutes a vision or model.

A solution to the model may be *specific* or *nonspecific*. A specific solution defines a *state* of the model: it is the set of values for the variables which results from a specific set of values for the data. A nonspecific solution to the model defines the set of values for the variables for any and every allowable set of values for the data.

Both the interrelationships among data and variables which are part of the structure of the model and the nonspecific solutions of the model may take the form of mathematical functions and should be distinguished from one another. For example, let us anticipate some of the analysis of Chapter 2 by stating that the conventional demand function is a nonspecific solution to a model of consumer choice, and relates the amount purchased of a commodity to the data of the model: prices of goods, consumer wherewithal, and consumer preferences. The structural interrelationships of the model relating variables and data are derived, in the usual interpretation, from the assumptions of maximizing behavior and of spending neither less nor more than one's income.

The "generalness" or ambition of such models must be defined in terms of the extent of conventionally-defined "economic" variation that is included in the variable category of the model as opposed to the amount placed in the data category. The greater the proportion of the whole field of variation "internal" to the model, i.e., whose values are to be determined by the model, the more "general" the model. The distinctive feature of the models developed and treated in this book, therefore, is that they are among the more ambitious visions of economic variation.

Another common structural feature of such models—apart from the fact that the number of variables is relatively large—is contained in the interrelationships of the model. More specifically, it is the complicated mutual interdependence among the *variables* of the model inherent in these relationships. This is a frequent mark of the general model, the source of much of the advantage it may possess over its less ambitious rivals, but the wellspring of its analytical impotence as well.

In strict logic, general economic systems need not display this interdependence of the variables that we have termed characteristic. Imagine a model concerned with three variables X_i, $i = 1, 2, 3$, and a three-element set of data, Q_k, $k = 1, 2, 3$. If the model related the variables directly to the data in a nonspecific solution without benefit of interrelationships among the variables, we should have:

$$(1) \qquad X_i = F_i(Q_1, Q_2, Q_3), \qquad i = 1, 2, 3$$

While this model might have great explanatory power, its several parts do not cohere. Each of the equations in (1) may be solved independently of the other two: for each equation there exists an unimpeded flow of causation from the data to a single variable. The system (1) is decomposable into its individual equation components, indicating a complete absence of interdependence among the variables. It is, however, a general system within our meaning of the term.

Suppose, however, that the structural interrelationships of the model were not as written in (1), but were instead:

$$
(2) \qquad
\begin{aligned}
&1. \quad X_1 = F_1(Q_k), \qquad\qquad k = 1, 2, 3 \\
&2. \quad X_2 = F_2(X_1;\, Q_k) \\
&3. \quad X_3 = F_3(X_1, X_2;\, Q_k)
\end{aligned}
$$

We have used a semicolon to separate variables from data in the functional interrelationships, a convention we shall follow throughout this book. Equation (2-1) reveals the same quality of separability from the system as that possessed by every equation of (1). Given the data set, it may be solved directly for X_1. However, from (2-2) it is clear that in addition to the set of data given it is necessary to know the value of X_1 to obtain the solution value of X_2. For the first time we have encountered an eddy in the flow of "causation" from Q_k to a variable in addition to the direct impact via their determination of X_1. We note, however, that while (2-1) and (2-2) must be solved together to obtain the value of X_2, (2-3) need not enter the computations. To obtain the solution value of X_3, on the other hand, it is necessary to know X_2 and X_1, in addition to the data set. The flow of "causation" from Q_k to X_3 is even more complicated than that to X_2: in addition to the "direct" impact of Q_k upon X_3, there is a first indirect effect from X_1, a second indirect effect from the indirect effect of X_1 upon X_2, and a third indirect effect upon X_3 from the presence in (2-3) of X_2.

System (2) is characterized by a type of interdependence among the variables termed "triangular" from the configuration of the X_i's on the right-hand side of the equations. The peculiarities of this form of interdependence are well illustrated if the system is "shocked" at a solution by a slight change in the value of one of the data (say Q_1). If we assume that the equations in system (2) are continuous and differentiable, at least in the neighborhood of a specific solution, the changes induced in the solution values of the variables may be obtained from the system in (3):

$$
(3) \qquad
\begin{bmatrix} 1 & 0 & 0 \\ -F_2^1 & 1 & 0 \\ -F_3^1 & -F_3^2 & 1 \end{bmatrix}
\begin{bmatrix} \dfrac{\partial X_1}{\partial Q_1} \\ \dfrac{\partial X_2}{\partial Q_1} \\ \dfrac{\partial X_3}{\partial Q_1} \end{bmatrix}
=
\begin{bmatrix} F_1^{Q_1} \\ F_2^{Q_1} \\ F_3^{Q_1} \end{bmatrix}
$$

where $F_i^j = \dfrac{\partial F_i}{\partial X_j}$, i and $j = 1, \ldots, 3$, and $F_i^{Q_1} = \dfrac{\partial F_i}{\partial Q_1}$, $i = 1, \ldots, 3$. These latter notations will be used throughout the book for partial derivatives. We may abbreviate (3) to

$$(4) \qquad [D_2][dV] = [dK]$$

where the subscript 2 identifies $[D]$ as derived from system (2), and the symbols V and K are used to denote vectors of variables and constants respectively.

The "triangularity" of the interdependence of the variables is revealed by the existence of zeros above the main diagonal of $[D_2]$. This implies, for example, that when Q_1 changes slightly, the impact of the induced changes upon X_2 and X_3 need not be taken into account when computing the induced change in X_1. This degree of interdependence contrasts with that revealed by $[D_1]$, the matrix obtained when (1) is differentiated with respect to Q_1, which is the identity matrix, all of whose off-diagonal elements are zero and whose diagonal terms are unity. This constellation reflects the need to consider only direct impacts of the change in Q_1 on every variable in the system.

Consider a third model, obtained from (2) by substituting the following equation for (2-1):

$$(5) \qquad X_1 = F_1(X_2, X_3; Q_k), \qquad k = 1, 2, 3$$

If this system were shocked in the same manner as the previous two, (4) would become

$$(6) \qquad [D_5][dV] = [dK]$$

where the subscript identifies the matrix as derived from the model containing (5). Further,

$$(7) \qquad [D_5] = \begin{bmatrix} 1 & -F_1^2 & -F_1^3 \\ -F_2^1 & 1 & 0 \\ -F_3^1 & -F_3^2 & 1 \end{bmatrix}$$

We have not reached what we might term "perfect interdependence" in the sense that every variable is directly dependent upon every other variable. Nevertheless, we have achieved a degree of interdependence which is qualitatively different from that of system (2), for it is now impossible to solve any subset of the three equations with fewer than three equations. This is true because even though X_2 does not depend directly upon X_3, it does depend upon X_1, which in turn is a function of X_3. Therefore, by virtue of indirect relationships, X_2 cannot be obtained independently of X_3: every variable in the system is linked, directly or indirectly or both, to every other variable.

We may express this property of such systems as (6) as that of "indecomposability." For linear systems of that type, it is an easy matter to establish whether the model does or does not possess it. If it does $[D_5]$ will be indecomposable. Let s symbolize a row in such a matrix, t a column, and a_{st} the element in the sth row and t^{th} column. For a square matrix to be indecomposable it is necessary and sufficient that there exist at least one chain of nonzero, nondiagonal elements of the form $a_{sk} \rightarrow a_{k1} \rightarrow a_{1m} \rightarrow a_{mn} \rightarrow \cdots a_{qs}$ with n or more elements, n being the number of rows (or columns) of the matrix, and with each subscript occurring at least once in the chain.[5] For example, from $[D_5]$ it is possible to form the chain $a_{21} \rightarrow a_{13} \rightarrow a_{31} \rightarrow a_{12}$. It is not possible to find similar chains for $[D_2]$ or, of course, $[D_1]$.

Further, let us form yet another model by substituting the following equation for (2-1):

$$X_1 = F_1(X_2; Q_k), \qquad k = 1, 2, 3 \tag{8}$$

Then, if the system were disturbed in the standard manner, we should obtain:

$$[D_8][dV] = [dK] \tag{9}$$

where

$$[D_8] = \begin{bmatrix} 1 & -F_1^2 & 0 \\ -F_2^1 & 1 & 0 \\ -F_3^1 & -F_3^2 & 1 \end{bmatrix} \tag{10}$$

In this model, at least one variable acts directly upon every variable, but $[D_8]$ fails to meet the conditions for indecomposable matrices. This is reflected in the ability to solve for $\frac{\partial X_1}{\partial Q_1}$ and $\frac{\partial X_2}{\partial Q_1}$ independently of $\frac{\partial X_3}{\partial Q_1}$.[6] Thus, merely including at least one variable in each structural relationship of the model is necessary but not sufficient to guarantee indecomposable interdependence.

Lastly, of course, we treat the case of perfect interdependence, where every variable is affected directly by every other variable in the system:

$$X_i = F_i(X_j; Q_k), \qquad i = 1, 2, 3; j \neq i; k = 1, 2, 3 \tag{11}$$

For a displacement of equilibrium similar to the previous cases, a system is obtained whose $[D]$ is the following:

$$[D_{11}] = \begin{bmatrix} 1 & -F_1^2 & -F_1^3 \\ -F_2^1 & 1 & -F_2^3 \\ -F_3^1 & -F_3^2 & 1 \end{bmatrix} \tag{12}$$

It, of course, meets the conditions of indecomposability.

[5] Cf. W. Evans, (1), pp. 60–2.

[6] This may be confirmed by solving for, say, $\frac{\partial X_1}{\partial Q_1}$ by Cramer's method. It will be seen that in both numerator and denominator determinants all products which include F_3^1, F_3^2, or $F_3^{Q_1}$ are uniformly zero.

Systems (1), (2), (5), (8), and (11), as well as the systems yielding $[D_1]$, $[D_2]$, $[D_5]$, $[D_8]$, and $[D_{11}]$, are general systems in our sense. Yet that feature of general systems which we have signalized as being of greatest interest is not possessed by system (1) or by that model from which $[D_1]$ was derived; is found in incomplete forms in systems (2) and the $[D_2]$-model, and in system (8) and the $[D_8]$-system; is contained only imperfectly in system (5) and the $[D_5]$-model; and is found in full measure only in system (11) and the $[D_{11}]$-system.

Modern general economic systems tend to stress the indecomposable variety of interdependence, of either the imperfect or perfect form. Models with this characteristic are believed to be more reflective of the circularity in the paths of association among realistic economic variables in modern complex economies. As an index of the strength of this characteristic, in the productive sector of the United States economy Chenery and Watanabe found that on the average, in 1947, about 43 cents of every dollar of gross output were fed back to intermediate uses by industries rather than devoted to final uses.[7]

3. The Uses of General Models

Let us now return to the questions posed at the end of Section 1. If, as we shall demonstrate below, most of the potentiality for yielding operational theorems is sacrificed in general models on the altar of interdependence, of what use are they to the economist?

A first benefit to a field of study derives from the "limiting" general model in that field: the closed model. Suppose the economist were to pose this question to himself: "If I were to essay the construction of a model whose variables encompassed every phenomenon I believe to be primarily and essentially economic in nature, what variables would I include in the model? Further, what explicit data would be required in my model, and what physical-behavioral assumptions might I employ, to determine this 'complete' set of variables?" In the case of the individual economist, of course, a good deal of arbitrariness would exist in his definition of the relevant field of variation, and, for economists collectively, the element of inertial convention in a consensus, if it could be achieved, would be a large one. Moreover, these conventional limits to the "field of economics" would be expected to change with the consensus, generation by generation. The English classical economists included the level of population as an economic variable in their systems, employing as they did a Malthusian population response to income change to determine changes in it. Today, few economists would regard population levels as predominantly economic in nature.

[7] H. Chenery, (1), pp. 202–11, 230. However, studies of the United States, Japanese, Italian, and Norwegian economies discussed in these pages disclose broad patterns of triangularity.

To the extent that a field of study can achieve a consensus on the "proper bounds" for its investigators, its workers gain a sense of coherence and unity not otherwise attainable. We shall term any model which seeks to cope with this *whole* field of variation a "closed" model, and we shall regard it as the limiting general model. In economics, for all practical purposes, the general models of Walras, Wicksell, and, to a lesser extent, Pareto, are closed models. They pushed the boundaries of economics outward to include within their variable-sets those phenomena economists are concerned with even today, and to exclude what are still regarded as predominantly extra-economic phenomena. In so doing, the authors of these models helped to determine important components in the visions of economists who followed them; their systems provide maps of the whole economic terrain, within which models of lesser ambition obtain position and scale.

A second advantage may spring from the existence of the closed model. In Schumpeter's terms,[8] the ambitious closed model may be the "Magna Charta" of a field of study, establishing it as a separate and self-contained body of variation, fully determinate from the data and interrelationships of the model. If, through the use of the techniques discussed in Chapter 9, it were possible to prove that with acceptable restrictions upon data and assumptions a solution to the closed model existed, then workers on less ambitious models would be assured that they *need* not go beyond the range of variation in the larger model for their data and assumptions.

Thirdly, the treatment of general models stresses the importance of prescientific acts in the search to understand variation. The vision provides the theorems which, if subject to testing by the scientific method, are grist for the mill of learning. But, in the social sciences, we are often doomed to shape our visions of reality with little hope of testing derived theorems objectively. In our discussion of the operational approach to model construction we did not touch upon the kinds of evidence acceptable in the validation of meaningful hypotheses. In the social sciences much of our evidence is of the "indirect" type—uncontrolled observation or introspective judgment.[9] If one asserts that he prefers coffee to tea by more than he prefers tea to cocoa, whether or not this is an operational hypothesis hinges upon the hearer's judgment of its intuitive plausibility and his willingness to accept such "evidence."

We should be romanticizing the fund of economic "knowledge" were we to imply that effort in the field was relentlessly subjecting our visions to objective, direct tests against reality, continuously winnowing out those models not found useful, accepting provisionally those whose theorems were not contradicted by such tests, and retesting these latter merci-

[8] J. Schumpeter, (1), Vol. I, pp. 41–2.

[9] For an interesting discussion of the relevance of indirect evidence see M. Friedman, (2), pp. 466–7.

lessly. Rather, the greater part of our analytical frameworks are untested visions—untested, that is, by nonintrospective, controlled methods.

Yet we continue to use these frameworks in analysis and the framing of policy. For example, the vision of the market economy as a vast complex of closely interconnected markets whose prices and quantities are *greatly* interdependent is still just that: a set of hypotheses that have not been subjected to any thoroughgoing objective testing, but so plausible in the light of indirect observation as to make it inconceivable that they are not useful.

We should be foolish, therefore, to ignore general models, including closed models, on the grounds that they yield few operational theorems. Pedagogically, if not analytically, their role is quite important. To teach that everything depends upon everything else may be a simple lesson, but it is an impressive one. Models designed to trace out the vastly complex interdependencies of economic sector with economic sector may yield few testable theorems, even if indirect evidence be accepted in validation, but they may throw brilliant light into dark corners. Consider, for example, the Slutsky-Hicks substitution-income effects concerning leisure and income and their implications for tax policy.

Finally, there exists the possibility that in the future these general systems will be able to yield operational theorems by virtue of some Newtonian breakthrough in the area of multivariable analysis, or, less fancifully, by simplifications of the interrelationships among the variables. While we are pessimistic about the future analytic uses of general systems with much ambition, the possibility of developments in these directions must not be dismissed out of hand. But merely to mention such potentialities leads one to ask what those analytic deficiencies are? Why must such models be approached with the expectation that few testable theorems will be derivable from them? To answer this question, as we shall do in Section 5, we must devote some time to an extensive examination of the more important properties of general models.

4. The Properties of General Models

It is clear from the discussion that the potential value of any vision lies in the insights it yields of realistic economic variation. Ideally, but as we have argued in Section 3 not necessarily, these insights should be operationally meaningful theorems, placing qualitative or quantitative restrictions upon empirical variation, and capable of validation by direct evidence. While we may employ a system to instill broader visions of economic process, and while such employments are of great importance, it is admitted that economic systems usually must yield theorems with empirical content before they can be of continuing analytical utility to the policymaker. Pareto and Osorio spoke of three separate levels of such knowledge concerning economic interdependence: (1) knowledge of its existence, (2) qualitative knowledge of the movements of variables with changes in the data, and (3) quantitative knowledge of such movements.[10] While each level of knowledge contributes useful insights, each of the three levels is on a different plane of importance. Failing the ability to rise from the first level, a system can assume pedagogical or "background" significance, but can seldom attain an active analytical significance.

The reason for this inability does not spring solely from the inapplicability of the scientific method, as we have defined it, to such models. It is simply that sooner or later we must arrive at the ultimate aim of any program developed to cope with variation—prediction. The ability to yield predictive theorems—to rise above Pareto's first level—springs from the properties of the model. We shall discuss, in turn, a group of the more important properties of economic systems as they relate to the ability to obtain operational theorems from such systems.

4.a. Static and Dynamic Models

Because this distinction will be treated at length in Chapter 8, we will limit the present introduction to a discussion of the types of theorems potentially derivable from models with these properties. The value of viewing the distinction from this angle is seen immediately in discussing the implications of a static system.

In the literature of economics, statics often seems to be treated as a framework for the study of equilibrium states in which motion has not only ceased to exist but in which change does not exist, even in a virtual sense.[11] In such treatments, dynamic properties are identified with fruitful analysis of change, characteristic of models that are not locked in time. The outlook developed in this chapter reveals that any economic model

[10] V. Pareto, (1), Vol. II, p. 6, and A. Osorio, (1), pp. 158–60.

[11] See, for example, Cassel's identification of statics with the explanation of how the data determine equilibrium values and dynamics with equilibrium displacements. G. Cassel, (1), pp. 153–4.

This same view is expressed explicitly and implicitly by Walras, in (3), pp. 319 and 377–81. In Walras, however, dynamics has the cast of a *medley* of comparative statics adjustments occurring with time lags. See also H. Moore, (1), pp. 21–3, for a repetition of this Walrasian outlook.

To J. B. Clark, statics dealt with economic systems whose factor quantities (among other data) were given and invariable, while dynamics coped with the laws of change of factors, technology, and wants. Robbins has shown a possibility of this interpretation in J. S. Mill's writings as well. See L. Robbins, (1), pp. 202–4.

Pareto, while holding views on the nature of statics which appear confused from the modern view, did depart from his contemporaries in defining two types of dynamics, the first of which is clearly comparative statics in modern terminology and the second of which is true dynamics. V. Pareto, (2), p. 147.

Thus, in classical and neo-classical economics, there was a widespread tendency to consider comparative statics a form of dynamics, with the implied treatment of statics discussed above.

designed to place limits on variation in the real world must be able to cope with change. Of course, this does not mean that it must yield meaningful theorems about the *time process* of change; but it does imply that it must be able to relate a new state of the model to a change in the data of the model, and thereby to present the old and new states for comparison. Statics, therefore, to be fruitful, cannot imply merely the study of conditions holding at a specific solution to the system.

From this viewpoint, even though statics and dynamics are concerned fundamentally *with the structure of the interrelationships among variables and data of models*, a description of statics and dynamics which compares the nature of the theorems derivable from systems structured in both ways is most useful at this point. In a purist sense, both types of model preclude the derivation of theorems relating to virtual states which are not specific solutions of them. Let us assume such solutions exist in the following discussion.

The differences begin to emerge when such specific solutions are interpreted as "positions of rest," i.e., as situations in which motion in the variables has ceased. Movement implies the existence of a medium through which it occurs, and therefore time is explicitly or implicitly present when states of models are interpreted in this sense. The fundamental difference between models characterized by these structures is that a specific solution to a static system yields a single solution vector (if the solution is unique), whereas a specific solution to a dynamic system is a set of such vectors linked in a path through time.[12] If we adopt the "position-of-rest" interpretation of a static specific solution, a time dimension is built into the space which contains the solution, and we move that solution in a repetitive fashion "parallel" to the time axis; on the other hand, the time dimension for the dynamic solution is integral to its representation, and the path of the variables through it need not be an unchanging one. In the dynamic case, no position of rest need exist in the solution, in that the variables need not approach limiting values as time goes on indefinitely. At this point in our consideration, however, let us assume that the dynamic systems with which we are concerned do yield specific solutions whose vectors do approach limiting values, at least "in the long-run."

A dynamic model contains the potential for the derivation of theorems concerning the values of the variables, or changes in those values, before the position of rest has been attained. It has this potential by virtue of the fact that these values are part of the specific solution: "solution" and "position of rest" are not synonomous. A static system can yield theorems about the values of the variables only in a state of rest, or theorems

[12] A dynamic system may have as solutions more than one path converging to the same or different positions of rest, if indeed one or more such paths do converge to such limiting positions.

about changes in the values of the variables only between two states of rest: "solution" and "position of rest" are synonomous.

It is not, then, the existence of time in a dynamic system and its nonexistence in a static system which is the distinguishing feature of the two types of models. Any realistic use of a static model must involve the interpretation of its solutions against time as a backdrop.[13] Rather, the difference is reflected in the above distinction between potentially derivable theorems. This distinction keeps clear terms which distinguish the properties of a *model*, and, specifically, the functional interrelationships of a model (static, dynamic), from those used to specify the behavior of its specific solutions through time (stationary, nonstationary).[14]

A stationary solution to a model is a specific solution which does not change through time, while a nonstationary solution is a specific solution which does not approach a position of rest. We have seen that an unchanged static model always yields a stationary specific solution (if a solution exists), while a dynamic model may yield stationary or nonstationary solutions.[15]

Comparative statics is a *method* of employing static models analytically by imposing changes upon the data of the model and tracing the changes imposed upon the specific solutions—the displacement of such solutions—by such data manipulation. It is useful to distinguish between changes in the data which are "infinitesimal" in size and which lead to a new solution in the neighborhood of the old, and changes in the data which are finite in size. Similarly, comparative dynamics is a *method* of using dynamic models with the same implications as those in the case of statics.

[13] As E. Schneider writes: " . . . It is essential to understand that in modern theory 'statics' and 'dynamics' refer to a particular *mode of treatment or type of analysis* of the phenomena observed, while the adjectives 'stationary' and 'changing' describe the actual economic phenomena. *A static or dynamic theory is a particular kind of explanation of economic phenomena; and, indeed, stationary and changing phenomena can be submitted either to a static or to a dynamic analysis.*" E. Schneider, (1), p. 185. Quoted by permission.

The neoclassical theorist who came closest to this distinction between static-dynamic vs. stationary-nonstationary systems and solutions respectively was Pareto, as pointed out in footnote 11. His distinctions were not clear, however; for example, he identifies a state of rest in a static system with a stationary state in a dynamic system. In effect, he defines static equilibrium in dynamic terms. See V. Pareto, (2), pp. 153–4.

Not all modern theorists would acquiesce in our interpretation of statics and dynamics. For example, M. Allais writes: "An economic system may be said to be static when all of its elements—production, consumption, prices, and so forth—do not introduce time. In the contrary case, the system may be said to be dynamic." M. Allais, (1), p. 28.

[14] Cf. P. Samuelson, (4), pp. 311–33.

[15] This statement holds even when the static model includes expectations of prices in the future among the data. In Week 0 a specific solution will include the magnitudes of variables in the future *n* weeks. If the same set of expectations and other data is repeated in Week 1, the same specific solution will emerge in Week 1, and so forth.

4.b. Extremum and Nonextremum Properties

Given the underlying data of the model, within whose constraints decisionmaking units are forced to operate, there remains the important task of specifying the motivation of these units. What are the criteria by which decisions among alternative strategies are made? Practically speaking, these assumptions of motivation for firms and consumers must be simple if they are to possess a workable generality. One of the most frequent and convenient of these assumptions in economic models is that decisions are taken as if the unit involved were attempting to reach an *extremum* point, i.e., a minimum or maximum. Such assumptions, together with the data of the model, may be combined to obtain the interrelationships among variables and data discussed in Section 2.

In the case of microeconomic models these extremum strivings are frequently interpreted as attempts to maximize consumers' "utility" and firms' profits. In general models, these assumptions are treated as occupying fully symmetrical roles: the consumer is assumed to act to maximize his subjective welfare, guided in his choices by considerations of more or less, subject to an expenditure constraint. At the same time, the firm is viewed as seeking to maximize profits, an objective magnitude. With the exception of the "subjective" *vs.* "objective" natures of the magnitudes, utility theory and production theory up to recent times stressed the essential similarity of these processes. However, modern theory does not view them as exact analogues. The modern concept of utility is that of a preference function which *defines* the consumer's tastes in the sense that, once derived, it allows the prediction of the consumer's choices. It does not purport that those choices were arrived at by the consumer in any extremum search, purposive or intuitive.

Thus, any "maximization of utility" which we adopt will be merely the specification of one of the data of the model—the consumer's preferences—rather than an actual motivating drive of the consumer. It is even misleading to say that the consumer acts *as if* he were maximizing satisfactions, because the satisfactions cannot exist in any form for maximizing before they have been defined. That is to say, the consumer's "utility" is maximized *by the economist* to find the alternative the consumer has indicated previously he would choose under the postulated conditions. The measure the model-builder has chosen is maximized because when this is done the consumer's tastes are defined. We may make the assumption in the case of the firm that it will always act to make the difference between revenues and costs a maximum, since both revenues and costs may be defined (at least ideally) independently of the state of mind of the decisionmaking unit.

Maximization and minimization techniques, therefore, like other components of our vision, are merely methodological conveniences whose value is measured in terms of usefulness in deriving the required interrelationships. Usefulness, in turn, is defined in terms of the insights yielded by the vision into real economic variation. When convenient, we may build choice into the consumer sector of the model without "maximizing utility:" it may be methodologically convenient to assume that under certain conditions the consumer will take a quantity of a good best predicted by other-than-maximization techniques. Whole systems may rest upon consumer choice which abstracts completely from maximization reasoning, as the models of Cassel or Keynes will illustrate.

The methodological convenience of extremum systems in framing models which will yield meaningful theorems goes beyond the initial derivation of interrelationships among the variables. So-called "second-order conditions" can frequently place restrictions upon the shapes of these interrelationship functions, and these restrictions make an independent contribution to the derivation of such theorems. The appeal to other methods for obtaining the functional interrelationships of the model may well sacrifice these sources of restrictions on the system.

The importance of obtaining such restrictions in the search for operational theorems will be stressed below, but frequently outright assumptions to obtain them may be no more objectionable than assuming an extremum position has been attained and deriving the restrictions from that assumption. For example, if Keynes had obtained his consumption function from a prior maximization analysis he might have been able to derive a marginal propensity to consume of less than unity and more than zero as an implication of the maximum position. As it was, he had to assume in quite arbitrary fashion that it fell within this range of values. Neither method is "right" or "sophisticated," "wrong" or "naïve": the criterion is one of convenience, and in this simple case there seems little reason to choose one method over the other.

But in general models it is frequently true that such restrictions *can* be obtained from second-order extremum conditions while intuitive methods fail wholly to provide substitute restrictions. For example, as we shall show in Chapter 2, the Slutsky-Hicks-Hotelling income-substitution effect analysis allows certain theorems to be framed from a general model because second-order maximization conditions are available to yield the sign of the substitution effect. Thus, we may rise from Pareto's first level of knowledge to the second level with these restrictions, while, in their absence, intuition would afford little justification for one assumption or the other about the relevant determinants' signs.

4.c. Equilibrium and Nonequilibrium Solutions

One of the most fruitful of the many economic adoptions from the field of mechanics is the concept of "economic equilibrium," or a specific solution characterized by a state of balance between opposed forces acting upon economic variables.[16] As we shall employ the term we shall not make it synonomous with "solution" but rather shall use it to distinguish one type of solution. Thus, for example, we shall not use the term to characterize a steady motion of a variable in a repetitive time path, as might emerge from a specific solution to a dynamic system, as we shall not interpret this type of behavior as reflecting a true equipoise of human motives and natural forces.[17] Therefore, given the existence of the forces described above, we use the term "equilibrium" as synonomous with "specific solution" for a static system, but to characterize *one type* of specific solution to a dynamic system, viz., one which attains a position of rest.

Our definition of economic equilibrium is that of Pareto:[18] a specific solution to an economic model describing a state of rest and resulting from the opposition between identifiable desires of men and obstacles to their fulfillment, including among these latter the desires of actors other than any one of the specific firms or consumers under consideration. A model constructed to obtain its solutions on the basis of such an opposition of identifiable forces is called an equilibrium model. Nonequilibrium systems are those whose solutions are not the results of such counteracting forces. For example, a model which predicts that tomorrow's price will be today's price plus a random element is a nonequilibrium system.

In our terminology, therefore, the equilibrium property is not a purely formal one: there must be identifiable and meaningful opposition of motives and/or forces tending toward a net balance as reflected in a position of rest before solutions are acceptable as equilibrium solutions. This is frequently a matter of the model-builder's choice of interpretation. For example, it will be shown in Chapter 7 that the Leontief static open input-output model may be interpreted as an equilibrium or nonequilibrium system. The theorems derivable from either system differ considerably from those obtainable from the other, so that the property with which we choose to endow the model is not unimportant.

Since most of the models with which we shall deal are in fact equilibrium models, we shall frequently use the terms "specific solution" and "equilibrium" interchangeably where no danger of confusion exists. With this in mind we shall assert an interest in four properties of the "equilibrium": (1) its existence, (2) its economic meaningfulness, (3) its unique-

[16] Cf. H. Moore, (1), pp. 19–23. For a discussion of the relationship of equilibrium in the social sciences to that in the physical sciences, and especially the analogous roles of motive and force in the respective areas, see F. Knight, (4), pp. 161–85, and especially p. 163. To Knight's way of thinking, economics is properly concerned with equilibrium not as a pure state of rest but as a state of a "process" in which the data are not truly constant but moving more slowly than the variables and enforcing a kind of moving tendency to a state of rest. See pp. 169–70. The relevance of this outlook for his capital theory will be made clear in Chapter 4.

[17] Cf. J. Sargan, (1), p. 382.

[18] V. Pareto, (2), pp. 150, 155.

ness or nonuniqueness, and (4) its stability. We shall treat the first three of these properties in great detail in Chapter 9, and the last in Chapter 8. In this introduction, however, we must indicate the nature of our concern with these concepts.

4.c.1. The Existence of an Equilibrium

It is truistic to say that we are interested in knowing if a solution to a system exists, both in the specific and nonspecific senses of that term. We have indicated in Section 3 that a model may have value even if we can frame no operational hypotheses from it, although, of course, such usefulness must be of somewhat restricted scope. Similarly, a system can be of value even if it should be impossible to prove the existence of a solution to it. This is not to deny the value of such a proof. Merely to state its implications in a negative fashion—that the data and assumptions of the model will yield a sufficient number of interrelationships among the variables and data which are not mutually inconsistent—is to see that an existence proof is a valuable assurance of potential usefulness for any purpose and may be indispensable if serious efforts to frame fruitful hypotheses are to be made. For example, modern welfare economics must be framed within the confines of a closed system for maximum usefulness, and therefore must concern itself with the properties of a general equilibrium. It is of utmost importance to be assured that the competitive equilibrium which is being described so airily can be shown to exist. In the area of normative economics such proofs would seem to be of extreme importance.[19]

But there is no need to be unbending on the need for this proof, particularly for non-normative uses of models. Quite apart from possible pedagogical uses of the model to fill in the canvas of interdependence, for which an existence proof is only a luxury, it is quite legitimate for the economist to *assume* that the equilibrium exists for acceptable restrictions upon the data of his model which will not disturb the theorems of his model. That such a procedure is less satisfactory intellectually does not

[19] R. Dorfman, P. Samuelson, and R. Solow, in R. Dorfman, (1), pp. 350–1, take a more positive position on the need for an existence proof than the one developed here. They assert, among other things, that "a system of equations whose assumptions do not guarantee the existence of a solution may fail to be a useful idealization of reality," and again that it is necessary to establish existence of equilibrium to be sure a model "really captures what is really important about economic reality."

They, themselves, point out that the existence question hinges on a property of the model, not reality. Merely to assert that the complicated dynamic system which describes reality functions and therefore an evolutionary path exists as a solution does not imply that a general static system approximating it grossly must have a solution under all conditions. Indeed, the assumptions concerning continuity of functions and correspondences which must be made to guarantee the existence of equilibrium in such static model approximations to reality may be more accurately described as a retreat from reality, not a guarantee that it has been approached.

establish its illegitimacy nor the nonapplicability of operational theorems derived in the absence of existence-of-equilibrium proofs.

4.c.2. The Economic Meaningfulness of the Equilibrium

Given the existence of an equilibrium solution to a model, it is of some interest to know the nature of it. In particular, negative prices and quantities in general have no economic content, although in certain situations they may have. Therefore, the equilibrium values of the variables, if they exist, must in addition meet any restrictions necessary to guarantee that they do not grossly violate economic reality.

4.c.3. The Uniqueness of the Equilibrium

Still another property of an equilibrium which holds an interest for the analyst is the number of states of the model consistent with a given set of data; i.e., how large is the set of specific solutions for a given data set? It is tempting to believe that only one state exists in the real economy for any given constellation of data. But no *a priori* argument can establish that if a solution to the real economy exists it is necessarily unique.[20] We have asserted that to be analytically useful a model must assert hypotheses which restrict the expected variation in the real economy under the stated conditions of the model. It is corollary that the number of solutions to a model consistent with a given data set must be small enough in number to yield useful restrictions, and in many cases this number need not necessarily be unity.

4.c.4. The Stability of the Equilibrium

The stability of an equilibrium solution is concerned with the time path followed by the values of the variables of a model when an equilibrium set of values is displaced by a change in the initial position of the model. Note that the stability analysis is fundamentally one of an equilibrium, i.e., a position of rest, not of a system. And note also that because it is concerned with a time path for values of variables in a model whose initial position has been changed, we are dealing with comparative dynamics. We begin with a dynamic model whose specific solution yields a position of rest, disturb this position of rest by a slight or large displacement which is equivalent to changing the initial position of the model, and find whether the specific solution germane to the new data set will lead to a reattainment of the old position of rest via the same or a new path, whether a new position of rest will be attained, or whether no position of rest will be attained.

A most important point is that a stability analysis is of necessity a

[20] Indeed, as we shall show in Chapter 9, the intuitive plausibility of the restrictions upon consumer preference functions for unique solutions to static approximations to reality is something less than compelling.

dynamic analysis: it can be accomplished only with explicit information about the behavior *through time* of a static or dynamic model in disequilibrium. The values of the variables must at all times be consistent with the data set ruling yet be capable of being in a position of non-rest. From our analysis of statics it is clear that the specific solutions will change instantaneously to equilibrium levels consistent with the nonspecific solutions, and the time paths of these operations will be sharp movements from one equilibrium point to another. In the strictest sense, it is impossible to get the system out of equilibrium since it yields information only about equilibrium states of the model, i.e., positions of rest.

This last point is not true of a dynamic system; among the data of such a system is its initial position, or the values of the variables in some arbitrarily denominated period 0. Therefore, in a dynamic system which yields a position of rest, it is possible to specify the set of values desired as the initial disequilibrium position relative to the first set of data, change the initial position of the system to those values without altering any other characteristic of the system, and compare the subsequent time path of the specific solution with that obtained for the original initial position.

Therefore, a dynamic system must be specified to answer questions essentially dynamic. If the stability properties of an equilibrium solution to a static system are to be investigated, an explicit supplementary dynamic model, specifying the mode of reaction through time to disequilibrium values of the system, must be given, as Samuelson has shown so well.[21] This has not prevented economists of the rank of Walras, Pareto, and Marshall from discussing the "stability" properties of static equilibria, as coming chapters will reveal. They were, of course, implicitly assuming certain dynamic properties for their models in disequilibrium situations which in strict logic could not be brought about. Walras spent pages trying to show, from the slopes of his interrelationship functions, that the time path of his general equilibrium system's values always approached a position of rest corresponding to the specific solution dictated by the given data and assumptions of the static model. Wicksell went so far as to combine the problems of the existence of an equilibrium solution and the stability of an equilibrium, holding that if "Walrasian stability conditions" (to be discussed below) do not hold at an equilibrium position, it is not truly an equilibrium, but merely a provisional equality of supply and demand.[22]

Of course, it is useless to quarrel over wholly definitional matters, but it is also confusing to move, however deftly, between pure static, quasi-

[21] P. Samuelson, (4), pp. 260–9. These dynamic supplementary models may be made to appear "timeless" by assuming (1) the directions of movements of variables are known and (2) the rates of movement are so rapid as to be essentially instantaneous.

[22] K. Wicksell, (1), p. 87.

static, dynamic, and pseudo-dynamic models in the manner of Marshall, Walras, and Pareto, or to mix problems concerning the existence of a solution to a static model and of the stability of some dynamic counterpart as Wicksell advocates. It is not to deny these giants of economic analysis their just claims to greatness for insightful analyses to adopt a more puristic approach to the questions of stability. We shall deny the meaningfulness of the term "stability" to the solution of a wholly static system with no explicitly defined dynamic interrelations among the variables for positions of disequilibrium. Instead of adopting the usual terminology in referring to static "stability conditions," to be discussed in the following section, we shall term them "slope conditions" to emphasize the distinction. When they may become true stability conditions is a question we shall pose of our dynamic analysis in Chapter 8.

5. The Derivation of Operational Theorems

We may now return to the question posed at the end of Section 3: wherein lie the difficulties of deriving useful theorems from general models? With the discussion of the more basic properties of economic systems completed, it is now possible to illustrate how these properties are employed in the construction and manipulation of the systems. We shall begin the analysis with a nongeneral system—a partial model—and then complicate it by increasing its ambition.

5.a. The Partial Model

From an analysis of consumer choice which we shall leave for consideration in Chapter 2 and of producers' behavior which will be studied in Chapter 3, the respective nonspecific solutions for the consumption of good Y_1 (symbolized X_1) and for the output of good Y_1 (symbolized $\bar{X}_1$) are obtained as functions of the data P_1 and Z, or the price of good Y_1 and consumers' incomes respectively. For consumers

$$X_1 = F_1(P_1, Z) \tag{13}$$

and for producers

$$\bar{X}_1 = F_2(P_1) \tag{14}$$

Each of these equations represents a set of nonspecific solutions to static, extremum, equilibrium models, each model independent of the others. In (13), for every specification of a price and an income level, consumers will desire to purchase the specific equilibrium value X_1 yielded by that function; similarly, for producers, and for a given price, (14) yields an equilibrium desire-to-supply. Merely from the nonspecific solutions of (13) and (14) we have no way of knowing how general or nongeneral were the models for which they are solutions, but from the paucity of the data we might suspect they were quite limited in ambition.

Let us step up the level of ambition of the analysis and attempt to determine P_1; that is, remove P_1 from the status of datum and convert it to a variable. Then, (13) and (14), which are nonspecific solutions in lesser models, now become the interrelationships among variables and datum (Z) of the grander model. As a condition for the solution of the new model, it will be necessary for consumers and producers simultaneously to be willing to accept the *status quo*. Therefore, equilibrium must be characterized by the condition or interrelationship:

$$X_1^\circ = \bar{X}_1^\circ \equiv X^\circ \tag{15}$$

The superscript ° indicates that this relationship need characterize the variables only for their solution values in the grand model. This notational procedure has been adopted from Pareto and will be used throughout this book to distinguish relationships holding only in the solution from relationships which may hold out of equilibrium. Thus, in general, for an allowable value of P_1 (given Z) picked at random, (13) will dictate a value for X_1 and (14) for $\bar{X}_1$, but they will not be equal, and (15) will not characterize these values. For simplicity, since the amount demanded in equilibrium must equal the amount supplied, we have defined the symbol X° to denote both equilibrium values.

If our interest lies only in the solution values of X_1, $\bar{X}_1$, and P_1, (i.e., X_1°, $\bar{X}_1^\circ$, P_1°) it is possible to reduce the three-equation system (plus one definitional identity) of (13), (14), and (15) to two equations:

(16)

1. $X^\circ = F_1(P_1; Z)$
2. $X^\circ = F_2(P_1)$

There are two unknowns in the model, X° and P_1°; one datum, Z; and two interrelationships (16-1) and (16-2) derived from certain psychological and physical constraints, motivational assumptions not presented explicitly, and conditions (15). Further, under certain assumptions, it is possible to solve (16) for the nonspecific solutions to the system which would be of the form:

(17)

1. $X^\circ = G_1(Z)$
2. $P_1^\circ = G_2(Z)$

In Section 4 we have indicated the properties of the equations of (17) that hold an interest for us: do they exist, are they meaningful, do they yield unique values, are these equilibrium values stable? But suppose we could answer "yes" to each of these questions. Of what value is this simplest of economic visions contained in (16)?

A first point to be made is that such values must be derivable from equations (16) in their nonstatistical form; in 999 cases out of 1000 it will prove impossible for one reason or another to fit these equations to realistic data and manipulate the statistical functions. The model-builder's task is to obtain insights into the reality which cannot be poured into the empty containers he has constructed. With this limitation upon his opportunities, the economist may well approach his tools with a good deal of skepticism. If—and this so far by assumption—he can merely assert that for any value of consumers' income stated by an inquiring policymaker there will exist a unique, meaningful, stable price-quantity which will satisfy all actors in the market, he would be wise to expect an "if so, so what" reaction from the policymaker. To be sure, the body which the model-builder must build upon the skeleton of (16) will be a useful representation of economic process for the policymaker: the isolation of the strategic variables involved, the market concept and a description of its operation, the notion of competition, and so forth, have their educating role. But the broadness of the education makes it of limited applicability to some specific problems in which the policy man might be vitally concerned.

For example, suppose the nation became involved in a limited war, and the policymaker anticipated a relatively small rise in consumers' income. Should he expect the quantity of Y_1 exchanged (equals the amount demanded in equilibrium equals the amount supplied in equilibrium) to rise or fall as a result? What of the equilibrium price of Y_1: will it rise or fall? Granted an inability to give quantitative answers to these questions and thus attain Pareto's third level of knowledge, is it possible to deduce from (16) together with any other information we may obtain about the system theorems which yield such qualitative predictions? If not, we must fall yet another level to Pareto's first stage and its implied "broad education."

One manner of proceeding is to start from an equilibrium solution of (16), displace it slightly by a small increase in income, $dZ > 0$, and, by assuming both functions are continuous and possess at least first derivatives, solve for $\frac{dX^\circ}{dZ}$ and $\frac{dP^\circ}{dZ}$.[23] This manner of equilibrium displacement has the disadvantage of yielding theorems for very small changes in the data, and is not applicable for finite changes: it can yield information about the values of the variables in a model only for two solutions which are quite close to each other. Also, its use implicitly assumes that in neither the beginning nor terminal equilibrium is the value of any variable zero. And, moreover, its use depends upon all of the interrelationships of the system being stated in the form of equalities rather than inequalities.

[23] Since only one price exists in this simple system, we may omit the subscript 1 for simplicity in the following operations.

Despite all these limitations, the technique remains a valuable method of obtaining testable theorems from economic models, and we shall rely heavily upon it throughout the book, although we shall not neglect other and more recent techniques for deriving theorems by equilibrium displacement when one or more of the above conditions are not met. By differentiating (16) with respect to Z we obtain the following system:

$$(18) \qquad \begin{bmatrix} 1 & -F_1^p \\ 1 & -F_2^p \end{bmatrix} \begin{bmatrix} \dfrac{dX^\circ}{dZ} \\ \dfrac{dP^\circ}{dZ} \end{bmatrix} = \begin{bmatrix} F_1^Z \\ 0 \end{bmatrix}$$

Note, for the sake of interest, that the matrix of the system is indecomposable, indicating that the changes in the equilibrium quantities and prices are interdependent.

Because this simple system is the first of many equilibrium displacement systems we shall present, it will be useful to spend a little time in interpreting (18) in an economic manner. The two equations of (18) indicate that if consumer income is changed slightly, there will be two independent paths of influence upon the variables of the system. Along the first path (the demand function) the change in the quantity exchanged from the first to the second equilibrium position will equal the direct impact of the income change on that quantity (F_1^Z) plus the indirect impact equal to the change in equilibrium price times the response of the demand function to a small change in price in this neighborhood. Similarly, along the second path (the supply function) the change in equilibrium quantity must equal the direct impact of the change in income on the quantity via the supply curve (in this case zero) plus the indirect impact of the equilibrium price change times the response of quantity supplied to price in this neighborhood of the supply function. The values of the variables change in response to the influences flowing along those paths until a set of values is achieved which lies on *every* path of influence in the system.

The terms F_j^i are the various "slopes" of the interrelationships in the system. Imagine a three-dimensional space with P along the x-axis, Z along the y-axis, and X_1 or $\bar{X}_1$ along the z-axis, and the demand and supply functions of (13) and (14) represented as three-dimensional functions in that space. For every value of Z, under our ideal assumptions, these functions will have an intersection at X° and P°. Then, choose a Z arbitrarily on the y-axis, and move to the corresponding point (P°, X°). Now, if we want to get to another equilibrium point (P°, X°)′, we can do so only by moving along the demand and supply functions. If (P°, X°)′ is very close to (P°, X°), then the slopes of the demand function in the P and Z directions at (P°, X°), or F_1^p and F_1^z, and of the supply function at the same point in the same directions, or F_2^p and 0, must be taken into account in the desired movement.

Let us solve system (18) for $\frac{dX^\circ}{dZ}$, to obtain

$$\frac{dX^\circ}{dZ} = F_1^z\left(\frac{F_2^p}{F_2^p - F_1^p}\right) \tag{19}$$

We know the direction of impact of income change upon the demand function: dZ is assumed positive, as is F_1^z. Therefore, the direction of change of X° with a slight rise in income depends upon the signs and relative magnitudes of the slopes of the demand and supply functions in the P-direction at (P°, X°). Similarly, if we solve for $\frac{dP^\circ}{dZ}$ we obtain from (18)

$$\frac{dP^\circ}{dZ} = F_1^z\left[\frac{1}{F_2^p - F_1^p}\right] \tag{20}$$

In this case, also, the sign of the change of equilibrium price depends upon the signs and magnitudes of the slopes of the demand and supply functions in the P-direction, although if the sign of the difference of the slopes is known the sign of the term can be determined—which is not true of $\frac{dX^\circ}{dZ}$, for which the sign of F_2^p is also needed.

Thus, the ability to answer the questions posed hinges upon knowledge of these slopes of the interrelationship functions—their absolute values, their relative values, their signs, the signs or values of their differences, and so forth. It is impossible to progress further in the derivation of theorems unless restrictions may be placed upon these slopes. In the recognition of this need at this simplest level of model building is the explanation of much of the work that lies ahead for more complicated models. What are the paths to follow to gain this needed information? In our work three such alternatives will be explored:

1. The Postulational Method. It is possible merely to assume information about the slopes in the neighborhood of the equilibrium. For example, we might assume that the slope of the demand function in the P-direction is negative and the slope of the supply function in the same direction is positive. On the basis of these assumptions we may evaluate the expressions in (19) and (20) to obtain unambiguous predictions: $\frac{dX^\circ}{dZ}$ will be positive, $\frac{dP^\circ}{dZ}$ will be positive. These are theorems potentially testable against reality and of some real value to the policymaker. Of course, the assumptions may prove to be incorrect, but at least the theorems derived from the assumptions are potentially capable of validation. A less powerful assumption about these slopes is that $F_2^p - F_1^p$ is positive

in the relevant neighborhood. With this information, $\frac{dP^\circ}{dZ}$ is predicted to be positive, but the sign of $\frac{dX^\circ}{dZ}$ is ambiguous in the absence of specific information about the sign of F_2^p.

2. The Extremum Method. In the discussion of extremum models in Section 4.b. it was indicated that their use to derive the needed interrelationships of the model frequently yielded a further dividend to the analysis by facilitating the derivation of operational theorems. We may now illustrate this point. If the demand function was indeed derived by "maximizing satisfactions," and if in fact maxima have been attained, certain characteristics of the utility surfaces where they touch the budget planes must hold true, for, by assumption, true maxima positions have been reached in the beginning and the terminal equilibrium points. With the implied characteristics of the utility surface in this neighborhood, for example, plus another assumption we may deduce the negative slope of the demand function in the P-direction. Similar maximization analyses permit the deduction of positive P-slopes for the supply function. The methods will be examined in greater detail in Chapters 2 and 3, but at this point this brief indication suffices.

For the simple model we are now treating, there seems little choice on grounds of analytical nicety between the postulational and extremum methods, when both are possible and yield equivalent information. We need not aspire to deal with models of much greater ambition before the first method, relying as it does upon intuitive guidance to the slope characteristics, becomes much less satisfactory, and, for all practical purposes, unusable.

3. The Stability Method. Frequently, particularly for models in whose construction extremum reasoning plays no explicit part, information about these slopes is obtained from an explicit stability analysis. That is, the equilibrium is *assumed* stable, and, from the conditions which must hold for this to be true, information is obtained limiting the values of the slopes. In most "stability" analysis of partial static models depicting price determination, the reasoning follows one of two routes:

(1) Walrasian slope conditions. If price rises above the equilibrium point to a slight extent, and if excess demand $(X_1 - \bar{X}_1)$ becomes negative, competition among the sellers will push price back toward its equilibrium value. Similarly, if price falls below the equilibrium, and if excess demand becomes positive, competition on the demand side will force price upwards toward the equilibrium. For small movements of price around an equilibrium, it is necessary and sufficient for stability of equilibrium that the difference between the slope of the demand curve and supply curve $(F_1^p - F_2^p)$ (which is the slope of the excess demand curve) in the neighborhood of equilibrium be negative.

(2) Marshallian slope conditions. Marshall tended to view the market adjustment in terms of prices adjusting to quantity movements, interested as he was in longer-term economic movements. Consequently, he framed his slope conditions on the inverse functions of those we have used in (13) and (14), defining price as a function of quantities demanded and supplied respectively. Following convention, we should graph P on the z-axis instead of X_1 and $\bar{X}_1$, and these latter on the x-axis. We should then speak of the slopes of these new functions in the X_1 or $\bar{X}_1$ direction, and these slopes would be the reciprocals of F_1^p and F_2^p, i.e., $\frac{1}{F_1^p}$ and $\frac{1}{F_2^p}$.

Then, if the quantity on the market fell below the equilibrium quantity, the price at which buyers would take this quantity off the market (demand price) would differ from the price which would just induce suppliers to bring it to the market (supply price). If excess demand price (demand price minus supply price) is positive in this case, the profit motive will lead suppliers to increase their outputs and move back to equilibrium. Also, in the neighborhood of equilibrium, if the quantity on the market rose above the equilibrium level, and if excess demand price were negative, suppliers would be led to reduce output and return to equilibrium. Therefore, it is necessary and sufficient for the stability of an equilibrium for small movements in its neighborhood for the slope of the excess demand price function $\left(\frac{1}{F_1^p} - \frac{1}{F_2^p}\right)$ to be negative.

The objection to these types of analyses is not that they are incorrect in a fundamental sense, but rather that they are implicitly expanding an explicit static model by the addition of dynamic relations. This procedure can be misleading in two important respects. First, the very fact that Walras and Marshall arrived at two different sets of slope conditions is an indication that their implicit dynamic analyses were quite different interpretations of the reactions of actors in a market to nonequilibrium states. If these interpretations are allowed to remain implicit, the differences may remain unnoticed and undiscussed. If one were wholly unrealistic, or acceptable only for certain well-defined market structures but not for others, then adoption of the wrong slope-conditions could yield incorrect operational theorems. The Walrasian outlook views demanders and suppliers as acting quickly upon price via competition whenever they cannot buy and sell the desired amounts. The Marshallian outlook puts the major emphasis for adjustment upon suppliers who are viewed as adjusting output to profit opportunities, while consumers tend to be passive. These are two different pictures of reality and they spring from meaningful differences in the construction of the dynamic models.

Second, whenever results are obtained implicitly rather than explicitly, there is a danger when more complicated models are constructed that these *results* will be generalized rather than the *methods*, with error resulting to a greater or lesser degree. In the case of stability analysis this has in fact occurred, in that Hicks's static stability conditions (slope conditions) for general models do not in general correspond to those derived by generalizing the implicit dynamic models of the partial static system.

It is fruitful, therefore, for the matter in hand as well as for the more complicated analysis to follow in Chapters 2 and 8, to derive these slope conditions as stability conditions from explicit dynamic models. In the case of Walrasian adjustment, the dynamic interrelationship which must be added to (16) is the following:

$$\text{(21)} \qquad \frac{dP}{dt} \equiv \dot{P} = G(X_1 - \bar{X}_1), \qquad G' > 0,\ G(0) = 0$$

That is, the time rate of change of price in the market is some function of the excess demand in the market such that when excess demand changes, the rate of change of price moves in the same direction, and when excess demand is zero price remains at rest through time. We may simplify (21) by the use of Maclaurin's variant of Taylor's series: we retain the linear portion of the expression and neglect all terms with derivatives of higher order than the first.[24] Then, (21) is approximated by

$$\text{(22)} \qquad \dot{P} = G(0) + G'(X_1 - \bar{X}_1) = G'(X_1 - \bar{X}_1)$$

where G' is the first derivative of the function evaluated at the point of equilibrium. Further, let us define excess demand,

$$\text{(23)} \qquad E = X_1 - \bar{X}_1$$

so that (22) becomes

$$\text{(24)} \qquad \dot{P} = G'E$$

But we may approximate E by Taylor's series. Since

$$\text{(25)} \qquad E = F_1(P; Z) - F_2(P) = H(P; Z)$$

we may approximate E at a point P very close to P° by the following expression, if we again ignore all expressions containing derivatives of H higher than the first order:

$$\text{(26)} \qquad E = H(P^\circ; Z) + H'(P - P^\circ) = 0 + H'(P - P^\circ)$$

where H' is the derivative of H at P°. Substituting from (26) we arrive at the final linear approximation of $\dot{P}$ from (24):

$$\text{(27)} \qquad \dot{P} = G'H'P - G'H'P^\circ$$

[24] Less pretentiously, and more honestly, we shall linearize (21).

This expression is a first order nonhomogeneous linear differential equation whose solution is

$$P_t = (P - P^\circ)e^{G'E't} + P^\circ \tag{28}$$

where P_t is the price at time-point t, P is the initial non-equilibrium price, t is the number of time-points away from $t = 0$, and e is the base of natural logarithms. But, from (25)

$$E' = F_1^p - F_2^p \tag{29}$$

and substituting

$$P_t = (P - P^\circ)e^{G'(F_1{}^p - F_2{}^p)t} + P^\circ \tag{30}$$

Now, from (21), $G' > 0$ and, of course, $t > 0$. For stability it is necessary and sufficient that $P_t \rightarrow P^\circ$ as $t \rightarrow \infty$, which will occur if and only if the first term approaches zero. For this to occur, however, it is necessary and sufficient that

$$(F_1^p - F_2^p) < 0 \tag{31}$$

Therefore, if we assume the equilibrium of our model to be stable in the sense of Walras, a market reaction function of the type in the dynamic equation (21) is implicit, with the set of corrective market adjustments represented by it, and (31) is implied.[25]

If the Marshallian market adjustment had been adopted, the dynamic equation counterpart to (21) would be

$$\frac{dX}{dt} \equiv \dot{X} = M(P_d - P_s), \qquad M' > 0, M(0) = 0 \tag{32}$$

where P_d is demand price and P_s supply price. Approximation by Maclaurin's and Taylor's series and solution of the differential equation would yield

$$X_t = (X - X^\circ)e^{M'\left(\frac{1}{F_1{}^p} - \frac{1}{F_2{}^p}\right)t} + X^\circ \tag{33}$$

where X is the initial disequilibrium quantity. For stability of the equilibrium it is required that $X_t \rightarrow X^\circ$ as $t \rightarrow \infty$, for which it is necessary and sufficient that

$$\left(\frac{1}{F_1^p} - \frac{1}{F_2^p}\right) < 0 \tag{34}$$

Therefore, if stability in the sense of Marshall is assumed, (34) is implied.

In the evaluation of (19) and (20) it may be seen that with the information gained from (31) it is possible to predict that $\frac{dP^\circ}{dZ}$ will be

[25] For an attempt to relate the dynamic market process to iterative processes for solving equations, see R. Goodwin, (1).

positive but it is impossible to obtain a theorem concerning the sign of $\frac{dX^\circ}{dZ}$, since this would require a knowledge of the sign of F_2^p which is not given. On the other hand, (34) yields much more ambiguous information. It says that $\frac{dX^\circ}{dZ} < 0$ if the demand curve is negatively sloped in the relevant neighborhood, $\frac{dX^\circ}{dZ} > 0$ if the demand curve is positively sloped in that neighborhood. Also, $\frac{dP^\circ}{dZ}$ will take the sign $(-F_1^p F_2^p)$, which may be positive or negative.

5.b. The General Model

The experiment in the derivation of operational theorems from the partial model was a relatively successful one, for in spite of the triviality of the results, it points the way to the treatment of more realistic variation with more sophisticated models. Specifically, let us introduce the phenomenon of market interdependence into our model by increasing the level of its ambition slightly. We shall merely introduce a second market into the analysis, in which good Y_2 is sold at P_2. From prior maximization analyses we derive the set of demand and supply functions given below:

$$(35)\qquad \begin{aligned} &1.\quad X_1 = F_1(P_1, P_2; Z) \\ &2.\quad \bar{X}_1 = F_2(P_1, P_2) \\ &3.\quad X_2 = F_3(P_1, P_2; Z) \\ &4.\quad \bar{X}_2 = F_4(P_1, P_2) \end{aligned}$$

where the additional symbols are simple extensions of those of our partial model. Further, it is required that in equilibrium excess demand be zero in both markets:

$$(36)\qquad \begin{aligned} &1.\quad X_1 = \bar{X}_1 \equiv X_1^\circ \\ &2.\quad X_2 = \bar{X}_2 \equiv X_2^\circ \end{aligned}$$

Substituting from (36) into (35) yields the simpler system,

$$(37)\qquad \begin{aligned} &1.\quad X_1^\circ = F_1(P_1, P_2; Z) \\ &2.\quad X_1^\circ = F_2(P_1, P_2) \\ &3.\quad X_2^\circ = F_3(P_1, P_2; Z) \\ &4.\quad X_2^\circ = F_4(P_1, P_2) \end{aligned}$$

Under assumptions wholly similar to those made about the functions of the simpler model, and beginning from an assumed equilibrium position, it is possible to displace the equilibrium by a very small increase in consumer income. The changes in equilibrium values of the variables will then be given by the following system of equations:

$$
\begin{bmatrix} 1 & 0 & -F_1^1 & -F_1^2 \\ 1 & 0 & -F_2^1 & -F_2^2 \\ 0 & 1 & -F_3^1 & -F_3^2 \\ 0 & 1 & -F_4^1 & -F_4^2 \end{bmatrix} \begin{bmatrix} \dfrac{dX_1^\circ}{dZ} \\ \dfrac{dX_2^\circ}{dZ} \\ \dfrac{dP_1^\circ}{dZ} \\ \dfrac{dP_2^\circ}{dZ} \end{bmatrix} = \begin{bmatrix} F_1^z \\ 0 \\ F_3^z \\ 0 \end{bmatrix} \tag{38}
$$

or

$$
[D][dV] = [dK] \tag{39}
$$

Then, for example,

$$
\frac{dX_1^\circ}{dZ} = F_1^z \frac{|D_{11}|}{|D|} + F_3^z \frac{|D_{31}|}{|D|} \tag{40}
$$

$$
\frac{dP_1^\circ}{dZ} = F_1^z \frac{|D_{13}|}{|D|} + F_3^z \frac{|D_{33}|}{|D|} \tag{41}
$$

where $|D|$ is the determinant formed from $[D]$ and $|D_{st}|$ is the minor of $|D|$ formed from the matrix obtained by crossing out the sth row and t^{th} column of $[D]$. Unless otherwise indicated, throughout the book such expressions as $|M_{st}|$ will denote minors formed in this way. Since the F_1^z and F_3^z terms are assumed to be positive, the signs of the expressions in (40) and (41) will depend upon the absolute values of F_1^z and F_3^z and the algebraic values of the ratios of determinants.

In order to get some idea of the complexity of these expressions as compared with their counterparts in the partial model, given in (19) and (20), they are expanded in full below:

$$
\begin{aligned}
\frac{dX_1^\circ}{dZ} &= F_1^z \left[\frac{1}{1 - \left(\dfrac{F_1^1F_3^2 + F_1^2F_4^1 - F_1^2F_3^1 - F_1^1F_4^2}{F_2^1F_3^2 + F_2^2F_4^1 - F_2^2F_3^1 - F_2^1F_4^2} \right)} \right] \\
&+ F_3^z \left[\frac{F_1^1F_2^2 - F_1^2F_2^1}{(F_2^1F_3^2 + F_2^2F_4^1 - F_2^2F_3^1 - F_2^1F_4^2) - (F_1^1F_3^2 + F_1^2F_4^1 - F_1^2F_3^1 - F_1^1F_4^2)} \right]
\end{aligned} \tag{42}
$$

$$
\begin{aligned}
\frac{dP_1^\circ}{dZ} &= F_1^z \left[\frac{F_3^2 - F_4^2}{(F_2^1F_3^2 + F_2^2F_4^1 - F_2^2F_3^1 - F_2^1F_4^2) - (F_1^1F_3^2 + F_1^2F_4^1 - F_1^2F_3^1 - F_1^1F_4^2)} \right] \\
&+ F_3^z \left[\frac{F_1^2 - F_2^2}{(F_2^1F_3^2 + F_2^2F_4^1 - F_2^2F_3^1 - F_2^1F_4^2) - (F_1^1F_3^2 + F_1^2F_4^1 - F_1^2F_3^1 - F_1^1F_4^2)} \right]
\end{aligned} \tag{43}
$$

If the reader is impressed with the complexity of these two equations, as compared with the neatness of their counterparts in the partial model, this clumsy method of expression will have served its purpose. It is a basic lesson in the difficulties of manipulating general systems.

By increasing the ambition of the model to the extent of including only one more market, the number of slopes involved in the expressions to be evaluated rose from 3 to 10. No longer will information about the sign of the difference between two slopes yield an operational theorem concerning the sign of $\frac{dP_1^\circ}{dZ}$, or this information plus the sign of one of the slopes suffice to obtain the sign of $\frac{dX_1^\circ}{dZ}$. The information now required includes knowledge about the absolute magnitudes as well as signs of all of these slopes. The problem of deriving theorems in this manner from the model has increased so sharply in difficulty as to have become qualitatively different from that of the partial model.

An increase in the number of equations of a model by one results in an increase in the elements of $[D]$ of $2n + 1$, where n is the previous number of equations. Against this rampant rise in complexity must be counterposed the ability of the economist to extend the methods employed to gain information about these slopes in the partial analysis to the general analysis. To date, as we shall demonstrate in the remainder of the book, this ability has proved quite limited. For obvious reasons less reliance can be put upon the postulational method: who would desire to depend upon his intuition to restrict the signs of the denominator in the terms of (42) and (43)? On the other hand, by appealing to the underlying maximization processes of this model, discoveries made by Slutsky, Hotelling, and Hicks and Allen do allow some restrictions to be placed upon some of the determinants in (40) and (41), but only seldom are they sufficient to yield completely unambiguous signs for the derivatives. Lastly, if one is willing to accept "static stability" analysis, other restrictions are possible, while if he insists upon dynamic stability conditions less information is forthcoming in general.

The lesson is a simple one. An increase in the ambition of a vision implies the removal of phenomena from the data category and their placement in the variable category. This requires an increase in the number of equations and a much larger increase in the number of "slope terms" which are the elements in the expressions that must be evaluated if operational theorems are to be forthcoming from the model. In the absence of specific statistical information about these slopes, the usefulness of models declines very quickly as more variables are added. With the present ability to restrict these slopes by plausible assumption one may conclude with reasonable confidence: *either the economist has a simple theory or he has no theory at all!*

6. The Closed General Model

If these lessons are apparent in the analysis of a general model with so little ambition, the limited analytical applicability of the closed model—the "general equilibrium model" of economic theory—with its ultimate pretensions will come as no shock. As Leontief writes:

"The comprehensive general equilibrium theories developed by the Lausanne school are essentially grand classificatory taxonomic devices. They define and stratify the basic types of economic phenomena and describe their mutual interrelationships in so general a form that very few, if any, operational propositions concerning the measurable properties of specific economic systems can actually be derived from them. Neither Walras nor Pareto made any stipulations concerning the possible empirical implementation of their explanatory schemes. The fact that at least one of the two—Pareto, with his well-known statistical "law of income distribution"—gave much thought to the role of measurement in economics seems to indicate that such reticence was not accidental. The theory of general interdependence—no less than the classical 'theory of value' to which it was generically related despite the many differences—was not intended by its creators to become a tool of factual analysis. . . ."[26]

As we have emphasized in Section 3, the more ambitious general model is most useful in its portrayal of interdependence, as Professor Leontief stresses for the case of the closed general model. The phenomenon of interdependence had been pointed out by John Stuart Mill in his statement of the demand schedule:

". . . the quantity demanded is not a fixed quantity, even at the same time and place; it varies according to the value; if the thing is cheap, there is usually a demand for more of it than when it is dear. The demand, therefore, partly depends on the value. But it was before laid down that the value depends on the demand. From this contradiction how shall we extricate ourselves? How solve the paradox, of two things, each depending on the other?"[27]

But the clearest vision of interdependence as a phenomenon making the economy a coherent whole, and the one which influenced most the thinking of Walras, was that of Cournot. His mathematical background facilitated an understanding of the simultaneity of determination of the values of variables and forestalled him from viewing it as paradox, as Mill had. At the same time it led him to see the complexity of general analysis:

[26] W. Leontief, (5), pp. 41–2. Quoted by permission.
[27] J. S. Mill, (1), Book III, Ch. 2, Section 3.

". . . the economic system is a whole of which all parts are connected and react on each other. . . . It would seem, therefore, as if, for a complete and rigorous solution of the problems relative to some parts of the economic system, it were indispensable to take the entire system into consideration. But this would surpass the powers of mathematical analysis and of our practical methods of calculation, even if the values of all the constants could be assigned to them numerically."[28]

Although both Walras and Pareto stressed the need for general economic analysis, the interdependence of economic variables, and the mutuality of such interdependence in the sense of Section 2, Pareto stressed interdependence more consistently than Walras. Even though no one can dissociate the name of Walras from the contribution that his general equilibrium model made in *depicting* mutual interdependence, nor deny that the latter lay at the heart of the former, Walras was quite ready to become a Marshallian pragmatist:

"Theoretically, all the unknowns of the economic problem depend upon all the equations of economic equilibrium. Nevertheless, even from the static, theoretical viewpoint, it is indeed permissible to consider certain of these unknowns as more especially dependent upon the equations which were introduced with them into the problem in order to determine them. . . ."[29]

Pareto, more rigid in his insistence upon a consistent recognition of mutual interdependence, took Walras to task for lapses from the outlook in the first sentence of the above quotation. He viewed the *whole* purpose of employing mathematics in economics to originate in the need to build models capable of coping with that phenomenon.[30] Indeed, some contemporary economists regard the concept of full economic equilibrium in a mutually interdependent system as a Paretian contribution rather than a Walrasian one.[31] And, unlike Walras, who always sought to convey the impression that the equations of the system had some potential for statistical fitting, Pareto was willing to base the value of the closed economic model on its "broader" lessons of interdependence:

". . . if the conditions that we have just enumerated are not able to serve us practically in numerical calculations of quantity and price, they are the unique method known at present to arrive at a notion of the manner in which prices and quantities vary, or more exactly, in a general fashion, to know how economic equilibrium is produced."[32]

[28] A. Cournot (1), p. 127. Quoted by permission of Miss Anne Ashley.

[29] L. Walras, (2), p. 289. Quoted by permission.

[30] V. Pareto, (2), p. 246, for the objection to Walras, and pp. 42–3, 146, 247, 557n, for the view on the role of mathematics in economics. See also V. Pareto, (3), pp. 60–2.

[31] See M. Brodsky, (1), pp. 135–47, and L. Einaudi, (1), pp. 14–6.

[32] Pareto, (2), p. 234. See also p. 665.

The desirability of deriving greater insights into economic reality from the closed model than those implicit at this "first level" of knowledge was made quite clear by Walras. He believed it to be a responsibility of the theorist to go beyond the mere derivation of models in order to strive for operational theorems of the type we sought in the less ambitious systems of (42) and (43). He termed these "laws of variation" and of them he wrote:

"The theorist has the right to assume that the underlying price determinants are invariant over the period he has chosen to use in his formulation of the law of equilibrium prices. But, once this formulation has been completed, it is his duty to remember that the forces that underlie prices are by their nature variable, and consequently he must formulate the law of variation of equilibrium prices. . . ."[33]

Walras made little progress down this tortuous route. The real beginning of the derivation of theorems from general systems in a workmanlike manner dates from Pareto. We shall study Pareto's initiating efforts in Chapter 2, but, from our analysis of Section 5, we should not be surprised if his success was somewhat limited. Walras and Pareto left the theory of general equilibrium resting on the first level of Pareto's classification of knowledge, with clearly perceived goals on the second level, but with only the beginnings of efforts to achieve them.

It was this lack of achievement in general equilibrium theory which led U. Ricci to remark that "The whole construction gives the effect of an enchanted palace which delights the fantasy but does not help to solve problems of housing. Or, to drop the metaphor, the theory remains abstract and intangible."[34] And Hicks would write in the 1930's:

"Now the reason for this sterility of the Walrasian system is largely, I believe, that he did not go on to work out the laws of change for his system of General Equilibrium. He could tell what conditions must be satisfied by the prices established with given resources and given preferences; but he did not explain what would happen if tastes or resources changed."[35]

[33] L. Walras, (3), p. 146. Quoted by permission of Richard Irwin, Inc., George Allen & Unwin, Ltd., and the American Economic Association.

[34] Quoted in H. Moore, (1), p. 28. The article has been translated and published in U. Ricci, (1), and the quotation may be found on p. 20.

[35] J. Hicks, (5), p. 61. Quoted by permission. This also seems to be the burden of the charge by F. Oulès that the extreme concentration upon equilibrium conditions by both Walras and Pareto led them to neglect certain "interdependences" in the system. See F. Oulès (1). So many charges are made, however, many of them badly taken (e.g., Walras's and Pareto's adoption of the mathematical method *interfered* with their handling of interdependence systems), that it is difficult to discern the relative weight assigned each by Oulès.

And, as a last example of this criticism, we may quote from Samuelson on the general aims of analysis:

"It is hardly enough, however, to show that under certain conditions we can name enough relations (equations) to determine the values of our unknowns. It is important that our analysis be developed in such terms that we are aided in determining how our variables change qualitatively or quantitatively with changes in explicit data. . . ."[36]

It is against this body of criticism and the orientation spelled out at such length in this chapter that the contributions of Slutsky, Hotelling, Hicks, Keynes, Lange, Samuelson, Patinkin, and others will be developed and viewed. What progress has been made in increasing the analytical power of general systems by working within the neoclassical framework of Walras-Pareto-Fisher-Wicksell to facilitate the derivation of operational theorems? Even the study of minor progress is of great value, for the vision of interdependence is too valuable to be thrown up before the most exhaustive efforts to derive information about the relevant slopes have been expended. We shall devote Part II to a succession of general models in the neoclassical tradition, building successively and cumulatively through exchange models (Chapter 2), production models (Chapter 3), investment models (Chapter 4), and money models (Chapter 5). We shall end Chapter 5 with a closed general model incorporating each of these aspects of a realistic economy.

In Chapter 7 an attempt will be made to extend this neoclassical analysis by building in an explicit spatial dimension; in Chapter 9 restrictions upon the data and the assumptions will be imposed which will assure that certain of these neoclassical systems will have solutions, and the conditions for uniqueness of solutions for some of these systems will be explored. In Chapter 8 general dynamic systems will be constructed with a primary goal being that of seeing what true dynamic stability analysis can contribute to the derivation of operational theorems from such systems as those contained in Part II.

The number of these general systems from which we can derive any operational theorems is relatively small, and the empirical content of these hypotheses quite disappointing in scope and restrictiveness. Having attained the high ground, however, it will be possible to discern three lower-lying alternative paths of analytical promise:

(a) *The Simplification of the Interrelationships of the General Model.* One route is that of retaining the generalness of the model by approximating the interrelationships in it with simple functions whose slopes may be fitted by simple statistical techniques. In this way not only may operational hypotheses be forthcoming but they may achieve Pareto's third level of knowledge: quantitative predictions. The rather recent tech-

[36] P. Samuelson, (4), p. 7. Quoted by permission. See also pp. 257–8.

niques of linear economics are relevant under this heading, and we shall study the Leontief static input-output system in Chapter 6, the dynamic system in Chapter 8, linear programming or activity analysis in Chapters 3, 6, and 7, and von Neumann's growth model in Chapter 8.

(b) *The Elimination of Variables from the Model by Aggregation.* Yet another path open to the model-builder in his strivings for meaningful systems is to reduce the number of equations in his model by aggregation techniques. Instead of n goods in the consumer's action space let there be one: "consumption goods." By such Gordian-knot approaches, the matrices of the systems can be drastically reduced in the number of slope-elements they contain, and, as we have seen, this is a large leap forward toward the theorems sought. Except in the trivial sense that every model is aggregated to some extent, we shall deal with only one aggregate general system in this book: the Keynesian model. It will be viewed as a contribution to the stream of neoclassical general equilibrium theory and will be analyzed in Chapter 5.

(c) *The Elimination of Variables from the Model by Converting Them to Data.* Lastly, we may tread the path of partial analysis, turning our backs (however reluctantly) upon the mutual interdependence of economic variables. Certainly we should be following a most persuasive leader:

> "It was not till the seventeenth century that the physical sciences appreciated the full importance of the fact that when several causes act together and mutually affect one another, then each cause produces two classes of effects: those which are direct, and those which result indirectly from the influence exerted by it on other causes: for indeed these direct and indirect effects are apt to become so intricately interwoven that they can by no means be disentangled. So far the results are negative: they seem to indicate that the task of following out and understanding the combined action of several causes, which are in various degrees mutually interdependent, is beyond the power of human faculty. But a way out of the difficulty was found, chiefly under the guidance of Leibnitz and Newton. An epoch-making process of reasoning showed that, though the indirect effects might grow cumulatively, and ere long become considerable, yet at first they would be very small indeed relatively to the direct effects. Hence it was concluded that a study of the tendency to change, resulting from each of several disturbing causes, might be made the starting point for a broad study of the influence of several factors acting together. This principle is the foundation of the victory of analytical methods in many fields of science. . . ."[37]

It is but a short step from this position to the assertion of the negligibility of the indirect effects and a full-blown partial analysis.[38] This is equiv-

[37] A. Marshall, (1), pp. 677–8. Quoted by permission.
[38] H. Moore, (1), pp. 24–5.

alent to substituting zeros for the off-diagonal terms in the matrix of a general system depicting an equilibrium displacement, or to eliminating interdependence of variables from the original interrelationships by placing most of the variables among the data and holding them constant.

Certainly this has proved to be a productive analytical method—indeed, to date, few have been the economic laws or hypotheses which have not been derived from its use. So great is its predominance in Anglo-American economics that we need not consider it in this work. Rather, we shall somewhat idealistically follow less well-known paths of a great deal less analytical promise, but with the compensating reward of leading to heights from which new perspectives and a panoramic view of the whole economic terrain may be attained.

PART II

THE NEOCLASSICAL CONSTRUCTION

CHAPTER 2

THE EXCHANGE ECONOMY

1. Simple Exchange

In the progression from simple to more complicated general models, a convenient starting point is the classic Robinson Crusoe economy. In the *Robinsonade*, a single decision-making unit must allocate given quantities of scarce wherewithal among desired ends whose attainment requires use of the means at known rates of transformation. Wicksell's view that such economies are in reality the simplest of exchange economies is adopted here as a useful one.[1] Böhm-Bawerk's famous pioneer, who had to allocate five sacks of grain among competing uses, was actually engaged in an exchange process with himself, transforming one set of satisfactions into another at fixed technological coefficients of transformation within the limits of his stock of means.

From one narrow point of view, the only essential differences between the decisionmaking of Robinson and that of the consumer in the social setting of the market place are that the coefficients of transformation are prices in the social economy rather than technological input ratios and that the means constraint has a value dimension. We may take advantage of this similarity by placing the consumer in the midst of a social economy rather than an isolated one to construct a model for the prediction of his choices under varying regimes of prices and quantities of wherewithal. The data of the model of simple exchange are the following:

1.a. The Preferences of the Consumer Among Alternative Uses of the Resources

Unless we desire to predict them from a grander system, it is necessary to begin the analysis with a statement of the consumer's preferences over his relevant "action space," i.e., the entire set of actions he may initiate to employ resources. It is requisite to specify preferences over actions rather than the outcomes of those actions in order to take into account the fact that the decisionmaker may not control all of the factors which will dictate the resultant outcome. It is possible to specify certain types of environment in which decisions must be made by distinguishing the various regimes ruling over the factors beyond the consumer's control.

1. The Environment of Perfect Certainty. In this situation one can relate the action and its consequence or outcome in a one-to-one manner, since all factors linking them are under the control of the consumer. This

[1] K. Wicksell, (1), p. 53. Also U. Ricci, (2), pp. 2, 32, reduces all economic acts to sets of exchanges in the sense defined above.

environment is the one for which the neoclassical theory of consumer choice was developed.

2. The Perfect Risk Environment. Under these circumstances each action of the consumer can lead to any one of a set of outcomes known in full detail to the consumer. Given a consumer's choice of action, which of these outcomes will in fact eventuate is determined by factors completely beyond the influence of the consumer, although he does possess a set of information allowing him to predict in the large but not in the small. This holds by virtue of the existence of an objective probability distribution over all possible outcomes of a given consumer action, which distribution is assumed to be known to the consumer for every action in the action space. In the simplest case, the action may be the purchase of a lottery ticket with three mutually exclusive outcomes: then, in the pure-risk environment, the probabilities of each outcome are fixed and known to the consumer.

A simplified tableau may be used to illustrate these two environments:

TABLE 2-1. A Tableau for Consumer Decisionmaking

		Opponent's Strategy Set S			
		S_1	S_2	. . . .	S_n
Consumer's Action	A_1	0_{11}	0_{12}	. . . .	0_{1n}
	A_2	0_{21}	0_{22}	. . . .	0_{2n}
Set A	.	.	.	. . . .	.
	.	.	.	. . . .	.
	.	.	.	. . . .	.
	.	.	.	. . . .	.
	A_m	0_{m1}	0_{m2}	. . . .	0_{mn}

In the tableau an "Opponent" has been created who is viewed as choosing a "state" from a known set S with n elements $S_1, \ldots, S_n$; the outcome to a consumer, symbolized by the 0-terms in the table, is a joint result of the choice of the consumer from his "action" set A with m elements $A_1, \ldots, A_m$, and the Opponent's choice of a state.

In the pure risk environment the Opponent may be viewed as "Nature," choosing among her states in a nonpurposive manner: for any A_i, her choices follow a probability distribution $(p_1, \ldots, p_n)_i$, such that $p_j \geqq 0$ and $\Sigma p_j = 1$. The case of pure certainty is the special case of pure risk when, for each A_i, the associated probability vector has only one non-zero p_j-element.

3. The Game-Theoretic Environment. In this environment there exists a purposive, cognitive, perceptive Opponent who recognizes that his welfare is opposed in greater or lesser degree to the welfare of the consumer. He is expected to choose from his strategy set in full anticipation of the consumer's imminent choice, and, therefore, the consumer's choice must be conditioned by this expectation. This environment represents a

sharp break from the patterns of predictability possible in the first two environments, akin to the difference between the game of solitaire and the game of poker. We may further complicate the environment by creating one or more additional opponents, all of whose interests are in conflict with the consumer's and each other's.

4. The Risk-Game-Theoretic Environment. In this environment both game-theoretic and risk elements are involved in the administration of the factors outside the consumer's control. For example, the outcomes in Table 2-1 might themselves be probability distributions over some set of payoffs, while the opponent or opponents choose a strategy in a game-theoretic environment.

5. The Imperfectly Uncertain Environment. This environment is a rather omnibus category, perhaps most representative of the typical environment in which the firm operates and in which no objective probability function can be said to characterize the opponent's choices, no game-theoretic opponent exists, or, if he does exist, dominates the control of factors external to the consumer sphere of discretion. On the other hand, from more or less vaguely held hypotheses, formed perhaps in an indirect, intuitive way from previous experiences, the decisionmaker does not act as if he were wholly ignorant of the likelihood of emergence of the various states of nature. It might be possible to quantify these vague hunches of the decisionmaker and thereby derive a subjective "probability" distribution, which, at least in a surface fashion, would convert the environment to one of risk. In most instances, however, it is more likely that new techniques will have to be adopted to cope with decisionmaking under its regime.

6. The Environment of Perfect Uncertainty. Lastly, as a polar analogue to the case of perfect certainty, we may define an environment where the consumer may be said to possess *absolutely* no information of the likelihood of the emergence of states from the set S. Perfect ignorance is not easy to come by, but it may be defined to exist if two conditions are met:

a. the consumer's choices are unaffected by any system of numbering the states S_j. If the consumer really has no ideas concerning the likelihood of occurrence of S_{15}, he must attach no significance to any labelling we may use to identify it. This would be true, however, not only if he were completely ignorant of the likelihood of emergence of every state, but also if he regarded each as equally likely—hardly a state of ignorance. Therefore, a second condition must be met before complete ignorance is attained.

b. if two states of nature have the same outcomes, row by row, in the tableau, the elimination of one of them must have no effect upon the consumer's choice of an action. Suppose S_1 and S_2 met these conditions:

then if we combined them into one state, $S_{1,2}$, by deleting, say, S_2, the new state would not be less likely to occur than S_1 or S_2 taken singly, but if the consumer were absolutely ignorant about the likelihood of either state he could not say it was more likely to occur.

This classification does not exhaust the possible environments in which the consumer might be viewed as operating. For example, there are environments in which not all of the actions he might take are known to him; not all the states of nature which may eventuate are known to him; not all outcomes are known to him, even in a probability sense; and so forth. Indeed, in the descriptions of these idealized environments, the consumer is uncommonly well-informed, knowing all of his own and the opponent's action potentials, as well as all of the outcomes eventuating from the conjunction of any pair of these actions. The case of absolute ignorance (perfect uncertainty) is defined to imply lack of information only about the likelihood of the known alternative states with their known outcomes—really a quite limited degree of ignorance! In this book, however, we shall limit ourselves to analyses of decisionmaking for environments appearing in the preceding listing, and specifically for environments (1), (2), (3), and (6).

Although we have defined these environments with the consumer as the decisionmaker, they are equally applicable to the firm's decision processes. Since environments (1) and (2) are of greatest interest in consumer theory, we shall treat them in this chapter. In Chapter 3, where we shall construct models of firm behavior, we shall treat environments (1) and (6). In Chapters 8 and 9 we shall have occasion to employ the game-theoretic model. The problem at hand, therefore, is how best to specify consumer preferences over his action space for environments of perfect certainty and of perfect risk.

The term "best" is given a wholly pragmatic definition. The manner of specifying—let us use the term "measuring"—consumer preference should be operational; i.e., we should be capable of specifying a set of operations by which preferences may be derived from information concerning the consumer. Also, the method of measurement must be of at least that degree of uniqueness required for the validity of the types of operations imposed by the models into which the preferences will fit as data. These two requirements alone are basic to the task of recording the consumer's preferences, but neoclassical and modern theorists have not always seen the task in these terms.

1.a.1. The Utility Function: Preference Measurement vs. Welfare Measurement

The neoclassical approach to the job of defining consumer preferences generally took a quite different tack, although it did obtain a measure of preferences from the process. The treatment of "utility" by Walras, Jevons, Menger, Böhm-Bawerk, Edgeworth, and Marshall left little doubt that they considered it not an index of preference-measurement but rather the measurement of a subjective psychological state associated with the consequences of taking certain consumption actions.[2] Wants were considered more or less intense on some scale of psychological calibration, and the elemental quantity in which interest centered was the unit of want-intensity existent within the individual. Utility measured the intensity of wants satisfied not only by differing amounts of the same good but by differing kinds of goods, metering the number of units of these wants-intensities a given basket of goods could satisfy.

This approach concentrates upon the level of welfare attained by an individual during a given period. It focusses upon the consequences of consumption choices rather than upon the acts of choice themselves. We may illustrate the type of reasoning which follows from this outlook by using an example of Böhm-Bawerk's which attempted to show, in the context of the simple exchange economy, that the line of causation in pricing runs from the "utility" of goods to the valuation of factor services, rather than in the opposite direction as implied in cost-of-production theories.[3]

[2] Cf. G. Stigler, (2), pp. 315–8, and especially: "Without exception, the founders accepted the existence of utility as a fact of common experience, congruent with the most casual introspection." (P. 316)

Even if we include the name of Pareto with those of the group above, Irving Fisher must be singled out as the one theorist most consistently opposed to linking utility to psychological concepts of pleasure:

> "The plane of contact between psychology and economics is *desire*. It is difficult to see why so many theorists endeavor to obliterate the distinction between pleasure and desire. No one has ever denied that economic acts have the invariable antecedent desire. Whether the necessary antecedent of desire is 'pleasure' or whether independently of pleasure it may sometimes be 'duty' or 'fear' concerns a phenomenon in the second remove from the economic act of choice and is completely within the realm of psychology." (P. 11)

Also:

> " . . . while utility has an original 'common sense' meaning related to feelings, when economics attempts to be a positive science, it must seek a definition which connects it with objective *commodity*." (P. 15)

These quotations are from I. Fisher, (1).

A vigorous dissent is raised by Antonelli to the inclusion of Walras as a utility theorist in the sense to which Fisher is objecting. Antonelli views Walras as reacting against the psychological school associated with the names of Gossen and the German psychologist, Herbart, to follow the lead of Cournot in emphasizing revealed exchanges in the market place. Antonelli also attempts to show, in support of this position, that Walras treated utility as ordinally measurable, largely on the grounds that Poincaré, in a letter to Walras in 1901, revealed to him the possibility of ordinal measurement. To the present author, both arguments are completely unconvincing. See E. Antonelli (1), pp. 17–9, 63, 66–70.

[3] The following analysis is based upon Book III, Chs. 7 and 10, of E. von Böhm-Bawerk, (1), pp. 162–5, and 179–89, especially pp. 185–9.

Böhm-Bawerk believed that if he worked with the total utility functions deriving from goods which were not infinitely divisible, i.e., "step" functions which are not smooth and everywhere differentiable, he could isolate this direction of causation. Suppose in a Robinson Crusoe economy, under conditions of certainty, a consumer can produce three goods Y_j, $j = 1, 2, 3$, using a given stock of scarce factor Z. Technology dictates

TABLE 2-2. TOTAL UTILITY SCHEDULES

Units of Y_j	Total Utility of:		
	Y_1	Y_2	Y_3
0	0	0	0
1	400	630	420
2	700	1130	780
. . . .	.	.	.
. . . .	.	.	.

that a unit of Y_1 requires 4 units of Z, Y_2 requires 5 units of Z, and Y_3 requires 6 units, while only 100 units of Z are available for the given time period. Lastly, assume independence of the utilities of the three goods, so that the satisfaction derived from Y_j depends only upon the amount of Y_j consumed. Let these total utility schedules be those depicted in Table 2-2. The marginal utilities of Y_j and the marginal utilities per unit of Z of the Y_j are shown in Table 2-3.

TABLE 2-3. MARGINAL UTILITY SCHEDULES

Units of Y_j	Marginal Utility of:			Marginal Utility Per Unit of Z of:		
	Y_1	Y_2	Y_3	Y_1	Y_2	Y_3
0	—	—	—	—	—	—
1	400	630	420	100	126	70
2	300	500	360	75	100	60
. . . . . .	.	.	.	.	.	.
. . . . . .	.	.	.	.	.	.
. . . . . .	.	.	**66**	.	.	**11**
. . . . . .	**40**	.	48	**10**	.	8
. . . . . .	36	.	.	9	.	.
. . . . . .	.	**70**	.	.	**14**	.
. . . . . .	.	40	.	.	8	.

The marginal utility of each quantity of Y_j is divided by the number of units of Z required to produce it to obtain the marginal utility per unit of Z; more properly, this last concept is the average incremental utility per unit of the factor.

Let a_{zj} be the unit resource requirement for Y_j. Then, assuming the consumer will not be satiated in all goods, and assuming the equilibrium allocation of Z just exhausts the amount available, the requirements for a maximum-of-utility equilibrium may be stated:

$$(1) \quad \begin{aligned} &1. \quad \frac{u_j^e}{a_{zj}} \geqq \frac{u_k^{e+1}}{a_{zk}}, \quad \text{for each } j, k = 1, \ldots, 3 \\ &\qquad\qquad\qquad\qquad\qquad j = 1, \ldots, 3 \\ &2. \quad \sum_j a_{zj} X_j^{\circ} = Z \end{aligned}$$

where u_j^e is the marginal utility of the last unit of Y_j purchased, u_j^{e+1} is the marginal utility of the next unit of Y_j, and X_j° is the equilibrium quantity of Y_j purchased. In Table 2-3 it is assumed that this equilibrium is reached where $\frac{u_1^e}{4} = 10$, $\frac{u_2^e}{5} = 14$, and $\frac{u_3^e}{6} = 11$. Had Böhm-Bawerk adopted utility functions which were smooth and an infinitely divisible resource service Z, these values would have been equal, of course. But, since the discrete steps in the functions yield these inequalities, he poses the question: what is the "true" utility value of a unit of Z? How should the consumer value a unit of factor service?

He answers: at the value 10, the least important of the equilibrium uses, since a loss of a unit of Z (neglecting the lumpiness of its uses) would lead consumers to sacrifice $\frac{1}{4}$ unit of Y_1. But, if the marginal unit of Z is worth 10, all units of Z are worth 10; if a unit of Z is worth 10, then the "true" marginal utility of Y_1 must be the value $a_{z1} \times 10$, of Y_2 the value $a_{z2} \times 10$, and of Y_3 the value $a_{z3} \times 10$, or 40, 50, and 60 units of utility respectively. These contrast with the values 40, 70, and 66 from which the boldface values in Table 2-3 were obtained.

Now the purpose served by the "true" marginal utility of a unit of factor in Böhm-Bawerk's scheme is to indicate the rates at which the consumer's measure of want-intensity would decline if one unit of Z were lost. "If we are estimating what amount of wellbeing a productive instrument brings us, we look, naturally, first of all to the product which we get from it, and then, beyond that, to the wellbeing which that product brings us."[4] In this, given the assumptions implicit in his measure of utility, his discussion is correct, since the "true" utility contingent upon having the 100th unit of Z is 10, not 11 or 14.

Let U_j denote the total utility schedules for Y_j as written in Table 2-2. Then, obviously, any other utility schedule which would have yielded the same marginal utility schedules as those of Table 2-3 would serve Böhm-Bawerk's purpose. For example, if to any or all of the Y_j columns in Table 2-2 a constant a_j had been added, the new schedules would yield the same marginal utility schedules and would therefore be acceptable. Moreover, if *all* of the Y_j columns were multiplied by some constant $k > 0$, the marginal utility values would be uniformly k times larger than their

[4] E. von Böhm-Bawerk, (1), p. 183.

values in Table 2-3. This would merely indicate that the unit of utility in which they were measured was $1/k^{th}$ as large as the original unit, but the measurements in both instances would be no more different than the same length expressed in yards or feet. Further, if both operations were performed—the addition of a constant to U_j and multiplication by a positive constant—the marginal utilities would be the same except for the change in unit of measurement. If U_j^* is defined as

$$U_j^* = a_j + kU_j, \qquad k > 0 \tag{2}$$

then U_j^* is as acceptable for Böhm-Bawerk's purposes as U_j—it is, indeed, the same welfare index except for origin and unit of calibration. Total utility schedules which are positive linear transformations of U_j possess the quality of being measures of welfare unique up to a linear transformation, yield marginal utility schedules which are unique up to a positive multiplicative constant, and allow Böhm-Bawerk's measurement of welfare adjustments at the margin to be meaningful. This kind of measurement we shall term "cardinal measurement" and the family of total utility functions defined by Equation (2) we shall term cardinal utility or preference functions.

But, for all his constructions, Böhm-Bawerk and his contemporaries were not really and essentially concerned with changes in the state of the consumer's psyche. Their requirement of a utility schedule was wholly pragmatic: they were interested in predicting *ex ante facto* the consumer's choices among alternatives from his utility function, not in measuring his differential welfare among these alternatives. In terms of Böhm-Bawerk's problem, what really interested him about the values of u_j^e was their ability to predict which of the goods Y_j would be reduced in quantity if the consumer lost a unit of Z. This realization, first seen by Fisher and Pareto, marked the beginning of a second phase of "utility" reasoning in economic theory.

1.a.2. The Utility Function: Cardinal Measurement vs. Ordinal Measurement

We return to Table 2-3 with this more limited aim in mind: to predict the good whose quantity would be reduced if the consumer lost a unit of Z. Certainly U_j and its marginal utilities u_j would yield the correct prediction—assuming that Böhm-Bawerk had somehow obtained a measurement of preference unique up to a linear transformation and that the consumer acted consistently with what he said he would do. It follows, also, that any U_j^* and their marginal preference schedules u_j^* would, under the same assumptions, yield the same prediction. However, except for the unrealistic case of independent utilities, neither Böhm-Bawerk nor his neoclassical contemporaries were able to define a set of operations by which cardinal preference functions could be derived from (1) the responses of the consumer to questions concerning his preferences among baskets of goods and (2) the assumption of transitivity of choice.

Operationally, to derive a preference function one must proceed as follows. Assume three baskets of goods, A, B, and C, were offered to the consumer. He must be asked, for example, if he prefers A to B, B to A, or is indifferent between them, and a similar procedure can be employed for B and C. Alternatively, this information may be obtained from his past actions. If he prefers A to B and B to C, if we assume that transitivity is an intuitively plausible axiom for a "rational" consumer to follow, we need not question him about A and C but may assume that he prefers A to C. Thus, in the interests of time-saving, the preference function obtained in this manner will contain in itself, as part of the data of the consumer choice model, a great deal of prediction as well as observation.[5]

If, however, the only purpose for "measuring" such preferences is to predict consumer actions in the situation depicted by Böhm-Bawerk's problem, it is possible to sacrifice a good deal of the "uniqueness" of the measurement. Indeed, any set of functions which keeps the measures of marginal preferences per unit of factor in the same *order* as the ranking revealed by $\frac{u_2^e}{a_{z2}} > \frac{u_3^e}{a_{z3}} > \frac{u_1^e}{a_{z1}}$ will yield the same solution as obtained in (1). Since the a_{zj} factors are constant, this implies that the ranking of the u_j^e in Table 2-3 (which have not been recorded there but are derivable) must be preserved to obtain the same prediction. And, since we are interested in the nonspecific solutions to (1) it will be necessary that the ranking of the u_j for all quantities of goods be preserved by any new index if predictions are to be the same for all relevant sets of data a_{zj} and Z.

Such an index will be defined by m_j, where

$$(3) \qquad m_j = m_j(u_j), \qquad m_j' > 0$$

which will hold if total preference functions are obtained for which the values, M_j, are related to U_j as

$$(4) \qquad M_j = M_j(U_j), \qquad M_j' > 0$$

For, by assumption,

$$(5) \qquad U_j = F_j(X_j)$$

and

$$(6) \qquad u_j = \frac{dU_j}{dX_j} = F_j'$$

[5] For the moment, we assume the existence of an ordinal index of preference. For three goods, if the consumer can always order baskets in terms of preference or indifference, and if transitivity holds at all times, the integrability conditions hold and an index exists. When more than three goods exist, the transitivity relation must be replaced by more complicated relations involving chains of baskets in order that the consumer's preferences be consistent and therefore describable by a preference function. See Section 2.b.2.a. of this chapter.

Substituting (5) into (4),

$$M_j = M_j(F_j(X_j)) \tag{7}$$

And

$$m_j = \frac{dM_j}{dX_j} = M_j'F_j' = M_j'u_j \tag{8}$$

Since $M_j' > 0$ by (4) it follows that $m_j' > 0$.

A total utility function such as that in (4) measures preferences unique up to a monotone transformation. Such functions retain the ordering of the preferences of the consumer and may be constructed from the consumer's answers to our questions plus the assumption of transitivity. As we shall see, the ability to derive operational theorems from the model of consumer choice to be constructed with such preference functions as data is only slightly less than that in models where cardinal measurement of these preferences is possible. Such functions, alternative for all practical purposes to cardinal measurement for the derivation of the same hypotheses from our models, are ordinal functions, and the measurement they yield is an ordinal measurement. In the two-commodity case, they yield the familiar two-dimensional indifference curves of economic theory.[6]

We may refer to "preference functions" rather than "utility functions," since the above analysis allows us to "precipitate out" the neoclassical assumption that there exists a meaningful subjective entity called "utility." Its assumed existence is not a requisite to perform the tasks for which a function describing consumer tastes is needed. The field of economics finds itself in the situation which Poincaré describes below:

"No theory seemed more solid than that of Fresnel which attributed light to the movements of the ether. Nevertheless, Maxwell's is now preferred. Does this mean the work of Fresnel has been in vain? No, for the goal of Fresnel was not to know if there really was an ether, if it was or was not made up of atoms, if these atoms really moved this or that direction; it was to predict optical phenomena. Now, Fresnel's theory

[6] Although Edgeworth put forward the concept of ordinal measurement and indifference varieties before Pareto, he derived the curves from an existent cardinal utility surface. It was Pareto, working in the opposite direction from indifference maps to the preference function, who broached the important questions concerning the measurability of preferences, although his answers, as in the case of the integrability conditions to be discussed shortly, were sometimes not satisfactory. For this analysis of indifference varieties, see V. Pareto (2), pp. 539–57, and also M. Brodsky (1), pp. 119–20.

Yet, it is interesting that Pareto retained the assumption of cardinal measurability of preferences by virtue of the second of two postulates in his analysis (V. Pareto (2), pp. 574–7). His first assumption is that the consumer is able to order baskets of goods by preference, and the second assumption is that the consumer can order the *increments* in preference indices between baskets of goods. This second assumption

permits this today as well as it did before Maxwell's theory. The differential equations are still true; they can still be interpreted by the same methods and the results retain their value forever."[7]

---

can be shown to be equivalent to the assumption of measurement of preferences unique up to a linear transformation.

Let X denote the set of baskets of goods in the consumer's action space and let X_1, X_2, and X_3 denote three different baskets from the set. Let

$$U = F(X) \tag{1}$$

be a cardinal utility function, and

$$M = G(X) = M(U), \qquad G' > 0 \tag{2}$$

an ordinal preference function over the same set.

If Pareto's second postulate holds, then

$$\text{sign}\,[(G(X_3) - G(X_2)) - (G(X_2) - G(X_1))] = \text{sign}\,[(F(X_3) - F(X_2)) - (F(X_2) - F(X_1))] \tag{3}$$

for all such comparisons between elements in X.

For k_1, $0 < k_1 < 1$, define a new basket of goods, $X_{1,2}$,

$$X_{1,2} = (1 - k_1)X_1 + k_1X_2 \tag{4}$$

and for k_2, $0 < k_2 < 1$, define $X_{2,3}$,

$$X_{2,3} = (1 - k_2)X_2 + k_2X_3 \tag{5}$$

By the mean value theorem, under the appropriate continuity assumptions for $F(X)$,

$$(F(X_3) - F(X_2)) - (F(X_2) - F(X_1)) = dF(X_{2,3}) - dF(X_{1,2}) \tag{6}$$

and

$$(G(X_3) - G(X_2)) - (G(X_2) - G(X_1)) = dG(X_{2,3}) - dG(X_{1,2}) \tag{7}$$

From (2), (7) may be written

$$(G(X_3) - G(X_2)) - (G(X_2) - G(X_1)) = M'F(X_{2,3})dF(X_{2,3}) - M'F(X_{1,2})dF(X_{1,2}) \tag{8}$$

Let

$$(G(X_3) - G(X_2)) - (G(X_2) - G(X_1)) = 0 \tag{9}$$

It follows from (8)

$$M'F(X_{2,3})dF(X_{2,3}) - M'F(X_{1,2})dF(X_{1,2}) = 0 \tag{10}$$

But, from (3) and (6), substituted into (10),

$$M'F(X_{2,3}) = M'F(X_{1,2}) \tag{11}$$

which implies that M' is a constant, and

$$M'F(X_{2,3})dF(X_{2,3}) - M'F(X_{1,2})\,dF(X_{1,2}) = dF(X_{2,3}) - dF(X_{1,2}) \tag{12}$$

can hold only if M' is a constant. Thus, (11) is necessary and sufficient. Integrating,

$$G(X) = a + bF(X) \tag{13}$$

where $b = M'$. Therefore, $G(X)$ is in fact unique up to a linear transformation by virtue of Pareto's second assumption. This proof is due to O. Lange, (1) and (2).

[7] H. Poincaré, (1), pp. 189–90. Quoted by permission.

Neoclassical "utility" was a kind of economic ether: an element whose assumed existence was merely a convenient medium for the analytical transmission of the observable phenomena of consumer choice. Since other means have proved capable of yielding the same predictions of these phenomena, the assumption of its existence is simply not needed. To assert this is not to deny that operational theorems about consumer behavior can be obtained from the neoclassical theory, nor that they can be tested against reality. We may merely derive most of these theorems without this subjective ether.

But, while it laid to rest the ghost of cardinal measurement of utility, the cardinalist-ordinalist controversy retained some of the superfluous assumptions inherited from the welfare interpretation of "utility." Cardinalists like Jevons had struggled with the belief that "utility" was "inherently" a nonmeasurable phenomenon in the cardinal sense, only to ignore such misgivings and to assume it to be so. The ordinalists, able to reject the need for such measurement, tended to justify their position on the grounds that the "desirability" of goods for consumers was inherently a matter of the consumer's ordering of such goods in terms of preference. Was "utility" quantitative in the cardinal sense or "qualitative" in this latter sense? Implicit in the arguments was Pareto's distinction between the existence of feelings of relative desirability in the consumer's psyche and practical methods of measuring such feelings.[8] Today economic theorists would respond that the question does not concern the inherent measurability or nonmeasurability in the cardinal sense of a property. Rather the question hinges upon the ingenuity of investigators in designing procedures to measure displayed preferences unique up to a linear transformation, the lack of ingenuity displayed in defining them "only" unique up to a monotone transformation, or whether the science has succeeded in obtaining any type of measurement of preferences.

1.a.3. *The Utility Function: The Operational View*

Tacitly, in this cardinalist-ordinalist discussion of the question, the existence of "utility" as a psychological property of the relation of goods-and-subject is accepted. But this hypothesis is part of the "economic ether" that can be eliminated along with the assumption of cardinal measurability. It leads to the view of the preference function as the depiction of a state of the consumer's psyche for use in a maximization model which yields choices by *imitating* the purposive or intuitive mental processes of the consumer. The consumer is viewed as being guided in his decisionmaking by the desire to maximize his well-being as indexed by the preference function.[9]

[8] V. Pareto, (1), I, p. 8.

[9] See, for example, the presentation of his "postulate of rationality" in Lange, (7), pp. 29–32.

The operational view of consumer's choice analysis begins from the position that a concept is synonomous with the operations defined to obtain it. Thus, "utility" is the designation of a numerical index to represent the preferential ordering relationships by the consumer over baskets of goods as revealed by his responses to questions (or his actions) plus any assumptions accepted by the analyst. The consumer is seen as doing what he desires to do, apart from any concept of psychological welfare maximization except the purely tautological one. This information is gathered *by the economist* in the form of a preference function, and, to predict the current actions of the consumer from the information contained in the function, *the economist maximizes* the function, subject to constraints, to find out what the consumer said or actually did before the current analysis, either directly or by implication.

The preference function thus becomes a repository of observed behavior, or of response to questions, or of these and assumptions such as transitivity which economize on the direct evidence needed to construct the function. The process of maximizing is a convention adopted for convenience by the economist, and the purpose of the models of consumer choice which we shall build is seen as the *definition* of the consumer's choices, not their prediction, except (1) to the extent that assumptions were used to fill gaps in the construction of the preference function, and (2) in the trivial sense that the consumer does what he said he would do or did in the past. The degree to which the models of consumer choice yield information which is wholly tautological or yield theorems for testing depends upon the extent to which assumptions have been made in the construction of the preference function.[10]

The consumer cannot be said to be consulting his preference function to attain some optimum; rather, the economist has constructed the function to be at a maximum when the desired prediction is at hand. The consumer is not acting "as if" he were maximizing the value of the index: the index is maximized because the consumer is doing what he said or implied he would do.

1.a.4. The Measurement of Preference

Having traced the development of the concept of utility, we now turn to the task of defining the consumer's preferences among a set of actions for (*a*) the pure certainty environment and (b) the pure risk environment.

1.a.4.a. The Preference Function For Pure Certainty

Let us now return to Böhm-Bawerk's problem and construct continuous, differentiable functions instead of the "step" functions used by Böhm-Bawerk. In the remainder of this book, we shall symbolize a

[10] See R. Luce, (1), Ch. 2, especially pp. 16–7, and A. Alchian, (1), p. 31.

preference function which yields cardinal measurements of the consumer's desires in the following manner:

$$U = F([X]) \tag{9}$$

where $[X]$ designates an element in the whole set of consumer actions. We shall assume $F([X])$ is continuous and differentiable, possessing derivatives at least of the first and second order, unless noted otherwise. The function will be interpreted with the operational meaning in mind.

Similarly, in the remainder of the book we shall designate a consumer preference function which yields only ordinal measurements of preference in the following manner:

$$M = G([X]) \tag{10}$$

The same conditions are assumed to hold as those stated immediately above for (9).

1.a.4.b. The Preference Function for Pure Risk

When the definition of the preference function is extended into the pure risk environment to define the consumer's preferences over a set of actions, several complications arise. First, we shall assume at the outset that an ordinal preference index over all the outcomes, treated as occurring with certainty, is available for the consumer. Further, it will be treated as an operational preference function, with the tautological significance this implies. However, when this ordinal function is used as the basis for deriving a preference function over the actions under known probability conditions, we shall treat this latter function as a predictive function. That is, the preference function for pure risk environments is *not* derived from the direct questioning of the individual about risky choices to obtain information which merely requires recording. Further assumptions, with much less intuitive plausibility than that of transitivity of preferences in conditions of certainty, must be made to obtain the desired function. The consumer will be treated *as if* he were maximizing the preference index in the sense to be defined, and an intensive study will be made of the characteristics of his decisionmaking which will lead to the *as if* behavior.

Note again that the distinction between the operational preference function and the preference function which is viewed as containing nonobserved phenomena is not a clear-cut one. The assumption of transitivity made in the construction of the preference function in perfect certainty injects, as we have seen, an element of the nonobserved into that function. Also, it would be possible conceptually to present all hypothetical situations of choice under risk in given circumstances to a consumer and ask him to indicate his choices, record them, and use the maximization convention to recollect this data in the future. The distinction revolves, therefore, about the interpreter's subjective evaluation of the "importance" of the role of any assumptions made in the definition of the function to lessen the task of data collection and of the intuitive plausibility of such assumptions.

Second, the function we seek must be of that degree of uniqueness characterized by cardinal measurability. It has proved to be impossible to date, except for the case of independent utilities, to construct such a preference function for conditions of perfect certainty. Fortunately, the ingenuity of von Neumann and Morgenstern has evolved a method for obtaining such a cardinal function for the risk environment.

In a *Robinsonade*, assume that some happy circumstance has freed one unit of Z (say labor) for one period from its current employment without lessening current output. The action space for Robinson contains three alternative uses for the unit of labor: A_1, which consists of using it on free land to grow more wheat; A_2, which denotes the use of it on free land to grow melons; and A_3, which indicates its use as leisure. We assume that all of the extra labor must be used in one of these pursuits, so that the alternative actions are mutually exclusive as well as exhaustive.

The outcomes of these actions, once initiated by Robinson, are wholly dependent upon the states of nature generated by "the weather." Robinson identifies two states of interest to him as composing Nature's strategy set: S_1, indicating a "rainy" period for the time span over which Robinson is planning, and S_2, a "dry" period. There are, therefore, six alternative outcomes in Robinson's tableau. We assume that wheat does well in a dry season but poorly in a wet season; that melons do poorly in a dry season but well in a wet season; and that leisure is quite enjoyable in a dry season but much less so in a rainy season.

The outcome resulting from the choice of A_i and S_j will be denoted O_{ij}. The first step in the analysis is to obtain from Robinson an ordinal index of preference over all the outcomes if they were received with certainty. We shall consider this decisionmaking as marginal, concerned as it is with the allocation of an extra unit of Z, and shall therefore symbolize the ordinal index values attached to the O_{ij} by the lower case letters m_{ij}. Suppose the outcomes were ranked by Robinson in the following order:

$$O_{21} > O_{32} > O_{12} > O_{22} > O_{11} > O_{31} \tag{11}$$

where (>) symbolizes the expression "is preferred to." Then, since we need only an ordinal index, any set of numerical values m_{ij} which retains this ordering will be acceptable as a preference index over the alternatives considered as certain outcomes. For example, let us adopt the m_{ij} values in Table 2-4.

A second set of data required is the set of probabilities over Nature's states; i.e., from Robinson's experience on his island, it is assumed that he can specify the probability that the coming period will be rainy or dry. Let p_1 be the probability that the period will be rainy and p_2 the probability it will be dry, $p_j \geqq 0$, $j = 1, 2$, $p_1 + p_2 = 1$. In this case it is assumed that the same probability distribution will rule over Nature's strategies regardless of Robinson's choice of an action, although in other contexts this need not be true.

TABLE 2-4. A First Ordinal Preference Function Over the Outcomes

		Nature's Strategy Set S	
		S_1 (rainy)	S_2 (dry)
Robinson's	A_1 (wheat)	5	22
Action Set A	A_2 (melons)	35	11
	A_3 (leisure)	3	25

From these two separate bodies of information we seek to construct a preference function *over the actions* A_i to allow us to predict Robinson's choices if the "play" of his "Opponent" were to change and follow any new probability distribution meeting the conditions $p_j \geqq 0$, $\Sigma p_j = 1$. We might hypothesize any of a number of simple methods for deriving an index over the actions for a given probability vector $[p]$. First, if Robinson were a more or less reckless person, as he might be at the margin, he may identify his preference for every action with the preference value for that outcome which is most-preferred for that action. Thus, he might adopt a preference value $m_{a_1} = 22$, since that is the highest value obtainable from choosing A_1, and similarly by this rule $m_{a_2} = 35$, and $m_{a_3} = 25$.

Second, if he were an extremely conservative person, he might go to the opposite extreme and identify his preference for each action with a preference value equal to the worst outcome's m_{ij}. In this case, $m_{a_1} = 5$, $m_{a_2} = 11$, and $m_{a_3} = 3$.

We may react negatively to both of these simple assumptions on the rather plausible grounds that they reflect a preoccupation with only one aspect of an explicitly two-dimensional problem. The consumer in both cases concentrates upon his preferences for outcomes under conditions of certainty, wholly neglecting probabilities. He is assumed to treat his decisions in the pure risk environment as of the same essence as those in the pure certainty environment, and it may be doubted that Robinson would do so.

Third, therefore, let us go to the other extreme and raise the probability element in the problem to predominance. Robinson may tag every action with the preference value of that outcome which occurs in the column of the most probable state of Nature. For example, suppose $p_1 = .1$ and $p_2 = .9$. Then, under this assumption, $m_{a_1} = 22$, $m_{a_2} = 11$, and $m_{a_3} = 25$. But such a procedure ignores the preference values for outcomes other than those in one column, and could lead to some intuitively implausible valuations of actions. For example, if $p_1 = .49$ and $p_2 = .51$, the valuation of A_2 at 11 might seem strange, and if $p_1 = .51$, the corresponding valuations of A_1 and A_3 would seem implausible.

It seems desirable, therefore, to derive the preference values over the actions from a set of assumptions which leads to a *joint* consideration of the m_{ij} and the p_j. A large number of ways to achieve this desideratum exists, but the most famous of them is to multiply a utility measure in the row A_i by its column p_j and to sum these products across the row to obtain the preference value for A_i. Let u_{ij} be this utility measure for 0_{ij} (instead of m_{ij} which, as will be shown, is not acceptable). Then, u_{a_i}, the corresponding preference measure for the action A_i, is

$$u_{a_i} = \sum_j u_{ij} p_j \tag{12}$$

This preference value for A_i is called the "expected utility" of A_i.[11]

Our notation in (12) indicates that the preference values that are to be weighted by probabilities must be unique up to a linear transformation rather than only up to a monotonic transformation. A further probing of the differences between the two types of indices will be valuable in itself, and, moreover, will help to give a greater understanding of the methods now being presented. Therefore, the analysis will now turn to a demonstration of the inapplicability of the m_{ij} values in an expected-utility construction.

Suppose the formula in (12) were applied to the m_{ij} values of Table 2-4 when $p_1 = .25$ and $p_2 = .75$. We should obtain the "expected-utility" values $m_{a_1} = 17.75$, $m_{a_2} = 17$, and $m_{a_3} = 19.50$, and these index values yield the prediction that for the given m_{ij} and $[p]$, $A_3 > A_1 > A_2$. But if the m_{ij} constitute an acceptable index, Robinson's preferences over the 0_{ij}, as indicated in Table 2-4, will be accurately rendered by any other set of numbers m_{ij}^* which retains that ranking. For example, let the m_{ij}^* values in Table 2-5 constitute an alternative ordinal index over the 0_{ij}.

TABLE 2-5.
A SECOND ORDINAL PREFERENCE FUNCTION OVER THE OUTCOMES

	S_1	S_2
A_1	2	24
A_2	100	3
A_3	1	25

Both the m_{ij} and m_{ij}^* constitute ordinal preference indices containing the same information about Robinson's choices in conditions of certainty, and no basis exists for choosing one over the other for this function. Therefore,

[11] The use of this measure dates back to D. Bernoulli's use of it to escape the so-called St. Petersburg Paradox, and even earlier to a prior use by G. Cramer. For further historical data see M. Friedman (2), and G. Stigler, (3), pp. 373–7.

if ordinal indices over the 0_{ij} are capable of use in the expected-utility construction, it must be demonstrated that the predictions yielded by the analysis are invariant with the choice of ordinal index. But it is possible to demonstrate that this is not true for the indices in Tables 2-4 and 2-5. We shall use the m^*_{ij} in the formula of (12) when $p_1 = .25$ and $p_2 = .75$, and then compare the results with those obtained when the same procedure is followed with the m_{ij}.

The values of $m^*_{a_i}$ are $m^*_{a_1} = 18.5$, $m^*_{a_2} = 27.25$, and $m^*_{a_3} = 19$, yielding the predictions $A_2 > A_3 > A_1$, which are quite different from the previous predictions. The reason for these differing results is not difficult to find. The ranking of the m_{a_i} values depends upon the probability-weighted differences between the m_{ij} in the rows taken column by column. For example, from Table 2-4, the rows for A_2 and A_3 are reproduced, and $m_{21} - m_{31}$ and $m_{22} - m_{32}$ calculated:

$$\begin{array}{rr} 35 & 11 \\ -3 & -25 \\ \hline 32 & -14 \end{array} \tag{13}$$

If these are weighted by $p_1 = .25$ and $p_2 = .75$ respectively and the resulting products are added, one obtains -2.5 as the increment of expected utility between m_{a_2} and m_{a_3}, which corresponds to the difference between the original computed values. If this same procedure is repeated for the same two actions using m^*-values, we obtain from Table 2-5:

$$\begin{array}{rr} 100 & 3 \\ -1 & -25 \\ \hline 99 & -22 \end{array} \tag{14}$$

Weighting by the probabilities and adding yields an increment of 8.25.

By using an incremental analysis, the source of the contradictory predictions of the two ordinal indices is revealed. An ordinal index, which retains a ranking of preferences, merely keeps the *signs* of the relevant differences in (13) and (14) the same. Thus,

$$\text{sign}(m_{21} - m_{31}) = \text{sign}(m^*_{21} - m^*_{31}) \tag{15}$$

and so forth. But, the *absolute* values of these increments are wholly meaningless, so that in (15) as long as both increments are positive, whether the absolute value is 32 or 99 makes no difference. But, of course, it makes a great difference to the weighted sums which determine the ranking of the preference indices over the actions.

Therefore, the requirement that the ordering of the preferences over actions be invariant with the particular values of the index over the 0_{ij}

is the requirement that the increments of the type in (15) be such as to yield the same ranking of the preferences over the A_i whatever these particular values. For example, if m_{ij} were the values in one index derived in acceptable fashion, then every other index m^*_{ij} which might have been obtained by this procedure must, when used in an expected-utility framework, yield the same ranking over the actions. *One* manner of meeting these conditions is to derive an index in such a way that it and every alternative index which might have been derived differ, value by value, by an additive constant and/or a positive multiplicative constant.

For example, assume the preference values recorded in (13) were one member of such a family of functions. Then, if any number (say) 17 is added to each of the four figures in (13), increments of the form in (15) will be unchanged in value. Similarly, if each index value in (13) is multiplied by a positive constant (say) 13, the increments will retain the same sign and will have absolute values which are 13 times their values in (13). A little thought will indicate that a second index which yields increments exactly 13 times all increments in the first index can never yield a different ordering of the A_i. Lastly, if (say) 17 is added to every value and also each value is multiplied by (say) 13, the increments will again differ only by being 13 times larger in the second case as compared to the first. Thus, if the manner of obtaining an initial preference index over the 0_{ij} yields indices unique up to a linear transformation, we will have the degree of uniqueness required for the operations we desire to perform.

It was the great contribution of von Neumann and Morgenstern to have devised a method of deriving such a cardinal preference function over the 0_{ij}. The method is discussed in five steps below:

Step 1. The process begins with an ordinal preference function obtained from the consumer over the 0_{ij}, let us say the m_{ij} values of Table 2-4.

Step 2. From the table of outcomes that with the highest m_{ij} value (in Table 2-4, 0_{21}) and that with the lowest value (0_{31}) are singled out to form mutually exclusive prizes in a "lottery." In further questioning of the consumer, he is offered a "lottery option" consisting of a q probability of obtaining the most preferred outcome in the tableau, and a $1 - q$ probability of obtaining the least preferred outcome. In our case, we may symbolize this lottery option by

$$L = \{0_{21}, 0_{31}; q\} \tag{16}$$

with most-preferred outcome, least-preferred outcome, and the probability of receiving the most-preferred outcome listed in that order. When this is done we have finished with the initial need of an ordinal index over the outcomes.

Step 3. An index value is specified arbitrarily for the least-preferred outcome, say

$$u_{31} = 0 \tag{17}$$

This is, in effect, setting the origin of the index at 0 (in (17)) or at any other value desired. In the same arbitrary manner, an index value for the most preferred outcome is specified, say

$$u_{21} = 10 \tag{18}$$

This sets the length of the entire interval over which the index will range as $u_{21} - u_{31}$, and uses up the second element of arbitrariness a cardinal index allows.

Step 4. A "certainty option" is selected, i.e., an opportunity for the consumer to receive one of the outcomes which lies between the most-preferred and least-preferred, say 0_{32}, with certainty. The consumer is offered, on the one hand, 0_{32} with certainty, or, on the other hand, the lottery with a probability q of getting the most-preferred outcome, 0_{21}. If, at q, the consumer prefers the lottery option to the certainty option, q is reduced; if at q he prefers the certainty option, q is raised. For that value of q, symbolized q_{32}, at which he is indifferent between the certainty option and the lottery option, the process of changing q is stopped. Then,

$$0_{32} = \{0_{21}, 0_{31}; q_{32}\} \tag{19}$$

where the equality sign stands for "is indifferent to" in this context. This operation is repeated for every other intermediate outcome in the matrix, in our case, for 0_{11}, 0_{12}, 0_{22}, and the values q_{11}, q_{12}, and q_{22} obtained.

Step 5. Since the consumer is indifferent between the receipt of any intermediate outcome and its equivalent lottery option, we may conclude from (19) that, for example:

$$u_{32} = u(L_{32}) \tag{20}$$

where L_{32} symbolizes the lottery option equivalent to 0_{32} in the consumer's preferences, and $u(L_{32})$ denotes the "utility" or preference value of that lottery option. But, by the hypothesis of expected utility,

$$u(L_{32}) = q_{32}u_{21} + (1 - q_{32})u_{31} \tag{21}$$

That is, the preference value of a specific lottery is equal to its expected utility. Suppose $q_{32} = .875$. Then,

$$u_{32} = u(L_{32}) = .875\ (10) + .125\ (0) = 8.75 \tag{22}$$

If we repeat this operation for the remaining three intermediate outcomes, we might obtain a set of von Neumann-Morgenstern index values for Robinson as shown in Table 2-6.

Any index that we might have derived for Robinson in these circumstances would have differed from that of Table 2-6 only by another origin (adopted by specifying the utility value of the least-preferred outcome) and/or the length of the interval (determined by the origin and the specification of the preference value for the most-preferred outcome).

TABLE 2-6.
HYPOTHETICAL VON NEUMANN-MORGENSTERN PREFERENCE INDEX

	S_1	S_2
A_1	4.3	7
A_2	10	5.25
A_3	0	8.75

That is, any other preference value, u^*_{ij}, will be related to u_{ij} as the following:

$$u^*_{ij} = a + bu_{ij} \tag{23}$$

The family of preference functions will be linear transformations of one another.[12]

The von Neumann-Morgenstern index will preserve, of course, the ranking of the ordinal index values, m_{ij}. Its important feature, however, is that its uniqueness up to a linear transformation preserves the meaningfulness of the absolute differences of the type in (15) as well as the signs of such differences. It obtains this degree of uniqueness by virtue of the fact that the u_{ij} are related linearly to probability values which range from 0 to 1, in the simplest case, as in (22), by the multiplicative constant u_{21}. It is a cardinal index, therefore, only in situations where probability plays a meaningful role; specifically, it cannot be used with confidence to predict choices under conditions of certainty except as an ordinal index.

For example, suppose we have a situation where it is known (1) that the individual's preferences are not a linear transformation of money payments for the range of choice being considered, and (2) that combining two outcomes into one yields no "interaction" effects, so that combining an outcome of \$10 and one of \$15 into a single outcome of \$25 is legitimate. This second condition is the specification of independent utilities, and does away with substitutionary and complementarity relationships among outcomes. The adoption of the last condition yields the case most favorable to the use of the von Neumann-Morgenstern index as a predictor of consumer choice in a cardinal fashion under the regime of certainty. Suppose there were four outcomes: $0_1 = \$10$, $0_2 = \$0$, $0_3 = -\$5$, and $0_4 = -\$20$. Suppose that the von Neumann-Morgenstern index values were $u_1 = 10$, $u_2 = 5$, $u_3 = 4$, and $u_4 = 0$. Now if two outcomes

[12] For the original presentation of the derivation of the index, see J. von Neumann, (2), pp. 15–31.

were defined, $0_1 + 0_4$ and $0_2 + 0_3$, adding the respective utilities together as if they could be treated as cardinal independent measurements would yield $u_1 + u_4 = 10$, $u_2 + u_3 = 9$, and the analysis would lead us to predict the consumer to prefer to lose \$10 to the alternative of losing only \$5. Therefore, quite apart from the complications of interdependent utilities, the use of the von Neumann-Morgenstern utility index out of the probability context in which it was derived as a cardinal index is not warranted. A new index must be constructed over the two new outcomes.[13]

The use of these five steps to obtain a preference function over outcomes which may in turn be used to predict the consumer's choices under risk is equivalent to endowing the consumer with a "pattern of rationality" which may be more or less intuitively plausible to the analyst. This pattern of rationality is defined by the set of axioms about the consumer's behavior that implies the ability to construct the index and predict his ordering over the actions in his action-space. It was another contribution of von Neumann and Morgenstern to have developed the axiomatic basis for the construction of their index.[14]

The individual who orders his preferences over his set of actions *as if* he were obtaining the expected utility of those actions from a von Neumann-Morgenstern index and ranking them, is acting *as if* he were reducing every outcome to a variant of a standard lottery, and then valuing the "lottery" that nature forces upon him by the probability weighting of standard lottery utilities. For the individual to act as if he were doing this, it is necessary that he act as if all risk situations whose ultimate result is to yield a single outcome can be reduced to an equivalent standard lottery variant. The following five axioms will guarantee that this can be done:

Axiom 1. There exists a preference ordering over the 0_{ij}, ordering them completely in terms of preference or indifference, and characterized by transitive preferences.

Axiom 2. Any compound lottery may be reduced to a single lottery whose probabilities are built up from those of the compound lottery. A compound lottery is a set of lotteries whose drawings, prior to the last one, are for prizes which are chances in further lotteries. To illustrate, suppose there were a compound lottery, C, made up of two separate simple lotteries, C_1 and C_2:

$$C = \{\{0_1, 0_2; q_1\}\{0_3, 0_4; q_2\}\} \tag{24}$$

0_1 is a chance in C_2, 0_2 is a loss of C_1 and the cessation of further play and q_1 is the probability of 0_1. 0_3 is a money prize, 0_4 is a loss of C_2 yielding no

[13] R. Luce, (1), p. 22.

[14] J. von Neumann, (2), pp. 617–32. These have been restated and simplified in several further treatments: I. Herstein, (1); M. Hausner, (1); and the simplest of these axiom systems, which is the one adopted here, in R. Luce, (1), pp. 23–31.

dollars, and q_2 is the probability of 0_3. Suppose $q_1 = .6$, 0_3 is \$100, and $q_2 = .2$. Then C is a lottery in which one has a .6 chance of winning the chance to draw from another lottery in which there is a .2 chance of winning \$100.

The probability of winning \$100 is the probability of winning the first lottery (.6) times the probability of winning the second (.2), or .12. Suppose the consumer were to be offered a choice between C or C', where

$$C' = \{\$100, 0; .12\} \tag{25}$$

A consumer who acts in accordance with the second axiom will be indifferent between C and C', since the only difference between them is that one has two lotteries and the other only one. This indifference indicates that he attaches no significance to the act of gambling; if he liked the act of gambling, he would prefer C to C' since it allows him to indulge his fancy, while if he disliked gambling he would prefer C' to C since the former allows him to escape one distasteful experience.

Axiom 3. It is always possible to find *some* probability q_{ij} for the lottery option which will make the latter equal to every certainty option in the analysis. This merely assures that there will be no "gaps" in the preference index caused by the existence of an outcome for which the consumer cannot name a standard lottery equivalent. It is not difficult to imagine situations in which this axiom might seem implausible: for example, if the most-preferred outcome in the standard lottery option were a prize of one dollar and the least-preferred outcome were death by hanging, it might seem quite plausible that no probability q would make this lottery indifferent to the receipt of a five-cent candy bar. But the axiom merely requires that some probability exist, perhaps .99999999999999999999999999999998, and it seems highly plausible that even for the least daring individual some such value could be found in these extreme circumstances. If this does not satisfy the reader, it may be asserted that although a more complicated utility function is required, the expected-utility approach may still be salvaged even if this axiom is rejected.

Axiom 4. If a variant of the standard lottery option is indifferent to a certainty option, the former may be substituted for the latter in any lottery containing the latter. With Axiom 3, which asserts that such an equivalent lottery option always exists, this axiom assures that if the certainty option and lottery option variant are equivalent taken by themselves, they will be so regardless of any other alternative outcomes in any other lottery.

Axiom 5. Among lotteries as well as certainty options, preference relationships are transitive.

These five axioms allow the analyst to (1) reduce every certainty option to a lottery option involving only the most- and least-preferred outcomes in a given choice situation, (2) reduce any compound lottery option to a lottery involving only the most- and least-preferred outcomes, and (3) by using the expected-utility hypothesis, derive a set of preference values unique up to a linear transformation over all actions.

With these axioms we finish our discussion of the construction of consumer preference functions under conditions of pure certainty and of pure risk. The first set of data is therefore assumed to have been obtained.

1.b. The Terms of Transformation Among Factors and Actions

A second set of data that must be specified for the consumer model is the set of coefficients which dictates the transformation possibilities between factors and actions, either via production in a Robinsonade or via exchange in a social economy. These terms may or may not vary with the scale of transformation: for example, if the scarce factor is a productive resource in a Robinsonade, economies or diseconomies of scale may cause changes in the marginal terms of transformation. If the scarce factor is "wealth" or "income" in an exchange economy, the marginal terms may or may not reflect the impact of the consumer's purchases or sales on markets.

In the second case—that of the social economy—we shall deal only with the case of constant terms of transformation, i.e., where the consumer has no impact upon market price.

1.c. The Stock of Resources Available for Allocation Among the Actions

A final explicit datum of the analysis is the amount of "wherewithal" or "means" available to support the consumer's actions. In both the primitive and social contexts we shall assume the existence of only one scarce factor which can be allocated on the fixed terms described in Section 1.b. above among all the actions designed to obtain consumption outcomes.

2. Simple Exchange Models

Given these data—a consumer preference function, the terms at which he transforms resources into actions, and the number of resources available—we may begin the construction of a "vision" or model, as discussed in Chapter 1. It will be easiest to deal with the case of pure risk first, since it is simplest in construction.

2.a. The Environment of Pure Risk

To the five axioms of Section 1.a.4.b. we need add only one more to obtain the basis for proceeding from the preference function over the actions, whose values are u_{a_i}, to the choice of an action. Note that in this analysis of consumer choice under risk both the terms of transformation between resources and actions and resource availability have been taken into account implicitly. These are reflected in the definition of the action-space of the consumer, all elements of which are assumed *feasible* and exclude no action which is not infeasible. The feasibility of the action-space implies, given the terms of transformation and the amount of resources available, a prior analysis.

The required axiom is self-evident: in our form of the preference index one variant of the lottery option is preferred to another if and only if the probability q is larger, while one variant is indifferent to another if their q's are equal. Since in the final analysis compound lotteries of the type faced by the consumer when he adopts any action are reducible to variants of the lottery option, it follows that that u_{a_i} which is a maximum will be chosen by the consumer—if the axioms truly characterize his behavior.

These results, therefore, are truly operational theorems, given our interpretation of the importance of the assumptions used in building the preference function over the actions. They are predictions which must be checked against the consumer's actions and which, at least ideally, are capable of such validation or lack of validation.

2.b. The Environment of Pure Certainty

Let us move into a model which lacks this theoretical potential except in almost trivial senses[15] and which possesses in much greater degree the character of merely yielding information held in store.

Three models of simple exchange will be constructed in this section, each distinguished by the character of the given preference function. Model I-1 contains a preference function which is (1) cardinal in its measurements and (2) characterized by independence of the preferences among goods. Model I-2 retains the first of these assumptions but drops the second, adopting instead the assumption that the preferences for the goods in the function are interdependent. Lastly, Model I-3 drops the assumption of a cardinal function in favor of an ordinal function, and assumes the interdependence of the preferences.

As indicated in Chapter 1, the economist is not merely interested in the specification of such general systems for their own essential value. He is interested in deriving information about the qualitative movements in the quantities taken of each good with changes in the data. We shall, therefore, impose upon each of these three models in turn small changes in certain of the data in order to gauge movements in the variables. The method to be employed is that illustrated in Section 5 of Chapter 1.

[15] Again, except in the sense that assumptions such as that of transitivity of consumer preferences were used to derive it and in the sense that the consumer may not do in the event what he said or indicated he would do *ex ante*.

2.b.1. Model I-1: Cardinal, Independent Preferences

Assume that there exist three goods, Y_j, $j = 1, 2, 3$, capable of consumer acquisition by production or exchange through a market at constant transformation coefficients P_j, measured in dollar units, through the use of Z, a fixed stock of resources measured in units worth one dollar. The preferences for varying quantities of goods, X_j, are specified by a continuous function whose first and second derivatives at least exist, and which yields preferences unique up to a linear transformation:

$$U = F_1(X_1) + F_2(X_2) + F_3(X_3) = F([X]) \tag{26}$$

Each of the F_j functions must be unique up to a linear transformation. A distinctive feature of this function is that the cross-derivatives are identically zero:

$$\frac{\partial^2 U}{\partial X_j \partial X_k} \equiv 0, \qquad j \neq k, j \text{ and } k = 1, 2, 3 \tag{27}$$

That is, the marginal preference value for one good is unaffected by the amounts of all other goods consumed. As we shall see, and as might be expected by the preliminary consideration of such systems in Chapter 1, the absence of these cross-relationships serves to simplify the matrices of derived systems. The utility function (26) was, therefore, a favorite in neoclassical presentations: among those theorists who used it were Gossen, Jevons, Menger, Walras, Böhm-Bawerk, Wicksell, Wicksteed, J. B. Clark, Pareto, Slutsky, and Marshall.[16] It was, indeed, the utility function in whose terms neoclassical consumer theory was developed. Marshall's earlier work was stated exclusively in the terms of an additive, cardinal function, and even though he introduced the Fisher-Edgeworth-Pareto complications into the third edition of the *Principles* in 1895, "He retained to the last a theory constructed on the assumption of an additive utility function."[17] Pareto also, though his name is identified with the introduction of an ordinal function, held to the additive function in the *Cours*, retained the cardinal measurement assumption in the *Manuel*, and defended the function of (26) as holding approximately for small movements about the equilibrium position.[18] Thus, the additive utility function had an impact upon neoclassical consumer analysis which extended well beyond the initial development of that theory.

[16] Cf. G. Stigler, (2), pp. 322–4; F. Edgeworth, (1), pp. 20, 24, 104, 108; V. Pareto, (2), pp. 581–4, although Pareto stressed the approximate nature of the independence-of-utilities assumption and the danger of using it except for dealing with small movements in the neighborhood of an equilibrium position, pp. 255–6; E. Slutsky, (1), pp. 45–7; and I. Fisher, (1), pp. 24, 33.

[17] G. Stigler, (2), p. 327.

[18] V. Pareto, (1), Vol. II, pp. 332 ff.; V. Pareto, (2), pp. 253ff, 274. See also footnotes 5 and 16 above.

The consumer will not in general choose that basket of goods for which U attains its *maximum maximorum*, if such exists, because the P_j are assumed to be positive and Z is finite; i.e., the consumer's resources are limited. These are the Paretian obstacles facing the consumer, enforcing upon the analyst the need to derive the consumer's choice by means of a constrained-maximum approach.[19] If it be assumed, quite illegitimately, that the basket of goods which the model yields as a solution will have the form $X_j^\circ > 0$ for all j, so that some of every good will appear in the solution basket, we may work with the convenient "interior maximum" model.[20] This assumption is "illegitimate" in that it assumes certain characteristics of the specific solution before that solution is obtained. We shall postpone further discussion of this matter until after the presentation of the interior maximum model, when its conditions will be generalized to cover the possibility of "end-point" or "corner" solutions.

2.b.1.a. The Interior Maximum

In order to maximize U subject to the constraint,

$$\sum_j X_j P_j - Z = 0 \tag{28}$$

the function, S, is formed with a Lagrangean constant, λ, whose value is determined in the solution:

$$S = U - \lambda\left(\sum_j X_j P_j - Z\right) \tag{I-1-1}$$

When S is differentiated partially with respect to the X_j and λ, and these derivatives are equated to zero, the following are obtained:

$$\text{(I-1-2)}\quad \begin{aligned} &1. \quad \frac{\partial S}{\partial X_j} = F_j^j - \lambda^\circ P_j = 0 \\ &2. \quad \frac{\partial S}{\partial \lambda} = \sum_j X_j^\circ P_j - Z = 0 \end{aligned}$$

Throughout this book, as we have already noted in Chapter 1, expressions

[19] Pareto dealt with the resource constraint as an important special case of a family of possible constraints upon the consumer, treating all such constraints as "paths" on the utility surface which the consumer was forced to follow. Modern theory has neglected all but the "budget path." V. Pareto, (2), pp. 183–4.

[20] The following terminology will be adopted in this book; if $[X]$ is a vector with elements X_j, $[X] > k$ denotes that every element X_j of the vector is larger than k. The expression $[X] \geq k$ denotes that every element is at least as large as k and at least one element is greater than k. The expression $[X] \geqq k$ denotes that every element is at least as large as k, including the possibility that all $X_j = k$. The same types of definitions are adopted when the inequality sign is reversed. Then, for an interior maximum, $[X^\circ] > 0$.

of the form F_j^i denote the partial derivative of F_j with respect to the ith variable.

Further, at the equilibrium point and subject to the consumer spending all of (but no more than) his budget, the consumer must find that he does have the basket he wants, i.e., that the economist has attained a true constrained maximum for a function constructed to yield desired information at such maxima:

$$d^2U = \sum_j F_j^{jj} dX_j^2 < 0 \qquad \text{(I-1-3)}$$

subject to (I-1-2-2), and where throughout this book F_j^{jk} denotes the partial derivative of F_j^j with respect to k.

The value of the Lagrangean multiplier in the solution, $\lambda°$, may be interpreted as the "marginal utility of income," or the preference index value obtained per unit of Z from a small change dZ in the neighborhood of the solution. For it is possible to write

$$\frac{dU}{dZ} = \sum_j F_j^j \frac{\partial X_j}{\partial Z} \qquad (29)$$

In the solution, from (I-1-2-1),

$$\frac{dU}{dZ} = \lambda° \sum_j \frac{\partial X_j^\circ}{\partial Z} P_j \qquad (30)$$

From (I-1-2-2) the summed terms must equal unity, so

$$\frac{dU}{dZ} = \lambda° \qquad (31)$$

Therefore, the conditions for obtaining the consumer's choice of a basket of goods, given prices and income, are that the marginal satisfaction derived from the unit-of-income's worth of each good be equal to the marginal satisfaction of income, when this latter variable is at the level reflected by the exhaustion of means on the goods.

2.b.1.b. The Kuhn-Tucker Generalization

We may now generalize the conditions of (I-1-2) to provide for the cases in which an interior maximum is not attainable. It may prove to be the case that (1) one or more goods up to a maximum of $n - 1$ may not in fact be taken by the consumer, or (2) the consumer may be satiated with all goods before he has exhausted his income. By writing the conditions of a solution in the form (I-1-2) we have *assumed* away the possibility of either of these eventualities. They may be included by the introduction of inequality signs into the conditions:

$$(32)\qquad \begin{aligned} &1. \quad F_j^j - \lambda^\circ P_j \leqq 0 \\ &2. \quad \sum_j X_j^\circ P_j - Z \leqq 0 \end{aligned}$$

The first set of these conditions recognizes that one or two (in the specific case at hand) of the goods may have marginal preference values per unit of income less than the marginal utility of income in the solution. That is, one or two goods may have preference functions such that the first unit of income spent on it or them does not yield the satisfaction derived from the last unit of income spent on other goods taken in the solution. The second condition recognizes that the consumer may not spend all of his income. This occurrence, however, implies that the consumer has been satiated in *all* of the goods available for consumption. It is necessary for the existence of this condition that λ° be zero if the inequality of (32-2) holds explicitly; therefore, we must have

$$(33)\qquad \lambda^\circ \left(\sum_j X_j^\circ P_j - Z\right) = 0$$

If all income is spent, λ° may be positive or zero, but if all income is not spent λ° must be zero; these are necessary conditions for a maximum.

But it is also necessary to make explicit the condition that the inequality of (32-1) can rule only if the corresponding quantity of good Y_j is zero:

$$(34)\qquad X_j^\circ (F_j^j - \lambda^\circ P_j) = 0$$

Also, of course,

$$(35)\qquad X_j^\circ \geqq 0, \qquad \lambda^\circ \geqq 0$$

Conditions (32-1), (33), (34), and (35) are necessary conditions for a constrained maximum when the constraint meets a certain qualification possessed by a linear constraint. They are a generalization of the Lagrange conditions for a constrained interior maximum and were derived by H. Kuhn and A. Tucker.[21] Kuhn and Tucker prove that when the function to be maximized and the constraint are *concave*, the necessary conditions will be sufficient as well. This concavity of the function exists when

$$(36)\qquad d^2U \leqq 0$$

and the freedom of the dX_j to vary is not constrained by any function.

The implications of concavity may be pointed out in this fashion. Imagine a utility function in $n + 1$ space. At a point on the surface,

[21] H. Kuhn, (1).

$F([X^\circ])$, imagine a hyperplane tangent to it. The equation of this hyperplane is

$$T = F([X^\circ]) + \sum_j F_j^j(X_j - X_j^\circ) \tag{37}$$

Global concavity implies that the utility surface lies below or on the tangent plane everywhere for all points $[X^\circ]$; local concavity implies that within a range of values in the neighborhood of $[X^\circ]$ the utility surface lies below or on the hyperplane. Strict concavity applies when the surface lies below the tangent plane globally or locally except at the point of tangency. The condition (I-1-3) is a necessary and sufficient condition for strict concavity; however, this condition is met by locally strict concavity, since $[X]$ is constrained to lie near $[X^\circ]$. Therefore, for $[X]$ in the neighborhood of $[X^\circ]$,

$$T > F([X]) \tag{38}$$

Condition (36), however, implies

$$T \geqq F([X]) \tag{39}$$

for any $[X]$ in the neighborhood of an $[X^\circ]$ which does not contradict (32-2) or (35). Graphically, the preference function may lie on the tangent hyperplane at some points $[X]$ other than $[X^\circ]$.

But, as will be pointed out below, concavity of the utility function is a stronger restriction than is needed, since (36) is required to be true only for movements of the variables along the budget plane. As will be shown, "quasi-concavity" of the preference function will suffice to yield a constrained maximum. Arrow and Enthoven have proved that if (a) $U = F([X])$ is differentiable and quasi-concave, (b) the budget constraint is differentiable and quasi-concave, as, being linear, it will be, (c) both functions are defined for $X_j \geqq 0$, while (d) X_j° and λ° satisfy (32-1), (33), (34), and (35): then, if the marginal utility of one good at equilibrium is positive, or all marginal utilities are non-zero and second derivatives of U exist at $[X^\circ]$, conditions (32-1) – (35) will be sufficient as well as necessary to achieve a constrained maximum.[22] Moreover, if (a) – (d) immediately above are met, and $U = F([X])$ is concave, (32-1) – (35) will be sufficient for a constrained maximum—a generalization of Kuhn and Tucker's requirement that the constraint be concave rather than the Arrow-Enthoven requirement that it be merely quasi-concave.

With the techniques of linear and nonlinear programming, it is now possible not only to state these more general conditions but to solve for specific solutions and to gain information about equilibrium displace-

[22] K. Arrow, (7).

ments by parametric programming when either ordinal or cardinal measurement of welfare is a possibility. We shall, indeed, study the methods of linear programming in some detail in Chapters 3 and 6. These techniques, however, are recent developments. Therefore, neoclassical theory was worked out in terms of the special case where none of the inequalities was assumed to hold in solution, and, because of the great ease with which models can be manipulated when these assumptions are held, we shall return to them.

2.b.1.c. Critics of the Utility Function Concept

Our interpretation of Model I-1 as a purely formal maximization procedure to exploit the "memory" of a preference function springs from the tautological interpretation given the latter in Section 1.a.3. It must be distinguished from Cassel's criticism of neoclassical consumer theory. Cassel denied the possibility of defining a function of the type discussed in Section 1.a.3. because he believed it impossible for the consumer to indicate his preferences without the specification of a set of prices. It is not generally realized that Cassel did not eliminate preference functions from his analysis: the demand functions which are among the data of his model *are* Cassel's preference functions. To him they are the only possible manner of stating the consumer's preferences, for they are the only possible way of recording answers to questions that must involve hypothetical prices: ". . . His [the consumer's] whole scale of reckoning is necessarily bound up with the actual prices. If we keep strictly to the simple facts, we can only say that men decide what they will buy when all the prices are given: decide, that is to say, upon the line to be drawn between those wants which they will satisfy and those which they will ignore. Further than that . . . economic science need not concern itself with the question."[23]

Henry Schultz went even beyond Cassel in objecting to the storage of information in preference functions of the type we have assumed possible. He wrote: "Most people simply *do not know* how their consumption of a given commodity would be affected if prices were to move much above or below their accustomed range, and even within the accustomed range there may be a great deal of uncertainty. They must *experience* a given set of price relations in its proper institutional setting in order to make up their minds as to the quantities they will purchase. . . ."[24] Strictly interpreted, Schultz's criticisms are a denial of any meaningfulness to the concept of virtual consumption information capable of storage, while Cassel's are less restrictive in their insistence that hypothetical price vectors be specified in the questioning of the consumer.

[23] G. Cassel, (1), p. 82. Quoted by permission of Ernest Benn, Ltd.

[24] H. Schultz, (2), p. 10. Copyright 1938 by The University of Chicago. Quoted by permission.

2.b.1.d. The Manipulation of Model I-1

The nonspecific solutions to equations (I-1-2), if they exist, will yield the X_j° as explicit functions of the P_j and Z:

$$(40)\qquad \begin{aligned} &1. \quad X_{j\neq 1}^\circ = H_{j\neq 1}(P_j, Z) \\ &2. \quad X_1^\circ = \frac{1}{P_1}\left(Z - \sum_{j\neq 1} X_j^\circ P_j\right) \end{aligned}$$

where one of the demand functions (in our case, arbitrarily, that for X_1°), follows as a residual from the others and the budget constraint of (I-1-2-2).

But merely to know (by assumption) that for any specified set of data there exists at least one optimal basket of goods for the consumer is to say little, as we have seen from the analysis of Chapter 1. Also, merely to write the solutions inherent in the conditions of (I-1-2) in the form of (40) is to gain no new insights into the nature of the consumer's preferences. On the other hand, as indicated in Chapter 1, we are interested in information about the slopes of the functions in (40) which depict the nonspecific solutions. These magnitudes, $\frac{\partial X_j^\circ}{\partial P_k}$, for each $j = 1, 2, 3$, and $k = 1, 2, 3$, and $\frac{\partial X_j^\circ}{\partial Z}$, $j = 1, 2, 3$, however, must be studied with the aid of system (I-1-2). To do so, let us shock this system by enforcing upon it a very small change in resources:

$$(41)\qquad \begin{bmatrix} F_1^{11} & 0 & 0 & -P_1 \\ 0 & F_2^{22} & 0 & -P_2 \\ 0 & 0 & F_3^{33} & -P_3 \\ P_1 & P_2 & P_3 & 0 \end{bmatrix} \begin{bmatrix} \frac{\partial X_1^\circ}{\partial Z} \\ \frac{\partial X_2^\circ}{\partial Z} \\ \frac{\partial X_3^\circ}{\partial Z} \\ \frac{\partial \lambda^\circ}{\partial Z} \end{bmatrix} = \begin{bmatrix} 0 \\ 0 \\ 0 \\ 1 \end{bmatrix}$$

(where the vector of unknowns is written as the slopes of (40)), or

$$(42)\qquad [D][dV] = [dZ]$$

Then, letting s denote rows and t columns of matrices, as we shall throughout this book,

$$(43)\qquad \frac{\partial X_j^\circ}{\partial Z} = (-1)^t \frac{|D_{4t}|}{|D|} \qquad j = t = 1, 2, 3$$

or, to fix our ideas, where $t = 1$,

$$(44)\qquad \frac{\partial X_1^\circ}{\partial Z} = -\frac{|D_{41}|}{|D|} = \frac{1}{P_1 - F_1^{11}\frac{|D_{11}|}{|D_{41}|}}$$

We may now fall back upon methods developed in Chapter 1. In order to obtain information about the second derivatives in $[D]$, which are the slopes of the interrelationship functions of Model I-1, it is possible to postulate such restrictions directly, employ second-order extremum conditions, or extract information from an explicit stability analysis. The last of these three methods will be employed for a consumer model in Chapter 8. Therefore, the present analysis will turn to the postulational basis and the use of second-order maximum conditions.

2.b.1.d.1. THE POSTULATIONAL BASIS: UNIVERSAL DIMINISHING MARGINAL UTILITY. Because measurement of preferences unique up to a linear transformation has been assumed, the signs of the second derivatives of the preference function are meaningful.[25] The usual neoclassical assumption, of course, was universal diminishing marginal utility to consumption, i.e., $F_j^{jj} < 0$ for all j. The extent to which the neoclassical writers availed themselves of Model I-1's additive utility function has already been referred to and provides an indication of the pervasiveness of universal diminishing marginal utility in neoclassical thought.[26]

In terms of the evaluation of (44), universal diminishing marginal utility is a powerful assumption. With it the sign of $\frac{\partial X_1^\circ}{\partial Z}$ depends upon the ratio $\frac{|D_{11}|}{|D_{41}|}$. This ratio, when expanded, is

$$\text{(45)} \qquad \frac{|D_{11}|}{|D_{41}|} = -\frac{P_2^2F_3^{33} + P_3^2F_2^{22}}{P_1F_2^{22}F_3^{33}} > 0$$

Universal diminishing marginal utility is sufficient to guarantee that any good will be consumed in greater quantity when income increases in Model I-1; i.e., $\frac{\partial X_j^\circ}{\partial Z} > 0$. Of course, it follows that

$$\text{(46)} \qquad \frac{\partial \lambda^\circ}{\partial Z} = \frac{|D_{44}|}{|D|} = \frac{F_1^{11}F_2^{22}F_3^{33}}{P_1^2F_2^{22}F_3^{33} + P_2^2F_1^{11}F_3^{33} + P_3^2F_1^{11}F_2^{22}} < 0$$

[25] That is, the ability to rank differences between marginal utilities is implied by the cardinal measurement of preference, and, as shown in the discussion of Section 1, the ability to rank magnitudes implies that the signs of differences between them are meaningful. Compare the proof of footnote 6 and the references to Lange's work cited there.

[26] In the present case the assumption of universal diminishing marginal utility is equivalent to the assumption of global strict concavity. That is, $d^2U < 0$ when the dX_j are unconstrained. For this quadratic form to be negative definite it is necessary and sufficient that the following expressions alternate in sign negative and positive:

$$F_1^{11}, \quad \begin{vmatrix} F_1^{11} & 0 \\ 0 & F_2^{22} \end{vmatrix}, \quad \begin{vmatrix} F_1^{11} & 0 & 0 \\ 0 & F_2^{22} & 0 \\ 0 & 0 & F_3^{33} \end{vmatrix}$$

We shall compare concavity with the less strict requirement of quasi-concavity in the next section.

The second set of equilibrium displacements which is of interest in the search for information about the consumer's reactions to changes in the data concerns price change. For example, suppose P_1 were to rise slightly, all other data being held constant. Then, instead of (42) we should obtain from the differentiation of (I-1-2) with respect to P_1:

$$[D][dW_1] = [dP_1] \tag{47}$$

where

$$[dW_1] = \left[\frac{\partial X_1^\circ}{\partial P_1}, \frac{\partial X_2^\circ}{\partial P_1}, \frac{\partial X_3^\circ}{\partial P_1}, \frac{\partial \lambda^\circ}{\partial P_1}\right] \tag{48}$$

Throughout the book all vectors will be assumed to be column vectors. Also,

$$[dP_1] = [\lambda^\circ, 0, 0, -X_1^\circ] \tag{49}$$

Solving,

$$\frac{\partial X_1^\circ}{\partial P_1} = \lambda^\circ \frac{|D_{11}|}{|D|} + X_1^\circ \frac{|D_{41}|}{|D|} \tag{50}$$

for an own-price change, and more generally:

$$\frac{\partial X_j^\circ}{\partial P_1} = (-1)^{t+1}\lambda^\circ \frac{|D_{1t}|}{|D|} - (-1)^t X_1^\circ \frac{|D_{4t}|}{|D|} \tag{51}$$

where t is the relevant column of $[D]$ for $\dfrac{\partial X_j^\circ}{\partial P_1}$.

From (44) we may substitute into (50) to get

$$\frac{\partial X_1^\circ}{\partial P_1} = \lambda^\circ \frac{|D_{11}|}{|D|} - X_1^\circ \left(\frac{\partial X_1^\circ}{\partial Z}\right) \tag{52}$$

Define

$$s_{11} = \lambda^\circ \frac{|D_{11}|}{|D|} \tag{53}$$

Then, the economic meaning of (52) is best presented if that equation is rewritten in differentials:

$$dX_1^\circ = s_{11}dP_1 - X_1^\circ dP_1 \left(\frac{\partial X_1^\circ}{\partial Z}\right) \tag{54}$$

If P_1 rises by dP_1, the consumer's effective change in real income is $-X_1^\circ dP_1$. That is, if in the first solution the consumer were purchasing 50 units of X_1, but price rose \$.05 per unit, his effective income has fallen by \$2.50, in the sense that only if he were given an extra \$2.50 would he be able, if he desired, to buy the same basket of goods that he purchased before the price change. In the absence of such a subsidy, neglecting for the moment any other price change effects, he will reduce his purchase of

Y_1 by this reduction in effective income times his "marginal propensity to consume Y_1 from income," $\frac{\partial X_1^\circ}{\partial Z}$.

If this were the only set of forces acting upon him, the consumer's change in consumption would equal this "income effect." To the extent that dX_1° does not correspond to it, s_{11} in (54) must be nonzero. This residual is Hicks's "substitution effect" and Slutsky's "residual variability of good Y_1 with respect to a compensated variation in its price," and its existence means that even if the consumer were given sufficient compensation to buy the same basket of goods as before the price change, he will choose to alter his purchases by virtue of the price change.[27]

If we define the income effect, r_{11}, as

$$r_{11} = -X_1^\circ \left(\frac{\partial X_1^\circ}{\partial Z}\right) \tag{55}$$

or the amount of change in X_1° per unit of change in P_1 due to the real income effects of the price change alone, then, from (52) and (54)

$$\frac{\partial X_1^\circ}{\partial P_1} = s_{11} + r_{11} \tag{56}$$

Now, under the assumptions of universal diminishing marginal utility as well as the additive utility function, it has been shown that $\frac{\partial X_1^\circ}{\partial Z} > 0$ (see (44) and (45)). From (55), therefore, it follows that

$$r_{11} < 0 \tag{57}$$

and more generally,

$$r_{jj} < 0 \tag{58}$$

That is, in Model I-1 the income effect will always push consumption of the good whose price has changed in the direction opposite to that of the price change.

It remains to evaluate s_{11}. From (53), since λ° is a positive term by assumption, and, with the assumption of universal diminishing marginal utility, $|D| > 0$ from (46), the sign of s_{11} depends upon the sign of $|D_{11}|$. Expanding this last expression, we get

$$D_{11} = P_2^2 F_3^{33} + P_3^2 F_2^{22} < 0 \tag{59}$$

and, therefore,

$$s_{11} < 0 \tag{60}$$

[27] E. Slutsky, (1), p. 42, and J. Hicks, (5), pp. 31–2.

Therefore, from (56), (57), and (60), generalized in (58) and (61),

$$s_{jj} < 0 \tag{61}$$

it follows

$$\frac{\partial X_1^\circ}{\partial P_1} < 0 \tag{62}$$

$$\frac{\partial X_j^\circ}{\partial P_j} < 0 \tag{63}$$

In this case, income and substitution effects will operate in the same direction to insure that the amount demanded of any good will fall with a rise in its price, all other prices and income remaining constant. The classic partial demand curve falls monotonically.[28]

Next, what may be said of the sign of $\frac{\partial X_j^\circ}{\partial P_k}$, say of $\frac{\partial X_2^\circ}{\partial P_1}$? From (51)

$$\frac{\partial X_2^\circ}{\partial P_1} = -\lambda^\circ \frac{|D_{12}|}{|D|} - X_1^\circ \frac{|D_{42}|}{|D|} \tag{64}$$

From (41), and by an obvious extension of (53), (55), and (56),

$$\frac{\partial X_2^\circ}{\partial P_1} = s_{21} + r_{21} \tag{65}$$

The sign of s_{21} must depend upon $|D_{12}|$ for reasons discussed in the evaluation of s_{11}. Expanded,

$$|D_{12}| = P_1 P_2 F_3^{33} < 0 \tag{66}$$

and

$$s_{21} > 0 \tag{67}$$

If we define net substitutability among goods as the rise in X_j° with a rise in P_k after the consumer's income has been increased sufficiently to allow

[28] Walras asserts that the negative inclination of the demand curve follows from the assumption of diminishing marginal utility, but he is implicitly assuming independence of the utilities. See L. Walras (3), p. 136n.

This result for the conditions of Model I-1 must be credited to Pareto, and, indeed, its derivation was the origin of the formal search for laws of change or operational theorems in general models, the need for which is stressed so frequently in this book. See V. Pareto, (1), Vol. II, p. 332n and V. Pareto, (2), pp. 272–3, 581–4. Although he made explicit the dependence of (63) upon the independence-of-utilities assumption, and warned that the cross-derivatives F_j^{jk}, $j \neq k$, can depart significantly from zero, Pareto failed to indicate in his further work the restrictions such assumptions place upon the usefulness of general equilibrium analysis.

Slutsky acknowledged Pareto's prior work in deriving (63) and says his own work is identical to it, but stressed the greater convenience of the statement of the results in terms of what we have termed s_{jj} and r_{jj}. Pareto had not discerned the existence of these effects, and, consequently, his analysis did not yield the insights into similar expressions for more complicated models which Slutsky's analysis provides. Cf. E. Slutsky, (1), p. 39n.

him to purchase the old basket of goods if he wishes, then when a cardinal utility function with independent utilities is assumed to be characterized by diminishing marginal utility for all goods, every good must be a net substitute for every other. That is,

$$s_{jk} > 0 \tag{68}$$

The sign of $|D_{42}|$ must determine the sign of r_{21}, given our knowledge of the signs of the other terms in r_{21}:

$$|D_{42}| = P_2 F_1^{11} F_3^{33} > 0 \tag{69}$$

and

$$r_{21} < 0 \tag{70}$$

In Model I-1, the income effect on any good of a rise in the price of any other good will always push the consumption of that good in a direction opposite to that of the price change:

$$r_{jk} < 0 \tag{71}$$

Therefore, from (65), (68), (70), (71), and the obvious generalization of (65),

$$\frac{\partial X_2^\circ}{\partial P_1} \gtreqless 0 \tag{72}$$

$$\frac{\partial X_j^\circ}{\partial P_k} \gtreqless 0 \tag{73}$$

Since the income and substitution effects operate in opposite directions it is not possible to evaluate the change in quantity purchased of one good when another good's price changes, under the assumptions of Model I-1 and universal diminishing marginal utility.

Lastly, what will happen to the marginal utility of income with a change in price, say P_1? From (47), (48), and (49),

$$\frac{\partial \lambda^\circ}{\partial P_1} = -\lambda^\circ \frac{|D_{14}|}{|D|} - X_1^\circ \frac{|D_{44}|}{|D|} \tag{74}$$

We may retain the symbols so useful to us above:

$$\frac{\partial \lambda}{\partial P_1} = s_{\lambda 1} + r_{\lambda 1} \tag{75}$$

From (58) and (70) we should suspect that if only the income effect were taken into account, the reduction in real income when $dP_1 > 0$ would raise λ° if all goods had diminishing marginal utility. Also, if sufficient income were given in compensation to allow the consumer to purchase his former basket of goods, we should suspect that the existence of alternatives on all sides would allow a rise in satisfaction and a fall in λ°. The sign of $s_{\lambda 1}$ hinges upon the sign of $|D_{14}|$:

(76) $$|D_{14}| = P_1 F_2^{22} F_3^{33} > 0$$

so

(77) $$s_{\lambda 1} < 0$$

Further,

(78) $$r_{\lambda 1} > 0$$

since

(79) $$|D_{44}| = F_1^{11} F_2^{22} F_3^{33} < 0$$

and (78) follows from (74). Therefore, from (78) and (77)

(80) $$\frac{\partial \lambda^\circ}{\partial P_1} \gtreqless 0$$

This generalizes to

(81) $$\frac{\partial \lambda^\circ}{\partial P_j} \gtreqless 0$$

since

(82) $$s_{\lambda j} < 0$$

(83) $$r_{\lambda j} > 0$$

When $|s_{\lambda 1}| = r_{\lambda 1}$, $\dfrac{\partial \lambda^\circ}{\partial P_1} = 0$, which implies that the elasticity of X_1° with respect to P_1 is minus one. Similarly, when $|s_{\lambda 1}| > r_{\lambda 1}$, $\dfrac{\partial \lambda^\circ}{\partial P_1} < 0$, the expenditure on Y_1 has fallen when P_1 rises, and the absolute value of elasticity of demand for Y_1 is greater than unity. When $|s_{\lambda 1}| < r_{\lambda 1}$, $\dfrac{\partial \lambda^\circ}{\partial P_1} > 0$, and the absolute value of the elasticity of demand is less than unity.[29]

These theorems may be proved in the following fashion, by use of the example at hand. If (74) is evaluated and simplified,

(84) $$\begin{aligned} \frac{\partial \lambda^\circ}{\partial P_1} &= -\lambda^\circ \frac{P_1 F_2^{22} F_3^{33}}{|D|} - X_1^\circ \frac{F_1^{11} F_2^{22} F_3^{33}}{|D|} \\ &= -\frac{F_2^{22} F_3^{33}}{|D|} (\lambda^\circ P_1 + F_1^{11} X_1^\circ) \\ &= K(\lambda^\circ P_1 + F_1^{11} X_1^\circ) \end{aligned}$$

[29] These results are due to Pareto, (2), pp. 581–4.

It is possible to substitute into the last expression in (84) from the first equation of (44) for F_1^{11}:

$$\frac{\partial\lambda^\circ}{\partial P_1} = K\left[\lambda^\circ P_1 + X_1^\circ\left(\lambda^\circ \frac{\partial P_1}{\partial X_1^\circ} + P_1 \frac{\partial\lambda^\circ}{\partial P_1}\frac{\partial P_1}{\partial X_1^\circ}\right)\right] \tag{85}$$

Let e_1 be the price elasticity of demand for Y_1:

$$e_1 = \frac{\partial X_1^\circ}{\partial P_1}\frac{P_1}{X_1^\circ} \tag{86}$$

Then

$$\frac{\partial\lambda^\circ}{\partial P_1} = \lambda^\circ\left[\frac{e_1 + 1}{\dfrac{e_1}{KP_1} - P_1}\right] \tag{87}$$

When $\dfrac{\partial\lambda^\circ}{\partial P_1} = 0,$

$$e_1 = -1 \tag{88}$$

To show the other propositions stated above, let us expand K from (84):

$$\begin{aligned} K &= -\frac{F_2^{22}F_3^{33}}{P_1^2F_2^{22}F_3^{33} + P_2^2F_1^{11}F_3^{33} + P_3^2F_1^{11}F_2^{22}} \\ &= -\frac{1}{P_1^2 + P_2^2\left(\dfrac{F_1^{11}}{F_2^{22}}\right) + P_3^2\left(\dfrac{F_1^{11}}{F_3^{33}}\right)} \\ &= -\frac{1}{P_1^2 + aF_1^{11}} \end{aligned} \tag{89}$$

We are free to choose the arbitrary unit in which Z is measured in such a manner as to make $P_1 = 1$, since, as we shall see, Model I-1 is homogeneous of degree zero in all prices and Z.[30] The marginal preference value of income, λ°, is homogeneous of degree minus one in all prices and income, but from (87) it is seen that we may deal with percentage changes in λ° by dividing (87) through by λ°, and these percentage changes will be unaffected by our choice of unit for Z. Then, making $P_1 = 1$, we obtain from (87),

$$\frac{\partial\lambda^\circ}{\partial P_1}\frac{1}{\lambda^\circ} = \frac{e_1 + 1}{\dfrac{e_1}{K} - 1} \tag{90}$$

[30] A function, $x = f(y, z)$, is homogeneous of degree n in its arguments y and z if, when these arguments are multiplied by an arbitrary positive term, θ, the value of the function increases to $\theta^n x$. If $f(y, z)$ is homogeneous of degree 0 in y and z, $f(\theta y, \theta z) = f(y, z)$, or the value of x is unchanged. In the case of Model I-1, the assertion is that if the nonspecific solutions of (40) are treated by multiplying the P_j and Z by (say) 2, the X_j° will be unaffected. This is equivalent to saying that if all prices and income are measured in half-dollar units instead of dollar units, the consumer's basket of goods will remain unchanged in the solution.

and, if we substitute simultaneously in the last expression of (89) for P_1 and F_1^{11} (see (85)),

$$K = -\frac{1}{1 + a\left(\lambda^\circ \dfrac{\partial P_1}{\partial X_1^\circ} + \dfrac{\partial \lambda^\circ}{\partial P_1}\dfrac{\partial P_1}{\partial X_1^\circ}\right)} \tag{91}$$

or

$$-\frac{1}{K} = 1 + a\left(\lambda^\circ \frac{\partial P_1}{\partial X_1^\circ} + \frac{\partial \lambda^\circ}{\partial P_1}\frac{\partial P_1}{\partial X_1^\circ}\right) \tag{92}$$

Multiply by X_1°:

$$-\frac{X_1^\circ}{K} = X_1^\circ + \frac{a}{e_1}\left(\lambda^\circ + \frac{\partial \lambda^\circ}{\partial P_1}\right) \tag{93}$$

Solve for e_1:

$$e_1 = -\frac{a}{X_1^\circ}\left(\frac{K}{K+1}\right)\left(\frac{\partial \lambda^\circ}{\partial P_1} + \lambda^\circ\right) \tag{94}$$

Substitute for $\dfrac{\partial \lambda^\circ}{\partial P_1}$ from (90) and simplify:

$$e_1 = K\left(1 - \frac{a\lambda^\circ}{X_1^\circ}\right) \tag{95}$$

Since $a < 0$ (see (89)), it follows from (95) that

$$|e_1| > |K| \tag{96}$$

i.e., the absolute value of e_1 will be greater than the absolute value of K. Since $K < 0$ (see (89)), $e_1 < 0$ from (95), and $\dfrac{e_1}{K} > 0$. From this and (96) it follows that the denominator of the right side of (90) will always be positive. Therefore, the sign of the relative change in λ° will depend on the absolute value of e_1, as will the sign of the absolute change in λ°. When $|e_1| > 1$, $\dfrac{\partial \lambda^\circ}{\partial P_1} < 0$, and when $|e_1| < 1$, $\dfrac{\partial \lambda^\circ}{\partial P_1} > 0$.

We may summarize the results of the analysis so far. Under the conditions of Model I-1 (cardinally-measured, independent preferences) the additional assumption of universal diminishing marginal preferences is a powerful tool for the derivation of information about the consumer's reactions to data changes. It has been shown that:

1. $\dfrac{\partial X_j}{\partial Z} > 0$: the consumption of all goods will rise with an increase in income, fall with a decrease in income.

2. $\dfrac{\partial \lambda^\circ}{\partial Z} < 0$: the marginal utility of income will fall when income rises, rise when income falls.

3. $s_{jj} < 0$: the "own-substitution effect" of a price change will be in the opposite sense of that change.

4. $r_{jj} < 0$: the "own-income effect" of a price change will also be in the opposite sense of that change.

5. $\frac{\partial X_j^\circ}{\partial P_j} < 0$: from 3 and 4, a rise in the price of a good will lower the quantity taken, and a fall in price will increase the quantity taken.

6. $s_{jk} > 0$: the "other-substitution effect" of a price change will be in the same sense as that of the price change.

7. $r_{jk} < 0$: the "other-income effect" of a price change will be in the opposite sense to that of the price change.

8. $\frac{\partial X_j^\circ}{\partial P_k} \gtreqless 0$: the "other-price effect" on the quantity of a good taken is ambiguous, depending upon the absolute magnitudes of s_{jk} and r_{jk}.

9. $s_{\lambda j} < 0$: the substitution effect of a price change upon the marginal utility of income will be opposite to the direction of movement of price.

10. $r_{\lambda j} > 0$: the income effect of a price change upon the marginal utility of income will move it in the same direction as the price movement.

11. $\frac{\partial \lambda^\circ}{\partial P_j} \gtreqless 0$: the total impact of a price change on the marginal utility of income is ambiguous, but depends wholly upon the price elasticity of demand for the good whose price changes.

Consideration of this list of reasonably clear-cut propositions, and a comparison of it with the lists of like conclusions to follow from Models I-2 and I-3, will convince the reader of the importance of this model in shaping the "ordinary" notions of consumer theory: the downward sloping demand curve, the increased consumption of a good with a rise in income, the all-pervading characteristic of substitution relations among goods. None of these propositions will be clear-cut in further models, or even in this model when an alternative basis for evaluation of the relevant expressions is employed.

2.b.1.d.2. THE EXTREMUM BASIS: SECOND-ORDER MAXIMUM CONDITIONS. An alternative basis for the evaluation of such expressions is to assume that the critical point attained by the economist in I-1-2 is a constrained maximum position; i.e., that I-1-3 does in fact hold. In order to use this assumption in the evaluation of the expressions in which we are interested, it is first necessary to draw out the implications of I-1-3 in a form which is of direct use to us. We will see that this condition implies and is implied by the requirement of strict quasi-concavity of the utility function at the point of equilibrium.

We must contrast the less strict requirement of quasi-concavity with concavity. Concavity indicates that (1) as one subset of goods is increased in consumption, the remaining goods being held constant in amounts consumed, the marginal rates of psychological transformation of groups of variable goods must be diminishing or constant, and (2) at constant values of the function, when all goods are allowed to vary, marginal rates of substitution between all pairs of goods must diminish. The first characteristic is that of non-increasing marginal utility to every good or group of goods, while the second characteristic is that of diminishing marginal rates of substitution. Concavity rules when the chord joining two points on any plane profile of the surface lies everywhere below or on the surface. Condition (36) is necessary and sufficient to guarantee this condition in the neighborhood of equilibrium, at least, or, if interpreted as holding at all points, to guarantee global concavity; (I-1-3) is necessary and sufficient to guarantee strict concavity (diminishing marginal returns to all goods and groups of goods) in the same situations.

Concavity of the utility function must be distinguished from quasi-concavity. A function (say $U = F([X])$) is quasi-concave at the point $[X^\circ]$ if the subset X' of X, where X' is that set of points $[X]$ defined by the condition that $F([X]) \geqq F([X^\circ])$, is convex. We may interpret this definition in the following manner. Select an arbitrary point in X, $[X^\circ]$, which yields a utility value $F([X^\circ])$. Define X' as the set of all baskets of goods $[X]$ which yield utility values at least as high as $F([X^\circ])$. Then, if any two points $[X^1]$ and $[X^2]$ be taken in X', and a straight line $\theta[X^1] + (1 - \theta)[X^2]$, $0 \leqq \theta \leqq 1$, be drawn connecting them, it is required that the line be wholly in X'; i.e., every basket of goods on the line yields at least as much utility as $[X^\circ]$.

This is best visualized in terms of the usual three-dimensional utility surface. Choose a point $[X_1^\circ, X_2^\circ]$ on the base plane and determine the utility value U°. Then, slicing the utility surface parallel to the base plane at U° will yield a profile, viewed from the top, of an "indifference curve," which, when projected onto the base plane, will define all baskets of goods yielding U° in utility. The set X' then will be that portion of the base plane, X, which is on and to the northeast of the indifference curve. A straight line connecting any two points of this set must lie wholly within the set. For example, two points on the indifference curve must yield a straight line which coincides with or lies above the indifference curve at all points. Thus, the second characteristic of concave functions is quasi-concavity, which will hold for utility surfaces when marginal rates of substitution between all pairs of goods, including all pairs of composite goods, diminish. It yields no information about the changes in the function when a good or groups of goods are increased while other goods are held constant. For this the considerations taken into account in the discussion of concavity are relevant. Concavity implies quasi-concavity, although the opposite is not true.

We shall deal first with the implications of strict quasi-concavity. To recall, the necessary and sufficient condition for this is that of (I-1-3),

$$d^2U = F_1^{11}dX_1^{\circ 2} + F_2^{22}dX_2^{\circ 2} + F_3^{33}dX_3^{\circ 2} < 0$$

subject to the restriction, derived from (I-1-2-2),

$$\sum_j dX_j^\circ P_j = 0 \tag{97}$$

(I-1-3) is a simple type of quadratic form subject to the linear constraint (97). Note that universal diminishing marginal utility is sufficient to insure (I-1-3), but it is not necessary. One good—and only one good, regardless of the number of goods in the analysis—may be characterized by rising marginal utility, without necessarily violating (I-1-3).[31] The use of second-order extremum conditions to evaluate expressions, therefore, is a weaker assumption than universal diminishing marginal utility, and we should suspect that its usefulness in the analysis would reflect this lesser power.

It is now necessary to draw the desired implications from (I-1-3) and (97). First, we may use the linear relation (97) to express one dX_j° in terms of the others, say dX_1° in terms of dX_2° and dX_3°. Doing so, substituting in (I-1-3), and simplifying, we obtain:

$$\left[\frac{P_2^2}{P_1^2}F_1^{11} + F_2^{22}\right]dX_2^{\circ 2} + \left[\frac{P_3^2}{P_1^2}F_1^{11} + F_3^{33}\right]dX_3^{\circ 2} + 2\left[\frac{P_2P_3}{P_1^2}F_1^{11}\right]dX_2^\circ dX_3^\circ < 0 \tag{98}$$

or, if we make the given substitutions for the bracketed expressions,

$$c_{22}dX_2^{\circ 2} + c_{33}dX_3^{\circ 2} + 2c_{23}dX_2^\circ dX_3^\circ < 0 \tag{99}$$

which may be rewritten

$$c_{22}\left[dX_2^\circ + \frac{c_{23}}{c_{22}}dX_3^\circ\right]^2 + \frac{c_{22}c_{33} - c_{23}^2}{c_{22}}[dX_3^\circ]^2 < 0 \tag{100}$$

The expression (100) has the advantage that all terms with differentials in them are included in the brackets which are squared. Therefore, the sign of the expression must depend upon the coefficients of the terms inside the brackets. These coefficients may be written in determinantal form:

$$c_{22}, \quad \frac{\begin{vmatrix} c_{22} & c_{23} \\ c_{23} & c_{33} \end{vmatrix}}{c_{22}} \tag{101}$$

Now (100) is a negative definite quadratic form, since for all admissible real values for the dX_j° it is required to be negative, except where all $dX_j^\circ = 0$. It may be seen that if both expressions in (101) are negative, which implies that the determinant in the numerator of the second

[31] The reason for the restriction to one good will be noted below. The theorem was originally due to Slutsky, (1), pp. 31–4, 45–7.

expression be positive, a sufficient condition for negative definiteness will be met. It also may be proved, however, that this is a necessary condition, for if we adjust dX_2° and dX_3° so that $\left[dX_2^\circ + \frac{c_{23}}{c_{22}} dX_3^\circ\right] = 0$, it is necessary that the second expression in (101) be negative to retain negative definiteness. This may be generalized for a quadratic form with any number of variables: it is necessary and sufficient for a quadratic form to be negative definite that the determinants of the form,

$$(102) \qquad c_{22}, \begin{vmatrix} c_{22} & c_{23} \\ c_{23} & c_{33} \end{vmatrix}, \begin{vmatrix} c_{22} & c_{23} & c_{24} \\ c_{23} & c_{33} & c_{34} \\ c_{24} & c_{34} & c_{44} \end{vmatrix}, \ldots \begin{vmatrix} c_{22} & \cdots & c_{2n} \\ c_{23} & \cdots & c_{3n} \\ \cdot & \cdots & \cdot \\ c_{2n} & \cdots & c_{nn} \end{vmatrix}$$

have the sign $(-1)^s$ where s denotes the number of rows.[32]

Let us now reconvert the determinants of (101) into determinants with the F_j^{ij} and P_j values as elements. If c_{22} is multiplied by P_1^2,

$$(103) \qquad P_1^2 c_{22} = P_2^2 F_1^{11} + P_1^2 F_2^{22}$$

which is seen to be

$$(104) \qquad \begin{vmatrix} F_1^{11} & 0 & -P_1 \\ 0 & F_2^{22} & -P_2 \\ P_1 & P_2 & 0 \end{vmatrix}$$

In similar fashion,

$$(105) \qquad P_1^2 \begin{vmatrix} c_{22} & c_{23} \\ c_{23} & c_{33} \end{vmatrix} = \begin{vmatrix} F_1^{11} & 0 & 0 & -P_1 \\ 0 & F_2^{22} & 0 & -P_2 \\ 0 & 0 & F_3^{33} & -P_3 \\ P_1 & P_2 & P_3 & 0 \end{vmatrix}$$

Therefore, the conditions upon c_{22} and the determinant in (103) become (since multiplying by P_1^2 does not change the signs)

$$(106) \qquad \begin{vmatrix} F_1^{11} & 0 & -P_1 \\ 0 & F_2^{22} & -P_2 \\ P_1 & P_2 & 0 \end{vmatrix} < 0, \quad \begin{vmatrix} F_1^{11} & 0 & 0 & -P_1 \\ 0 & F_2^{22} & 0 & -P_2 \\ 0 & 0 & F_3^{33} & -P_3 \\ P_1 & P_2 & P_3 & 0 \end{vmatrix} > 0$$

or that these determinants must have the sign $(-1)^s$, $s > 2$, where s is the number of rows. Since the numbering of the goods in our problem is completely arbitrary, any good could be Y_1 and any other Y_2, so that the first determinant in fact constrains the relevant terms for *any* pair of goods.[33]

The last determinant in (106), however, is $|D|$, and the first determi-

[32] H. Hancock, (1), pp. 19–21, 86–91.

[33] We may now prove Slutsky's theorem that no more than one good may exhibit increasing marginal utility. If two goods did so, at least one of the 3×3 determinants of (106) would be positive and violate the second-order equilibrium conditions.

nant is a principal minor $|D_{ss}|$. Thus, it is seen, the second-order maximum conditions (I-1-3), when assumed to hold, place restrictions upon the determinants which contain the slopes upon whose values the signs of the expressions we seek depend. With this information it is possible to attempt to evaluate the same expressions listed in the summary of the analysis under the assumption of universal diminishing marginal utility.

1. $\frac{\partial X_j^\circ}{\partial Z}$. From (43) and (106) for our example this will be positive if $(-1)^t|D_{4t}|$ is positive, negative if this expression is negative. But the information in (106) provides us no information about such determinants as $|D_{4t}|$. If it is multiplied out, say for $\frac{\partial X_1}{\partial Z}$,

$$-|D_{41}| = P_1F_2^{22}F_3^{33} \tag{107}$$

As we have seen, it is possible that either F_2^{22} or F_3^{33} (but not both) could be positive without violating (106). Suppose, in fact, F_2^{22} were known to be positive and consistent with (106). Then, if income rose slightly, the consumer would reduce his purchases of Y_1 (and all other goods but Y_2). We conclude: $\frac{\partial X_j^\circ}{\partial Z} \gtreqless 0$.

2. $\frac{\partial \lambda^\circ}{\partial Z}$. From (46) and (106) the sign of this expression will be positive when $|D_{44}| > 0$, negative if this determinant is negative. From (46), again, it is clear that if any of the three goods exhibits increasing marginal utility, λ° will move in the same direction as income, and if none does, it will move in the opposite direction. Therefore: $\frac{\partial \lambda^\circ}{\partial Z} \gtreqless 0$.

3. s_{jj}. From (50), (51), (53), and (106), it may be seen that second-order equilibrium conditions yield unambiguous information about the signs of the two determinants involved, and $s_{jj} < 0$.

4. r_{jj}. From (55) and the analysis of $\frac{\partial X_j^\circ}{\partial Z}$ in paragraph 1 above, it will be clear that $r_{jj} \gtreqless 0$.

5. $\frac{\partial X_j^\circ}{\partial P_j}$. From (56), 3 and 4 above, this expression may be positive, negative, or zero. Therefore, if the price of a good rises, given the assumption of a constrained maximum having been attained on the utility surface, it is not certain that the quantity consumed of that good will fall. This by virtue of the possibility of a positive income effect; however, it may be seen from the analysis that such perverseness will occur only if one good possesses increasing marginal utility at the equilibrium in question.

6. s_{jk}. From (64), (65), and (106), it is clear that information about the sign of such determinants as $|D_{kj}|$ is not obtainable. For the case of

$|D_{12}|$, (66) indicates that if Y_3 demonstrates increasing marginal utility, $s_{jk} < 0$, and, generalizing, if any other good but that whose quantity change or price is being analyzed shows increasing marginal utility, this result will hold. If all of these other goods exhibit diminishing marginal utility, $s_{jk} > 0$. It is interesting to note that whether good Y_j exhibits increasing or diminishing marginal utility has no impact upon the sign of s_{jk}. We conclude: $s_{jk} \gtreqless 0$.

7. r_{jk}. From (64), (65), and (106), no information is yielded by the second-order maximum conditions about such determinants as $|D_{4j}|$. For $|D_{42}|$, from (69), if either Y_1 or Y_2 exhibits increasing marginal utility in this neighborhood, $r_{jk} > 0$, and, more generally, if any good other than Y_j does so, $r_{jk} > 0$. Otherwise, $r_{jk} < 0$. Therefore: $r_{jk} \gtreqless 0$.

8. $\frac{\partial X_j^\circ}{\partial P_k}$. From (64) and 6 and 7 above, $\frac{\partial X_j^\circ}{\partial P_k} \gtreqless 0$, depending (1) upon the existence of a good with increasing marginal utility, (2) whether that good is Y_j or Y_k, or a good which is neither, and (3) upon the magnitudes of s_{jk} and r_{jk} in absolute value.

9. $s_{\lambda j}$. From (74) and (75), as well as (106), no information on determinants of the type $|D_{j4}|$ is obtainable. For $j = 1$, from (76) it is seen that if any good other than the one whose price has changed exhibits increasing marginal utility, $s_{\lambda 1} > 0$; if not, it is negative or zero. Therefore, $s_{\lambda j} \gtreqless 0$.

10. $r_{\lambda j}$. From (74), (75), and (106), once more the secondary equilibrium conditions may be seen to offer no aid in evaluation of such determinants as $|D_{44}|$. From (79), however, this is seen to be positive if any good exhibits increasing marginal utility, negative otherwise. Therefore, $r_{\lambda j} \gtreqless 0$.

11. $\frac{\partial \lambda^\circ}{\partial P_j}$. From (75) and 9 and 10 above, it may be seen that $\frac{\partial \lambda^\circ}{\partial P_j} \gtreqless 0$.

The second-order equilibrium conditions, therefore, provide a much less powerful basis for the derivation of the directions of movements of the variables with price and income changes than does the postulational basis. Nevertheless, the nature of the ambiguities and their cause are clear: one good, and only one good, may yield increasing marginal utility in the neighborhood of equilibrium. Consequently, the analyst may make intuitive judgments about the likelihood of such departures from the expected, given the initial equilibrium position, and eliminate many of the ambiguities as not likely. Most importantly, in the evaluation of $\frac{\partial X_j^\circ}{\partial P_j}$, nonnegativity can arise only with the existence of a good exhibiting increasing marginal utility.

Model I-1, with its simple form of preference function, therefore, regardless of which basis is adopted, yields rather clear insights into the consumer's reactions to data changes. However, the assumption that preferences among goods are independent—that the preference of a consumer for beef steak is independent of the amount of pork chops he consumes or the amount of potatoes he enjoys—cannot be accepted as realistic. Therefore, we move a step closer to the real world in consideration of Model I-2.

2.b.2. Model I-2: Cardinal, Interdependent Preferences

All of the assumptions of Model I-1 are retained except that of independence of the consumer's preferences. In this complication we follow the innovation of Edgeworth, who in 1881 proposed that the consumer's preference function, assumed to be unique up to a linear transformation, be written in the form

$$U = F(X_1, X_2, X_3) \tag{108}$$

instead of the additive version of (26).[34] This version implies that the identities of (27) do not hold; that is,

$$\frac{\partial^2 U}{\partial X_j \partial X_k} \neq 0 \tag{109}$$

Pareto was the most energetic in opening up the fruitful analysis of consumer choice under these conditions, thereby taking a major step forward in models of simple exchange.[35]

In a straightforward repetition of the method used in Model I-1, the following equations of Model I-2 are derived by maximization of (108) subject to a budget constraint:

$$S = U - \lambda\left(\sum_j X_j P_j - Z\right) \tag{I-2-1}$$

(I-2-2)

$$1. \quad \frac{\partial S}{\partial X_j} = F^j - \lambda^\circ P_j = 0, \qquad j = 1, 2, 3$$

$$2. \quad \frac{\partial S}{\partial \lambda} = \sum_j X_j^\circ P_j - Z = 0$$

$$d^2U = \sum_j F^{jj} dX_j^{\circ 2} + 2 \sum_j \sum_k F^{jk} dX_j^\circ dX_k^\circ < 0, \quad j = 1, 2, 3 \quad j \neq k \tag{I-2-3}$$

Moreover, the nonspecific solutions to the model will be of the form in (40).

[34] F. Edgeworth, (1), pp. 20, 104.
[35] V. Pareto, (2), pp. 252–63.

System (I-2-2) will now be shocked by a small change in Z. The resulting equations in matrix form will be:

$$(110) \qquad \begin{bmatrix} F^{11} & F^{12} & F^{13} & -P_1 \\ F^{12} & F^{22} & F^{23} & -P_2 \\ F^{13} & F^{23} & F^{33} & -P_3 \\ P_1 & P_2 & P_3 & 0 \end{bmatrix} \begin{bmatrix} \frac{\partial X_1^\circ}{\partial Z} \\ \frac{\partial X_2^\circ}{\partial Z} \\ \frac{\partial X_3^\circ}{\partial Z} \\ \frac{\partial \lambda^\circ}{\partial Z} \end{bmatrix} = \begin{bmatrix} 0 \\ 0 \\ 0 \\ 1 \end{bmatrix}$$

No longer are zeros found in the off-diagonal elements of the matrix, and, from previous analyses, it is to be expected that the relevant expressions will prove to be more resistant to evaluation.

2.b.2.a. Integrability of the Utility Function and the Symmetry of the Matrix of the System

The F^{jk} terms in (110) form a symmetric submatrix, no longer trivial in its symmetry by virtue of off-diagonal elements being zero. If we merely assume the function (108) to exist and be given to us in revelatory fashion, the ability to assume the equality $F^{jk} = F^{kj}$ derives from the assumed continuity of the F-function.[36] However, if we remain with the operational view, we must begin with the information collected from the consumer as described by a set of differential equations, and the ability to write these equalities then depends on the "integrability conditions" for the utility surface; we shall discuss these briefly here, to return to them in Model I-3.

Pareto was misled into believing that these conditions were concerned with the order of consumption of a given basket of goods, and that the existence of the function (108) implied that the order of consumption had been determined in a nonexplicit but optimal manner.[37] However, as Samuelson has shown, even in the case of two goods, where no integrability problem arises if the partial derivatives are continuous, the order-of-consumption problem would still exist, while in a three-good case even if the soup-steak-pie order of consumption were given, the problem of the integrability of the indifference varieties would still exist.[38] Therefore, though the equalities $F^{jk} = F^{kj}$ tempt one into the Paretian interpretation, it is not relevant.

As we have seen in Section 1, the derivation of the indifference contours of such functions as those of (108) must be done by integrating slope

[36] The conditions are stated in precise terms in Young's Theorem.
[37] V. Pareto, (2), pp. 555–6. See also J. Mosak, (1), p. 6.
[38] P. Samuelson, (5).

relationships derived from observations which are written as linear differential equations of the type

$$\sum_j F^j dX_j = 0 \tag{111}$$

The problem arises because it is not at all certain that differential equations of the form of (111) can be integrated into indifference contours. In the case where only two goods are involved (as in (111)), and where F^1 and F^2 are continuous and differentiable, no problem is met. Under these conditions the preference function will always exist. The problem is encountered in its troublesome form only when three or more goods are included. Its meaning may be illustrated in the following way.

Suppose a basket of goods, $[X^1]$, is offered the consumer with specific amounts of three goods. Then, $[X^1] = (X_1^1, X_2^1, X_3^1)$. Now, move the consumer to a second basket, $[X^2]$, equally as desirable to him as $[X^1]$, and which contains the same amount of Y_1, but differing amounts of Y_2 and Y_3. Then, $[X^2] = (X_1^1, X_2^2, X_3^2)$. Next, move him to a third basket of goods, $[X^3]$, equal in desirability to $[X^1]$ and $[X^2]$, and obtained from $[X^2]$ by holding Y_2 constant but changing the amounts of Y_1 and Y_3 contained therein. Thus, $[X^3] = (X_1^3, X_2^2, X_3^3)$. Lastly, from $[X^3]$ the consumer is moved to $[X^4]$, indifferent to $[X^3]$, defined as (X_1^1, X_2^1, X_3^4). Thus, we have moved the consumer in a "circle," at each step holding one or two goods constant at a prior level, and varying the remaining good or goods. If $X_3^4 = X_3^1$ the circle is closed, and the integrability conditions are met. If $X_3^4 \neq X_3^1$, the circle is not closed, and the consumer has revealed a contradiction in his preferences, since he has indicated indifference between $[X^1]$ and $[X^1 + \Delta X]$, where $[\Delta X]$ is the vector $[0, 0, X_3^4 - X_3^1]$. The integrability conditions are not met in this last case. In the case of three goods, if the consumer can order his preferences, and transitivity holds among the orderings, the integrability conditions do hold and the indifference surfaces exist.[39]

For the three-good case the circle will be closed if and only if the following restrictions are met:

$$F^1(F^{23} - F^{32}) + F^2(F^{31} - F^{13}) + F^3(F^{12} - F^{21}) = 0 \tag{112}$$

[39] P. Samuelson, (5). Houthakker, by extending Samuelson's Weak Axiom of Revealed Preference to a chain of more than two baskets of goods, provided the necessary and sufficient conditions for integrability. For two baskets, if $[X^1]$ is revealed to be preferred to $[X^2]$, or if

$$[P^1] \cdot [X^2] \leqq [P^1] \cdot [X^1] \tag{1}$$

then the Weak Axiom states that $[X^2]$ can never be revealed to be preferable to $[X^1]$, i.e.,

$$[P^2] \cdot [X^1] > [P^2] \cdot [X^2] \tag{2}$$

If the consumer bought basket 1 when he might have bought basket 2, he will

Obviously, if the F^j can take all nonnegative values, including zero, it is necessary and sufficient for (112) to hold that $F^{jk} = F^{kj}$ for all j and k, $j \neq k$. Therefore, if (112) is met, the indifference varieties can be obtained by integration. Further, when $n > 3$, at most $\frac{(n-1)(n-2)}{2}$ such equations as (112) must hold for integrability. Note that for the case of independent utilities (112) is satisfied trivially.

It must be stressed that the assumption of integrability is a behavioral assumption: it implies that the consumer cannot, by judicious choices of baskets, be led into indifference between two baskets alike in all respects except for a quantitative difference in a good. He *cares* about what he obtains and he is *perceptive* enough to realize when such differences exist in the choices offered him.

2.b.2.b. Manipulation of Model I-2

We shall represent system (110) in the following symbols:

(113) $$[D^*][dV] = [dZ]$$

We may evaluate the impacts of a small change in income upon equilibrium amounts consumed in similar fashion to (44):

(114) $$\frac{\partial X_j^\circ}{\partial Z} = (-1)^t \frac{|D_{4t}^*|}{|D^*|}$$

More specifically,

(115) $$\frac{\partial X_1^\circ}{\partial Z} = -\frac{|D_{41}^*|}{|D^*|}$$

No longer may we appeal to any simple postulational basis for evaluation, for even if we wished to assume universal diminishing marginal

---

buy basket 2 in another situation only when he cannot afford basket 1, if the Weak Axiom holds. The Weak Axiom is only a necessary condition for integrability, since if $[X^1]$ is revealed preferable to $[X^2]$, and $[X^2]$ to $[X^3]$, it is not implied that $[X^1]$ is revealed preferable to $[X^3]$ in general.

If the Weak Axiom holds for a chain of baskets at least two of which are different, so that if

(3) $$[P^2] \cdot [X^3] \leqq [P^2] \cdot [X^2], \text{ then } [P^3] \cdot [X^2] > [P^3] \cdot [X^3]$$

and so forth, to

(4) $$[P^{n-1}] \cdot [X^n] \leqq [P^{n-1}] \cdot [X^{n-1}], \text{ then } [P^n] \cdot [X^{n-1}] > [P^n] \cdot [X^n]$$

the Strong Axiom of Revealed Preference states that $[X^1]$ will never be revealed to be inferior to $X^n]$, or

(5) $$[P^n] \cdot [X^1] > [P^n] \cdot [X^n]$$

If these conditions are met, the "circle" will always be closed and integrability conditions will be satisfied. H. Houthakker, (1).

utility the cross-effects of substitutability and complementarity will nullify any aid this assumption yields. For example, let us expand $|D^*_{41}|$:

$$(116)\quad |D^*_{41}| = P_1(F^{23^2} - F^{22}F^{33}) + P_2(F^{12}F^{33} - F^{13}F^{23}) + P_3(F^{13}F^{22} - F^{12}F^{23})$$

This expression should be compared in its complexity with the denominator of (45) to obtain an index of the complications introduced by interdependence of the utilities. Given diminishing marginal utility for all goods, we should have to know the algebraic values of all the F-terms before the sign of this expression would be given unambiguously.

For whatever restrictions we may place upon the F-terms, therefore, it will be necessary to resort to the second-order maximization conditions. By the same reasoning as that used to derive (106), the necessary and sufficient conditions for the strict quasi-concavity of U expressed in (I-2-3) subject to (I-2-2) to hold are

$$(117)\quad \begin{vmatrix} F^{11} & F^{12} & -P_1 \\ F^{12} & F^{22} & -P_2 \\ P_1 & P_2 & 0 \end{vmatrix} < 0, \quad \begin{vmatrix} F^{11} & F^{12} & F^{13} & -P_1 \\ F^{12} & F^{22} & F^{23} & -P_2 \\ F^{13} & F^{23} & F^{33} & -P_3 \\ P_1 & P_2 & P_3 & 0 \end{vmatrix} > 0$$

Again, these may be generalized to n goods. Let $|D^*_s|$ be the principal minor of $|D^*|$ with s rows and columns. Then, for $2 < s \leqq n$ and for all *bordered* principal minors, it is required that $|D^*_s|$ have the sign $(-1)^s$.[40]

The conclusions about the signs of the eleven magnitudes in which we are interested are the same as those given by the analysis of Model I-1 using second-order maximization conditions as a basis for evaluation. In this formal sense, then, if we were unwilling to specify universal diminishing marginal utility in Model I-1, the complication of the analysis by interdependent utilities does not result in any loss of analytical power. In actual fact, however, there is a considerable gain in complexity between the two models. The ambiguities of signs in Model I-1's conclusions from the evaluation by second-order maximum conditions resulted entirely from the possible presence of a single good with increasing marginal utility. In Model I-2 these ambiguities are much more complex in origin, springing as they do from this first cause plus the complex substitutionary-complementarity relations among goods.

If the analyst were willing to make the further assumption that while the F^{jk} are not identically zero they are small enough to be neglected, he may return to the analysis of Model I-1 with the second-order equilibrium conditions as a basis for evaluation. If he went further to assume none of the goods in this neighborhood exhibited increasing marginal utility, he could obtain the propositions developed from Model

[40] These conditions (for ordinal preference functions) were given explicit formulation by H. Hotelling, (3), and J. Hicks and R. G. D. Allen in J. Hicks, (3).

I-1 with the postulational basis for evaluation. The first of these steps, of course, is a good illustration of the analysis of general models of Chapter 1 and of its conclusions about the difficulties arising with too much interdependence among the variables. Once more the source of the attractiveness of the simplicities of Model I-1 for the analyst has been described, with its consequent impact upon the body of economic propositions in the tool kit of the working economist.

2.b.3. Model I-3: Ordinal, Interdependent Preferences

There remains but one more task in the analysis of simple exchange: to take account of the empirical fact that economists have not yet devised methods of measuring interdependent preferences unique up to a positive linear transformation, and must count upon using measurements unique up to a monotone transformation. We may now proceed to the demonstration that the use of such a preference function does nothing to lessen the economist's analytical power, as reflected in the derivable propositions from Model I-3. They are *exactly* the same as those derivable from Model I-2, with the exception of the treatment of $\lambda^{*\circ}$ as the marginal "utility" of income. Since "utility" is not measured cardinally, the absolute value of $\lambda^{*\circ}$ has no particular significance although propositions concerning its direction of movement are still derivable.

We assume a set of information in the form of differential equations derived from empirical analysis of the consumer's preferences; moreover, it is assumed that the integrability conditions are met, and that there exists a function:

(118) $$M = G(X_1, X_2, X_3) = M[F(X_1, X_2, X_3)], \qquad M' > 0$$

where $F(X_1, X_2, X_3)$ is the preference function of (108) which we shall assume exists for our analysis.

Then, once more we shall repeat the methods of Model I-1 to derive the conditions for the solution of Model I-3:

(I-3-1) $$S = M - \lambda^*\left(\sum_j X_jP_j - Z\right)$$

(I-3-2)
$$1.\quad \frac{\partial S}{\partial X_j} = G^j - \lambda^{*\circ}P_j = 0, \qquad j = 1, 2, 3$$
$$2.\quad \frac{\partial S}{\partial \lambda^*} = \sum_j X_j^\circ P_j - Z = 0$$

(I-3-3) $$d^2M = \sum_j G^{jj}dX_j^{\circ 2} + 2\sum_j\sum_k G^{jk}dX_j^\circ dX_k^\circ < 0, \quad \text{for every } j,\ j \neq k$$

If the system is shocked, say by a slight change in income, the following equations would be obtained:

(119)
$$\begin{bmatrix} G^{11} & G^{12} & G^{13} & -P_1 \\ G^{12} & G^{22} & G^{23} & -P_2 \\ G^{13} & G^{23} & G^{33} & -P_3 \\ P_1 & P_2 & P_3 & 0 \end{bmatrix} \begin{bmatrix} \dfrac{\partial X_1^\circ}{\partial Z} \\ \dfrac{\partial X_2^\circ}{\partial Z} \\ \dfrac{\partial X_3^\circ}{\partial Z} \\ \dfrac{\partial \lambda^{*\circ}}{\partial Z} \end{bmatrix} = \begin{bmatrix} 0 \\ 0 \\ 0 \\ 1 \end{bmatrix}$$

or

(120)
$$[H][dV] = [dZ]$$

Now, from (118) it is possible to rewrite (I-3-2) in the form:

(121)
$$1.\quad M'F^j - \lambda^{*\circ}P_j = 0$$
$$2.\quad \sum_j X_j^\circ P_j - Z = 0$$

Then, $[H]$ may be rewritten,

(122)
$$\begin{bmatrix} M'F^{11} + M'^1F^1 & M'F^{12} + M'^2F^1 & M'F^{13} + M'^3F^1 & -P_1 \\ M'F^{12} + M'^1F^2 & M'F^{22} + M'^2F^2 & M'F^{23} + M'^3F^2 & -P_2 \\ M'F^{13} + M'^1F^3 & M'F^{23} + M'^2F^3 & M'F^{33} + M'^3F^3 & -P_3 \\ P_1 & P_2 & P_3 & 0 \end{bmatrix}$$

But, since

(123)
$$M'^j = \frac{\partial M'}{\partial X_j^\circ} = \frac{\partial M'}{\partial U}\frac{\partial U}{\partial X_j^\circ} = M''F^j$$

we may substitute to obtain[41]

(124) $[H] =$
$$\begin{bmatrix} M'F^{11} + M''(F^1)^2 & M'F^{12} + M''F^1F^2 & M'F^{13} + M''F^1F^3 & -P_1 \\ M'F^{12} + M''F^1F^2 & M'F^{22} + M''(F^2)^2 & M'F^{23} + M''F^2F^3 & -P_2 \\ M'F^{13} + M''F^1F^3 & M'F^{23} + M''F^2F^3 & M'F^{33} + M''(F^3)^2 & -P_3 \\ P_1 & P_2 & P_3 & 0 \end{bmatrix}$$

It may now be shown that $|H|$ is reducible to a positive constant times $|D^*|$ and, therefore, that the same propositions which depend upon the

[41] Thus, $G^{jk} = M'F^{jk} + M''F^jF^k$. Since M'' is not restricted as to sign, for reasons examined in Section 1, this second term, except when F^j or F^k equals zero by virtue of satiation, is arbitrary as to sign. This explains why, when $j = k$, it is impossible with this monotone function to specify the equivalent of diminishing marginal preference. Cf. J. Mosak, (1), pp. 6–7.

sign of the latter can be derived from the former. First, substitute for P_j into (124) from (121):

$$(125)\quad [H] = \begin{bmatrix} M'F^{11} + M''(F^1)^2 & M'F^{12} + M''F^1F^2 & M'F^{13} + M''F^1F^3 & \dfrac{-M'F^1}{\lambda^{*o}} \\ M'F^{12} + M''F^1F^2 & M'F^{22} + M''(F^2)^2 & M'F^{23} + M''F^2F^3 & \dfrac{-M'F^2}{\lambda^{*o}} \\ M'F^{13} + M''F^1F^3 & M'F^{23} + M''F^2F^3 & M'F^{33} + M''(F^3)^2 & \dfrac{-M'F^3}{\lambda^{*o}} \\ \dfrac{M'F^1}{\lambda^{*o}} & \dfrac{M'F^2}{\lambda^{*o}} & \dfrac{M'F^3}{\lambda^{*o}} & 0 \end{bmatrix}$$

Second, in the determinant formed from $[H]$, multiply the last column and row by $\left(\dfrac{\lambda^{*o}}{M'}\right)$:

$$(126)\quad |H| = \frac{(M')^2}{(\lambda^{*o})^2} \begin{vmatrix} M'F^{11} + M''(F^1)^2 & M'F^{12} + M''F^1F^2 & M'F^{13} + M''F^1F^3 & -F^1 \\ M'F^{12} + M''F^1F^2 & M'F^{22} + M''(F^2)^2 & M'F^{23} + M''F^2F^3 & -F^2 \\ M'F^{13} + M''F^1F^3 & M'F^{23} + M''F^2F^3 & M'F^{33} + M''(F^3)^2 & -F^3 \\ F^1 & F^2 & F^3 & 0 \end{vmatrix}$$

Third, since multiplying a row or column of a determinant by a constant and adding the resulting terms to another row or column does not alter the value of the determinant, we may multiply the last column of (126) by $M''F^1$ and add the result to the first column, then multiply the last column by $M''F^2$ and add the result to the second column, and then multiply the last column by $M''F^3$ and add the result to the third column:

$$(127)\quad |H| = \left(\frac{M'}{\lambda^{*o}}\right)^2 \begin{vmatrix} M'F^{11} & M'F^{12} & M'F^{13} & -F^1 \\ M'F^{12} & M'F^{22} & M'F^{23} & -F^2 \\ M'F^{13} & M'F^{23} & M'F^{33} & -F^3 \\ F^1 & F^2 & F^3 & 0 \end{vmatrix}$$

Fourth, multiply the last row and column by M':

$$(128)\quad |H| = \left(\frac{1}{\lambda^{*o}}\right)^2 \begin{vmatrix} M'F^{11} & M'F^{12} & M'F^{13} & -M'F^1 \\ M'F^{12} & M'F^{22} & M'F^{23} & -M'F^2 \\ M'F^{13} & M'F^{23} & M'F^{33} & -M'F^3 \\ M'F^1 & M'F^2 & M'F^3 & 0 \end{vmatrix}$$

Fifth, divide out M' from each column:

$$(129) \qquad |H| = \frac{(M')^4}{(\lambda^{*\circ})^2} \begin{vmatrix} F^{11} & F^{12} & F^{13} & -F^1 \\ F^{12} & F^{22} & F^{23} & -F^2 \\ F^{13} & F^{23} & F^{33} & -F^3 \\ F^1 & F^2 & F^3 & 0 \end{vmatrix}$$

Lastly, multiply the last row and column by $\frac{M'}{\lambda^{*\circ}}$:

$$(130) \qquad |H| = (M')^2 \begin{vmatrix} F^{11} & F^{12} & F^{13} & \frac{-M'F^1}{\lambda^{*\circ}} \\ F^{12} & F^{22} & F^{23} & \frac{-M'F^2}{\lambda^{*\circ}} \\ F^{13} & F^{23} & F^{33} & \frac{-M'F^3}{\lambda^{*\circ}} \\ \frac{M'F^1}{\lambda^{*\circ}} & \frac{M'F^2}{\lambda^{*\circ}} & \frac{M'F^3}{\lambda^{*\circ}} & 0 \end{vmatrix}$$

or, from (121)

$$(131) \qquad |H| = (M')^2|D^*|$$

Since $M' > 0$, regardless of the power to which it is raised, it cannot affect the sign of $|H|$. In the general case, for an $[H]$ with n goods,

$$(132) \qquad |H| = (M')^{n-1}|D^*|$$

and thus the sign of $|H|$ is the same as the sign of $|D^*|$ whatever n is.

Further, all minors of $|H|$ which retain a "price border," may be written

$$(133) \qquad |H_{jk}| = (M')^{n-2}|D^*_{jk}|$$

The second-order equilibrium conditions, necessary and sufficient for (I-3-3) subject to (I-3-2-2) to hold, are

$$(134) \qquad \begin{vmatrix} G^{11} & G^{12} & -P_1 \\ G^{12} & G^{22} & -P_2 \\ P_1 & P_2 & 0 \end{vmatrix} < 0, \quad \begin{vmatrix} G^{11} & G^{12} & G^{13} & -P_1 \\ G^{12} & G^{22} & G^{23} & -P_2 \\ G^{13} & G^{23} & G^{33} & -P_3 \\ P_1 & P_2 & P_3 & 0 \end{vmatrix} > 0$$

and, from (131) and (133), that all *bordered* principal minors $|H_s|$ with s rows, $s = 3, \ldots, n + 1$ have the sign $(-1)^s$.

From (121-1) and (I-2-2-1),

$$(135) \qquad \lambda^{*\circ} = M'\lambda^\circ$$

Also,

$$\frac{\partial \lambda^{*\circ}}{\partial Z} = M' \frac{\partial \lambda^\circ}{\partial Z} \tag{136}$$

$$\frac{\partial \lambda^{*\circ}}{\partial P_j} = M' \frac{\partial \lambda^\circ}{\partial P_j} = s_{\lambda^* j} + r_{\lambda^* j} = M' s_{\lambda j} + M' r_{\lambda j} \tag{137}$$

It follows that Model I-3 yields the same propositions about signs as paragraphs 2, 9, 10, 11, in the discussion of Model I-1 with second-order maximum conditions as a basis for evaluation and of Model I-2.

Further,

$$\frac{\partial X_j^\circ}{\partial Z} = (-1)^t \frac{|H_{4t}|}{|H|} = (-1)^t \frac{M'^2 |D_{4t}^*|}{M'^2 |D^*|} = (-1)^t \frac{|D_{4t}^*|}{|D^*|} \tag{138}$$

Therefore, the conclusions of paragraph 1 hold.

And, as far as price changes are concerned:

$$\begin{aligned} \frac{\partial X_j^\circ}{\partial P_j} &= \lambda^{*\circ} \frac{|H_{tt}|}{|H|} - (-1)^t X_j^\circ \frac{|H_{4t}|}{|H|} \\ &= s_{jj}^* + r_{jj}^* \\ &= \lambda^\circ \frac{|D_{jj}^*|}{|D^*|} - (-1)^t X_j^\circ \frac{|D_{4j}^*|}{|D^*|} \\ &= s_{jj} + r_{jj} \end{aligned} \tag{139}$$

Therefore, the conclusions of paragraphs 3, 4, and 5 hold true for Model I-3.

Also,

$$\begin{aligned} \frac{\partial X_j^\circ}{\partial P_k} &= (-1)^{j+k} \lambda^{*\circ} \frac{|H_{kj}|}{|H|} - (-1)^{j+k} X_k^\circ \frac{|H_{4j}|}{|H|} \\ &= s_{jk}^* + r_{jk}^* \\ &= (-1)^{j+k} \lambda^\circ \frac{|D_{kj}^*|}{|D^*|} - (-1)^{j+k} X_k^\circ \frac{|D_{4j}^*|}{|D^*|} \\ &= s_{jk} + r_{jk} \end{aligned} \tag{140}$$

Therefore, the conclusions of paragraphs 6, 7, and 8 hold for Model I-3. We have shown, therefore, that every proposition derived from Model I-2, with its cardinal preference function and interdependent utilities, can be obtained from the ordinal function of Model I-3.

2.b.4. Further Propositions in Consumer Theory

It is possible to derive further propositions relating to consumer behavior, and we now shall do so in concluding our consideration of simple exchange theory.

2.b.4.a. The Homogeneity of the Demand Functions

We may eliminate λ° from I-1-2 and I-2-2, and $\lambda^{*\circ}$ from I-3-2, to obtain, in the case of I-3-2,

$$\frac{G^j}{P_j} = \frac{G^k}{P_k} = \cdots \tag{141}$$

$$\sum_j X_j^\circ P_j = Z \tag{142}$$

Let θ be any positive constant: then it is readily seen that equations (141) and (142) are homogeneous of degree zero in P_j and Z.[42] This implies that the demand functions, or nonspecific solutions to these equations, enjoy the same properties, for if all P_j and Z are multiplied by θ, none of the above equations will have changed. What this means in economic terms is that the interrelationships of Models I-1, I-2, and I-3 are functions of relative prices and income only. That is, the set of prices and income ($P_1 = 5$, $P_2 = 7$, $P_3 = 2$, $Z = 10$) will lead to the same X_j° as the set ($P_1 = 10$, $P_2 = 14$, $P_3 = 4$, $Z = 20$), since the relative values are the same.

In our models we have been measuring prices and income in terms of the "dollar." Such a good is termed the *numéraire*, and an arbitrary quantity of this good is taken as the unit of measurement for prices and income.[43] If the *numéraire* is external to the model, as in our cases, the fixing of the standard unit of it is equivalent to the specification of an absolute price level: if the "dollar" is the unit of the commodity "cash" whose price is equated to unity, then all P_j and Z are specified in dollars, not half-dollars, and (say) the first price-income set above is relevant, not the second. If the unit were changed to the "half-dollar," and its price were thereby equated to unity, the second price-income set would become relevant.

A second way in which this single degree of freedom which exists because prices and income are expressed in relative rather than absolute terms may be expended is by selecting one of the P_j or Z as the *numéraire* good's price, thereby arbitrarily setting it at unity. To do this is to select an internal *numéraire*, and it is the procedure we shall follow in most instances in this book. For example, if Z is selected as *numéraire* and adopted as a unit, so that $Z \equiv 1$, all prices would be expressed in income

[42] See footnote 30 for the definition of homogeneity.

[43] The specification of the *numéraire* good and the quantity of it used as a unit of measurement are explicit Walrasian innovations, although they had been used implicitly by many economists before him. It was the virtue of Walras's introduction of it, however, that he demonstrates the emergence of a *numéraire* in a system of complex exchange as of such importance in the attainment of a solution to the system as almost to make of that emergence a theorem of market behavior. See L. Walras, (3), pp. 153–63.

units, or the proportion of income required for unit purchases of all goods. A doubling of income must then be expressed as a halving of all prices, since $Z \equiv 1$ by definition. More frequently, a good is chosen as *numéraire* (in this book, good Y_1 is selected) as a mere convention, a unit of it is defined, and its price $P_1 \equiv 1$. If Y_1 is wheat and the standard unit is one bushel, all prices and income are measured in bushels of wheat. It is important to see that the specification of any one good as *numéraire* is a wholly arbitrary decision; most particularly, the specification of the good "money," where it exists in a model or the real world, as the *numéraire* commodity, is no less an arbitrary action than the specification of wheat for that role. It is just as possible to have a wheat price of money as a money price of wheat. Indeed, in Chapter 5 we shall employ throughout a *numéraire* other than money in order to clarify the role of money in a general system.

A third way of "anchoring" the price-income system is to enforce some other restriction upon prices and income, most frequently for reasons of convenience of analysis. The normalization of prices or of prices and income—enforcing the condition that they sum to unity—is, for example, a convenient restriction in the proof of the existence of a solution of a model, and will be used in Chapter 9.

When the use of an internal *numéraire* is employed, it is customary not to include the price of the unit of *numéraire* (equals unity) in the analysis. Thus, for example, the nonspecific solutions to (141) and (142) would be written

(143)

1. $$X_j^\circ = H_j(P_2, P_3, \ldots, P_n, Z) \quad j = 2, \ldots, n$$

2. $$X_1^\circ = Z - \sum_{j=2}^{n} X_j^\circ P_j$$

The expression of the *numéraire's* demand function as a residual is wholly arbitrary, any other good being equally subject to such residuary treatment.

2.b.4.b. Restrictions Upon the Substitution Effects

It has been demonstrated for all three models that the own-substitution effects of price changes are negative; i.e.,

(144) $$s_{jj} < 0$$

Further, from (139)

(145) $$s_{jj}^* < 0$$

where the asterisk indicates their derivation from Model I-3. Since the equivalence of these substitution terms has been established in the above analysis, we shall henceforth omit the asterisk.

Another restriction upon the substitution terms concerns the "other-substitution" effects. Since

$$(146) \qquad s_{jk} = (-1)^{j+k}\lambda^{\circ} \frac{|H_{kj}|}{|H|}$$

and since, by virtue of the essential symmetry of $[H]$, $|H_{kj}| = |H_{jk}|$, it follows that

$$(147) \qquad s_{jk} = s_{kj}$$

This result is of prime importance for the further analysis of general systems, and is not intuitively obvious. It states that if price changes were compensated to eliminate the income effect, the residual variation due to the substitution effect of X_j° per unit of change in P_k would be equal to the residual variation of X_k° per unit of change in P_j. From this, the matrix of substitution effects for the consumer is seen to be symmetric:

$$(148) \qquad [s] = \begin{bmatrix} s_{11} & s_{12} & \cdots & s_{1n} \\ s_{12} & s_{22} & \cdots & s_{2n} \\ \cdot & \cdot & \cdots & \cdot \\ s_{1n} & s_{2n} & \cdots & s_{nn} \end{bmatrix}$$

Further, $[-s]$ is positive semi-definite: $|s| = 0$ by virtue of the third condition discussed below, while all principal minors of $[-s]$ will be positive. Also, not only is the symmetry of $[s]$ implied by the integrability conditions on the consumer's preferences, but it implies them. Therefore, the symmetry of $[s]$ is a necessary and sufficient condition for the integrability of consumer preferences.[44] Therefore this symmetry implies and is implied by the Strong Axiom of Revealed Preference.

A third condition follows from the zero degree homogeneity of the demand functions in the P_j and Z. Euler's theorem on homogeneous functions states that if $x = f(y, z)$ is homogeneous of degree n, then

$$(149) \qquad nx = f^y y + f^z z$$

or in the case of the demand functions of our three models with an external *numéraire* as written in (40)

$$(150) \qquad \begin{aligned} &1. \quad 0 = \sum_k H^k_{j \neq 1} P_k + H^z_{j \neq 1} Z, \qquad k = 1, \ldots, n \\ &2. \quad 0 = Z - \sum_j X_j^{\circ} P_j, \qquad j = 1, \ldots, n \end{aligned}$$

But, of course, $H_j^k = \dfrac{\partial X_j^{\circ}}{\partial P_k} = s_{jk} + r_{jk}$, and substituting in (150–1),

$$(151) \qquad 0 = \sum_k s_{jk} P_k + \sum_k r_{jk} P_k + H_j^z Z, \quad j \neq 1,\ k = 1, \ldots, n$$

[44] P. Samuelson, (5), p. 378.

But, $r_{jk} = -X_k^\circ \dfrac{\partial X_j^\circ}{\partial Z} = -X_k^\circ H_j^z$. Therefore,

(152) $$\sum_k r_{jk}P_k = \sum_k - X_k^\circ P_k H_j^z$$

or, by (150–2),

(153) $$\sum_k r_{jk}P_k = -ZH_j^z$$

Therefore, (151) becomes

(154) $$0 = \sum_k s_{jk}P_k, \qquad j \neq 1,\ k = 1, \ldots, n$$

We shall now show this holds for $\Sigma_k s_{1k}P_k$ as well. Into (150–2) substitute for the X_j°, $j = 1, \ldots, n$, from the equations:

(155) $$-X_j^\circ = \frac{r_{1j}}{H_1^z}$$

to obtain

(156) $$0 = Z + \frac{1}{H_1^z}\left[\sum_j r_{1j}P_j\right], \qquad j = 1, \ldots, n$$

But,

(157) $$r_{1j} = H_1^j - s_{1j}$$

Substituting,

(158) $$0 = Z + \frac{1}{H_1^z}\left[\sum_j H_1^j P_j - \sum_j s_{1j}P_j\right],$$

or

(159) $$0 = H_1^z Z + \sum_j H_1^j P_j - \sum_j s_{1j}P_j$$

But (150–2) made explicit for X_1°, is the function H_1. Differentiating it as indicated in (159), and adding the terms, yields,

(160) $$0 = \sum_j s_{1j}P_j$$

Therefore, from (154) and (160) it follows that

(161) $$\sum_k s_{jk}P_k = 0, \qquad k = 1, \ldots, n;\ j = 1, \ldots, n$$

Since $s_{jj} < 0$, this implies that for every Y_j there must exist at least one positive s_{jk}; that is, every good must have at least one good for which it is a net substitute.[45]

These first three conditions on the s_{jk}, contained in (144), (147), and (161), were originally stated by Slutsky in his classic article. The next proposition concerning the substitution effects is due to Hotelling. It is that

$$\sum_{j=1}^{m} \sum_{k=1}^{m} P_j P_k s_{jk} < 0 \qquad m < n \tag{162}$$

This states that for any set of positive prices, a subset of the equilibrium substitution effects up to but not including all goods when multiplied by the respective prices and added will always be negative.[46] For example, let $j = 1$, $k = 1$; then

$$P_1^2 s_{11} < 0 \tag{163}$$

so that (145) is a special case of (162). Or, let the subset of goods be Y_2 and Y_3. Then

$$P_2^2 s_{22} + 2P_2P_3s_{23} + P_3^2 s_{33} < 0 \tag{164}$$

This is a quadratic form and we have the requirement that it be negative definite. By a process of reasoning which resembles that used to derive the second-order equilibrium conditions as restrictions upon the determinants in (106), (117), and (134), and which differs only in the fact that no linear constraint binds (162) or (164) as the restriction (97) constrains the previous forms, a necessary and sufficient condition for (162) to hold is that expressions of the type

$$s_{jj}, \begin{vmatrix} s_{jj} & s_{jk} \\ s_{jk} & s_{kk} \end{vmatrix}, \ldots, \begin{vmatrix} s_{jj} & s_{jk} & \cdots & s_{jm} \\ s_{jk} & s_{kk} & \cdots & s_{km} \\ \cdot & \cdot & \cdots & \cdot \\ s_{jm} & s_{km} & \cdots & s_{mm} \end{vmatrix} \tag{165}$$

[45] In one of Hick's definitions of the terms, substitution relations existed between two goods if $s_{jk} > 0$, complementary relations if $s_{jk} < 0$, in a given neighborhood of equilibrium. See J. Hicks, (5), p. 311. We shall term these *net* relationships, and those same relations defined in terms of $\frac{\partial X_j^\circ}{\partial P_k}$ *gross* relationships, since these latter are gross of income effects. These distinctions were introduced by Mosak.

[46] The expression in (162) is more general than we are interpreting it. Indeed, it may be shown that for any arbitrary values, b_j, b_k, not all zero, $\sum_{j=1}^{m} \sum_{k=1}^{m} b_j b_k s_{jk} < 0$ for $m < n$, which are the necessary and sufficient conditions for the quadratic form to be negative semi-definite, from which the conditions stated in (162) derive. See J. Hicks, (5), pp. 310–1.

alternate in sign negative and positive. In the case of (164),

$$\text{(166)} \qquad 1.\quad s_{22} < 0,\ s_{33} < 0 \qquad 2.\quad \begin{vmatrix} s_{22} & s_{23} \\ s_{23} & s_{33} \end{vmatrix} > 0$$

Now, from (146), (166) may be written:

$$\text{(167)} \quad \lambda^{*\circ}\frac{|H_{jj}|}{|H|},\ \left(\frac{\lambda^{*\circ}}{|H|}\right)^2 \begin{vmatrix} |H_{jj}| & |H_{jk}| \\ |H_{jk}| & |H_{kk}| \end{vmatrix},$$

$$\cdots \left(\frac{\lambda^{*\circ}}{|H|}\right)^m \begin{vmatrix} |H_{jj}| & |H_{jk}| & \cdots & |H_{jm}| \\ |H_{jk}| & |H_{kk}| & \cdots & |H_{km}| \\ \cdot & \cdot & \cdots & \cdot \\ |H_{jm}| & |H_{km}| & \cdots & |H_{mm}| \end{vmatrix}$$

From the second-order maximum conditions for Model I-3, as given for the three-good case in (134) and subject to straightforward generalization in the manner discussed immediately following (117) it is implied that

$$\text{(168)} \qquad \lambda^{*\circ}\frac{|H_{jj}|}{|H|} < 0,\ \lambda^{*\circ}\frac{|H_{jj,kk}|}{|H|} > 0, \text{ and so forth,}$$

where $|H_{jj,kk}|$ is the principal minor of $|H|$ formed by deleting the jth and k^{th} rows and columns. It may be shown that (168) implies that the expressions of (167) are alternately negative and positive.[47] Therefore, by virtue of the second-order equilibrium conditions (162) holds.[48]

Lastly, from (160) and (162), it follows that

$$\text{(169)} \qquad \sum_{j=1}^{m}\sum_{k=m+1}^{n} P_jP_ks_{jk} > 0$$

[47] W. Burnside, (1), Vol. II, p. 42.

[48] Cf. J. Hicks, (5), pp. 310–1. These results were first obtained by H. Hotelling (2), (3). Hotelling developed the analysis first in terms of a consumer who faced no budget constraint; in this case no income effect exists and $\frac{\partial X_j^\circ}{\partial P_k} \equiv s_{jk}$. In the later analysis, he extended this to the consumer with a budget constraint to prove that if the second-order maximization conditions hold it must be true that

$$\text{(1)} \qquad \begin{vmatrix} \frac{\partial X_1^\circ}{\partial P_1} & \frac{\partial X_1^\circ}{\partial P_2} & \cdots & \frac{\partial X_1^\circ}{\partial P_n} & -P_1 \\ \frac{\partial X_2^\circ}{\partial P_1} & \frac{\partial X_2^\circ}{\partial P_2} & \cdots & \frac{\partial X_2^\circ}{\partial P_n} & -P_2 \\ \cdots & \cdots & \cdots & \cdots & \cdots \\ \frac{\partial X_n^\circ}{\partial P_1} & \frac{\partial X_n^\circ}{\partial P_2} & \cdots & \frac{\partial X_n^\circ}{\partial P_n} & -P_n \\ P_1 & P_2 & \cdots & P_n & 0 \end{vmatrix}$$

must have the sign $(-1)^s$ where s is the number of rows and all bordered principal

That is, if the n goods are divided into two mutually exclusive groups, and if the terms $P_jP_ks_{jk}$ are formed and added, the results must be positive.[49]

3. Complex Exchange

With the introduction of complex exchange the analysis introduces explicitly the market economy, for by the term "complex" is meant the interaction of individuals' decisions. The ambition of the analysis is, therefore, enhanced to include prices as variables rather than data; moreover, the budget constraint will be stated in terms of the value of given stocks of goods in the hands of the individual consumer rather than a given magnitude termed "income." We shall construct two models of this type: Model II-1, featuring the exchange of two goods (i.e., $n = 2$) and Model II-2, where $n > 2$. For both models Walras's analysis will be drawn upon heavily, since it is largely to him that economic theory owes the first thoroughgoing treatment of a barter economy.[50]

A set of consumers, $c = 1, \ldots, s$, is now assumed to exist, where s is taken to be "large," and where large is defined as a number which makes the impact of any consumer's actions upon prices negligible.

3.a. Model II-I: Complex Exchange, n = 2

Assume that in lieu of Z, income, consumer c is endowed with Q_{cj} of Y_j. For analytical ease, assume that only goods Y_1 and Y_2 exist, and that consumers enter the period having positive stocks *either* of Y_1 or Y_2, but not both.

Further, and for every model in Part II, the following is the specific institutional framework within which economic functions occur. The time period for which current decisions are relevant is "the week." On Monday, all decisionmaking units in the economy enter a set of markets in which goods and services are exchanged. By the end of this "market day," equilibrium prices for all goods and services have been determined,

---

minors must have the sign $(-1)^s$ where $s > 2$ is the number of rows in them.

In a separate proof, Hotelling showed that if the second-order maximization conditions held, it is also true that

$$(2) \qquad \begin{vmatrix} \frac{\partial X_1^\circ}{\partial P_1} & \frac{\partial X_1^\circ}{\partial P_2} & \cdots & \frac{\partial X_1^\circ}{\partial P_n} \\ \frac{\partial X_2^\circ}{\partial P_1} & \frac{\partial X_2^\circ}{\partial P_2} & \cdots & \frac{\partial X_2^\circ}{\partial P_n} \\ \cdots & \cdots & \cdots & \cdots \\ \frac{\partial X_n^\circ}{\partial P_1} & \frac{\partial X_n^\circ}{\partial P_2} & \cdots & \frac{\partial X_n^\circ}{\partial P_n} \end{vmatrix}$$

has the sign $(-1)^s$.

[49] This proposition is due to J. Hicks, (5), p. 311.

[50] L. Walras, (3), Lessons 9–15.

at which all transactions occur for that week. These transactions are fixed at the end of Monday in a set of contracts among decisionmaking units to deliver specific amounts of commodities to specific firms or consumers at specific places on specific days in the coming week. This "contract-fulfillment" week includes the days Tuesday through Sunday, and all contracts are completed by this last day. This is the Walrasian framework for the analysis of the market economy.

In Models II-1 and II-2 we assume that the two relevant dimensions through which an economy must move—time and space—have no economically meaningful implications. Thus, goods delivered Thursday cost no less than goods delivered Tuesday, implying either that the "price of time-movement" (the "interest rate") is zero, or the "length of movement" in days is so small as to make cost negligible. Similarly, either the "price of space-movement" (the transport rate) is zero, or the market economy is effectively a point in space, and delivery distances zero in length. The first of these assumptions will be relaxed in Chapters 4, 5, and 8, by degrees, and the second will be relaxed in Chapter 7.

Using an external *numéraire,* and rewriting the budget constraint in the form

$$(170) \qquad \sum_j X_{cj}P_j - Q_{cj}P_j = 0$$

we obtain the following nonspecific solution for a Model I-3 analysis for consumer c:

$$(171) \qquad \begin{aligned} &1. \quad X^{\circ}_{c2} = H_{c2}(P_1, P_2; Q_{cj}) \\ &2. \quad X^{\circ}_{c1}P_1 = Q_{cj}P_j - X^{\circ}_{c2}P_2 \end{aligned}$$

These functions are homogeneous of degree zero in prices alone. We may, therefore, set P_1 equal to unity in order to obtain an internal *numéraire.* Further, each consumer will belong to one of the two groups we defined, depending upon his initial possession of Y_1 or Y_2, and we shall add over all consumers in each group to obtain aggregate functions from (171):

$$(172) \qquad \begin{aligned} &1. \quad {}_1X_2 = {}_1H_2(P_2; Q_{11}, Q_{21}, \ldots, Q_{s1}) = {}_1H_2(P_2; [Q_1]) \\ &2. \quad {}_1X_1 = \sum_c Q_{c1} - {}_1X_2P_2 \\ &3. \quad {}_2X_2 = {}_2H_2(P_2; Q_{12}, Q_{22}, \ldots, Q_{s2}) = {}_2H_2(P_2; [Q_2]) \\ &4. \quad {}_2X_1 = \sum_c Q_{c2}P_2 - {}_2X_2P_2 \end{aligned}$$

where $[Q_j] = [Q_{1j}, Q_{2j}, \ldots, Q_{sj}]$.

No longer are the values of the variables in (172) written as equilibrium quantities, since these relations will hold whether the prices given are or are not the solution values for the larger model we now seek to build. The subscripts ${}_1$ and ${}_2$ written before the symbols denote the first and second groups of consumers, as defined above.

The interrelationships among the variables which must be added to these are the requirements that the demands for each good, over both groups, be equal to the supply. These make Model II-1 an equilibrium model, in the sense of Chapter 1, and these relationships are derived as conditions for its existence:

$$(173)\qquad \begin{aligned} &1. \quad {}_1X_1^{\circ} + {}_2X_1^{\circ} = \sum_c Q_{c1} \\ &2. \quad {}_1X_2^{\circ} + {}_2X_2^{\circ} = \sum_c Q_{c2} \end{aligned}$$

The *six* equations of (172) and (173) have been derived to determine the equilibrium values of only *five* variables: ${}_1X_1^{\circ}$, ${}_1X_2^{\circ}$, ${}_2X_1^{\circ}$, ${}_2X_2^{\circ}$, and P_2°. In general, this indicates that the analyst has become involved in one of two difficulties with the model. First, the model may be overdetermined, in that the variables have been forced to fulfill too many conditions, not all of which in general can be fulfilled simultaneously. Second, the model may contain a relationship which is not independent of the others; that is, there may be functional dependence in the system.

Our model is in fact characterized by the second type of difficulty: a relationship is redundant. The reason for this is simply that every consumer and therefore each of the two groups is subject to budget constraints. Thus, once prices and three of the four quantities in (173) are determined, the fourth quantity must follow identically. This may be shown as follows. First, for an equilibrium, substitute from (173) into (172-2 and 172-4) to eliminate the Q_{cj} terms:

$$(174)\qquad \begin{aligned} &1. \quad {}_1X_1^{\circ} + {}_1X_2^{\circ}P_2^{\circ} = {}_1X_1^{\circ} + {}_2X_1^{\circ} \\ &2. \quad {}_2X_1^{\circ} + {}_2X_2^{\circ}P_2^{\circ} = {}_1X_2^{\circ}P_2^{\circ} + {}_2X_2^{\circ}P_2^{\circ} \end{aligned}$$

These reduce to the same equation:

$$(175)\qquad \begin{aligned} &1. \quad {}_1X_2^{\circ}P_2^{\circ} = {}_2X_1^{\circ} \\ &2. \quad {}_2X_1^{\circ} = {}_1X_2^{\circ}P_2^{\circ} \end{aligned}$$

Thus, the four equations of (172) and (173) from which these results were obtained impose the same condition twice. They contain, in effect, only three independent conditions at most, not four, and it is therefore possible to eliminate any one of the four equations.

If this eliminated equation be (173-1), the definite implication of the procedure is that if the market for Y_2 is cleared, and units in the market are constrained by budget equations, the clearance of the market for Y_1 follows identically. This is because, of course, the equilibrium demand by the first group for Y_2 must equal the amount supplied of that good, and this will be the Y_1 value of the demand of the second group for Y_1. If the eliminated equation be (172-2), the procedure implies that if demand and supply for both goods are equal and one group is satisfied with the *status quo,* it must follow that the other group is also satisfied.

Therefore, we have reduced the model to a set of five independent equations in five unknowns, and this equality is, generally speaking, a condition for the solution of the system.[51] Before leaving this model, however, we may simplify it and develop some elementary concepts which will stand us in good stead when we treat more complex systems. First, (172-2 and 172-4) are *identities,* in the sense that the equality they state holds, whatever the ruling values of the price variables. Under no conceivable condition of the system can either group spend more (or less) than the market value of their goods endowments. This fact brings out the simple but important economic lesson that demand for one good implies a supply of another. Define the desire to supply a commodity as the quantity one possesses of it less the quantity one desires to consume, or, for the groups,

(176)

$$1.\quad {}_1\bar{X}_1 = \sum_c Q_{c1} - {}_1X_1$$

$$2.\quad {}_2\bar{X}_2 = \sum_c Q_{c2} - {}_2X_2$$

where the $\bar{X}$-terms symbolize here and throughout the book the desire to supply.

Then, if these terms are substituted in (172-2 and 172-4), the identities become

(177)

$$1.\quad {}_1X_2P_2 \equiv {}_1\bar{X}_1$$

$$2.\quad {}_2X_1 \equiv {}_2\bar{X}_2P_2$$

These indicate that whatever P_2 is, the desire to supply Y_1 is identically equal to the value of the desire of group 1 to consume Y_2, and the desire to consume Y_1 on the part of the second group is identical to the value of Y_2 the group desires to supply. These identities are immediately understood if Y_1 is conceived as a paper money and Y_2 is (say) apples. Then, a group desiring to consume 50 bushels of apples at 3 per bushel must identically desire to supply 150 units of paper money at 1 per unit, while the suppliers of apples at 3 per bushel might be desirous of selling 40 bushels and therefore would demand 120 units of money.

A market, therefore, is a place where two goods are traded, so that

[51] In strict truth, this equality is neither necessary nor sufficient for solubility. The necessary and sufficient conditions are much more complicated than the mere equality of unknowns and independent equations, and will be developed at length in Chapter 9.

Model II-1 contains two goods but only one market. Since demands and supplies of one good follow in or out of equilibrium identically from supplies and demands for the other, it is a waste of time to deal with more than one of the goods. If we are interested in the equilibrium price and amount exchanged of apples, why worry about the amounts of money exchanged in this equilibrium, for they merely form the obverse of the apple transactions? If we should be desirous of knowing them, we do know that they follow identically for equilibrium or nonequilibrium values from such identities as those in (177). Therefore, Model II-1 may limit itself to the study of demands and supplies as they concern one of the two goods.

Thus, we may reduce the equations to three to determine only three unknowns, ${}_1X_2^\circ$, ${}_2X_2^\circ$, and P_2°:

$$\text{(II-1)}\qquad \begin{aligned} &1. \quad {}_1X_2 = {}_1H_2(P_2; [Q_1]) \\ &2. \quad {}_2X_2 = {}_2H_2(P_2; [Q_2]) \\ &3. \quad {}_1X_2^\circ + {}_2X_2^\circ = \sum_c Q_{c2} \end{aligned}$$

We must now turn our attention to evaluating the expressions $\frac{\partial_1X_2^\circ}{\partial Q_{c1}}$, $\frac{\partial_2X_2^\circ}{\partial Q_{c1}}$, $\frac{\partial_1X_2^\circ}{\partial Q_{c2}}$, $\frac{\partial_2X_2^\circ}{\partial Q_{c2}}$, $\frac{\partial P_2^\circ}{\partial Q_{c1}}$, and $\frac{\partial P_2^\circ}{\partial Q_{c2}}$. For example, let us assume that a small increase occurs in the holdings of Y_1 by consumer 1, all other consumer endowments remaining unchanged. Then, the equilibrium displacement system which interests us is:

$$\text{(178)}\qquad \begin{bmatrix} 1 & 0 & -{}_1H_2^p \\ 0 & 1 & -{}_2H_2^p \\ 1 & 1 & 0 \end{bmatrix} \begin{bmatrix} \frac{\partial_1X_2^\circ}{\partial Q_{11}} \\ \frac{\partial_2X_2^\circ}{\partial Q_{11}} \\ \frac{\partial P_2^\circ}{\partial Q_{11}} \end{bmatrix} = \begin{bmatrix} {}_1H_2^q \\ 0 \\ 0 \end{bmatrix}$$

where the p (symbolizing P_2) and q (symbolizing Q_{11}) superscripts have been abbreviated for simplicity. Denote system (178) by

$$\text{(179)}\qquad [H][dV] = [dQ]$$

Since the aggregate functions are simply sums over the individual demand functions, it follows that

$$\text{(180)}\qquad {}_1H_2^p = H_{12}^p, \qquad {}_1H_2^q = H_{12}^q$$

from (171). We return for the moment to the case of simple exchange to find that

(181) $$\frac{dX_{12}^{\circ}}{dQ_{11}} = H_{12}^{q}$$

which is the slope of the individual's demand curve for Y_2 in the Q_{11} direction.

We have already solved for the sign of this term in Models I-1, I-2, and I-3, but only in an implicit sense, since $Q_{11} = Z$ in these models. Our conclusions from that analysis are unaltered, however, when Q_{11} is substituted for Z. But we must re-examine the analysis for the case of an individual in group 2 to take account of a complication which now exists and did not in the former analysis. This complication arises from the fact that any individual who holds Y_2 has a $Z = Q_{c2}P_2$, and the complicating price factor must be taken into account. If price remains constant and Q_{c2} increases, then the analysis of the simple exchange model for a change in Z holds unaltered. But let us now change P_2 and determine the impact this will have upon an individual consumer in group 2 as far as his demand for Y_2 is concerned. Suppose individual 2 holds Y_2: then we seek

(182) $$\frac{\partial X_{22}^{\circ}}{\partial P_2} = H_{22}^{p}$$

To evaluate this we must return to a simple exchange model, say I-3. Now that we have identified the individual in question as consumer 2, we may drop that subscript as superfluous in the analysis that follows. Then (I-3-2) is altered by virtue of the new budget constraint to

(183)
1. $G^j - \lambda^{*\circ}P_j = 0, \qquad j = 1, 2$
2. $X_1^{\circ} + X_2^{\circ}P_2 - Q_2P_2 = 0$

Then, if P_2 varies slightly, we obtain

(184) $$[H_{33}]\left[\frac{\partial X_1^{\circ}}{\partial P_2}, \frac{\partial X_2^{\circ}}{\partial P_2}, \frac{\partial \lambda^{*\circ}}{\partial P_2}\right] = [0, \lambda^{*\circ}, Q_2 - X_2^{\circ}]$$

where $[H_{33}]$ is the matrix formed by eliminating the third row and column from $[H]$. Then,

(185) $$\frac{\partial X_2^{\circ}}{\partial P_2} = \lambda^{*\circ}\frac{|H_{33,22}|}{|H_{33}|} - (Q_2 - X_2^{\circ})\frac{|H_{33,42}|}{|H_{33}|}$$

where all subscripts on the determinants refer to rows and columns of $[H]$. Or,

(186) $$\frac{\partial X_2^{\circ}}{\partial P_2} = s_{22} + \bar{X}_2\frac{\partial X_2^{\circ}}{\partial Z} = s_{22} + r_{22}$$

Now, if the marginal propensity to consume Y_2 is positive, i.e., if the income elasticity of demand for Y_2 is positive, as is normally assumed, then

(187) $$r_{22} > 0$$

That is, a rise in P_2 will lead to an income effect which will be expected to *raise* the demand for Y_2 on the part of consumers who *supply* the good to the market, because a rise in the price of the good they supply raises their incomes. On the other hand, when $Q_2 = 0$, so that the consumer is a demander of the good, it is seen from (185) that the income effect would be negative under the assumption of a positive income elasticity of demand.

On the supply side of the market, therefore, since $s_{jj} < 0$, and in the normal case $r_{jj} > 0$, the chance for a "backward bending" supply function for the individual is quite large in an exchange economy. It does not depend, as does the demand curve of an individual who holds no Y_j, upon a perverse income elasticity to yield an $r_{jj} > 0$. Hence the greater likelihood of backward bending supply curves than of perverse demand curves.[52]

Now, with this analysis of the individual's demand for Y_1 and Y_2, we may move forward to the aggregate demand curves of Model II-1. We may define

(188) $$\frac{\partial_1 X_2}{\partial P_2} = {}_1S_{22} + {}_1R_{22} = \sum_{c'} {}_{c'}s_{22} + \sum_{c'} {}_{c'}r_{22}$$

where ${}_1R_{22}$ is the aggregate income effect and ${}_1S_{22}$ the aggregate substitution effect. Similarly,

(189) $$\frac{\partial_2 X_2}{\partial P_2} = {}_2S_{22} + {}_2R_{22} = \sum_{c''} {}_{c''}s_{22} + \sum_{c''} {}_{c''}r_{22}$$

In (188) c' is taken to be the group of individuals possessing the first good and in (189) c'' is the second group of consumers, who possess only Y_2.

We may return to (178) and specify the expectation that

(190) $${}_1H_2^p < 0, \ {}_2H_2^p \gtreqless 0$$

By virtue of the expectation that ${}_1R_{22} < 0$ and ${}_2R_{22} > 0$,[53]

(191) $${}_1H_2^p + {}_2H_2^p < 0$$

if demanders and suppliers have about the same marginal propensities to consume Y_2.

Since we are interested only in the *directions* of equilibrium move-

[52] J. Hicks, (5), pp. 35–7.

[53] The netting out of the income effects on both sides of the market in an exchange economy is a Hicksian contribution to the derivation of operational propositions from general systems. See J. Hicks, (5), pp. 316–7.

ments, let us now assume that although the impact of an increase in a consumer's holdings is small it is still capable of having a perceptible impact upon P_2 and therefore ${}_1X_2^\circ$ and ${}_2X_2^\circ$. We may solve (178) to obtain:

$$(192)\qquad \begin{aligned} &1.\quad \frac{\partial\,{}_1X_2^\circ}{\partial Q_{11}} = \frac{{}_1H_2^q\,{}_2H_2^p}{{}_1H_2^p + {}_2H_2^p} \\ &2.\quad \frac{\partial\,{}_2X_2^\circ}{\partial Q_{11}} = -\frac{{}_1H_2^q\,{}_2H_2^p}{{}_1H_2^p + {}_2H_2^p} \\ &3.\quad \frac{\partial P_2^\circ}{\partial Q_{11}} = -\frac{{}_1H_2^q}{{}_1H_2^p + {}_2H_2^p} \end{aligned}$$

From (191) we may conclude that the new equilibrium P_2 will always lie above the old when the quantity of Y_1 increases. If suppliers of Y_2 decrease their demand (increase their supply), then holders of Y_1 will take the amount of Y_2 given up by suppliers. If suppliers increase their desire to consume Y_2, the reverse will occur. These are the same results deduced in Chapter 1, Section 5.a. by the use of an explicit dynamic model. In this section it has been demonstrated that information gained from the second-order maximization conditions on the individual plus the assumption of compensating income effects in the aggregate provide an alternative route to the derivation of these theorems. The analysis also reveals the high probability that the slope conditions required to yield Walrasian stability will indeed prevail. It shows that if consumers on both sides of the market are rather alike in their desires to consume Y_2, in the sense that their marginal propensities to consume it from income are positive (or negative) to the same degree, income effects should cancel out and substitution effects guarantee the holding of Walrasian stability conditions. Practically speaking, only if individuals in group 1 or group 2 were markedly different in these respects from their counterparts in the other group would an unstable situation be likely to arise. Thus, we may in this first exchange model featuring market functions make the Walrasian stability assumptions (${}_1H_2^p + {}_2H_2^p < 0$) with a great deal more confidence than dependence upon a wholly postulated basis would have afforded.

Sooner or later, however, we must recognize that the retention of the individual demand functions and the ability to appeal to them for information about the aggregate demand functions are impractical. At this juncture, then, we may reluctantly move away from the individual simple exchange model and resolve to seek information about the relevant slopes of the aggregate functions from sources other than second-order maximization conditions. This implies the acceptance of the aggregate demand functions as data of the models rather than the nonspecific solutions of prior simple exchange models which have been summed. To do so is to seek the rules of market behavior abstracted from the individuals who in fact generate it, much as the physicist develops a theory of thermodynamics in abstraction from the movements of molecules of matter.

3.b. Model II-2: Complex Exchange, n > 2

Let us begin with the aggregate demand curves of Model II-1, this time including a third good, Y_3, in the hands of yet a third group. Further, since we are now to leave the molecular units of decisionmaking behind us, we shall assume that $\Sigma_c Q_{cj} = Q_j$, where Q_j, $j = 1, 2, 3$, is an aggregate endowment of Y_j to the group which possesses it exclusively. The distribution of this stock among individuals in the group, as well as the distributional impacts of changes in the stock, are simply abstracted from, although Q_j as a datum is directly related to the relevant group's demands via the demand functions.

A naïve projection of Model II-1 into the world of more than two goods would envision a separate market for each pair of goods, or $.5(n)(n - 1)$ markets in general. In the case in hand, where $n = 3$, there would be 3 separate markets, where Y_1 and Y_2, Y_1 and Y_3, and Y_2 and Y_3 are exchanged. We shall select a separate *numéraire* for each market, quite arbitrarily of course: let us designate Y_1 as *numéraire* in the Y_1-Y_2 market, Y_2 in the Y_2-Y_3 market, and Y_3 in the Y_1-Y_3 market.

Then, in this naïve projection, group 1 consumers, who possess Q_1, enter the Y_1-Y_2 and Y_1-Y_3 markets to exchange Y_1 for the other two goods. This group is interested in the Y_1 value of other goods, i.e., in the prices of Y_2 and Y_3 in terms of Y_1 as *numéraire*. Let us designate such prices as $P_{2;1}$ and $P_{3;1}$ with the figure behind the semicolon denoting the *numéraire*. Then, group 1's demand functions are

(193)
1. $${}_1X_2 = {}_1H_2(P_{2;1}, P_{3;1}; Q_1)$$
2. $${}_1X_3 = {}_1H_3(P_{2;1}, P_{3;1}; Q_1)$$
3. $${}_1X_1 = Q_1 - {}_1X_2P_{2;1} - {}_1X_3P_{3;1}$$

Similarly, for groups 2 and 3,

(194)
1. $${}_2X_1 = {}_2H_1(P_{1;2}, P_{3;2}; Q_2)$$
2. $${}_2X_3 = {}_2H_3(P_{1;2}, P_{3;2}; Q_2)$$
3. $${}_2X_2 = Q_2 - {}_2X_1P_{1;2} - {}_2X_3P_{3;2}$$

(195)
1. $${}_3X_1 = {}_3H_1(P_{1;3}, P_{2;3}; Q_3)$$
2. $${}_3X_2 = {}_3H_2(P_{1;3}, P_{2;3}; Q_3)$$
3. $${}_3X_3 = Q_3 - {}_3X_1P_{1;3} - {}_3X_2P_{2;3}$$

As an equilibrium condition, it is required that the total demand for each good equal the quantity available:

(196)
1. $${}_1X_1^\circ + {}_2X_1^\circ + {}_3X_1^\circ = Q_1$$
2. $${}_1X_2^\circ + {}_2X_2^\circ + {}_3X_2^\circ = Q_2$$
3. $${}_1X_3^\circ + {}_2X_3^\circ + {}_3X_3^\circ = Q_3$$

These 12 equations contain 15 unknowns—three quantities demanded and two prices per group—and therefore the system is "underdetermined." The difficulty is speedily corrected, however; it will be recalled that only three prices will emerge from the three markets: $P_{2;1}$, $P_{3;2}$, and $P_{1;3}$. However, the following identities hold from the very definition of a price:

$$(197)\qquad \begin{aligned} &1. \quad P_{1;2} \equiv \frac{1}{P_{2;1}} \\ &2. \quad P_{2;3} \equiv \frac{1}{P_{3;2}} \\ &3. \quad P_{3;1} \equiv \frac{1}{P_{1;3}} \end{aligned}$$

With these relationships the equality of equations and unknowns is attained. With them also we have extended the two-good complex exchange system to a three-good case, with *three* markets functioning side by side, equilibrium prices emerging from each, and with all groups satisfied with the *status quo* within the limits of the budget constraints. As Wicksell points out, this model with equation systems (193)–(197) is as far as Jevons carried the general theory of exchange.[54]

But we can sense that something is amiss with this model from the discussion of Model II-1, where there existed two goods but only one market. Why is not one of the three goods in balance as far as supply and demand are concerned when the other two goods are in that state? This does not occur in this larger model because each consuming group enters only two of the three markets, so that the price determined in the omitted market does not enter into its calculations. For example, consider group 1: it considers only $P_{2;1}$ and $P_{3;1}$, and ignores $P_{2;3}$. Therefore, nothing in the model prevents the following from ruling in equilibrium:

$$(198)\qquad \frac{P^{\circ}_{2;1}}{P^{\circ}_{3;1}} \neq P^{\circ}_{2;3}$$

But suppose $\frac{P^{\circ}_{2;1}}{P^{\circ}_{3;1}} < P^{\circ}_{2;3}$; could it really be expected that this price solution would continue to rule? It would pay holders of Y_1 to obtain ${}_1X_3$ indirectly by selling Y_1 for Y_2 and then entering the Y_2-Y_3 market to barter Y_2 for Y_3, rather than obtaining Y_3 directly for Y_1. If any of these arbitrage opportunities exist—and nothing prevents them from arising—market behavior which does not exploit them seems peculiarly blind. Therefore, we are compelled to add the condition that indirect exchange of Y_2 for Y_3 yield a price equal to that yielded by direct exchange:

$$(199)\qquad \frac{P^{\circ}_{2;1}}{P^{\circ}_{3;1}} = P^{\circ}_{2;3}$$

With the specification of this condition, it is possible to prove, using

[54] K. Wicksell, (1), pp. 18, 81–2.

the definitions of (197), that all other indirect exchange ratios will be equal to direct exchange ratios. That is, we may prove that $\frac{P^{\circ}_{2;3}}{P^{\circ}_{1;3}} = P^{\circ}_{2;1}$ and $\frac{P^{\circ}_{1;2}}{P^{\circ}_{3;2}} = P^{\circ}_{1;3}$. The first follows from the substitution of the left-hand side of (199) for $P^{\circ}_{2;3}$ and (197-3), and the second follows by multiplying the first through by $P^{\circ}_{1;3}$ and inverting terms by virtue of (197). But we may now seem to be overdetermined by one equation, since we have 16 of them and only 15 unknowns.

The key, of course, is that (199) makes one equation of (193-3), (194-3), (195-3), and (196) redundant. This is true because it is now possible to express every price in terms of one good, the *numéraire* for all markets. For from the designated *numéraires*

$$(200) \qquad \begin{aligned} &1. \quad P_{2;1} \text{ exists} \\ &2. \quad P_{3;1} = \frac{1}{P_{1;3}} \text{ by (197)} \\ &3. \quad P_{2;3} = \frac{P_{2;1}}{P_{3;1}} \text{ by (199)} \end{aligned}$$

If Y_1 is used as *numéraire* in all markets (199) holds not only in equilibrium but as an identity, as stated in (200), because then the *numéraire* forms the obverse of every one of the $n - 1$ goods markets in the economy. Arbitrage can occur only when the standards of measurement differ. Therefore, (199) is brought about identically by a market society with the adoption of an internal *numéraire*.

All prices are then understood to be measured in units of Y_1, $P_1 \equiv 1$. This does not imply that Y_1 is in fact traded against Y_2 in the market for Y_2: it means merely that transactions are recorded in prices of Y_2 measured in units of Y_1. Units of *numéraire* need not be exchanged in fulfillment of any bargain: group 2, for example, obtains Y_3 by delivering Y_2, but pays in Y_2 the Y_1 equivalent of Y_3. The reader is warned, therefore, in the pre-money models, to avoid the temptation of interpreting the *numéraire* as a medium of exchange instead of a mere unit of account. Nevertheless, because of the useful function a *numéraire* of this type performs in the complex exchange economy, we should expect it to emerge quickly. The demonstration of its usefulness, and the improvement of the Jevons type of exchange theory as a result, was, as we said earlier, a Walrasian contribution.

We demonstrate for the case where equilibrium price relations have emerged by arbitrage that one equilibrium condition can be eliminated. Convert (193-3) to its equilibrium state, transform (194-3) and (195-3) similarly and at the same time convert their equilibrium prices to *numéraire* prices:

(201)

$$1.\quad {}_1X_1^\circ + {}_1X_2^\circ P_{2;1}^\circ + {}_1X_3^\circ P_{3;1}^\circ = Q_1$$

$$2.\quad \frac{{}_2X_1^\circ}{P_{2;1}^\circ} + {}_2X_2^\circ\frac{P_{2;1}^\circ}{P_{2;1}^\circ} + {}_2X_3^\circ\frac{P_{3;1}^\circ}{P_{2;1}^\circ} = Q_2$$

$$3.\quad \frac{{}_3X_1^\circ}{P_{3;1}^\circ} + {}_3X_2^\circ\frac{P_{2;1}^\circ}{P_{3;1}^\circ} + {}_3X_3^\circ\frac{P_{3;1}^\circ}{P_{3;1}^\circ} = Q_3$$

Substitute for Q_1 and Q_2 from (196) to obtain:

(202)

$$1.\quad {}_1X_2^\circ P_{2;1}^\circ + {}_1X_3^\circ P_{3;1}^\circ - {}_2X_1^\circ - {}_3X_1^\circ = 0$$

$$2.\quad {}_2X_1^\circ + {}_2X_3^\circ P_{3;1}^\circ - {}_1X_2^\circ P_{2;1}^\circ - {}_3X_2^\circ P_{2;1}^\circ = 0$$

Adding (202-1) and (202-2),

(203)

$$ {}_1X_3^\circ P_{3;1}^\circ + {}_2X_3^\circ P_{3;1}^\circ - {}_3X_1^\circ - {}_3X_2^\circ P_{2;1}^\circ = 0$$

Divide (203) by $P_{3;1}^\circ$:

(204)

$$ {}_1X_3^\circ + {}_2X_3^\circ - \frac{{}_3X_1^\circ}{P_{3;1}^\circ} - {}_3X_2^\circ\frac{P_{2;1}^\circ}{P_{3;1}^\circ} = 0$$

And, lastly, add (204) to (201-3) to obtain:

(205)

$$ {}_1X_3^\circ + {}_2X_3^\circ + {}_3X_3^\circ = Q_3$$

which is (196-3). Therefore, for equilibrium values of the variables, (196-3) is implied by the five equations used above, and may be dropped. It must be understood, however, that these substitutions could not have been made without the arbitrage equilibrium condition (199) and therefore without (199) the three equilibrium conditions of (196) are independent.

In similar fashion, but without the need for equilibrium price solutions in the budget constraints, the same dependence follows when one internal *numéraire* is used. Thus it is shown once more that if the two *markets* of the economy are in equilibrium, demand must equal supply for the three goods, and more generally, if $n - 1$ markets are equilibrated, demand must equal supply for the n goods.

We are finally ready to construct Model II-2. Letting Y_1 be *numéraire*, we are given

(II-2-1)

$$1.\quad {}_1X_1 = Q_1 - {}_1X_2P_2 - {}_1X_3P_3$$

$$2.\quad {}_1X_2 = {}_1H_2(P_2, P_3; Q_1)$$

$$3.\quad {}_1X_3 = {}_1H_3(P_2, P_3; Q_1)$$

$$4.\quad {}_2X_1 = Q_2P_2 - {}_2X_2P_2 - {}_2X_3P_3$$

$$5.\quad {}_2X_2 = {}_2H_2(P_2, P_3; Q_2)$$

$$6.\quad {}_2X_3 = {}_2H_3(P_2, P_3; Q_2)$$

$$7.\quad {}_3X_1 = Q_3P_3 - {}_3X_2P_2 - {}_3X_3P_3$$

$$8.\quad {}_3X_2 = {}_3H_2(P_2, P_3; Q_3)$$

$$9.\quad {}_3X_3 = {}_3H_3(P_2, P_3; Q_3)$$

We define

$$\text{(II-2-2)}\qquad \begin{aligned} &1. \quad \bar{X}_1 \equiv Q_1 - {}_1X_1 \\ &2. \quad \bar{X}_2 \equiv Q_2 - {}_2X_2 \\ &3. \quad \bar{X}_3 \equiv Q_3 - {}_3X_3 \end{aligned}$$

and require[55]

$$\text{(II-2-3)}\qquad \begin{aligned} &1. \quad {}_1X_2^\circ + {}_3X_2^\circ = \bar{X}_2^\circ \\ &2. \quad {}_1X_3^\circ + {}_2X_3^\circ = \bar{X}_3^\circ \end{aligned}$$

Model II-2 contains 14 independent equations to determine 14 unknowns—the 9 ${}_kX_j$, 3 $\bar{X}_j$, and 2 P_j.

This model is the Walrasian complex exchange model, but it is also the abstract counterpart of Irving Fisher's famous hydrostatic model of general equilibrium when the following amendments are made: (1) cardinal, independent utilities underlie the individuals' demand functions from which the aggregate functions are obtained; (2) an external *numéraire* is employed; and (3) incomes are defined as fixed amounts of this *numéraire*. In addition to the sheer ingenuity of its construction, a basic reason for this physical model's interest lay in the series of valves which could be opened or closed to change individuals' incomes or the amounts of goods available. The observed changes in prices and individuals' market baskets were recorded by changes in water levels. Thus, the model put great emphasis upon equilibrium displacement, and its construction was designed to facilitate such evaluation. This gives to Fisher a first-rate claim to share with Pareto the prestige of having first perceived the importance of deriving laws of change from general models.[56]

The assumption that was adopted in both complex exchange models to the effect that each consumer possessed a pre-exchange stock of only one good may now be dropped since we have found in the *numéraire* a method of reducing all goods to a common denominator. An "equilibrium displacement" which consists of redistributing initial stocks among individuals in such fashion as to keep the *numéraire* value of stocks the same is no displacement at all, as Walras proved rigorously.[57] Nor do com-

[55] Pareto asserts that the equations of (II-2-3) hold, as do the individual budget equations behind the market demand curves, for all values of the X's, with only the equilibrium relations behind the demand equations valid for an equilibrium condition. See V. Pareto, (2), p. 592. But this cannot be. The X-terms in (II-2-3) must be interpreted as desired quantities in order to obtain a set of equilibrium prices, for if the arbitrary price set $[P]$ yields X-terms satisfying (II-2-3) so would any other set of prices $[P'] > 0$. Thus, Pareto's *ex post* interpretation of these equations is incorrect. In his analysis of the production model the analogous equations that demand equal supply for goods and services are not explicitly interpreted as equilibrium requirements. V. Pareto, (2), p. 610.

[56] I. Fisher, (1), pp. 35–54.

[57] L. Walras, (3), pp. 182–5.

plications result from splitting each individual among the groups used so that he supplies more than one good.

3.b.1. Manipulation of the Model

We may now return to the framing of operational theorems from Model II-2. As shown in Chapter 1, Walras recognized the theorist's duty to obtain these propositions, but did not go far in deriving them from any of his models. The state in which he left this task for the complex exchange model is indicated in the quotation below; it is in answer to the query about the response of the system to an increase in the "utility" of Y_2 for a group of consumers. He answers that P_2 will rise and that it ". . . may also result in a change in P_3, P_4, ... These secondary effects, however, will be less appreciable than the primary effect if there are a great many commodities other than Y_2 on the market and if, in consequence, the quantity of each commodity exchanged for Y_2 is very small. Besides, there is no way of knowing whether the prices P_3, P_4, . . . will rise or fall, nor can we even know that they will change at all."[58]

If we can go no farther than this in evaluation of displacements, we must be disappointed indeed. Walras' basis of reasoning is rough-and-ready, appealing as it does to the nonexistence of close substitutes or complements, to a large number of goods, and, in other places, to a large number of indirect effects striking prices with positive and negative impact rather randomly.[59] Pareto did little to improve the methods of dealing with complex exchange economies, and, while Fisher built the

[58] L. Walras, (3), p. 179. Quoted by permission of Richard Irwin, Inc., George Allen & Unwin, Ltd., and the American Economic Association. Walras' symbols have been changed to correspond to those used in this book. This quotation should be compared with the passage from Marshall cited in Chapter 1, pp. 38. Walras appealed to the direct-indirect effect dichotomy throughout his book, and was probably influenced in its use by Cournot's prior appeal to it:

" . . . in general . . . it must be the case, that a perturbation experienced by one element of the system [of prices] makes itself felt from that to the next, and by reaction throughout the entire system. Nevertheless, since the variation occurring in the price of commodity Y_1, and in the income of its producers, leaves intact the sum total of the funds applicable to the demand for the other commodities Y_2, Y_3, Y_4, etc., it is evident that the sum diverted, by hypothesis, from Y_2, by reason of the new direction of demands, will necessarily be applied to the demand for one or several of the goods Y_3, Y_4, etc. Strictly speaking, this perturbation of the second degree, which occurs in the incomes of the producers of Y_2, Y_3, Y_4, etc. would react on the system in turn until a new equilibrium is established; but, although we are unable to calculate this series of reactions, *the general principles of analysis will show us that they must go on with gradually decreasing amplitude,* so that it may be admitted, as an approximation, that a variation occurring in the incomes of the producers of Y_1, while modifying the distribution of the remainder of the social income among the producers of Y_2, Y_3, etc., does not alter the total value of it, or only alters it by a quantity which is negligible in comparison with the variation . . . which is experienced by the incomes of the producers of Y_1." A. Cournot, (1), pp. 130–1. Italics supplied. Quoted by permission of Miss Anne Ashley. Symbols have been changed to conform to the conventions of this book.

[59] See, for example, his discussion of the *tâtonnement* process in L. Walras, (3), p. 172.

hydrostatic model referred to above, he made no progress toward obtaining results with less concrete methods.

As we have seen from prior analysis, we should expect any progress in methods of deriving operational theorems from exchange models to come from three directions: (1) new postulational bases yielding information about the slopes of the relevant interrelationships; (2) new information springing from second-order extremum assumptions, either from the viewpoint of the individual or from the casting of the aggregate analysis into a fictitious extremum problem; and (3) new bases deriving from restrictions upon the slopes imposed by stability assumptions.

The names most closely associated with the development of these methods are those of Slutsky, Hotelling, and Hicks. The basic work of derivation of the substitution and income effects for the individual by Slutsky, as well as the restrictions placed upon the substitution effects by second-order maximum conditions and such features as the zero-degree homogeneity of the demand functions, has already been discussed. Before going further into the work of Hotelling and Hicks, however, we shall proceed as formerly to the displacement of Model II-2's equilibrium.

First, we may simplify the model by defining total demands for the Y_j over all groups:

$$X_j = \sum_k {}_kX_j, \qquad j = 1, \ldots, n \tag{206}$$

Second, we define the term Z to be the value, at the given prices, of the stocks of Q_j held, or $Z = \Sigma_j Q_jP_j$, so that it enters the aggregate demand functions in the manner indicated in (207) below. Third, we define the excess demand for Y_j, E_j, as

$$E_j \equiv X_j - Q_j = H_j(P_2, \ldots, P_n, Z) - Q_j, \qquad j = 1, \ldots, n \tag{207}$$

Then, from (II-2-2) and (II-2-3), we obtain as a set of equilibrium conditions,

$$E_j^\circ = 0, \qquad j = 2, \ldots, n \tag{208}$$

where one excess demand (E_1 in the present case) has been eliminated as redundant. To fix our ideas, let $n = 4$.

Suppose that a Q_j, say Q_2, changes slightly. We assume, as usual, that the demand functions are continuous and differentiable to at least the second order. Then, from (208) and letting $\dfrac{\partial X_j^\circ}{\partial P_k} = H_j^k$,

$$\begin{aligned}
&1. \quad \frac{\partial E_2^\circ}{\partial Q_2} = H_2^2 \frac{\partial P_2^\circ}{\partial Q_2} + H_2^3 \frac{\partial P_3^\circ}{\partial Q_2} + H_2^4 \frac{\partial P_4^\circ}{\partial Q_2} + H_2^z P_2^\circ - 1 = 0 \\
(209) \quad &2. \quad \frac{\partial E_3^\circ}{\partial Q_2} = H_3^2 \frac{\partial P_2^\circ}{\partial Q_2} + H_3^3 \frac{\partial P_3^\circ}{\partial Q_2} + H_3^4 \frac{\partial P_4^\circ}{\partial Q_2} + H_3^z P_2^\circ = 0 \\
&3. \quad \frac{\partial E_4^\circ}{\partial Q_2} = H_4^2 \frac{\partial P_2^\circ}{\partial Q_2} + H_4^3 \frac{\partial P_3^\circ}{\partial Q_2} + H_4^4 \frac{\partial P_4^\circ}{\partial Q_2} + H_4^z P_2^\circ = 0
\end{aligned}$$

In matrix form,

$$(210)\qquad \begin{bmatrix} H_2^2 & H_2^3 & H_2^4 \\ H_3^2 & H_3^3 & H_3^4 \\ H_4^2 & H_4^3 & H_4^4 \end{bmatrix} \begin{bmatrix} \dfrac{\partial P_2^\circ}{\partial Q_2} \\ \dfrac{\partial P_3^\circ}{\partial Q_2} \\ \dfrac{\partial P_4^\circ}{\partial Q_2} \end{bmatrix} = \begin{bmatrix} 1 - H_2^z P_2^\circ \\ - H_3^z P_2^\circ \\ - H_4^z P_2^\circ \end{bmatrix}$$

or

$$(211)\qquad [X][dV] = [dQ]$$

Then, it follows that

$$(212)\qquad \frac{\partial P_2^\circ}{\partial Q_2} = \frac{|X_{11}|}{|X|} - \frac{P_2^\circ}{|X|}(H_2^z|X_{11}| - H_3^z|X_{21}| + H_4^z|X_{31}|)$$

But, from (209),

$$(213)\qquad \frac{\partial P_2^\circ}{\partial Z} = -\frac{1}{|X|}[H_2^z|X_{11}| - H_3^z|X_{21}| + H_4^z|X_{31}|]$$

where dZ may be viewed as an injection of *numéraire* good from external sources.

$$(214)\qquad \frac{\partial P_2^\circ}{\partial Q_2} = \frac{|X_{11}|}{|X|} + P_2^\circ \frac{\partial P_2^\circ}{\partial Z}$$

then follows.

With a small unit increase in Q_2, P_2° will change for two separable reasons. First, a rise in Q_2 acts as a rise in income, or as an increase in the number of *numéraire* units available to the community. The amount

$$(215)\qquad P_2^\circ dQ_2 \frac{\partial P_2^\circ}{\partial Z}$$

is the change in price ascribable to the income change. If this be subtracted from $\frac{\partial P_2^\circ}{\partial Q_2}$, we should have the net rise or fall in price in the sense that this change in price would have resulted if Q_2 had increased and $P_2^\circ dQ_2$ in income had been withdrawn from the economy. We shall term this net effect the "compensated price effect of a quantity change," and symbolize it T_{jk}, for the net effect on P_j° of a change in Q_k. Then,

$$(216)\qquad T_{22} = \frac{|X_{11}|}{|X|}$$

In wholly similar fashion

$$(217)\qquad \frac{\partial P_3^\circ}{\partial Q_2} = -\frac{|X_{12}|}{|X|} + \frac{P_2}{|X|}[H_2^z|X_{12}| - H_3^z|X_{22}| + H_4^z|X_{32}|]$$

$$(218)\qquad \frac{\partial P_3^\circ}{\partial Z} = \frac{1}{|X|}[H_2^z|X_{12}| - H_3^z|X_{22}| + H_4^z|X_{32}|]$$

And, therefore,

(219) $$T_{32} = -\frac{|X_{12}|}{|X|}$$

and, more generally

(220) $$T_{kj} = (-1)^{s+t}\frac{|X_{st}|}{|X|}$$

where the s and t subscripts refer to the row and column of $[X]$ which are relevant to Q_j and P_k respectively.

From (II-2-1) it is clear that the terms in $[X]$ are the slopes of the aggregate demand curves defined there and in (206); thus, we must seek information about them to evaluate relevant terms. Hotelling sought this basis by an analysis of the individual demand functions from which the aggregates are assumed to be derived, as shown in (2) of footnote 48 of this chapter.[60]

As we have seen from the analysis of restrictions on the individual's substitution effects, Hicks has generalized Hotelling's analysis to show that the determinants of (165) alternate negative and positive in sign, if second-order maximization conditions hold. Since the total substitution effect is the sum of the individual substitution effects, it follows that the aggregate substitution effects, S_{jk}, follow the conditions on (165) if all individuals' choices have been derived from true maximum positions. Also, since we have seen that if all exchangers have about the same marginal propensities to consume all goods, and if these propensities are in the same direction, income effects will be in opposite directions on either side of the markets. If we go even further and assume that these income effects cancel to zero, then $\frac{\partial X_j^\circ}{\partial P_k} = S_{jk}$, and the conditions on (165) will hold again for $|X|$, $|X_{11}|$, $|X_{11,22}|$, . . . , $|X_{11,22,\ldots,n-2n-2}|$. Hicks, therefore, eliminates the aggregate income effect by adding what are assumed to be negative and positive individual income effects of about the same magnitude.

These Hotelling and Hicks restrictions on the slopes of the aggregate demand curves follow from properties of the individual demand curves plus some auxiliary assumptions discussed above. When employed to evaluate (216) they yield the theorem that the "own compensated price effect of a change in quantity" must be negative, while they do not yield enough information to allow the evaluation of the numerator Jacobian determinant in (219). Therefore, the "other price effect" of a quantity change may be positive, negative, or zero.

The income effect of a quantity increase on prices, as stated in (213) and (218) is not evaluable from this information. Even if it be assumed that $H_j^z > 0$ for all j, all of the Jacobians cannot be evaluated as to sign.

[60] See the references in footnote 48 of this chapter.

Thus, $\frac{\partial P_k^\circ}{\partial Z} \gtreqless 0$, and therefore,

$$\frac{\partial P_k^\circ}{\partial Q_j} \gtreqless 0, \qquad j = 2, \ldots, n, k = 2, \ldots, n \tag{221}$$

We may attack a second type of displacement with these restrictions. Into the demand functions, as they are written in (207), we introduce a new parameter, u_j:

$$X_j = H_j(P_2, P_3, \ldots, P_n; Z, u_j) \tag{222}$$

This term is a "parameter of shift" which allows us to increase or decrease the amount demanded at every price and value-of-stocks level by increasing or decreasing u_j. Thus, an increase in preferences of the community for Y_j would be depicted as an increase in u_j. Assume that (say) u_2 increases slightly. Then

$$[X]\left[\frac{\partial P_2^\circ}{\partial u_2}, \frac{\partial P_3^\circ}{\partial u_2}, \frac{\partial P_4^\circ}{\partial u_2}\right] = [-H_2^u, 0, 0] \tag{223}$$

Then

$$\frac{\partial P_2^\circ}{\partial u_2} = -H_2^u \frac{|X_{11}|}{|X|} = -H_2^u T_{22} \tag{224}$$

$$\frac{\partial P_3^\circ}{\partial u_2} = H_2^u \frac{|X_{12}|}{|X|} = -H_2^u T_{32} \tag{225}$$

It is interesting, therefore, that it is possible to find shifts in demand which are the exact equivalents of compensated quantity changes. An increase in u_j effects changes in P_k° at the same rate as a decrease in Q_j, and a decrease in u_j at the same rate as an increase in Q_j. The evaluation of (224) and (225) from the restrictions follows immediately.

These Hotelling-Hicks restrictions spring from the second of the three directions from which we expect information about functional slopes. They are, moreover, grounded in the *individual's* maximization process and therefore, as we have interpreted simple exchange, in the nature of his preferences. The maximization procedure appealed to has *not* been a fictitious one into which the market process can be fitted to obtain an analytical basis for new restrictions.[61] Moreover, the linkages from individual to market demand curves are not entirely satisfactory even in Hicks's procedure, based as it is upon a cancellation of income effects among net demanders and net suppliers. Once the analysis has left the

[61] As an example of our meaning of a fictitious market maximization model, Arrow and Debreu cast the general production model into the format of an n-person game, creating a fictitious third type of player. By so doing, they gained the analytical advantage of being able to avail themselves of Nash's proof of a solution for the n-person game, and went on to specify the implied restrictions on the data of the production economy necessary for its application to that economy. They dealt in similar fashion with a pure exchange economy as a subcase. We shall deal at length with the Arrow-Debreu existence proof in Chapter 9. See K. Arrow, (2).

confines of an exchange economy for a production economy the income effect on the supply side of the market will disappear and this neat cancellation will no longer be possible.

What, then, of the third direction—a derivation of slope restrictions on the market functions from an assumption of the stability of the equilibrium solution? This would finally cut the analysis free from molecular decisions if it succeeded. It will be recalled from Chapter 1 that we were most insistent upon the inherent dynamic nature of any stability analysis. Therefore, the derivation of the dynamic stability conditions will be postponed until Chapter 8, where the so-called Routhian conditions will be employed.

An alternative route—illegitimate in a purist sense and treacherous in a practical context—to the derivation of stability conditions is to generalize and develop not the method demonstrated in Chapter 1 but the *results*. This is the means Hicks has chosen and we shall turn to its rationale now, reserving until Chapter 8 extensive criticism of it and a comparison with the slope conditions resulting from a dynamic analysis of Model II-2.[62]

3.b.2. The Hicksian Slope Conditions for Complex Exchange

The analysis of Chapter 1, Section 5.a.3, led us to conclude that for a Model II-1 world in which exchangers were following a Walrasian pattern of reaction to disequilibrium, it is necessary and sufficient for the market to be stable that the difference between the slopes of the demand curve and supply curve be negative. In the conditions of Model II-1, as expressed in (II-1-3), this translates into

$$(226) \qquad {}_1H_2^2 + {}_2H_2^2 < 0$$

Conversely, (226) holds, from the analysis of Chapter 1, if the market in Model II-1 is assumed dynamically stable in the sense of Walras.

In a model with more than one market, however, the projection of this reasoning encounters complications. If we specify restrictions upon the demand functions for Y_2, what state do we assume to rule in the market for Y_3? If excess demand for Y_2 must fall with a rise in P_2, as a projection of Walrasian restrictions, must the markets for $Y_3, Y_4, \ldots, Y_n$ be in equilibrium? May a subset be in disequilibrium?

Since the function of a general analysis is to take into account explicitly the interdependence of all markets, the logic implied by the selection of the general model would impel one to require that all markets but that for Y_2 and one other market reflecting the disequilibrium be in equilibrium. Hicks, indeed, affirms that "it is what happens when all other prices are adjusted that is really most important."[63] That is, assume that demand equals supply for every good but Y_1 and Y_2, and that

[62] J. Hicks, (5), pp. 315–9.

[63] J. Hicks, (5), p. 66. See also P. Samuelson, (4), pp. 272–3.

$E_2 < 0$; assume further $P_3, P_4, \ldots, P_n$ are readjusted to bring about equilibrium again in their respective markets. Then, according to Hicks, if, in the second position, excess demand for Y_2 is negative when P_2 is above its equilibrium point, the Walrasian slope conditions have been generalized in their most meaningful form. But he also asserts an interest in the sign of E_2 when only the market for Y_3 is re-equilibrated; when only the markets for Y_3 and Y_4 are; when only the markets for Y_3, Y_4, and Y_5 are in equilibrium, and so forth until the final and most important state is reached. Consequently, Hicks's search for the generalized Walrasian conditions takes the form of a succession of "readings" of E_2 as the number of markets in equilibrium increases from 0 to $n - 2$.

We may return to (208) for the development of Hicks's slope conditions. The model is in full equilibrium in the initial state. Assume now that P_2 rises slightly above P_2°, throwing the entire system into disequilibrium. Now, holding all other prices at former levels, record the excess demand in the market for Y_2, denoting it $(E_2)_0$, the subscript 0 symbolizing the fact that no markets have been returned to equilibrium. Next, allow P_3 to return to a level which returns its market to equilibrium, and denote the corresponding excess demand in the market for Y_2 by the symbol $(E_2)_3$. Now, vary P_3 and P_4 simultaneously until the markets for Y_3 and Y_4 are back in equilibrium, and observe the excess demand for Y_2, $(E_2)_{3,4}$. In this same manner derive $(E)_{3,4,5}$, and so forth, until $(E)_{3,4,5,\ldots,n}$ is obtained.

If, at every step of this succession of adjustments, the excess demand for Y_2 is negative—that is, if $(E_2)_0$, $(E_2)_3$, $(E_2)_{3,4,\ldots}$ $(E_2)_{3,4,5,\ldots,n}$ are without exception less than zero and these same conditions hold for Y_3, $Y_4, \ldots, Y_n$—Hicks terms the equilibrium point one characterized by perfect stability. If one or more of these terms are positive, but $(E_2)_{3,4,5,\ldots,n}$ is negative, or the same condition holds for one or more of the other goods under analysis, Hicks terms the equilibrium point "imperfectly stable," providing an ultimate sort of stability. Further, the succession of adjustments for which these conditions must hold must be for every possible ordering of the markets. For example, Y_2 may have a market revealing "perfectly stable" behavior for the sequence of adjustments 3; 3 and 4; 3, 4, and 5; and so forth, to 3, 4, 5, . . . , n. But this does not imply that it will reveal the same perfectly stable characteristics for the sequence 4; 4, 5; 4, 5, 3; 4, 5, 3, 8; and so forth. Every such sequence for all markets but the one in question and the excluded market must meet the requirements of perfect stability if the latter is to rule.[64]

What conditions must hold for the slopes of the excess demand functions E_j in order for perfect stability or imperfect stability to characterize an equilibrium point of Model II-2? We may develop these conditions for a four-good system again, with Y_1 the excluded equation in (208).

[64] See R. Kuenne, (8).

Then, with a change in P_2, the changes in *excess* demand may be written $\left(\text{since } \frac{dQ_2}{dP_2} = 0\right)$,

$$
(227)\qquad
\begin{aligned}
&1. \quad \frac{dX_2}{dP_2} = \frac{\partial X_2}{\partial P_2} + \frac{\partial X_2}{\partial P_3}\frac{dP_3}{dP_2} + \frac{\partial X_2}{\partial P_4}\frac{dP_4}{dP_2} \\
&2. \quad \frac{dX_3}{dP_2} = \frac{\partial X_3}{\partial P_2} + \frac{\partial X_3}{\partial P_3}\frac{dP_3}{dP_2} + \frac{\partial X_3}{\partial P_4}\frac{dP_4}{dP_2} \\
&3. \quad \frac{dX_4}{dP_2} = \frac{\partial X_4}{\partial P_2} + \frac{\partial X_4}{dP_3}\frac{dP_3}{dP_2} + \frac{\partial X_4}{\partial P_4}\frac{dP_4}{dP_2}
\end{aligned}
$$

Then, allowing neither P_3 nor P_4 to change from the disequilibrium levels they now represent, we impose thereby zero values for $\frac{dP_j}{dP_2}$, $j = 3$, 4, and (227-1) reduces to

$$
(228)\qquad \frac{dX_2}{dP_2} = \frac{\partial X_2}{\partial P_2} < 0
$$

and if perfect stability is to hold, it is necessary that the slope of the partial demand function for X_2 be negative. Next, allow $\frac{dP_3}{dP_2}$ to attain the level necessary for P_3 to make $E_3 = 0$. Then, (227) becomes, in its relevant portions,

$$
(229)\qquad
\begin{aligned}
&1. \quad \frac{dX_2}{dP_2} = \frac{\partial X_2}{\partial P_2} + \frac{\partial X_2}{\partial P_3}\frac{dP_3}{dP_2} \\
&2. \quad 0 = \frac{\partial X_3}{\partial P_2} + \frac{\partial X_3}{\partial P_3}\frac{dP_3}{dP_2}
\end{aligned}
$$

which yields as a solution

$$
(230)\qquad \left(\frac{dX_2}{dP_2}\right)_3 = \frac{|X_{33}|}{|X_{11,33}|}
$$

which must be negative for perfect stability.

Finally, if we allow P_3 and P_4 to equilibrate their markets, (227) becomes

$$
(231)\qquad
\begin{aligned}
&1. \quad \frac{dX_2}{dP_2} = \frac{\partial X_2}{\partial P_2} + \frac{\partial X_2}{\partial P_3}\frac{dP_3}{dP_2} + \frac{\partial X_2}{\partial P_4}\frac{dP_4}{dP_2} \\
&2. \quad 0 = \frac{\partial X_3}{\partial P_2} + \frac{\partial X_3}{\partial P_3}\frac{dP_3}{dP_2} + \frac{\partial X_3}{\partial P_4}\frac{dP_4}{dP_2} \\
&3. \quad 0 = \frac{\partial X_4}{\partial P_2} + \frac{\partial X_4}{\partial P_3}\frac{dP_3}{dP_2} + \frac{\partial X_4}{\partial P_4}\frac{dP_4}{dP_2}
\end{aligned}
$$

and

(232) $$\left(\frac{dX_2}{dP_2}\right)_{3,4} = \frac{|X|}{|X_{11}|}$$

which must be negative as a necessary condition for perfect stability.

If like conditions hold for the analogous expressions for goods Y_3 and Y_4, perfect stability will characterize this equilibrium. For these conditions to hold it is necessary and sufficient that all Jacobian determinants of the forms

(233) $$|X_{jj,kk,\ldots,n-1n-1}|,\ |X_{jj,kk,\ldots,n-2n-2}|,\ \ldots,\ |X|$$

alternate in sign negative and positive; i.e., that these Jacobians have the sign $(-1)^s$ where s is the number of rows in them.

If imperfect stability is to characterize the equilibrium position, it is necessary and sufficient that the expressions

(234) $$|X_{jj}|,\ |X|, \qquad j = 2, \ldots, n$$

be of sign $(-1)^s$, where the subscript j denotes both goods and rows and columns in the matrix $[X]$.

Lange has extended Hicks's definition of types of stability to the case of "partial stability of order m," where $m \leqq n - 1$, for which the conditions for imperfect stability are met when at least one subset of m prices is adjusted to re-equilibrate their markets. Note that it need not meet these conditions for *all* subsets of m prices. When a system possesses partial stability of order m and no higher for an equilibrium point, Lange defines partial stability of *rank* m as holding. It will be perfect if partial stability of all lower orders and all prices holds. Where $m = n - 1$, Lange's definition of perfect partial stability corresponds to Hicks's perfect stability, but where $m < n - 1$, the conditions for Lange's perfect partial stability are that the following Jacobians of rank s ($s = 1, \ldots, m$) have the sign $(-1)^s$:

(235) $$|X_{jj,kk,\ldots m-1m-1,m+1m+1\ldots n-1n-1}|,$$
$$|X_{jj,kk,\ldots m-2m-2,\ldots m+1m+1\ldots n-1n-1}|,\ \ldots\ |X_{m+1m+1,\ldots n-1n-1}|$$

for all possible subsets with m goods, and for each such subset for all orderings of the goods in $[X]$.[65]

As we have seen, $[X]$ consists of elements which are the sum of individuals' substitution and income effects, and the aggregate substitution effects, like the individual's if true maximum positions are reached, will form determinants which alternate in sign in like manner to those of Hicks's perfect stability determinants. (See (165)). Therefore, if income effects cancel out in the aggregate, conditions (233) will hold by virtue of second-order maximization conditions. Only if income effects are not

[65] O. Lange, (6), pp. 93–4.

well-behaved can Hicks's perfect stability conditions fail to be met in the general case.[66]

F. Hahn and T. Negishi[67] have proved that if all goods in the model are gross substitutes, i.e., $\frac{\partial X_j}{\partial P_j} < 0$, $\frac{\partial X_j}{\partial P_k} > 0$, $j = 2, \ldots, n$, $k = 2, \ldots, n$, $j \neq k$,[68] the sufficiency conditions for Hicksian perfect stability will be met. Negishi's proof of this proposition is a simple one. Since the demand functions are homogeneous of degree zero in all prices, it follows from Euler's theorem on homogeneous functions that

$$(236) \quad \sum_j \frac{\partial X_k}{\partial P_j} P_j = -\frac{\partial X_k}{\partial P_1} P_1, \quad \text{for every } k = 2, \ldots, n, j = 2, \ldots, n$$

assuming all prices are measured in an external *numéraire.* Letting $P_1 = 1$, and multiplying both sides by (-1), we obtain

$$(237) \qquad \sum_j -\frac{\partial X_k}{\partial P_j} P_j = \frac{\partial X_k}{\partial P_1}$$

or

$$(238) \qquad [-X][P_2, P_3, \ldots P_n] = \left[\frac{\partial X_2}{\partial P_1}, \frac{\partial X_3}{\partial P_1}, \ldots \frac{\partial X_n}{\partial P_1}\right]$$

If gross substitutability holds for the system, $\frac{\partial X_k}{\partial P_k} < 0$; $\frac{\partial X_k}{\partial P_j} > 0$, $j \neq k$; $\frac{\partial X_k}{\partial P_1} > 0$. Therefore, all diagonal elements of $[-X]$ will be positive, and all nondiagonal terms negative. For such a matrix, an inverse will exist and all of its elements will be positive. Since this is true, the Hawkins-Simon conditions[69] imply that all determinants of the type in (233) will alternate in sign negative and positive, since the like subdeterminants of $[-X]$ will all be positive. Therefore, the Hicksian perfect stability conditions are met. In similar fashion, the same theorem is proved if some $\frac{\partial X_k}{\partial P_j} = 0$ and $[-X]$ is indecomposable.

Once more we pose the most important question, analytically speaking: of what aid are these Hicksian slope conditions for the derivation of

[66] J. Hicks, (5), pp. 310–11, 316–17. In the first edition of the work Hicks asserted that complementarity among goods might destroy stability even if income effects could be neglected. Mosak pointed out that if every individual's system met the second-order equilibrium conditions the entire system would be stable in Hicks's sense of perfect stability, and complementarity would not be capable of disturbing it. Cf. J. Mosak, (1), p. 42. Hicks caught the error himself as a result of his discovery of (162). See J. Hicks, (5), pp. 77, 316–7.

[67] F. Hahn, (2) and T. Negishi, (1). For a third statement of this theorem see K. Arrow, (6), p. 546.

[68] If the matrix is indecomposable (see Chapter 1, Section 2) off-diagonal elements may be non-negative for the theorem to apply.

[69] See the discussion in Chapter 6.

operational theorems? In practice, little use can be made of the restrictions on the Hicksian Jacobians except for those which must rule for imperfect stability, i.e., those on $|X_{jj}|$ and $|X|$. These, of course, enable us to evaluate, with the same results as those obtained previously, such expressions as (216), (219), (224), and (225). We have seen that it is possible to handle shifts in demand for a commodity by (1) shifting a parameter, u_j, in the demand functions, and (2) by using a compensated change in Q_j in the opposite direction of the shift in demand. Hicks illustrates yet a third manner in which this can be done through the use of such equations as those of (231). If the analysis centers upon an increase in the aggregate demand for Y_2, the question may be asked in this manner: when prices in all other markets but that for Y_2 are allowed to adjust as required to maintain equilibrium (the market for Y_1 being excluded), by how much must P_2 rise to induce the increase in E_2 equivalent to the shift in demand for Y_2 whose impact is to be investigated? It is possible, where we define

(239) $$\frac{dP_2}{dX_2} = \frac{|X_{11}|}{|X|} = T_{22}$$

to obtain expressions for $\frac{dP_j}{dP_2}$:

(240) $$\frac{dP_3}{dP_2} = -\frac{dX_2}{dP_2}\left[\frac{|X_{12}|}{|X|}\right] = \frac{dX_2}{dP_2}T_{32}$$

or

(241) $$\frac{dP_3}{dP_2} = -\frac{|X_{12}|}{|X_{11}|}$$

The denominator of this expression will be positive by the Hicksian slope conditions, but the numerator will be indeterminate as to sign. Once more we must, with Hicks, fall back upon the assumption that income effects may be neglected and aggregate substitution effects substituted for the terms in $[X_{11}]$ and $[X_{12}]$, to yield the expression

(242) $$\frac{dP_3}{dP_2} = -\frac{S_{23}S_{44} - S_{24}S_{34}}{S_{33}S_{44} - S_{34}^2}$$

If Y_2, Y_3, and Y_4 are net substitutes for one another, the numerator of (241) will be negative, and P_3 must rise along with P_2 following an increase in demand for Y_2. If Y_2 and Y_3 are substitutes, while Y_4 is a complement of both, the same direction of movement of P_3 must occur.

It is possible to go farther in peculiar cases. Morishima has shown that when the sign of $\frac{\partial X_i}{\partial P_j}$ is the same as the sign of $\frac{\partial X_j}{\partial P_i}$, while at the same time the sign of $\left(\frac{\partial X_i}{\partial P_k}\frac{\partial X_k}{\partial P_j}\right)$ equals the sign of $\frac{\partial X_i}{\partial P_j}$, then a rise in demand for any product will raise its price, while the prices of all goods which are substitutes for the good will rise and the prices of all goods which are complements will fall. The latter condition may be interpreted in the following way: when Y_k is a gross substitute for Y_j, and Y_j is a gross substitute for Y_i, then Y_i and Y_k must be gross substitutes to meet the condition. When Y_k is a gross complement for Y_j, and Y_j is a gross complement for Y_i, then Y_i and Y_k must be gross substitutes if the condition is met. More ponderously, if Y_k is a complement (substitute) of Y_j, and Y_j is a substitute (complement) for Y_i, then Y_i and Y_k must be gross complements for the condition to be met. These results for the Morishima case hinge upon the existence of Hicksian perfect stability of the given equilibrium.[70]

Lastly, Hicks has shown that in a system in which all goods are net substitutes and for an equilibrium characterized by perfect stability, when u_j rises *all* prices will rise, but that the percentage rise for P_j will be greatest.[71]

What independent contribution do the Hicksian slope conditions or, as they are usually termed, the Hicksian "static stability conditions," make to the task of deriving meaningful theorems? The answer must surely be "very little, if any." All of the theorems derived in the analysis of Model II-2 can either be derived equally well from the conditions obtained from second-order equilibrium conditions, or depend upon these conditions at some stage of the reasoning. The independent contribution to analysis of the concept of and conditions for perfect stability has been nil to date. In those instances where either basis for evaluation might be used—those derived from maximization conditions or those from Hick's slope conditions—seemingly the choice might be decided on grounds of theoretical plausibility.

But it is on this ground that Hicks's "stability" analysis is most vulnerable. It is not based upon an explicit dynamic model, and, as we shall see in Chapter 8, only in special cases do we know the structure of dynamic general models which would yield the conditions for Hicksian stability as necessary or necessary and sufficient conditions for dynamic stability. The theoretical advantage of the use of a stability analysis is that it affords some basis for a theory of market behavior cut free in important analytical respects from the individuals who compose the market. This makes it mandatory that this theory of market behavior be spelled out in explicit detail and the conditions for its attaining a position of rest be derived as theorems, not assumed definitionally.

4. A Recapitulation

Much analytical ground has been covered in this chapter. We have spent some time defining the data of the neoclassical theory of exchange, the greater part in exploring the problems arising in the definition of

[70] M. Morishima, (1).
[71] J. Hicks, (5), pp. 317–8.

consumer tastes for choices among actions under conditions of pure certainty and pure risk. The most distinctive feature of our treatment was its adoption of a wholly tautological interpretation of the preference function and an analytical as opposed to a behavioral outlook upon its constrained maximization.

Three models of simple exchange were developed to deal with cardinal, independent preferences; cardinal, interdependent preferences; and ordinal, interdependent preferences. It was demonstrated that although the first model offered advantages over the second and third for the derivation of theorems, the second afforded no advantage over the third. Moreover, the first possessed such intuitively objectionable assumptions and, like the second, could not, given the current state of technique, be constructed from an observational preference function. The third model, therefore, was selected as the simple exchange model to form the basis for the complex exchange model.

Concern over the derivation of "laws of change" from general models began with Pareto and Fisher, who confined themselves largely to the first type of model for these purposes. The greatest single step forward was taken by Slutsky with his classic analysis of what Hicks came to call the substitution and income effects of price changes. Most of our ability to obtain general propositions from simple exchange models derives from their manipulation. Even where ambiguities springing from interdependent preferences cloud the results, these Slutsky effects yield powerful insights into the nature of the complicating forces and afford the analyst an ability to gauge subjectively the likelihood of their occurrence in any specific problem.

In stepping up the analysis one level to models of complex exchange, we saw that these ambiguities increased more rapidly than the variables of the models, as the analysis of Chapter 1 would lead us to expect. Two models were presented, one with only one market and two goods, the other with more than two goods. In the latter the concept of the *numéraire* and its function were illustrated.

In the evaluation of equilibrium displacements we found once more that the most fruitful aid was rendered by the Slutsky effects, by specific restrictions upon the substitution effect first obtained by Hotelling but generalized by Hicks, and the further advance by Hicks in moving from the individual effects to the aggregate effects. We found the Hicksian attempt to generalize the results of a Walrasian dynamic one-market model to be less satisfying both in theoretical as well as practical terms.

CHAPTER 3

THE PRODUCTION ECONOMY

1. The Data and Assumptions of the Models

It is now necessary to ascend to a more ambitious level in recognizing that goods which are exchanged are largely the result of prior productive efforts. Consequently, in this chapter we shall build into Model II-2 a productive sector from which the supplies $\bar{X}_j$ emerge. To the data and assumptions of this model in Chapter 2 it is necessary to introduce the addenda and amendments which follow.

1.a. The Stock of Resources Available to the Consumer

The assumption that each consumer begins the week with a given set of Y_j endowments, $[Q_c]$, with elements Q_{cj}, is withdrawn. Substituted for it is the assumption that he is endowed with given amounts of primary inputs, Z_i, $i = 1, \ldots, m$, denoted Q_{ci} for consumer c. These are *stocks* of productive resources which came into existence before the week whose market day and contract-fulfillment period are under study. Moreover, in this chapter it will be assumed that they are eternal, indestructible, and nonaugmentable.

A unit of primary input Z_i yields a *flow* of primary input service whose width is one unit per unit of Z_i and whose duration is one week. These factor services we denote z_i, in lower case, to distinguish them from their generating factors, Z_i, in capitals. Thus, a given stock of Z_i in the possession of a consumer c, Q_{ci}, will yield a weekly flow of Q_{ci} units of factor service z_i. For each factor service, z_i, there exists a market in which it is sold for price P_i. The aggregate amount of it, $Q_i = \Sigma_c Q_{ci}$, is in the hands of consumers who bring what remains after satisfying their own demands for it to the market on Monday and sell it to enterpreneurs (primarily). All such transactions are viewed as occurring exactly as they did in the exchange economy: contracts are signed at the end of the market day on Monday to deliver given amounts of factor service z_i at P_i° on given days of the following six-day period. At the end of the fulfillment week, i.e., on Sunday, those who have bought such services by leasing amounts of Z_i for one week return these factors to the persons from whom they obtained them, and so, on the following Monday, the same process begins again.[1]

[1] This clear-cut distinction between stocks and flows, resources and resource services, explicitly made and consistently maintained, was a Walrasian innovation of the greatest importance to economic theory. Its "rediscovery" by Cannan and Fisher and its application by them to capital theory at the turn of the century was one of the most important steps taken on that thorny path. Cf. I. Fisher, (2) and (3). Fisher also used the distinction to great advantage in his work with national income, as, for example, in Fisher, (4).

As noted above, we shall adopt the Walrasian assumption that factor services can be consumed by consumers. Walras postulated this in the belief that by so doing, under conditions of fixed coefficients of production it would be possible to guarantee that no P_i would become zero.[2] We shall retain it because it is a simple method of including leisure in the consumer's market basket. If z_1 represents labor-weeks, then P_{z_1} is the wage rate and the price of a week of leisure. Since the same consumer attraction may exist for other factor services, we place all such services in the consumer's preference function, and *assume* that he takes some of each, no matter how small the amount, at any constellation of prices. The preference function for Model I-3 is then modified to read, instead of (118) of Chapter 2,

$$M = G(X_1, \ldots, X_n, X_{z_1}, \ldots, X_{z_m}) \tag{1}$$

and the new variables are treated exactly as the old to obtain specific and nonspecific solutions to Model I-3. The new nonspecific solutions, which include demand equations for every consumer for every factor service, are assumed to be projected forward into Model II-2.

1.b. The State of the Productive Arts

The act of production consists in the combination of factor services z_i and of intermediate goods Y_j produced during the week into final outputs of Y_j. The terms "intermediate" and "final" are interpreted from the viewpoint of the productive unit. Thus, a firm which uses electrical power to produce cement for sale to other firms is viewed as absorbing electricity on intermediate account and producing cement on final account, even though the cement will enter some other firm's productive activity as an intermediate good.

This process of transformation of factor service and intermediate good inputs into outputs is organized and supervised by individuals called "entrepreneurs." We may, in the Marshallian tradition, split off their "hiring-selling" function from their "organizing-managing" function, treating the latter as a factor service of the labor type for which a market-determined price is paid.[3] In Walras' treatment of production, the entrepreneur seems to be conceived wholly as a "hirer-seller," with abilities possessed so widely that they will be free goods under all conceivable circumstances. Pareto attempted to explain the failure of the Walrasian entrepreneur to obtain any gains ("profits") in equilibrium on the basis of the assumption of free competition among them, since they do not possess any factor service or other productive opportunities in their role as entrepreneurs. However, to this mechanism must be added the assumption that entrepreneurial skills are so plentiful that it may be taken for

[2] These matters are discussed in detail in Chapter 9, Section 3.

[3] Cf. A. Pigou, (1), p. 201.

granted before equilibrium is attained that they will be free goods in that state.[4]

This Walrasian entrepreneur *"faisant ni bénéfices ni pertes"* has the virtue of allowing the vision of the productive process to abstract from aspects of production rooted in dynamics or uncertainty and in whose existence more recent economic theory, as that of Knight or of Schumpeter, grounds the existence of profits. Risk, uncertainty, technological change, innovation, and speculation are either nonexistent in the models of Part II or present in neutral fashion, and so the Walrasian entrepreneur is peculiarly at home in his environment.

The technological constraints within which the entrepreneur must accomplish his functions are written in the following form in the general case:

$$(2) \qquad J_v(\bar{X}_{v1}, \ldots, \bar{X}_{vn}; X_{vz_1}, \ldots, X_{vz_m}; X_{v1}, \ldots, X_{vn}) = 0$$

where $v = 1, \ldots, o$ denotes the firm, and o is the number of firms actually and *potentially* capable of being in existence. As in Chapters 1 and 2, $\bar{X}$-terms denote supplies (outputs in this case), up to $n - 1$ of which may be zero for a specific firm's "transformation function" J_v. The symbols X_{vz_i} (we shall use X_{vi} whenever possible) denote firm v's demands for productive services, and X_{vj} symbolize the firm's demand for intermediate goods. As we have written and will write the functions in (2), it is quite possible for a firm to produce (say) coal as an output and to absorb coal as an intermediate good input; we shall keep the gross output of coal as an $\bar{X}$-term and the input of coal as an X-term rather than netting out the input to treat output as net of internal firm uses. We shall occasionally write the transformation function in explicit form; as an example, if one or more J_v contain only one output, we shall write the transformation relations as

$$(3) \qquad \bar{X}_{vj} = T_{vj}(X_{vz_1}, \ldots, X_{vz_m}, X_{v1}, \ldots, X_{vn})$$

In this form we will term the function a "production function," to conform to current usage.[5]

The function J_v is a datum of our models and is derived in the following manner from engineering information. Every possible combination of $2n + m - 1$ arguments of (2) is specified: if the remaining argument is an output, that manner of combining inputs is selected which, given the level of all other outputs, maximizes the remaining one whose output level is unspecified. This set of values for the $2n + m$ arguments of (2) then satisfies (2). If the remaining unspecified argument is an input, the small-

[4] V. Pareto, (1), Vol. II, p. 79.

[5] Among the first to write the transformation relationships in the form of (3) was A. Aupetit, (1), p. 64.

est quantity of it which will yield the specified outputs with the other specified inputs is that value chosen for the amount of unspecified input, and again the values of the $2n + m$ arguments will satisfy (2). When inputs are treated as negative outputs, we may state in general that every point in $2n + m$-Euclidean space which satisfies (2) has been obtained in a prior extremum analysis by specifying all but one of the coordinates and maximizing the value the last can attain under current technological constraints.

In this transformation process time is once more sterilized in that the entrepreneur is assumed never to have problems in financing any level of production he chooses: he has no budget constraint, since he can pay for all of his inputs from the value of his outputs, and we abstract from any impediments that might arise because the need to pay for inputs may precede the receipts of payments from outputs. Further, during the market day, each entrepreneur is assumed to hold firmly to fixed expectations of future prices for every future period in his planning horizon, and, at the end of the day, he is absolutely certain that the contracts to which he is a party will be fulfilled.

We shall assume that the motivating force behind entrepreneurial decisionmaking is that of profit maximization, and that this force exists in the entrepreneur's psychological drives. This is quite different from the role of "utility" or "preference" maximization in the analysis of consumer decisionmaking of Chapter 2. The transformation function is not an analytical creation of the economist, although it also serves as a repository of information. Points on the production surface were obtained, not by inquiring of entrepreneurs their preferences among baskets of inputs and outputs, but by making the assumption that the entrepreneur prefers larger net returns to smaller. If the economist, using this function in a given set of circumstances, predicts that the firm will choose a given point on the function, and the firm in fact does not, the firm has not revealed an inconsistency between what it said it would do and what it did. It is simply not following a profit-maximization strategy, and, if this motivation is one of the economist's assumptions, it is being violated for one reason or another. Thus, the economist's propositions about the firm's choices have a real predictive content, not contained, in our interpretation, by similar propositions about the consumer's behavior.

1.c. Zero Investment Levels

The further sterilization of time as a meaningful analytical entity requires that we eliminate any changes in the stocks of productive factors Z_i which exist. All forms of investment—gross and net, individual and aggregate—are assumed to be identically zero. There are, therefore, no markets in which the assets Z_i are sold, and, since we shall insist that every price in our models emerge from an identifiable market, P_{Z_i} are nonexistent.[6] As asserted in Section 1.a. above, the stocks of primary factors are given as data *in physical terms*, or as inventories of the various types of Z_i defined in physical categories. We follow Walras in this manner of specifying the data, even in the face of criticism by those who view the concept of capital as inseparable from value definition.[7]

Therefore, in the models of Chapter 3, where our interest focusses upon the complications introduced by production into the exchange mechanism, the assets Z_i are neither produced nor destroyed. The only reason why consumers would seek to sell their stocks of Z_i would be to acquire more present goods than their current flow of asset services would provide them; therefore, our denial of asset markets and individual disinvestment is a denial to the individual of the ability to rearrange his consumption through time, freezing him within the flow of income dictated by his initial stocks of assets.

Lastly, as our interpretation of paper money in Chapter 5 will indicate, this denial of individual investment and disinvestment effectively eliminates the possibility of the existence of money in these production models. For those who will object to this interpretation, however, we shall explicitly exclude a paper money from them.

[6] F. H. Knight discusses an economy where capital goods are not exchanged, but asserts that a value of capital will emerge from such a system, i.e., that the P_{Z_i} will be determined. As will be seen from the discussion of Chapter 4, this implies the determination of an interest rate. But no market for loans exists in the Knight economy. He seems to obtain the interest rate from his interpretation of capital as the value of primary and intermediate inputs invested in production, *plus the growth in value during the period of construction*. See, for example, F. Knight, (11), p. 70. This growth in value to Knight is a technological factor depending upon the size of the capital stock and dictating the interest rate. This would require, if we accepted Knight's theory of the interest rate, that goods emerging on Friday be valued more highly than goods emerging on Tuesday. We have explicitly assumed them to be perfect substitutes, however, thereby either (1) denying Knight's theoretical construction or (2) accepting it but ignoring the differences in value by virtue of the short duration of time. For Knight's economy with no markets for capital goods see his (7), pp. 438–9.

[7] Apart from this school of thought, Koopmans believes that in a static model, "to make sense," the constraints which produced primary resources place upon production must be stated in terms of value of capital rather than in physical terms. The reason is not made clear. See T. Koopmans, (2), p. 42.

It is interesting that Hayek, in his reconstruction of Austrian capital theory, explicitly adopts the Walrasian method of defining resource constraints:

" . . . This stock of non-permanent resources in the form in which it exists as a datum is not some definite quantity of capital; for it can be expressed as a single magnitude only after the relative values of the items of which it is composed have been determined. And these values are clearly a resultant of the same equilibrating forces as determine the investment periods. The initial datum from which we have to start is simply an enumeration of all the items of which this stock of non-permanent resources is composed, and of all their technical attributes . . . the quantity of capital as a value magnitude, no less than the different investment periods, are not data, but among the unknowns which have to be determined." F. Hayek, (2), pp. 191–2. Copyright 1941 by The University of Chicago. Quoted by permission. See also pp. 266–7.

2. The Models of Production

With these additions and alterations, we are prepared to construct the production models. These models will be distinguished by the technological conditions of production assumed to rule in each case. In Model III-1 the primitive case of fixed coefficients of production will be discussed. Model III-2 is developed for the linear homogeneous production function and the single output. Model III-3 generalizes the single output case to production under conditions of the generalized production function. And, lastly, Model III-4 undertakes an analysis of the case of the multiple-output, generalized transformation function. These models will assume perfect certainty; however, in Section 3 we shall spend some time analyzing aspects of entrepreneurial behavior in conditions of uncertainty.

2.a. Model III-1: Single Output, Fixed Input Coefficients

The simplest conditions of production which have any degree of credibility are those in which each firm (or entrepreneur) produces a single output—$\bar{X}_{vj}$—with given inputs per unit of output—a_{ij}, a_{jJ}—which do not vary with scale of output. The term a_{ij}, therefore, is the amount of z_i required per unit of $\bar{X}_{vj}$ regardless of the amount of output, and a_{jJ} the unit requirement of intermediate good Y_j per production of output Y_J. At this point, and throughout the book, we shall use a capital J when the need arises to distinguish Y_j as intermediate good from Y_j as an output. When it is used, it will always distinguish Y_j as an output.

These a_{ij}, a_{jJ} coefficients are *minimum* coefficients, which means that each is the minimum amount of input which must be put into the production process to obtain a unit of output. In this sense, then, there exists only one *activity* which the firm may use to produce an arbitrarily defined unit of output. This activity may be designated by the vector $[1, -a_{ij}, -a_{jJ}]$, the elements indicating that at a unit level of operation of the activity the indicated inputs are required to yield a unit of output. We assume that this activity is wholly divisible, so that any fraction of the unit level of operation may be obtained. And, as we have said above, we assume the elements in the vector do not change with the level at which it is operated, so that if $\bar{X}_{vj}$ is the level of operation, output levels and input levels may be obtained by multiplying the unit activity vector by $\bar{X}_{vj}$. For a single output process, we may speak of level of output or level of operation of the activity synonomously. Lastly, it must be emphasized that in the analysis above these a-coefficients are Walrasian average-and-marginal coefficients, rather than Paretian marginal coefficients.[8]

[8] V. Pareto, (2), pp. 607–8. We shall deal at length with the Paretian theory of production in the construction of Model III-3 below.

With the additional assumption that each firm produces only one good, the firm's total cost function may be written:

$$C_v = \sum_i a_{ij}\bar{X}_{vj}P_i + \sum_j a_{jJ}\bar{X}_{vJ}P_j \tag{4}$$

which is a minimum for every value $\bar{X}_{vj}$, given P_i and P_j, by virtue of the prior minimization of the a-coefficients. Total costs are linear and homogeneous (1) in output, (2) in all prices, and (3) in all a-coefficients. It follows that average cost, $\frac{C_v}{\bar{X}_{vj}}$, equals marginal cost, $\frac{dC_v}{d\bar{X}_{vj}}$, and that they are constant. It should be noted explicitly that (4) implies that no fixed costs exist, since the entrepreneur brings to the task of combining the inputs no factors which are peculiarly his own except his valueless services. *All* economic inputs are literally hired in the markets.

In an environment in which the firm views all prices as independent of its purchases and sales, its revenue, R_v, is, of course,

$$R_v = \bar{X}_{vj}P_j \tag{5}$$

and profits, π_v,

$$\pi_v = R_v - C_v \tag{6}$$

If $P_J - \frac{C_v}{\bar{X}_{vj}} > 0$, π_v has no finite maximum; if $P_J - \frac{C_v}{\bar{X}_{vj}} < 0$, π_v reaches a maximum at $\bar{X}_{vj} = 0$; and if $P_J - \frac{C_v}{\bar{X}_{vj}} = 0$, its maximum equals its minimum equals zero at any nonnegative output. In the first case the firm has no determinate output level; in the second case it produces nothing; and in the third case again its output is indeterminate. If we assume for the moment that there exists a determinate positive total (or "industry") output, which must rule out the second case as an equilibrium solution, it is necessary to seek further conditions for the allocation of the equilibrium output among an indeterminate number of firms. Walras' assumption was that if $\bar{X}_j^\circ$ was the equilibrium industry output, each of the o firms produced $\frac{\bar{X}_j^\circ}{o}$ of that output.[9] But what determines o? After all, Walras' theory of competitive adjustment assumes that entrepreneurs are wholly mobile among the various transformation functions that exist in a particular week for exploitation.

Model III-1's production conditions, therefore, rather effectively remove the spotlight from the firm's decisionmaking and place it upon the

[9] Cf. G. Stigler, (1), p. 240n.

"industry" and the decisions emerging from the latter. If only aggregate output is determinate, some theorists argue that the firm's output is not only indeterminate but of no interest.[10] But are we so ready to beg the question of the method by which the only operational decisionmaking unit in the analysis reaches a determinate output level? The aggregate of firms, after all, is a mere analytical category with no realistic decision-making power. If the focus is on the theory of the firm the question is far from being an uninteresting one, though it may be unanswerable.

It was no accident, then, that in the Walrasian body of analysis, whose core was Model III-1, the firm was not the subject of intensive study. Indeed, one has the feeling in reading Walras, and other representatives of the Lausanne school, that the firm was never really integrated into the models constructed by the group. Walras gives no evidence of ever having satisfied himself of the motivation of the firm in models where equilibrium profits must be zero. He is quite explicit, for example, in referring to the consumer's motivation as one of maximizing utility, but even in the cases where the lack of symmetry in his statement must have forced itself upon his awareness he backs away from the assumption of profit maximization as the goal of the entrepreneur. The asymmetry is brought out well in the following passage:

"Let us note, then, that we find here, in the desire to avoid losses and make profits, the determining reason for the demand for productive services and the supply of products by entrepreneurs, as we have already seen in the desire to obtain maximum satisfaction of desires the determining reason for the supply of factor services and demand for products by (consumers)."[11] Thus, Edgeworth's belief that Walras intended the

[10] See R. Dorfman, (1), p. 348n, and also P. Samuelson, (8), p. 1.

[11] L. Walras, (2), p. 194. Quoted by permission. See also the postscript to "Note on Mr. Wicksteed's Refutation of the English Theory of Rent," reprinted in L. Walras, (3), pp. 494–5, for an equally obvious avoidance of profit-maximization interpretation.

The clearest statement of profit maximization for the case of pure competition that the present author could locate in a survey of the Lausanne school from Walras through Boninsegni is the following quotation from Pareto's *Cours:* "We suppose entrepreneurs who produce with no other care than that of their own self-interest. . . . The entrepreneur will increase a factor of production's consumption as long as the cost of it is less than the revenue he derives from the product obtained. . . ." V. Pareto, (1), Vol. II, pp. 84–5. He then asserts that these considerations lead to the same conditions of equilibrium as an earlier production model he developed, but the only condition expressed there is the equality of average cost and price. Although one might be led to believe that he is failing to distinguish between marginal and average costs, Pareto is dealing with a linear homogeneous production function, in which case, by Euler's theorem, setting prices of inputs equal to marginal value products leads to zero profits.

However, (on p. 90n) in dealing with a-coefficients which are functions of the quantity produced, Pareto states that optimal output in pure competition will occur where average cost reaches its minimum, but he does not make it clear that the forces of competition will force the firm to that point. This failure to develop a clear-cut model of profit maximization for the firm contrasts vividly with the clear model of profit maximization Pareto developed for the monopolist. See, for example, the analysis of monopoly in V. Pareto, (2), p. 615.

This ambiguity in the writings of the two leaders of the Lausanne school tempts to the conclusion that profit maximization was never really reconciled with constant costs for the firm and/or zero profits in equilibrium in the analysis of that school. Even though we shall anticipate the analysis of Models III-2 and III-3 to some extent, it will pay us to pursue this point further to demonstrate the manner in which confusion was reflected in the difficulties the school had in distinguishing between minimum cost conditions for the firm on the one hand and maximum profit conditions on the other. The frequent confusion of the two has already been marked by P. Samuelson, (4), pp. 82–3.

In Pareto's model of production under pure competition, the firm's production functions are of the following types:

$$\text{(1)} \qquad \begin{aligned} &1. \quad X_{vi} = T_{vi}(\bar{X}_{v1}, \ldots, \bar{X}_{vn}), \qquad i = 1, \ldots, m \\ &2. \quad X_{vj} = T_{vj}(\bar{X}_{v1}, \ldots, \bar{X}_{vn}), \qquad j = 1, \ldots, n \end{aligned}$$

These relations state that given a constellation of firm outputs, there is one and only one (minimal) quantity of each input given by current technology. This is clearly not implied by such relations as (3) above. System (1), for the case of the single output, Pareto's usual case, when differentiated with respect to that output, yielded the following *marginal* coefficients of production:

$$\text{(2)} \qquad a'_{ij} = \frac{\partial T_{vi}}{\partial \bar{X}_{vj}}, \qquad a'_{jJ} = \frac{\partial T_{vj}}{\partial \bar{X}_{vj}}$$

Then marginal costs will be

$$\text{(3)} \qquad c'_v d\bar{X}_{vj} = \left(\sum_i a'_{ij} P_i + \sum_j a'_{jJ} P_j\right) d\bar{X}_{vj}$$

Where no fixed costs exist, total costs will then be

$$\text{(4)} \qquad C_v = \int_0^{\bar{X}_{vj}} c'_v d\bar{X}_{vj}$$

Since pure competition is characterized by the equality of price and cost of production, "we suppose that this equality holds for the total receipts and expenditures. When prices are fixed and there are no fixed costs, this equality implies also the equality of cost of production and sales price of the marginal production." V. Pareto, (2), p. 611.

This last sentence seems to imply or assume that the equality of total revenue and costs when all costs are variable is equivalent to linear homogeneity of the functions (1) in output. Indeed, at one point (p. 620), he assumes that marginal cost is constant explicitly. The conditions for equilibrium in his model are (1) the equality of total revenue and costs for the firm and (2) that the firm sell all it produces. Therefore, in the presentation of his basic production model in pure competition, Pareto: a. does not rely upon a maximization-of-profit motivation in any clear, explicit fashion; b. does not distinguish clearly between average and marginal costs of production; c. seems to believe that the absence of fixed costs spelled linear homogeneity in the production conditions (pp. 605–16).

Later, in discussing his famous optimality conditions, Pareto derives the condition that price equal marginal cost, but he interprets it not as a maximum-profit condition but indeed as an indication that no profit exists in equilibrium to interfere with a consumer optimum.

Why did Pareto assume marginal costs were constant with scale in all of this discussion? Did he not explicitly reject Walras' constant production coefficients as unrealistic? He did recognize the possibility of changes in the coefficients with the

entrepreneur to maximize profits may well have sprung from Pareto's *Cours* rather than Walras' *Elements*.[12]

In this slighting of the firm and the lack of clarity as to its decision-making in its relation to the adjustments of the industry we find one of the most fundamental differences between Walrasian and Marshallian economics. Triffin's assertion that Walras placed the individual entrepreneur in the foreground, and thereby made his analysis an ideal starting place for monopolistic competition analysis, seems misleading. This is particularly true when Marshall's analysis is compared unfavorably with that of Walras in its preoccupation with the industry, for Marshall's substitutional theory of necessity requires a great deal more analysis of the firm than Walras' theory which subordinated such considerations in his basic model.[13]

We may, therefore, turn immediately to the industry and conditions for its equilibrium in Model III-1. Before doing so we list the aggregate consumer demand and supply functions of the economy, derived by summing over like individual functions which are nonspecific solutions

---

scale of production, both in V. Pareto, (2), pp. 631, 636–8, and in (3), p. 85. Indeed, there is a reference to such potentialities in (1), Vol. II, pp. 82–4. But these were essentially qualifications to his major assumption. The variability of the a-coefficients was a variability with respect to *price changes*, not scale: the former are the changing conditions to which inputs respond within a linear, homogeneous production function.

In his later work, such as (3), which appeared in 1911, he did come to see that price had to equal marginal as well as average cost in the purely competitive equilibrium of the Walrasian type, and indeed stressed that in certain conditions the double equality might not be possible. Although he refers back to his work in (2), he adds apologetically that "there still remain many points to be studied" (p. 99). The possibility that it might be impossible to impose equality of price to both costs was noted by Pareto's disciples and served to add to the existing confusion in the absence of a clear distinction between minimum cost-maximum profit conditions for the zero profits case, which conditions are not identical when linear homogeneous production functions are no longer assumed. For example, Zawadzki simply says that when both costs cannot be equal to price it is "most probable" that the no-profit condition holds, and goes on to include it in his system. See W. Zawadzki, (1), pp. 216–7.

Pietri-Tonelli, a faithful follower of Pareto, followed this lapse of the master from linear homogeneity, and, more clearly than other Paretians, saw that when the a'-coefficients varied with scale a maximum-profit approach rather than a minimum-cost motivation is necessary. Nevertheless, he persisted in describing the firm's behavior exclusively in terms of cost minimization under the regime of pure competition. Yet, in his monopoly analysis, he followed Pareto in requiring that marginal profit be zero, giving further proof of the proposition that even in the late 1920's the role of profit maximization in pure competition was only beginning to be integrated into the Lausanne school's models. For all its defects, Pietri-Tonelli's production model is an attempt to build scale economies into a Paretian model and to obtain a meaningful theory of the firm for pure competition. See A. de Pietri-Tonelli, (1), pp. 254–66, 279. See also the unclear treatment of marginal cost by J. Åkerman as late as 1936 in J. Åkerman, (1), p. 103.

[12] F. Edgeworth, (2), pp. 174–83. He also wrongly interprets Walras to mean that the entrepreneur paid a normal salary to himself, *qua* entrepreneur, then goes on to criticize Barone who did treat entrepreneurial labor as another factor of production.

[13] Cf. R. Triffin, (1), pp. 6–12. See also J. Schumpeter, (5), pp. 974–5, 997.

to Model I-3, modified as indicated in Section 1.a. above:

(III-1-1) 1. $$X_{j \neq 1} = H_{j \neq 1}(P_2, \ldots, P_n, P_{z_1}, \ldots, P_{z_m}; [Q_1], \ldots, [Q_m])$$
$$= H_{j \neq 1}([P]; [Q])$$

where $[Q_i] = [Q_{1i}, Q_{2i}, \ldots, Q_{si}]$ and $[Q] = [[Q_1], [Q_2], \ldots, [Q_m]]$.

2. $$\bar{X}_i = Q_i - H_i([P]; [Q]), \qquad i = 1, \ldots, m$$

where $Q_i = \Sigma_c Q_{ci}$.

3. $$X_1 = \sum_i \bar{X}_i P_i - \sum_{j \neq 1} X_j P_j$$

Industrial demands for primary and intermediate inputs are readily defined as follows:

(III-1-2)

1. $$X_i \equiv \sum_j a_{ij} \bar{X}_j, \qquad i = 1, \ldots, m$$

2. $$X_j^* \equiv \sum_J a_{jJ} \bar{X}_J, \qquad j = 1, \ldots, n$$

Competition among firms will lead to increased production of any good which enjoys a positive profit, zero output of any good with a negative profit. This competition among entrepreneurs leads to price changes in products and in factor services until the zero profit point is reached for every good:

(III-1-3) $$P_J^\circ = \sum_i a_{iJ} P_i^\circ + \sum_j a_{jJ} P_j^\circ, \qquad J = 1, \ldots, n$$

Lastly, we may impose the necessity that every market in the model be cleared:

(III-1-4)

1. $$X_i^\circ = \bar{X}_i^\circ, \qquad i = 1, \ldots, m$$

2. $$X_j^\circ + X_j^{*\circ} = \bar{X}_j^\circ \qquad j = 1, \ldots, n$$

The number of equations in Model III-1 is $3m + 4n$, but the unknowns are only $3m + 4n - 1$ in number: (a) nX_j°, (b) $m\bar{X}_i^\circ$, (c) $nX_j^{*\circ}$, (d) mX_i°, (e) $n - 1P_j^\circ$, since $P_1 \equiv 1$, (f) mP_i°, and (g) $n\bar{X}_j^\circ$. But in the analysis of Model II-2 it was indicated how the use of a *numéraire* enables us to view one good as the obverse of the markets in which every good and service other than the *numéraire* is traded. Explicitly, to show the functional dependence of one equation of the model upon the others:

1. multiply the equations of (III-1-4) by their respective prices and add;

2. multiply the equations of (III-1-3) by their respective supplies, substitute from (III-1-2), and add;

3. subtract the result of (2) from the result of (1). The difference will be (III-1-1-3). Therefore, one equation may be eliminated from (III-1-1-3), (III-1-3), or (III-1-4).

Model III-1 is a step upward in complication from the complex exchange model with more than two commodities.[14] In the latter model we saw that the complexity was becoming great enough to constitute a serious impediment to the derivation of operational theorems. How far can we go in evaluating equilibrium displacements for such systems as Model III-1, which is even more complex? If we are frustrated in our efforts, at least it will be possible to study simplifications which may make it more amenable to manipulation for such purposes.

As in Chapter 1, we may simplify Model III-1 for purposes of equilibrium displacement by letting one symbol stand for equilibrium aggregate demand and supply. Let $x_i \equiv X_i^\circ = \bar{X}_i^\circ$ and $x_j \equiv X_j^\circ + X_j^{*\circ} = \bar{X}_j^\circ$. Then, the equations of Model III-1 may be written as follows:

$$(7)\qquad \begin{aligned}
&1. \quad X_{j\neq 1}^\circ - H_j([P^\circ];[Q]) = 0\\
&2. \quad X_1^\circ - \sum_i x_i P_i^\circ + \sum_{j\neq 1} X_j^\circ P_j^\circ = 0\\
&3. \quad X_j^{*\circ} - \sum_J a_{jJ} x_J = 0\\
&4. \quad x_j - X_j^\circ - X_j^{*\circ} = 0\\
&5. \quad x_i + H_i([P^\circ];[Q]) - Q_i = 0\\
&6. \quad x_i - \sum_j a_{ij} x_j = 0\\
&7. \quad P_{j\neq 1}^\circ - \sum_i a_{ij} P_i^\circ - \sum_j a_{jJ} P_j^\circ = 0
\end{aligned}$$

To fix our ideas let $n = 2$, $i = 1$. The data of this model in which we shall profess an interest are the Q_i and the a-coefficients. Note that we are interested in the total amounts of resources, Q_i, abstracting from the implicit distribution of these resources among individuals in $[Q]$. There-

[14] Actually there exists between these two models an intermediate step which we have omitted. It is Irving Fisher's "disutility production" model, in which the sole cost of producing each Y_j is the (cardinally measured, independent) disutilities undergone by the o individuals in fabricating them from free resources. The conditions for the solution of the model as Fisher gave them are:

1. aggregate output of each Y_j equals aggregate demand for it;
2. for the individual, the value of his output equals the value of his consumption;
3. for the individual, the marginal utilities of his consumption of Y_j divided by P_j, and the marginal disutilities of Y_j divided by $-P_j$, must be equal.

Where $P_1 \equiv 1$, one equation is functionally dependent. A fourth system defines marginal utilities and disutilities. See I. Fisher, (1), pp. 54–9.

fore, we substitute for $[Q]$ in the equations of (7) the vector $[Q^*] = [Q_1, Q_2, \ldots, Q_m]$, and assume that the functional changes are duly recorded in the H_j and H_i.

We suppose Q_1 to change slightly. Then the system of equations determining the changes in equilibrium quantities and prices is given below. Let $[D]$ be defined as

$$(8)\quad [D] = \begin{bmatrix} 0 & 1 & 0 & 0 & 0 & 0 & 0 & -H_2^2 & -H_2^z \\ 1 & P_2^\circ & 0 & 0 & 0 & 0 & -P_z & X_2^\circ & -x_z \\ 0 & 0 & -a_{11} & -a_{12} & 1 & 0 & 0 & 0 & 0 \\ 0 & 0 & -a_{21} & -a_{22} & 0 & 1 & 0 & 0 & 0 \\ -1 & 0 & 1 & 0 & -1 & 0 & 0 & 0 & 0 \\ 0 & -1 & 0 & 1 & 0 & -1 & 0 & 0 & 0 \\ 0 & 0 & 0 & 0 & 0 & 0 & 1 & H_z^2 & H_z^z \\ 0 & 0 & -a_{z1} & -a_{z2} & 0 & 0 & 1 & 0 & 0 \\ 0 & 0 & 0 & 0 & 0 & 0 & 0 & 1 - a_{22} & -a_{z2} \end{bmatrix}$$

and $[dV]$ and $[dQ]$ be defined as

$$(9)\quad \begin{aligned} &1. \quad [dV] = \left[\frac{\partial X_1^\circ}{\partial Q_1}, \frac{\partial X_2^\circ}{\partial Q_1}, \frac{\partial x_1}{\partial Q_1}, \frac{\partial x_2}{\partial Q_1}, \frac{\partial X_1^{*\circ}}{\partial Q_1}, \frac{\partial X_2^{*\circ}}{\partial Q_1}, \frac{\partial x_z}{\partial Q_1}, \frac{\partial P_2^\circ}{\partial Q_1}, \frac{\partial P_z^\circ}{\partial Q_1}\right] \\ &2. \quad [dQ] = [H_2^q, 0, 0, 0, 0, 0, 1 - H_z^q, 0, 0] \end{aligned}$$

The equations may then be written

$$(10)\qquad [D][dV] = [dQ]$$

It is quickly seen that even for as few goods and services as we have included in this system $[D]$ has become quite large. Nevertheless, it is a simple matrix in the sense that it is replete with zero and unity values, and with a-coefficients which are conceptually ideal for statistical derivation. The troublesome magnitudes are the slopes of the demand functions in the price and quantity directions. Indeed, one is struck by the ease with which (8) could be filled in with realistic data which might be relatively unchanged no matter what the beginning equilibrium point were. In Model III-1, the constancy of the production coefficients means that once a set of a-coefficients was obtained statistically, that set would hold no matter what the initial or terminal equilibrium points were. Even finite changes in outputs might be accommodated as far as these a-coefficients were concerned. Unfortunately, this is not true of the demand function slopes: they would have to be computed for every initial equilibrium and they would be strictly relevant only for slight changes. These factors and the difficulty of acquiring information on aggregate demand functions raise the question of whether it would not be possible to eliminate them from Model III-1, thus simplifying $[D]$, making it capable of rendering not only qualitative responses but quantitative ones as well.

In Chapter 6 we shall begin at this point with system (10) and by following this line of simplification derive the Leontief open static input-output system.

Until that time, however, we shall drop the consideration of Model III-1 as a source of operational theorems. We turn now to a new, non-Walrasian view of the entrepreneur and of the firm which allows us to resurrect them from the limbo to which Model III-1 relegates them.

2.a.1. The Firm Under Capacity Limitations: Linear Programming

In the Walrasian view, which we have adopted, the firm owns no scarce factors and therefore all of its costs are variable, rising proportionately with output in Model III-1 with its single, divisible activity for every Y_j. The zero-profit constraint is not, in the Walrasian model, as in the Marshallian, a long-run resultant: it occurs in the "weekly" short-run by virtue of the perfect mobility of all factors among all uses even in the short period. If, with Marshall, we recognize that the firm may, in the short period, control wholly immobile resources, it is possible to give the firm an isolable existence from the industry, even within the production conditions of Model III-1.

Having recognized the existence of these "capacities" in the firm's complex of inputs, traditional economic theory relegated them to the background to concentrate upon the firm's choice of variable factors and output mix. The capacity restrictions were relied upon primarily to account for the U-shaped cost curves so desirable under conditions of continuous, differentiable production functions. The so-called "linear programming" approach to the theory of the firm, however, changes this view of the firm's problems. It brings these capacity restrictions to the foreground of the analysis and deals only implicitly with the amounts of the variable factors employed. More important, however, than its recognition of a limit to the firm's output capabilities and this change in outlook on its problems, is the ability that linear programming affords to solve a whole new range of problems in economic theory which were previously not capable of solution by systematic algorithms.

The set of problems which can now be attacked by the methods to be described contains two types of situation which are in fact capable of being made one. The first of these may be described as an underdetermined system of linear equations. Suppose a set of n linear equalities, functionally independent, constrains m variables, $m > n$. In the terminology of Chapter 2, such a system is underdetermined and cannot in general yield a unique solution in which all of the variables have nonzero values. However, every set of n variables of the m will yield a solution in which, of course, only those n variables will be nonzero. Thus there will exist $\frac{m!}{n!(m-n)!}$ different solutions in which sets of n variables are nonzero.

Now, if there exists a criterion for choice among these solutions which is linear in the variables, then the problem is to choose the "best" solution from among the total number (or from among this total number reduced by those which fail to meet certain secondary criteria).

Conceptually, this is a straightforward problem: one need merely obtain the total set of solutions by straightforward algebraic algorithms, evaluate these solutions in terms of the secondary and primary criteria,[15] and choose that which is best according to their standards. The problem is wholly a computational one: this direct approach to the ultimate solution speedily leads the analyst into astronomical expenditures of time, even with modern computers. The body of linear programming techniques, therefore, is a set of methods for obtaining a single acceptable n-variable solution and moving from it in an efficient manner toward the optimal solution, if it exists.

A second type of problem which is amenable to the methods of linear programming is one in which the constraints are stated in the form of linear *inequalities*, while the criterion or "objective" function is again linear in the variables. As will be shown below, these inequalities may be converted into equalities through the use of "slack variables," and the problem thereby converted into the first type of problem.

Let us now turn again to the firm, removing the constraint that it produce only one output and recognizing the existing limits set upon its production by the capacity factors C_k, $k = 1, \ldots, p$. These might be, for example, limits upon the amount of output set by the number of lathes or drill presses held by the firm during the week, or the number of units of product which the shipping department is prepared to handle each week, and so forth. We define the coefficients, a_{kj}, as the requirement of capacity C_k per unit level of operation of the jth activity. If we continue the assumptions of Model III-1 to the effect that each activity yields one unit of a single output, and each output can be obtained from only one activity, we may identify activities by the outputs resulting from them. Then, a typical activity, the jth, may be defined at the unit level as a vector of inputs yielding a unit of Y_j:

$$(11) \quad [1, -a_{z_1j}, \ldots, -a_{z_mj}, -a_{1j}, \ldots, -a_{nj}; -a_{c_1j}, \ldots, -a_{c_pj}]$$

where the unity element denotes a unit of ouput of Y_j.

But the firm can obtain all of the variable factors that it desires at

[15] These criteria may be so restrictive as to specify which m–n variables may be removed, in which case the problem is made simple. They may insist upon all m variables being nonzero in the solution, in which case an infinite number of solutions exist to the problem. Thus, linear programming techniques deal with intermediate cases, where at most n variables need to be nonzero in the solution and more than one set of n variables is potentially capable of yielding the solution. It should be noted that linear programming techniques usually apply to problems where the solution values are constrained to be nonnegative.

fixed prices; moreover, it may sell all of the outputs it produces at fixed prices. Therefore, it is possible to define for the unit level of each activity a net revenue, r_j,

$$(12) \quad r_j = [1, -a_{z_1j}, \ldots, -a_{z_mj}, -a_{1j}, \ldots, -a_{nj}] \cdot [P_j, P_{z_1}, \ldots, P_{z_m}, P_1, \ldots, P_n]$$

In so doing, we may abstract from the variable inputs and view the firm's problem as that of deciding how its limited capacity levels, given in the vector $[K] = [K_1, \ldots, K_p]$, can be most profitably employed in support of the alternative activities. In formal terms, the firm seeks to maximize

$$(13) \qquad \pi_v = \sum_j r_j \bar{X}_{vj}$$

subject to the conditions that operation of the activities chosen be at nonnegative levels,

$$(14) \qquad \bar{X}^{\circ}_{vj} \geqq 0 \qquad j = 1, \ldots, n$$

which will not violate the capacity constraints:

$$(15) \qquad \sum_j a_{c_kj} \bar{X}^{\circ}_{vj} \leqq K_k, \qquad k = 1, \ldots, p$$

We shall term (13) the objective function, since it defines the objective of the firm and the criterion by which to select the optimal solution. We shall refer to the conditions in (14) as secondary constraints on the problem, and to the conditions in (15) as the primary constraints. The $\bar{X}_{vj}$ we shall term "activity levels" although they correspond under the conditions of this model to output levels. We seek an equilibrium vector $[\bar{X}^{\circ}_v] = [\bar{X}^{\circ}_{v1}, \ldots, \bar{X}^{\circ}_{vn}]$ which defines that activity- and product-mix which is consistent with (14) and (15) and maximizes (13).

The distinctive feature of (15), of course, is the fact that the constraints are inequalities, not equalities. It is, therefore, explicitly recognized that the optimal solution may not use all of the firm's capacities at the maximum level. Indeed, with linear activities, even if infinitely divisible, it may not be possible to find any vector of activity levels which exhausts every capacity which the firm has at its disposal. Therefore, in the optimal solution, when $n > p$, the firm *may* find it to its advantage to use all of its capacities to full employment, but when $n \leqq p$ it will generally pay the firm not to do so.

We may convert the inequalities of (15) to equalities by creating a set of "disposal activities," whose unit level of operation absorbs one unit of the relevant capacity and produces no output. Thus, we create p more activities, with levels of operation d_{vc_1} through d_{vc_p} (which we shall abbreviate to $d_1, \ldots, d_p$), whose unit vector is $[0, \ldots 0, 0, \ldots 0, -1, \ldots 0]$ where the unity element occurs as the $m + 2n + k + 1$th element for activity $n + k$. In so obtaining a set of equalities, it is necessary to recognize a new set of activity levels described immediately above whose symbols may be simplified as indicated below:

$$\sum_j a_{c_kj}\bar{X}_{vj} + d_k = K_k, \qquad k = 1, \ldots, p \tag{16}$$

The net revenues, r_k, of these new activities, are zero if the unit of capacity can be disposed of costlessly, negative to the extent it absorbs resources for such disposal. In all of the cases with which we shall deal it will be assumed that free disposal is possible.

2.a.1.a. An Interpretation in Vector Spaces

Let us now fix our ideas with an actual example. Suppose a firm had a technological opportunity with three alternative productive activities, yielding Y_1, Y_2, and Y_3 respectively as unique outputs. The firm is also assumed to have two limited capacities, C_1 and C_2, where $K_1 = 100$, $K_2 = 50$. The net returns on the productive activities are $r_1 = 2$, $r_2 = 3$, and $r_3 = 6$. The vectors of capacity requirements for unit operation of the productive activities are [2, 3], [4, 3], and [6, 5] respectively. The problem of the firm is, then, to maximize

$$\pi_v = 2\bar{X}_{v1} + 3\bar{X}_{v2} + 6\bar{X}_{v3} \tag{17}$$

subject to

$$\begin{bmatrix} 2 & 4 & 6 & 1 & 0 \\ 3 & 3 & 5 & 0 & 1 \end{bmatrix} \begin{bmatrix} \bar{X}_{v1} \\ \bar{X}_{v2} \\ \bar{X}_{v3} \\ d_1 \\ d_2 \end{bmatrix} = \begin{bmatrix} 100 \\ 50 \end{bmatrix} \tag{18}$$

and

$$\bar{X}^{\circ}_{vj} \geqq 0, \qquad d^{\circ}_k \geqq 0, \qquad j = 1, 2, 3,\ k = 1, 2 \tag{19}$$

2.a.1.a.1. STRAIGHTFORWARD SOLUTION. There are several ways to describe the economic meaning of this system, but we shall choose to interpret it in terms of vector spaces. A vector in n-dimensional space, for our purposes, can be viewed as a directed line segment from the origin of that space to the terminal point $(x, y, z, \ldots)$ as given by the n coordinates of the vector. For example, in our problem, capacity space[16] is a two-

[16] Capacity space is that vector space each of whose axes charts quantities of one of the scarce factors or capacities of the problem. A point or vector in that space, therefore, is a set of factor magnitudes, one for each capacity involved in the problem.

dimensional Euclidean space, with units of C_1 on the x-axis and units of C_2 on the y-axis, and origin at (0, 0); activity space is a five-dimensional space with units of activity 1 graphed on the first axis, activity 2 on the second, activity 3 on the third, the first disposal activity on the fourth, and the second disposal activity on the last; while profits space is a one-dimensional space, with profits on the axis.

In capacity space we are given one vector—the vector of capacities, (100, 50). This is graphed in Fig. 3-1 as $[K]$. Also, we may graph the "unit vectors" of capacity space; i.e., those vectors which include successively one unit of one capacity and zero of all others. In our case the unit vectors of capacity space, u_1 and u_2, are, respectively, (1, 0) and (0, 1) and are graphed in Fig. 3-1.

In activity space, we may define the five unit vectors of the space, v_1 through v_5, which are (1, 0, 0, 0, 0), (0, 1, 0, 0, 0), (0, 0, 1, 0, 0), (0, 0, 0, 1, 0), and (0, 0, 0, 0, 1). These are, of course, the vectors which denote one unit of each activity successively and zero of all others. Now, symbolize (18) by

$$[D][\bar{X}, d] = [K] \tag{20}$$

Then, given any real vector $[\bar{X}, d]$, it will be a point in activity space.

Any vector in a space of n dimensions may be derived as a weighted sum of *any n* independent vectors in that space. For example, the $[\bar{X}, d]$ may be viewed as the sum of the products $\bar{X}_{v1}v_1$, $\bar{X}_{v2}v_2$, $\bar{X}_{v3}v_3$, d_1v_4, and d_2v_5. The n vectors in terms of which the desired vector is expressed is called a *basis* of the space. In the case above, the five unit vectors are the basis of activity space, but only one possible basis.

Now, any vector $[\bar{X}, d]$ is "mapped" or "carried" onto capacity space from activity space by $[D]$. That is, $[D]$ transforms $[\bar{X}, d]$ in a linear fashion from a set of activity levels (a point in activity space) into the capacity requirements of that set (a point in capacity space). For example, choose the five $[\bar{X}, d]$ represented by v_1 through v_5, and map them onto capacity space with $[D]$. These yield the five two-dimensional vectors V_1 through V_5 in capacity space graphed in Fig. 3-1. Note that V_4 and u_1 coincide and V_5 and u_2 are the same: this of course is true by definition, since a unit level of the disposal activities is defined to require a unit of one capacity, or, in present terminology, to map onto capacity space as a unit vector of that space.

Consider the system (20): it states that a solution is a vector $[\bar{X}, d]$ which is mapped by $[D]$ into the given capacity vector $[K]$. That is, we seek a set of weights given by the elements of $[\bar{X}, d]$ which, when applied to the vectors V_1 through V_5 in capacity space, represented by the columns of $[D]$, will sum to the capacity vector [100, 50]. Our search, therefore, may be confined to a search for these weights.

Capacity space is two-dimensional, and therefore, a basis of only two independent vectors will provide all the vectors we need to get to any point in the space by applying the appropriate set of weights. Therefore, from the five vectors V_1 through V_5 which we have in this space, we have 10 different bases composed of pairs of the vectors. It is, of course, possible to choose 3, or 4, or all 5 of the vectors and to find weights which when applied to them will sum to $[K]$: the point to be made is that we

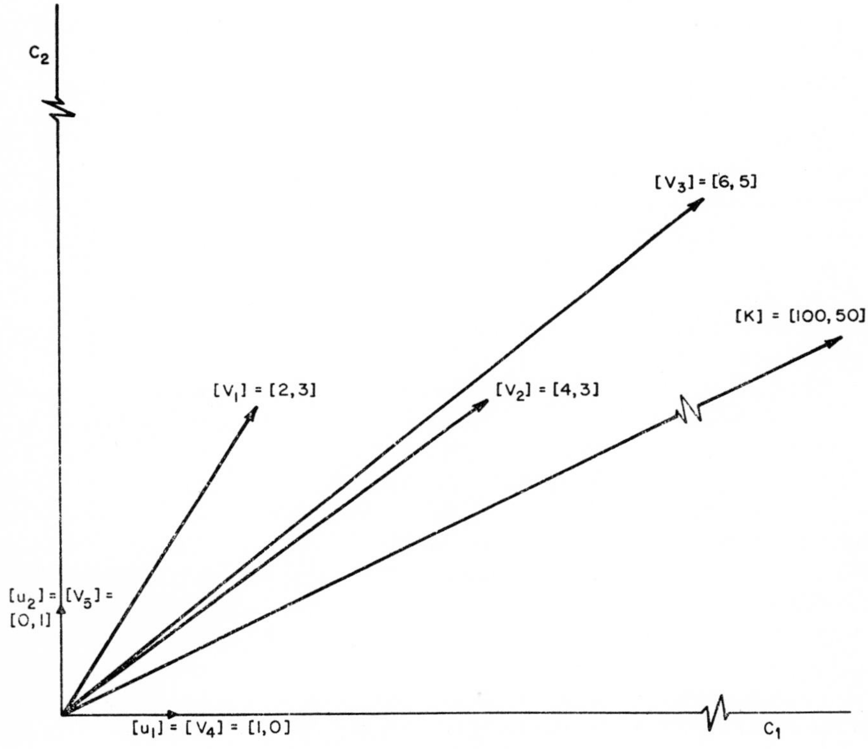

Figure 3-1. Capacity Space.

need only two vectors. Therefore, we propose to consider in our search for an optimal solution only *basic* solutions, i.e., solutions which are the weights applied to two of the five vectors mapped onto capacity space from activity space. If, from all these solutions (ten in our case) we can find the optimal one, we shall have only the optimal *basic* solution. It might be thought that there may exist a set of weights for three vectors which would yield higher profits. But we shall prove that if we have found an optimal basic feasible solution, no other solution with a larger number of vectors can be better than this optimal basic solution. Anticipating this theorem, therefore, we shall confine our attention to basic solutions.

The straightforward method of solving this system is clear: to form systems of two linear equations each by placing zeros in [D] for all but two columns, solving, repeating for every possible pair of columns, and then choosing that solution which yields the highest π_v. Moreover, the graphing of the vectors in Fig. 3-1 can help us in rejecting certain of these possible bases: if [K] falls outside the angle formed by the two vectors of a basis, one of the vectors will have to be weighted negatively in the solution. That is, with such a basis it will be necessary for the system to "generate" more of one capacity by operating one activity at a negative level. For example, if the first disposal activity absorbs a unit of C_1, the mathematics imply that by producing at $d_1 = -1$ it is possible to generate a unit of C_1. The economic restrictions of (19) forbid this, of course, and therefore we reject any solution which does not yield nonnegative values for the elements of [$\bar{X}$, d]. Such solutions are called *feasible* solutions; i.e., that subset of the solutions of (18) which meet the restrictions of (19). Basic feasible solutions are that subset of the feasible subset of solutions which are the weighted sums of only that number of vectors which forms a basis for the system—in our case, two.

The use of this test leads us to reject those bases formed by V_1 and V_2, V_1 and V_3, V_1 and V_5, V_2 and V_3, and V_3 and V_5, from the fact that the angles formed by them do not include [K]. Moreover, we may reject the basis formed by the image of the disposal processes in capacity space, or V_4 and V_5, since no profits would be obtained through such a usage of capacities, and it is easy to see that this cannot be optimal. We have, then, three bases remaining which will yield basic feasible solutions not *prima facie* infeasible or suboptimal. These are the bases formed by V_1 and V_4, V_2 and V_4, and V_3 and V_4. Obviously, then, it will pay the firm to use only one productive activity up to the point where C_2 is used up; whichever of the three productive activities is used in the optimal solution, C_1 will be in excess supply. The solutions for these bases are, respectively: [16.7, 0, 0, 66.7, 0], [0, 16.7, 0, 33.3, 0], and [0, 0, 10, 40, 0]. These yield three points in profits space—33.4, 50.1, and 60 respectively. Therefore, the optimal activity mix for the firm is to employ the third activity at the level $\bar{X}^\circ_{v3} = 10$ and the first disposal process at $d^\circ_1 = 40$.

This is the solution to the set of equations

$$(21) \qquad \begin{bmatrix} 6 & 1 \\ 5 & 0 \end{bmatrix} \begin{bmatrix} \bar{X}_{v3} \\ d_1 \end{bmatrix} = \begin{bmatrix} 100 \\ 50 \end{bmatrix}$$

Let us note once more the vector space interpretation of the unknowns: they are the weights which, when applied to the vectors [6, 5] and [1, 0]—

the images of the third and fourth activities operated at unit level in capacity space—and added yield the capacity-availability vector, (100, 50). Our straightforward method of solution has been to obtain this last vector from a set of weights obtained for each basis which would yield a feasible result, and to compare the images of them in profits space. These sets of weights are themselves vectors in activity space, and can be viewed as the weighted sums of the unit vectors in that space, v_1 through v_5.

Let us employ a method of writing the vectors of givens in a "tableau" in order to indicate the vectors they depict (column headings) and the vectors which form the basis for their expression (row headings). Note that we have included u_1 and u_2 to the right of the double-bars, for purposes to be shown directly. Then the tableau of (21) is

(22)

	v_3	v_4	K	u_1	u_2
u_1	6	1	100	1	0
u_2	5	0	50	0	1

Thus, $v_3 = [0, 0, 1, 0, 0]$ in activity space maps into commodity space as 6, 5, which are viewed as the weights applied to $u_1 = [1, 0]$ and $u_2 = [0, 1]$ to obtain [6, 5]; and so forth.

We have seen that for the solution to (21), which we already know to be optimal, we seek to put [K] on a basis which is formed from v_3 and v_4; therefore, we desire to shift the basis of tableau (22) from u_1 and u_2 to v_3 and v_4. We desire, as a final result, a tableau whose headings will be

(23)

	v_3	v_4	K	u_1	u_2
v_3					
v_4					

We may obtain this shift by obtaining a vector of [1, 0] in the first column and [0, 1] in the second in a series of row operations. To do this, it will be convenient to multiply the first row in (22) by 1 and add it to the second row:

(24)

	v_3	v_4	K	u_1	u_2
u_1	6	1	100	1	0
u_2	11	1	150	1	1

It will be recalled that such a procedure does not alter the determinants which could be formed from these vectors; this condition is crucial in this procedure. Next, subtract the second row of (24) from the first row, and replace the first row with the results:

(25)

	v_3	v_4	K	u_1	u_2
u_1	-5	0	-50	0	-1
u_2	11	1	150	1	1

Divide the first row of (25) by (-5) and we shall have converted the first row to a set of weights on a v_3 component of a v_3 and u_2 basis:

(26)

	v_3	v_4	K	u_1	u_2
v_3	1	0	10	0	.2
u_2	11	1	150	1	1

Next, multiply the first row by 11, subtract it from the second, and replace the second row with the result:

(27)

	v_3	v_4	K	u_1	u_2
v_3	1	0	10	0	.2
v_4	0	1	40	1	−1.2

We have now succeeded in putting all the vectors on the basis of vectors which we know to constitute the optimal basis. The vector $[K]$, now expressed in that basis, contains the components which are the optimal activity levels of activities 3 and 4. But what are the u_1 and u_2 columns in (27)? For the activities with positive levels in the optimal solution, they are the unit vectors in capacity space expressed in terms of (on the basis of) the unit vectors in activity space. A unit of capacity C_1 is the equivalent of $0[1, 0, 0, 0, 0] + 0[0, 1, 0, 0, 0] + 0[0, 0, 1, 0, 0] + 1[0, 0, 0, 1, 0] + 0[0, 0, 0, 0, 1]$. We may interpret these in marginal terms: a reduction in C_1's availability by one unit will result in a reduction of zero in $\bar{X}^\circ_{v3}$ and one of d°_1, and a reduction in C_2 availability by one unit would result in a reduction of .2 in $\bar{X}^\circ_{v3}$ and an *increase* of d°_1 by 1.2 units. These are the "marginal activity products" of the capacities and are the analogues of the marginal physical products of variable factors. If, for each capacity, we multiply the activity components of these marginal products by the "values" of those activities, r_j, and sum, we may obtain the marginal value productivity of each capacity. In our case, C_1 has a marginal value productivity of $6(0) + 0(1) = 0$ units of *numéraire*, while C_2 has the value $6(.2) + 0(-1.2) = 1.2$ units of *numéraire*. Thus, the firm, if it values its scarce factors at their marginal values, should view the "price" to the firm of the use of a unit of C_1 as zero, since it is in excess supply at the optimal usage, and should value C_2 at 1.2. The value of its scarce factors, then—the value of the firm this week—is $100(0) + 50(1.2) = 60$. This also represents the profits of the firm, π_v, and, thus, by valuing the scarce factors at their marginal value products we have exhausted the net returns of the firm.

Let us go a bit further with the u_1 and u_2 columns. We began the analysis with the system in (21), which we may abbreviate as

(28) $$[F][\bar{X}^\circ, d^\circ] = [K]$$

It has been said above that $[F]$ maps the vector $[\bar{X}^\circ, d^\circ]$ from activity space into $[K]$ in capacity space. We have seen, however, that what we really want is a transformation which takes $[K]$ from capacity space into $[\bar{X}°, d°]$ in the activity subspace formed from the unit vectors of the activities which form the optimal basis. We know that if $[F]$ is nonsingular, as we have assured ourselves it must be, we may rewrite (28) as

$$[\bar{X}°, d°] = [F]^{-1}[K] \tag{29}$$

The inverse of $[F]$ does in fact transform $[K]$ linearly into a point in the desired subspace. That is, if we map u_1 into activity space, u_2 into that space, and view $[K]$ as weights to be applied to them, the result will be that combination of activities in optimal subspace which is the image of $[K]$. But we have these mappings of u_1 and u_2 in (27), and thus it is seen that these columns are in fact the inverse of $[F]$. That is,

$$[F]^{-1} = \begin{bmatrix} 6 & 1 \\ 5 & 0 \end{bmatrix}^{-1} = \begin{bmatrix} 0 & .2 \\ 1 & -1.2 \end{bmatrix} \tag{30}$$

Thus, in the solution we have, with the inclusion of the u_1 and u_2 columns, merely inverted the $[F]$-matrix, and the economic interpretation of the inversion follows.

2.a.1.a.2. THE SIMPLEX METHOD. So much for the method of solution by shifting bases when we already know which vectors will exist in the optimal basis. The straightforward method for determining this is obviously time-consuming for problems with any number of constraints and activities. How can the problem be solved without having to obtain every basic solution that exists? There is no direct method of so doing; one of several iterative, trial-and-error algorithms must be employed. We shall employ the "pivot" method of shifting bases in a "simplex" algorithm to obtain the solution. Let us therefore go back to the statement of the problem in (17), (18), and (19), and forget that we have already solved this simple system.

It is necessary to begin with a basic feasible solution. It is possible in the present case to obtain a basis which will yield a feasible solution by using only disposal activites. This implies that the firm allows all of its capacities to run to waste, but it does yield a solution vector of activity levels which is nonnegative. Therefore, we shall begin with a tableau containing activities 4 and 5 as the "included" activities (included in the basis) and 1, 2, and 3 as the "excluded" activities. We shall separate these two groups with $[K]$, and shall also include u_1 and u_2 at the extreme right:

(31)

	v_4	v_5	K	v_1	v_2	v_3	u_1	u_2
u_1	1	0	100	2	4	6	1	0
u_2	0	1	50	3	3	5	0	1

Since v_4 maps into $V_4 = u_1$ and v_5 maps into $V_5 = u_2$, (31) has all vectors on a v_4 and v_5 basis immediately, and thus the K column states the level of activities 4 and 5 which would be the mapping of [K] into the subspace formed by the disposal activities.

The question is "Can the firm do any better than this?". Operating at $d_1 = 100$ and $d_2 = 50$ yields, from (17), profits of zero. Now, on the basis of v_4 and v_5, v_1 yields the weights which, when applied to the basis, are the equivalent combination of activities 4 and 5 in resource absorption. That is, in (31), operating the first activity at a unit level will absorb the same quantity of capacities as operating the first disposal process at a level of 2 and the second disposal process at a level of 3. Similarly, the v_2 and v_3 columns in (31) can be interpreted in like manner.

Starting from the full employment of C_1 and C_2 by the included activities, how much could be gained by operating activity 1 at a unit level? From (17) it will be seen that $r_1 = 2$, which is the contribution to profits of a unit level of operation of activity 1. But, to obtain the C_1 and C_2 necessary to operate activity 1 at unit level, it is necessary to reduce activity 4 by 2 units and activity 5 by 3 units. The "cost" of this substitution, c_1, is the value of the processes in the included sector which have to be sacrificed, or $c_1 = r_4(2) + r_5(3) = 0(2) + 0(3) = 0$. The net profit to be obtained from this substitution will be $r_1 - c_1$, or $2 - 0 = 2$. Therefore, it will pay the firm to substitute a unit level of activity 1 for the equivalent combination of included activities. But this is a linear system: if it pays to substitute a unit level of activity 1, it will pay to substitute as many units of operation as the capacity restrictions will allow. Similarly, if we test unit levels of activites 2 and 3 against their equivalent combinations, we obtain $r_2 - c_2 = 3$ and $r_3 - c_3 = 6$. Thus, we learn that it will pay the firm to substitute any one of the excluded processes for either of the included processes.

By convention, let us substitute the most profitable of the excluded activities for one of the included processes, and shift the basis to the unit vectors of this new pair. If this is done, experience suggests that about $2m$ iterations will be required, m being the dimension of the capacity space, though no rigorous bound can be set. But which of the activities in the present basis should be dropped? This is easily decided. The limitation to the number of units of the new activity will be set by the first of the two capacity limits it hits. For activity 3, the most profitable of the excluded processes, the availability of C_1 sets a limit of $\frac{100}{6}$ as a maximum activity level, while C_2 sets the limit $\frac{50}{5}$.[17] Therefore, in order to prevent negative

[17] Only those ratios which are positive and finite should be considered in this decision. If all ratios are negative or infinite, the problem has no finite solution, for this is an indication that there exists an activity which can be substituted for the included activities and at the same time free all capacities for use, indefinitely. If the minimum ratio is zero, the substitution of the respective activity may not result in a more profitable basis of activities, and, theoretically, a "cycling" process could start which would result in the same sequence of bases recurring indefinitely. In practice, however, it has been found that if the substitution is made, the process, after one or several failures to better the solutions will start once more to move toward the optimum.

levels of operation of the activity, we substitute activity 3 for that included activity whose element in the vector of the equivalent combination of activity 3 when divided into the relevant K_k is a minimum. (If the minimum is not unique, some of the solution values in the new solution will be zero, and "degeneracy" results. We shall not discuss these complications.) In the present example we substitute activity 3 for activity 5, and rearrange the tableau to obtain:

(32)

	v_3	v_4	K	v_1	v_2	v_5	u_1	u_2
u_1	6	1	100	2	4	0	1	0
u_2	5	0	50	3	3	1	0	1

We have, to the left of the v_1 column, the tableau we previously dealt with in (22). By a similar series of operations, we obtain finally

(33)

	v_3	v_4	K	v_1	v_2	v_5	u_1	u_2
v_3	1	0	10	.6	.6	.2	0	.2
v_4	0	1	40	−1.6	.4	−1.2	1	−1.2

Actually, we know from our previous analysis that the activities included in this basis are indeed those with nonzero levels in the optimal solution. But we can demonstrate this by obtaining $r_j - c_j$ for $j = 1, 2, 5$. For the first activity, this value is $2 - .6(6) + 1.6(0) = -1.6$. Thus, a substitution of one unit of activity 1 for the equivalent combination of included vectors would result in a loss of profits. For activity 2, $3 - .6(6) - .4(0) = -.6$, and again a loss would result from such a substitution. Lastly, for activity 5, profits are $0 - .2(6) + 1.2(0) = -1.2$. If any of these excluded activities had yielded a value of zero for $r_j - c_j$, that activity could be included in the optimal solution without loss of profits. We have attained an optimal basic solution, in that no activity in the excluded sector could be substituted for the included activities and profits increased. Thus, by the method of shifting bases and use of the simplex criterion to evaluate the impact upon profits of a substitution of an excluded activity for an included one we have arrived at the optimal result obtained previously by the straightforward method.

2.a.1.a.3. PROPERTIES OF THE OPTIMAL BASIC SOLUTION. We have merely shown thus far that it will be possible by the use of these methods to obtain an optimal *basic* solution, if such a solution exists. However, we have not shown that there does not exist a nonbasic feasible solution which is more profitable than the basic solution. It is easy to demonstrate, however, that this cannot be true. We have seen from the straightforward solution that [0, 16.7, 0, 33.3, 0] and [0, 0, 10, 40, 0] are basic feasible solutions. Now, if these two solutions are multiplied by positive weights which sum to unity and added, the result will also be a solution. For example, let $w_1 = .7$ and $w_2 = .3$. Then,

$$(34) \quad .7[0, 16.7, 0, 33.3, 0] + .3[0, 0, 10, 40, 0] = [0, 11.7, 3, 35.31, 0]$$

will exhaust the capacities available, as may be seen by multiplying these activity levels by the respective unit requirements of capacities. Conversely, any nonbasic feasible solution may be broken down into a weighted sum of basic feasible solutions.

It follows from the above that no nonbasic solution can ever be more profitable than the optimal basic feasible solution, for a weighted average of profits associated with each solution can, at most, be as large as the largest element in its construction. Therefore, we need concern ourselves only with basic solutions. This allows us to formulate a most important basic theorem of *linear* programming: given m linear equality primary constraints upon $n + m$ production and disposal activity levels, the basic optimal solution will contain, at most, m nonzero activity levels, and it will yield a value for the objective function at least as high as any nonbasic solution. Therefore, we may begin the attack upon the firm's maximization problem with knowledge beforehand that in the final solution it will use at most the number of activities whose unit images are required to form a basis in capacity space.

2.a.1.a.4. THE DUAL PROBLEM. It has already been shown that the solution to the firm's maximization program contains within it an implicit pricing of the capacities of the firm, and, therewith, an imputation of the net profits of the firm to these capacities. This being the case, we may solve the firm's problem by setting up the linear programming framework to yield these imputed "shadow prices" rather than optimal activity levels. This is the "dual" problem of the "primal" problem we have just solved, and, in addition to its basic economic interest, it is often used to solve the linear programming problem because it saves time in computation.

In the dual problem we seek to *minimize* Z, the value of the capacities available to the firm priced at shadow prices:

$$(35) \qquad Z = K_1 P_{c_1} + K_2 P_{c_2}$$

where P_{c_k} are the prices of the capacities. We shall drop the c subscripts hereafter to simplify notation. We may view this minimization as a mock competitive result; i.e., if the capacities were mobile, the force of pure competition would drive their prices down to minimum values. In our problem, the firm seeks to attain the same result; or, as we shall see, in seeking the maximum return from the use of his capacities, the entrepreneur is *implicitly* seeking shadow prices for his capacities which minimize their value subject to other considerations.

This minimum is subject to the primary constraint that the values of the capacities used in each productive activity be at least as great as the r_j return from the use of each at unit level:

$$
(36) \qquad \begin{aligned} &1. \quad 2P_1^\circ + 3P_2^\circ \geqq 2 \\ &2. \quad 4P_1^\circ + 3P_2^\circ \geqq 3 \\ &3. \quad 6P_1^\circ + 5P_2^\circ \geqq 6 \end{aligned}
$$

Again, this is a mock competitive result, for in pure competition no process could remain less costly than the value of the process, for this would imply a net return over costs. Either a process must cost more than its value, in which case it would not be used, or it must equal its value and be used. Lastly, the secondary constraints hold:

$$
(37) \qquad P_k \geqq 0
$$

It is possible to convert (36) into a set of equalities by adding in "net potential loss" variables, t_j, which represent the amounts by which the cost of a process exceeds its value:

$$
(38) \qquad \begin{aligned} &1. \quad 2P_1^\circ + 3P_2^\circ - t_1^\circ = 2 \\ &2. \quad 4P_1^\circ + 3P_2^\circ - t_2^\circ = 3 \\ &3. \quad 6P_1^\circ + 5P_2^\circ - t_3^\circ = 6 \end{aligned}
$$

where

$$
(39) \qquad t_j^\circ \geqq 0
$$

Then

$$
(40) \qquad \begin{bmatrix} 2 & 3 & -1 & 0 & 0 \\ 4 & 3 & 0 & -1 & 0 \\ 6 & 5 & 0 & 0 & -1 \end{bmatrix} \begin{bmatrix} P_1 \\ P_2 \\ t_1 \\ t_2 \\ t_3 \end{bmatrix} = \begin{bmatrix} 2 \\ 3 \\ 6 \end{bmatrix}
$$

We may interpret this system in a manner similar to the way in which the primal problem was presented. Two spaces exist: a net revenue space, points in which denote net returns from unit levels of operation of the activities, and prices-of-capacities space. This latter space has axes for prices of three fictitious capacities, the t_j, as well as for prices of the two real capacities. The column vectors in the large matrix of (40) are the mappings of the respective unit vectors of price space into revenue space. Note that the unit vectors for the t_j are mapped into the negative orthant of revenue space. If we view the P_k as payments to the firm, the t_j must be seen as payments by the firm; they are potential and must be paid if a given activity is used when its cost exceeds its value.

The problem is to find an optimal set of weights for the unit vectors in price space which will be mapped into the given point in revenue space. We have three dimensions in this latter space and five vectors from which bases may be obtained. Thus, our firm's problem in this dual or "shadow price" form has been cast into the same framework as the primal problem.

A difference is that we may not use the vectors of fictitious capacities' prices to form a basis yielding a basic feasible solution, as we used the disposal processes in the primal problem. Because these fictitious prices are outpayments, they cannot be positive and yield the net revenue vector. By trial and error (and more generally through use of a set of techniques which we shall not take time to discuss)[18] we find that the use of the column vectors in the first, second, and fourth positions in the matrix of (40) will yield a basic feasible solution which we obtain below. Let w_1, w_2, and w_3 be the unit vectors in revenue space, and x_1, x_2, x_3, x_4, and x_5 the unit vectors in price space. Then the initial tableau is

(41)

	x_1	x_2	x_4	r	x_3	x_5	w_1	w_2	w_3
w_1	2	3	0	2	-1	0	1	0	0
w_2	4	3	-1	3	0	0	0	1	0
w_3	6	5	0	6	0	-1	0	0	1

We choose element a_{11} in the above tableau as "pivot element," by which we mean that we shall convert it to unity by operations on the rows of the tableau and the remaining elements in the column a_{i1}, $i = 2, 3$, to zeros. Multiply the first row by 2 and subtract it from the second, to get a new second row

(42) $$0 \quad -3 \quad -1 \quad -1 \quad 2 \quad 0 \quad -2 \quad 1 \quad 0$$

Again, multiply the first row in (41) by 3 and subtract it from the third row to obtain as a new third row:

(43) $$0 \quad -4 \quad 0 \quad 0 \quad 3 \quad -1 \quad -3 \quad 0 \quad 1$$

And, lastly, divide the first row of (41) by 2 to obtain a new first row, which, together with (42) and (43) yields:

(44)

	x_1	x_2	x_4	r	x_3	x_5	w_1	w_2	w_3
w_1	1	1.5	0	1	$-.5$	0	.5	0	0
w_2	0	-3	-1	-1	2	0	-2	1	0
w_3	0	-4	0	0	3	-1	-3	0	1

Next choose element a_{22} as pivot element, divide the second row by 2 and add to the first row for a new first row:

(45) $$1 \quad 0 \quad -.5 \quad .5 \quad .5 \quad 0 \quad -.5 \quad .5 \quad 0$$

Multiply the second row by 1.33 and subtract from the third row:

(46) $$0 \quad 0 \quad 1.33 \quad 1.33 \quad .33 \quad -1 \quad -.33 \quad -1.33 \quad 1$$

[18]For an exposition of these techniques for finding an initial basic feasible solution, see D. Gale, (1), pp. 119–21.

And, lastly, divide the second row by −3, to get, along with (45) and (46)

(47)

	x_1	x_2	x_4	r	x_3	x_5	w_1	w_2	w_3
w_1	1	0	−.5	.5	.5	0	−.5	.5	0
w_2	0	1	.33	.33	−.67	0	−.67	−.33	0
w_3	0	0	1.33	1.33	.33	−1	−.33	−1.33	1

Now, choose a_{33} as pivot element, multiply the third row by .375 and add to the first row to get as a new first row

(48) 1 0 0 1 .625 −.375 −.625 0 .375

Divide the third row of (47) by 4 and subtract from the second row to obtain as a new second row

(49) 0 1 0 0 −.75 .25 .75 0 −.25

And, lastly, divide the third row by 1.33 to obtain, with (48) and (49), the tableau

(50)

	x_1	x_2	x_4	r	x_3	x_5	w_1	w_2	w_3
x_1	1	0	0	1	.625	−.375	−.625	0	.375
x_2	0	1	0	0	−.75	.25	.75	0	−.25
x_4	0	0	1	1	.25	−.71	−.25	−1	.71

The initial feasible basic solution, then, is to price C_1 at one unit of *numéraire*, set P_2 at 0, and t_2 at 1. This would yield a Z of 100, from (35) and the values of C_1 and C_2. Would it be possible, however, to price either or both t_1 and t_3 at nonzero prices and by so doing reduce Z? If so, obviously Z has not attained a minimum with the above basic solution. Suppose we priced t_1 at a value of one. We should increase Z by zero, but because of the net revenue constraints we should have to reduce P_1 by .625, increase P_2 to .75, and reduce t_2 to .75. Putting $P_1 = .375$ and $P_2 = .75$, into Z, we obtain $Z = 75$, which is smaller than 100. Therefore, it will be profitable to put x_3 in the basis. This will not be true of a substitution of x_5, which would require a negative P_2. Therefore, we shall substitute x_3 for that included activity for which the element in the r column divided by the corresponding element in the x_3 column, when positive, is a minimum, i.e., for the first activity. Therefore, our new tableau is

(51)

	x_2	x_3	x_4	r	x_1	x_5	w_1	w_2	w_3
x_2	1	−.75	0	0	0	.25	.75	0	−.25
x_1	0	.625	0	1	1	−.375	−.625	0	.375
x_4	0	.25	1	1	0	−.71	−.25	−1	.71

First, we divide the second row by .625, to obtain as a new second row

$$(52) \qquad 0 \quad 1 \quad 0 \quad 1.6 \quad 1.6 \quad -.6 \quad -1 \quad 0 \quad .6$$

Next, multiply (52) by .75 and add to the first row of (51) to get as a new first row

$$(53) \qquad 1 \quad 0 \quad 0 \quad 1.2 \quad 1.2 \quad -.2 \quad 0 \quad 0 \quad .2$$

And, lastly, multiply (52) by .25, subtract from the third row of (51) to get as a third row, together with (52) and (53),

(54)

	x_2	x_3	x_4	r	x_1	x_5	w_1	w_2	w_3
x_2	1	0	0	1.2	1.2	−.2	0	0	.2
x_3	0	1	0	1.6	1.6	−.6	−1	0	.6
x_4	0	0	1	.6	−.4	−.56	0	−1	.56

This is the solution we obtained from the inverse of the solution of the primal problem: $P_1 = 0$, $P_2 = 1.2$ (see (33)). Thus we need not work out the dual problem in a separate computation, but we may obtain it from the solution of the primal problem if the unit vectors from capacity space are included in the tableau. We also may note these correspondences, which hold not only for the example, but in general:

1. If the primal problem is a maximum problem, the dual problem is defined as a minimum problem, and *vice versa.*

2. $\pi_v^\circ = Z^\circ$; i.e., the optimal value of the objective function in the primal problem will equal the optimal value of the objective function in the dual. In our example of the firm, this translates economically into the statement that the optimal profits of the firm will be exhausted when the firm imputes the optimal shadow prices of the dual to the capacities.

3. The direction of the inequalities in the statement of the primary constraints of the primal and dual problems will be opposite to one another.

4. The elements in the vector of data to the right of the inequality signs in the primary constraints of both problems will appear in the objective function of the other. Thus, the values K_1 and K_2 are in the objective function of the dual, and the values r_1, r_2, and r_3 appear in the objective function of the primal problem.

5. Each problem will have the number of primary constraints equal to the number of nondisposal activities of the other.

6. In the statements of both problems' primary constraints as inequalities, the matrices of a-coefficients will be the transposes of one another.

As we should suspect, if we elect to solve the dual problem of the firm, it is not necessary to solve the primal problem in a separate calculation. If the unit vectors of revenue space are included in the tableau, the solution to the primal problem will be found when these vectors are stated in terms of the basis of vectors of the optimal dual solution. In (54), w_1 on the basis x_2, x_3, and x_4, tells us that a unit of net revenue from productive activity 1 could occur only if the price of "other capacity" were negative 1, i.e., only if external sources, instead of receiving outpayments from the firm, subsidized the firm instead. A similar statement holds for w_2 on the optimal basis. On the other hand, a unit of net profit from productive activity 3 implies a price of .2 for C_2 (and 6 units of profit a price of 1.2), outpayments of .6 for productive activity 1 if used (or 3.6 units of outpayments with a net revenue of 6), and outpayments of (approximately) .6 if productive activity 2 is used (or about 3.6 units of outpayments since net revenue on productive activity 3 is 6).

Then, column 3 in this inverse sector of the tableau has elements of the form $\frac{P_2}{r_3}$, $\frac{P_{t_1}}{r_3}$, and $\frac{P_{t_2}}{r_3}$. When this column vector is multiplied by the row vector $[K_2, 0, 0]'$ whose elements are the coefficients of the prices in the objective function we obtain

$$\frac{K_2 P_2}{r_3} = \bar{X}_{v3} \tag{55}$$

or, in the case at hand,

$$(50)(.2) = 10 \tag{56}$$

Thus, the values for the optimal nonzero activity levels will be obtained from the inverse in the dual solution. This leads to a seventh proposition:

7. In the usual (nondegenerate) case, every capacity fully employed in the primal problem's optimal solution will receive a nonzero price in the dual problem's optimal solution. Every capacity not fully used in the primal problem's optimal solution will receive a zero price in the dual solution. These merely reflect the economic relation between marginal value products of factors and scarcity: any factor of which there exists a remainder after all possible uses have been exhausted is a free good.

We have accomplished a variety of purposes in presenting this body of linear programming techniques. First, it has allowed us to introduce the firm into a production environment of fixed coefficients. Second, it has shown methods of solving for optimal solutions when more unknowns than linear equations are present, or when constraints of linear form must be written as inequalities. Third, it has introduced the concept of vector spaces and the interpretation of solutions as weightings of bases in such spaces, the concept of mappings from one space onto another, and the view of the inverse of a matrix as the unit vectors of the space of the givens of an equation system expressed in a basis of the vectors in the space of the unknowns. All of these concepts will prove valuable in Part III of this book as we go further with linear systems and wrestle with the problems of the existence and uniqueness of solutions to general models. Fourth, it introduced methods of solving a set of linear equations equal in number to the unknowns in such a way as to obtain an inversion of the matrix of the system as well; i.e., to obtain a nonspecific solution to the linear system as well as a specific solution. Fifth, it has introduced the concept of the dual, with its implications that maximization of profits implies a specific type of pricing of factors without market prices.

Building the firm into Model III-1 calls for obvious changes in the assumptions of the model, the most important of which is that change allowing the entrepreneur to control a new set of factors and factor services—capacities. The derivation of supply curves from firm behavior and the manipulation of the model to derive theorems about the system's response to equilibrium displacements requires the use of a set of programming techniques called "parametric programming." With these changes, however, we should have a reconstructed Model III-1 with the firm as a meaningful decisionmaking unit, rather than a mere shadow.

2.b. Model III-2: Single Output, Linear Homogeneous Production Function

We shall now introduce substitution among the inputs of the production process in Model III-1 while retaining the assumptions that only one output is involved in every production, that all costs are variable, and that average costs are constant. We shall do this by assuming that the production conditions of the firm are summarized by a production function which is homogeneous of degree one in all inputs. The more important features of such a function are best visualized by constructing a three-dimensional surface of this type. Let the horizontal plane be defined by the x- and y-axes against which two inputs are measured, and let the z-axis denote amounts of output. Then, if an end of a pencil is placed at the origin of the space, and the pencil is moved through the three-dimensional space from the x-axis to the y-axis, the surface traced out by the pencil will be that of a linear homogeneous function.

Note, first, that such a surface need not be concave globally: for example, the pencil might be moved in a U-shaped sweep from one axis to the other, in which case the surface would have the shape of an inclined valley. And, of course, it might have much more complicated shapes if the pencil were moved with abandon. Thus, we shall have to worry about the shape of the surface: to specify that the function is linear and homogeneous is not to specify, for example, that it is concave at some or all points.

Lay the pencil on the xy plane, end at the origin, so that it lies as a ray from the origin. It will then trace out points in which the two inputs are combined in the same proportions. If, holding the end at the origin, we lift the pencil to touch the surface, keeping its angles with the x- and y-axes as they were when it lay on the base plane, the pencil will be tangent to the surface throughout its length. Therefore, for any given ratio of inputs, there is no single best output, which is to say that the minimum average cost of production for such a ratio of inputs will be the same for any absolute output in the range of the function. Since this will be true for all factor proportions, scale economies are absent over all relevant output levels.

Now imagine the pencil to lie on the production surface, one end at the origin. From the initial point of rest move the pencil over the surface slightly, pivoting it about the origin. Of course, the path traced out by any point on the pencil will have the same configuration as that traced out by any other point; i.e., the slopes in the input directions will be the same. This would indicate that all isoquants are scale models of one another.

Lastly, from Euler's theorem on homogeneous functions, we know that if

$$(57) \qquad \bar{X}_{vj} = T_{vj}(X_{vz_1}, \ldots, X_{vz_m}, X_{v1}, \ldots, X_{vn})$$

is linear and homogeneous, we may write (dropping the v subscript as unnecessary),

$$(58) \qquad \bar{X}_j \equiv T_j^{z_1}X_{z_1} + \cdots T_j^{z_m}X_{z_m} + T_j^1X_1 + \cdots T_j^nX_n$$

while, from the definition of linear homogeneity,

$$(59) \qquad \theta\bar{X}_j = T_j(\theta X_{z_1}, \ldots \theta X_{z_m}, \theta X_1, \ldots, \theta X_n), \qquad \theta > 0$$

This set of production conditions should be distinguished clearly from the set first employed. The fixed coefficients of Model III-1 may be viewed, if desired, as a "degenerate" linear homogeneous production function, in the sense that in the example used above only one ray from the origin is economically meaningful. At every point along this single line the surface forms a 90° angle with the point as apex when a slice through the point parallel to the base plane is made. Any plane of expenditure at a set of positive prices for the inputs will touch the surface at its highest attainable point on this line. No substitution with varying relative input prices can occur. This is obviously not true of the continuous function (57) when (59) holds.

The output of the firm must be indeterminate in this set of production conditions, as it was in Model III-1. However, the prior minimization-of-costs procedure in that model, inherent in the definition of the given a-coefficients as minimum amounts of input per unit of output, does not exist for this model. Therefore, we may view the firm as having a profit function constrained by production conditions:

$$(60) \qquad S = \bar{X}_jP_j - \sum_i X_iP_i - \sum_j X_jP_j - \lambda(\bar{X}_j - T_j([X_i], [X_j]))$$

where, for simplicity, we view it as producing only one output.

If the P_i and P_j are given, and *the firm's output is given*, maximization of profits implies that the following conditions must hold in order to satisfy the necessary conditions for an interior maximum:

$$(61)\quad \begin{aligned} &1. \quad \frac{\partial S}{\partial X_i} = P_i - \lambda^\circ T_j^i = 0, \qquad i = 1, \ldots, m \\ &2. \quad \frac{\partial S}{\partial X_j} = P_j - \lambda^\circ T_j^j = 0, \qquad j = 1, \ldots, n \\ &3. \quad \frac{\partial S}{\partial \lambda} = \bar{X}_j - T_j([X_i], [X_j]) = 0 \end{aligned}$$

where we have assumed all z_i and Y_j to enter the production function as inputs; where they do not, the indices to the right of (61-1) and (61-2) are suitably altered. Also, it is required that

$$(62)\quad d^2S = \sum_{i=1}^{m} \sum_{h=1}^{m} T_j^{ih} dX_i dX_h + \sum_{j=1}^{n} \sum_{k=1}^{n} T_J^{jk} dX_j dX_k + \sum_{i=1}^{m} \sum_{j=1}^{n} T_j^{ij} dX_i dX_j < 0$$

This last requirement (taken in conjunction with the fixed output constraint) is that the production function be locally strictly quasi-concave in the neighborhood of equilibrium.[19]

These are the familiar minimum-cost conditions of the theory of the firm: they state that in order that the firm produce a given output most cheaply it must make the dollar cost of the marginal product rate for every variable input equal to a common factor of proportionality, λ°, subject to the requirement that it stay on the production function. The value, λ°, then, is the marginal cost of production at the equilibrium point for small variations in every factor when all others are held constant. However, we may go further to show that λ° will also be the marginal cost when all factors may vary simultaneously. Total cost is defined as

$$(63)\quad C = \sum_i X_i P_i + \sum_j X_j P_j$$

and, for small increases in total cost,

$$(64)\quad dC = \sum_i dX_i P_i + \sum_j dX_j P_j$$

From (57), which is not necessarily linear and homogeneous,

$$(65)\quad d\bar{X}_j = \sum_i dX_i T_j^i + \sum_j dX_j T_j^j$$

[19] See the discussion of quasi-concavity in Section 2.b.1.b., Chapter 2. Of course, if the linear homogeneous function is globally quasi-concave or strictly quasi-concave, the function will be globally concave.

may be used as a linear approximation. Marginal costs, when all variables are free to vary, are defined as

$$\text{(66)} \qquad \frac{dC}{d\bar{X}_j} = \frac{\sum_i dX_i P_i + \sum_j dX_j P_j}{\sum_i dX_i T_j^i + \sum_j dX_j T_j^j}$$

Substituting from (61) into the numerator,

$$\text{(67)} \qquad \frac{dC}{d\bar{X}_j} = \frac{\left(\sum_i dX_i T_j^i + \sum_j dX_j T_j^j\right) \lambda^\circ}{\sum_i dX_i T_j^i + \sum_j dX_j T_j^j} = \lambda^\circ$$

Therefore, for very small movements in the neighborhood of equilibrium, a given small value of any factor is a perfect substitute for the same small value of any other, and whether a small amount of increased output is obtained by varying any one of them by the necessary amount or varying two or more makes no cost difference. It is emphasized again that the validity of this result is not restricted to the case of a linear homogeneous production function, although only for this latter case does it hold as an exact rather than linear approximative relation.

Condition (62) requires that, subject to the restriction

$$\text{(68)} \qquad d\bar{X}_j = \sum_i T_j^i dX_i + \sum_j T_j^j dX_j = 0$$

the quadratic form in (62) be negative definite. If we substitute from (61) for the marginal productivity terms in (68), and multiply through by λ°, we may convert this expression to

$$\text{(69)} \qquad \lambda^\circ d\bar{X}_j^\circ = \sum_i P_i dX_i^\circ + \sum_j P_j dX_j^\circ = 0$$

which is the same form for this linear constraint as that upon the consumer in (97) of Chapter 2. We need not, then, repeat that analysis to derive the necessary and sufficient conditions for (62) to hold subject to (69)

$$\text{(70)} \qquad \begin{vmatrix} T_j^{z_1 z_1} & \cdots & T_j^{z_1 z_m} & T_j^{z_1 1} & \cdots & T_j^{z_1 n} & -P_{z_1} \\ T_j^{z_1 z_2} & \cdots & T_j^{z_2 z_m} & T_j^{z_2 1} & \cdots & T_j^{z_2 n} & -P_{z_2} \\ \cdot & \cdots & \cdot & \cdot & \cdots & \cdot & \cdot \\ \cdot & \cdots & \cdot & \cdot & \cdots & \cdot & \cdot \\ T_j^{z_1 n} & \cdots & T_j^{z_m n} & T_j^{1n} & \cdots & T_j^{nn} & -P_n \\ P_{z_1} & \cdots & P_{z_m} & P_1 & \cdots & P_n & 0 \end{vmatrix} = |T^*|$$

This bordered Hessian and all of its bordered principal minors with more than two rows must have the sign $(-1)^s$ where s is the number of rows and columns a specific determinant has. Again it is emphasized that these sign conditions must hold for all possible numberings of the inputs.

We may proceed to displace the equilibrium of the submodel (61). To fix our ideas suppose $n = 3$ and $m = 2$. Then, if P_2 is changed slightly, we obtain the following system for the evaluation of changes in the equilibrium inputs:

$$(71) \qquad \begin{bmatrix} \lambda^\circ T_1^{z_1z_1} & \lambda^\circ T_1^{z_1z_2} & \lambda^\circ T_1^{z_11} & \lambda^\circ T_1^{z_12} & \lambda^\circ T_1^{z_13} & T_1^{z_1} \\ \lambda^\circ T_1^{z_1z_2} & \lambda^\circ T_1^{z_2z_2} & \lambda^\circ T_1^{z_21} & \lambda^\circ T_1^{z_22} & \lambda^\circ T_1^{z_23} & T_1^{z_2} \\ \lambda^\circ T_1^{z_11} & \lambda^\circ T_1^{z_21} & \lambda^\circ T_1^{11} & \lambda^\circ T_1^{12} & \lambda^\circ T_1^{13} & T_1^{1} \\ \lambda^\circ T_1^{z_12} & \lambda^\circ T_1^{z_22} & \lambda^\circ T_1^{12} & \lambda^\circ T_1^{22} & \lambda^\circ T_1^{23} & T_1^{2} \\ \lambda^\circ T_1^{z_13} & \lambda^\circ T_1^{z_23} & \lambda^\circ T_1^{13} & \lambda^\circ T_1^{23} & \lambda^\circ T_1^{33} & T_1^{3} \\ -T_1^{z_1} & -T_1^{z_2} & -T_1^{1} & -T_1^{2} & -T_1^{3} & 0 \end{bmatrix} \begin{bmatrix} \dfrac{\partial X_{z_1}^\circ}{\partial P_2} \\ \dfrac{\partial X_{z_2}^\circ}{\partial P_2} \\ \dfrac{\partial X_1^\circ}{\partial P_2} \\ \dfrac{\partial X_2^\circ}{\partial P_2} \\ \dfrac{\partial X_3^\circ}{\partial P_2} \\ \dfrac{\partial \lambda^\circ}{\partial P_2} \end{bmatrix} = \begin{bmatrix} 0 \\ 0 \\ 0 \\ 1 \\ 0 \\ 0 \end{bmatrix}$$

or

$$(72) \qquad [T'][dX] = [dP_2]$$

If the system were similarly shocked by a small change in $\bar{X}_1$, then in (72) we should substitute for the two column vectors:

$$(73) \qquad \begin{aligned} &1. \quad [dX] = \left[\frac{\partial X_{z_1}^\circ}{\partial \bar{X}_1}, \frac{\partial X_{z_2}^\circ}{\partial \bar{X}_1}, \ldots, \frac{\partial \lambda^\circ}{\partial \bar{X}_1}\right] \\ &2. \quad [d\bar{X}] = [0, 0, 0, 0, 0, -1] \end{aligned}$$

to obtain

$$(74) \qquad [T'] \, [dX] = [d\bar{X}]$$

We may proceed to derive the expressions:

$$(75) \qquad \begin{aligned} &1. \quad \frac{\partial X_2^\circ}{\partial P_2} = \frac{|T'_{44}|}{|T'|} = \bar{s}'_{22} \\ &2. \quad \frac{\partial X_3^\circ}{\partial P_2} = -\frac{|T'_{45}|}{|T'|} = \bar{s}'_{32} \\ &3. \quad \frac{\partial \lambda^\circ}{\partial P_2} = \frac{|T'_{46}|}{|T'|} = \bar{s}'_{\lambda 2} \end{aligned}$$

It will be recalled that these expressions depict the impact of the change in price of an input upon the demands for inputs and on marginal cost, *given a level of output.* This limited maximization-of-profits capability is denoted by the prime signs on the substitution effect symbols in (75). The bars denote the fact that these are firms' substitution effects. Also:

(76)

$$1.\quad \frac{\partial X_2^\circ}{\partial \bar{X}_1} = -\frac{|T'_{64}|}{|T'|} = e_{21} = \bar{s}'_{\lambda 2}$$

$$2.\quad \frac{\partial \lambda^\circ}{\partial \bar{X}_1} = -\frac{|T'_{66}|}{|T'|} = e_{\lambda 1}$$

We have symbolized these two expressions by e-terms to denote the fact that they are "expansion effects" of an output change upon input demands and marginal cost. Note that by virtue of the symmetry of $[T']$ except for the signs of the elements in the last column, $|T'_{st}| = |T'_{ts}|$, $s = 1, \ldots, 5$, $t = 1, \ldots, 5$, and $|T'_{st}| = -|T'_{ts}|$, when the minor involves removal of the last row or column. By virtue of this, the expansion effect on an input is equal to the impact of the price of that input on marginal cost.[20]

As an aid to the evaluation of these expressions, we may perform a series of operations upon $|T'|$ and its minors which will make the bordered Hessians of (70) directly relevant. First, eliminate the λ° terms from the $s-1$ columns of $|T'|$ and its bordered minors, and compensate by multiplying the determinant by $(\lambda^\circ)^{s-1}$. Second, eliminate the $\frac{1}{\lambda^\circ}$ terms from the last row of the determinant and compensate by multiplying the determinant by $\frac{1}{\lambda^\circ}$, which reduces the expression multiplying the determinant to $(\lambda^\circ)^{s-2}$. Third, multiply the last column and the last row of the determinant by $-\lambda^\circ$, and compensate by multiplying the determinant by $\left(\frac{1}{\lambda^\circ}\right)^2$, making the expression multiplying the determinant $(\lambda^\circ)^{s-4}$. Lastly, substitute from (61) to obtain the price elements in the last row and column. For $|T'|$ we should have

$$(77)\qquad (\lambda^\circ)^{s-4}|T^*| = |T'|$$

where $|T^*|$ is the corresponding bordered Hessian of (70). Then, the expressions of (75) and (76) may be written:

(78)

$$1.\quad \bar{s}'_{22} = \frac{|T^*_{44}|}{\lambda^\circ|T^*|}$$

$$2.\quad \bar{s}'_{32} = -\frac{|T^*_{45}|}{\lambda^\circ|T^*|}$$

$$3.\quad \bar{s}'_{\lambda 2} = \lambda^\circ \frac{|T^*_{46}|}{|T^*|}$$

[20] The theorem was first derived in P. Samuelson, (4), p. 67.

Note that in (78-3) the bordering column of $[T^*]$ is eliminated, which raises the multiplying expression to $(\lambda^\circ)^3$ in the numerator. Also

$$(79) \quad \begin{aligned} &1. \quad e_{21} = -\lambda^\circ \frac{|T^*_{64}|}{|T^*|} \\ &2. \quad e_{\lambda 1} = -(\lambda^\circ)^3 \frac{|T^*_{66}|}{|T^*|} \end{aligned}$$

From the restrictions upon the bordered Hessians of (70), then it follows that

$$(80) \quad \begin{aligned} &1. \quad \bar{s}'_{22} < 0 \\ &2. \quad \bar{s}'_{32} \gtreqless 0 \\ &3. \quad \bar{s}'_{\lambda 2} \gtreqless 0 \end{aligned}$$

The rise in price of an input, given a constant output level, must always restrict that input's use, but will have ambiguous impacts upon the use of other inputs and upon marginal cost.

Further, from this body of restrictions obtained from the second-order maximization conditions:

$$(81) \quad \begin{aligned} &1. \quad e_{21} \gtreqless 0 \\ &2. \quad e_{\lambda 1} \gtreqless 0 \end{aligned}$$

For the general production function, quasi-concave in the strict sense at the point of equilibrium, a rise in the amount supplied of output may increase, decrease, or leave unaffected the equilibrium amount demanded of any input, and increase, decrease, or leave unaffected the equilibrium marginal cost.

It is possible to evaluate e_{21} $(= \bar{s}'_{\lambda 2})$ and $e_{\lambda 1}$ on the basis of knowledge that the production function (57) is linear and homogeneous. It must be emphasized that none of the results of (80) or (81) depends upon this quality, but merely upon the second-order maximization conditions when output is taken as constant. But from (58) and (59), letting $\theta \bar{X}_j = d\bar{X}_j$, it follows that

$$(82) \quad \theta \bar{X}_j = \sum_i T^i_j \theta X_i + \sum_j T^j_j \theta X_j$$

since

$$(83) \quad d\bar{X}_j = \sum_i T^i_j dX_i + \sum_j T^j_j dX_j$$

From (63)-(67), it must follow that

$$(84) \quad d\bar{X}_j = \frac{\theta C^\circ}{\lambda^\circ}$$

Since all factors are taken in positive amounts in the initial equilibrium, it follows that $\frac{dX_2}{d\bar{X}_1} = e_{21} = \bar{s}'_{\lambda 2} > 0$. Not only is an equi-proportionate increase in all inputs a possible way of increasing output when prices are constant, it is the optimal way for linear homogeneous functions. From this follows the theorem that an increase in P_2 will always increase the marginal cost of production.

Also, (84) establishes that $e_{\lambda 1} = 0$, since marginal cost is unchanged. This can be shown in the following manner as well. We differentiate (58) to obtain

$$(85) \qquad d\bar{X}_j \equiv \sum_i T_j^i dX_i + \sum_j T_j^j dX_j$$

and yet again

$$(86) \quad d^2\bar{X}_j \equiv \sum_{i=1}^{m} \sum_{h=1}^{m} T_j^{ih} dX_i dX_h + \sum_{j=1}^{n} \sum_{k=1}^{n} T_j^{jk} dX_j dX_k + 2 \sum_i \sum_j T_j^{ij} dX_i dX_j \leqq 0$$

When all inputs are changed proportionately, this quadratic form vanishes at any point on the surface at which one starts, when that surface is linear and homogeneous. Since (86) is a semi-definite quadratic form and since such forms are singular, the determinant formed by the matrix of its coefficients will vanish. It will be seen that this matrix is $[T^*_{ss}]$, so $|T^*_{ss}| = 0$, and for the case in hand $|T^*_{66}| = 0$. Thus, $e_{\lambda 1} = 0$.

We may obtain the nonspecific solutions to the equations of (61) in the form of demand functions for inputs as functions of prices, given output as a datum. They may be seen, from the underlying relations in (61), to be homogeneous of degree zero in all prices, while λ° is homogeneous of degree one in all prices. The demands for inputs may be written, once more introducing the firm's subscript which we dropped for simplicity,

$$(87) \quad \begin{array}{lll} 1. & X^\circ_{vi} = G_{vi}([P]; \bar{X}_{vj}), & i = 1, \ldots, m \\ 2. & X^\circ_{vj} = G_{vj}([P]; \bar{X}_{vj}), & j = 1, \ldots, n \end{array}$$

We may rely upon the prior analysis of the consumer's substitution effects to save time in stating the restrictions upon the firm's substitution effects. Letting u, v, w, etc., symbolize inputs of either the primary or intermediate type, we have seen that

$$(88) \qquad \bar{s}'_{uu} < 0$$

From Young's theorem, given a continuous, differentiable production function, the symmetry of $[T']$ follows and from it

$$(89) \qquad \bar{s}'_{uv} = \bar{s}'_{vu}$$

From the homogeneity of degree zero in prices of (87) it follows, for a given output level, that

$$\sum_v \bar{s}'_{uv} P_v = 0, \quad u = z_1, \ldots, z_m, 1, \ldots, n \tag{90}$$

Therefore, every input must have at least one substitute. And,

$$\sum_{u=1}^{t} \sum_{v=1}^{t} P_u P_v \bar{s}'_{uv} < 0, \qquad t < m + n \tag{91}$$

from which it follows that the following determinants must have the sign $(-1)^s$:

$$\bar{s}'_{uu}, \begin{vmatrix} \bar{s}'_{uu} & \bar{s}'_{uv} \\ \bar{s}'_{uv} & \bar{s}'_{vv} \end{vmatrix}, \ldots, \begin{vmatrix} \bar{s}'_{uu} & \bar{s}'_{uv} & \cdots & \bar{s}'_{um+n-1} \\ \bar{s}'_{uv} & \bar{s}'_{vv} & \cdots & \bar{s}'_{vm+n-1} \\ \cdot & \cdot & \cdots & \cdot \\ \bar{s}'_{um+n-1} & \bar{s}'_{vm+n-1} & \cdot & \bar{s}'_{m+nm+n-1} \end{vmatrix} \tag{92}$$

Further:

$$\sum_{u=1}^{t} \sum_{v=t+1}^{m+n} P_u P_v \bar{s}'_{uv} > 0 \tag{93}$$

With the theory of the individual firm's minimization of cost behind us, it is possible to proceed with the construction of Model III-2. First, we repeat the consumer equations of supply and demand unchanged from Model III-1:

(III-2-1) = (III-1-1)

Industrial demands for inputs are now the sums of firms' demands, as written in (87):

(III-2-2)

$$1. \quad X_i = \sum_v X_{vi} = G_i([P]; \bar{X}_1, \ldots, \bar{X}_n), \ i = 1, \ldots, m$$

$$2. \quad X_j^* = \sum_v X_{vj} = G_j([P]; \bar{X}_1, \ldots, \bar{X}_n), \ j = 1, \ldots, n$$

Let v_j be that subset of firms producing Y_j in equilibrium. Then it is required that profits for every good be zero on an industry basis:

$$\bar{X}_j^\circ P_j^\circ - \sum_{v_j} \sum_i X_{v_ji}^\circ P_i^\circ - \sum_{v_j} \sum_j X_{v_jj}^\circ P_j^\circ = 0, \quad j = 1, \ldots, n \tag{III-2-3}$$

And, in equilibrium, every market must be cleared:

(III-2-4)

$$1. \quad X_i^\circ = \bar{X}_i^\circ \qquad i = 1, \ldots, m$$

$$2. \quad X_j^\circ + X_j^{*\circ} = \bar{X}_j^\circ \qquad j = 1, \ldots, n$$

Again, v_j and the corresponding input demands are not determinate *ex ante.*

It is possible to eliminate one equation from (III-2-3) as redundant for reasons by now familiar, and, if this is done, the number of unknowns and equations are equal, given the qualification in the previous sentence. The only difference between Models III-1 and III-2 is that while minimum costs were given in the former, in the present model the firm must perform this minimization. It is still true that the firm is in an unclear light, since it cannot be presented as explicitly attempting to derive an optimal output by profit maximization.[21]

This model is the one used by Walras to introduce variable coefficients of production into the third edition of the *Éléments* and is frequently interpreted as the model employed for the same presentation in the definitive edition. In this last edition, the explicit equilibrium conditions are stated as the proportionality of marginal products and factor service prices. We have already commented, with regard to the Lausanne school, upon the lack of understanding of the relations between minimum-cost and maximum-profit conditions in pure competition, between profit-maximizing by the firm and zero profits in equilibrium, and between linear homogeneity and the mere lack of fixed costs.[22] By stating the firm's equilibrium conditions in this form, Walras seems to be assuming that the production function of his model is linear and homogeneous in the inputs. This hypothesis gains further support because he used the following "production equation" in *illustrating* the concept of substitutability among inputs:

$$(94) \qquad \phi(a_{z_1j}, \ . \ . \ . \ , a_{z_mj}, a_{1j}, \ . \ . \ . \ , a_{nj}) = 0$$

where the a-coefficients are not fixed. Schultz proved that writing these conditions in this form implied linear homogeneity in that the ϕ-function does not explicitly contain a scale-of-output argument.[23] However, in the *formal presentation* of his theory, Walras writes the production function in the form

$$(95) \qquad \bar{X}_j = \phi(\bar{X}_j a_{z_1j}, \ . \ . \ . \ , \bar{X}_j a_{z_mj}, \bar{X}_j a_{1j}, \ . \ . \ . \ , \bar{X}_j a_{nj})$$

which clearly brings in the scale factor. Further, he explicitly mentions the possibility of fixed coefficients existing for some inputs.[24] This would

[21] For a depiction of Models III-1 and III-2 in simple form, with numerical examples and solutions, see E. H. Phelps Brown, (1).

[22] See footnote 11.

[23] H. Schultz, (1), pp. 543–4. More recently, P. Samuelson in (8), p. 2, and Dorfman, Samuelson, and Solow, in R. Dorfman, (1), p. 348, have followed Schultz in accepting Walras' analysis of variable coefficients as one for a linear, homogeneous production function.

[24] L. Walras, (2), pp. 374–5. See also H. Neisser, (2), pp. 254, 256n, and C. Phipps, (1), pp. 31–8.

give some support to the hypothesis that Walras believed himself to be stating conditions for the firm's equilibrium under general conditions of production. In this he was influenced by Pareto, who, as we have seen, spent some time in denying the generality of the linear homogeneous production function, although he retained it through much of his analysis of variable coefficients. Further, in his postscript to the "Note on Mr. Wicksteed's Refutation of the English Theory of Rent," Walras stated his belief that Barone had freed his own production analysis from the Wicksteedian assumption of linear homogeneity. Still more evidence is added in support of this hypothesis by the fact that Walras dropped the "exhaustion-of-product" proposition (which follows from Euler's theorem) from the fourth edition of the *Éléments* although it was included in the third edition.[25] Therefore, we conclude that further evidence of the confusion in the theory of the firm as found in the work of the Lausanne school is apparent, and that Walras' general statement of the conditions of production was incorrect, although it is valid, as in Model III-2, for linear homogeneous production functions.

We shall conclude the discussion of Model III-2 with the statement of two fundamental propositions about linear homogeneous production functions. We have already seen that marginal costs are constant. We may now show that average costs will also be constant and equal to marginal costs:

$$(96) \qquad C^\circ = \sum_i X_i^\circ P_i + \sum_j X_j^\circ P_j = \lambda^\circ \left[\sum_i X_i^\circ T_j^i + \sum_j X_j^\circ T_j^j \right]$$

If this is divided by the identity of (58) average cost is seen to equal marginal cost in equilibrium.

Lastly, linear homogeneity implies that if every input receives its marginal physical product or marginal value product as a return, all product or revenue will be exhausted and no residual factor return will remain to be explained. This follows from (58). To show that each input does in fact receive its marginal value product we can see that (61) requires that the price of each input be equal to marginal cost times marginal physical product. But marginal cost equals average cost when the firm is in equilibrium, and (III-2-3) requires average cost to equal price in full general equilibrium. Therefore, each factor service does indeed receive its marginal value product in every employment.

2.c. Model III-3: Single Output, General Production Function

We shall now assume that there exists some element in production—be it the possession of a fixed amount of immobile factor by the firm, such as the entrepreneur's ability to supervise the hiring-selling process, or

[25] See L. Walras, (3), pp. 382–7 and 493–5, and R. Kuenne, (2), pp. 339–40.

the fact that the efficiency of factors is a function of the absolute numbers employed as well as their relative numbers[26]—which leads to a U-shaped average cost curve and a rising marginal cost curve. We shall assume that as output increases from zero, average costs fall smoothly and continuously to a minimum, then rise smoothly and continuously indefinitely.

With these assumptions we may work with the firm in pure competition as a full-bodied decisionmaking unit whose output will be a determinate result of profit maximization. To the firm's equilibrium conditions in (61) we add the condition obtained by differentiating S with respect to $\bar{X}_j$, now assumed variable and to be determined by profit maximization conditions:

$$\frac{\partial S}{\partial \bar{X}_j} = P_j - \lambda^\circ = 0 \tag{97}$$

That is, price of the unit of output, or marginal revenue in the purely competitive context, must be equated to marginal cost in the solution. Substituting from (97) into (61-1) and (61-2), we obtain

$$(98)\qquad \begin{aligned} &1. \quad P_i - P_j T_j^i = 0, && i = 1, \ldots, m \\ &2. \quad P_j - P_J T_J^{j} = 0, && j = 1, \ldots, n \end{aligned}$$

These combined conditions indicate that in equilibrium the firm will hire each variable input up to the point where its marginal value product equals price. If the firm desires to maximize profits under conditions of variable output, it may be told to do either of the following equivalent things: (a) for that output which makes price equal to optimal marginal cost, hire factor services until the ratios of their prices to their marginal physical products are equal, or (b) hire every variable input until its marginal value product is equal to its price.

The second-order equilibrium conditions of (62) are changed in that the same quadratic form is required to be negative definite subject only to the conditions that marginal movements conform to the production function. No longer is it required that output be unchanged, as it was by (68). The form must be negative definite for zero *and for nonzero* changes in output in the neighborhood of equilibrium:

$$d\bar{X}_j^\circ - \sum_i T_j^i dX_i^\circ - \sum_j T_j^j dX_j^\circ = 0 \tag{99}$$

or from (61) and (98)

$$P_j d\bar{X}_j^\circ - \sum_i P_i dX_i^\circ - \sum_j P_j dX_j^\circ = 0 \tag{100}$$

[26] For a discussion of the recent controversy over the mutual implications of divisibility of factor services, efficiency of factor services, and constant costs, see E. Chamberlin, (1), Appendix B.

To meet this new condition—that S be locally strictly concave—we must add to the requirements of (70) the further requirements that the unbordered principal minors of $|T^*|$ have the sign $(-1)^s$, where s is the number of rows in the determinant, and $1 \leqq s \leqq n + m$.

Now, let us shock this new expanded system of the firm's maximization process by changing, say, P_2, by a very small amount. Then the system of changes can be depicted as follows:

$$(101) \quad \begin{bmatrix} \lambda^\circ T_1^{z_1z_1} & \lambda^\circ T_1^{z_1z_2} & \lambda^\circ T_1^{z_11} & \lambda^\circ T_1^{z_12} & \lambda^\circ T_1^{z_13} & 0 & T_1^{z_1} \\ \lambda^\circ T_1^{z_1z_2} & \lambda^\circ T_1^{z_2z_2} & \lambda^\circ T_1^{z_21} & \lambda^\circ T_1^{z_22} & \lambda^\circ T_1^{z_23} & 0 & T_1^{z_2} \\ \lambda^\circ T_1^{z_11} & \lambda^\circ T_1^{z_21} & \lambda^\circ T_1^{11} & \lambda^\circ T_1^{12} & \lambda^\circ T_1^{13} & 0 & T_1^{1} \\ \lambda^\circ T_1^{z_12} & \lambda^\circ T_1^{z_22} & \lambda^\circ T_1^{12} & \lambda^\circ T_1^{22} & \lambda^\circ T_1^{23} & 0 & T_1^{2} \\ \lambda^\circ T_1^{z_13} & \lambda^\circ T_1^{z_23} & \lambda^\circ T_1^{13} & \lambda^\circ T_1^{23} & \lambda^\circ T_1^{33} & 0 & T_1^{3} \\ 0 & 0 & 0 & 0 & 0 & 0 & -1 \\ -T_1^{z_1} & -T_1^{z_2} & -T_1^{1} & -T_1^{2} & -T_1^{3} & 1 & 0 \end{bmatrix} \begin{bmatrix} \dfrac{\partial X^\circ_{z_1}}{\partial P_2} \\ \dfrac{\partial X^\circ_{z_2}}{\partial P_2} \\ \dfrac{\partial X^\circ_1}{\partial P_2} \\ \dfrac{\partial X^\circ_2}{\partial P_2} \\ \dfrac{\partial X^\circ_3}{\partial P_2} \\ \dfrac{\partial \bar{X}^\circ_1}{\partial P_2} \\ \dfrac{\partial \lambda^\circ}{\partial P_2} \end{bmatrix} = \begin{bmatrix} 0 \\ 0 \\ 0 \\ 1 \\ 0 \\ 0 \\ 0 \end{bmatrix}$$

where $m = 2$, $n = 3$, and output is good Y_1; abbreviating,

$$(102) \qquad [T''][dX] = [dP_2]$$

We may note for future analysis that

$$(103) \quad \begin{array}{lll} 1. & [T''_{66}] = [T'] & \\ 2. & |T''| = |T''_{67,76}| & \\ 3. & |T''| = |T'_{66}| = \lambda^{\circ 5}|T^*_{66}| & \\ 4. & |T''_{ss}| = |T'_{66,ss}| = \lambda^{\circ 4}|T^*_{66,ss}|, & s = 1, \ldots, 5 \\ 5. & |T''_{st}| = |T'_{66,st}| = \lambda^{\circ 4}|T^*_{66,st}|, & s = 1, \ldots, 5, t = 1, \ldots, 5 \\ 6. & |T''_{s6}| = -|T'_{s6}| = -\lambda^{\circ 4}|T^*_{s6}|, & s = 1, \ldots, 5 \\ 7. & |T''_{76}| = |T'_{66}| = \lambda^{\circ 5}|T^*_{66}| & \end{array}$$

Then, we may evaluate:

$$(104) \quad \begin{array}{ll} 1. & \dfrac{\partial X^\circ_2}{\partial P_2} \equiv \bar{s}_{22} = \dfrac{|T''_{44}|}{|T''|} = \dfrac{|T^*_{66,44}|}{\lambda^\circ|T^*_{66}|} \\ 2. & \dfrac{\partial X^\circ_3}{\partial P_2} \equiv \bar{s}_{32} = -\dfrac{|T''_{45}|}{|T''|} = -\dfrac{|T^*_{66,45}|}{\lambda^\circ|T^*_{66}|} \\ 3. & \dfrac{\partial \lambda^\circ}{\partial P_2} \equiv \bar{s}_{\lambda 2} = -\dfrac{|T''_{47}|}{|T''|} \end{array}$$

The conclusions of (80) and (81) will hold for equilibrium displacements in this model when output is held fixed. The expressions in (104) differ from the substitution terms in these systems by their failure to have a prime sign. This indicates that the substitution terms in (104) include the impacts upon input demands and marginal cost of induced output changes; that is, the substitution effects include implicitly the expansion effects of changes in $\bar{X}_1^\circ$ induced by the change in input price.

From (103), (104), and the additions to (70) it follows that

$$(105) \qquad \begin{aligned} &1. \quad \bar{s}_{22} < 0 \\ &2. \quad \bar{s}_{32} \gtreqless 0 \end{aligned}$$

Note that it is now possible to say that when a true maximum profit position has been attained, with output variable, the Hessian of the production function, $|T^*_{66}|$, will be negative. As shown in (79-2), this is the restriction needed to insure that marginal cost will rise with output at minimum cost for that output ($e_{\lambda j} > 0$). Therefore, at our equilibrium positions we are assured that marginal cost rises in function of output.

How, then, do we explain

$$(106) \qquad \bar{s}_{\lambda 2} = 0$$

This occurs because we are constrained by (97) to keep marginal costs constant between equilibrium levels, since the price of output does not rise. Thus, though the fall in price of input may affect the marginal cost of the initial output in a downward direction, output expands until marginal cost rises once more to the old level.

It may appear clear, then, what sign the following expression must bear:

$$(107) \qquad \frac{\partial \bar{X}_1}{\partial P_2} = \frac{|T''_{46}|}{|T''|} = \underline{\bar{s}}_{12} = -\frac{|T^*_{46}|}{\lambda^\circ\, |T^*_{66}|}$$

where the lower bar is used to denote that the first subscript in the $\bar{s}$-term symbolizes an output. But (107) may be seen to be

$$(108) \qquad -\underline{\bar{s}}_{12} = \frac{\bar{s}'_{\lambda 2}}{e_{\lambda 1}}$$

or

$$(109) \qquad \bar{s}'_{\lambda 2} = -\underline{\bar{s}}_{12} e_{\lambda 1}$$

That is, an increase in P_2 will change $\bar{X}_1$ by the negative of the amount the marginal costs of the previous output change divided by the impact of a change in $\bar{X}_1$ upon marginal costs. This is the result discussed in the previous paragraph. We know that $e_{\lambda 1}$ is positive, and so the sign of $\underline{\bar{s}}_{12}$ will be opposite to the sign of $\bar{s}'_{\lambda 2}$. But this last expression is not derivable for the general production function. It is possible for the firm maximizing its profits, even when marginal costs are rising with output, to undergo a drop in marginal costs with a rise in the price of an input. In this case output would rise, not fall.

A last type of equilibrium displacement is that caused by a price change for the output rather than one of the inputs. We have assumed throughout the discussion of Models III-2 and III-3 that an external *numéraire* is used (see (70)). If the system is displaced by a small change in P_1, we should obtain:

$$(110) \qquad [T''][dX'] = [dP_1]$$

where

$$(111) \qquad \begin{aligned} &1. \quad [dX'] = \left[\frac{\partial X^\circ_{z_1}}{\partial P_1}, \ldots, \frac{\partial \lambda^\circ}{\partial P_1}\right] \\ &2. \quad [dP_1] = [0, 0, 1, 0, 0, -1, 0] \end{aligned}$$

Therefore:

$$(112) \qquad \begin{aligned} &1. \quad \frac{\partial X^\circ_1}{\partial P_1} = \bar{s}^*_{11} = \frac{|T''_{33}|}{|T''|} + \frac{|T''_{63}|}{|T''|} = \bar{s}_{11} + \underline{\bar{\bar{s}}}_{11} \\ &2. \quad \frac{\partial \bar{X}^\circ_1}{\partial P_1} = \underline{\bar{s}}^*_{11} = -\frac{|T''_{36}|}{|T''|} - \frac{|T''_{66}|}{|T''|} = \underline{\bar{\bar{s}}}_{11} + \underline{\bar{s}}_{11} \\ &3. \quad \frac{\partial X^\circ_2}{\partial P_1} = \bar{s}^*_{21} = -\frac{|T''_{34}|}{|T''|} - \frac{|T''_{64}|}{|T''|} = \bar{s}_{21} - \underline{\bar{s}}_{12} \\ &4. \quad \frac{\partial \lambda^\circ}{\partial P_1} = \bar{s}_{\lambda 1} = \frac{|T''_{37}|}{|T''|} + \frac{|T''_{67}|}{|T''|} \end{aligned}$$

Each of these substitution effects includes a term through which the impact of Y_1 as an input is felt and a second term through which the effect of Y_1 as an output is transmitted. These gross effects have been decomposed into net effects on the basis of the following translations:

$$(113) \qquad \begin{aligned} &1. \quad \bar{s}^*_{11} = \frac{|T^*_{66,33}|}{\lambda^\circ |T^*_{66}|} - \frac{|T^*_{36}|}{(\lambda^\circ)^2 |T^*_{66}|} \\ &2. \quad \underline{\bar{s}}^*_{11} = -\frac{|T^*_{36}|}{(\lambda^\circ)^2 |T^*_{66}|} - \frac{|T^*|}{(\lambda^\circ)^3 |T^*_{66}|} \\ &3. \quad \bar{s}^*_{21} = \frac{|T^*_{46}|}{(\lambda^\circ)^2 |T^*_{66}|} - \frac{|T^*_{66,34}|}{\lambda^\circ |T^*_{66}|} \\ &4. \quad \bar{s}^*_{\lambda 1} = 0 + 1 \end{aligned}$$

But, as in the case of $\underline{\bar{s}}_{12}$, it is possible to break down $\underline{\bar{\bar{s}}}_{11}$:

$$(114) \qquad \underline{\bar{\bar{s}}}_{11} = -\frac{\bar{s}'_{\lambda 1}}{e_{\lambda 1}}$$

and so (113-1) and (113-2) become:

$$(115)\qquad \begin{aligned} &1. \quad \bar{s}^*_{11} = \bar{s}_{11} - \frac{\bar{s}'_{\lambda 1}}{e_{\lambda 1}} \\ &2. \quad \underline{\bar{s}}^*_{11} = \frac{-\bar{s}'_{\lambda 1}}{e_{\lambda 1}} + \underline{\bar{s}}_{11} \end{aligned}$$

In the first case, the direct input effects of the price change will be negative ((105-1)); the indirect effects caused by an induced expansion have a positive denominator, but an indeterminate numerator. If marginal costs rise when P_1 rises, the induced expansion effect will be negative and reinforce the direct input effect; if it falls, this latter effect will move contrary to the indirect effect which if powerful enough will outweigh the direct effect.

Similar considerations hold in the second case. The direct impact of an own-price change upon output, $\underline{\bar{s}}_{jj}$, will be positive by virtue of the opposition of signs of $|T^*|$ and $|T^*_{66}|$ in our case. When P_1 rises, from the viewpoint of output changes there exists a direct impact, marginal costs held constant ($\underline{\bar{s}}_{11}$), and an indirect effect due to the rise or fall in marginal costs. This latter term is capable of analysis in terms of the previous paragraph. Gross output of Y_1, or $\bar{X}_1$, minus intermediate output of Y_1, or X_1, equals net output, or final demand, and is, of course, affected in the following way by a price change:

$$(116)\qquad \frac{\partial y_1^\circ}{\partial P_1} = \underline{\bar{s}}_{11} - \bar{s}_{11}$$

where y_1 symbolizes net output. Thus net output must increase with a price change when a true maximum profit position has been attained. This obviously implies that $\frac{\partial \bar{X}_1^\circ}{\partial P_1} - \frac{\partial X_1^\circ}{\partial P_1} > 0$, else we should have an "autophagous" (self-consuming) system; we shall treat this problem further in the simpler systems of Chapter 6.

In similar fashion the gross effect of a change in price of an input which is also an output upon another input is composed of two effects: a direct impact, output constant, plus the indirect impact via induced expansion; or,

$$(117)\qquad \begin{aligned} \bar{s}^*_{21} &= -\frac{\bar{s}'_{\underline{\lambda 2}}}{e_{\lambda 1}} + \bar{s}_{21} \\ &= \bar{s}_{21} - \frac{e_{21}}{e_{\lambda 1}} \end{aligned}$$

Thus, $\bar{s}_{21}$ is the effect of a change in P_1 upon X_2°, output held constant; the ratio term is the effect upon X_2° of the expansion of $\bar{X}_1$.

Lastly, as shown in (113-4) equilibrium marginal cost must rise by the whole of the price change in output in order for equilibrium to be reattained.

The equation system of (61) and (97) may be solved for the firm's nonspecific solutions, of the form:

$$(118)\quad \begin{aligned} &1. \quad X^{\circ}_{vi} = G^{\circ}_{vi}([P]), && i = 1, \ldots, m \\ &2. \quad X^{\circ}_{vj} = G^{*}_{vj}([P]), && j = 1, \ldots, n \\ &3. \quad \bar{X}^{\circ}_{vJ} = G^{*}_{vJ}([P]), && J = 1, \ldots, n \end{aligned}$$

The restrictions upon the $\bar{s}$-terms may be quickly stated. We have seen that

$$(119)\quad \begin{aligned} &1. \quad \bar{s}_{uu} < 0, && u = 1, \ldots, m, j = 1, \ldots, n \\ &2. \quad -\underline{\bar{s}}_{jj} < 0, && j = 1, \ldots, n \end{aligned}$$

From the symmetry conditions

$$(120)\quad \begin{aligned} &1. \quad \bar{s}_{uv} = \bar{s}_{vu}, && u, v = i = 1, \ldots, m, j = 1, \ldots, n \\ &2. \quad \underline{\bar{s}}_{jk} = -\underline{\bar{s}}_{kj}, && \\ & && \text{for each output } j, k = z_1, \ldots, z_m, 1, \ldots, n \end{aligned}$$

From the homogeneity of degree zero of the functions of (118):

$$(121)\quad \begin{aligned} &1. \quad \sum_u \bar{s}_{iu}P_u + \underline{\bar{s}}_{Ji}P_i = 0, && u = z_1, \ldots, z_m, 1, \ldots, n \\ &2. \quad \sum_u \bar{s}_{ju}P_u + \underline{\bar{s}}_{Jj}P_j = 0, && u = z_1, \ldots, z_m, 1, \ldots, n \\ &3. \quad \sum_u \underline{\bar{s}}_{Ju}P_u - \underline{\bar{s}}_{JJ}P_J = 0, && u = z_1, \ldots, z_m, 1, \ldots, n \end{aligned}$$

The conditions derived by Hotelling for the "consumer" without budgetary restrictions are directly applicable to this case, for as already pointed out,[27] he derived them for the case of profit maximization with variable output. Therefore, the principal minors of the following determinant must have the sign $(-1)^s$, while the determinant itself will disappear:

$$(122)\quad \begin{vmatrix} -\underline{\bar{s}}_{uu} & \underline{\bar{\bar{s}}}_{uu} & \underline{\bar{s}}_{uv} & \cdots & \underline{\bar{s}}_{um+n} \\ \underline{\bar{\bar{s}}}_{uu} & \bar{s}_{uu} & \bar{s}_{uv} & \cdots & \bar{s}_{um+n} \\ \cdot & \cdot & \cdot & \cdots & \cdot \\ \underline{\bar{s}}_{um+n} & \bar{s}_{um+n} & \bar{s}_{vm+n} & \cdots & \bar{s}_{m+nm+n} \end{vmatrix}$$

These assure that the following quadratic form is negative definite:

$$(123)\quad \sum_{u=1}^{t} \sum_{v=1}^{t} P_u P_v s_{uv}, \qquad t < m + n + 1$$

[27] See footnote 48, Chapter 2.

where the s-terms have been left unbarred to indicate that they may take all barred values, all of which values are positive except for $\bar{s}_{uu}$ which is negative. Lastly, from (121) and (123),

$$(124) \qquad \sum_{u=1}^{t} \sum_{v=t+1}^{m+n} P_u P_v s_{uv} > 0$$

We may now construct Model III-3 quickly. The consumers' equations remain unchanged:

(III-3-1) = (III-2-1) = (III-1-1)

Industrial demands for inputs are, once more, the sum of firms' demands as given in the nonspecific solutions of (118). To them it is now possible to add market supply functions for each output, or the sum of firms' output functions:

$$\text{(III-3-2)} \quad \begin{aligned} &1. \quad X_i = \sum_v X_{vi} = G_i([P]), \qquad i = 1, \ldots, m \\ &2. \quad X_j^* = \sum_v X_{vj} = G_j([P]), \qquad j = 1, \ldots, n \\ &3. \quad \bar{X}_j = \sum_v \bar{X}_{vj} = G_J([P]), \qquad J = 1, \ldots, n \end{aligned}$$

Since the firm exists in this model in every sense of the word, we state the restrictions on profits in terms of the firm:

$$\text{(III-3-3)} \qquad \bar{X}_{vj}^{\circ} P_j^{\circ} - \sum_i X_{vi}^{\circ} P_i^{\circ} - \sum_j X_{vj}^{\circ} P_j^{\circ} = 0, \qquad v = 1, \ldots, o$$

As before, all markets must be cleared in equilibrium:

(III-3-4) = (III-2-4)

And, finally, we repeat (118) to determine firms' input demands and outputs:

$$\text{(III-3-5)} \quad \begin{aligned} &1. \quad X_{vi} = G_{vi}^*([P]), \qquad i = 1, \ldots, m, \qquad v = 1, \ldots, o \\ &2. \quad X_{vj} = G_{vj}^*([P]), \qquad j = 1, \ldots, n, \qquad v = 1, \ldots, o \\ &3. \quad \bar{X}_{vJ} = G_{vJ}^*([P]), \qquad v = 1, \ldots, o \end{aligned}$$

In this model, the following unknowns exist in the listed quantities: (a) X_j°, $X_j^{*\circ}$, $\bar{X}_j^{\circ}: 3n$; (b) X_i°, $\bar{X}_i^{\circ}: 2m$; (c) P_j°, $P_i^{\circ}: n + m - 1$; and (d) X_{vi}°, X_{vj}°, $\bar{X}_{vj}^{\circ}: om + on + o$. These total $4n + 3m + om + on + o - 1$. The equations number $m + n$ in (III-3-1); $m + 2n$ in (III-3-2); o in (III-3-3); $m + n$ in (III-3-4); and $om + on + o$ in (III-3-5), for a total of $4n + 3m + om + on + 2o$. We may show that if all markets are in equilibrium and all but one firm are earning zero profits, the last firm must also be earning zero profits. We eliminate one equation (say for firm 1) from (III-3-3), leaving us with an excess of o equations.

By the assumption of U-shaped cost curves for all firms, equilibrium will occur at the minimum point of the average cost curve and at this point the exhaustion-of-product proposition will hold, exactly as if linear homogeneity characterized the production function. If every firm pays each input its marginal value product, total product will be exhausted in factor service payments; and in full equilibrium each factor service will receive its marginal value product in all occupations.[28] At the minimum cost point average and marginal costs are equal and constant for a very small interval. Thus, in the neighborhood of the full general equilibrium output for the firm, the conditions of linear homogeneity of the production function hold. We may therefore eliminate one equation for each firm from (III-3-5), for if the firm is constrained to earn zero profit and all but one of the input demands and output value are determined, the remaining value follows from the homogeneity of the function at the equilibrium. The removal of these o equations eliminates the excess of equations over unknowns. Moreover, the effective industry production function will be linear and homogeneous.

Thus, Model III-3 yields a system which may be envisioned as a set of industries with linear homogeneous production functions acting to obtain minimum cost for that output which makes price equal to marginal cost. In this manner, the industry can be converted into a fictitious decision maker. Unlike the case of the firm under similar conditions, the slope of the total demand function $X_j + X_j^*$ is negative in the P_j-direction and ultimately sets a limit to output. Therefore, the industry functions as a constant cost monopolist who neglects the impact of his output upon the price of his product.

2.d. Model III-4: Multiple Output, General Production Function

We shall make one final generalization: assume that the firm has a transformation function which allows it to produce more than one output per activity. For convenience, let us assume that we have a fully general transformation function which allows all outputs to be produced from all inputs:

$$(125) \quad J_v(\bar{X}_{v1}, \ldots, \bar{X}_{vn}, X_{vz_1}, \ldots, X_{vz_m}, X_{v1}, \ldots, X_{vn}) = 0$$

where outputs are treated as negative inputs.

We shall drop the subscript v from the function for simplicity. Further, in order to compare the analysis to better advantage with that of Model

[28] This proposition was derived by Wicksell in (3), Vol. I, p. 129, and by Walras in (3), pp. 489–95. See H. Neisser, (2), p. 257. See also J. Viner, (1), p. 28; P. Samuelson, (4), pp. 85–7; and G. Stigler, (1), pp. 380–7.

III-3, it will be best to convert the implicit function J into an explicit function with an arbitrary good (say Y_1) chosen as dependent variable. We shall write the function in the form:

$$(126) \quad \bar{X}_1 = V(\bar{X}_2, \ldots, \bar{X}_n, X_{z_1}, \ldots, X_{z_m}, X_1, \ldots, X_n)$$

where outputs are considered negative inputs. We generalize the assumption of the U-shaped cost curve derived from the production function of Model III-3. For every set of positive P_i and P_j, assume that the minimum cost of producing every feasible set of outputs is obtained. Now, beginning with any initial basket of outputs, multiply each output level by all values $\theta > 0$ which yield feasible baskets, and trace out the minimum average cost curve for all feasible amounts of the fictitious commodity made up of the bundle-of-goods at unit level. It is required in our analysis that every such average cost curve be U-shaped in the sense defined in Model III-3. This will assure us, as it did in the earlier model, that a maximum profit equilibrium at zero profits can exist, whatever the ratios in which the community desires to produce goods.

The firm may be seen to be maximizing profits subject to the production constraint (126):

$$(127) \quad S = \sum_j \bar{X}_j P_j - \sum_i X_i P_i - \sum_j X_j P_j - \lambda(\bar{X}_1 - V(\bar{X}_2, \ldots, \bar{X}_n, X_{z_1}, \ldots, X_{z_m}, X_1, \ldots, X_n))$$

This is maximized when:

$$(128) \quad \begin{aligned}
&1. \quad \frac{\partial S}{\partial X_i} = -P_i + \lambda V^i = 0, && i = 1, \ldots, m \\
&2. \quad \frac{\partial S}{\partial X_j} = -P_j + \lambda V^j = 0, && j = 1, \ldots, n \\
&3. \quad \frac{\partial S}{\partial \bar{X}_j} = P_j + \lambda \bar{V}^j = 0, && j = 2, \ldots, n \\
&4. \quad \frac{\partial S}{\partial \bar{X}_1} = P_1 - \lambda = 0, && \\
&5. \quad \frac{\partial S}{\partial \lambda} = -\bar{X}_1 + V(\bar{X}_2, \ldots, \bar{X}_n, X_{z_1}, \ldots, X_{z_m}, X_1, \ldots, X_n) = 0 &&
\end{aligned}$$

when an interior maximum is assumed. Also, the second-order conditions require that

$$(129) \quad d^2S = \sum_u \sum_v V^{uv} dX_u dX_v < 0, \qquad u, v = i, j, J \neq 1$$

subject to (128), i.e., $dS = 0$.

Four sets of conditions are set forth in (128) for the multi-output firm which wants to maximize profits: (a) in equilibrium, the ratios of prices to marginal products for all inputs must be equal; (b) the ratios of prices to marginal outputs must be equal; (c) the factor of proportionality in (a) must be equal and opposite in sign to the factor of proportionality in (b); and (d) the factor of proportionality in (b) must equal the price of Y_1. These translate further into the conditions that the marginal cost of any output be equal to a common value whatever input is used to produce the marginal output, and that the marginal output of every good yield a zero marginal profit.

For the case where $m = 1$, $n = 2$, a small rise in P_2 will yield the following set of displacement equations, where we drop the subscript 1 on z:

$$
(130) \quad \begin{bmatrix} \lambda^\circ V^{zz} & \lambda^\circ V^{z1} & \lambda^\circ V^{z2} & 0 & \lambda^\circ \bar{V}^{z2} & V^z \\ \lambda^\circ V^{z1} & \lambda^\circ V^{11} & \lambda^\circ V^{12} & 0 & \lambda^\circ \bar{V}^{12} & V^1 \\ \lambda^\circ V^{z2} & \lambda^\circ V^{12} & \lambda^\circ V^{22} & 0 & \lambda^\circ \bar{V}^{22} & V^2 \\ 0 & 0 & 0 & 0 & 0 & -1 \\ \lambda^\circ \bar{V}^{z2} & \lambda^\circ \bar{V}^{12} & \lambda^\circ \bar{V}^{22} & 0 & \lambda^\circ \bar{\bar{V}}^{22} & \bar{V}^2 \\ V^z & V^1 & V^2 & -1 & \bar{V}^2 & 0 \end{bmatrix} \begin{bmatrix} \dfrac{\partial X_z^\circ}{\partial P_2} \\ \dfrac{\partial X_1^\circ}{\partial P_2} \\ \dfrac{\partial X_2^\circ}{\partial P_2} \\ \dfrac{\partial \bar{X}_1^\circ}{\partial P_2} \\ \dfrac{\partial \bar{X}_2^\circ}{\partial P_2} \\ \dfrac{\partial \lambda^\circ}{\partial P_2} \end{bmatrix} = \begin{bmatrix} 0 \\ 0 \\ 1 \\ 0 \\ -1 \\ 0 \end{bmatrix}
$$

and where single- and double-barred V-terms denote differentiation with respect to output once and twice respectively. We abbreviate (130) to

$$
(131) \qquad [V][dX] = [dP_2]
$$

The now familiar conditions for (129) to hold are that all bordered Hessians of the forms

$$
(132) \qquad \begin{vmatrix} \lambda^\circ V^{zz} & \lambda^\circ V^{z1} & V^z \\ \lambda^\circ V^{z1} & \lambda^\circ V^{11} & V^1 \\ V^z & V^1 & 0 \end{vmatrix}, \ldots, |V|
$$

have sign $(-1)^{s+1}$, where s is the number of columns or rows in the determinant, while, in addition, all unbordered Hessians of the forms

$$
(133) \quad \lambda^\circ V^{zz}, \begin{vmatrix} \lambda^\circ V^{zz} & \lambda^\circ V^{z1} \\ \lambda^\circ V^{z1} & \lambda^\circ V^{11} \end{vmatrix}, \ldots, \begin{vmatrix} \lambda^\circ V^{zz} & \lambda^\circ V^{z1} & \lambda^\circ V^{z2} & \lambda^\circ \bar{V}^{z2} \\ \lambda^\circ V^{z1} & \lambda^\circ V^{11} & \lambda^\circ V^{12} & \lambda^\circ \bar{V}^{12} \\ \lambda^\circ V^{z2} & \lambda^\circ V^{12} & \lambda^\circ V^{22} & \lambda^\circ \bar{V}^{22} \\ \lambda^\circ \bar{V}^{z2} & \lambda^\circ \bar{V}^{12} & \lambda^\circ \bar{V}^{22} & \lambda^\circ \bar{\bar{V}}^{22} \end{vmatrix}
$$

have the sign $(-1)^s$, as a consequence of the conditions on the bordered Hessians. As we have done in Models III-2 and III-3, we may prefer to maintain the symmetry of these conditions with those of consumer theory by eliminating from these determinants the λ° terms and converting the borders to prices by substitution from (128). Denoting $[V]$ thus altered by $[V^*]$, we obtain

$$(134) \qquad (\lambda^\circ)^{s-5}|V^*| = |V|$$

Obviously, these V^*-determinants must obey the same restrictions as to sign as the V-determinants.

When both outputs are held fixed, the conclusions of (80) and (81) hold. When the output of Y_2 is held constant, the theorems of (105), (106), (115), and (117) hold true.

One change occurs in the system by virtue of the multiple outputs now produced by the firm. In Models III-2 and III-3 there was only one marginal cost magnitude while in the present model there are two. In equilibrium, the marginal contribution to revenue of units of goods obtained for the same marginal cost must be the same. In the single output case, marginal cost was defined for a unit of the single product, but in the multiproduct case this unique unit no longer exists. Our choice of Y_1 as the dependent variable in the analysis implicitly defined marginal cost as units of *numéraire* per marginal unit of this good. If $\frac{1}{\lambda^\circ}$ is interpreted as the unit of "product" per value unit of marginal revenue, then $P_j\left(\frac{1}{P_1}\right) = \bar{V}^j$, or $\bar{V}^j$ is the effective number of units of "product" in terms of the unit of marginal revenue defined in the analysis. The marginal cost of the analysis, λ°, is the marginal cost of Y_1, and must always equal in equilibrium the price of Y_1. It can change only if P_1 changes. Thus, from (130),

$$(135) \qquad \frac{\partial \lambda^\circ}{\partial P_2} = -\frac{|V_{36}|}{|V|} + \frac{|V_{56}|}{|V|} = 0$$

However, the effective number of units of product contained by a unit of Y_2 will now rise and, taking account only of Y_2 as an output, its level of production must expand to obtain a new equilibrium.

The evaluations of the $\bar{s}_{z2}$, $\bar{s}_{12}$, $\bar{s}_{22}$, $\underline{\bar{s}}_{22}$, $\underline{\bar{\bar{s}}}_{22}$, $\underline{\bar{s}}^*_{22}$, $\underline{\bar{s}}^*_{21}$, and $\bar{s}^*_{22}$, are the same as those of Model III-3, as is $\bar{s}^*_{\lambda 1}$. Moreover, as we have just seen, $\bar{s}^*_{\lambda 2} = 0$. These s-terms must follow the conditions in (119), (120), (121), (122), and (124). The nonspecific solutions are of the same form as those of (118), with of course the addition to (118-3) of an output function for the firm for every output it produces.

Model III-4 is then speedily constructed. The consumer sector once more is unchanged:

(III-4-1) = (III-3-1) = (III-2-1) = (III-1-1)

Also, the aggregate demands for inputs and supplies of outputs are unchanged from those of Model III-3, when it is understood that they are derived from the model of the firm's decisionmaking in (127), (128), and (129):

(III-4-2) = (III-3-2)

The profits restriction on the firm is changed only in that the revenue term is now a sum of the value of outputs of the firm, not merely the value of one output:

$$\text{(III-4-3)} \qquad \sum_j \bar{X}^{\circ}_{vj} P^{\circ}_j - \sum_i X^{\circ}_{vi} P^{\circ}_i - \sum_j X^{\circ}_{vj} P^{\circ}_j = 0, \quad v = 1, \ldots, o$$

As before, all markets are cleared:

(III-4-4) = (III-3-4)

And firms' demands and supplies are defined, when the latter now include more than one good:

(III-4-5) = (III-3-5)

The only additions to the unknowns and equations of this model are firms' outputs of more than one good, and sufficient equations have been added to (III-4-5) to determine them. With the development of this most general Walrasian type of model, we have completed the task of depicting a production economy.

In building Model III-4, we have followed the Walrasian construction in requiring the elimination of profits in equilibrium. The economic interpretation of the role of the entrepreneur and the restrictions it places upon the supply of entrepreneurial ability have already been developed. It should be noted that it is quite allowable to build the possibility of positive profits into this type of general production equilibrium model. Depending upon the degree of mobility assumed among the production possibilities for firms, all firms in equilibrium may or may not be earning the same positive profits. These profits will have to be distributed to consumers in some determined manner, enter their budget constraints, and be used in the purchase of goods. This type of model is less puristic than the Walrasian, in that it does not compartmentalize all agents in the productive process by functional categories: the entrepreneur or other claimants are assumed to control some unspecified resources which entitle them to the receipt of the firm's profits. However, the major reason for not adopting such a model for our purposes—the derivation of operational theorems concerning the *directions* of movement of variables with equilibrium displacements—is that it makes no difference whether positive or zero profits are earned at the maximum-profit position. Whether external conditions beyond the firm's control do or do not, in the final result, nullify the initial movement of profits has no effect upon the firm's response to such stimuli.

Except for the postponed consideration of a simplified Model III-1, we have already given up the hope of being able to manipulate such models as III-4 as a whole—apart, that is, from its consumer and producer sub-systems. Therefore, our interest in the bases for evaluating the signs of expressions for the movement of variables with changes in the data of the large model is considerably lessened. Specifically, we shall again postpone consideration of the stability of the equilibrium of Model III-4 until Chapter 8. It will be interesting, however, to consider briefly the Hicksian slope conditions on the excess demand functions of the markets in this model, even though we shall not attempt to employ the restrictions they imply for the derivation of operational theorems.

3. The Hicksian Slope Conditions for a Production Model

Let E_i and E_j denote the excess demand for services z_i and goods Y_j respectively; i.e.,

$$(136)\qquad \begin{aligned} &1. \quad E_i = X_i - \bar{X}_i, && i = 1, \ldots, m \\ &2. \quad E_j = X_j + X_j^* - \bar{X}_j, && j = 1, \ldots, n \end{aligned}$$

From Model III-4, in equilibrium,

$$(137)\qquad \begin{aligned} &1. \quad E_i^\circ = 0, && i = 1, \ldots, m \\ &2. \quad E_j^\circ = 0, && j = 1, \ldots, n \end{aligned}$$

Now, let us exclude one equation, say that for E_1, the *numéraire,* in order to allow excess demand for a good to be nonzero when the other $n + m - 2$ markets are in equilibrium. Then, starting from a position of full general equilibrium, assume that P_2 is increased slightly, all other prices remaining constant, and that all markets depart from equilibrium as a result. Then, we may draw upon the analysis of Chapter 2, and if we denote markets generally by u, v, w, and so forth, for perfect Hicksian "stability" it is necessary and sufficient that

$$(138)\qquad E_2^2, \quad \begin{vmatrix} E_2^2 & E_2^u \\ E_u^2 & E_u^u \end{vmatrix}, \ldots, \begin{vmatrix} E_2^2 & E_2^u & E_2^v & \cdots & E_2^{m+n} \\ E_u^2 & E_u^u & E_u^v & \cdots & E_u^{m+n} \\ E_v^2 & E_v^u & E_v^v & \cdots & E_v^{m+n} \\ \cdot & \cdot & \cdot & \cdots & \cdot \\ E_{m+n}^2 & \cdot & \cdot & \cdots & E_{m+n}^{m+n} \end{vmatrix}$$

possess the sign $(-1)^s$, where s is the number of rows or columns in the determinant. If these same conditions hold for all configurations of included markets, then the equilibrium of Model III-4 is stable in the perfect Hicksian sense. If only imperfect stability is to characterize the equilibrium position, it is necessary and sufficient for every market that the last determinant in (138) and all of the principal minors with $m + n - 2$ rows and columns have signs $(-1)^s$. Now

$$\text{(139)} \qquad \begin{aligned} &1. \quad E_i^u = \frac{\partial X_i}{\partial P_u} - \frac{\partial \bar{X}_i}{\partial P_u} \\ &2. \quad E_j^u = \frac{\partial X_j}{\partial P_u} + \frac{\partial X_j^*}{\partial P_u} - \frac{\partial \bar{X}_j}{\partial P_u} \end{aligned}$$

The distinctive difference between the present economy and the complex exchange economy of Model II-2 is that income effects no longer exist on both sides of markets to allow the easy assumption that they tend strongly to counteract one another. Therefore, we must expect net aggregate income effects on the supply side of the markets for factor services z_i to tend normally to be positive: a rise in P_i will lead consumers in the aggregate in the case of a noninferior service to tend to take more of the factor service for their own consumption by virtue of the operation of the income effect, since a rise in its price increases their incomes and leads to larger purchases of all noninferior goods. Also, in the normal case, negative income effects will exist on the demand side of the markets for Y_j. The first type of income effect will move in the "destabilizing" direction, militating against the Hicksian adjustments, while the second type will tend to be "stabilizing."

If these income effects may be ignored, and only the substitution effects considered, then (139) becomes

$$\text{(140)} \qquad \begin{aligned} &1. \quad E_i^u = \sum_v \bar{s}_{iu} + \sum_c s_{iu} = \bar{S}_{iu} + S_{iu}, \qquad u = z_1, \ldots, z_m \\ &2. \quad E_i^u = \sum_v \bar{s}_{iu}^* + \sum_c s_{iu} = \bar{S}_{iu} + S_{iu}, \qquad u = 1, \ldots, n \\ &3. \quad E_j^u = \sum_c s_{ju} + \sum_v \bar{s}_{ju} - \sum_v \underline{\bar{s}}_{ju} = S_{ju} + \bar{S}_{ju} - \underline{\bar{S}}_{ju} \end{aligned}$$

The first and second of these sets of equations are sums of positive terms because the supply term is a quantity *less* consumer demand. Since s_{iu} and $\bar{s}_{ij}$ meet the same set of restrictions in (165) of Chapter 2 and (122) of this chapter, their sums over consumers and over firms will also meet these restrictions, as will the sums of these aggregate substitution effects. Therefore, since the restrictions on the substitution effects are those required for Hicksian perfect stability, if income effects can be neglected, the factor service markets will be perfectly stable. An exactly similar statement may be made about product markets when it is recalled that the $\bar{\bar{s}}$-terms are negative. Therefore, the economy should be perfectly "stable" in Hicks's sense unless income effects in one or more markets, and more especially in the factor service markets, interfere with the conformity of the substitution effects to the requirements.[29] Thus, once more, as in the case of the complex exchange economy, the only potential disturber of the stability of equilibrium of the Model III-4 type is the income effect, although in this case it need not be in an "abnormal" direction to effect this disturbance, nor can compensating income effects in the opposite direction be relied upon to damp down these sources of disturbance.

It is possible, of course, to apply the Negishi-Hahn theorem for gross substitutes, the Morishima theorem, and the Hicks net substitutes theorem on prices to the case of production theory, keeping in mind the treatment of outputs as negative inputs. Further, all the objections to the Hicksian slope conditions which were developed in Chapter 2 are applicable without change in the context of the production economy.

4. The Firm's Decisionmaking in an Uncertainty Environment

Up to this point we have been discussing the decisionmaking of the purely competitive firm in a perfect certainty environment: all exchanges were contract-certain and occurred at given equilibrium prices in a framework where tomorrow had no analytical meaning. The firm's choice of a strategy from its strategy space, therefore, was tantamount to the selection of an outcome, and it was never disappointed.

We shall ignore the game-theoretic environment, with its purposive, malevolent opponent, whose welfare is to a greater or lesser extent dependent upon the losses of the firm. We shall, therefore, move to the environment described in Chapter 2 as that of pure uncertainty for a brief consideration. Once more we shall have recourse to the most abstract "pure" case, as we did in the analysis of pure competition under perfect certainty, in frank acceptance of the reason that it is easier to handle analytically.

We may project from the analysis of consumer behavior the firm's behavior in an environment of risk. But absolute uncertainty is at once more difficult and more challenging. Can we speak of "the probability" of a state of nature ruling when we have no *a priori* basis for obtaining a probability distribution? Even if we are willing to adopt a "frequency-of-occurrence" outlook upon probability, does an event which will happen only once have a definable probability connotation? Or should we adopt a subjectivistic definition of probability, making of it a measure of the degree of likelihood we confer upon some "one-shot" event, given

[29] J. Hicks, (5), pp. 323–5.

a body of evidence, knowledge, and prejudice? Those who adopt the objectivistic or frequency-of-occurrence outlook upon probability might well reject any such approach to the problems of uncertainty, while those who adopt the subjectivistic attitude might seek to attach probabilities to states of nature and reduce the problem to a special case of risk.

Let us begin with a concrete problem that might face the firm in this environment. Suppose it is engaged in a highly style-dominated type of production—say women's fashions. For simplicity, let us say that the states of nature that might rule next market-day *when already produced goods are brought to the market for sale* are S_1 or "excellent business," S_2 or "good business," and S_3 or "poor business." Which of these states will indeed emerge on the market day is completely beyond the control of the firm, and the knowledge possessed by the firm about the relative likelihood of the states meets the two postulates for absolute ignorance described in Chapter 2, Section 6.

The firm's productive set-up is geared to the adoption of one line of womens' dresses for sale on the market-day. We shall delimit the firm's action space by describing three actions which compose it: A_1, the production of a line of dresses which, if business is good, will make large profits, but will do quite poorly if business is bad; A_2, the production of a line of dresses which will do less well if business is good, but which will limit losses if business is not excellent; and A_3, the production of a line of dresses which will make losses whichever state of nature occurs, but which makes more losses when business is excellent than when it is poor or good. This would happen, for example, if revenue were less than average variable costs per dress, so that the firm lost on every dress sold, but in the short-run might be better off to sustain the losses than to cease production and lose its personnel, its liaison with the market, and so forth.

Suppose the firm views its profits under all combinations of states of nature and of its own actions as in Table 3-1:

TABLE 3-1. THE FIRM'S PAYOFF MATRIX

		Nature's Strategies		
		S_1	S_2	S_3
	A_1	3	−1	−5
Firm's Strategies	A_2	2	0	−4
	A_3	−3	−2	−1

These figures may denote hundreds or thousands of units of *numéraire*.

The firm is engaged in a type of "game against Nature," an opponent which is really not a malevolent, maximizing rival acting purposively to thwart the firm's designs. Yet, one possible approach to the firm's decisionmaking is to assume it acts as if the criterion for optimal solutions were that for a game in which Nature did indeed have those attributes.

Obviously, this would be an assumption which would lead to very conservative behavior on the part of the entrepreneur. The maximin criterion rests upon this basis.

4.a. The Maximin Criterion

The payoffs in the cells of Table 3-1 are in units of *numéraire;* yet, as we have seen in Chapter 2, we really require some measure of preference among the outcomes which is unique up to a linear transformation. If we perform our operations upon the magnitudes of Table 3-1 we are implicitly assuming that money is linear with such utilities. That is, if u_{ij} is a von Neumann-Morgenstern utility value, we are assuming that

$$\pi_{ij} = a + bu_{ij}, \qquad b > 0 \tag{141}$$

It will be noted in our analysis of the firm's actions under perfect certainty, even though we employed a measure of firm "welfare" capable of measurement up to a linear transformation, that none of our results depended upon the assumption that the firm's preferences were linear with profits. Any ordinal function of profits which rose when profits rose and fell when profits fell could have been substituted in the S-function and, when maximized subject to the production function constraint, would have yielded the same results we obtained. We implicitly assumed that the firm preferrred more profits to less—an ordinal measurement suffices to allow decisionmaking on this assumption—without any need to specify by how much it prefers one level of profits to another. Thus, though we have at our disposal a more conveniently measured unit of input into the entrepreneur's psyche, we are still faced with the need to measure preference "outputs" and, similarly to our assumptions about the consumer, we required only an ordinal measure of these.

As in the case of risk in Chapter 2, our methods for attacking the decisionmaking of the firm in the present environment will depend upon a cardinal preference measurement. It is most convenient to assume that preferences are linear with *numéraire*, and, while it may be true in some range about zero profits, it probably would become grossly misleading if losses approached the moderately large or profits became extremely large. Evidence seems to be quite marked that gains are more heavily discounted than equivalent losses are, so that the firm will tend not to take a fifty-fifty chance of losing $1000 or making $1000. Losses endanger the firm's very existence, its credit standing, and perhaps the honor or self-esteem of the entrepreneur.[30] If, nevertheless, we introduce the assumption of linearity of preferences and *numéraire*, we introduce a bias toward

[30] Cf. F. Mosteller, (1), p. 400, for some experimental evidence that subjects were more inclined to take risks when they were net winners than when net losers, indicating a possible bias toward conservatism when "customary wealth" was threatened.

risk-taking which experience and intuition warn us not to expect in the real world.

If the losses became quite heavy, it might make excellent sense to adopt criteria for choosing a strategy which would protect against further losses, since their disutility would be far higher than their *numéraire* value would indicate. Thus, a firm which had in past market-days sustained large losses that began to encroach upon its capital base might well approach today's decisions for tomorrow's market-day with a most conservative pattern of rationality. Under such conditions the "maximin" criterion for choice in game-theoretic situations might have some appeal. That is, we might predict that the entrepreneur will adopt that strategy which yields the maximum of the minimum payoffs of each act available to him. For example, in Table 3-1, if he chose A_1, the maximum losses he might sustain would be 5; if he chose A_2, the maximum losses would be 4; and if he chose A_3, the maximum losses would be 3. Thus, the maximum of these three minimum gains would be -3, and under the maximin criterion we should predict that the firm would choose A_3. In so doing the firm is limiting the losses which would occur under any choice of Nature, and is implicitly acting as if Nature were a purposive opponent whose welfare depended upon the poor performance of the firm.

But, generally speaking, if these losses were not of tremendous significance relative to the existence of the firm as an entity, we should expect the entrepreneur to look upon such a pattern of rationality as overly conservative. For example, by choosing A_2 the firm puts itself into the position of being able to make a profit or at least avoid a loss merely by taking on the risk of losing 1 more than A_3's minimum loss. The fact of the matter is that Nature is not involved in a game against the firm, and the only justification for acting as if she were would exist under conditions which called for the degree of conservative thinking implicit in the criterion.

4.b. The Maximax Criterion

Suppose, then, that the firm went to the opposite extreme to choose that strategy which contained the largest payoff. In our case it would choose A_1 which, if Nature played S_1 would yield the entrepreneur 3 of *numéraire*. But this does subject the firm to the possibility of a loss of 5. Once more our judgment of the intuitive plausibility of such behavior would be related to the significance of such potential gains and losses to those "threshold" levels of losses and profits as may exist. In most cases, perhaps, most of us would brand the pattern of action implied by the maximax criterion overly rash.

We may use these two criteria as the upper and lower bounds of conservatism or pessimism: to assume that the worst will happen or that the best will happen, assign either state of Nature a probability of 1, and maximize on that basis seems to warrant these descriptions. Also, we have asserted that both of them may well have a place in the tool kit of the model builder under conditions which hinge upon the "critical" level of the firm's current losses or profits. But what of the more "normal" cases when these are neither potentially capable of threatening the firm's existence nor of becoming so large in the positive direction as to inspire a fervor to gamble? Are there any alternatives in this case of perfect uncertainty which would seem to offer a pattern of rationality more intermediate in its conservatism? Of all the possible alternatives we shall focus upon two: the criterion of insufficient reason and the minimax-regret criterion.

4.c. The Criterion of Insufficient Reason

One rule states that in the absence of knowledge about the likelihood of occurrence of each of a set of events, rational decisionmaking requires that all events be considered equally likely. The ability to use this rule with any degree of plausibility depends upon some satisfactory definition of the states of nature. Suppose, for example, that S_1 were the existence of a gross national product in excess of $560 billion at annual rates, S_2 were the existence of this magnitude in excess of $540 billion but less than $559 billion, while S_3 implied an annual rate between $0 and $539 billion. Following Bayes' lead we should assign to each of these states a .33 probability. But introduce now a fourth state, S_4, with a gross national product of between $520 billion and $539 billion. This introduction reduces the probability of S_1 to .25, even though nothing substantive in the problem has changed. Therefore, if this criterion is used, the states of nature must be defined to minimize this degree of variability of the probabilities with the arbitrariness of definition of the states.

Application of the criterion of insufficient reason in this manner to our problem means, in essence, that each state of nature receives a probability measure equal to $\frac{1}{n}$, where n is the number of strategies in Nature's set, and that these probabilities are used in a straightforward expected-value analysis exactly as that described in the discussion of consumer decisionmaking under risk. Thus, the expected value of A_1 is -1, of A_2 is $-.67$, and of A_3 is -2, and, therefore, under the rule that the expected value be maximized, the firm would be expected to choose A_2. In this case the result is the yielding of a more moderate type of strategy.

4.d. The Minimax-Regret Criterion

Another criterion designed to meet the conditions of the uncertainty environment is the Wald-Savage minimax-regret criterion. The concept of "regret" is not mere negative profits but rather a measure of the degree of "inappropriateness" a specific strategy entails if a given state of nature should rule *ex post*. For example, to use the case of the dress manufacturer, we ask, "If S_1 rules in the event, how inappropriate would have been the choice by the firm of A_1, A_2, and A_3?" Savage obtains the degree of "risk" or "regret" by subtracting each entry in the S_1 column from that column's maximum. Letting L denote the regret payoff, and P the *numéraire* payoff, Savage defines

$$L_{i\bar{j}} = \max_i P_{i\bar{j}} - P_{i\bar{j}} \tag{142}$$

where the barred subscript indicates that a specific column is the subject of the definition, and the first term on the right indicates that the maximum entry in the column is to be taken. If this is done for every column in Table 3-1, we obtain, for the problem in hand, the regret matrix shown in Table 3-2.

TABLE 3-2. THE REGRET MATRIX

	S_1	S_2	S_3
A_1	0	1	4
A_2	1	0	3
A_3	6	2	0

Basing the prediction of the firm's behavior upon this matrix rather than the payoff matrix of Table 3-1 implicitly takes into account the fact that often the best the firm can do is not very attractive, yet, if it must make a decision, it should concentrate upon what lies within its power. For example, compare column 3 in Table 3-2 with the same column in Table 3-1. In the latter the best the firm can hope to do is to lose 1. In Table 3-2, this is indicated by a zero entry, as is the "best" outcome in every other column. Thus, row by row, the absolute values of the outcomes are sacrificed in an emphasis upon the desirability of concentrating upon the best to be done in any situation, instead of upon those absolute values.[31]

This feature of the analysis can prove to be a disadvantage, of course, for reasons we have already discussed. The minimax-regret criterion treats equal positive and negative "losses" as equal in the firm's preferences. It postulates that the firm will have an equal amount of regret in obtaining 12 when it might have had 14, and in obtaining -4 when it might have had -2. In this fashion the asymmetry of gains and losses noted in the previous analysis is lost; in cases where the payoffs are both negative and positive, widely scattered about some moderate level, this

[31] L. Savage, (2), and (4), pp. 163–4.

symmetry of treatment can be quite troublesome. For example, suppose a firm faced the following payoff matrix:

TABLE 3-3. A PAYOFF MATRIX

	S_1	S_2
A_1	−40	52
A_2	−20	32

The regret matrix would be

TABLE 3-4. THE REGRET MATRIX

	S_1	S_2
A_1	20	0
A_2	0	20

If the entrepreneur follows the minimax-regret criterion by choosing that strategy whose maximum is the minimum maximum, he would find these two strategies equally attractive. However, the larger potential negative profits of the first strategy might well bias the firm against it. Let it be pointed out, however, that in this case the criterion of insufficient reason would lead to the same indifference among the strategies. This is merely to emphasize the fact that the basic problem is that of measuring preferences in a cardinal manner, and that such a measure need not vary in linear fashion with quantities of money. In seeking techniques which counterbias against this assumption, we are involved in an inefficient procedure, and their ability to do so or not to do so under certain conditions is only one facet of the criterion's intuitive plausibility.

A more serious objection to the intuitive plausibility of the minimax-regret criterion is its failure to meet the test of independence from non-optimal solutions. That is, it would appear plausible to expect that if a fourth strategy were introduced into the action space of the dress manufacturer which was not in itself the optimal one under a criterion, it should not make a previously nonoptimal strategy optimal. The adoption of the minimax-regret criterion can lead to just such an occurrence, however. For example, into the payoff matrix of Table 3-3 let us introduce a third strategy of the firm, A_3, with payoffs $(-10, 12)$. The regret matrix then becomes

TABLE 3-5. THE REGRET MATRIX

	S_1	S_2
A_1	30	0
A_2	10	20
A_3	0	40

Now A_1 has become nonoptimal, A_2 is clearly optimal, while A_3, which has had this impact upon the situation is not optimal. This is a questionable result of structuring the effective payoffs of the model—the regret payoffs—in columnar fashion.

In the dress manufacturing example, the criterion would lead to the choice of A_2 as that strategy which would minimize the maximum regret sustainable from the model. This is, as is the result of the criterion of insufficient reason, the intermediate solution.

It may well be that this method of approach to the problem of decisionmaking under absolute uncertainty for the firm and/or the criteria discussed above are not fruitful ones. Yet, the models resulting from their use are simple models yielding operational theorems which can be tested. As such they are worthy of further development and experimental use.

5. A Recapitulation

Throughout our treatment of the firm's decisionmaking, and frequently with lengthier treatments than otherwise required, we have sought to keep the symmetry of the entrepreneur's problem-solving and that of the consumer to the fore. This is true even though the analysis began with two different interpretations of the maximization processes involved in the two theories. Each decisionmaker is viewed as absorbing inputs with a view of obtaining outputs subject to a constraint: a budget constraint in the case of the consumer, a technological constraint in the case of the entrepreneur.

For the perfectly certain environment, the differences in the models analyzed were, as in the case of the consumer, dictated by differences in the form of the given informational functions. In the case of the theory of the firm these differences were not concerned with the uniqueness of measurability, since it is possible to assume cardinal measurability of the necessary magnitudes and develop the theory for this degree of arbitrariness. Rather, the differences were those of the technological nature of the interrelatedness of inputs and outputs.

The major difference between the form of the theorems derived from the four models and those derived from the consumer models was the lack of the income effect of price changes in the former. Only the substitution effect exists in the production model since the entrepreneur is under no budget constraint. Even with this simplification of the form of the expressions for evaluation, however, we were struck once again by the relatively short distance which the second-order maximization conditions take us in obtaining general information about the nature of responses of the variables in the models to changes in the data. The "own-price" impacts upon both inputs and outputs were evaluable while the "other-price" impacts were not in general evaluable. Where the nature of the profit maximization is merely that of cost-minimization, the own-price substitution effects upon inputs are similarly evaluable, and, in addition, the impacts upon marginal cost and the expansion effects upon inputs when outputs are increased may be restricted to some extent depending upon some further assumptions.

The only attempt we shall make to derive operational theorems from the complete production models will occur in Chapter 6; yet the application of the Hicksian "stability conditions" to the production model was examined; they were found to be exactly like those conditions for the exchange model, with the exception that compensating income effects on both sides of the market could no longer be assumed.

Lastly, a brief overview of some decisionmaking models for the uncertainty environment was taken, the nature of some of the difficulties in their use discussed, and the differences in their predictions demonstrated.

CHAPTER 4

THE INVESTMENT ECONOMY

1. The Introduction of the Time Dimension

Up to this point, every step has been taken to eliminate any meaningful impact of time upon the models presented. In current economic theory the movement of economic activity through the time dimension is meaningful in three ways: (a) time separates the responses of decision-makers from the emergence of the stimuli which inspire these responses, and the results of such actions from the actions themselves; (b) time distinguishes different types of information on the basis of which actions are taken, in that past, current, and future information are quite different in significant ways; and (c) time differentiates between the preferences of a consumer for a given bundle of goods available at different points of time and between the productivities of like bundles of inputs at different points of time. These three implications of temporal movement—leads and lags, expectations, time preference in the consumption and production senses—give rise to the most troublesome problems of economic theory. We must, therefore, alter the general equilibrium models we have been constructing and attempt to cope with some of these complexities.

We shall postpone any treatment of the first set of such problems, dealing with rates of change in responses of individuals or of groups, until the consideration of dynamic models in Chapter 8. To cope properly with these leads and lags implies the need for introducing dynamic forms of the variables into the equations of the model—an introduction which was not done explicitly to any degree by the earlier neoclassical theorists. Further, as we have seen, in order to attack the question of stability of equilibrium it is necessary to concern ourselves with the rates of change of responses to stimuli. For both reasons, therefore, we shall postpone this consideration of the first set of time-inspired problems.

Also, by virtue of the broad definition in which the first type of problem has been framed above, the money phenomenon may be subsumed in it. The use of money in purest form originates when a lag arises between the delivery of some good or service and the counterflow of other goods or services. The specific difficulties incurred analytically when the emergence of these money instruments is taken into explicit account will be discussed in great detail in Chapter 5.

The second type of problem, concerned as it is with expectations of the unknowable, has been to some extent dealt with in the discussion of the pure risk and pure uncertainty environments. We shall go further to discuss the general problem of multiperiod planning, although no attempt will be made to exhaust the analytical treatments in the literature.

2. The Investment Models

The greatest part of this chapter will concentrate upon the "classic" time problems grouped under the third heading, or those concerned with the nature of capital, the existence of interest, the determination of investment levels, and the emergence of a determinate rate of interest. We shall move from the simple statics of Model III-4 to a Model IV-1 which simply repeats the solutions of the former model on every subsequent market day. That is to say, the first model in this chapter consists simply in turning on a time switch to allow an unchanged specific solution to recur through time. In Model IV-2 we merely introduce the possibility of exchange of the eternal capital goods of Models III-4 and IV-1, to see how the phenomenon of consumer time preference is reflected in the markets for these assets. Model IV-3 introduces depreciating or wasting of the capital assets, removing the simplifying assumption of eternal asset life. And, lastly, in Model IV-4, we consider briefly the question of a progressive economy with positive net investment, rather than the zero net investment of Model IV-3.

In the presentation of Model IV-3—the core of the neoclassical investment analysis, with producible and wasting assets in full stationary equilibrium with zero net investment—we will pause to spend some time on the theories of capital and interest presently existing. Much effort will be devoted to analysis of Böhm-Bawerk's, Wicksell's, and Knight's theories, as they contrast with the straightforward Walrasian "productive" theory of capital and interest. Further, the insights obtained from Schumpeter's and Kaldor's work will be used to illumine some of the more difficult conundrums in this area of theoretical analysis. Finally, we shall again seek operational theorems from the submodels constructed to cope with the third set of problems.

2.a. Model IV-1: Eternal Capital Goods in the Stationary State

A stationary state is an analytical construction in which a particular or specific solution to a model (say Model III-4) repeats itself "week after week" without change. This implies that the data of the model are effectively constant: either rigorously fixed—individual by individual, piece of equipment by piece of equipment, and so forth—or immutable in the manner of Marshall's "motionless economy full of movement," in which individuals are born, mature, and die, and equipment is produced and wastes away, but without net changes of any type.[1] We shall, however, view the stationary state as a strictly analytical concept and not worry

[1] A. Marshall, (2), pp. 366–7.

about building into it a degree of movement for the sake of "realism" we do not need.[2]

As defined in Chapter 1, stationarity implies the movement of an economy through time, or, in terms of our models, a succession of market days whose outcomes are compared with previous outcomes and will be compared with succeeding outcomes by consumers and firms. These specific solutions are the results, ultimately, of the data underlying them, and, to the extent that the solutions are related to one another serially through time, such relationships must be reflected in the data of each market day. Which of the data of Model III-4 could form the bridges over time by means of which the values of the variables move "sideways" through time?

Consumer tastes are obviously phenomena which link one market day with another and provide two sources of possible temporal changes in the model: the consumer's preferences among the various bundles of goods on any market day may vary from one market day to the next, and his preferences among the same bundles at different points in time, seen from the vantage point of a specific market day, may vary. Viewed from the time axis, the first of these types of potential change is cross-sectional, while the latter is longitudinal.

Transformation functions similarly contain the potential for changes in time which can lead to changes in the specific solutions on any market day. As in the case of the consumer's taste functions, a cross-sectional type of change is that type which, for any market day, alters the relations of inputs and outputs which satisfy the function, and a longitudinal type of change is one which does the same thing for the relations of inputs and outputs of different market days. This latter type of movement presumes, of course, as the analogous consumer movement implies for preference functions, that the transformation function differs from those presented in Chapter 3 by including intertemporal relations among inputs and outputs.

Factor services may fail to be available in a constant flow through time by virtue of changes in the stocks available to the economy market day by market day. These obviously occur with new discoveries of resources or increases in the labor force for one or another reason. Also, however, when resources are not of infinite durability, and when their flows of factor service may be altered so that it is possible to use them more intensively one period than another, the temporal use pattern of the resources may vary.

Each of the three sets of explicit data in Model III-4, therefore, reconstructed to take into account the movement of the economy through time, contains the potential for displacement of a stationary solution. We may symbolize the three sets of data by U(Utility), T(Technology),

[2] Compare the similar position taken by Pigou in (1), p. 5.

and R(Resources), and the set ruling at a particular market day, t, as $(U, T, R)^t$. The current week we denote $t = 0$, the previous week $t = -1$, and all future weeks within the time horizon of the economy's decision-makers as $0 < t \leqq h$. Let us now ask: if we impose a time pattern of constancy upon the specific solutions of the model, what implications are involved concerning these data sets and what further data must we introduce into these sets?

Fortunately, all influences upon the behavior of consumers and firms not flowing from the three elements in the data set must originate in their price expectations. Current price expectations for any given consumer or firm include the prices expected to rule in every period $0 < t \leqq h$, and are most importantly influenced by the historical record of prices in the specific solutions of previous market days and by the current prices emerging on the present market day. It is most important to see, however, in our models, that no matter how expectations of the prices which will rule at the end of the current market day are influenced by the solutions of $t < 0$, such expectations can have no influence upon the solution for $t = 0$ unless the state of the data $(U, T, R)^0 \neq (U, T, R)^{-1}$. In this respect, our model, with its market day and fulfillment week, differs from the Hicksian model.[3] The solution for the current market day is independent of that body of influence which springs from past solutions and which shapes price expectations for the current market day except insofar as those solutions induce changes in the data sets. As long as we do not allow the path of the approach to an equilibrium to have any effect upon the equilibrium attained—by adoption of the Edgeworth recontracting technique or the Walrasian "bidding-by-chit" assumption, by which either party may break a provisional agreement if it is to his advantage—we need not worry about price expectations for market day 0 as a new element in the individual's data set. Therefore, in seeking to impose restrictions upon our data sufficient to yield stationary solutions for Model III-4, we may abstract from all paths of influence from the past upon present and future solutions by assuming that

$$(1) \qquad (U, T, R)^{t<0} = (U, T, R)^0$$

Insofar as the R-element in (1) is concerned, we have construed this strictly in the construction of Model III-4 by ruling out explicitly the

[3] These Walrasian markets are futures markets, with contracts made on the market day having relevance to consumption and production for the forthcoming week. Hicks's markets are constructed so that the previous week's production is sold for consumption and further production in the current week. In the Walrasian economy, planned production and consumption always equal realized production and consumption; consequently, on the succeeding market days, plans do not have to be altered in view of disappointed expectations as they do in Hicks's spot markets. Therefore, an important source of uncertainty in Hicks's model is eliminated in the models to be constructed in this chapter, allowing us to abstract in simpler form the complications of investment. See J. Hicks, (5), Ch. X, and R. Kuenne, (2), p. 346.

possibility of wasting capital assets, production of new assets, and any change in the distribution of existing assets among consumers.

But we have not yet considered the impact upon the current market day's solution of the influences flowing from the future, as vaguely perceived and registered in price expectations. If a consumer on market day $t = 0$ changes his expectation of the prices which will rule on $t = 1$ from the expectations he held on $t = -1$, since all such changes which materialize in the markets must in the event reflect changes in the data sets (U, T, R), it might seem that changes in expectations must be linked to expected changes in these data sets. But, of course, for the firm and the consumer, prices are data with an independent existence, and, in the thinking of the decisionmaker, expectations of them need not be tied rigorously to expected data changes. While this was also true of the impacts of past prices upon expectations of current prices at the start of the market day for $t = 0$, any such influence was eliminated by the natural unfolding of equilibrium forces during that market day. But this is not true of expectations of future prices and their impact upon current equilibrium prices, since $(U, T, R)^1$ does not yet exist. Therefore, for every consumer and every firm, we must specify a set of price expectations $\bar{P}$ with elements $[\bar{P}^1]$, $[\bar{P}^2]$, . . . , $[\bar{P}^h]$, for every period in the time horizon of the unit, and where the components of $[\bar{P}^t]$ are the prices of every good and factor service expected for that period.

Thus, the new complete data set for the economy may be written $(U, T, R, \bar{P})^t$, where these sets include, for every decisionmaker in the economy, his expectations of tastes, technological alternatives, resource ownership, and prices which rule on market day t. We assume that the elements in such data sets are unchanged throughout the current market day, even though current market prices are in a state of flux until the end of the market day.

We must ask, regarding this new element in the data set, what assumptions must be made concerning it in order to obtain stationary solutions. Of course, the requirement for stationarity is effective constancy, as in the case of the other elements of the data set.[4] That is, the

[4] E. Fossati seems to challenge this reasoning. He views general equilibrium as occurring instantaneously and simultaneously in all markets, and, to project such solutions through time, he believes two sets of assumptions are necessary: (a) one set to neutralize the time factor, with the holding of all objective data (in our analysis, (U, T, R)) constant, and the further assumption that every decisionmaker knows them to be constant; and (b) a second set to neutralize time's effects by making every decisionmaker's predictions perfect *ex post*. Every unit's plans must include every other's in order to anticipate the future exactly.

We would quarrel with the manner in which expectations are assumed to be formed in the first set of assumptions, as will be clear from the above discussion, and would substitute for the full-knowledge assumption that of constant price expectations. Except for this, the first set of assumptions is our own. But the second set is not a necessary set of conditions from our point of view until we introduce depreciation in the stationary flow. If the objective data are held constant, any set of price expecta-

elasticity of price expectations held in period $t = 1$ with respect to the discrepancies between price expectations held in period $t = 0$ and realized prices of that period must be zero. We should have little confidence in the stationarity of an economic equilibrium where expectations were not confirmed by events, but if the former were held constant, they would be no bar to such stationarity in Models IV-1 and IV-2.

Now that Model III-4 has been given an explicit time dimension, and before introducing markets for the exchange of assets, let us indicate how effectively time has been sterilized as an economic agent in this model by changing the price expectation element in the data set for period 0. That is, assume that full stationary equilibrium is disturbed by a rise in the expectations of an individual or firm of prices in period 1. How might these decisionmaking units readjust their purchases and sales to upset the ruling equilibrium? The consumer might act to change the time pattern of his sales of factor services and/or his purchases of goods, while the firm might act to change the pattern of input absorption and/or its output or sales pattern through time. Let us consider the potential actions of the consumer first under the assumption that he expects all prices in period 1 to rise a given percentage, k:

1. If the consumer postpones sales of factor services today, his inability to store such services and the eternal character of the assets that yield them imply that he will have wasted his resources. The consumer cannot shift the sale of resource services through time.

2. If the consumer increases his sales of factor services by decreasing his own consumption of such services and uses the increased revenue to buy consumption goods for storage until period 1, he would violate the prohibition of investment in our model. Similar restrictions would prevent him from reducing his consumption of goods Y_j today and storing for use tomorrow.

3. He cannot borrow from or lend to other spending units, nor can he sell or exchange any of his inheritance of assets.

From the viewpoint of the firm:

1. The firm would desire to increase current inputs at the expense of inputs in period 1 and to increase current outputs to hold for sale in period 1. But in Model IV-1, no process of production lasts beyond the current period, so that the first type of substitution cannot exist. Further, all output produced in period 0 must be sold in period 0 by virtue of the

---

tions that is held constant through time, even in the event of their continuous nonfulfillment, is consistent with stationary equilibrium in the present model. Of course, the stationarity would be more precarious than if the expectations were realized period after period, but it would none the less exist. Lastly, the implication that every unit must include the plans of every other unit in its own is overly demanding: we have shown that use of its own planning parameters is all that the unit need consider. Cf. E. Fossati, (2), p. 8, and (3), pp. 212–4.

constraints on the model, since the firm's value of product must equal its value of inputs and no borrowing facilities exist, nor does the firm own assets it could sell.

2. Under the restriction of (1), if the firm owned some scarce and depreciating factor, it would desire to postpone its use until period 1 with the purpose of increasing the net yield from that factor. But, of course, the firm does not own such resources, and therefore has no motive on this score to alter its current production pattern.

Suppose, now, that any subset of prices was expected to increase k per cent during the next period. Then it is easily seen that all of the above reasoning holds true and that no consumer or firm would have any reason for upsetting the status quo.

Thus, Model IV-1, which does not as yet possess capital goods markets, is inherently stationary since, even though price expectations exist explicitly, we have so structured the model that changes in them cannot upset the stationary equilibrium. All decisionmaking units are captives of time.

2.b. Model IV-2: Eternal Capital Goods, the Stationary State, and Asset Exchange

We shall now relax the assumption that the individual can neither invest nor disinvest, i.e., that he can neither buy nor sell capital goods Z_i, $i = 1, \ldots, m$, although we maintain the assumption that these goods are eternal and fixed in quantity for the economy under study. We create markets where the individual may exchange such assets, and, since he may purchase the services of these capital goods in factor service markets, the only reason why he would enter this first type of market is to adjust his holdings of current and future wealth.

It is to Irving Fisher that we owe the first, clear-cut mathematical statement of the essential sub-model in Model IV-2. We have taken some liberties with his presentation, but the analysis below is essentially Fisherian. He assumed a time horizon of $h + 1$ periods, $t = 0, \ldots, h$, over which consumers distribute a set of fixed period incomes, Z_{ct}, $c = 1, \ldots, s$, $t = 0, \ldots, h$, where c denotes the consumer. In the current period contracts may be made in week 0 to borrow or lend for the current week and any week in the future except the last. This gives rise to h markets for funds—one spot market and $h - 1$ futures markets—where the interest rates i_t, $t = 0, \ldots, h - 1$, are determined. Fisher showed that such transactions among individuals can be reduced to the sale and purchase of assets in these markets if such an interpretation is desired.

The individual's preferences for income over time may be transformed, for the given pattern of receipts $[Z_{ct}]$, to the function

$$M_c = M_c(X_{c0}, X_{c1}, \ldots, X_{ch}) \tag{2}$$

where the X_{ct} are the proceeds of loans made in period t when positive, or the payment of principal and interest on loans made in week $t - 1$ when negative. Then the maximization of satisfaction over time demands that for any two periods t and t^*, the following hold true:

$$\text{(3)} \qquad \frac{\dfrac{\partial M_c}{\partial X_{ct}}}{\dfrac{\partial M_c}{\partial X_{ct^*}}} = \frac{(1 + i_0)(1 + i_1) \cdots (1 + i_{t^*})}{(1 + i_0)(1 + i_1) \cdots (1 + i_t)}$$

subject to the constraint that the consumer not exceed in expenditure the present value of the income of the $h + 1$ weeks:

$$\text{(4)} \qquad \sum_t X'_{ct} = 0$$

where X'_{ct}, the present value of loans or borrowings and repayments in period t, is defined as

$$\text{(5)} \qquad X'_{ct} = \frac{X_{ct}}{(1 + i_0)(1 + i_1) \cdots (1 + i_t)}$$

Lastly, in each market for funds, demand and supply must be equated:

$$\text{(6)} \qquad \sum_c X_{ct} = 0, \qquad t = 0, 1, \ldots, h - 1$$

The unknowns in Fisher's system are: (a) the i_t which are h in number; (b) the $hs + s$ X_{ct}-terms; (c) the $hs + s$ X'_{ct}-terms; and (d) the M_c-values, s in number.

The number of equations is: (a) s in system (2); (b) hs in system (3); (c) s in system (4); (d) $hs + s$ in system (5); and (e) h in system (6). But one of the equations in (4) or (6) is redundant, since if all but one fund market is equilibrated and all individuals are remaining within the limits of the present value of their present and prospective incomes, the remaining fund market must be in equilibrium.

The excess of one unknown over the number of equations is eliminated by recognizing the relative nature of the terms on the right-hand side of equation (3). The expression $1/(1 + i_0) \cdots (1 + i_t)$ is the present *numéraire* value of a unit of *numéraire* on the market day of week $t + 1$. We may write such expressions P_t, and rewrite (3):

$$\text{(7)} \qquad \frac{\dfrac{\partial M_c}{\partial X_{ct}}}{\dfrac{\partial M_c}{\partial X_{ct^*}}} = \frac{P_t}{P_{t^*}}$$

It is then obvious, as in the simple exchange models of Chapter 2, that only the ratios P_t/P_{t^*} have significance, and only h of these exist; therefore $(1 + i_0)$ which is contained in all P_t terms may be arbitrarily set equal to unity, so that $P_0 \equiv 1$. When this is done the desired equality of unknowns and equations is obtained.

This simplest Fisherian model is a mere extension of the simple exchange Models I-1, I-2, and I-3, and the theorems of those models may be derived for it, depending upon the nature of the preference function. The fundamental magnitude is income—a keynote of Fisher's work—and the fundamental decision the allocation of a constant present value of income over time. The only opportunity available to the consumer is to borrow or lend at varying maturities (sell or buy assets on spot and futures markets.).

In a second model, Fisher allowed the present value of the income stream to vary by virtue of "investment" opportunities open to the individual. At a fixed set of interest rates i_t, $t = 0, \ldots, h$, a given stock of resources owned in period 0 will yield different streams of earnings and different present values of these streams depending upon the exact time pattern of "investment." Therefore, the individual may be seen as (1) seeking the maximum present value of earnings from all possible investment patterns, and (2) using the loan markets as in the first model to allocate this pattern of earnings optimally in consumption. The analysis for (1) is therefore grafted to the simpler model to obtain the second model. The Z_{ct}, or income in period t, are unknowns, and are related by the following function:

$$(8) \qquad Z_c(Z_{c0}, Z_{c1}, \ldots, Z_{ch}) = 0$$

This function describes all Pareto-optimal patterns of income receipts available to the consumer. That is, if h of the income terms are specified arbitrarily, the $h + 1$st is the maximum possible income obtainable for the given period. Thus, the function describes optimal investment patterns for the consumer for any pattern of interest rates which might rule, and includes implicitly the constraints upon his earning abilities set by his initial resource limitations. If it be assumed that (8) is continuous and differentiable, and that the investment opportunities in each period lead to identifiable streams of marginal returns, then the consumer may be assumed to maximize

$$(9) \qquad V_c = Z_{c0} + (1 + i_0)^{-1}Z_{c1} + [(1 + i_0)(1 + i_1)]^{-1}Z_{c2} + \cdots$$

subject to (8) as a constraint. This maximization leads to the conditions

$$(10) \quad \begin{aligned} &1. \quad 1 - \lambda^\circ Z_c^0 = 0 \\ &2. \quad [(1 + i_0)(1 + i_1) \cdots (1 + i_{t-1})]^{-1} - \lambda^\circ Z_c^t = 0, \\ &\qquad\qquad t = 1, \ldots, h \end{aligned}$$

in addition to (8), where λ is a Lagrangean multiplier. We add (a) $hs + s$ new unknowns in the Z_{ct} to the simple model, and (b) the s present value magnitudes V_c. To determine these we add the (a) s equations of (8), (b) the s equations of (9), and (c) the $s(h + 1) - s$ equations of (10), when the s λ° terms are eliminated.[5]

Our introduction of individual investment into the theory of simple exchange will follow the Walrasian path rather than that of Fisher, since it is believed that the former will possess some advantages when money is integrated into the system in Model V. Fisher has indicated that his theory of interest is similar to that of Walras and Pareto but he criticizes them for not developing a theory of income.[6] Pareto did, however, discuss the substitution of one income stream for another as a case of substitution in general, although Walras did not conceive of the investment opportunity as the substitution of income streams. Wicksell's criticisms of Walras center about the latter's rather superficial consideration of the nature of the consumer's problem, as we shall see below. The simplicity of the Walrasian "vision" of individual investment, however, makes it attractive as the starting point of our discussion of difficult material.

2.b.1. The Net Rate of Return

Let us consider "an investment" of some sort which yields g units of *numéraire* per week as a gross return and requires m units of *numéraire* per week as a maintenance cost to enable the gross return to be made. Suppose, further, that this "investment" is not eternal, but must be replaced at the end of t weeks of use. Then, from the gross return, in addition to maintenance, an amortization charge must be subtracted every week in order to calculate the net return per week on the investment. If a denotes this amortization cost, and C denotes the cost of the investment, we may write the rate of return over initial cost as

$$r = \frac{g - m - a}{C} \tag{11}$$

A problem arises, however, in that the amortization allowances are not merely held until the end of the t weeks, but are, week by week, invested themselves at some rate of return. Therefore, the rate of return on the investment, as given in (11), in being a function of amortization payments, is a function of the rate of return earned on amortization payments, for the higher this latter rate the smaller the amount that must be deducted week by week to replace the investment at the end of its life. Let r^* be this rate of return on amortization payments; then we seek some value, a, such that t such installments invested successively will

[5] I. Fisher, (7), pp. 288–315.
[6] I. Fisher, (7), pp. 518–9.

yield the cost of the good:

$$C = a \sum_{n=0}^{t-1} (1 + r^*)^n \tag{12}$$

But this is merely the requirement that the *amount* of a t-year annuity add to cost. From the formula for the amount of an annuity, therefore,

$$C = a\left[\frac{(1 + r^*)^t - 1}{r^*}\right] \tag{13}$$

or

$$a = \frac{Cr^*}{(1 + r^*)^t - 1} \tag{14}$$

Substituting into (11)

$$r = \frac{g - m}{C} - \frac{r^*}{(1 + r^*)^t - 1} \tag{15}$$

In the special case, and only in the special case, where $r = r^*$, so that amortization allowances earn the same net return as that earned on the investment, (15) becomes

$$r = \frac{g - m}{C} - \frac{r}{(1 + r)^t - 1} \tag{16}$$

or

$$Cr = (g - m) - \frac{Cr}{(1 + r)^t - 1} \tag{17}$$

and

$$C = (g - m)\left[\frac{(1 + r)^t - 1}{r(1 + r)^t}\right] \tag{18}$$

In this fashion, the cost of an investment is expressed in terms of the weekly return net of maintenance fees, the rate of return net of amortization and maintenance fees, and the life of the investment, on the assumption that amortization fees are reinvested for the period of their accumulation in projects which return exactly the same net return as the investment itself. Suppose that t approached infinity, so that $g - m$ were a perpetuity. If the numerator and denominator of the expression in brackets in (18) are divided by $(1 + r)^t$, and $t \to \infty$, (18) simplifies to

$$C = (g - m)\left(\frac{1}{r}\right) \tag{19}$$

Thus, given the cost of a perpetuity yielding $g - m$ units of *numéraire* per week forever, the rate of return is calculable from (19). Further, given the net rate of return r and the amount of the weekly payment

$g - m$, the *value* of the investment is given by (19). By this it is meant that if r is a general rate of return available to the investor, and if the specific investment in question yields $g - m$ units of *numéraire* per week in perpetuity, the investor should pay no more than C for it, for should he do so he would be neglecting more profitable alternatives.

It was Walras who saw that all investments could be reduced to dealings in perpetuities, although Fisher developed this viewpoint at greatest length. Walras created a fictitious commodity, E, embodied in securities which sold for P_e per unit, and whose unit of holding guaranteed the riskless receipt in perpetuity of one unit of *numéraire*. In (19), $m = 0$, $g = 1$ (unit of *numéraire*), and for r we may substitute the "net rate of return on capital goods," i_k. Then, in the securities market a price, P_e, is established for a unit of "net perpetual revenue," and from it and (19) follows the common net rate of return on assets:

$$P_e \equiv \frac{1}{i_k} \tag{20}$$

By means of these constructions, Walras was able under stationary conditions to reduce all capital goods to varying amounts of a homogeneous good on the basis of their earning power, since only this last quality is of importance in the consumer's decisions to invest or disinvest in them. Since it is eternal in Model II-2, a capital good Z_i earning P_i per week in stationary equilibrium will have a price P_{Z_i} equal to $\frac{P_i}{i_k}$, and Z_i will be the equivalent of $\frac{P_{Z_i}}{P_e}$ units of the security.

We interpret the mechanics of the investment-disinvestment process in the following terms: on the market day consumers desiring to buy or sell capital goods for current purchasing power enter the securities market and buy or sell securities at P_e. At the end of the week, these securities are redeemed by the individuals who sold them in capital goods to an equivalent value. No securities survive their week of issue.

Fisher used this device to illustrate the nature of all borrowing and lending as the purchase and sale of perpetual annuities. For example, a bond maturing in 20 years with a \$1000 redemption value and a coupon rate of 5 per cent can be reduced to the purchase of a perpetuity yielding \$50 per year and its sale 20 years later for \$1000. The present value of this investment opportunity is

$$V = \frac{\$50}{.05} - \frac{\$1000}{(1.05)^{20}} \cong \$623 \tag{21}$$

By (18) this may be seen to be the present value of \$50 per year for 20 years when the interest rate is 5 per cent. In similar fashion, the loan of

\$1000 at 5 per cent for one year is equivalent to the purchase of a perpetuity and the sale of it one year later for \$1000:[7]

$$V = \frac{\$50}{.05} - \frac{\$1000}{1.05} \cong \$47.62 \tag{22}$$

To introduce individual investment and disinvestment into the simple exchange model in a Walrasian manner, we assume that the consumer at the start of the market day of week 0 possesses a stock of capital goods, Q_{i0}, (we omit the consumer's subscript), and a set of price expectations $[\bar{P}] = [\bar{P}_{z_11}, \ldots, \bar{P}_{z_m1}, \bar{P}_{21}, \ldots, \bar{P}_{n1}, \bar{P}_{e1}; \bar{P}_{z_12}, \ldots, \bar{P}_{z_m2}, \bar{P}_{22}, \ldots, \bar{P}_{n2}, \bar{P}_{e2}; \ldots, \bar{P}_{z_1h}, \ldots, \bar{P}_{z_mh}, \bar{P}_{2h}, \ldots, \bar{P}_{nh}, \bar{P}_{eh}]$, where the second subscript denotes the time period for which the price is expected to rule. The consumer buys or sells capital goods week by week in the form of "securities" in such fashion as to plan to obtain that pattern of consumption over the $h + 1$-week period which is optimal for him. We shall allow the consumer to plan to disinvest completely over the $h + 1$-week period, so that he conceives his problem to be the distribution of his initial assets plus income over the whole period.

In the manner of specifying expectations, we have assumed implicitly that the consumer is sufficiently perspicacious to foresee that in future equilibria all capital goods will continue to be homogeneous in their ability to create purchasing power, and will be priced proportionately to their P_i. The factor of proportionality will be i_k, the rate of return on capital goods, which from (20) is seen to be the reciprocal of security prices. The possibility of expected changes in the value of factor services creates problems for us in using the Walrasian method, since it may destroy the consumer's willingness to receive the value equivalent of his securities or pay the value equivalent of his security sales in equal value amounts of *any* capital good. If he expects the price of machine tool services to rise in period 1 while all other factor services and the interest rate remain unchanged, he will obviously desire to shift his asset holdings into lathes and out of other factors. If we are not to introduce price expectations for every capital good in the system, therefore, we must enforce the assumption that the expectations of factor service prices for every consumer move in the same proportion from one future period to the next.

The value of the consumer's capital stock on the market day of week 0 is defined as

$$V_{e0} = \sum_i Q_{i0}P_{i0}P_{e0} \tag{23}$$

Let X_{e0} be the number of securities bought (if positive) or sold (if negative) during period 0, and $X_{e0}P_{e0}$ the change in capital stock value in

[7] I. Fisher, (4), pp. 194–5.

current prices accomplished in period 0. Then, the value of capital stock available in period 1 in period 0's prices is $V_{e0} + X_{e0}P_{e0}$. But this value may be expected to change by virtue of changes in the consumer's price expectations of (a) factor prices and/or (b) the price of securities. The first change may be introduced by multiplying the value by the ratio of period 1's and period 0's factor service prices; since all factor service price expectations move proportionately, any factor service price, say P_{z_1}, will serve in the ratio. In similar fashion, the current value of capital stocks available in week 1 must be multiplied by the ratio $\frac{P_{e1}}{P_{e0}}$. Then,

$$(24) \qquad V_{e1} = (V_{e0} + X_{e0}P_{e0})\left(\frac{P_{z_1 1}}{P_{z_1 0}}\right)\left(\frac{P_{e1}}{P_{e0}}\right)$$

and, more generally,

$$(25) \qquad V_{et} = (V_{et-1} + X_{et-1}P_{et-1})\left(\frac{P_{z_1 t}}{P_{z_1 t-1}}\right)\left(\frac{P_{et}}{P_{et-1}}\right)$$

where V_{e0} is defined in (23) and $X_{eh} = 0$.

Let us assume for simplicity that the seller of a security receives payment for it during the period and redeems it in capital goods at the end of the period. The buyer, therefore, does not earn income on the capital goods involved in the investment until the following period. Then, the income received in period t must be

$$(26) \qquad q_{et} = \frac{V_{et}}{P_{et}}$$

The consumer has a preference function for factor services and goods Y_j for every period in the planning horizon, and it is further assumed that the Y_j are not storable from one period to the next:

$$(27) \qquad M = M(X_{it}, X_{jt}), \qquad i = 1, \ldots, m \quad j = 1, \ldots, n \quad t = 0, \ldots, h$$

He is assumed to plan his investments and purchases over time in such manner that the economist, by maximizing (27) subject to the following constraints can predict his choices:

$$(28) \qquad T_t = V_{et} + q_{et} = \sum X_{it}P_{it} + \sum_j X_{jt}P_{jt} + V_{et+1}\left(\frac{P_{z_1 t}}{P_{z_1 t+1}}\right)\left(\frac{P_{et}}{P_{et+1}}\right) = 0$$

or

$$\text{(29)}\quad \begin{aligned} &1.\quad T_t = q_{et} - \sum_i X_{it}P_{it} - \sum_j X_{jt}P_{jt} - X_{et}P_{et} = 0, \qquad t = 0, \ldots, h-1 \\ &2.\quad T_h = V_{eh} + q_{eh} - \sum_i X_{ih}P_{ih} - \sum_j X_{jh}P_{jh} = 0 \end{aligned}$$

We multiply each of these $h + 1$ constraints by a different Lagrangean multiplier, λ_t, form the function,

$$\text{(30)}\qquad S = M(X_{it}, X_{jt}) + \sum_t \lambda_t T_t$$

and maximize S. We obtain the $h + 1$ equations of (29) in differentiating S with respect to the λ_t terms and, in addition, the following:

$$\text{(31)}\quad \begin{aligned} &1.\quad \frac{\partial S}{\partial X_{et}} = \sum_{t'=t+1}^{h-1} \lambda_{t'}^{\circ}\left(\frac{P_{z_1t'}}{P_{z_1t}}\right) - \lambda_t^{\circ}P_{et} + \lambda_h^{\circ}\left(\frac{P_{z_1h}}{P_{z_1t}}\right)(1 + P_{et}) = 0, \qquad t = 0, \ldots, h-1 \\ &2.\quad \frac{\partial S}{\partial X_{it}} = M^{it} + \lambda_t^{\circ}P_{it} = 0, \qquad t = 0, \ldots, h \\ &3.\quad \frac{\partial S}{\partial X_{jt}} = M^{jt} - \lambda_t^{\circ}P_{jt} = 0, \qquad t = 0, \ldots, h \end{aligned}$$

Lastly,

$$\text{(32)}\qquad d^2S < 0$$

The conditions of (31-2) and (31-3) are the familiar equilibrium conditions of Models I-1, I-2, and I-3, with a modification. They instruct the decisionmaker to make the last unit of each factor service and consumer good divided by price equal to a common factor, period by period. However, the same good in two different periods, even if its price were equal in both, must be adjusted to two different λ-values. We shall term these λ-terms "discount factors" in the present context, and will now derive their relative values from the conditions of (31-1).

We may rewrite these conditions as follows for $\frac{\lambda_h^{\circ}}{\lambda_{h-1}^{\circ}}$

$$\text{(33)}\qquad \frac{\lambda_h^{\circ}}{\lambda_{h-1}^{\circ}} = \frac{P_{z_1h-1}\,P_{eh-1}}{P_{z_1h}(1 + P_{eh-1})}$$

Under the assumptions (a) that the expected prices of factor services are constant from period to period and equal to current prices, and (b) that the expected prices of securities are constant at the current level, (33) becomes

$$\frac{\lambda_h^\circ}{\lambda_{h-1}^\circ} = \frac{P_e}{1 + P_e} = \frac{1}{1 + i_k} \tag{34}$$

Further, since

$$\lambda_{h-2}^\circ P_e = \lambda_{h-1}^\circ + \lambda_h^\circ(1 + P_e) \tag{35}$$

it follows that

$$\frac{\lambda_{h-2}^\circ}{\lambda_{h-1}^\circ} = 1 + i_k \tag{36}$$

and

(37)

$$1. \quad \frac{\lambda_{h-3}^\circ}{\lambda_{h-1}^\circ} = (1 + i_k)^2$$

$$2. \quad \frac{\lambda_{h-n}^\circ}{\lambda_{h-m}^\circ} = (1 + i_k)^{n-m}$$

These relationships state that the marginal preference value of a unit of expenditure on goods in period $t + b$ should be, in equilibrium, $\frac{1}{(1 + i_k)^b}$ times that of period t, since a price in period t is, in terms of the prices of period $t + b$, effectively $P_{jt}(1 + i_k)^b$, because P_{jt} units of *numéraire* invested in period t will have grown to this amount by period $t + b$; prices in period $t + b$ are related to prices in period t as $P_j(1 + i_k)^{-b}$.

We may form the ratios $\frac{\lambda_1^\circ}{\lambda_0^\circ}, \frac{\lambda_2^\circ}{\lambda_0^\circ}, \ldots, \frac{\lambda_h^\circ}{\lambda_0^\circ}$, since only relative values are needed in system (31). Then, for example, from (31-3) we may illustrate the equilibrium conditions for inter-period purchases as follows:

$$\frac{M^{jt}}{M^{j0}} = \frac{P_{jt}}{P_{j0}(1 + i_k)^t} \tag{38}$$

Thus, in equilibrium, the marginal preference ratios must be equal to the ratio of the discounted prices.

We may solve out system (31) to obtain the nonspecific solutions for the consumer. Since we are interested only in his current choices, i.e., his choices in period 0, we include only these variables. For simplicity, we shall omit the time subscript 0 from any magnitude referring to the current period. Then, for individual c, where $[\bar{P}_c]$ denotes the vector of price expectations over his whole time horizon, we may write these nonspecific solutions as:

(39)

$$1. \quad X_{cj\neq 1}^\circ = H_{cj\neq 1}(P_2, \ldots, P_n, P_{z_1}, \ldots, P_{z_m}, P_e; [Q_c], [\bar{P}_c]) = H_{cj\neq 1}([P]; [Q_c], [\bar{P}_c])$$

$$2. \quad \bar{X}_{ci}^\circ = Q_{ci} - H_{ci}([P]; [Q_c], [\bar{P}_c])$$

$$3. \quad X_{ce}^\circ = H_{ce}([P]; [Q_c], [\bar{P}_c])$$

$$4. \quad X_{c1}^\circ = \sum_i \bar{X}_{ci}^\circ P_i - \sum_{j\neq 1} X_{cj}^\circ P_j - X_{ce}^\circ P_e$$

There is a seeming anomaly in this system which should be pointed out explicitly. The individual is planning to reduce his holdings of wealth to zero at the end of period h. As of period 0, therefore, he is looking forward to disinvestment over a shorter or longer period $h + 1$ weeks in length. Suppose his initial stocks of wealth, current prices, expected prices, and his tastes dictate that $X_e = 0$ in period zero. Now, when period 0 has become history and the current period is period 1, he will plan again to liquidate all of his holdings by the end of week $h + 1$, and if current prices are the same as period 0's prices, expected prices are the same for all future periods through $h + 1$, and his tastes are constant, he will once more be led to $X_e = 0$. Thus, this individual and every individual in the economy may plan continuously in a framework of disinvestment and yet be led to a stationary income level through time. The assumption that the individual so plans over a period $h + 1$ weeks in length, where h need not approach infinity, is not inconsistent with individual and aggregate stationarity.

We may now proceed to the construction of Model IV-2. The first set of equations is one for which no need was found in earlier models but which was in fact available. It is the set of individual demand and supply equations:

(IV-2-0) = (39), $\qquad c = 1, \ldots, s$

The aggregate consumer functions are obtained by summation:

(IV-2-1)

$$
\begin{aligned}
&1. \quad X_{j\neq 1} = H_{j\neq 1}([P]; [Q_1], \ldots, [Q_s], [\bar{P}_1], \ldots, [\bar{P}_s]) \\
&\qquad\quad\;\, = H_{j\neq 1}[P]; [Q], [\bar{P}]) \\
&2. \quad \bar{X}_i = Q_i - H_i([P]; [Q], [\bar{P}]) \\
&3. \quad X_e = H_e([P]; [Q], [\bar{P}]) \\
&4. \quad X_1 = \sum_i \bar{X}_i P_i - \sum_{j\neq 1} X_j P_j - X_e P_e
\end{aligned}
$$

Industrial demands for inputs and supplies of outputs are repeated unchanged:

(IV-2-2) = (III-4-2)

Profits of all firms must be zero:

(IV-2-3) = (III-4-3)

We require that all markets except that for securities, to be dealt with in (IV-2-6), be cleared:

(IV-2-4) = (III-4-4)

The definition of firms' input demands and output supplies is unaltered:

(IV-2-5) = (III-4-5)

Market equilibrium in period 0 requires that aggregate net investment be zero:

$$X_e^\circ = 0 \qquad \text{(IV-2-6)}$$

However, for true stationarity, it is further required that every individual net investment magnitude be zero, since if within the requirement (IV-2-6) individuals are net investors and disinvestors, the *status quo* will be upset period after period. Of course, it is possible to imagine two groups of consumers, one of which is investing and the other disinvesting equivalently, forming exact mirror images of each other period by period in terms of goods consumed. But this obviously imposes severe and unacceptable restrictions upon the nature of the taste functions of both groups. Therefore, for our Model IV-2 in stationary equilibrium, the economy is assumed to have evolved through a sufficient number of periods that every consumer has had time to adjust his stock of wealth to that level which he will maintain indefinitely, even with a finite planning period.

But the fact that no exchanges of capital goods or securities occur in equilibrium does not mean that the prices of capital goods and securities fail to emerge from these markets. The price P_e° is determined at that level where demand for securities equals supply of securities at a zero magnitude. In two dimensions, the demand and supply curves meet at P_e° on the vertical axis, the supply curve rising and the demand curve falling from this point. Any departure of price from P_e° would lead to a non-zero excess demand for securities. Further, the redemption value of securities in terms of capital goods implies the price of each capital good. If the capacity to earn one unit of *numéraire* in perpetuity is valued at P_e, the capacity to earn a net of P_i units per week in perpetuity must be valued at

$$P_{Z_i}^\circ = P_i^\circ P_e^\circ \qquad \text{(IV-2-7)}$$

To the equations of Model III-4 (and Model IV-1) we have added (a) the $sm + sn + s$ equations of (IV-2-0); (b) one investment equation to (IV-2-1); (c) the one equation of (IV-2-6); and (d) the m equations of (IV-2-7). To the unknowns of the earlier models we have added (a) the $sm + sn + s$ individual demand and supply terms, X_{cj}°, $\bar{X}_{ci}^\circ$, and X_{ce}; (b) the single X_e° variable; (c) the single P_e° variable; and (d) the m capital good prices $P_{Z_i}^\circ$. The net balance is maintained.

The further conditions necessary to make this equilibrium a stationary one are discussed throughout this chapter but may be summarized as the following: (1) the consumers must plan in the current period on the basis of price expectations of h future periods, where h may vary among individuals, but is constant for all individuals as time evolves; (2) the consumers must, period after period, plan in the same manner as discussed in (1), pushing one period ahead the terminal period of their planning horizon; (3) prices for the h future periods must be fixed in each consumer's mind and, good by good, service by service, need not be identical for all periods in the future, although factor service prices must be expected to change in the same proportion by all individuals; (4) capital goods must be eternal and fixed in the aggregate for each type, including in the definition of capital goods all assets yielding factor services; (5) technology must be constant; and (6) consumer tastes over time, including attitudes to future goods, must be unchanged and meet certain conditions of the type discussed in Chapter 9 to guarantee that every consumer will approach a zero net investment expenditure.

2.b.2. Displacement of Equilibrium in the Consumer Sub-Model

We shall now separate from Model IV-2 the individual consumer's sub-model contained in (31) and (32) and operate upon it to derive operational theorems. Let $m = 1$, $n = 1$, $t = 2$, $P_{z0} = P_{z1}$, $P_{10} = P_{11} \equiv 1$, and $P_{e0} = P_{e1}$, so that we may use P_z and P_e to symbolize current and expected prices. These assumptions are made because we shall be concerned for the most part in the theory of investment with the stationary state, and, although the assumptions are not necessary to obtain it in the present model, they are plausible for such a state and will become necessary for stationarity in future models. We shall assume P_z (the current *and expected* price of the factor service) changes slightly. The system of equilibrium displacement equations becomes:

$$(40)\quad \begin{bmatrix} M^{z0,z0} & M^{z0,z1} & M^{z0,10} & M^{z0,11} & 0 & -P_z & 0 \\ M^{z0,z1} & M^{z1,z1} & M^{z1,10} & M^{z1,11} & 0 & 0 & -P_z \\ M^{z0,10} & M^{z1,10} & M^{10,10} & M^{10,11} & 0 & -1 & 0 \\ M^{z0,11} & M^{z1,11} & M^{10,11} & M^{11,11} & 0 & 0 & -1 \\ 0 & 0 & 0 & 0 & 0 & -P_e & 1+P_e \\ -P_z & 0 & -1 & 0 & -P_e & 0 & 0 \\ 0 & -P_z & 0 & -1 & 1+P_e & 0 & 0 \end{bmatrix} \begin{bmatrix} \dfrac{\partial X^{\circ}_{z0}}{\partial P_z} \\ \dfrac{\partial X^{\circ}_{z1}}{\partial P_z} \\ \dfrac{\partial X^{\circ}_{10}}{\partial P_z} \\ \dfrac{\partial X^{\circ}_{11}}{\partial P_z} \\ \dfrac{\partial X^{\circ}_{e0}}{\partial P_z} \\ \dfrac{\partial \lambda^{\circ}_{0}}{\partial P_z} \\ \dfrac{\partial \lambda^{\circ}_{1}}{\partial P_z} \end{bmatrix} = \begin{bmatrix} \lambda^{\circ}_0 \\ \lambda^{\circ}_1 \\ 0 \\ 0 \\ 0 \\ X_{z0} \\ X_{z1} \end{bmatrix}$$

Let us designate the matrix of (40) as $[M]$. Then, from the analysis of Model I-4, it is clear that the impact of a change in current and expected prices upon consumer demands is simply the sum of $h + 1$ substitution and $h + 1$ income effects. In the present case, a change in P_z implies a change in P_{z0} and P_{z1}, and the total effects will include substitution and income effects for both price changes:

$$(41)\quad \begin{aligned} &1. \quad \frac{\partial X_{z0}^{\circ}}{\partial P_z} = \lambda_0^{\circ}\frac{|M_{11}|}{|M|} - \lambda_1^{\circ}\frac{|M_{21}|}{|M|} - X_{z0}\frac{|M_{61}|}{|M|} + X_{z1}\frac{|M_{71}|}{|M|} \\ &\qquad = s_{z0,z0} + s_{z0,z1} + r_{z0,z0} + r_{z0,z1} \\ &2. \quad \frac{\partial X_{z1}^{\circ}}{\partial P_z} = -\lambda_0^{\circ}\frac{|M_{12}|}{|M|} + \lambda_1^{\circ}\frac{|M_{22}|}{|M|} + X_{z0}\frac{|M_{62}|}{|M|} - X_{z1}\frac{|M_{72}|}{|M|} \\ &\qquad = s_{z1,z0} + s_{z1,z1} + r_{z1,z0} + r_{z1,z1} \end{aligned}$$

Also:

$$(42)\quad \begin{aligned} &1. \quad \frac{\partial X_{e0}}{\partial P_z} = \lambda_0^{\circ}\frac{|M_{15}|}{|M|} - \lambda_1^{\circ}\frac{|M_{25}|}{|M|} - X_{z0}\frac{|M_{65}|}{|M|} + X_{z1}\frac{|M_{75}|}{|M|} \\ &\qquad = s_{e0,z0} + s_{e0,z1} + r_{e0,z0} + r_{e0,z1} \\ &2. \quad \frac{\partial \lambda_0^{\circ}}{\partial P_z} = -\lambda_0^{\circ}\frac{|M_{16}|}{|M|} + \lambda_1^{\circ}\frac{|M_{26}|}{|M|} + X_{z0}\frac{|M_{66}|}{|M|} - X_{z1}\frac{|M_{67}|}{|M|} \\ &\qquad = s_{\lambda 0,z0} + s_{\lambda 0,z1} + r_{\lambda 0,z0} + r_{\lambda 0,z1} \end{aligned}$$

The necessary and sufficient conditions that $d^2S < 0$ subject to $dS = 0$ are that all bordered Hessian determinants of the forms $|M_{33,44,55}|$, $|M_{44,55}|$, $|M_{55}|$, and $|M|$, alternate in sign negative and positive. From these we may generalize the conclusions of Model I-4 for (41) and (42-2), treating these expressions exactly as if two prices had changed in our equilibrium displacement of those models rather than only one.

Also, from (29-2),

$$(43)\qquad (1 + P_e)\frac{\partial X_{e0}}{\partial P_z} = X_{z1} + P_z\frac{\partial X_{z1}^{\circ}}{\partial P_z} + \frac{\partial X_{11}^{\circ}}{\partial P_z}$$

from which we may derive the relationships between the substitution and income effects involved, although they prove to have little value in evaluating (42-1).

Further, had we continued the distinction between current and expected prices, we could have treated changes in expected prices exactly as we treated changes in the prices of Model I-4. Thus the introduction of future time periods into the analysis may be absorbed with the tools already at hand.

What of a change in P_e? If P_e changes, the two column vectors of (40) are modified accordingly, and we obtain:

(44)

$$1.\quad \frac{\partial X^{\circ}_{z0}}{\partial P_e} = (\lambda^{\circ}_0 - \lambda^{\circ}_1)\frac{|M_{51}|}{|M|} - \left(\frac{q_{e0}}{P_e} + X_{e0}\right)\frac{|M_{61}|}{|M|} + \left(\frac{q_{e0}}{P_e} - X_{e0}\right)\frac{|M_{71}|}{|M|}$$

$$2.\quad \frac{\partial X^{\circ}_{z1}}{\partial P_e} = (\lambda^{\circ}_1 - \lambda^{\circ}_0)\frac{|M_{52}|}{|M|} + \left(\frac{q_{e0}}{P_e} + X_{e0}\right)\frac{|M_{62}|}{|M|} - \left(\frac{q_{e0}}{P_e} - X_{e0}\right)\frac{|M_{72}|}{|M|}$$

$$3.\quad \frac{\partial X_{e0}}{\partial P_e} = (\lambda^{\circ}_0 - \lambda^{\circ}_1)\frac{|M_{55}|}{|M|} - \left(\frac{q_{e0}}{P_e} + X_{e0}\right)\frac{|M_{65}|}{|M|} + \left(\frac{q_{e0}}{P_e} - X_{e0}\right)\frac{|M_{75}|}{|M|}$$

or

(45)

$$1.\quad \frac{\partial X^{\circ}_{z0}}{\partial P_e} = s_{z0,e} + r_{z0,e} = s_{z0,e0} + s_{z0,e1} + r_{z0,e0} + r_{z0,e1}$$

$$2.\quad \frac{\partial X^{\circ}_{z1}}{\partial P_e} = s_{z1,e} + r_{z1,e} = s_{z1,e0} + s_{z1,e1} + r_{z1,e0} + r_{z1,e1}$$

$$3.\quad \frac{\partial X^{\circ}_{e0}}{\partial P_e} = s_{e0,e} + r_{e0,e} = s_{e0,e0} + s_{e0,e1} + r_{e0,e0} + r_{e0,e1}$$

A rise in P_e is equivalent to a uniform percentage rise in all prices in a future period. If we treat the two goods in the consumer's budget in period 1 as one good, since a single good cannot be inferior, less of this fictitious single good must be expected to be purchased in the consumer's plans. At constant expected prices of the goods, this implies a fall in expected spending in week 1 and a rise in expenditure in week 0. This may be proved as follows.

The determinant $|M|$, when evaluated by cofactors, may be written

$$(46)\qquad M = P_e|M_{56}| + (1 + P_e)|M_{57}|$$

or, by virtue of the symmetry of $[M]$

$$(47)\qquad \begin{aligned} M &= P_e|M_{65}| + (1 + P_e)|M_{75}| \\ &= P_e(|M_{65}| + |M_{75}|) + |M_{75}| \end{aligned}$$

But it is easily shown that $|M_{65}| = |M_{75}|$.[8] Therefore, since $|M| < 0$ it

[8] In $[M_{65}]$ add the second column to the first column to get a new first column, and the fourth column to the third column to obtain a new third column. In $[M_{75}]$ add the first to the second column for a new second column and the third to the fourth column for a new fourth column. The two new matrices may be made identical by interchanging two pairs of columns in one of them.

follows that $|M_{65}| = |M_{75}| < 0$; and, from (44-3), that $r_{e0,e} < 0$. From the second-order equilibrium conditions, $s_{e0,e} < 0$. Therefore, $\dfrac{\partial X_e^\circ}{\partial P_e} < 0$ when $P_e > 0$.

But it must also be shown that the elasticity of investment with respect to P_e is greater than unity, so that the amount invested, not only X_e°, does in fact fall when P_e rises. The elasticity of demand for securities is

$$(48) \qquad \frac{\partial X_{e0}^\circ}{\partial P_e}\frac{P_e}{X_{e0}^\circ} = \left[(\lambda_0^\circ - \lambda_1^\circ)\frac{P_e}{X_{e0}^\circ}\right]\left[\frac{|M_{55}|}{|M|}\right] - 2P_e\left[\frac{|M_{65}| + |M_{75}|}{|M|}\right] = e_e$$

From (31-1)

$$(49) \qquad e_e = \frac{\lambda_1^\circ}{X_{e0}^\circ}\left(\frac{|M_{55}|}{|M|}\right) - 4P_e\frac{|M_{65}|}{|M|}$$

To show that $e_e < -1$, it is required to show that the right-hand side of (49) < -1. Rewriting, we must show that

$$(50) \qquad \lambda_1^\circ|M_{55}| - 4X_{e0}^\circ P_e|M_{65}| < -X_{e0}|M|$$

But $|M| < 0$, $|M_{55}| < 0$, and we have just shown $|M_{65}| < 0$; therefore,

$$(51) \qquad e_e < -1$$

when

$$(52) \qquad \lambda_1^\circ > 0,\ P_e \geqq 0$$

We conclude, therefore, that under the conditions of our simple two-period model, the consumer will always reduce the number of securities he purchases and the value of such investment when the price of securities rises.

The impact of a rise in P_e upon current consumption of (say) z will lead to a larger expenditure on current goods taken as a whole if the fall in interest rate does not reduce income more than the fall in $X_{e0}P_e^\circ$ raises current spending; whether or not X_{z0} rises will depend upon its substitution and "wherewithal" effects. The r-terms in the analysis of this investment subsystem of Model IV-2 are no longer the "income effects of price changes" as they were in Models I-1, I-2, and I-3, but are "income-wealth" or "wherewithal" effects, since the consumer may be disinvesting as well as consuming income.

2.b.3. The Walrasian Use of Net Perpetual Revenue, E

Although Walras introduced the concept of net perpetual revenue, E, with a unit price, P_e, into economic theorizing, his use of the construct was somewhat different from its use in Model IV-2. Walras simply introduced amounts of perpetual revenue, X_e, measured in units of *numéraire* per period, into the utility function, and made this new good fully coordinate with current Y_j and z_i. Thus, all of the complications of time and expectations with which we had to cope were simply abstracted from with the facile assumption that the consumer sought to make the marginal utility of X_e divided by its price, P_e, equal to the marginal utility of income, $\lambda°$.

To introduce savings in this way is to assume implicitly the existence of stationary conditions: it is to postulate that the consumer expects P_{e0} and all other prices to continue indefinitely, unless of course the utility of present purchases of net perpetual revenue is a function of the expected prices in some nonexplicit manner. Moreover, although this is not a weakness inherent in the concept of net perpetual revenue or in Walras' handling of it, such a method does permit Walras to ignore in his discussion of investment models one of the most important theoretical debates of his time—that concerning the existence and role of time preference. We shall discuss this fully below.

Drawing upon the theoretical constructions of F. H. Knight, Friedman has criticized the Walrasian model in yet another respect. As we noted, Walras' treatment requires the introduction of q_{e0} and X_{e0} (in our terminology) into the preference functions of consumers, since the consumer varies X_{e0} marginally to arrive at the equilibrium amount $q_{e0} + X_{e0}$ of net perpetual revenue. Friedman contends that this is not a valid procedure because these two magnitudes have different dimensions: the second, he says, has the dimension "income per time period per time period," while the first has the dimension "income per time period." It is difficult to see how Friedman derives these interpretations, but it is possible that his criticism implies that while the choice of a time period is arbitrary it nevertheless affects the decisions of the consumer. But since q_{eo} is a flow it may be readily adjusted to any time period chosen.

A further but related criticism of Friedman is that Walras' preference function asserts that given the choice of a basket containing, on the one hand, $q_{e0} = 10{,}000$ units of *numéraire* and $X_{e0} = 100$, and, on the other hand, $q_{e0} = 9700$, $X_{e0} = 400$, the consumer will be indifferent between them. (In actuality, he will not, since current investment earns a first return only in period 1 while q_{e0} pays a return in period 0 as well, but we shall neglect this and adopt Friedman's interpretation.) If the consumer were *given* one or the other of these two baskets, it is difficult to see why he would not be indifferent; indifference in preferences is ordinarily defined to be independent of the conditions of sacrifice under which the consumer must in fact make his choices. Friedman's assertion that the consumer would not be indifferent is based upon the fact that the first basket at some given P_{e0} requires a smaller current sacrifice than the second, and therefore would be preferred. But to say this is merely to say that when the conditions of acquisition are such as to require current sacrifices by consumers, it is better to have larger initial holdings than smaller. If apples cost 50¢ per pound, who would not prefer beginning the period with 4 pounds and buying only one pound to buying 5 pounds? The preference function of the consumer would not contradict this by asserting that both situations produce the same result.[9]

Although Friedman's objections to the Walrasian treatment of individual investment and disinvestment are difficult to accept, the superficial quality of Walras' analysis of the consumer's attitudes toward consumption in the future vs. current consumption and of his expectations of prices in the future is most marked. It leads us to include him in the "productivity" school of interest theory, imperfect as such overly sharp distinctions must be. Much of the blame for his poor performance in this area of consumer preferences—a sector in which Walras' pioneering as a utility theorist has won him permanent recognition as a major innovator in economic theory—must be placed upon the very brilliance of his concept of net perpetual revenue. Its neat simplicity and symmetry in conception with current consumer goods permitted him too facile a projection of the reasoning of Models I-1, I-2, and I-3 into Model IV-2.

Pareto contributed little to the analysis of consumer attitudes toward the future, except to emphasize in both earlier and later work that at least a portion of the consumer's investment springs from the instinct man possesses along with other animals to save, so that even if the interest rate were zero, such savings could continue.[10] These were in the nature of *obiter dicta*, however, and no formal theory was based upon them.

Important advances in the theory of capital and interest must be ascribed primarily to Böhm-Bawerk and Fisher, although it is possible to name other neoclassicists who made contributions: T. N. Carver,[11] F. Fetter,[12] and L. von Mises,[13] for example. Carver developed a theory of interest which stressed the coordinate roles of productivity and time preference, while Fetter and von Mises developed their theories of interest on a purely time preference basis. The considerations springing from these theoretical developments are best taken up, however, in a model where capital goods are wasting assets. Therefore, we shall move on to Model IV-3.

2.c. Model IV-3: Depreciation in the Stationary State

We shall now relax the assumption that the capital goods, Z_i, are eternal and assume instead that u_i is the proportion of the useful life of the good which wears out weekly. Further, it is now necessary to enforce upon price expectations the requirement that all consumers have the

[9] M. Friedman, (3), pp. 907–8.
[10] V. Pareto, (1), Vol. I, p. 302, and (2), p. 438.
[11] T. Carver, (1) and (2).
[12] F. Fetter, (1).
[13] F. Knight, (12).

same expectations about $P_{z_{i}t}$ and P_{et}, that they be constant through time, and that they be correct *ex post*. Thus, the model about to be presented, which is Walrasian in inspiration, is implicitly stationary, and stationary in the special sense that everyone's price expectations are correct after the event.

Between two market days the price of a capital good, P_{Z_i}, may alter either by physical change in the asset through use, by change in P_i, or both. Therefore, the price of its service, P_i, must, when these value changes are foreseen, equal interest on the value of the good minus any appreciation in its value plus any depreciation in its value. That is, during period 0,

$$P_i^{\circ} = i_k^{\circ} P_{Z_i}^{\circ} - \Delta P_{Z_i}^{\circ} \tag{53}$$

where ΔP_{Z_i} is the change in value of the asset over the period. This may be rewritten

$$i_k^{\circ} = \frac{P_i^{\circ}}{P_{Z_i}^{\circ}} + \frac{\Delta P_{Z_i}^{\circ}}{P_{Z_i}^{\circ}} \tag{54}$$

This formulation has the important advantage of stressing that the rate of interest involves a comparison between the values of an asset at two points in time.[14]

In the stationary state, of course, the only change in value of the asset which can occur is the physical wastage called depreciation. Therefore, (54) may be rewritten for stationary states,

$$i_k^{\circ} = \frac{P_i^{\circ} - u_i P_{Z_i}^{\circ}}{P_{Z_i}^{\circ}} \tag{55}$$

Note that we have defined a "rate of return on capital goods" which once more makes of them homogeneous goods in the eyes of consumers, since in equilibrium *net* rates of return will be equal. Depreciation allowances, in effect, convert each good to an eternal good. Also, it should be pointed out for later reference, that we have defined a rate of return on capital goods for an economy in which no money yet exists; i.e., an economy in which no "interest rate," in our definition of that term as the net rate of return on money, occurs. We stress, as does Hayek, that,

> "The rate of return on investment as determined by the price relationships between capital goods and consumers' goods is thus prior to, and in principle independent of, the interest on money loans, although, of course, where money loans are possible, the rate of return on these money loans will tend to correspond to the rate of return on other investments. The fundamental price relationships are the result of a demand for capital goods in terms of consumer goods or of an exchange of present consumers' goods for future consumers' goods."[15]

[14] See I. Fisher, (5), Ch. V and pp. 369–73, and M. Allais, (1), pp. 70–1.

[15] F. Hayek, (2), p. 266. Copyright 1941 by The University of Chicago. Quoted by permission.

This outlook, developed in the presentation of Model IV-2 and exploited also in the analysis of Model IV-3, is the basis for treating money as a particular type of capital good in the models of Chapter 5.

From equations (12)-(19), the ability to write the depreciation formula in the form of (55) assumes that the amortization quotas are reinvested, week by week, in investments earning the same rate of return as i_k. The simplest assumption to make is that the age structure of the existing stock of each Z_i is such in the stationary equilibrium that the proportion u_i of Q_{Z_i} is junked each week and replaced by new machines, for there is no way to hold amortization quotas from one period to the next.

Into the consumer analysis of the new model we need merely introduce the receipt of these depreciation allowances by each consumer as part of his weekly wherewithal. Remembering the stationarity assumptions we have explicitly assumed, we may change the definition of (26) to

$$(56) \qquad q_{et} = \frac{V_{et}}{P_e} + \sum_i p_{Z_i} u_i$$

The terms X_{et} are now interpreted as gross investment rather than net investment from the individual's viewpoint, but the analysis is not changed from that of Model IV-2.

By virtue of these depreciation allowances the economy of Model IV-3 can be in stationary equilibrium only when the stock of assets has been re-shaped from its initial structure to that configuration most desired by the market. Then period 0 must be taken to be a period in which the stationary equilibrium of the economy is ruling: the data $[Q_i]$ are equilibrium values in a sense that they were not in Models III, IV-1, and IV-2, since the Q_i are variables in the dynamic model whose stationary equilibrium we depict.

A basic change from the previous model is the producibility of capital goods: into the firms' transformation functions depicted in equation (122) of Chapter 3 we may now introduce outputs of Z_i. Concomitantly we must introduce markets in which each of these goods is sold, and somehow link these markets to the securities market. We will postpone a discussion of the exact nature of these relations until Chapter 5, and merely assert at this stage that the markets are purely competitive.

Another change which may be introduced at this point, if desired, is a replacement of the assumption that all goods require one week for their construction, so that no semi-finished goods exist at the end of the period. This is the Walrasian assumption that has been used to this point. The model to be presented below may be interpreted in its light. In this case, the firm's planning horizon is limited to one week, expected prices have no place in the model of producer behavior, and the only types of goods Z_i sold in their respective markets are finished forms.

We may, however, move one step closer to an Austrian interpretation of the problems of capital with the assumption that every Y_j and Z_i have definable and rigidly fixed periods of construction which are not necessarily one week in length. For example, suppose in stationary conditions $\bar{X}_j$ units of Y_j are produced and consumed, and that this good requires h weeks to construct. Then, in any one week, the economy must produce $\bar{X}_j$ units which are 1 week along in semi-finished form, $\bar{X}_j$ units which are 2 weeks along, $\bar{X}_j$ units 3 weeks along, and so forth, up to the currently produced finished goods. Similar time-phasing must hold, of course, for the Z_i.

Under these conditions we must add to the list of Z_i one new good for each Y_j which takes more than one period to construct, and capital goods may now be assumed to include these semi-finished goods. We may differentiate among these new capital goods as to their nearness to completion by adding the subscript $d = 1, 2, \ldots, h - 1$, denoting the number of weeks of work that has been completed on them at the start of the current market day. Thus, $Z_{m+3,5}$ would denote a stock of goods which is 5 weeks along in construction on the current market day. Its price would be $P_{Z_{m+3,5}}$. In our model, unfinished Y_j and Z_i will be given to savers at the end of the period in redemption of securities in similar fashion to the redemption process of Model IV-2, and consumers will sell them (i.e., their services) to firms in the current period at prices $P_{z_{m+3,5}}$. Thus, a unit of $Z_{m+3,6}$ requires a unit of "factor service" $z_{m+3,5}$ in its manufacture. Also, in equilibrium, if all types of capital goods are to be homogeneous in the eyes of the consumer, and since depreciation of these semi-finished goods is complete ($u_{m+3,5} = 1$),

$$P^\circ_{Z_{m+3,5}} = [P^\circ_{z_{m+3,5}} - P^\circ_{Z_{m+3,5}}]P^\circ_e \tag{57}$$

When $Z_{m+3,5}$ enters into the production of $Z_{m+3,6}$, interest will enter directly into the production process, and the essential likeness between "the productivity of durable capital goods" in the single period-of-construction model and the "cost of waiting" in multi-period construction models is brought out.[16]

Lastly, we may eliminate the rigid period of construction assumed for every output and assume instead that these periods are continuously variable at the option of the entrepreneur. There is given the firm a transformation function linking inputs and outputs at all dates over the $h + 1$ period planning horizon:

$$\begin{aligned} J_v(&\bar{X}_{10}, \ldots, \bar{X}_{n0}, \bar{X}_{Z_10}, \ldots, \bar{X}_{Z_m0}, \bar{X}_{Z_{m+1,0,1}}, \bar{X}_{Z_{m+1,0,2}}, \ldots; \\ &X_{z_10}, \ldots, X_{z_m0}, X_{z_{m+1,0,1}}, X_{z_{m+1,0,2}}, \ldots, X_{10}, \ldots, X_{n0}) = 0 \end{aligned} \tag{58}$$

We require that it yield U-shaped cost functions, exactly as its counterpart of (125), Chapter 3, in Model III-4.

[16] G. Mackenroth, (1).

But we may simplify this function by including in it as inputs only primary factors and intermediate completed goods. That is, even though the firm in our model yields up the unfinished goods of the week's production at the end of the week, only to reacquire them at the start of the following week, we need not take cognizance of these institutional arrangements. We need merely consider the transformation function

$$(59)\quad J(\bar{X}_{1t}, \ldots, \bar{X}_{nt}, \bar{X}_{Z_1t}, \ldots, \bar{X}_{Z_mt}, X_{z_1t}, \ldots, X_{z_mt}, X_{1t}, \ldots, X_{nt}) = 0$$

where the firm subscript has been dropped for simplicity, and where $t = 0, 1, \ldots, h$. By charging the firm P_{it} and P_{jt} for all input services used in period t, we are implicitly charging it "interest." In this sense interest is taken as the cost of movement through time, when we deal with discounted values. The current value (the value in the period in question) of total costs in period t is

$$(60)\qquad C_t = \sum_i X_{z_it}P_{it} + \sum_j X_{jt}P_{jt}, \qquad t = 0, \ldots, h$$

where all prices but those for $t = 0$ are expectations in the entrepreneur's mind. For the purposes of this sub-model we shall allow these expectations to assume nonstationary values. Also, the current values of revenue are

$$(61)\qquad R_t = \sum_j \bar{X}_{jt}P_{jt} + \sum_i \bar{X}_{Z_it}P_{Z_it}, \qquad t = 0, \ldots, h$$

and current profits are

$$(62)\qquad \pi_t = R_t - C_t, \qquad t = 0, \ldots, h$$

To the entrepreneur, a unit of *numéraire* in profit in period $t + 1$ is worth only $1/(1 + i_{k0})(1 + i_{k1}), \ldots, (1 + i_{kt})$ units of *numéraire* in period 0's profits, since this amount of *numéraire* invested in capital goods in period 0 would grow to a unit of *numéraire* in period $t + 1$'s market day. If we impose the constraint of constant interest rate expectations upon the entrepreneur, we may define these discount factors as in the case of consumer theory:

$$(63)\qquad b_t = (1 + i_k)^{-t}, \qquad t = 0, \ldots, h$$

The firm may then be viewed as maximizing the present value of its profits over the $h + 1$ week time period, or, since it owns no salable resources of its own, the present value of the firm itself. This it does subject to the transformation function as a constraint. Therefore, we may once more set up the Lagrangean function S and maximize it:

$$(64) \quad S = \sum_t b_t\pi_t + \lambda J(\bar{X}_{1t}, \ldots, \bar{X}_{nt}, \bar{X}_{Z_1t}, \ldots, \bar{X}_{Z_mt}, X_{z_1t}, \ldots, X_{z_mt}, X_{1t}, \ldots, X_{nt})$$

which leads to

$$(65) \quad \begin{aligned} &1. \quad \frac{\partial S}{\partial X_{z_it}} = -b_tP_{it} + \lambda^\circ J^{z_it} = 0, \qquad t = 0, \ldots, h \\ &2. \quad \frac{\partial S}{\partial X_{jt}} = -b_tP_{jt} + \lambda^\circ J^{jt} = 0, \\ &3. \quad \frac{\partial S}{\partial \bar{X}_{jt}} = b_tP_{jt} + \lambda^\circ J^{jt} = 0, \\ &4. \quad \frac{\partial S}{\partial \bar{X}_{Z_it}} = b_tP_{Z_it} + \lambda^\circ J^{Z_it} = 0, \\ &5. \quad \frac{\partial S}{\partial \lambda} = J(\bar{X}_{1t}, \ldots, \bar{X}_{nt}, \bar{X}_{Z_1t}, \ldots, \bar{X}_{Z_mt}, X_{z_1t}, \ldots, X_{z_mt}, X_{1t}, \ldots, X_{nt}) = 0 \end{aligned}$$

when

$$(66) \qquad d^2S < 0$$

Briefly, the firm will plan to produce each output in each period up to the point where its discounted marginal revenue equals discounted marginal cost, and, for the production of these outputs, it will use each input up to the point where, for a given period, marginal products are proportional to prices, and, between periods, marginal products are proportional to discounted prices.

The nonspecific solutions to the equations of (66) for the firm may be written:

$$(67) \quad \begin{aligned} &1. \quad X_{vit} = G_{vit}(P_2, \ldots, P_n, P_{z_1}, \ldots, P_{z_m}, P_{Z_1}, \ldots, P_{Z_m}, P_e, [\bar{P}^*_v]) \\ &\qquad\quad = G_{vit}([P], [\bar{P}^*_v]) \\ &2. \quad X_{vjt} = G_{vjt}([P], [\bar{P}^*_v]) \\ &3. \quad \bar{X}_{vjt} = G_{vjt}([P], [\bar{P}^*_v]) \\ &4. \quad X_{vZ_it} = G_{vZ_it}([P], [\bar{P}^*_v]) \end{aligned}$$

where v denotes the firm, prices without time subscripts are those for the current week, and $[\bar{P}^*_v]$ is the vector of the firm's price expectations over the planning horizon.[17]

[17] Compare Samuelson's intertemporal model of the firm's decisionmaking in (1), and J. Hicks's in (5), pp. 325–6.

To save space, we shall not manipulate the firm's set of equations (67) to derive operational theorems, since these theorems will be projections of the results of the model of the firm in Model III-4, as we have shown for its consumer counterpart. Specifically, of the propositions about substitution effects contained in Chapter 3, (119) and (120) will hold for inputs and outputs at a given time period, (121) will hold when discounted prices are used and the summation is taken over time as well, (122) will hold when discounted prices are employed and the summations include inputs and outputs at different points in time, as will (124).

Let us therefore proceed to the construction of Model IV-3. Since it is the core of the neoclassical investment analysis, we shall present it in some detail.

First, we are given the demand and supply functions for each consumer in the economy:

$$\text{(IV-3-0)}\quad \begin{aligned} &1. \quad X_{cj\neq 1} = H_{cj\neq 1}([P]; [Q_c], [\bar{P}_c]), \qquad c = 1, \ldots, s \\ &2. \quad \bar{X}_{ci} = Q_{ci} - H_{ci}([P]; [Q_c], [\bar{P}_c]) \\ &3. \quad X_{ce} = H_{ce}([P]; [Q_c], [\bar{P}_c]) \\ &4. \quad X_{c1} = \sum_i \bar{X}_{ci}P_i - \sum_{j\neq 1} X_{cj}P_j - X_{ce}P_e \end{aligned}$$

Next, the aggregate functions are given by summing over the individual functions:

$$\text{(IV-3-1)}\quad \begin{aligned} &1. \quad X_{j\neq 1} = H_{j\neq 1}([P]; [Q], [\bar{P}]) \\ &2. \quad \bar{X}_i = Q_i - H_i([P]; [Q], [\bar{P}]) \\ &3. \quad X_e = H_e([P]; [Q], [\bar{P}]) \\ &4. \quad X_1 = \sum_i \bar{X}_iP_i - \sum_{j\neq 1} X_jP_j - X_eP_e \end{aligned}$$

Aggregate entrepreneurial input demands and output supplies may be defined by summation of the individual firm functions:

$$\text{(IV-3-2)}\quad \begin{aligned} &1. \quad X_i = G_i(P_2, \ldots, P_n, P_{z_1}, \ldots, P_{z_m}, P_{Z_1}, \ldots, P_{Z_m}, P_e; [\bar{P}^*]) \\ &\qquad\;\; = G_i([P^*]; [\bar{P}^*]) \\ &2. \quad X_j^* = G_j([P^*]; [\bar{P}^*]) \\ &3. \quad \bar{X}_j = G_J([P^*]; [\bar{P}^*]) \\ &4. \quad \bar{X}_{Z_i} = G_I([P^*]; [\bar{P}^*]) \end{aligned}$$

Firm by firm, profits are constrained to be zero:

$$\text{(IV-3-3)}\quad \sum_j \bar{X}_{vj}^{\circ}P_j + \sum_i \bar{X}_{vZ_i}P_{Z_i} - \sum_i X_{vi}^{\circ}P_i - \sum_j X_{vj}^{\circ}P_j = 0$$

All markets are cleared in equilibrium; once more we exclude the market for securities for a later statement:

$$\text{(IV-3-4)} \qquad \begin{aligned} &1. \quad X_i^{\circ} = \bar{X}_i^{\circ} \\ &2. \quad X_j^{\circ} + X_j^{*\circ} = \bar{X}_j^{\circ} \\ &3. \quad X_{Z_i}^{\circ} = \bar{X}_{Z_i}^{\circ} \end{aligned}$$

We must define the firms' individual demand and supply functions:

$$\text{(IV-3-5)} \qquad \begin{aligned} &1. \quad X_{vi} = G_{vi}([P^*]; [\bar{P}_v^*]), \qquad v = 1, \ldots, o \\ &2. \quad X_{vj} = G_{vj}([P^*]; [\bar{P}_v^*]) \\ &3. \quad \bar{X}_{vj} = G_{vJ}([P^*]; [\bar{P}_v^*]) \\ &4. \quad \bar{X}_{vZ_i} = G_{vI}([P^*]; [\bar{P}_v^*]) \end{aligned}$$

In the securities market, the value of securities at equilibrium price must equal the value of gross investment *when the capital goods are valued at equilibrium prices:*

$$\text{(IV-3-6)} \qquad X_e^{\circ}P_e^{\circ} = \sum_i X_{Z_i}^{\circ}P_{Z_i}^{\circ}$$

And, lastly, capital goods must exchange in equilibrium at the capitalized value of their *net* revenue:

$$\text{(IV-3-7)} \qquad P_{Z_i}^{\circ} = [P_i^{\circ} - u_iP_{Z_i}^{\circ}]P_e^{\circ}, \qquad i = 1, \ldots, m$$

To the equations of Model IV-2 we have added (a) the m new equations of (IV-3-2-4); (b) m new equations in (IV-3-4-3); and (c) the om equations of (IV-3-5-4); to its unknowns have been added (a) m $\bar{X}_{Z_i}$ terms; (b) m X_{Z_i} terms; and (c) om $\bar{X}_{vZ_i}$ terms. Therefore the equality of equations and unknowns has been maintained.

Walras' achievement in the field of investment theory must be pointed out as a highlight of his economic theory. The difficulties he faced can be seen by assuming in straightforward fashion that the consumer had a demand function for each capital good; aggregate consumer demand could be obtained by summing over these functions; and the price of each capital good determined by the interaction of supply and demand in the market for the capital good. This would add $sm + m$ equations to the model, but allow the removal of the s individual demands for securities, the aggregate demand for securities, and the equilibrium condition in (IV-3-6). Thus, the number of equations would rise by $sm + m - s - 2$. Further, we could eliminate one equation from (IV-3-7) by merely requiring that the bracketed term divided by P_{Z_i} be equal to all other such ratios. Finally, then, we would have removed $sm + m - s - 3$ equations. We would have lost s X_{ce} terms, 1 X_e term, and 1 P_e term, and would have gained sm X_{cZ_i} terms. After adjusting for these changes, we would find that we had $m - 1$ too many equations: the system would be overdetermined. We cannot allow consumers to follow their preferences for the various types of capital goods, equate supply and demand, *and* force net rates of return on these goods to be equal, unless, of course, there were only one type of capital good, in which case the equality-of-net-rates-of-return condition disappears.

Walras succeeds in eliminating this net excess of $m - 1$ equations by creating a single "capital good," E, for consumers to buy, since they would logically have no basis for choosing one specific capital good over another if the net rates of return were equal. With one stroke the overdeterminacy disappears: the equilibrium value of savings is distributed over the production of capital goods in such a way as to make net returns in equilibrium equal prices of the capital goods and capital good services.[18]

Unlike Model IV-2, for which there could be defined a static equilibrium which was not stationary, the existence of depreciation allowances makes it extremely difficult to interpret Model IV-3 for any but stationary conditions. Moreover, we shall be most interested in the stationary solution in the discussion of the problems of capital and interest that follows in Section 3. Therefore, we shall assume further (a) that each consumer expects every future period's price solution to be exactly the same as the current period's solutions; (b) that each firm expects every future period's price solution to be exactly the same as the current period's solution; and (c) that $X^{\circ}_{ce}P^{\circ}_{e} = \Sigma_i\ Q_{ci}P^{\circ}_{Z_i}u_i$ for all c. With the constancy of the objective data of the economy, these assumptions will yield the stationary solution we seek, assuming always that it can indeed exist.

2.d. Model IV-4: Depreciation and the Progressive State

The inherent stationarity of Model IV-3 did not deter Walras, with his simplistic analysis of the savings process, from constructing a progressive state by merely assuming $X^{\circ}_{e}P^{\circ}_{e} > \Sigma_i\ Q_iP^{\circ}_{Z_i}u_i$, so that net investment occurred.[19] In fact, Walras pointed out the role of consumer and entre-

[18] Cf. P. Rocher, (1), pp. 301–5.

[19] Walras was guilty of ambiguous analysis in his presentation of the progressive state. The difficulty begins in a curious passage on pp. 244–5 of (2) in which he expresses the opinion that in a stationary state no sales or purchases of capital goods would occur since such goods could be exchanged only in the ratios of their net returns over cost, and no benefit would accrue to either party to the exchange. He thus assumes that replacement of capital goods is automatic and occurs without exchanges (or that such goods are eternal—but he had just finished discussing depreciation), and unnecessarily imposes the condition of positive net savings before an interest rate can exist. Compare the discussions of Hicks in (2), pp. 345–7; C. Bresciani-Turroni, (1), pp. 3–8; and G. Stigler, (1), p. 249.

Walras then defines net savings as gross savings less depreciation allowances, refers to gross savings (defined as X_eP_e in (2), p. 251) as "positive savings" ((2), p. 252), and later in the same paragraph imposes the condition that the demand for new capital goods be positive. He continues, "in making this assumption we restrict ourselves to

preneurial expectations but makes no suggestion of methods to include them in the analysis.[20]

Continuous displacement of Model IV-3 to obtain net investment must have disturbing impacts upon expectations and disrupt the simple depreciation analysis of that model. More recently, Allais, in his rejection of the stationary for the progressive state, includes a risk premium for changes in the value of money in his concept of interest, but abstracts from the possibility that changes in the prices of goods under progressive conditions will alter the real value of assets. His concern is the study of rates of return on capital in a framework where there exists a liquidity function for money as a hedge against uncertainty.[21]

The "progressive state" model is, then, at best an imprecise and informal one, measured against the precise models constructed in this book. Since most of our uses of investment models will involve Model IV-3, for reasons to be presented in Section 3, we shall go no further in presenting the progressive model until Chapter 8.

3. A Critique of the Investment Models

In Models IV-1 through IV-4, we have built into our production systems individual and aggregate investment. Somehow, however, we must feel a sense of not having come to grips with the basic problems of capital and interest. The simple projection of consumer tastes into time and of production theory into the realm of capital goods fails to yield any profound insights into the fundamental essence of the phenomena with which we are concerned. The models are valuable in providing the bare ribs of the fuller theories we seek, however, and we shall organize our discussion about them.

The essential problem of interest and capital has been well stated by Wicksell, if we ignore the exclusive concern with consumer goods as capital which he corrected in his later work:

"The seemingly paradoxical phenomenon, that consumable goods—that is to say, goods which exhaust or seem to exhaust their whole content of usefulness in a limited series of acts of use—can nevertheless be

---

the study of the production of new capital goods in a progressive society and we neglect that of the consumption of existing capital goods in a retrogressive society." Since the condition that gross saving be positive is not sufficient to guarantee that a society's capital is being maintained, the passage is unclear. Are "new capital goods" to be only those purchased over and above automatic depreciation demands? If this is not his meaning there is no reason why $X_e P_e$ should not include depreciation allowances, free for investment in any direction, and the reinvestment of such allowances allows the determination of the interest rate in a stationary flow. The present writer pointed out this error in Walras in R. Kuenne, (2), but has since discovered that it was found earlier by E. Lindahl, (1), p. 294.

[20] L. Walras, (2), p. 293.

[21] M. Allais, (1), p. 32.

employed 'capitalistically,' so that their entire value remains stored up for the owner, and yet provides him with an income—this *perpetuum mobile* of the economic mechanism forms, as was said previously, the real pith of the theory of capital . . . ."[22]

If capital goods are augmentable factors of production, they must consist in final analysis of nonaugmentable factors, the latter being defined as goods either fixed in amount or following laws of variation in quantity essentially noneconomic in character. But if they are merely nonaugmentable factor services in another form, why should there be any return to them over and above their content of nonaugmentable factor services? If, as our production theory of Chapter 3 informs us, maximum profits are obtained when every input is employed to the point where its price equals its marginal physical product times price of that product, it would seem to be implied that if transfigured nonaugmentable factor services yield more in marginal value product than nonaugmentable factors not transfigured, more of them should be put into the transfigured or capital goods form, until their marginal value products in both forms are the same. Why should there exist, in the stationary flow and therefore without tendency to elimination, a permanent difference between the marginal value products of a fixed basket of nonaugmentable factor services in direct form on the one hand and in capital goods form on the other?

This question itself may be divided into two questions. First, why are nonaugmentable factor services transfigured at all, and, second, if a reason exists, why does the payment for this superiority accrue to the holder of the transfigured factors? Why is this advantage not passed on to the owners of the nonaugmentable factors, so that the owner of the capital goods receives back only the value of the nonaugmentable resource services contained in them? More succinctly, why are capital goods produced and why does a positive rate of interest emerge in the free market economy?

3.a. The Theory of Model IV-2

The answers to these questions are at their simplest in the stationary solution of the economy where capital goods are nonaugmentable and nondepreciating, and may therefore be treated as gifts of nature capable of appropriation by the individual. Since our theory of production says that any factor service which is scarce in the sense of having a positive marginal value productivity will earn it as a return in equilibrium, the explanation of a net return over the zero amounts of constituent resources used up each week is readily explained. Indeed, we are merely dealing with the theory of rent.

It follows that if we may broadly neglect the differences in tastes for

[22] K. Wicksell, (1), p. 99. Quoted by permission of George Allen & Unwin Ltd.

current goods among individuals, the values P_i° would be about the same whether consumers were or were not constrained to hold all of the capital goods with which they began the period. But there could be no *rate* of return on capital goods in the first case, since the P_{Z_i} could not exist, as we have discussed in Section 2.b. Once we have released consumers from this constraint, however, Model IV-2 determines *a rate of return on capital goods directly in the securities market by a pricing of future* numéraire *in terms of present* numéraire. The prices of capital goods are derivative from this rate: the rate of return, or, for present purposes, the rate of interest, exists because of different attitudes among consumers, in Fisherian terms, between different income streams over time. In stationary equilibrium every consumer will have had time to adjust the flow of present income as compared with future income to the level he desires to maintain.

3.a.1. Knight's Crusonia and Fisher's Island: Active Technology and Passive Consumer Preferences

Professor Knight has depicted the stationary equilibrium of Model IV-2 as a Robinsonade with some interest for us. He imagines an island with a miraculous plant. In Crusonia, this plant expands by i_k per cent per week. Every pound of plant left on the vine in period 0 will be $1 + i_k$ pounds in period 1, $(1 + i_k)^2$ pounds in period 2, and so on. In week 0, therefore, Robinson has the simplest decision to make: that adjustment of the stream of the income plant which yields the optimal pattern of present and future income. If the price of a unit of plant in period 0 is taken to be 1, the price of the same unit in period 1 in week 0 product is only $[(1 + i_k)]^{-1}$, in week 2, $[(1 + i_k)]^{-2}$, and so forth. If the plant grew not at all, prices of a unit of plant would be the same in all periods. If the plant declined by i_k per cent per period, price in period t in terms of period 0's product would be $(1 - i_k)^{-t}$, future plant being more expensive than present.

These three possibilities have been presented by Fisher in his case of the shipwrecked sailors with (a) sheep whose wool and mutton expands at 10 per cent per year, (b) fixed stocks of hardtack, and (c) figs which deteriorate with time.[23] In Crusonia and on Fisher's Island, the individual consumer is in the position of the consumer of Model IV-2: he is faced with a set of prices of future goods in terms of present goods to which he must adjust his purchases. As in the Robinsonades of Models I, the positive, zero, or negative discount in the rates of transformation between present and future goods are technologically determined. The "rate of interest" in these simple exchange economies is wholly a result of productivity considerations, and consumers are forced to adjust their preferences to it. In the case of the market economy, again as in Models I, these rates of transformation are not so simply determined, emerging as they do

[23] F. Knight, (13), and I. Fisher, (7), pp. 184–94.

from the interaction between consumer time preferences and productivities. The conditions of equilibrium for the consumer in Crusonia have already been given in the presentation of Fisher's model in equations (2)-(6) of this chapter.

Giammaria Ortes, in the late 18th century, formulated the following relationship which sought to attach a present utility value to a constant flow of "utility" over an h-week period beginning in week 1. We shall follow Pantaleoni and call it Ortes' Rule. Let $D < 1$ be the "psychological rate of discount of the future" in the mind of the consumer. Then, when u is the weekly flow of "utility," the present utility value of the flow is[24]

$$(68) \quad U = Du + D^2u + D^3u + \cdots D^h_u = u(D - D^{h+1})(1 - D)^{-1}$$

Quite apart from the assumption of cardinal measurability of preferences, Ortes assumes the psychological discount of the consumer can be closely approximated by a simple compounding formula, and, implicitly, assumes D to be independent of the size of u if u is total income, or of the existing income flow if u is a marginal increment.

Böhm-Bawerk, in his classical treatment of consumer attitudes toward consumption in the present vs. the future, dealt primarily with marginal time preference, and we need concern ourselves in the theory of interest rate determination only with this marginal concept.[25] Suppose the consumer to be at equilibrium in Crusonia; i.e., where

$$(69) \quad \frac{\partial M}{\partial X^{\circ}_{c0}} = \frac{\partial M}{\partial X^{\circ}_{c1}}(1 + i_k) = \cdots \frac{\partial M}{\partial X^{\circ}_{ch}}(1 + i_k)^h$$

At this point, let the consumer be asked what increase in income *for consumption* in period 1 would just compensate him for a small reduction in period 0 consumption income; similarly, obtain the amounts for every period from 2 to h which would just compensate him for a small loss in consumption in period 0. Obviously, the pattern of these h increments could be quite varied, but let us follow Ortes and assume that the pattern could be reasonably approximated by a compounding formula. Let θ_c be a factor and assume that it turns out the increment of consumption in period t which just compensates for a unit loss in week 0 at a given equilibrium point is

$$(70) \quad dX_{ct} = (1 + \theta_c)^t dX_{c0}$$

Then θ_c may be termed the "marginal rate of psychological discount" for consumer c, and $(1 + \theta_c)$ the "marginal discount factor." When $\theta_c = 0$, the consumer may be said to demonstrate zero marginal time preference; when $\theta_c > 0$, he may be said to demonstrate a positive mar-

[24] M. Pantaleoni, (1), pp. 91–3. The formal expression is Launhardt's.
[25] E. von Böhm-Bawerk, (1), pp. 249–81.

ginal time preference; and when $\theta_c < 0$, he may be termed as revealing negative marginal time preference.

The marginal time preference pattern may differ drastically from initial equilibrium to initial equilibrium: if with a given interest rate a consumer starts with equilibrium values of \$10,000 in week 0 and \$15,000 in week 1, θ_c can be quite different from that for initial values of \$13,000 in week 0 and \$11,000 in week 1. In investment and capital theory, however, we are interested primarily in the stationary equilibrium, because only in that state will the interest rate have achieved a position of rest. In this state, each individual in Crusonia will have had sufficient time to adjust his stock of plant to the point where he is consuming optimally when he takes the "income" week by week from the plant, or $Q_{ct}i_k$. In this state, therefore, each consumer will have adjusted his current and expected weekly consumption to a constant magnitude.

Marginal time preference of the consumer in such a position is of greatest interest to the economist working with the abstract questions posed at the beginning of this section. In the world of Crusonia or on Fisher's Island, for every individual in this stationary equilibrium, $\theta_c = i_k$.

There exist interesting contrasts among economists' views regarding the "legitimacy" or "rationality" of the marginal attitudes of consumers toward goods at various points of time as compared with the "legitimacy" of their marginal choices among goods at one period of time, both sets of phenomena considered from the viewpoint of optimal resource allocation. Böhm-Bawerk's discussion of time preference is studded with the "irrational" implications of the second ground for the existence of interest. Among modern theorists, this nonsymmetry of treatment reaches its peak in Allais's work. In his discussion of Pareto optimality, he gives full recognition to static consumer preferences and the essential "rightness" of allowing the consumer freedom of choice to attain the proportionality of marginal preferences and prices which must rule to obtain such an optimum. However, he believes individual rates of time preference are "arbitrary" in a sense that static preferences are not, and asserts that a stationary state where the interest rate has attained a zero level by virtue of state interference with consumer allocation over time can be "justified" on welfare grounds. The grounds for the justification are: (1) the consumer can only see his future wants in light of wants that exist today, while the state, being able to foresee his future wants more clearly, is in a better position to make more rational decisions; and (2) since the accumulation of capital raises the marginal productivity of labor services and, therefore, wages over time—a result not foreseen by the laborer in his allocation over time—individual savings are less than those which would emerge if the laborer correctly foresaw this long-term rise in income. On both grounds the state has the "right" to overrule the individual and lead the economy toward the stationary equilibrium with a zero rate of interest; i.e., force the economy to accumulate all the units of transfigured nonaugmentable factors whose services yield any surplus above the value of these factors used up in capital goods employment.[26] We shall return to the conditions for the emergence of such a stationary equilibrium and the implications of its existence for a market economy in our discussion of Model IV-3.

3.a.2. Model IV-2: Active Consumer Preferences and Passive Technology

In a stationary flow, it is obvious that every consumer must adjust his constant weekly income flow until the ratio of the psychological discount factors for any two periods is equal to the ratio of the market's discount factors for those periods. In the more realistic economy of Model IV-3, as we shall see, it is the interaction of two factors—the "productivity" of capital and the "time preference" of consumers—which leads to a stationary state with constant interest rate. In Crusonia or on Fisher's Island, as we have already indicated, the productivity element is dominant, and the time preference element passive, in the sense that if a stationary equilibrium is to emerge the marginal discount factors of individuals must adjust to a rigid i_k.

But, in Model IV-2, consumer time preference has an active role to play in the determination of i_k, while productivity considerations are passive. Of course, it was Böhm-Bawerk's position that at any feasible equilibrium position for Model IV-2, stationary or nonstationary, by far most $\theta_c > 0$, and therefore an $i_k^{\circ} > 0$ would emerge in the market, since the productivity element in capitalistic production would allow such a position to be reached; i.e., Crusonia's miracle plant or Fisher's Island populated with sheep was the true analogy with Model IV-2 insofar as productivity aspects were concerned. Yet, given these potentialities, productivity considerations can be allowed to recede into the background, and the polar analogue of Crusonia and Fisher's Island can be presented before we move to an eclectic analysis.

Those economists whose theories of interest and capital are grounded predominantly in the productivity of capital tend to take negative or ambiguous positions toward the existence of predominant positive marginal time preference and its role in the theory of interest. For example, John Bates Clark, in his famous debate with Böhm-Bawerk at the turn of the century, wrote: ". . . In deciding to 'save' wealth rather than to spend it, a capitalist looks forward to the *unending* series of accretions of interest, and sets a subjective value on them. The remoteness of most of them in time is one fact to be considered . . . ."[27] Frank H. Knight,

[26] M. Allais, (1), pp. 179–228.

[27] J. B. Clark, (1), p. 261. Quoted by permission of Harvard University Press. Italics have been supplied.

the leading modern proponent of a productivity theory of interest, is even more forceful in his rejection of positive time preference. He views saving, as did Pareto, as a product largely of instinctive or compulsive factors, and as being by its nature (we shall clarify this aspect of Knight's theory subsequently) the purchase of an infinite number of periodic income installments. It is not, as in Clark's view, that the consumer actually plans over an infinite horizon, but that his actions lead him to the same results by virtue of the inherent nature of the investment process. He writes:

"The fact that the investor typically plans on the basis of maintaining the investment in perpetuity does not by any means imply that he consciously looks forward to infinity or over any particular distance in time. As long as he plans to be a little better off, or at least as well off, in the immediate future, however narrowly defined, as he is at the moment, and does not explicitly plan to the contrary with regard to the more remote future, the effect is the same, even in a Crusoe economy, as if he did literally look ahead to infinity."[28]

It is the desire to "get ahead" which stirs a Paretian drive to save in Knight's theory:

"Certainly, what we call the 'economic interest,' in the context of modern civilization, includes as an apparently essential factor the interest in getting ahead, both for the individual during his own life and for his successors or heirs of some kind. In the aggregate people are as much interested in this getting ahead, which does not look forward to any cessation of getting ahead, as they are in maximizing their consumption in relation to the economic resources momentarily available. They save in order to save more in the future as well as to consume more . . . ."[29]

It might seem to follow from these positions that in an economy where no further investment possibility could be profitably exploited, as in Model IV-2, the interest rate would be negative with the operation of this blind drive to get ahead. Knight makes a bow toward this position, but essentially rules it out as an interesting proposition by asserting that the existence of the productivity element is of such dominant interest in any realistic theory of interest that the question is of little but academic importance:

"There is no reason to assume that, other things equal, normal human psychology contains any general tendency to underestimate the future, and it is as easy to argue for the predominance of the opposite irrational-

[28] F. Knight, (7), p. 458. Copyright 1936 by the University of Chicago. Quoted by permission.

[29] F. Knight, (7), pp. 457–8. See also (8), p. 627. Copyright 1936 by The University of Chicago. Quoted by permission.

ity. It is impossible to know whether the interest rate would be positive or negative in the absence of opportunity for productive investment. . . ."[30]

Thus, positive time preference does not set a limit to the effective planning horizon in Knight's theory, since the consumer's actions are in essence taken in perpetuity. The drive to better one's position would lead the consumer to accumulate, presumably, in the face of a zero or negative interest rate. It is, then, the never-ending ability to invest in productive uses of resources which leads to the positive interest rate that we know, and it may exist even in the face of generalized negative or zero time preference.

Knight holds explicitly that, properly defined, time preference concerns itself with the consumer's choices at a position of uniform consumption through time; i.e., such as would exist in a stationary state. At such a point, would the individual prefer more present consumption and a lower rate in the future? Knight argues once more that the real world offers, by virtue of investment opportunity, a premium on postponement: in the absence of such opportunity, debates about what the "rational" consumer would do are academic and no agreement is to be expected.[31]

But if we are to probe the nature of interest, the question is not so easily shoved aside: in a world where saving would be forthcoming even in the face of a zero or negative interest rate, would not the stationary state be approached with a zero or negative rate of interest? Knight himself is forced to wrestle with this conundrum at various points in his theory. Holding technology constant, sooner or later we should have exploited investment opportunities fully, and, since no investments yielding a negative rate of return would be undertaken unless the interest rate became negative, would (1) investment and saving stop at $i_k = 0$, or (2) continue at $i_k < 0$? Professor Knight's theory of the interest rate provides no apparent stationary equilibrium at a determinate rate of interest. He asserts that since stocks of capital goods would not be maintained if $i_k = 0$ (why not, if the impulse to save existed at that interest rate or even below?) the services of capital goods would be free goods in such a state[32] (more exactly, the services would sell for the value of the primary factors used up in their rendering). Indeed, at another point, Professor Knight asserts that i_k could be zero only if a complete satiation with goods occurs in the economy, and that this state could never be reached, "For it is certainly inadmissible to assume that society could reach a state in which no additional capacity could be employed to any advantage whatever, before all other factors or their services

[30] F. Knight, (8), p. 636. Copyright 1936 by The University of Chicago. Quoted by permission.

[31] F. Knight, (12), pp. 413–4.

[32] F. Knight, (12), pp. 414–5.

became free goods."[33] It is not at all clear how his reasoning has led him to these conclusions. Nevertheless, he concludes that "The insatiability of wants, and the unlimited technical opportunities for investment, make it unthinkable that all services of producible productive capacity, including all that requires maintenance [i.e., even nonaugmentable factors] should ever become free goods."[34] Thus, by a chain of reasoning which is unclear, Knight adds to the inexhaustible potentialities of technology the insatiability of human wants as a bar to the zero rate of interest and the stationary state.

In summary, Professor Knight avoids the implications of his rejection of positive marginal time preference—a nonpositive rate of return on capital goods in stationary equilibrium, if the latter could exist—by simply refusing to discuss the possibility of a stationary state. This is quite explicit in one of his articles[35] and implicit in the arguments presented above. For reasons which are uncertain, his long-term economic position is that of an economy with $i_k > 0$ by virtue of investment productivity, at worst approaching zero asymptotically but attaining it only in the impossible state of complete societal satiation.

It is difficult to see what Professor Knight gains by not accepting the implications of a rejection of positive marginal time preference. The major sacrifice is that of a stationary equilibrium by virtue of the assumption of the savings drive and the continuous availability of investment opportunities. Model IV-2, with its lack of new investment opportunity, is simply not a framework within which Knight's theory of interest can be presented. Crusonia, with its miraculous expanding plant, contains a *sine qua non* of a positive rate of interest in a Knightian world: the force of investment productivity. Indeed, in his theory, the rate of return on capital is a function of the stock of capital, does not vary with investment during any period, and, therefore, if we modify the miraculous plant so that i_k varies negatively with the stock of plant but is given during any one period, we see that Knight's interest theory differs very little from the Crusonia construction. An interest rate must exist in an economy in which any non-free good expands in physical quantity at a positive rate without any expenditure of the services of nonaugmentable factor services.

In Model IV-2 we have assumed a kind of Crusonia, in that the stocks of capital goods are assumed to be small enough that the service of each has a positive marginal revenue product. In this model there is no way to obtain future income, or more exactly, income tomorrow, other than

[33] F. Knight, (8), pp. 623–4. Cf. also J. Weston, (1), p. 142.

[34] F. Knight, (12), p. 426. Quoted by permission.

[35] F. Knight, (10), pp. 223–4. His definition of the "stationary state" allows new "forms" of final product to emerge and new forms of capital equipment to make old types of product.

by buying securities today; nor is there any manner of obtaining income today other than by selling securities today. It follows that P_e can never fall below 0, for suppose all consumers in the economy were to have very strong positive time preference, and threw all of their currently held assets on the securities market. Then, P_e would fall toward zero, $i_k \rightarrow \infty$, and capital goods would become free goods, even though their marginal value productivities, P_{z_i}, were positive. On the other hand, suppose all consumers were to have very strong negative time preferences, rushing into the securities market to buy, sending P_e toward infinity and i_k toward zero. Capital goods would not be exchanged at a price approaching infinity. In more realistic cases, where some consumers may be supposed to have positive and others negative marginal time preferences at current income levels, and where these preferences may be supposed responsive to changes in income levels, a finite positive rate of interest may be expected week by week in the approach to a stationary state with positive finite i_k.

But our interest in Model IV-2 with no depreciation or production of capital goods must have its limits. What of the role of time preference and productivity in an economy with depreciation and the possibility of net investment?

3.a.3. Model IV-3: Coordinate Consumer Preferences and Technology

It is clear that even in Model IV-2 the mere existence of an average productivity of capital is not sufficient to yield a determinate interest rate greater than zero. Time preference must be brought in as an added consideration. That neither Walras nor Pareto gave deep consideration to this necessary ingredient for a positive interest rate we have already noted. In Model IV-3, where the marginal productivity of the capital stock may be changed by investment and disinvestment, Walras freed the second of the two forces interacting in the market for securities to secure the price of securities and a rate of return on capital goods.

3.a.3.a. The Austrian Theories of Capital and Interest and Their Critics

With the introduction of the concept of the mortality of capital goods we take the first large step toward the Austrian outlook upon capital. To the Austrian theorist, capital consists of concrete capital goods which enter the production process, combine with the services of nonaugmentable factors, undergo physical change, and emerge from that process after a calculable period of time in the form of consumable goods. Wastage or transformation of capital goods week by week characterizes—indeed, forms the essence of —capitalistic production to the Austrian school, and to explain the length of time over which this wastage or maturation occurs is a major aim of the theory. On the other hand, Walras and subsequent members of the productivity school are anxious to abstract from the admitted wastage of individual capital goods by going immediately to the stationary state, where their "automatic" replacement and maintenance endows them with an appearance of permanence.[36]

To the Austrian, the fundamental dichotomy is that between "permanent factors" *vs.* "nonpermanent factors," or, as Kaldor points out, between "producible" *vs.* "nonproducible" factors.[37] While nonproducible factors contribute services to the production of goods, producible factors contribute themselves, and, in a stationary state, are periodically extinguished. The desire of the Austrian to focus upon this periodicity—to measure its length, to find in that length for the economy as a whole a meaningful concept with which to measure the capital stock of the society, and to associate the productivity of capital with its length—contrasts, generally speaking, with the desire of the productivity school to abstract from it, to deal with capital as a wholly coordinate factor yielding services endlessly in the production process. Thus, Knight writes: "In the 'stationary' view, the productive equipment of society, material and human, yields want-satisfying services which are consumed as they are rendered.[38]

[36] Böhm-Bawerk treats this as the one point on which he and John B. Clark disagree—a fundamental point. It is Clark's contention that Böhm-Bawerk deals only with capital goods which enter and emerge from the production process and fails to treat "true" capital—that permanent fund of productive wealth which may be viewed as merely contributing services, not itself, to production. Böhm-Bawerk compares his own approach to a "natural history" of capital, while that of Clark he terms a "mythology of capital." See E. von Böhm-Bawerk, (2).

Compare also J. B. Clark's following definition of the problem: ". . . Is the problem of accounting for the current rate of interest anything else than the problem of discovering why a certain permanent fund of producers' wealth annually creates and secures for its owners an income that is equal to a certain fraction of the fund itself? If this is true, the conception of capital as a permanent thing, existing and acting in its entirety, is introduced in the statement of the interest problem." J. B. Clark, (1), p. 258. Quoted by permission of Harvard University Press.

[37] Kaldor is supporting Knight's position that, practically speaking, all factors would wear out if maintenance and replacement expenditures were not made period by period, and that the distinction between maintenance and replacement may be murky at best. The Austrian school, in drawing too clear a line between permanent factors and nonpermanent factors, was clearly subject to Knight's criticism, and redefinition of the line clouds the simpler Austrian cases. It is possible to imagine permanent, produced factors in which the period of investment of the nonproduced factors would be infinite. The typical Austrian case is one of nonpermanent, produced capital goods. Cf. N. Kaldor, (1).

[38] F. Knight, (3), p. 328. Or again:

"Thus the basic issue is the old and familiar one of choice between two conceptions of capital. In one view it consists of 'things' of limited life which are periodically worn out or used up and reproduced; in the other, it is a 'fund' which is maintained intact though the things in which it is invested may come and go to any extent. In the second view, which of course is the one advocated here, the capital 'fund' may be thought of as either a value or a 'capacity' to produce a perpetual flow of value . . . ." F. Knight, (9), p. 38. Quoted by permission of Harvard University Press. Also:

". . . wealth, which is identical with capital, can be treated quantitatively only by viewing it as capacity to render services." F. Knight, (5), p. 86n. Quoted by permission. Cf. also J. Hicks, (4), pp. 456–7.

Lastly, compare the following statement by Knight:

"The basic fallacy of the Böhm-Bawerk theory of capital is a two-fold one which

The effective conversion of capital goods into a permanent fund of capital whose services are priced by the market mechanism was achieved by Walras merely by going to the stationary state and including a fixed depreciation charge in the price of the use of the asset. To the Austrian, this depreciation charge, being a function of the useful life of the good, is a variable of the analysis, not a fundamental datum of the model. But, in the stationary state, time in the Austrian sense may have the appearance of being unmeaningful: in the terms of J. B. Clark's analysis, nonaugmentable factor services fed into the production process in week 0 may be viewed as yielding today's product, the mystical eternal fund of capital serving to synchronize current inputs and current outputs. To this, of course, the Austrian responds that it is merely the appearance of timelessness that Clark obtains from the stationary state; the economy is potentially capable of drawing down its capital stock and thus consuming more than the input of current nonaugmentable services alone would permit.

This difference in outlook may be compared in these terms. Let K be the volume of a container, and let Y be the constant rate of inflow and outflow of water. When this hydraulic model is in a stationary condition, the average period of time t which a molecule of water spends in the container is given by the formula:

$$t = \frac{K}{Y} \tag{71}$$

Any particular molecule of water may eddy about in the container forever or may enter and exit in short order. If we view the constant input as the volume of services of nonaugmentable resources flowing in during week 0 to cooperate with the stock K of factors in the reservoir, and if we term t the "period of investment of the nonaugmentable factor services," then t is obviously the *average* time period required in the stationary state for current services of nonaugmentable resources to enter the production process and leave it as consumers' goods. If within K eddies are set up through the use of augmentable goods to produce augmentable goods, then some nonaugmentable factor services could remain within the capital stock forever; yet, under the simplified conditions of this hydraulic model, the average period of investment of nonaugmentable services would remain determinate.[39]

To the Clark school of productivity theorists, the function of the

---

has vitiated the entire theoretical system of classical economics. Production is viewed as production of wealth, and wealth is viewed as concrete things. In reality, what is produced *and consumed* is services. The production of any service includes the maintenance of things used in the process, and this includes *re*production of any which are used up. Apart from such reproduction, really a detail of maintenance, things are 'produced' only when added to a total stock." F. Knight, (5), p. 85n.

[39] Compare K. Boulding's hydraulic analogy in F. Knight, (9), p. 38, and for an explicit statement and proof of (71) see R. Dorfman, (3), pp. 353, 367–9.

reservoir is, by virtue of its services of storage, to permit an inflow of Y in services to yield immediately an outflow of Y in goods. In so doing, time is telescoped to negligible lengths. To the Austrian school, t is a measure of K under stationary conditions, given the flow of nonaugmentable factor services available and typically fixed in the Austrian stationary flow;[40] and, more importantly, the *value* of the physical outflow Y from the process was a rising function of the amount of time the nonaugmentable factor services remained invested, i.e., in K. Time, or, from the viewpoint of the owners of the nonaugmentable services, the willingness to "wait" for consumer goods, may be viewed as a factor of production with a service possessing a marginal value product.

It was this failure to capture the essence of time and capital in the production process—if we may continue to employ the overly simple reservoir example used above—which led Wicksell to rebel in his early work against Walras' investment models, though he had fully accepted the exchange and production models of the master. In his first book, Wicksell wrote:

> "In this connection Walras has made an extremely praiseworthy attempt to summarize the phenomena of the production of goods in actual equations, according to the same principles as the phenomena of exchange before. According to him, economic production would be nothing else but an exchange between the products and the "productive services" of labor, land, and capital; and in the last instance production would even be an exchange between these productive services themselves. In this field Walras' investigations probably belong to the most abstract and difficult ever written about economic questions, and it is no easy task to estimate exactly the importance of his assumptions concerning these questions, and the correctness of his conclusions.
>
> "I have, however, been able to convince myself that his theory of production suffers from a fundamental mistake connected with his old-fashioned and one-sided interpretation of the concept of capital, which could only be removed by a thorough revision of his presentation. I have therefore left Walras at this point, in order to side with the more recent theory of capital, the beginnings of which we already find in Jevons, but which was fully developed in Böhm-Bawerk's outstanding work, *Positive Theorie des Kapitals*."[41]

Wicksell's interpretation of Walras' capital model underwent considerable change during his lifetime; in particular, his feeling that Walras' saving function, $X_e = H_e([P]; [Q], [\bar{P}])$ in Model IV-3, was a sterile stationarity requirement that net savings be zero, was rescinded by him. But in his later work the basic criticism contained in the quotation from his early effort is repeated. In essence it is that Walras' theory hinges

[40] See the classic article by L. Robbins, (1).
[41] K. Wicksell, (1), pp. 20–1. Quoted by permission of George Allen & Unwin Ltd.

upon the productivity of capital goods, divorced from time, so that in fact they become, after depreciation allowances, wholly coordinate with nonaugmentable factors:

". . . It [Walras' investment model] affords no answer to the question why a given amount of existing social capital gives rise to a certain rate of interest, neither higher nor lower. The importance of the time element in production was never properly appreciated by Walras and his school. The idea of a *period* of production or of capital investment does not . . . exist in the Walras-Pareto theory; in it capital and interest rank equally with land and rent; in other words, it remains a theory of production under essentially noncapitalistic conditions, even though the existence of durable but apparently indestructible, instruments is taken into account."[42]

It must be emphasized that both Austrian and productivity schools stress the "productivity" aspect of capital: Wicksell, as we shall see, placed this consideration to the fore, almost to the exclusion of the time preference aspects of the problem. It is rather that the "productivity" referred to by the Austrians is the "productivity" of time or waiting, or of nonaugmentable factor services transfigured by time; in the productivity school this time aspect is abstracted from as not meaningful and the treatment of capital as a coordinate factor is characteristic.

This distinction may be made clearer in the following fashion, and Wicksell's criticism of Walras illustrated at the same time. If we neglect intermediate goods by assuming they have been reduced to their component nonaugmentable factors, the Austrians would insist that the production function for a good include the time structure of the inputs:

$$\bar{X}_{jt} = T_j(X_i, t_i) \tag{72}$$

where the t_i are the number of weeks required for the inputs to turn over and where, in relevant ranges, $\frac{\partial \bar{X}_{jt}}{\partial t_i} > 0$.[43] It is the crucial role of these t_i factors which in Walras may be (1) viewed as identically equal to unity, as Walras himself interpreted them, or (2) in the stationary flow, where, as we have discussed, perfect phasing of unfinished goods has been achieved, they may be abstracted from. To Walras, the production process represented by (72) is a series of cross-sections through time, a capital good with a life (however determined) of 10 weeks being viewed as yielding up one tenth of its life in each cross-section. To the Austrians, the production process is a longitudinal slice of time, with focus upon the outputs and inputs over the span of the 10 week period, if this capital

[42] K. Wicksell, (3), Vol. I, p. 171. Quoted by permission.
[43] Cf. W. Leontief, (1), pp. 151–2, and E. Theiss, (1).

good's demise spells the end of the production process. Even in the stationary flow, where week by week the same inputs and outputs are derived, the Austrians never lose sight of the longitudinal axis.

In view of these considerations the appeal of the productivity school to the stationary state is an understandable one: only in this way can the abstraction from time that these theorists need be obtained. But the appeal of the Austrian to the same stationary equilibrium appears self-defeating. Yet, only in this state, as in the simple hydraulic model, can the determinate period of investment of resource services be forthcoming, and only in this state can certain other features of the Austrian system be rendered unambiguously.[44]

But Knight, for whom the stationary state is an unacceptable analytical construct, obtains the permanent character of the capital stock by a different route from Walras and Clark. Knight admits consistently that the Austrian analysis is a valid one for the conditions they postulate, but objects that the conditions are so unrealistic as to rule it from the realm of reality:

"The main conclusion of my argument . . . is that a theory of the general character of that of Jevons, Böhm-Bawerk, and Wicksell . . . is valid under conditions so far contrary to the facts of real life as to deprive the theory of all interpretative value. Most important are two assumptions: (1) that capital goods are produced by the services of agencies which are not capital goods but belong to a distinct class; and (2) that the individual capital good typically has a history of periodic, rhythmical production, consumption, and reproduction, or investment (of noncapital services) and disinvestment (in consumption). The expressions in parentheses will suggest that the two false assumptions are closely interconnected and that it is the first which is primary, and fatal to the argument."[45]

Knight categorically denies the possibility of distinguishing among factors on the basis of permanence or even augmentability: human capabilities, for example, are developed by resource expenditure. This dichotomy is "the ultimate and crucial fallacy in the time-period theory of capital."[46] All factors require maintenance and replacement expenditures. The entire economy may be viewed in week 0 as an organic combination

[44] For example, the period of investment of nonaugmentable resources will be correlated, in nonstationary conditions, with the changes in *investment,* not the capital stock, so that if investment merely slows down, resources will be freed from the construction of longer time processes and the period of investment for the economy could fall even though the capital stock were continuing to rise. This is Kaldor's criticism, in (1), pp. 206–7.

[45] F. Knight, (11), p. 65. Quoted by permission. See also pp. 70–1, and (5), pp. 80–1.

[46] F. Knight, (11), p. 74.

of factors, indistinguishable from one another in any relevant way, delivering services to the body of capital as a maintenance expense to obtain an output, national income, used either to maintain and replace capital or build up the capital stock:

"It is surely axiomatic that any 'production' of material things in any period either represents replacement and hence maintenance of capital (however these concepts are given precise definition) or else it represents a net addition to capital, which is not in accord with stationary conditions. If production is consistently treated as the rendering of services by a given 'plant,' it will be recognized that it does not and cannot require time at all, since consumable services must be consumed in the same instant that they are rendered (produced). And services which add to capital also yield 'instantly' their product, which is an increase in the value of the capital goods on which they are expended."[47]

To Knight, the investment process consists of devoting a stream of factor services to the construction of a capital good instead of consumer goods over a period of construction, t''. At the end of this period of construction, the good, combined with weekly maintenance and replacement expenditures, begins to produce a perpetual flow of consumer goods. Investment includes (1) the devotion of resource services diverted from the production of consumer goods plus (2) the Crusonia-like growth in value of the invested resources over the construction period:

". . . the instant any investment whatever is made, it must be assumed to begin to yield a return which, since it is not instantly consumed, must be added to the investment itself. That is, if an investor begins to sacrifice (invest) consumption income at a rate U_1 . . . , he is after the first instant really investing it at a higher rate of speed, because he could have had some consumption income by stopping the investment process at the first instant."[48]

If U_1 is the "intensity" of consumption sacrificed uniformly per week over a t''-week period of construction, and if U_2 is the weekly stream of consumption goods which begins to flow at the end of t'' weeks and which includes the previously diverted U_1, the internal growth rate on the investment, i_k, is determined by the formula[49]

$$U_2 = U_1(1 + i_k)^{t''} \qquad (73)$$

[47] F. Knight, (6), p. 405. Quoted by permission. It must be pointed out that the Austrians would not dispute the proposition that capital goods gain in value period by period. Knight is discussing time in a different sense from that of an average period of investment of resources.

[48] F. Knight, (7), pp. 445–6. See also (10), pp. 224–5.

[49] To validate this derivation consider the following. Suppose $U_1 = 1$ and were invested at the start of each week for t'' weeks. Then the value of principal and accumulated interest at a rate of return i_k over t'' weeks is:

It must be stressed that the Knightian vision of the investment process is that of a consumer who saves U_1 each week for t'' weeks, then stops all investing and receives a perpetual flow of U_2 if no maintenance and replacement expenditures are made (although they will be generally in Knight's system), plus the U_1 previously diverted. It is *not* the case of the farmer planting U_1 in trees for harvest in week t'', U_1 in trees in period 2 for harvest in week $t'' + 1$, and so forth indefinitely. In the second interpretation it is possible to calculate a period of investment of the foregone consumption income, while in Knight's interpretation it is not possible to do so.[50]

The quantity of capital in any such investment, and in all investments, is the capitalized value of the net perpetual revenue, i.e., U_2 less depreciation and maintenance: "Under competitive conditions, where alone quantity of capital is at all definite, the quantity is the capitalized perpetual net income of any capital good (after full maintenance, including replacements) and is *also* its cost of production, which includes a capital charge."[51]

With the above as background, we may now turn to the question with which we began: how does Knight insure the permanence of the capital stock in his theory? To Knight, even though periodic replacement of the individual investment is necessary, the certainty of replacement is a technological fact inherent in the very concept of a net rate of return, i_k. This is the meaning of such statements as the following, which, at first sight, seem to smack of the mystical analysis of J. B. Clark:

> "It cannot now escape observation that 'capital' is an integrated, organic conception, and the notion that the investment in a particular instrument comes back periodically in the form of product, giving the owner freedom to choose whether he will reinvest or not, is largely a fiction and a delusion. To show this conclusively it should suffice to mention the case of a part of a machine. The part cannot be liquidated without liquidating the machine. And the machine as a unit is in a similar sense a 'part' of an integrated productive organization which is not bounded by the scope of 'plant' or firm, but extends outward indefinitely to indeterminate limits. Moreover, the capital structure and every unit in it is typically planned to perpetuate itself, and not for liquidation . . . ."[52]

---

(1) $$1 + (1 + i_k) + (1 + i_k)^2 + \cdots (1 + i_k)^{t''-1}$$

which, by the formula for the amount of an annuity is

(2) $$\frac{(1 + i_k)^{t''} - 1}{i_k}$$

This sum is to yield a flow of i_k times the sum, or $(1 + i_k)^{t''} - 1$ plus the previously diverted $U_1 = 1$, for a total of $(1 + i_k)^{t''}$.

[50] Cf. F. Knight, (11), p. 70.

[51] F. Knight, (5), p. 82. Quoted by permission.

[52] F. Knight, (5), p. 83. Quoted by permission.

The first part of the paragraph lays stress upon maintenance expenditures to keep the machine operating and similar inflexibilities within larger economic units. Knight has emphasized the difficulties of distinguishing between maintenance and replacement expenditures, and the technological pressure to retain investment by replacing parts to prevent the loss of the larger unit. In extending the organic conception beyond the firm to subsystems of the economy and to the economy as a whole, Knight becomes less convincing, in that maintenance-replacement procedures will be the results of separate suboptimizing managements which do not recognize spillover or external effects in their own decisionmaking.

The last sentence, however, is more important to the Knightian theory. As we have seen in deriving the present value of an investment opportunity, and, implicitly, the internal rate of return on that opportunity, in (11) through (19), it is assumed that the rate of return at which the amortization funds are accumulated is the same as that being earned on the investment in question. That is, for all practical purposes, the very term "net rate of return over cost" defined thusly implies that amortization payments are deducted to perpetuate the investment at the end of its life by the continuous reinvestment in the same type of capital good. Ideally, then, in the stationary flow, if an entrepreneur invests in lathes which last ten years, the age structure of the capital stock will be adjusted so that he will replace one tenth of the lathes each year. One need not accept a smaller rate of return than that being earned on the lathes, and one cannot get more or else (under stationary conditions) the original investment would not have been made. *De facto,* therefore, the investment is converted into a perpetual one.[53]

Thus, there exists a peculiar ambivalence regarding the stationary state in Knight's theory. Because of his attitudes toward time preference and the savings process, Knight is reluctant to discuss an economy whose savings drive ultimately exhausts the investment opportunities afforded by a fixed technological horizon. However, instead of appealing to the forces extant in a progressive state for technological advancement and to the savings drive to make of investments effectively permanent commitments of potential present enjoyment in changing forms, Knight chooses to seek this permanence in a characteristic which can only hold rigorously in the stationary flow.

Under Knight's interpretation of capital and the investment process the Austrian period of investment of nonaugmentable resources disappears: "The production period for consumed services, if the expression is to be used at all, is zero, while the production period for the capital equipment of society is all past economic history."[54]
That is, if we view the economy as an organic combination of factors,

[53] See F. Knight, (1), pp. 211–2. Also see I. Fisher, (3), pp. 527–37.
[54] F. Knight, (5), p. 88. Quoted by permission.

and if we let W depict the value of the services rendered weekly on depreciation and replacement account to maintain the capital stock in the stationary flow, then weekly income may be viewed as W plus net return:

$$Y = W + i_k K \tag{74}$$

where K is the quantity (value) of capital. Let g be the gross return from it, m be the maintenance cost per week on it, and a be the amortization charge. Then

$$i_k K = g - m - a = Y - m - a \tag{75}$$

from the analysis of (11)-(19). Since, in Knight's analysis, m and a are difficult to separate, and both are included in W,

$$K = \frac{Y - W}{i_k} \tag{76}$$

which is the limit of

$$V = (Y - W)[(1 + i_k)^t - 1][i_k(1 + i_k)^t]^{-1} \tag{77}$$

as $t \to \infty$, where t is interpreted as the period over which the net return is earned, or what may be interpreted as the period of investment of non-augmentable resources. Therefore, in the stationary flow, Knight's "period of investment" may be taken as infinite.

A difficulty with Knight's theory is that he does not effectively bring together the productivity and the savings analyses to describe the manner in which the "interest rate," i_k, is determined in a general system. In Knight's organic conception of the economy, of what does W consist? How is the net return on investment computed? Knight indicates that the instantaneous rate of interest in his system, from which the effective rate for any period can be obtained, is the rate of change in capital, or investment (including the internal growth discussed above) divided into the rate of change of consumer goods potentially obtainable if desired at the moment.[55] But how this is determined in just these terms in a market economy is not made clear. One cannot escape the conclusion that i_k is given and fixed (*à la* Crusonia) or given as a function of the existing capital stock which no feasible amount of investment (or saving) in the current period can alter.

3.a.3.a.1. THE PERIOD OF INVESTMENT IN THE AUSTRIAN THEORY. Let us now turn to the work of Wicksell, who accepted the groundwork of Böhm-Bawerk but improved upon it and must be credited with casting the Austrian theory in a rigorous, general model.

Wicksell concentrated upon the third ground for interest in Böhm-Bawerk's system—the so-called "technological superiority of present

[55] F. Knight, (7), pp. 433–5.

goods,"[56] or, more accurately, the productivity of roundabout processes—with such single-mindedness that he is best considered a productivity theorist of the Austrian stripe. His attitudes toward the role of time preference in the determination of the interest rate are atypically ambiguous. Wicksell makes a great point of "separating" the time preference from the productivity aspects of interest determination by going to the stationary state. Time preference, he asserted, affects the accumulation of capital, but if the theorist proceeds to the circular flow where accumulation has ceased, it may be ignored as a factor.[57] In this easy abstraction from marginal time preferences in the stationary state, Wicksell adopts either the Clarkian *assumption* of a constant amount of capital or the level of *t*, the period of investment for the economy as a whole.[58] Yet, at one point, he implies that, in the stationary flow, marginal time preferences would be zero and would take the interest rate with them: ". . . if we consider society as a whole, and regard the average economic conditions as *approximately* stationary, the progressive accumulation of capital must be regarded as economical so long as any rate of interest, however, low, exists . . . . Under such conditions we should, therefore, expect the continued accumulation of capital—though at a diminishing rate—and at the same time a continued fall in the rate of interest."[59]

In Wicksell's early work capital was defined as the value of goods, in existence and to come into existence, which contribute directly to the making of advances to workers and landlords during a period. True interest was earned only on this type of "capital good," while durable man-made goods earned rents.[60] Although in his later work Wicksell formally abolished this distinction between forms of capital, and included durable capital in the wages-rent fund, the "vision" of capital as a fund of advances to non-interest earners is a keynote of his treatment.[61]

[56] We shall discuss and criticize the concept of the technological superiority of present goods in the presentation of the Fisherian model below.

[57] K. Wicksell, (1), pp. 20–2, 111–3, and (3), Vol. I, p. 150.

[58] Compare L. Robbins, (1), pp. 204–6.

[59] K. Wicksell, (3), Vol. I, p. 209. Quoted by permission.

[60] K. Wicksell, (1), pp. 96, 105–6.

[61] Compare Ohlin's preface, pp. xviii–xix, in K. Wicksell, (2). Also, in the early work, *Value, Capital, and Rent,* Wicksell declares that the definition of capital goods is not important in understanding the nature of interest. See K. Wicksell, (1), pp. 105–6. Nevertheless, he writes:

". . . Practically, however, the difference is a highly important one. The volume of circulating capital determines the level of wage, rent, and capital-interest. Upon these the highly durable goods merely exercise the same influence as, say, the size of the cultivated area of land. But their *capital* value is, at least in the stationary economy, an entirely secondary phenomenon and has for the exchange values of consumable goods no importance whatsoever." K. Wicksell, (1), p. 163. Quoted by permission of George Allen & Unwin Ltd.

This basic point about Wicksell's capital theory is important to emphasize because, in the *Lectures,* his treatment of capital begins with the presentation of a straightforward marginal productivity analysis of current land-and-labor and of stored land-

To describe the capital problem, Wicksell sets up the following simple explanation, which, as noted in footnote 61, is in some respects misleading as to the nature of the analysis to follow. Assume a stationary equilibrium in a production economy with a capital stock of which all is consumed in a one-week period. Let Q_1 be the number of labor-weeks available, Q_2 the number of land-weeks available, and K the stock of capital. Then, symbolically,

$$K = [Q_1, Q_2] \tag{78}$$

and the value of capital is

$$Q_1 P_{z_1} + Q_2 P_{z_2} = V \tag{79}$$

Thus, the value of the capital stock available to the economy is the value of the subsistence of nonaugmentable factors for the period in question. The firm has a production function relating current and past land and labor to current output:

$$\bar{X}_{vj} = T_{vj}(X_{10}, X_{20}, X_{1,-1}, X_{2,-1}) \tag{80}$$

In equilibrium,

$$\begin{aligned} &1. \quad T_{vj}^{10} = P_{z_1 0} \\ &2. \quad T_{vj}^{20} = P_{z_2 0} \\ &3. \quad T_{vj}^{1,-1} = P_{z_1,-1} \\ &4. \quad T_{vj}^{2,-1} = P_{z_2,-1} \end{aligned} \tag{81}$$

where the price of the product Y_j is taken as *numéraire,* and where all prices of factor services are prices in the current week; i.e., $P_{z_1,-1}$ is the current price of a unit of last week's labor. Usually, however, $P_{z_1,-1} >$ $P_{z_1,0}$, and

$$\frac{P_{z_i,-1} - P_{z_i 0}}{P_{z_i 0}} = i_k \tag{82}$$

The current scarcity of past land and labor services (in capital goods form, of course) leads to a higher marginal productivity for them, and the difference in marginal productivities between past and current resource services is the interest payment on a unit of that factor service.

If the society saved land and labor services in capital form to the extent that their marginal products were no higher than their marginal productivities in current form, no interest rate would exist. As pointed out in the beginning of the discussion of Model IV-3, a basic question that must be answered in interest theory is why any portion of the admitted boost in total productivity of resources brought about by the use of capi-

---

and-labor in capital good form. This is to some extent a misleading simplification of the essence of his productivity theory, which is Austrian rather than Walrasian.

tal goods accrues to the owners of such goods. The return to a factor depends upon its *marginal* product: if $P_{z_i,-1} = P_{z_i0}$, owners of capital goods would receive for their use only the value of their costs of production. The hike in total product brought about by their use would accrue to the benefit of owners of current labor and current land services.

It is a simple point, but an important one, and it is taught well by Wicksell's simple symbolism: it is a necessary but not a sufficient condition for the payment of interest in a production economy that capital goods be "productive" in the sense that they yield, over their lifetimes, a greater value of finished goods than their cost of production. This fact could hold true but marginal products of the incorporated past factor services could be zero, in which case interest could not exist. Obviously, then, the constraints upon the supply of past land and labor services must be brought in to explain a positive, negative, or zero rate of interest—a lesson Wicksell himself essentially ignored.

It was the *value* phenomenon that had to be explained in Wicksell's capital theory: why does the product of capital at the prices ruling when it is forthcoming have a greater value than the value of the capital good sacrificed? That is the question posed by (81) and (82). Being a value problem, capital theory is subject under nonstationary conditions to changes in the prices of the product produced by the capital goods, and therefore one of the reasons Wicksell (and others) deals consistently with stationary equilibrium is to escape the nettles of value measurement under other regimes.[62]

[62] Three alternatives exist for the measurement of the capital stock of an economy: (1) the Walrasian method of presenting a physical inventory of all capital goods in the economy among the data of the economy; (2) the Austrian "period of investment" for the economy as a whole, as illustrated in simple terms in equation (71) and the accompanying discussion; and (3) as a fund of value, either of the potential value of the consumer goods contained in the stock or of the cost of production of the stock of capital goods.

The ambiguities inherent in the Austrian concept of an average period of investment for the economy as a whole, mercilessly revealed by such critics as Knight, have led modern Austrian theorists to reject the concept as unfruitful. For example, Hayek writes:

"This approach suffers from two fundamental defects, which not only make the conclusions inapplicable to any real phenomena, but even deprive it of value as an initial simplification. For the unrealistic assumptions which it makes do not merely refer to incidental circumstances; they touch the very core of the problem and consequently make it impossible to proceed from them to more realistic cases. The *first* of these two defects is the assumption that the variety of waiting periods which are involved in any given structure of production can be described in terms of a single aggregate which has an unequivocal meaning. The *second* defect is the assumption that the extent to which we are in a position to wait for part of the product of the existing resources, without reducing consumption below the level at which it can be permanently maintained, can similarly be expressed in terms of a single 'amount of waiting,' a kind of product of the volume of commodities for which we have to wait and the time we have to wait for them . . . ." F. Hayek, (2), p. 141. Copyright 1941 by The University of Chicago. Quoted by permission. Hayek reverts to the Walrasian method of inventorying capital goods as a method of describing the capital stock of an

Let us now postulate the simplest conditions of production: an economy where land and rent-goods are free, in which every laborer is his own entrepreneur, and in which only one good, wine, is produced. The wine is sold in an external market, and the price of the given quantity produced by *one worker* rises in function of time:

$$P_j = F_j(t), \qquad F_j^t > 0, F_j^{tt} < 0 \tag{83}$$

where t is the number of weeks the wine is allowed to age. The marginal value product of time within the relevant domain of the function is assumed to be positive, but the slope of the marginal value product function is negative. We have in this case the classic Austrian point-input, point-output example: the services of nonaugmentable resources are expended at one point of time (although labor must be supported during the period of waiting), they ripen into consumable products simultaneously at another well-defined point in time, and only time at the cost of waiting operates upon the unfinished product between the two dates. Further, the results of time's operations on the value of consumer products eventuating are described by a function with the characteristics of (83).

The period of investment of the nonaugmentable resource services in such a case may be unambiguously designated as t weeks: all inputs were introduced into the production process at the same point of time, the product to which they ultimately give rise is unmistakably imputable to the inputs, and the outputs emerge from the process at a single and identifiable point of time.

---

economy, in some places. Usually however, he measures capital by enumerating all of the alternative time flows of consumer goods to which it can give rise.

Metzler has elaborated upon and extended Wicksell's comments upon the difficulties of measuring capital in value terms, particularly in that the act of saving leads to a redefinition in value terms of the society's capital stock. Nevertheless, Metzler rejects Walras' method because he believes it fails to explain the interest rate as a ratio to value of goods, it offers no explanation of the equalization of interest rates among different investments, and neglects the relation of capital goods supply as a whole to the desire of consumers to hold assets. These would seem to be limitations of a partial approach to capital theory, since a general equilibrium approach such as that of Model IV-3, contains such relationships, although, it is true, a deeper analysis must be used to illuminate them. See L. Metzler, (2).

Lerner denies the possibility of measuring capital in units homogeneous with outputs or other inputs, but distinguishes capital in this respect from investment in a Knightian manner. That is, investment is a sacrifice of current goods and therefore its marginal product in terms of future goods can be compared with the required sacrifice in present goods, and a pure number comparable with the interest rate computed from such ratios. Further, since all questions concerning capital changes must occur as questions of investment, the marginal product of investment is the important concept. A. Lerner, (1). Knight has used this method of computation of a pure number to escape a circularity in the definition of the interest rate as a return on a cost-of-production value of capital stock which includes interest. In Knight, however, Lerner's measure *is* the interest rate, definitionally, not only in equilibrium. We have used it above to define i_k in Knight's system. See F. Knight, (7), pp. 433–5.

The total outpayments by the firm over the period t, assuming that the firm must pay interest on the capital it borrows each week as it accrues, will be

$$C = X_z P_z t + K \sum_t (1 + i_k)^t - K \tag{84}$$

where X_z is the amount of labor employed by the firm, P_z is the weekly wage rate, K is the amount of capital borrowed in week 1, i_k is the given interest rate per week, and t is the number of weeks for which resources are invested. We may make $X_z = 1$, where the firm employs only one laborer as in Wicksell's example; moreover, if we assume that simple interest rules instead of compound interest, we will simplify our calculations considerably without affecting the operation of the forces we seek to uncover. Therefore, we may substitute for (84) the simpler expression

$$C = P_z t + K i_k t \tag{85}$$

Now, K is the value of "subsistence goods" which the firm must borrow "effectively" to finance the production process. It is most readily interpreted under the circumstances that the entrepreneur can borrow only in period 1 for t weeks, and must borrow in period 1 *all* of the wage and interest outpayments he will make over the course of t weeks. Then

$$K = P_z t + P_z t^2 i_k \tag{86}$$

is the capital which must be borrowed in period 1. Note that although the laborer gives services only in the first week, he must be supported (receive wages) over the whole period—a peculiarity of this model.

Once more let us simplify and assume that interest need not be paid out as it accrues, week by week, but may rather be paid in lump sum from the proceeds of the sale in period t. Then, (86) simplifies to

$$K = P_z t \tag{87}$$

and the total costs from (85) become

$$C = P_z t + P_z t^2 i_k \tag{88}$$

We may consider the entrepreneur to choose that value for t which (1) returns to him at the end of the period a sufficient revenue to equal C when (2) the wage payments he makes to himself period by period are a maximum. That is, the first condition is that

$$F_j(t) - P_z t - P_z t^2 i_k = 0 \tag{89}$$

If we differentiate this with respect to t, and set $\frac{dP_z}{dt} = 0$ as it must be if

P_z° is to be a maximum, we obtain as a condition

(90) $$F_j^t = P_z + 2P_z i_k t$$

when

(91) $$F_j^{tt} - 2P_z i_k < 0$$

as it will be under the conditions of (83) when $i_k > 0$. We may rewrite (90) as

(92) $$F_j^t = P_z + 2Ki_k$$

Had the entrepreneur chosen to substitute for condition 2 the maximization of the rate of return i_k over the period for a given P_z the same conditions (90) and (91) would have been obtained. And, indeed, had the entrepreneur accepted both P_z and i_k as given and attempted to maximize the difference between total receipts and total costs, conditions (90) and (91) would have to hold in equilibrium.

The left-hand term in (92) may be seen to be the marginal product of time, and the right-hand expression the marginal cost of time. The conditions for equilibrium, then, are that the marginal product of time equal its marginal cost when total revenue equals total cost.

But we have dealt with our firm as if it were isolated, rather than a unit of a functioning economy. It has long been recognized that the firm need not, in week 1, acquire all the capital needed over the investment period.[63] It may instead borrow each week the capital needs of that week if the structure of the economy's production enables it to do so. To illustrate this let us expand the number of firms in the analysis to 39, each producing "consumer goods" in a process with a duration of 13 weeks at the end of which all product emerges. We define:

1. K°: the stock of capital borrowed by the firm on the market day of week 1.

2. K^m: the stock of capital invested in the product of the firm just before consumer goods are sold at the end of week 13.

[63] Compare Senior's comment on the wages-fund theory:

". . . Nor is it absolutely necessary in any case, though, if Adam Smith's words were taken literally, such a necessity might be inferred, that, before a man dedicates himself to a peculiar brand of production, a stock of goods should be stored up to supply him with subsistence, materials, and tools, till his own product has been completed and sold. That he must be kept supplied with those articles is true; but they need not have been stored up before he first sets to work, they may have been produced while his work was in progress . . . ." N. Senior, (1), pp. 78–9.

It was this consideration which led Taussig to suggest the revision of the name of the theory to "wages-flow" instead of "wages-fund" in F. Taussig, (1) pp. 346–7. Fisher credits Newcomb with the first clear vision of wages as coming from a flow rather than a fund. See I. Fisher, (2), p. 526.

Pareto, in (2), p. 309, and Cassel, in (1), pp. 196–9, stressing the continuous nature of production, also noted that current needs were not all met from previously accumulated stocks of necessities.

3. K^*: the "effective stock of capital," or that value which, when multiplied by the interest rate and the number of weeks in the period of investment yields the actual interest payments of the firm over that period.

4. t: the period of construction of the consumer goods, in our case fixed at 13 weeks.

5. P_z: the fixed wage rate per week per unit of labor service. Again we assume that the firm need only borrow to advance its wage payments.

Now, assume that all firms began production in week 1 and poured out product in week 13, began the cycle again in week 14 and completed production in week 26, and so forth. Then, assuming no external sources of financing are available, each firm must have on hand in week 1 the entire capital needed to advance labor its wages over the whole production period. To fix our ideas, assume $P_z = 20$; then

(93) $$K^\circ = P_z t = 20 \times 13 = 260 = K^m$$

The firm must have on hand in period 1 the consumer goods equal in value to the maximum capital stock, K^m, or 260 units of *numéraire* in the example. Then,

(94) $$t = \frac{K^\circ}{P_z} = 13 \text{ weeks}$$

It follows that t is (1) the actual period of production of the goods; (2) the actual period of investment of *all* units of *numéraire* comprising K^m; (3) a measure of the capital required, with given wages and employment in the firm, to finance production; and (4) the turnover period of the firm's capital as wages.

Since all firms are exact replicas of each other, it follows that

(95) $$\bar{K}^\circ = K^\circ \times 39 = 10{,}140 = \bar{K}^m$$

and that

(96) $$\bar{t} = \frac{\bar{K}^\circ}{P_z \times 39} = 13 \text{ weeks}$$

where barred terms are used to denote like concepts for the economy as a whole. The investment period for society as a whole in this simple case is calculable, and, for constant labor force and given wages, measures exactly the capital stock of society.

As a next example we merely assume that the 39 firms do not begin and end their processes simultaneously, but that 3 of the firms finish their 13-week investment periods each week, so that production is even through time. Under such conditions it is no longer necessary for the firm to acquire the maximum capital stock K^m in week 1, since it may now borrow each market day to meet its needs for advances that week. That is,

(97) $$K^\circ \neq K^m$$

The effective capital stock, K^*, is the fictitious magnitude which, if borrowed in period 1 and interest paid on it for the 13 week period, would yield the actual interest paid during the period of production. From this definition, and using the formula $.5(t)(t + 1)$ to obtain the sum of the first t integers, we obtain

$$\begin{aligned}(13i_k)K^* &= P_z i_k + 2P_z i_k + 3P_z i_k + \cdots 13P_z i_k \\ &= .5P_z i_k(t)(t+1) = P_z i_k(91) \\ K^* &= 140\end{aligned} \tag{98}$$

Because of the time phasing of production in this new economy, the firm is *effectively* borrowing 140 instead of 260 in week 1. We may define t^* as the effective investment period of labor services, or the period for which the average *numéraire* unit of labor is invested in the firm's production:

$$t^* = \frac{K^*}{P_z} = 7 \text{ weeks} \tag{99}$$

The average unit of *numéraire* stays in the production "reservoir" 7 weeks; once again we may extend it and the other value, K^*, to the economy as a whole:

$$\bar{t}^* = \frac{\bar{K}^*}{P_z \times 39} = \frac{5460}{780} = 7 \text{ weeks} \tag{100}$$

Thus, the economy as a whole is effectively employing only 5460 units of capital instead of 10,140 units employed in the first example. Merely by phasing production of the economy differently, the society can finance the same national production with smaller capital stocks.

If the period for which wages were paid were the half-week, and the firm could borrow for each half-week, K^* would fall to 135; if the period were to decline to a quarter-week, K^* would fall to 132.5; if the period were allowed to continue to shrink in this manner without limit, $K^* \rightarrow .5K^m$, or in our case, $K^* \rightarrow 130$, and $t^* \rightarrow .5t \rightarrow 6.5$. Therefore, we shall use the approximations

$$\begin{aligned}&1. \quad K^* = .5K^m, \ t^* = .5t \\ &2. \quad \bar{K}^* = .5\bar{K}^m, \ \bar{t}^* = .5\bar{t}\end{aligned} \tag{101}$$

in the formulae to follow.[64]

[64] We may use the firm in this example to illustrate a useful measure of an "average period of investment," T, developed by Boulding. The firms in our economy make 13 weekly payments of wages and receive one payment at the end of the 13th week which includes wage costs plus interest. In the general case let C_t be a cost payment in the tth week and R_t a receipt in the tth period. Then, we define r, the internal rate of return, as that value which equates the sum of the discounted receipts to the sum

It follows that:

1. $\bar{t}^*$ is a calculable measure under these conditions, so that it is meaningful to speak of a period of investment, not only for the firm but for the economy as a whole.

2. $\bar{t}^*$ is the period the average unit of labor service is invested in the economy as a whole.

3. $\bar{t}^*$ is about one half of the period of construction of the consumer goods, $\bar{t}$.

4. $\bar{t}^*$ is the period of turnover of the firm's and nation's capital stock as wages.

5. if $\bar{K}^*$ is viewed as the effective size of the capital reservoir in the economy, $P_z \times 39$ is the weekly inflow of labor services as well as the weekly outflow of goods valued at labor content, then $\bar{t}^*$ is the time it takes a unit of labor to move through the production process. Now, if

---

of the discounted costs:

$$\sum_t R_t(1 + r)^{-t} = \sum_t C_t(1 + r)^{-t} \tag{1}$$

Define an average date of payments and an average date of receipts in the following manner. Let t_c be the week which is the time center of the cost payments. It is defined by the equation:

$$\sum_t C_t = \sum_t C_t(1 + r)^{t_c - t} \tag{2}$$

In the same fashion, the time center for receipts, t_r, is given by:

$$\sum_t R_t = \sum_t R_t(1 + r)^{t_r - t} \tag{3}$$

Multiply both sides of (2) by $(1 + r)^{t_r - t_c}$:

$$\left(\sum_t C_t\right)(1 + r)^{t_r - t_c} = (1 + r)^{t_r} \sum_t C_t(1 + r)^{-t} \tag{4}$$

And (3) may be rewritten:

$$\sum_t R_t = \left(\sum_t C_t\right)(1 + r)^{t_r - t_c} \tag{5}$$

Boulding defines $t_r - t_c = T$ as the "time spread of the investment." Given an internal rate of return, it is the time required for the sum of costs to grow to equality with the sum of receipts—a period-of-investment concept. Letting R be the sum of receipts and C the sum of costs, we may rewrite (5) as

$$T = \frac{\log R - \log C}{\log (1 + r)} \tag{6}$$

Suppose that the firm in our example sold its product in the 13th week for 278.20. This would lead to an internal rate of return of $r = .01$ per week. Substituting this into (2) yields $t_c = 6.8$ and substituting into (3) yields $t_r = 13$, so that $T = 6.2$. See K. Boulding, (1).

wages and the size of the labor force remain fixed, and $\bar{K}^*$ increases, the economy is using more capital per unit of labor, the average time period the typical unit of labor is invested rises, and $\bar{t}^*$ rises: these statements are equivalent.

6. time itself may be treated as a factor of production with a price, which is what the Austrians sought, as noted above.

Every week, the 39 firms require $P_z \times 39 = 780$ to finance their investment; this is the labor value of the gross increment in capital contributed by their operations that week. But, each week, three firms finish their processes, with a product whose labor value is $20 \times 13 \times 3 = 780$, which is the economy's gross disinvestment. The excess in value accrues each week to lenders as interest if, as we suppose, competition eliminates all surpluses.

Let us now follow the lead given in point (6) above and assume that $\bar{t}$ (and therefore $\bar{t}^*$) is variable and that the value $\bar{t} = 13$ is an optimal value rather than fixed. We define the per-worker-value-of-product function for the firm, as we did in (83), showing the value of output emerging from a construction period of any length in a relevant domain:

(102) $$V = F(t),\ F' > 0,\ F'' < 0$$

The marginal revenue product of time is therefore positive in that domain of t.

The total cost to the firm of a production period of length t will be, on the assumption that one unit of labor is used per week,

(103) $$C = P_z t + K^*(1 + i_k)^t - K^*$$

where compound interest is used, or, with simple interest assumed for simplicity,

(104) $$C = P_z t + K^* i_k t = K^m + K^* i_k t \cong 2K^* + K^* i_k t$$

The last approximation follows from (101).

The firm, given i_k and P_z will attempt to maximize the difference between V and C by choosing an appropriate t. This will occur when

(105) $$F^t = P_z + 2K^* i_k - .5P_z i_k$$

But competition will have forced the total costs of the firm to equality with the value of product at fruition, so that in equilibrium:

(106) $$\begin{aligned} F(t) &= P_z t + K^* i_k t \\ &= (F^t - K^* i_k + .5P_z i_k)t \end{aligned}$$

and

(107) $$d^2(V - C)/dt^2 = F^{tt} - P_z i_k < 0$$

which will hold for $i_k \geqq 0$ when the conditions on V stated in (102) hold.

We shall now return to the world of compound interest. We have defined K^* as that fictitious amount of capital which, if borrowed by the firm in the current period and accumulated at i_k for t weeks would yield the interest payments actually made by the firm when it sells its product in week t. That is, when $A = (1 + i_k)$,

$$(108) \quad K^*A^t - K^* = P_z\left(\sum_{h=1}^{t} A^h - t\right)$$

$$= P_z\left(\frac{A}{A-1}\right)\left(A^t - 1 - \frac{A-1}{A}t\right)$$

which may be reduced to

$$(109) \qquad K^* = K^m\left(\frac{A}{A-1}\right)\left(\frac{1}{t} - \frac{(A-1)}{A(A^t-1)}\right)$$

In a stationary flow, where $t = 13$, and the number of firms, o, is 39, there will be 13 groups of 3 firms each in different stages of completion of their final product. For such an economy we may measure capital as a value-measure in several ways. As of the market day of the current period, we may define capital as (1) the present value of the surplus over labor value of the product of 13 groups of firms; (2) the value of a fund of capital which will yield the present surplus over labor value in perpetuity; and (3) the labor value of the product currently held by the 13 groups accumulated at the current interest rate to the current period.

1. *Capital as Present Value of the Surplus.* The net value of product for a firm, $V - P_zt$, or $V - K^m$, will be equal in stationary equilibrium, when $V = C$, to the interest payments of the firm. This may be written from (108) and (109)

$$(110) \qquad K^*(A^t - 1) = K^m\left(\frac{A}{A-1}\right)\left(\frac{A^t-1}{t} - \frac{A-1}{A}\right)$$

One group of $\frac{o}{t}$ firms will, on the market day of week 0, be one week away from realizing this interest payment, and the present value of this group's surplus will be

$$(111) \qquad \frac{o}{t}\left(\frac{K^*(A^t-1)}{A}\right)$$

A second group will be two weeks away from realization, so the present value of its surplus will be

$$(112) \qquad \frac{o}{t}\left(\frac{K^*(A^t-1)}{A^2}\right)$$

and so forth to the last group whose present value of surplus will be

$$(113) \qquad \frac{o}{t}\left(\frac{K^*(A^t-1)}{A^t}\right)$$

For the economy as a whole, therefore, the present value of surpluses from operations of existing firms will be

$$\bar{N} = \frac{\bar{K}^m}{t}\left(\frac{A}{A-1}\right)\left(\frac{A^t - 1}{t} - \frac{A-1}{A}\right)\left(\sum_{h=1}^{t} A^{-h}\right) \tag{114}$$

or

$$\bar{N} = \frac{\bar{K}^m}{t}\left(\frac{A}{A-1}\right)\left(\frac{A^t - 1}{t} - \frac{(A-1)}{A}\right)\left(\frac{A^t - 1}{A^t(A-1)}\right) \tag{115}$$

and

$$\bar{N} = \frac{\bar{K}^m}{t^2}\left(\frac{A(A^t - 1)}{A-1} - t\right)\left(\frac{A^t - 1}{A^t(A-1)}\right) \tag{116}$$

2. *Capital as the Present Value of a Perpetuity.* One difficulty with the first value concept is the element of arbitrariness in the selection of t as the period over which to sum present values. For example, $\frac{o}{t}$ of the firms in the current week have invested nothing in unfinished product, having just sold their finished product the period before. Why not, then, in this stationary flow, sum the present values of surpluses which other groups of firms have not yet begun to produce—those of period $t + 1$, $t + 2$, and so forth?

In Knightian fashion, let us simply forget t, the construction period of the capital goods, and treat the economy as an organic system, which is yielding a weekly income of

$$Y = k^m + s \tag{117}$$

where k^m is the labor cost of the week's output and s the interest costs of that output. We view the total value of labor services expended this period as a maintenance-plus-replacement expenditure so that net revenue is defined as

$$Y - oP_z = s \tag{118}$$

Then, we may define capital as that fund of value which, when invested at i_k, yields s in perpetuity:

$$\bar{N}' = \frac{s}{i_k} \tag{119}$$

In the symbols of the Wicksellian model, we may write this

$$\begin{aligned} \bar{N}' &= \frac{o}{t}\left(\frac{K^*(A^t - 1)}{A-1}\right) \\ &= \frac{\bar{K}^m}{t^2}\left(\frac{A(A^t - 1)}{A-1} - t\right)\left(\frac{1}{A-1}\right) \\ &= \bar{N}\left(\frac{A^t}{A^t - 1}\right) \end{aligned} \tag{120}$$

Obviously, as t, the period over which $\bar{N}$ is computed, becomes very large, these two capital measures approach one another.

Indeed, we may interpret (119) in a Knightian manner. From (116) and (110) it may be seen that $\frac{\bar{K}^m}{t^2}\left(\frac{A(A^t - 1)}{A - 1} - t\right)$ in (120) represents the surplus accruing in any one week. In this expression t may be interpreted as a construction period in the Knight sense, and i_k the equilibrium internal growth rate of investment in his theory. The second bracketed expression in (116) is merely that for the present value of one unit of *numéraire* earned for t periods beginning in one week. It is this period which Knight allows to approach infinity, in which case the expression becomes $\frac{1}{i_k}$, as in (119).

3. Capital as Accumulated Value of Nonaugmentable Factor Services. Another value-of-capital measure is the current value on the market day of the current week of all unfinished goods existing on the market day. This is obtained in the stationary flow by accumulating the labor services contained in these goods. In the present market day, there will be $\frac{o}{t}$ firms whose goods will be equal in value to finished value less one week's labor and interest, $\frac{o}{t}$ firms with goods whose value is final value less two weeks labor and interest, and so forth, to the set which has no goods at all:

$$
\begin{aligned}
&1. \quad \frac{o}{t}[K^*(A^t - 1) + K^m] - P_z \sum_{h=1}^{13} A^h \\
(121)\quad &2. \quad \frac{o}{t}[K^*(A^t - 1) + K^m] - P_z \sum_{h=2}^{13} A^h \\
&\quad\vdots \\
&12. \quad \frac{o}{t}[K^*(A^t - 1) + K^m] - P_z A^{13}
\end{aligned}
$$

If we reduce the geometric progressions to amounts of annuities, we obtain by summing over all firms:

$$(122)\quad \bar{N}'' = \bar{K}^*(A^t - 1) + \bar{K}^m - P_z\left(\frac{A}{A-1}\right)\left(tA^t - \frac{A^t - 1}{A - 1}\right)$$

which reduces to[65]

$$(123)\qquad \bar{N}'' = P_z\left(\frac{A(A^t - 1)}{A - 1}\right)\left(o + \frac{1}{A - 1} - \frac{A^t}{A^t - 1}t\right)$$

[65] Dorfman has derived a similar measure in his presentation of Böhm-Bawerk's model, in R. Dorfman, (2), pp. 157–8.

We have seen that the Austrian measure of capital, $\bar{N}$, is quite close to the Knightian $\bar{N}'$ for large values of t (see (120)). It follows that the Austrian measure of capital, t^*, and its related value, $\bar{K}^*$, are, under stationary conditions, also quite close to the Knightian measure of capital, $\bar{N}'$. If we substitute from (109) into (116), and this new equation into (120), we obtain the following relationship:

$$(124) \qquad \bar{N}' = \bar{K}^* \left(\frac{A^t - 1}{A - 1}\right)\left(\frac{1}{t}\right) = \bar{K}^* \left(\frac{(1 + i_k)^t - 1}{i_k}\right)\left(\frac{1}{t}\right)$$

If simple interest were used, or if i_k is small enough and/or t is short enough so that all terms involving powers of i_k are ignored, the two capital measures are identical. In those situations in which the compounding effects are significant, this is no longer true, but the approximation is reasonably correct. For example, if $i_k = .06$ and $t = 10$, so that $A = 1.06$, $\bar{N}' = \frac{.7905}{.6000}\bar{K}^*$. When $t = 5$, $A = 1.06$, $\bar{N}' = \frac{.338}{.300}\bar{K}^*$.

In the current period, the magnitude of K in our example has a direct meaning which even Knight is willing to accept. It is the clearly marked period over which all labor inputs were invested; this began, for the product that matures in week 0 in week -12, and no inputs precede that date. Let us now retain the assumption that only one nonaugmentable factor exists, but also assume that, looking back from week 0 to the origins of the product of the 3 firms whose product is maturing in the current week, it is impossible to find a finite cutoff point in time for such inputs. We shall assume that for every period between $-\infty$ and week 0 it is possible to identify the amount of input into the product and that from -1 to $-\infty$ these amounts fall successively toward zero as a limit. Let $X_{z,-g}$ be the input for week $t = -g$. Then we may define for the firm

$$(125) \qquad K^m = P_z \sum_{g=\infty}^{0} X_{z,-g}$$

In similar fashion, effective capital for the economy is defined, for compound interest conditions, as

$$(126) \qquad \bar{K}^* = \frac{\sum_{g=\infty}^{0} P_z X_{z,-g}(A^{g+1} - 1)}{A^{h+1} - 1}$$

At this point our concept of "effective capital" fails us, since the denominator does not approach a limit: obviously, for any positive interest rate, and an infinite period, it takes an amount of capital indistinguishable from zero to compound to very large amounts.

Moreover, it will be noted that we did not use the concept of K^* under compound interest conditions to define a t^* as we did in our earlier models with simple interest. The term, t^*, is the Austrian period of production, or the average period of time in which a given *numéraire* unit of nonaugmentable resources flowed through a production process. For a set of inputs structured through time, the computation of such a summary technological datum, when it can be measured, should be unaffected by the interest rate which happens to rule. Böhm-Bawerk obtained the measure by weighting the inputs during each week of the t-week production period by the number of weeks that input was from the date of completion of the product, and divided this weighted total by the total number of units of inputs employed during the whole process. Thus, for a firm in the economy with which we have been dealing, t^* was obtained by the formula

$$t^* = \frac{\sum_{g=1}^{t} (1)g}{t} \tag{127}$$

or, more generally, where each period may have employed a constant flow of more than one unit of labor

$$t^* = \frac{\sum_{g=1}^{t} (X_z)g}{X_z t} \tag{128}$$

When, in stationary conditions, the wage rate remains constant, we will alter nothing by dealing with the value of labor rather than physical quantities of it:

$$t^* = \frac{\sum_{g=1}^{t} (P_z X_z)g}{P_z X_z t} = \frac{.5(t)(t+1)}{t} = .5(t+1) \tag{129}$$

From (98) it will be noted that K^* is unaffected by the value of i_k, which can indeed be cancelled out, so that

$$K^* = \frac{\sum_{g=1}^{t} (P_z X_z)g}{t} = \frac{.5P_z X_z(t)(t+1)}{t} = .5P_z X_z(t+1) \tag{130}$$

Dividing this by the weekly wage bill, $X_z P_z$, as shown in (99), reveals the same definition of t^* as that in (129).

Weighting inputs by simple interest implicitly weights them by the number of weeks away from fruition of the product: compound interest, rising faster than the arithmetic progression of time, obviously will not do so, nor will the interest rate wash out without trace. For example, from (109) and for our example, when $i_k = .05$, $P_z = 20$, $K^* = 284$, and when $i_k = .02$, $K^* = 133$, as compared with the $K^* = 140$ obtained with simple interest weighting.

Let us therefore revert to the Austrian period of investment for the problem in hand. From (129),

$$(131) \qquad t^* = \frac{\sum_{g=\infty}^{0} (P_z)(X_{z,-g})(g+1)}{K^m}$$

where K^m is defined in (125). Since both numerator and denominator of (131) approach a limit, the Austrian period of investment is determinate even though the "period of construction," t, is infinite in length.[66]

But, as we may discern from the criticisms of Knight of the Austrian period of investment, the ability to define t^* for the firm and the society under the conditions assumed in Gifford's analysis is not an answer to the major strictures of the critics. The heart of that criticism is the asserted inability to interpret production as periodic; i.e., to find a meaningful t.

To illustrate the difference in interpretations, let us use the following example. Kaldor initially understood Knight's vision of investment to be a process in which resources, X_zP_z in value, are invested in the production of a capital good yielding all of its value in t weeks. For example, the farmer plants X_zP_z in trees in week 0 to mature in week $t - 1$, X_zP_z in trees in week 1 to mature in week t, and so forth. In stationarity, it is possible to look upon X_zP_z as an input for maintenance and replacement, and the value of the trees maturing each week, P_j, as a gross value return. Then,

$$(132) \qquad X_zP_z(1 + i_k)^t = P_j$$

or, simplifying the symbols,

$$(133) \qquad m(1 + i)^t = g$$

which is a special case of the example we have been using.

On the basis of compound interest, however, in stationary equilibrium, C_j, or total cost, will equal P_j (or g), and, in addition, the perpetuity $P_j - X_zP_z$ (or $g - m$), the weekly interest payment, will have a value, equal to cost, of

$$(134) \qquad C_j = \frac{P_j - X_zP_z}{i_k} = \frac{g - m}{i}$$

[66] This analysis is that of C. Gifford, (1).

Then, substituting,

$$(1 + i)^t = \left(1 + \frac{iC_j}{m}\right) \tag{135}$$

and

$$\frac{C_j}{m} = \frac{(1 + i)^t - 1}{i} \tag{136}$$

Or, $\frac{C_j}{m}$ will be the amount of an annuity of one unit of *numéraire* invested at i each week of a t-week period.[67]

If construction costs rise relative to maintenance costs, in conditions of fixed i_k, t must rise, and, in the opposite case, t must fall. Thus, if the cost of time, i_k, is constant, so that t reflects only the "method of production" in its substitution of initial for subsequent inputs, t varies directly with the value of initial resources employed relative to subsequent. If i_k rises when C_j and m are constrained to remain constant, equilibrium requires that t fall. The Austrian theorist can simplify these statements by converting "time" or "waiting" into a separate factor of production whose price is the interest rate, and refer to a rise in t with a fall in i_k and a fall in t with a rise in i_k in a straightforward marginal revenue productivity analysis, assuming the prices of future inputs to be constant. In Kaldor's view, this Austrian use of the period of investment —in (136) the average time a unit of *numéraire* in nonaugmentable factor services takes to "move through" the reservoir of capital value in the $\bar{N}'$ sense—was the mere adaptation of the marginal productivity doctrine to the problems of capital. We shall expand these arguments in the presentation of the Kaldor model below.

The dispute over the calculability of t arises, however, in the view of the investment process. As we have seen, and as Knight pointed out to Kaldor,[68] t in the Knightian analysis is a period of construction of capital goods (we have symbolized it t'' in our previous analysis) after which, with maintenance and replacement expenditures, an eternal stream of goods enters the weekly flow together with the previously diverted flow of goods into investment. The analogy is not that of the farmer planting trees, but that of the same farmer employing the services of nonaugmentable and augmentable factors alike (to use a terminology not accepted by Knight as accurate) for t'' weeks to drill a well which then,

[67] N. Kaldor, (1), pp. 211–4. In this article, Kaldor derives a simpler measure of t which he pointed out later was illegitimate because it employed both simple and compound interest assumptions. See N. Kaldor, (2), p. 167. Further, Kaldor's present thinking concerning the analysis which follows is to be found in N. Kaldor, (3), pp. 6–7.

[68] See F. Knight, (11), p. 70. This interpretation was accepted by Kaldor in N. Kaldor, (2), p. 167.

with weekly maintenance-replacement expenditures of the same types of resource services, yields an eternal stream of water for consumption along with the consumption product of the previously invested factor services. Even if it were possible to discern the value of inputs from $-\infty$ to the end of the construction period—which Knight denies—who can tell when a "construction" input emerges from the investment and when a "maintenance" input emerges? Without some ability to construct a period of entry and exit for resources, if only in marginal terms, it simply is impossible to determine the size of the capital reservoir. When t is calculable, as Knight agrees, the Austrian t^* may be used in the productivity analysis; in most circumstances, Knight believes, and presumably most economists would agree with him, it is not possible to calculate it and another form of productivity analysis must be employed.[69]

We shall complete this section, concerned with the presentation and criticism of the Austrian type of production theory, with the assumption, implicit up to this point, that conditions are such as to make t and t^* calculable for the firm's production processes. Two general models will interest us: the first is a grafting of the Wicksellian capital analysis on to a Walrasian model of the type of Model IV-3. The distinguishing feature of this model is its ability to denote some resources as augmentable and others as nonaugmentable. The second model is Kaldor's model of an economy in which all factors are augmentable under linear homogeneous production conditions.

4. Models Featuring the Austrian Productivity Approach

We shall now generalize the simple Wicksellian model presented in the previous section within the context of Model IV-3.

4.a. Model IV-5: The Wicksellian-Walrasian Model

We shall revert to the option discussed in the presentation of Model IV-3 of perfect time-phasing of production in an economy where productive processes extend beyond one week in duration. Capital goods are held by consumers at the start of the week in the form of durable "rent-goods" in Wicksell's sense and of "unfinished" goods of the rent-good and consumer good type. No finished stocks of consumer goods exist in the economy, so that consumers must be supported entirely in week 0 from the consumer goods that emerge in that week. We assume that we break into a stationary equilibrium where all price expectations are the same as current prices and where all expectations will, in the event, prove correct.

The conditions of production are such that all firms are single product firms who initiate processes in a given week, invest resources for some variable period t_j, and obtain all of the product at the end of that period. During the period t_j, the firm ends each week with unfinished product

[69] See footnote 45 above and its referend.

which it returns to those consumers who have leased the unfinished goods to the firm or have bought its securities that week, and at the beginning of the following week it leases the unfinished goods one stage further along from consumers.

For example, in the first week of its construction period a firm enters the security market and sells 5 of securities, with which it buys 5 of current resources. It ends the week with an unfinished good worth 5 with which it redeems its securities. At the start of the second week the firm leases the unfinished good at a price which includes depreciation (100 per cent) plus a net return which in effect is interest. To the unfinished good it adds (say) 8 in current resources, to obtain an unfinished good whose value is $(5 + 8 + 5i_k)$. The firm has sold securities during the week to obtain advances with which to pay for the services of current factors ("rent goods" and labor), or a total of 8. It returns $5(1 + i_k)$ of the unfinished product to the lessors and 8 to redeem its securities, and clears its books at the end of the week. Note that the firm does not make advances to the "capitalist"—the lessor of unfinished goods—in this model. If he desires to consume interest in the period, as he would in the stationary state, he may sell $5i_k$ in securities, consume this amount in current goods, and redeem the securities in unfinished product at the end of the week. Thus, ultimately, advances are made each week at the expense of the "saver."

But, as we have seen in the discussion of Model IV-3, we may escape from this clumsy process by abstracting from these unfinished goods and dealing only with current resource services. Into the production function, however, we may introduce a new variable, t. The firm's production function may be written

$$(137) \quad \bar{X}_{vj} = T_{vj}(X_{z_1 0}, \ldots, X_{z_m 0}, \ldots, X_{z_1 h}, \ldots, X_{z_m h}, X_{10}, \ldots, X_{n0}, \ldots, X_{1h}, \ldots, X_{nh}, t)$$

where h is the end of the potential planning horizon.

The model may then be constructed. The conditions of individual consumer equilibrium are unchanged from those of Model IV-3 when one interprets Q_{ci} as including unfinished goods—an interpretation we have already indicated is possible in that earlier model:

(IV-5-0) = (IV-3-0)

And similarly for the aggregate consumer functions:

(IV-5-1) = (IV-3-1)

Aggregate functions for all firms' demands for and supplies of current rent-good services, intermediate goods, and final consumer and rent-goods are unchanged from the previous model:

(IV-5-2) = (IV-3-2)

Each period, for each firm, the realized and *potential* profits obtainable if unfinished product were sold must be zero:

(IV-5-3)

1. $$\bar{X}_{vjt_f}P_j = \sum_{g=t_0}^{t_f} C_{vjg} + K^*_{vjo}(A^{1-t_0} - 1) + K^*_{vjf}(A^{t_f} - 1)$$

2. $$\bar{X}_{vZ_it_f}P_{Z_i} = \sum_{g=t_0}^{t_f} C_{vZ_ig} + K^*_{vZ_io}(A^{1-t_0} - 1) + K^*_{vZ_if}(A^{t_f} - 1)$$

where t_0 is defined as the given period in which production was started and t_f the period in which it is scheduled to be finished and sold. Further definitions are:

3. $$C_{vjg} = \sum_i X_{viJ_g}P_i + \sum_j X_{vjJ_g} P_j, \quad g = t_0, \ldots, -1, 0, 1, \ldots, t_f$$

4. $$C_{vZ_ig} = \sum_i X_{viZ_ig} P_i + \sum_j X_{vjZ_ig}P_j, \quad g = t_0, \ldots, -1, 0, 1, \ldots, t_f$$

5. $$K^*_{vjo} = \frac{\sum_{g=t_0}^{0} C_{vjg}(A^g - 1)}{(A^{-t_0} - 1)}$$

6. $$K^*_{vZ_io} = \frac{\sum_{g=t_0}^{0} C_{vZ_ig}(A^g - 1)}{(A^{-t_0} - 1)}$$

7. $$K^*_{vjf} = \frac{\sum_{g=1}^{t_f} C_{vjg}(A^g - 1)}{(A^{t_f} - 1)}$$

8. $$K^*_{vZ_if} = \frac{\sum_{g=1}^{t_f} C_{vZ_ig}(A^g - 1)}{(A^{t_f} - 1)}$$

9. $$A = \left(1 + \frac{1}{P_e}\right)$$

That is, for each firm, the value of its past and future cost payments for resource services and intermediate products accumulated or discounted to the present must equal the sale price of its product discounted back to the present.

All product and service markets must be cleared in the current market day:

(IV-5-4) = (IV-3-4)

Each period each firm will enter the fulfillment week with partially completed product or no product. In either case, we may define the firm's production function as of the current week, including in it inputs from past as well as future periods; t_0, the number of weeks invested in the unfinished product; and t_{f+1}, the number of periods from the market day of the present to the end of the completion week. For the firm, then

(IV-5-5)

1. $$\bar{X}_{vj} = T_{vj}(X_{z_1g}, \ldots, X_{z_mg}, X_{1g}, \ldots, X_{ng}, t)$$
$$g = -t_0, \ldots, -1, 0, 1, \ldots, t_f$$

2. $$\bar{X}_{vZ_i} = T_{vi}(X_{z_1g}, \ldots, X_{z_mg}, X_{1g}, \ldots, X_{ng}, t)$$
$$g = -t_0, \ldots, -1, 0, 1, \ldots, t_f$$

where the t-inputs denote the productivity of time alone in some processes, e.g., agricultural. In week 0, for all $g > -1$, the prospective discounted marginal revenue productivity of each input, discounted to the period of its input, must equal its discounted price:

3. $$T^{ig}_{vj} \frac{P_j}{A^{t_f - g}} = \frac{P_i}{A^g}$$

4. $$T^{jg}_{vj} \frac{P_J}{A^{t_f - g}} = \frac{P_j}{A^g}$$

5. $$T^{ig}_{vZ_i} \frac{P_{Z_i}}{A^{t_f - g}} = \frac{P_i}{A^g}$$

6. $$T^{jg}_{vZ_i} \frac{P_{Z_i}}{A^{t_f - g}} = \frac{P_j}{A^g}$$

Lastly, as of the current week, the amount of additional time which the firm plans to invest, in the sense of merely holding product without expenditures on current resources, will be determined by the requirement that the present value of the marginal revenue product of time be equal to the present value of the cost of the time, where we treat time as continuous and indefinitely divisible as an approximation to reality:

7. $$\frac{T^t_{vj} P_j}{A^{t_f}} = \frac{P_j(A - 1)}{A^{t_f}}$$

8. $$\frac{T^t_{vi} P_{Z_i}}{A^{t_f}} = \frac{P_{Z_i}(A - 1)}{A^{t_f}}$$

For the firm, the addition to capital in period 0 may be defined as the sum of its payments over the period:

$$\text{(IV-5-6)} \quad 1. \qquad \Delta K_v = \sum_i X_{vi}P_i + \sum_j X_{vj}P_j + K^*_{vo}(A - 1)$$

where K^*_{vo} is K^*_{vjo} or K^*_{vZio} as relevant.

For all firms

$$2. \qquad \Delta K = \sum_v \Delta K_v$$

Then, for the economy, gross savings must equal all additions to unfinished stocks over the period, including finished capital goods in this category as unfinished consumer goods:

$$3. \qquad X^\circ_e P^\circ_e = \Delta K^\circ + X^\circ_{Z_i} P^\circ_{Z_i}$$

Since ΔK is national income, our conditions state that the economy must be willing to add to its stocks of unfinished goods, in a gross sense, one week's income. Since one week's income is released in finished product, net investment is zero, assuming of course that depreciation of rent-goods equals new investment in them.

(IV-5-7) = (IV-3-7)

To the data of Model IV-3 we have added that $X_{vi,g}$ and $X_{vj,g}$ for $g < 0$, as well as the t_0 terms. To the unknowns we have added: (a) $om(t_f)$ $X_{vi,g}$ terms, $g \geqq 0$; (b) $on(t_f)$ $X_{vj,g}$ terms, $g \geqq 0$; (c) A; (d) the o K^*_{ov} terms; (e) the o K^*_{vf} terms; (f) the o ΔK_v terms; (g) ΔK; and (h) the o t_f terms. This is a total of $4o + ot_f\ (m + n) + 2$ new unknowns. The net addition to equations is (a) $2o + 1$ in (IV-5-3-3, -4, and -5); (b) $t_f(m + n)$ in (IV-5-5-3, -4, -5, and -6), and o in (IV-5-5-7 and -8); and (c) the $o + 1$ in (IV-5-6-1 and -2).

This model differs somewhat from Wicksell's in that no inventories of finished consumer goods exist at the start of the week: all "capital" in the Wicksellian sense emerges from current production. We have not introduced such stocks because we shall postpone until Chapter 5 the consideration of "synchronization" media. With this unimportant exception, however, it contains the essence of the Wicksellian performance. Every firm's period of production is a variable in the model, time or waiting is a productive factor, and the price of time, as well as the firm's period of production, is strongly influenced by the willingness of savers to save. If, for example, savers were willing only to replace rent-goods which depreciate, all firms would have to adopt periods of production of one week.

4.b. The Kaldor Model

Kaldor has constructed an economy[70] where all factors are augmentable in accordance with economic motivation, and, in addition, are non-perpetual. He uses slaves and machines (Z_1 and Z_2 respectively) as such factors, and bread, Y_1, as the only consumer good produced. The services z_1 and z_2 of both factors enter into the production functions of each of the three goods:

(IV-6-1)

$$1.\quad \bar{X}_1 = T_1(X_{z_1 1}, X_{z_2 1})$$

$$2.\quad \bar{X}_{Z_1} = T_{Z_1}(X_{z_1 Z_1}, X_{z_2 Z_1})$$

$$3.\quad \bar{X}_{Z_2} = T_{Z_2}(X_{z_1 Z_2}, X_{z_2 Z_2})$$

Kaldor assumes that because no factor is limitational, efficiency of factors will be a function of relative combinations only, and, therefore, that each of the functions in (IV-6-1) is linear and homogeneous.[71]

Letting Y_1 be the *numéraire*, we impose the conditions in equilibrium that price of each product equal average cost:

(IV-6-2)

$$1.\quad \bar{X}_1^\circ = X^\circ_{z_1 1} P^\circ_{z_1} + X^\circ_{z_2 1} P^\circ_{z_2}$$

$$2.\quad \bar{X}^\circ_{Z_1} P^\circ_{Z_1} = X^\circ_{z_1 Z_1} P^\circ_{z_1} + X^\circ_{z_2 Z_1} P^\circ_{z_2}$$

$$3.\quad X^\circ_{Z_2} P^\circ_{Z_2} = X^\circ_{z_1 Z_2} P^\circ_{z_1} + X^\circ_{z_2 Z_2} P^\circ_{z_2}$$

Also, costs in each industry are minimized:

(IV-6-3)

$$1.\quad \frac{T_1^1}{P_{z_1}} = \frac{T_1^2}{P_{z_2}}$$

$$2.\quad \frac{T_{Z_1}^1}{P_{z_1}} = \frac{T_{Z_1}^2}{P_{z_2}}$$

$$3.\quad \frac{T_{Z_2}^1}{P_{z_1}} = \frac{T_{Z_2}^2}{P_{z_2}}$$

The net rate of return on capital goods must be equal for both factors:

(IV-6-4)

$$1.\quad \frac{P^\circ_{z_1} - u_1 P^\circ_{Z_1}}{P^\circ_{Z_1}} = i^\circ_k$$

$$2.\quad \frac{P^\circ_{z_2} - u_2 P^\circ_{Z_2}}{P^\circ_{Z_2}} = i^\circ_k$$

[70] This model is similar to the von Neumann model of an expanding economy which we shall analyze in Chapter 8, and Kaldor reaches the same conclusion about the interest rate when all final product is reinvested. It was derived independently by Kaldor in (1). Von Neumann's model was first presented in Princeton in 1932, but was not published in English until 1945. See Section 3.d. of Chapter 8, below. Also, see N. Kaldor, (3), p. 7.

[71] See the reference to the controversy over this point in footnote 26, Chapter 3.

Demand for inputs in equilibrium must equal supply:

(IV-6-5)
$$1.\quad X^{\circ}_{z_1 1} + X^{\circ}_{z_1 Z_1} + X^{\circ}_{z_1 Z_2} = Q_{z_1}$$
$$2.\quad X^{\circ}_{z_2 1} + X^{\circ}_{z_2 Z_1} + X^{\circ}_{z_2 Z_2} = Q_{z_2}$$

The depreciation allowances may be defined as

(IV-6-6)
$$D = u_1 Q_{Z_1} P_{Z_1} + u_2 Q_{Z_2} P_{Z_2}$$

Net savings may be simply defined as a constant proportion of the net product:

(IV-6-7)
$$I = s(\bar{X}_1 - D)$$

Then, the value of new machines and slaves each period must equal gross savings:

(IV-6-8)
$$D^{\circ} + I^{\circ} = \bar{X}^{\circ}_{Z_1} P^{\circ}_{Z_1} + \bar{X}^{\circ}_{Z_2} P^{\circ}_{Z_2}$$

The system has 16 unknowns and 16 equations.

Since production conditions are linear and homogeneous, only the relative availabilities of slaves and machines have any impact upon the marginal revenue productivities of their services. From an initial set of available slaves and machines, the capital stock will be reshaped by investment of depreciation allowances and new savings to maximize the net rate of return on both capital goods. When this optimal stock is reached, gross investment each period will have the same relative structure as the optimal stock; i.e., $\dfrac{\bar{X}^{\circ}_{Z_1}}{\bar{X}^{\circ}_{Z_2}} = \dfrac{Q^{\circ}_{Z_1}}{Q^{\circ}_{Z_2}}$.

Unlike the usual case where nonaugmentable resources exist, these new accretions to capital stocks will have no effect upon the marginal productivities of the capital good factor services, and therefore cannot affect the interest rate. If net savings are indeed a fixed proportion of net income, this economy will expand indefinitely with the interest rate locked in time.

Now, interest payments, as a percentage of the value of capital, are defined as

(138)
$$i^{\circ}_k = \frac{\bar{X}^{\circ}_1 - D^{\circ}}{Q^{\circ}_{Z_1} P^{\circ}_{Z_1} + Q^{\circ}_{Z_2} P^{\circ}_{Z_2}}$$

and g, the rate of growth of capital, as

(139)
$$g = \frac{s(\bar{X}^{\circ}_1 - D^{\circ})}{Q^{\circ}_{Z_1} P^{\circ}_{Z_1} + Q^{\circ}_{Z_2} P^{\circ}_{Z_2}}$$

If $s = 1$, so that all net product were reinvested, g would equal i_k: thus, the maximum rate of growth in this economy is the interest rate.[72]

[72] Compare the same theorem derived from the von Neumann model of a moving equilibrium economy, Section 3.d., Chapter 8.

Only if one of the two factors becomes nonaugmentable does the Austrian concept of a period of investment become relevant. For example, if we remove slaves from the augmentable category by manumission, the accumulation of machinery would raise the marginal revenue productivity of labor, and the marginal productivity of machinery services would decline. With savings unresponsive to the fall in i_k, presumably the economy would approach $i_k^\circ = 0$ with a Schumpeterian circular flow, at which point savings would cease. On the other hand, if slaves were augmentable but machines were nonaugmentable, the economy (presumably) would approach a Ricardian circular flow in which labor services were priced at subsistence (i.e., depreciation allowance).

Now, assume that slaves are nonaugmentable, so that their "maintenance" expenditures are included in the $(1 - s)$ proportion of the net product consumed. Assume, further, that bread is produced wholly by machine services and machines wholly by labor services. Then, we may regard this economy as a stock of machines, Q_{Z_2}, whose value of gross product is $u_2Q_{Z_2}P_{Z_2}$ per week, with a flow of inputs $u_2Q_{Z_2}P_{Z_2}$. This is a Knightian framework, and Kaldor, using the analysis discussed above, attempts the measurement of a period of investment for slaves. Since this is based upon a chain of reasoning which includes both simple and compound interest, and is disowned by Kaldor himself in a later article, we shall not discuss it.[73]

5. Time Preference and Productivity: The Determination of the Interest Rate

We have discussed at rather great length the theories of interest and capital which stress one or the other of the coordinate elements in interest rate determination. Indeed, one is surprised, in studying the literature of capital theory, at the manner in which theorists would stress one or the other aspect of the problem to the subordination or denial of the role of the other. Böhm-Bawerk stressed the psychological factors, and, although he introduced the productivity element into the process, he did so in a backhanded manner which, as we shall see, made productivity dependent upon time preferences. We have stressed at length Wicksell's strong emphasis upon productivity. Clark and Knight are cases of such emphasis in the productivity direction, while, on the other hand, we have mentioned von Mises and Fetter who stressed the psychological factor to an exclusion of the productivity element.

There were theorists before Irving Fisher who were explicit in developing the psychological and the technological bases for a positive interest rate. T. N. Carver, in 1893, published a clear-cut theory of interest along these lines, as we have had previous cause to mention. And, indeed, the

[73] See footnote 67 above.

early Fisher placed such a strong emphasis upon the psychological factor that he was widely regarded as a time-preference theorist of the interest rate.[74] Yet, particularly in the later work, Fisher consistently stressed the interaction of "impatience" and "investment opportunity" in the determination of the interest rate.

We may illustrate Fisher's theory with a diagram adapted from Hayek.[75] Along the X-axis in Fig. 4-1 we measure units of actual and potential consumption in the current period. Along the Y-axis we measure the maximum attainable weekly rate of consumption which could be maintained in perpetuity. The transformation curves, T_0 and T_1, depict,

[74] We agree with G. Haberler that the productivity element existed in Fisher's earlier works, and that the *Theory of Interest*, published in 1930, merely gave it stronger emphasis. See G. Haberler, (1), p. 500. Yet, it is not hard to find instances in this earlier work where the emphasis upon time preference becomes almost exclusive. For example, at one point he appears to assert that productivity affects the interest rate via time preference:

". . . the only way in which the existence of long processes of production acts on interest is by overendowing the future and underendowing the present, thus creating a 'scarcity-value' of present goods." I. Fisher, (5), p. 72. See also pp. 186, 187, 195–6. Although this seems to be denying a coordinate status to productivity, it may be seen to be a special view of a process in which this is not true. One might say, for example, that the only way in which supply affects the price of a good is by affecting the "scarcity-value" of the commodity for which the demand curve is defined.

But Fisher, in answering Böhm-Bawerk, asserts that "To abstract both the underestimate of the future and underprovision for the present is to abstract the *whole* basis for interest and not a part merely." I. Fisher, (5), p. 65. This would seem to deny the "third ground" for interest in Böhm-Bawerk's system, but again there are extenuating circumstances. As we shall develop below, it is not an easy thing to free the "technological superiority of present goods" from time preference, and Fisher criticizes the presentation of Böhm-Bawerk quite justifiably. Therefore, it may very well have been this specific introduction of the productivity element into interest theory that Fisher had in mind in this statement.

Nevertheless, it cannot be denied that among his contemporaries Fisher was viewed as an "impatience" theorist of the interest rate. His student, H. G. Brown, was an early critic of this emphasis, in (1), but acknowledged the productivity element in his work. Seager, on the other hand, was frankly amazed at the claim of Fisher to the productivity element, and drew the following response from Fisher:

"Professor Seager's criticism came to me as a great surprise and seems very *mal à propos*; for what Professor Seager calls the 'productivity' or 'technique' element, so far from being lacking in my theory, is one of its cardinal features and the one the treatment of which I flattered myself was most original!" I. Fisher, (6), p. 610. Quoted by permission. The impact of this statement upon the profession may be gauged from Fetter's reaction:

". . . This reply comes as a surprise even to those who were aware of certain ambiguous expressions on this point in Fisher's writings. For if he has not meant to deny, in his previous writings, the validity of productivity theories, one knows not what to believe." F. Fetter, (1), p. 69. Fetter quotes from Fisher's *The Rate of Interest* to cast doubt upon the belief that Fisher had integrated the concept of the *marginal* productivity of capital into his theory.

Despite this early ambiguity, the clear and unsurpassed exposition of a theory of interest treating the psychological and technological bases in a marginal manner in *The Theory of Interest*, pp. 312–3, 467–70, is the basis of our treatment of Fisher as the most important of the theorists stressing both elements.

[75] F. Hayek, (1), pp. 50–1.

for two different levels of initial capital stock, the technological terms on which it is possible to convert current consumption into perpetual *consumption* in the future. The intersections of these transformation curves with the X-axis, M_0 and M_1, therefore denote maximum current consumption for the society with two different levels of initial stocks. C_0

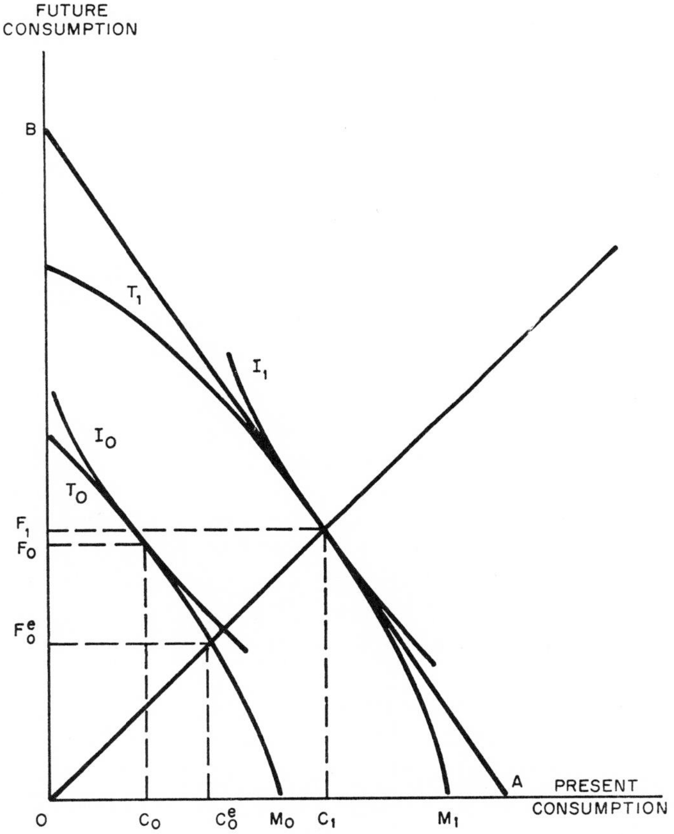

Figure 4-1. The Determination of the Rate of Interest.

denotes the level of consumption in week 0 chosen by virtue of the tangency of the "community indifference curve," I_0, with T_0. We shall dodge those difficult questions implied by the concept of the community indifference curve by assuming a Robinsonade economy—if the reader insists.

The choice of C_0 implies the possibility of a perpetual weekly basket of consumption goods of F_0. The levels of present consumption and weekly flows to future consumption which would yield the stationary state are C_0^e and F_0^e respectively, since these magnitudes are equal. Since the economy has not achieved a stationary equilibrium in week 0, maximum present consumption potential rises, say, to M_1 in week 1. Y_1 is tangent to T_1 at the point where consumption is steady through time. At the point of tangency, the marginal rate of substitution of present consumption for future consumption will be equal to the marginal technological terms of converting present consumption into perpetual future consumption; i.e., if the community preference function is

$$M_t = M(C_t, F_t) \tag{140}$$

and the transformation function is

$$F_t = T(C_t; K_0, I_1, \ldots, I_{t-1}) \tag{141}$$

where K_0 is initial capital stock, then at the stationary equilibrium

$$\frac{dF_t}{dC_t} = \frac{M^c}{M^f} \tag{142}$$

while, at the same time

$$C_t = F_t \tag{143}$$

Henceforth, let us assume for simplicity that the future contains only one week. Then, in a stationary equilibrium, the "price" of future goods in the market place in terms of current goods as *numéraire* is depicted by the slope of the line AB. If this slope is greater than unity (neglecting the minus sign on slope and dealing with absolute values), it will take more than a unit of future goods to obtain a unit of current goods, or $P_f = 1 + i_k$, where $i_k > 0$. In like manner, if the slope of the line is unity, the interest rate is zero, and if less than unity, the interest rate is less than zero.

The interaction of marginal time preference and marginal productivity of present resources to determine the value of the interest rate that emerges is apparent. If, for one reason or another, the transformation or indifference curve is linear in relevant ranges (i.e., in the neighborhood of the 45° line), we may speak of the interest rate as being "determined" by one or the other of the two elements. For example, in Knight's Crusonia each transformation curve would be linear with identical slopes. In the context of the diagram, current consumption must then expand to the point along the 45° line where the marginal time preference equals this fixed rate of transformation of present into future goods. We may then speak loosely of a "productivity" theory of interest.[76] On the other hand,

[76] It follows that if one good expands by virtue of time alone, a stationary state interest rate, if it exists, must be positive, for the transformation curve's slope must be greater than 1, if the physical productivity is not counterbalanced by changes in the value of the good. Let Y_j be a good which increases by $\lambda = \frac{\Delta \bar{X}_j}{\bar{X}_j}$ in amount in one

in Allais' recommended economy, the state imposes the constraint that all indifference curves have the slope of -1 in the neighborhood of the 45° line. Then capital accumulation must continue until the marginal productivity of present goods in manufacturing future sustainable consumption is one, and we may speak of a "pure time preference" theory of interest. In the intermediate cases, we may speak of mutual determination, in terms more evident but no more accurate than those relevant to the limiting cases just discussed.

5.a. The Zero Rate of Interest in a Stationary State

Under what conditions will the rate of interest in the stationary state be reduced to zero? Clearly, if technological functions are such as to allow the marginal productivity of capital to fall to zero and marginal time preferences are zero at a point of tangency on the 45° line in Fig. 4-1. We have already seen that at one place Wicksell writes as if the stationary state would indeed be characterized by a zero interest rate; at other points, however, he recognized the possibility of a positive interest rate in stationarity.[77] Moreover, Carver explained clearly that the marginal productivity of capital would decline to zero in the absence of the supply constraints inflicted by abstinence.[78] But the theorist who asserted a belief that in the circular flow the rate of interest *would* fall to zero was Schumpeter, in his classic *Theory of Economic Development.*

---

week, with a total cost of C_j. Then, when C_j includes land and labor resources,

$$P_j \Delta \bar{X}_j = C_j + i_k(P_j \bar{X}_j) \tag{1}$$

in purely competitive equilibrium. Or,

$$i_k = \lambda - \frac{C_j}{P_j \bar{X}_j}, \qquad \text{where} \tag{2}$$

$$\lambda = \frac{\Delta \bar{X}_j}{\bar{X}_j} \tag{3}$$

If $C_j = 0$, the interest rate equals the rate of growth of product. This is an "own" rate of interest which may be converted into a general rate by multiplying by the *numéraire* prices of the increment and the initial stock:

$$i_k = \frac{\Delta \bar{X}_j P_j}{\bar{X}_j P_J} \tag{4}$$

where P_j is the price per unit of the increment and P_J the price per unit of the stock. If $\frac{P_j}{P_J} = \frac{1}{\lambda}$, the interest rate is 1. If the interest rate were 0, and $C_j = 0$, for this commodity it would have to be true that $\Delta \bar{X}_j P_j = 0$ and therefore that $\bar{X}_j P_J + \Delta \bar{X}_j P_j = \bar{X}_j P_J$, which implies that the value of two cows today equals the value of three cows next year—a result valid in the stationary state with marginal time preference of zero only if cows are free goods.

[77] See K. Wicksell, (3), Vol. I, pp. 202–3, 207.

[78] T. Carver, (1), p. 46.

Our analysis leads us to expect that to maintain this position, Schumpeter must (a) assert that marginal time preferences in the neighborhood of the 45° line ultimately reveal no bias toward the present, and (b) assert that no good multiplies in value by virtue of time alone. The essence of his arguments, therefore, must involve these two points, and we shall discuss his assertions under both heads.

5.a.1. Zero Marginal Time Preference

Schumpeter writes:

". . . Someone enjoys a life-annuity. His wants remain absolutely constant in kind as well as in intensity throughout the rest of his life. The annuity is big and secure enough to relieve him of the necessity of creating funds for special emergencies and for the possibility of loss. He knows himself secure from responsibilities arising toward others and proof against sudden desires. No possibility of investing savings at interest exists—for if we were to grant this we should assume the element of interest beforehand and come dangerously near to circular reasoning. Now will a man in such a position esteem future instalments of his annuity less than those nearer in time? Would he—always abstracting from the personal risk of life—give up future more easily than present instalments? Obviously not, for if he did, that is if he gave up a future instalment for smaller compensation than one nearer in time, he would discover in due course that he had obtained a smaller total satisfaction than he might have done. His conduct would therefore cause him loss; it would be uneconomic. Such a course may nevertheless be taken, just as in other respects offences against the rules of economic reason frequently occur. . . ."[79]

The existence or nonexistence of zero marginal time preference in stationary equilibrium is an empirical question, as Schumpeter recognizes in the last sentence of the quotation, and such *a priori* arguments can merely frame hypotheses, not establish them. Böhm-Bawerk, of course, in spite of Schumpeter's effective elimination of his first ground for interest (differences in want and provision in present and future) would assert that his second ground ("irrational" discount of the future) is sufficient in Schumpeter's example to guarantee a positive rate of interest.

No "waiting" is involved in Schumpeter's example, therefore no temptation exists to shorten periods of investment: ". . . the necessity of waiting does not recur every time a process of production is repeated. One need not "wait" for the regular returns, since one receives them as a matter of course just when they are needed. In the normal circular flow one has not periodically to withstand a temptation to instantaneous

[79] J. Schumpeter, (2), p. 35. Quoted by permission.

production, because one would *immediately* fare worse by succumbing . . . ."[80]

M. Allais raises an objection to the Schumpeterian stationary state with zero interest rate which questions Schumpeter's view of rational behavior in the quotation above. As the economy approached the zero interest rate, capital goods would sell at their costs of production but nonaugmentable resources (i.e., land) would rise in value without limit. Sooner or later, therefore, landlords should attempt to increase their current consumption by sale of small portions of their assets. This constitutes an obstacle to the state's reduction of the interest rate to zero, and therefore leads Allais to the conclusion that, in his economy, land must be nationalized. That is to say, a real-wealth effect should operate upon landlords' consumption.

Would not the landlord be revealing an inordinate *negative* time preference if he did not seek to convert some of his wealth to present consumption? Schumpeter's example avoids this question by implicitly assuming that the individual involved has power only to consume or save a weekly income. Such an assumption allows Schumpeter to abstract merely from the "personal risk of life," without having to cope with the individual's realization of the certainty of his death. In the more realistic situation, where the individual receives an annual income from ownership of a stock of wealth, he has an option not afforded him by Schumpeter: to purchase streams of current and future income at the expense of capital. But the landlords' desire to sell land would continuously depress its price and prevent the attainment of the zero interest rate.[81]

Suppose the economy were in stationary equilibrium at zero interest rate, with landlords receiving a steady income flow over time and possess-

[80] J. Schumpeter, (2), p. 38. Quoted by permission. The word "immediately" here is difficult to understand. Should a consumer succumb to a temptation to consume more today than his income and be led to disinvest, switching resources from capital good production to consumer good production, it is difficult to understand why the consumer should "*immediately* fare worse." Samuelson has suggested that Schumpeter meant that the current reckoning of the utility *to be* enjoyed is lessened, not the immediate enjoyment. See P. Samuelson, (2), p. 64.

[81] G. Cassel, (1), pp. 233–8, has stressed the increasing attractiveness of purchasing annuities with capital as an alternative to investing it at the going rate of interest as that rate declines toward zero. At 5 per cent, a 20-year annuity of $100 a year would cost $1246, while it would require $2000 in capital to yield the annual sum as an income. At an interest rate of .5 per cent, the same annuity would cost about $1900, while it would take $20,000 invested to achieve the same income. The attraction of the annuity rises as the number of years of its receipt decreases, interest rate constant. Thus, as the interest rate fell toward zero in the Schumpeterian state, the older landlord would be particularly attracted toward the sale of current capital for increased consumption.

All such advantages disappear, of course, if the individual desires a perpetuity, i.e., if he plans as if he were going to live forever or if his heirs' welfare is as important to him as his own. Thus, if Schumpeter's annuitant is viewed as owning salable wealth, some such assumption as this is implied in the example he gives.

ing stocks of wealth approaching infinity. Not to offer pieces of land at finite prices in terms of present goods would imply an infinite time preference for goods after death. As far as non-landowners are concerned, even though at the margin the preferences of each for future and present goods are equilibrated, the effective offer of land leads to a reduction in the price of future income and should lead to purchases. Therefore, the level of $i_k^\circ = 0$ cannot be maintained.[82]

The same types of questions may be posed of Pigou's analysis of the possibility of a stationary state with zero (or negative) interest rates in a non-money economy.[83] Pigou recognized that the "representative man" would probably have marginal time preferences which are positive in the tradition of Böhm-Bawerk. However, he felt that savings which springs from "arational" drives, uninfluenced by the interest rate, might push the rate of interest to zero or below, and lead to the coexistence of a nonpositive interest rate and positive marginal time preferences. It is difficult to see why the wealth-effect in such a state would not lead to much greater induced consumption than induced savings, following the lines of the analysis above, indeed, in the very manner of the "Pigou effect" for non-money assets.

5.a.2. The Absence of a Value-Increment Ascribable to Time

If we accept Schumpeter's implicit assumption that the consumer plans over an infinite horizon with zero marginal time preference, there remains the possibility that one or more of the goods in the economy may be subject to value increases due to the operation of time alone.[84] Schumpeter recognizes two possibilities on this score: that time actually works a change upon goods making them more valuable, in the classic Austrian wine or timber cases, or that time increases the value of the good without affecting the good physically. As we have seen, unless a compensating downward movement in the value of time's increment occurs, either of these effects would rule out a zero interest rate.

But this is exactly what will happen, Schumpeter argues. Only changes such as these which are foreseen can occur if we are to have a stationary state, and, if they are foreseen, the changes will have been

[82] See M. Allais, (1), pp. 468–77, for his line of reasoning, which is similar to, but not identical with, the one above. Since we shall treat money in Chapter 5 exactly as a capital good, it might seem that similar conclusions hold in a world where money exists, but if the rate of interest attained zero, money would disappear from our economy, as will be shown.

[83] A. Pigou, (2), pp. 345–7. In an economy where money continued to exist, the floor to the interest rate would be at zero, since money can be held costlessly.

[84] One kind of physical change can be ruled out immediately: that in which time alone multiplies the number of goods of like kind available. Equilibrium requires, as mentioned in footnote 76, that two cows today equal three cows tomorrow and therefore today in value—a result which can occur only if cows are free goods. Therefore, such temporal multiplications must have proceeded to the point where the goods are free if the stationary state exists.

taken into account in the price of the uncompleted product. In Schumpeter's example, the value of the seedling planted today will equal the value of the 50-year old tree cut down today. We encounter here the difficulty noted by Wicksell and discussed above: the productivity of capital is a value concept which includes the cost of moving through time. If that cost of movement is zero, any increase in value of product imputable to the action of time must accrue to the other factors. Thus, the transformation curves in Fig. 4-1 are *value-of-product* curves *dependent* upon the very interest rate determined partially by them. As such they are illegitimate in the strictest sense, as would be any attempt to determine the interest rate in a nongeneral system.

Therefore, Schumpeter is perfectly correct: if the interest rate were zero, technological forces would not operate to push it to positive levels. Samuelson's spatial analogy is a most useful one: if the transport rate were zero, the price of wheat in New York must equal that in Chicago. If the mere movement of the wheat between the two cities somehow enhanced its value, i.e., if space had a productivity but was a free good, this would be reflected in the Chicago price as well as the New York price, since the owner of the wheat in Chicago could obtain this increment costlessly by movement of his crop to New York.[85]

Therefore, the crucial assumption of Schumpeter is that of zero marginal time preference in the stationary state. He has not established a strong case for its existence in the typical case, in our opinion, having failed to deal with the case of the owner of capital who has the option of selling portions of it for current consumption.

5.b. The Productivity Component as the Technological Superiority of Present Goods

Böhm-Bawerk, reluctant to admit the "productivity" of capital goods, introduced this aspect into his theory in the third ground for the existence of interest: the technological superiority of present goods over future goods. It is a notable feature of the theories of Böhm-Bawerk's successors that they did not adopt this tenet of the theory; workers such as Wicksell, Fisher, Schumpeter, and Hayek chose instead to ground the technological basis for the existence of interest in the greater "productivity" of roundabout processes or in innovation. There exists a temptation, however, to believe either (1) that the greater productivity of roundabout processes is identical with the proposition that present goods are superior technically to future goods, or (2) that while these two are not identical propositions the technical superiority of present goods may be shown to follow in simple fashion from the roundaboutness postulate conjoined with certain assumptions which are independent of time preference.

The first of these temptations claimed Böhm-Bawerk himself as a

[85] P. Samuelson, (2), p. 65. See also L. Robbins, (1).

victim at times. For example, in answering Fisher's criticism, he wrote: "When a timber dealer simultaneously clears a 100-year-old and an 80-year-old forest, he will value the older forest higher simply because it actually yields more timber. And when we drink "old" and "young" wine, we value the older wine higher simply because it is superior in quality. Is this or is this not a real technical superiority?"[86] In this passage, Böhm-Bawerk identifies falsely the preferability of the results available today of longer processes to those of shorter processes available today, with the problem of preferences between the results of equally long processes available in week n or in week $n + 1$. Fisher, too, in his earlier works, makes the same error in asserting that in demonstrating the falsity of the technological superiority dictum as presented by Böhm-Bawerk he had destroyed the entire productivity base of Böhm-Bawerk's theory.

The independence of the doctrine from time preference assumptions has been explicitly challenged by Bortkiewicz, Fisher, and Landry,[87] and Böhm-Bawerk's response to the first two authors' criticisms forms the famous Excursus 12 in the *Further Essays on Capital and Interest.* In reading this famous debate, one has the feeling that the issues were left hanging in mid-air, with Böhm-Bawerk yielding most ground but unconvinced that in so doing he had surrendered the field.

5.b.1. *Definitions of Neutral Time Preference*

Let us once more adopt the concept of a community indifference curve and refer to the nation as the decisionmaker. We shall then say that present goods are technologically superior to future goods if, after abstracting from time preference in ways shortly to be discussed, a nation decides in week 0 that it prefers a gift in week 0 to an equivalent gift in week 1.

In order to neutralize the impact of time preference on the discussion of the technological aspects of capital and investment, it is necessary to make explicit alternative definitions of neutral time preference. It would seem that three of these might qualify as implying a type of neutrality:

Definition 1. The time of consumption is completely ignored in the utility function, as is the possibility of satiation, more goods at any time always being preferred to fewer goods at any time. This might be the outlook adopted by an underdeveloped nation's policy-makers were

[86] E. von Böhm-Bawerk, (5), Vol. III, p. 178. Quoted by permission.

[87] L. von Bortkiewicz, (1); I. Fisher, (5), pp. 53–74, and (7), pp. 473–85; and A. Landry, (1), pp. 197ff. Also, at my request, Professor Viner granted me access to his lecture notes, which were written in the late 1920's, in which some of the analysis to follow was anticipated. He criticized Böhm-Bawerk for "elaborate arithmetical illustrations to show that the earlier you acquire productive capital the greater its product, since this is proving the obvious" once a monotonically rising productivity curve in function of time is granted. Beyond this, Viner noted the strategic importance in the analysis of neutral time preference and dealt explicitly with the interdependence of time preference and technological superiority.

they to put the maximum social emphasis upon growth in the uses of an increment of investible resources. One difficulty with this definition is that its pattern of time preference may be approximated in given situations by patterns of *negative* time preference, with the discount factors for future goods falling continuously through time. Thus, what appears to be neutral time preference has a close kinship with negative time preference. We may identify this concept with that implicitly defined by Allais in his state, discussed above.

Definition 2. Let us assume that it is possible to approximate any pattern of social time preference we might wish to deal with by the discount factor $d_t = (1 + \theta)^t$, where t is the time period and θ the psychological rate of time discount. Then, if the preference function for the alternative receipts of consumer goods over time which could arise from the increment of capital goods is defined as $M = M(X_1, \ldots, X_h)$, where $M(X_s) = M(X_u)$ when $X_s = X_u$, for all s, u, we may consider the society to maximize its welfare by choosing a set of optimal annual consumptions X_t. We may regard time preference as neutral if $\theta = 0$ for $0 \leqq t \leqq n$, where n may approach infinity. That is, if the society attempts to maximize its satisfaction from the investment gift over a possibly infinite time period, we shall consider time preference to be neutral in the second sense. This definition of neutrality seems to be "purest" in that its affinities with negative or positive time preference are the least of the three alternatives presented. This is not to say that it is most "useful," "realistic," or "natural." It is, as we have seen above, the definition implied by Schumpeter's stationary state analysis.

Definition 3. Under the same conditions as those of Definition 2, we shall merely recognize the possibility that the society may choose to maximize satisfaction over a finite time period, so that $\theta = 0$ for $0 \leqq t \leqq m$, where m is finite, and $\theta \rightarrow \infty$ for $t > m$. In this definition, of course, we may view the finite cutoff point as being dictated by a break in the regime of neutral time preference for the institution of a regime of positive time preference. In this sense, it resembles Definition 1 in its non-purist quality.

5.b.2. Böhm-Bawerk's Analysis

Suppose an underdeveloped nation were offered either (1) a unit of wheat at the beginning of week 0 or (2) a unit of wheat at the start of week 1.[88] On the basis of "technological superiority" alone, would the nation prefer (1) to (2), (2) to (1), or be indifferent between them. If it is assumed that the unit of wheat will purchase a unit of labor which, working with free land, will in one week's time produce a given quantity of capital goods, or, instead, be consumed, we have an elementary capital problem. Let us further assume that these capital goods, after mainte-

[88] Compare the example in R. Dorfman, (3).

nance and replacement expenditures, if any, can produce a weekly net output of (say) .1 unit of wheat indefinitely.

Before we attempt to answer this problem let us briefly consider a somewhat different attempt to prove the technological superiority proposition. Suppose this nation had a unit of labor in week 0 and faced the alternatives of using it to produce wheat for consumption in week 0, or week 1, or week 2, and so forth. If the nation elected to use the labor in processes whose investment period was greater than one week, it would have to add labor in future years to that invested in week 0, but we shall imagine that it is always possible to impute to week 0 labor its share of the ultimate product.

In Böhm-Bawerk's presentation[89] the amount of product imputed to a unit of week 0's labor invested for increasing lengths of time rose without limit within the time span illustrated in his tables.[90] This being the case, at whatever week one wishes to halt for consideration (say week 12), the product imputed to a unit of labor of week 0 is always larger than that imputed to a unit of labor of week 1 for a period of investment ending in week 12. Consequently, he argues, present goods are technologically superior to future goods.

A fundamental assumption of Böhm-Bawerk's analysis was that of "capital scarcity." By virtue of it he obtained an assurance that the marginal product of time at the point chosen for the length of investment period would be positive. He argued that the case of technological superiority of present goods held only for those realistic cases where the community's stock of present goods prevented it from approaching the limit of the curve.[91]

A difficulty with this assumption is that it may be viewed as introducing, to a debatable degree, a nonneutral time preference, since one of the major reasons why sufficient present goods do not exist to finance such investment periods is found in the existence of positive time preference, as Böhm-Bawerk himself asserts. Further, while such an assumption may

[89] E. von Böhm-Bawerk, (1), pp. 260–8.

[90] While he denies the practical existence of a point on this curve where it turns down (the marginal product of time becomes zero and then negative), Böhm-Bawerk does admit that the curve approaches a finite limit. For example, in somewhat ambiguous language, he says:

"Fisher remarks correctly that 'the limited earth can never produce unlimited products', and that, therefore, these do not grow to an infinite maximum by an infinite process of increasing productivity, but can only infinitely approach an ultimate maximum. The latter situation would be mathematically fully compatible with my opinion that higher productivity shows a successive tendency to lessen. However, I have neither an inclination nor a theoretical interest in asserting an 'infinite' continuation of my law in this physical and mathematical sense." E. von Böhm-Bawerk, (5), Vol. III, p. 215, note 27. Quoted by permission. See also pp. 170, 176.

[91] E. von Böhm-Bawerk, (5), Vol. III, p. 162. Hence the lack of "theoretical interest" in whether or not the period-of-investment curve approaches a limit, referred to in the quotation in footnote 90. See also his response to White in (4), p. 127.

be acceptable when the totality of investment is under consideration, it hardly seems appropriate to such examples as the present one where only a small portion of the total labor supply is in question.

We shall therefore generalize the Böhm-Bawerk case in the following way. Suppose the underdeveloped nation were told by a wealthy nation of the latter's willingness to underwrite the use of a unit of labor in a process of any length the recipient nation might wish to undertake. That is, if it chose to invest a unit of week 0 labor for five weeks, the underdeveloped nation would receive all the aid necessary to finance the total labor to sustain such a period of investment. However, at the end of the period, the lending nation would reclaim all of the product except the amount imputed to one unit of labor invested for the whole of the period. We should therefore be dealing with a "quasi-point input, point output" case, and Böhm-Bawerk's tables could be considered to be the net returns to the underdeveloped nation from the investment of one unit of labor for variable lengths of time.

It is assumed that this offer is made in week 0 and that the underdeveloped nation is forced to make an irrevocable decision in that year concerning the amount of the gift it will consume and the amount it will invest, as well as the length of the period of investment. Further, we shall consider two relevant circumstances: (1) whether the returns to a unit of labor through time rise without limit or approach a limit, and (2) whether the underdeveloped nation is constrained to consume the wheat at the end of the investment period or may commit itself, in week 0, to reinvest it in a new process at the end of the initial period, and, if desired, reinvest it periodically in the future.

For each of the four cases obtained by pairing these two sets of circumstances, and for each of the definitions of neutral time preference, would the recipient nation prefer the initial delivery of wheat to begin in week 0 rather than week 1, or would it be indifferent between these alternatives? In the first case we shall speak of present (week 0) goods being technologically superior to future (week 1) goods; in the second case, no such technological superiority exists. Let us consider each case in turn.

Case 1. Returns to Time Rise Without Limit, Enforced Terminal Consumption.

Definition 1. Goods in week 0 would be technologically superior to goods in week 1, since all of the gift would be invested in an indefinitely long time period. The amount of the goods available from an investment in the earlier year would always be larger and therefore preferable to the amounts available from investment begun in the later year.

Definition 2. The investment period would be terminated in week n when the returns to the units of labor invested would satiate the community and the marginal satisfaction derived from a lengthening of the period to week $n + 1$ would be zero. In this case the marginal productivity of time would still be positive. Further, no technological superiority of present goods would exist since the same amount of wheat would be obtainable from the process, whether begun in week 0 or week 1, the only difference being the receipt of the product in week n or week $n + 1$; this is of no importance to the community.

Definition 3. In this case the investment period will terminate in week m if started in week 0, the fruition week being dictated by the "cutoff point" in the community's pattern of discount rates. Were the process to be started in week 1 the cutoff point would be week $m + 1$. But, in week 0, when the offer is made, the community prefers the first option, since goods receivable in week $m + 1$ possess negligible utility for the society. Therefore, the logic of our framework leads us to declare present goods "technologically superior" to future goods, but no doubt will leave the reader disturbed about the true neutrality of time preference in obtaining this result.

CASE 2. RETURNS TO TIME RISE TO AN UPPER LIMIT, ENFORCED TERMINAL CONSUMPTION.

Definition 1. For an implicit assumption of this definition of time preference neutrality, Bortkiewicz and Fisher demonstrated that present goods would not be superior to future goods, since the investment period would terminate at week n when the marginal product of time was zero. The community would be indifferent to the receipt of the same quantity of goods in week n or week $n + 1$. Böhm-Bawerk admits his critics are correct but denies the relevance of the case by asserting that Definition 3 is alone valid and, moreover, that under his definition the cutoff point will always occur before week n, the year of zero marginal product.[92]

Definition 2. The terminal week will occur at the earlier of two possibilities: week n or the week at which satiation occurs. In either case, present goods will not possess a technological superiority.

Definition 3. In this case the terminal week m will be greater than, equal to, or less than $n + 1$, the number of weeks' investment before the zero marginal product point is reached. If $n + 1 < m$, then goods receivable in weeks 0 through $m - n + 1$ are perfect substitutes, but goods received thereafter are inferior "technologically." If $n + 1 = m$ or if $n + 1 > m$, goods in week 0 will be technologically superior to those available in week 1, in the first case for the same reason as in Case 1, Definition 3, and in the second because fewer goods will be available in the cutoff year.

Böhm-Bawerk's examples belong to Case 2 and assume time preference to be neutral in the sense of Definition 3 when $n > m$. Consider the following statement:

"Therefore, it certainly was neither 'arbitrary' nor 'unsuitable for the problem,' but rather required by its very nature, that I mentioned

[92] E. von Böhm-Bawerk, (5), Vol. III, pp. 155–7.

the case in question in my suppositions and that in the unavoidable 'interruption' of my series I assumed the border of the higher productivity zone to lie beyond and not before my point of interruption. For in reality the period of time for whose wants we plan to provide through the use of our means of production and which can exert an influence on our valuations of producers' goods never and nowhere extends beyond the zone of higher productivity of longer roundabout methods. We will observe that in economic calculations we never make investments for the sake of wants that lie beyond this zone."[93]

CASE 3. RETURNS TO TIME RISE WITHOUT LIMIT, REINVESTMENT POSSIBLE. In these cases where the nation may commit itself to reinvest the net returns at the end of investment periods, certain modifications in these conclusions occur.

Definition 1. No change from Case 1.

Definition 2. A succession of investment periods will be selected such that in week t, for t sufficiently large, a satiation output is produced with sufficient surplus to produce, in a one-week investment period, a satiation output in week $t + 1$ and a similar surplus. Since goods in week 0 will allow this state to be reached a week earlier than goods in week 1, and therefore will produce a greater flow of goods over any time period selected, they will be superior technologically to goods available in week 1.

Definition 3. A pattern of investment and consumption will be selected to maximize satisfaction over the period from week 0 to week m. Abstracting from satiation, we conclude that goods in week 0 will be preferred to goods in week 1 as a result of the community's discounting in week 0 of goods receivable in week $m + 1$.

CASE 4. RETURNS TO TIME RISE TO AN UPPER LIMIT, REINVESTMENT POSSIBLE.

Definition 1. If returns to successive investments were constant, the society would select the optimal investment period, reinvest the gross proceeds upon its completion in an investment period of similar length, and enjoy an indefinite rise in product. However, the ultimate limitations on nonproducible factors will lead to a point where reinvestment in a period of any length will yield no enhancement of product. This is the point of maximum product and it will be achieved and maintained indefinitely. Since a beginning in week 0 would allow its attainment one week earlier than a start in week 1, goods in the earlier year will be superior technologically.

Definition 2. No change from Case 3.[94]

93 E. von Böhm-Bawerk, (5), Vol. III, p. 156. See also G. Haberler, (1), pp. 510–1. Quoted by permission.

94 Given the whole context of Knight's theory, with its "automatic" reinvestment to achieve a perpetual flow of net income, we suggest that this case is closest to his own statement of the technological superiority of present goods, although Definition 2 is not quite his view of time preference. Nonetheless, it is closest. He says: "The

Definition 3. No change from Case 3.

We may conclude from this analysis that the independence of time preference assumptions and technological superiority of present goods is a complicated thing to establish. Böhm-Bawerk, Fisher, and Bortkiewicz remained with the cases of enforced terminal consumption, all three ultimately agreeing upon the reality of the bounded-returns-to-time condition. Thus, Case 2 was relevant to their analyses, and disagreement centered upon the acceptance of Definition 1 by Bortkiewicz and Fisher and of Definition 3 with $n + 1 > m$ by Böhm-Bawerk. Both of these definitions of neutral time preference are tinged with nonneutral impurities, but perhaps these are strongest in the latter case, implying as it does a cutoff point in the planning period. Be it noted that if the "purest" definition of time preference neutrality, Definition 2, be adopted for Case 2, Fisher and Bortkiewicz would still be correct in maintaining the nonsuperiority of present goods.

On the other hand, if Böhm-Bawerk had chosen to extend the analysis to the cases of reinvestment, his position would be correct for all definitions of neutral time preference whether or not time were limitlessly productive.

In view of these ambiguities in the nature of the concept of technological superiority of present goods, it seems much more fruitful to follow the lead of later theorists and employ the productivity of roundabout processes exclusively as the productive component of a theory of interest. We have seen that, in any productivity concept in the theory of interest and capital, we encounter the need to measure "product" in value rather than physical terms, which leads to an indirect impact of time preference upon the technical transformation of present into future goods. The technical superiority concept does not allow us to escape this dependence between the preference and transformation functions of Fig. 4-1. But we may escape the second type of dependence this form of the productivity-of-capital assumption introduces by merely asserting that in any week 0 there exist opportunities for investing current resources in roundabout processes which will yield streams of physical product of greater magnitude than will like amounts of current resources used in direct processes.[95] Unsatisfying as this simple statement may seem, it is difficult to define the "productivity" of capital in any more useful manner.

---

psychological preference of present to future wealth is merely the reflection of a fact that wealth in hand now will grow into a larger amount of wealth in the future." F. Knight, (7), p. 435.

[95] Compare Böhm-Bawerk's and Wicksell's concern to show in what sense a capital good is "productive" with Pareto's footnote dismissal of the topic: "To ask 'why a capital good is productive' is to ask why a cherry tree produces cherries. Political economy need not resolve this problem." V. Pareto, (1), Vol. I, p. 304.

6. A Recapitulation

The introduction of an analytically meaningful concept of time into our models opens a Pandora's box of complications for the general equilibrium models which are our present concern. It is rather simple to introduce intertemporal elements into the consumer's preferences and decisionmaking procedures, and to make identical alterations in the firm's processes. From such models emerges the role of time discount in an economy with a positive interest rate, and the need for the discussion of the possibility of a general theory of the consumer's treatment of present and future.

General equilibrium models based upon such consumer and firm submodels, with the altered equation systems they imply for markets, while they may set out the conditions for static and stationary equilibrium sufficiently well, do not afford deeper insights into the nature of capital and interest. In spite of one's knowledge that the Austrian period of investment is nonoperational, it is difficult to escape the feeling that the "vision" of economic process contained in the Austrians' productivity analysis comes closer to capturing the essence of capital than the analyses of the pure productivity school.

The determination of the interest rate must be treated in the context of a general equilibrium system which can accommodate the interdependence of productivity and preference functions implicit in the treatment of capital and its net return. Moreover, this general system is best studied in a position of stationary rest, where prices are constant over time, and many of the value complications are reduced to a minimum. Any partial analysis must contain its portion of inaccuracy, but the Fisher theory of interest rate determination as the joint product of a transformation curve and consumer preferences is a most useful simplification of the general model in which the process can alone be handled in full methodological purity.

CHAPTER 5

THE MONEY ECONOMY

1. The Problems of Current Synchronization

In our presentation of the Wicksellian-Walrasian system, Model IV-5, we explicitly abstracted from the problems of supporting the population between the close of the market day and the beginning of the flow of final consumer goods from the processes of the current week. Essentially, therefore, the current week was compressed into a point of time, and no problems arising from the lack of synchronization between consumer needs and the flow of products to satisfy them were allowed to intrude. Although this body of what we shall term "current synchronization capital" assumed a fundamental importance in the crude wage-fund theories of classical economics, we have seen that in the more sophisticated "advances" theories they were viewed as a portion only of the capital which would be necessary to support long processes.

Even if the period of investment of resource services were one week identically in all processes, as we may interpret them to be in the earlier models of Chapter 4, the need for this type of capital would arise. We may introduce it as Walras did, in a manner wholly symmetrical with other forms of capital goods: consumers hold, among the stocks of factors with which they begin a market day, inventories of finished consumer goods, Q_{cj}, which yield flows of services, $Q_{cj'}$, where $Y_{j'}$ is the service involved. These services are sold to entrepreneurs and consumers at equilibrium prices, $P^{\circ}_{j'}$, which will include a "depreciation" charge of 100 per cent plus a net return which, in equilibrium, will have to equal the net rate of return on all capital goods:

$$(1) \qquad i^{\circ}_{k}P^{\circ}_{j} = P^{\circ}_{j'} - P^{\circ}_{j}u_{j'} = P^{\circ}_{j'} - P^{\circ}_{j}$$

Thus, in a Walrasian economy with unit periods of production for each good, the stationary level of national product depends upon the willingness of savers to maintain and replace stocks of durable capital goods with lifetimes in excess of one period, and to maintain and replace stocks of inventories with a lifetime of one week. Current consumption is supported by this stock of resources plus the consumer goods flowing in final form during the week. This type of analysis is changed in the Wicksellian model only insofar as periods of production are variable in length and the stocks of durable goods which must be maintained include unfinished goods of all forms: but current consumption is financed out of inventories plus the consumption goods ripening in the current week.

Both the theory of capital and the theory of the determination of a common rate of return on capital for stationary conditions may be viewed "cross-sectionally," or period by period, rather than longitudinally over time. Wicksell, in the *Lectures*, came to recognize the validity of both approaches:

". . . For my part I cannot feel myself bound to any particular terminology, but have often declared that as long as the *time-element* is given its appropriate place, the starting-point for the construction of a theory of interest can be chosen almost at random; it does not really matter whether we start from the productivity theory, or from use, or abstinence, or even from the theory of money. The only important thing is to be consistent. . . . We can *either* adopt Walras's method of taking a *cross-section* through social production at a moment of time, and thus consider only the cooperation of the factors of production existing at the moment. In this case, no doubt, the demand for finished products constitutes an indirect demand for raw materials and the factors of production, by means of which the finished products are produced. At the same time there is a demand for new capital goods, and their present yield is the basis for their estimated future yield. We thus gain a clear insight into the mechanism by which loan-interest is determined at each moment of time. In this method of procedure we have no use for 'waiting as a factor of production' (though it enters to some extent as the regulator of savings). *Or else* we can refer everything back to the original factors of production in conjunction with waiting (or preferably *time*). Here we make a *longitudinal section*, instead, and this construction is also admissible. . . ."[1]

In this mature statement of his outlook upon capital theory, Wicksell accepts the validity of Walras' approach to that subject—a position explicitly denied in his earlier work on capital theory. We suggest that the combination of the Walrasian and the Wicksellian models in Model IV-5, complicated in obvious ways by the introduction of inventory capital, provides the best static capital theory for a general model. Because it is primarily a cross-sectional model, we preserve the advantages Wicksell refers to above in incorporating savings and the determination of the interest rate. On the other hand, in deriving the conditions for a cross-sectional stationary system from "longitudinal" consumer and firm suboptimization models, the role of time in these two vital areas may be clearly discerned.

At the same time that we introduce inventories of consumer goods into the model we may also recognize a second type of synchronization asset and a third type of "capital good:" money. Its existence raises

[1] K. Wicksell, (3), Vol. I, pp. 236–7. Quoted by permission.

fundamentally new and different problems from those of Chapter 4, and will form the subject matter of this chapter. Money is, in the analysis of this chapter, an asset in every sense, like Q_{cz_i} or $Q_{cj'}$; we shall symbolize stocks of it held by consumer c as Q_{cu}. It has a price in *numéraire*, P_u, and yields services, U', whose price is $P_{u'}$ per week per unit of money. Its return must be equal in equilibrium to the common rate of return for all capital goods plus depreciation in both the physical and the value sense, both of which are zero in the stationary state. It is a synchronization medium in the sense that it affords the consumer and firm a method of holding control over current goods in the absence of current receipts. Indeed, goods inventories and cash balances are substitutes to a large degree, so that they should be introduced into the models simultaneously. They differ, of course, in that while money balances provide synchronization services only for the individual decisionmaker, goods inventories provide them for the society as well.

We should point up a fundamental departure from Wicksell's analysis which we shall adopt for reasons to be made clear below. It is believed best to keep the concept of money and the concept of capital in the sense of Chapter 4 distinct, even at the cost of some sacrifice of realism. Wicksell, to the contrary, writes of the money economy: "It is not true that 'money is only one form of capital,' that the lending of money constitutes 'a lending of real capital goods in the form of money,' etc. Liquid real capital, (*i.e.*, goods) are never lent (not even in a system of simple merchandise credit); it is money which is lent, and the commodity capital is then *sold* in exchange for this money."[2] Of course, we do not dispute this, but we shall continue to assume that markets in the economy exist to price inventory services which are borrowed in kind, and to assume that securities are redeemed each week in capital goods (including now money and inventories of finished as well as unfinished goods if the latter exist in the economy). In Chapter 8 of *Interest and Prices* Wicksell's model does begin with the assumption that entrepreneurs borrow capital goods in kind from capitalists—which we of course retain—and repay it in kind at the end of the period. In order to gain deeper insights into the phenomena involved, we follow Walras in retaining this "barter" aspect of even complicated economic systems.

There is, therefore, no "money capital" market in our models where money is borrowed to buy capital goods and inventories for ownership by firms. All capital assets—including money and inventories of consumer goods—are leased week by week by the firm. Since neither inventories nor money can be lent for shorter periods than a week, and since only if they are delivered to the hirer of their services at the start of the

[2] K. Wicksell, (2), p. xxvi. Quoted by permission. See also pp. 102, 108. An interesting modern development is the leasing of capital equipment by the using firm from firms set up to own it.

fulfillment week can they render maximum service, we assume these two types of resources are delivered to their users at this time.

Other goods and services are delivered throughout the week—specifically, contract dates are set at the end of the market day—to firms and consumers at specified times, and payment for all deliveries is assumed to be made at the time of delivery. The prices of goods and services are the same regardless of the day of delivery within the week. Our economy remains one of effective certainty in the areas of goods delivery, prices at time of delivery, and price expectations, and, of course, full stationarity is also assumed.

2. The Preconditions of Money in a Stationary State

If we define money as a *stock* of good with no inherent utility, acceptable in the discharge of obligations, whose use does not involve the recording and clearing of debit and credit accounts for economic units, we shall have captured the essence of money. This last characteristic of a true money has been little stressed in the literature, but it forms a major distinction of an impersonal means of transacting from any type of personal instrument for so doing. Throughout our treatment of money, we shall accept the familiar hypothesis that barter, in the sense of an exchange of spot goods for spot goods, is so inefficient a method of transacting that its costs effectively rule it out of the realm of relevance.

Demand deposits may be seen to fall somewhere in between money and personal credit instruments, but since they require clearing between units we shall term them credit instruments. Although we shall treat them as a sort of riskless bill purchased by units at par, and although we shall assume that they circulate at no discount, we shall also consider the demand depositor to be receiving earnings in the form of clearing services to a full or partial extent of their costs.

Given these conditions, then, we ask: under what circumstances will there arise a stock of money, a market for money services, and a market for the asset "money," in the circular flow? What conditions must be fulfilled to assure the continuance of this stock and these markets?

2.a. The Case of Perfect Knowledge

Let us suppose initially that every firm and consumer in the economy will engage in "understandings" only to the extent that its stock of wealth plus the willing loans of others allow, and that it will honor all its understandings as to quantity and time of delivery. This is true, we shall assume, because the state of knowledge in all markets at all times is such that each unit foresees that any such inconsistency in its overall weekly plan would be apparent immediately to every other unit in the economy, it would be deprived of access to markets for the week, and other severe penalties would follow. The risk, therefore, that any individual will default in any respect is nil.[3]

Under such conditions, it may be argued that the market-day becomes superfluous, since, if foresight is sufficiently acute to discern the preceding, it should be true that equilibrium prices and quantities are immediately apparent to all in the economy.[4] Nevertheless, "understandings" between individual units will be required to assure the coordination of deliveries of inputs and outputs, if one refuses, as we shall, to admit the possibility of foreseeing the purely stochastic variation in the economy. In the absence of these undertakings between units, all units will tend to move together immediately to correct imbalances, since the cognisance of such defects would be instantaneous and action immediate. We should be in the situation, to use Pareto's analogy, of inhabiting a frictionless world in which *all* heat moves immediately to correct the slightest departure from an even distribution, and thereby renders the world uninhabitable at the first lapse from the ideal state. Of course, we could assume a pluperfect foresight in which all units foresee that all other units will move to create further disequilibrium, and therefore no unit will move. However, there is no end to this ponderous gavotte, and we shall not begin it.

But despite the need for undertakings, so that coordination of units can occur, they are not necessary to insure against the default of these units. We may look upon the economy as a series of open stockpiles upon which units place their supplies at agreed-upon intervals and from which they take a socially-condoned value of desired goods and services. No need for any medium of exchange will arise: there is no use for money or open-book credit, checks, bills of exchange, receipts, and so forth.[5]

[3] See S. Chambers, (1), p. 39, and J. Gilbert (1), pp. 150–1. This seems to be the degree of perfection of knowledge implied by Knight when he discussed the nonexistence of money in a circular flow. See F. Knight, (2), p. xxii.

[4] Cf. O. Morgenstern, (1), p. 17. This paper considers the game theoretic aspects of the assumption of perfect foresight and demonstrates the impossibility of its existence.

[5] The literature reveals that others have discussed the nonexistence of money in a "perfect foresight" context which was not "perfect" enough to rule out other media of exchange. Marget, for example, argues that no cash balances would exist, but that units would have to convert all goods into some acceptable commodity before obtaining the goods they desire. He suggested that units might go to a "public treasury" to obtain a "certificate" to spend immediately, so that "money" would not be absent. Quite apart from the fact that this is not "money" in our sense (since it is not a stock of good), no such need would arise under the conditions we hypothesize. See A. Marget, (1), p. 159.

Similarly, Rosenstein-Rodan puts much stress on the absence of money rather than of *any* transactions medium, making his "certain" foresight ambiguous:

". . . it is inconsistent to assume at the same time a state of general certain foresight and the existence of money: they are mutually incompatible. Money (as cash balance) exists only and insofar as general foresight is not certain, it is a function of the individual's feeling of uncertainty, a means of meeting it: a good satisfying the want for certainty. Since certain foresight is assumed in a static equilibrium money

A medium of exchange (of whatever type) arises only when there exists a need to "identify" transactions—to keep track in some way, or to make a note of, the deposits of units upon and their withdrawals from society's stores. Under the state of perfection of knowledge here assumed, no "personal" or "impersonal" type of instrument (distinguished by the existence or non-existence of an economic unit's pledge) will arise for "identifying" transactions.

2.b. The Case of Imperfect Knowledge

Let us now move to an economy in which potential default by units is not ruled out by perfect foresight. Suppose it to be possible in the conditions of "open stockpiles" for units to withdraw goods without ever replacing them. Under these conditions, explicit notice must be taken of transactions: withdrawal must be accompanied by a token which has the function either of (1) explicitly identifying the person who obtained the goods, or (2) noting the nonnecessity of identifying the unit by assuring the deliverer of the goods that the receiving unit has a valid claim to them.[6]

In this case, however, it is assumed that personal credit instruments arise to deny the possibility of default, *but that once the identification of units has been made, default once more becomes nil.* In such circumstances, the credit instuments would be needed in order to deter default, but no clearing between units at the end of the period would be necessary. If it be assumed that the costs of such credit instruments—let us say simple receipts signed by agencies of the economic units receiving goods—are negligible, once more we find that no additional burden to the real (inventory) costs of synchronization is borne by society. These credit instruments would be kept by the force of competition at face value, and any attempt to exchange via a stock of impersonal instruments could not succeed if a *sine qua non* of its continued existence was a positive price for the services of these instruments.

This type of credit instrument has an important kinship with money as defined above. Although it is literally a personal credit instrument, the fact that it is not cleared makes it impersonal in a *de facto* sense. It is one of the important features of money, as will be apparent later, that it

---

and static equilibrium are incompatible." P. Rosenstein-Rodan, (1), pp. 271–2. Quoted by permission.

[6] Pigou asserts that in a one-good production economy no need for money arises, since all factors can be paid in the good. With imperfect foresight assumed, this solution neglects completely the need to "identify" deliverers of services and receivers of the good when such deliveries are not perfectly synchronized. A. Pigou, (1), p. 70. Pigou seems to combine money and credit instruments in his considerations, and therefore abstracts from the problems that concern us. See, for example, his conclusions about money on pp. 74–5, which are phrased in terms of barter or no barter, not money vs. credit instruments.

serves as a token of transactions that requires no clearing between individuals. It would not be far-fetched therefore if we stepped outside the rigorous definition of money and looked upon this type of economy as one in which the price of the services of "money," and therefore the price of "money" itself, is zero.

2.c. The Case of Imperfect Knowledge and Clearing

But the mere existence of uncleared personal credit instruments could not for long continue to guarantee the nonexistence of default under conditions of imperfect foresight. Sooner or later, individual units would take advantage of this lack of clearing to draw more from the stockpile than they deserved, and a need for clearing instruments would arise.[7] We may suppose that all transactions are conducted by the signing of receipts, and assume further that a prior cost-minimization decision by society has led to a central clearing agency where individual units' accounts are cleared at the end of each fulfillment week. Assume, finally, to keep the new institution Walrasian, that it is forced to price at average cost for its clearing function in an as yet unspecified manner. At last, then, we have arrived at conditions in a circular flow in which the services of a "transactions identification" instrument entail a real charge against the economy—a real cost necessitated by the need to obviate the possibility of default by clearing credit instruments.

As soon as the need for clearing comes into being, and its cost becomes greater than zero, there is need to consider the possibility of substitutes as methods of "identifying" transactions. Specifically, an *impersonal* credit instrument whose mere possession is sufficient evidence of the validity of a claim upon society's goods can (1) eliminate the cost of clearing while it (2) identifies transactions.[8] If we assume that it provides these services costlessly, then holders of a given stock of it may sell its services period after period at prices that just entice the marginal economic unit

[7] This need may not be continuous. If penalties for default are made severe enough and the probability of being caught high enough, randomized clearing-or-no-clearing decisions at the end of each week may be sufficient, but costs may not be greatly reduced under those of continuous clearing. We shall assume that clearing is necessary period by period in this chapter.

[8] This role of money is close to, but not identical with, Pareto's "guaranty role" of a true (commodity) money. See V. Pareto, (2), p. 451. Pareto's work in money was neither very extensive nor original. He had a relatively simple quantity theory approach to the determination of the price level, and said little about the determination of desired cash balances by economic units. See (2), pp. 368–71.

His predecessor, Pantaleoni, however, did emphasize the fact that not only is money's function instrumental but that it performs this task without the need of complementary factor services. See M. Pantaleoni, (1), p. 221.

Pigou also stresses the fact that money is not neutral in the deeper sense that its use frees resources for greater social output because of the freer exchange conditions it creates. However, as previously noted, he contrasts a money state to a barter state, not to a credit state with *numéraire*, in which many of his advantages could also be obtained. See A. Pigou, (1), pp. 74–5.

to transact with it rather than use the credit mechanism.[9] The upper limit to the price of the service rendered by money must be the cost of transacting a unit of *numéraire's* business with the cheapest personal credit instrument requiring clearing.

It must not be forgotten that there was no default in the credit instrument economy before we introduced money. *Actual* default is zero and is recognized to be such by every unit in the economy as long as regular clearing is carried on. Thus, in our economy, the costs of actual default do not enter into the price of credit instruments, although, of course, the basic reason for their existence (as well as that of money) and for their being cleared is to *prevent potential default.* This distinction is vital in understanding the reason for the existence of money, for the individual in deciding to transact by purchasing the services of money in the market or availing himself of the use of his personal credit pledge, is absolutely certain that payment in both will be accepted, although a discount will rule on the latter.

Although it is an awkward approach that leads its user into difficulties, let us follow Hicks in assuming the existence of money before we establish that it will arise in a personal credit instrument economy. Assume that money is borrowed by the delivery of personal credit instruments (bills) which are riskless in the credit sense and on which the interest rate cannot change since they are redeemable at the end of the fulfillment-week. Then, Hicks says, ". . . If bills stand at a discount, and consequently earn interest, is there anything to stop any individual from investing all his surplus funds in bills, and holding them during the week in that form? If there is nothing to stop him, then money has no superiority over bills, and therefore cannot stand at a premium to bills. The rate of interest must be nil."[10] But, Hicks continues, ". . . If people receive payment for the things they sell in the form of money, to convert this money into bills requires a separate transaction, and the trouble of making that transaction may offset the gain in interest. It is only if this obstacle were removed, if safe bills could be acquired without any trouble at all, that people would become willing to convert all their money into bills, so long as any interest whatever was offered. Under the conditions of our model, it must be the trouble of making transactions which explains the short rate of interest."[11]

While this explanation can be used to show why money can continue in existence, once born, it cannot answer the question why it came into existence.[12] This can be seen more clearly if, unlike Hicks, we start with

[9] Hicks has indicated that no monopoly bank could have a free hand in the pricing of its services, since substitutes as media of exchange would arise to limit its pricing power. See J. Hicks, (1), pp. 448n.

[10] J. Hicks, (5), p. 164.

[11] J. Hicks, (5), pp. 164–5. Quoted by permission.

[12] See F. Modigliani, (1), pp. 82–3, for the first discussion of this point. But he

an economy where only a credit instrument of a personal type is being used, and ask if money will come into being. The cost of converting money into bills cannot now be used to explain the interest rate, for the "bills" are being used as circulating media already without conversion to money. Hicks comes to this point and says: ". . . If this were to happen generally, there would be no cost of investment, and therefore, so it would appear, no reason for bills to fall to a discount. . . ."[13] And further: ". . . If default risk is so generally ruled out, that all traders reckon, and are known to reckon, a particular bill as perfectly safe, then there is no reason why that bill should stand at a discount, for the obstacle of cost of investment can be circumvented. . . ."[14]

Thus, the existence of money, and with it, the interest rate, cannot be explained by the costs of converting personal credit instruments to impersonal ones. By the logic of Hicks's own arguments, in the absence of default risk, money cannot exist in these circumstances. But he never comes to grips with the question of why credit does not replace money. He concedes the possibility, but shrugs it off by refusing to admit of the general acceptability of personal credit instruments: "But this general acceptability is something different from the mere absence of default risk, which we assumed previously. A class of bills may be regarded as perfectly safe by those who actually take them up, and yet these persons may be different from those to whom the borrower has to make payments. These latter would not accept his bills, so he has to pay *cash;* the former are perfectly willing to lend, but require interest to compensate for their cost of investment."[15] Therefore, when the question is finally posed by Hicks's analysis—when under conditions of a regime of personal credit instruments which are riskless methods of identifying transactions, will money come into existence?—Hicks backs away from answering it. As we shall see, his investment impediments are a separate condition for the existence of money, but he has omitted a prior one.

That condition we have found in the need to clear personal credit instruments which circulate to prevent potential default (when actual

---

substitutes for Hicks's reasoning an unsatisfactory theory of interest:

". . . for certain categories of people (entrepreneurs as well as spendthrifts) it is worth while to pay a premium to obtain spot cash against a promise to pay cash in the future."

Here, too, the reason why credit instruments cannot be used and money dispensed with is begged. Later, in his attempt to show that the disappearance of money in a stationary state, and the substitution of existing securities for money, would not lead to a zero interest rate, Modigliani limits his analysis to bonds and stocks. But if the "securities" used were the "receipts" we have been dealing with (because, for example, securities of the bond-type do not exist beyond the fulfillment week in a Walrasian system) no need to use bonds and stocks would arise, and the interest rate would decline to zero.

[13] J. Hicks, (5), p. 165. Quoted by permission.

[14] J. Hicks, (5), p. 165.

[15] J. Hicks, (5), pp. 165–6. Quoted by permission.

default is zero). But, of course, our singling out of this expense because of our belief that it would be major should not blind us to the disadvantages inherent in such an instrument as money (the need to transport it physically, risk of loss or theft, and so forth). Only if the costs of using an impersonal instrument which obviates the need for clearing are cheaper than those of using a personal instrument can money come into existence: but this cost advantage may be complete, in which case money would completely replace credit instruments, or it may be only partial, in which case credit instruments may be used along with money.

But what of the twilight case: bank deposits? Why should economic units which can transact with money or pay the costs of clearing their receipts purchase stocks of personal-impersonal credit instruments which require clearing? If the cost advantage of a non-clearing instrument were absolute, bank deposits could not exist in these circumstances. Similarly, if the cost advantages of a personal instrument requiring clearing were absolute, no such stocks of instruments need arise, for surely the need to clear current transactions and account for stocks as well cannot be any cheaper than merely clearing transactions. They *can* come into existence, therefore, only when neither of our pure methods has an absolute advantage, so that economic units may desire to use clearing or nonclearing at will. But will they come into existence? It would seem to us that our assumptions allow no middle ground: bank deposits, which possess the disadvantages of both media, would always be at a disadvantage to one or the other, whatever the nature of the transaction. Bank deposits cannot exist.[16]

Next, let us assume that the existence of a credit instrument plus clearing, and the provision of societal penalties, do not eliminate the occurrence of default entirely. If the clearing agency does not assume the responsibility and charges the loss to the seller of the goods, then the *numéraire* value of the credit instrument will be reduced further by this percentage charge that will just cover the individuals' defaults. If the clearing house sets up an insurance fund, the risks must enter into the

[16] Therefore the defense that the following writers were thinking of money in terms of demand deposits cannot fully excuse their neglect of the costs of clearing personal credit instruments. Patinkin has failed to provide an explanation of why credit cannot drive money from his own model in (4); G. Becker and W. Baumol, in G. Becker (1), p. 367, make the point that if no investment frictions exist, money and securities will circulate at par, neglecting any need for and costs of clearing, and Baumol repeats the assertion in W. Baumol, (3), p. 550; Rosenstein-Rodan stresses repeatedly that it is the "store of value" function of money—the "want for certainty" —that explains the existence of money, in (1); and J. Gilbert, in (1), pp. 146–54, distinguishes the inconveniences of time from uncertainty as a cause of the existence of money, but does not attempt to prove that money furnishes a cheaper method of coping with these than credit. Similarly, J. Marschak, in (2), rules out barter as a means of transacting, but does not discuss credit substitutes, although his provision that only money has a perfect market in the sense of zero transactions costs contains our concept of zero clearing costs implicitly. See pp. 87–100.

costs of clearing in order to keep profits zero. Therefore, the existence of *actual* default among the units of an economy does not introduce novel elements into our analysis, for the roots of the latter continue to lie in the costs of successful elimination of *potential* default of much greater magnitude: the former merely adds an additional burden.

2.d. The Case of Imperfect Lending Facilities

Given these two preconditions for the holding of money—the need to identify transactions and the existence of cost advantages in its use for this purpose—two relevant considerations arise: (1) economic units will seek to hold it, and to purchase it for holding, between the end of the fulfillment week and the beginning of the following market day, as they would seek to purchase and hold any other asset that yields a salable service; (2) economic units will seek to economize their use of its services.

From the first of these springs the assurance that individuals will not, even in a stationary state where the good, money, has no direct utility for consumers, seek to reduce their stocks of it to zero at the end of the market day. This is true for money as for any other stock of asset: inventories of consumption goods, for example. If no reason exists for the unit to liquidate its holdings of other stocks, no reason exists for it to seek to reduce its stock of money to zero.

The second consideration leads to an objection many economists have raised. Since money is a good whose service is required only at a set of discrete points for each economic unit in the fulfillment week, individuals will seek to lend it to other units between payment dates, or even to make contracts to rent durable consumption goods with cash balances—between such payment dates. Imagine, first, that the distribution of the *numéraire* value of transactions to be made throughout the fulfillment week is a uniform one at discrete points, so that, for example, $\frac{1}{10}$ of the total value of transactions occurs at each of 10 time points in the week. Between these points, demand for the services of money will be zero, so that units will seek to lend or rent goods until the next payment date. Thus, its velocity tends toward infinity, and the price level rises with it until it becomes useless as a medium of exchange.

If payment dates may occur continuously throughout the week, the same result will occur. Some method of preventing the use of cash balances between payment dates must be devised as a third condition for the holding of money balances, and, therefore, the continued use of money as a medium of exchange.

Two solutions have been advanced. First, the Wicksell-Hicks-Marget investment impediments, which assume that the costs of making extremely short-run investments outweigh their returns, can be looked upon as forcing the economic units to hold cash balances instead of securities between payment dates. Baumol has worked out a model based upon the impediments of brokerage charges in the broadest sense of the term, and Marschak has generalized the concept to one of perfect markets for goods and discusses such frictions for a pure exchange economy.[17]

A second method is that developed by Patinkin by which the payment dates for economic units are fixed in time, but the amounts of goods received and delivered, with attendant payments and receipts, at any given payment time, are randomized. The hope is that such a scheme will force economic units to hold cash if the drawings for receipts and payments are made just before the payment time, insofar as economic units will be unable to foresee accurately their net requirements of cash until it is needed. If our analysis is correct, however, it is difficult to see the need for randomization: even if payments and receipts at each fixed payment date are foreseen with certainty in Patinkin's system, the demand to hold money will arise, and since no need for it exists between payment dates, it will lie idle in balances.[18]

In our own model, delivery dates occur continuously through the fulfillment week, every economic unit foreseeing with certainty the times and amounts of its net payments. However, since all contracts for borrowing cash balances are signed on the market day for the whole week, the inability to lend for portions of the week rules out the attempt to get rid of money when it is not needed.

Some have objected that under the circumstances, where money is held by default, there cannot be a true demand for cash balances. For example, Schumpeter wrote: ". . . If people got their 'incomes' each Saturday and spend them on consumers' goods each succeeding Monday —transactions between firms being excluded—then the money will lie about in the vaults of firms from Monday to Saturday, not because there is any demand for cash holdings, but because the institutional arrangement wills it. . . ."[19] We shall take this criticism somewhat into account in our statement of the form of the demand functions for cash balances; yet, the performance of the necessary identification of transactions most cheaply gives money a utility, and the mere fact that it is not in continuous use—just as the tractor on the farm is only intermittently useful—does nothing to lessen this usefulness.

2.e. Conclusions

Given (1) the need to identify individual units' withdrawals and deposits of goods and services, (2) the cheaper cost of doing so with a nonclearing type of instrument than with one that must be cleared, with

[17] K. Wicksell, (3), Vol. II, p. 71; J. Hicks, (3), pp. 6–7, and (5), p. 165; A. Marget, (1), pp. 159–61; W. Baumol, (3); J. Marschak, (2). See also D. Patinkin, (1), p. 136, and (4), pp. 62–95; G. Becker and W. Baumol, in G. Becker, (1), p. 367; P. Rosenstein-Rodan, (1), pp. 269–72; F. Modigliani, (1), p. 51; and F. Hayek, (2), p. 357.

[18] D. Patinkin, (4), pp. 86–95.

[19] J. Schumpeter, (1), Vol. II, p. 547. Quoted by permission.

or without actual default occurring, and (3) some inhibition or inducement to hold it between payment dates, money will exist in a stationary economy.

Its services will sell for a price which can be no higher than the cost of the cheapest alternative method of clearing. Therefore, it becomes an asset in which consumers can invest to obtain a yield in futurity, and a market for it as an asset will exist in which it will be priced—an "unorganized" market formed of the obverses of all other markets.

From the price of its services and its price as an asset can be reckoned the "rate of interest," which is, as for any other asset, the net yield of a good, durable and limited in quantity, which provides a salable service. In this case it is the ability to perform most cheaply the necessary task of identifying transactions. Since the price of its service will always be above zero in the conditions envisioned, the interest rate will be positive and less than infinite as long as future income has a utility. Since an equilibrium condition in asset markets is the equality of all net rates of return, the rate of return on real assets can never drop below that on money. Therefore, as long as money exists in the stationary flow, the interest rate and return on capital goods can never, à la Schumpeter, decline to zero.[20]

Lastly, we have not asserted the probability of the preconditions for the existence of money, but merely the necessity of their existence in order for money to come into being and remain extant in the stationary state. To investigate these relative costs more closely, let us turn to Wicksell's famous credit systems of exchange. His basic position is that, ". . . in a pure cash economy the most essential cash holdings are those which are destined for definite payments at given points of time in the future. It is precisely these which in an advanced credit economy can most easily be dispensed with, for loans or commodity credits falling due on definite dates provide a perfect substitute."[21] Wicksell does not argue the disappearance of money in a stationary state, for money and merchandise credits are complete substitutes. The latter serves to magnify the velocity of circulation of the former without limit, allowing the stock of money to shrink to small amounts. Implicitly behind such reasoning is the proposition that the costs of extending merchandise credit to identify transactions and *then of clearing these credits by a limited stock of money* are less than either using money for identification or of using a personal clearing system. In other words, Wicksell's simple credit system does away almost entirely with the holding of cash balances by assuming credit instruments to be cheaper when the latter are cleared with money.

For example, suppose that, within the week, sellers extend credit to buyers, and that on Friday the clearing time arrives. With a sufficiently

[20] Cf. M. Allais, (1), p. 371.

[21] K. Wicksell, (2), p. 57. Quoted by permission.

large velocity, a $1 bill could be passed between hands to clear all of the account books. Money must always be somewhere in this simple credit system, but holdings of it are minimal during the week. We should not deny the possibility of the system, but would argue that merchandise credit is not costless, that direct clearing is a substitute for money clearing, and that the holder of money would be foolish to use it at par. Given these conditions, larger stocks of money and the holding of cash balances may well become a cheaper clearing method—say by the conversion of some commodity to stocks of money.

Wicksell's organized credit economy is more complex than the simple credit schema, but is fundamentally the same. In it bills of exchange or centralized lending by monetary institutions are employed to clear accounts between individuals. To the extent all individuals clear through banks, this system approaches Wicksell's pure credit economy in which all persons hold balances in one bank. We have already indicated our belief that this system would possess disadvantages when compared with a clearing system in which stocks of money did not have to be accounted for.[22]

2.f. The Compatibility of Money and Nondynamic Systems

The discussion of the preconditions for the existence of money which we have just concluded rejects the argument that money cannot exist in frameworks which are static and stationary. A leading proponent of this viewpoint is Fossati, and we shall take special care to discuss his arguments.[23] First, we would stress the fact that the models of this chapter, as of the last, are not only static but stationary. Time does exist in them, as we have emphasized. Fossati asserts that the study of general equilibrium is the study of an economy at a *point* in time, and that dynamic analysis converts this to a *period* of time. He explicitly compares the point of statics and the period of dynamics to the spatial analogues of point and area.[24] As we have discussed in Chapter 1, we must deny the association of movement through time exclusively with dynamics. These are, of course, matters of definition: to the extent Fossati is merely saying that a time dimension is necessary before any stock-of-money concept is meaningful, we should agree.[25]

A second point with which we must also take issue concerns more substantive terrain. Fossati, as well as Patinkin in his earlier articles, insists that money must be introduced in the preference function of the individual and treated in a marginal fashion if it is to be truly integrated

[22] K. Wicksell, (2), pp. 59–62.

[23] See E. Fossati, (3), (2), and (1).

[24] E. Fossati, (3), pp. 10n, 116, and (2), pp. 18–23.

[25] Henderson and Quandt also make this point, but term this introduction of stationarity "implicit dynamics." Again, we should disagree over definitions, but accept the need for a time dimension. See J. Henderson, (1), and R. Kuenne, (3).

into the model: "The theory of equilibrium springs from a general theory of choice based on the marginal analysis, which is applicable wherever choice takes place between alternatives capable of quantitative expression. Money is evidently capable of quantitative expression. The individual *chooses* between the possibility of keeping the money and the possibility of buying other goods, and therefore money must have a marginal utility.

"But how can we find a measure of this marginal utility? This question implicitly includes the problem whether the demand for money can be introduced into the equations of general equilibrium or not."[26] This criticism of the peculiarities of money and its lack of direct utility has had a long history. Del Vecchio used it against the Walrasian formulation of monetary theory in the early part of this century. The Walrasian introduction of money *services* into the utility function was the source of a great deal of opposition. For example, Divisia, interpreting money wholly as a claim on goods with no direct utility itself, devoted a special appendix to "proving" his implicit assumption that money could not enter the utility function.[27] This reflected Pareto's uneasiness with the Walrasian assumption, and Divisia quite properly criticizes Walras' superficiality of treatment of money and savings, as well as Pareto's feeling that money could be treated as a commodity money with a direct utility for some but not all persons. Pareto seems to have included the cash balances of the individual in his "savings," but is very unclear on this, as we shall see later in the chapter.

We have already mentioned the exception taken to this Walrasian assumption by many economists, most recently Nogaro, who argues that a demand and supply curve for money can only be drawn for the savings market: it is not the object of demand or supply as a medium of exchange.[28] We have also noted that part of Patinkin's earlier criticism revolved around the failure of money to have a direct utility and its "consequent" disappearance from the system.

It was Walras who first established the "utility" of money services to the consumer and introduced them formally into the utility function in the following manner. Just as the consumer derived satisfactions from the holding of real goods inventories, so could he be viewed as deriving "utility" from holding command over goods in money form. These, for all practical purposes, are "postponable" inventories, and we may allow $Y_{j''}$ to symbolize them. We may measure a unit of such services in the same units in which we measure the consumption of the goods involved,

[26] E. Fossati, (3), p. 210. Quoted by permission.

[27] F. Divisia, (1), pp. 399–413, 423–33.

[28] B. Nogaro, (1), p. 184. His position springs from a desire to see effects of monetary changes ramify through all markets, and thus avoid what has come to be known as Patinkin's Invalid Dichotomy, to be discussed below. See p. 186.

introduce them into the utility function, and obtain demand functions for them as we would for any other desirable good or service. Also, the service E'' may be defined in order that the consumer can hold cash balances against the delivery of securities. The prices of $Y_{j''}$ and E'' must be the income sacrificed for a week by tying up cash balances instead of lending their services; that is,

$$(2) \qquad P_{j''} = \left(\frac{P_j}{P_u}\right) P_{u'}, \qquad P_{e'} = \left(\frac{P_e}{P_u}\right) P_{u'}$$

Then, the consumer adjusts the marginal preference for these services divided by the respective prices to the marginal utility of income to obtain an equilibrium. The system for a given consumer derived as non-specific solutions to a simple exchange model would be:

$$(3) \quad \begin{aligned}
&1. \quad X_{cj\neq 1} = H_{cj\neq 1}(P_{j\neq 1}, P_i, P_e, P_{u'}, P_u, P_{j'}, P_{j''}, P_{e''}; Q_{cZ_i}, Q_{cj}, Q_{cu}) \\
&\qquad\quad = H_{cj\neq 1}([P]; [Q_c]) \\
&2. \quad \bar{X}_{ci} = Q_{cZ_i} - H_{ci}([P]; [Q_c]) \\
&3. \quad X_{ce} = H_{ce}([P]; [Q_c]) \\
&4. \quad \bar{X}_{cj'} = Q_{cj} - H_{cj'}([P]; [Q_c]) \\
&5. \quad X_{cj''} = H_{cj''}([P]; [Q_c]) \\
&6. \quad X_{ce''} = H_{ce''}([P]; [Q_c]) \\
&7. \quad \bar{X}_{cu} = Q_{cu} - \frac{\left(\sum_j X_{cj''}P_j + X_{ce''}P_e\right)}{P_u} \\
&8. \quad X_{c1} = \sum_i \bar{X}_{ci}P_i + \sum_j \bar{X}_{cj'}P_{j'} + \bar{X}_{cu}P_{u'} - \sum_{j\neq 1} X_{cj}P_j - X_{ce}P_e
\end{aligned}$$

Real inventories and money have been integrated into the simple exchange model: both have a "marginal utility" or a marginal rate of substitution for other commodities, and we should be able to obtain substitution and income effects of price changes upon both types of synchronization media. The mere fact that the marginal usefulness of money depends upon prices directly is not a crucial difference between it and other goods.[29]

Such an effort to integrate these commodities, and particularly money, into the general equilibrium system was a commendable stroke of brilliance, and much superior to the attempts of others of Walras' contemporaries to integrate money. Pareto, for example, suffers from a non-

[29] This dependence of the utility of money upon prices bothered, among others, Divisia. See P. Samuelson, (4), pp. 117–24 for a demonstration that it is not of fundamental importance.

typical lack of clarity in his treatment of money. He explicitly recognizes that a "true" money, i.e., a commodity like gold, is merely another form of capital good and that savings can be transformed into "locomotives, livestock, etc., or money of circulation."[30] But the fact that it was a good with alternative uses as a commodity was central to Pareto's theory: by virtue of this it had a cost of production and weekly increments to the money stock could be determined by enforcing equality of price and cost. In Walras' treatment, on the other hand, the money involved was a pure paper money, and the utility that of money services, not of the services of a good which may be consumed in lieu of using it for money.

But must we introduce money into the preference function and treat it in marginal terms? The removal of money from the function is not a denial that money has a "utility" for consumers. Nor, conversely, does the existence of such usefulness necessarily imply that it must enter the preference function used in the analysis. It is a methodological decision whether the consumer's demand may best be treated on a "marginal" basis or some other—say "institutional"—basis. In some transcendental sense a function exists in which money may be included—in the sense that it has a usefulness for the consumer—but this is not the analytical preference function constructed by the economist to predict the consumer's behavior. The strange position of those who, like Fossati and Marschak,[31] argue this necessity is not projected into the entrepreneurial sector to require a marginal productivity of money before it can be integrated into production theory.

Is not the "postponable" inventory approach of Walras to the demand for cash balances too pretentious for its surroundings? Did not Walras' desire for mathematical symmetry lead to an overwrought design for money? Does the concept of "postponable inventory services of perpetual net revenue" (E'') have any but mathematical meaning? It is meant to determine, of course, the cash balance one must hold against the delivery of securities during the week. In this Walrasian circular flow, with its certainty of delivery and delivery time, money is a mere flywheel converting discontinuous income receipts into a smoother path of consumption through time. That is, assuming a consumption pattern has been decided upon for the week, money serves a passive role in such an economy and cannot properly be envisaged as a vehicle for services which are conceptually capable of a continuous utility function.[32]

In view of these objections and the unnecessary complications of the model to which they are addressed, a disaggregated Marshallian-k approach seems preferable. It was the approach of Walras himself in the

[30] V. Pareto, (1), Vol. I, pp. 181–3.

[31] See J. Marschak, (2), pp. 74–9.

[32] For a somewhat similar criticism of a different concept having relevance to the spatial dimension, see footnote 8, Chapter 7, and its reference.

second and third editions of the *Éléments*, and, on the entrepreneurial side, he never did abandon the assumption of fixed coefficients for real balances. In Patinkin's view, the decisionmaker holds money, not because he maximizes his satisfaction level in doing so, but because the nature of the system requires him to, as in Schumpeter's example above. This smacks somewhat of Pareto's example of nations in which the state monopoly of salt production led to the requirement that each individual buy a stated amount of salt each period.[33]

Under these assumptions, we eliminate "postponable inventory services" as goods, thereby dropping (3-5) and (3-6) from the set of consumer equations, eliminating the corresponding prices from the price vector [P], and substituting for (3-7) the following:

$$\bar{X}_{cu} = Q_{cu} - \frac{\left(k_c \left[\sum_j X_{cj}P_j + X_{ce}P_e\right]\right)}{P_u} \tag{4}$$

where the k_c are institutionally determined, in the sense that the preferences of the consumer for delivery dates and the receipts of payment for his own factor service deliveries dictate the size of balance he must carry.

Fossati's third point gets to the heart of the matter: money cannot exist in the absence of uncertainty, he argues, and imperfect knowledge is the essence of "dynamics." He believes that static analysis is defined either as constancy of parameters through time or as a context wherein all economic units have perfect foresight. A known law of change of parameters implies to Fossati a nondynamic framework. Only in imperfect foresight—and therefore dynamic analysis—can money become a liquid reserve with a marginal utility.[34] We have attempted to show that the existence of money is possible even with perfect foresight.

In Section 2, therefore, we have attempted to establish the preconditions for money in a static, stationary equilibrium, and, in so doing, to cope with a variety of arguments against the possibility of the existence of money. On the assumption that we have been successful in this effort, we may now proceed to equilibrium conditions under the assumption of stationarity in models which do contain money.

3. Model V-1: A Money Model with Say's Identity

For simplicity let us return to the Walrasian type of model with periods of production of one week for each process. Then, for our revised consumer's nonspecific solution yielding demand and supply functions,

[33] D. Patinkin, (4), p. 160 and R. Kuenne, (7), p. 10. Walras' treatment of money does have the advantage of making the proof of an equilibrium for the general equilibrium model easier. See Chapter 9.

[34] E. Fossati, (3), pp. 209–22.

we obtain:

(V-1-0)

$$
\begin{aligned}
&1. \quad X_{cj\neq 1} = H_{cj\neq 1}(P_{j\neq 1}, P_i, P_e, P_{u'}, P_u, P_{j'}; [\bar{P}_c], Q_{cZ_i}, Q_{cj}, Q_{cu}) \\
&\qquad\quad = H_{cj\neq 1}([P]; [\bar{P}_c], [Q_c]) \\
&2. \quad \bar{X}_{ci} = Q_{cZ_i} - H_{ci}([P]; [\bar{P}_c], [Q_c]) \\
&3. \quad X_{ce} = H_{ce}([P]; [\bar{P}_c], [Q_c]) \\
&4. \quad \bar{X}_{cj'} = Q_{cj'} - H_{cj'}([P]; [\bar{P}_c], [Q_c]) \\
&5. \quad \bar{X}_{cu} = Q_{cu} - \frac{k_c\left(\sum_j X_{cj}P_j + X_{ce}P_e\right)}{P_u} \\
&6. \quad X_{c1} = \sum_i \bar{X}_{ci}P_i + \sum_j \bar{X}_{cj'}P_{j'} + \bar{X}_{cu}P_{u'} \\
&\qquad\qquad - \sum_{j\neq 1} X_{cj}P_j - X_{ce}P_e
\end{aligned}
$$

The aggregate functions are obtained by summing over the individuals' functions:

(V-1-1)

$$
\begin{aligned}
&1. \quad X_{j\neq 1} = H_{j\neq 1}([P]; [\bar{P}_c], [Q]) \\
&2. \quad \bar{X}_i = Q_{Z_i} - H_i([P]; [\bar{P}], [Q]) \\
&3. \quad X_e = H_e([P]; [\bar{P}], [Q]) \\
&4. \quad \bar{X}_{j'} = Q_{j'} - H_{j'}([P]; [\bar{P}], [Q]) \\
&5. \quad X_u = Q_u - \frac{\sum_c k_c\left(\sum_j X_{cj}P_j + X_{ce}P_e\right)}{P_u} \\
&6. \quad X_1 = \sum_i \bar{X}_i P_i + \sum_j \bar{X}_{j'}P_{j'} + \bar{X}_u P_{u'} - \sum_{j\neq 1} X_j P_j - X_e P_e
\end{aligned}
$$

We may define the aggregate entrepreneurial demands and supplies as aggregates over the firms' functions:

(V-1-2)

$$
\begin{aligned}
&1. \quad X_i = G_i(P_{j\neq 1}, P_i, P_{Z_i}, P_e, P_{j'}, P_{u'}, P_u; [\bar{P}^*]) \\
&\qquad\quad = G_i([P^*]; [\bar{P}^*]) \\
&2. \quad X_j^* = G_j([P^*]; [\bar{P}^*]) \\
&3. \quad \bar{X}_j = G_J([P^*]; [\bar{P}^*]) \\
&4. \quad \bar{X}_{Z_i} = G_{Z_i}([P^*]; [\bar{P}^*]) \\
&5. \quad X_{j'} = \sum_v \left(\sum_j k_{vj'j}\bar{X}_{vj} + \sum_i k_{vj'Zi}\bar{X}_{vZ_i}\right) \\
&6. \quad X_u = \sum_v \left(\frac{k_{vu}}{P_u}\right)\left(\sum_j \bar{X}_{vj}P_j + \sum_i \bar{X}_{vZi}P_{Z_i}\right)
\end{aligned}
$$

where it will be noted that inventories are assumed to be held by the firms that produce the goods and where it is further assumed that the demand for money is a linear function of the value of outputs.

Profits for every firm are zero:

$$\text{(V-1-3)} \quad \sum_j \bar{X}^{\circ}_{vj}P^{\circ}_j + \sum_i \bar{X}^{\circ}_{vZ_i}P^{\circ}_{Z_i} - \sum_i X^{\circ}_{vi}P^{\circ}_i - \sum_j X^{\circ}_{vj}P^{\circ}_j - \sum_j X^{\circ}_{vj'}P^{\circ}_{j'} - X^{\circ}_{vu}P^{\circ}_{u'} = 0$$

All real goods and factor service markets must be cleared in equilibrium:

$$\text{(V-1-4)} \quad \begin{aligned} &1. \quad X^{\circ}_i = \bar{X}^{\circ}_i \\ &2. \quad X^{\circ}_j + X^{*\circ}_j + X''^{\circ}_j = \bar{X}^{\circ}_j \\ &3. \quad X^{\circ}_{Z_i} = \bar{X}^{\circ}_{Z_i} \\ &4. \quad X^{\circ}_{j'} = \bar{X}^{\circ}_{j'} \\ &5. \quad X^{\circ}_u = \bar{X}^{\circ}_u \end{aligned}$$

We define the individual firm's demand and supply functions as follows:

$$\text{(V-1-5)} \quad \begin{aligned} &1. \quad X_{vi} = G_{vi}([P^*]; [\bar{P}^*_v]) \\ &2. \quad X_{vj} = G_{vj}([P^*]; [\bar{P}^*_v]) \\ &3. \quad \bar{X}_{vj} = G_{vJ}([P^*]; [\bar{P}^*_v]) \\ &4. \quad \bar{X}_{vZ_i} = G_{vI}([P^*]; [\bar{P}^*_v]) \\ &5. \quad X_{vj'} = \sum_j k_{vj'j}\bar{X}_{vj} + \sum_i k_{vj'Z_i}\bar{X}_{vZ_i} \\ &6. \quad X_{vu} = \frac{k_{vu}}{P_u}\left(\sum_j \bar{X}_{vj}P_j + \sum_i \bar{X}_{vZ_i}P_{Z_i}\right) \end{aligned}$$

In the securities market, once more, the equilibrium value of savings must equal the equilibrium value of capital goods plus produced goods Y_j going into inventories:

$$\text{(V-1-6)} \quad X^{\circ}_e P^{\circ}_e = \sum_i X^{\circ}_{Z_i}P^{\circ}_{Z_i} + \sum_j X''^{\circ}_j P^{\circ}_j$$

But, also, the three types of capital goods—capital goods proper, inventories, and money—must be homogeneous to the consumer, so that he will take an equivalent value of any of them in redemption of his security holdings. Therefore, net rates of return on each type must be equal to that on all others:

$$\text{(V-1-7)}\qquad \begin{aligned} &1. \quad P^{\circ}_{Z_i} = (P^{\circ}_{i} - u_i P^{\circ}_{Z_i})P^{\circ}_{e} \\ &2. \quad P^{\circ}_{j} = (P^{\circ}_{j'} - P^{\circ}_{j})P^{\circ}_{e} \\ &3. \quad P^{\circ}_{u} = P^{\circ}_{u'}P^{\circ}_{e} \end{aligned}$$

To the unknowns of Model IV-3 we have added the following: (a) $ns\ \bar{X}_{cj'}$ terms; (b) $s\ \bar{X}_{cu}$ terms; (c) $n\ \bar{X}_{j'}$ terms; (d) 1 $\bar{X}_u$ term; (e) $n\ P_{j'}$ terms; (f) 1 $P_{u'}$ term; (g) 1 P_u term; (h) $on\ X_{vj'}$ terms; (i) $o\ X_{vu}$ terms; (j) $n\ X_{j'}$ terms; (k) 1 X_u term; and (l) $n\ X_j''$ terms. To the equations we have added: (a) $ns + s$ in (V-1-0, -4, and -5); (b) $n + 1$ in (V-1-1, -4, and -5); (c) $n + 1$ in (V-1-2, -5, and -6); (d) $n + 1$ in (V-1-4-4 and -5); (e) $o + on$ in (V-1-5, -5, and -6); and (f) $n + 1$ in (V-1-7, -2 and -3). The additional equations are equal to the additional unknowns.

4. Say's Identity

If the equations of (V-1-0) are viewed as the results of nonspecific solutions to consumer simple exchange models yielding demands and supplies for any specified set of data, including prices, then there exists a basic difficulty with such systems as Model V-1. This fault is that money is not truly integrated into the system: indeed, it cannot exist in the system. This was first pointed out in Lange's classic article, which described the indeterminacy of the price of money and the essential barter nature of such models.[35] Although the specific nature of the indeterminacy in Model V-1 is a bit different from that uncovered by Lange, we shall use his criticism as the starting point of our own.

In (V-1-0-6) it is stated that for every individual, demand for goods and new capital assets must equal income plus disinvestment in capital goods and inventories. No room exists for the purchase or sale of money as an asset—in or out of equilibrium. Any excess supply of factor services must be balanced by an equivalent value of excess demand for consumption or investment goods other than money. This is "Say's Identity:" each individual is desirous of holding his existing stock of cash as an asset, no more and no less. Let us illustrate the difficulties this leads to with a simpler system than Model V-1.

For the individual, let $\bar{X}_{cz}$ be the supply of the only factor service in the economy, with price P_z, and let X_{c1} be the demand by the consumer for the only consumer good in the economy; let $P_u = 1$. The consumer's endowment of cash at the start of the market day is Q_{cu}, and the amount he desires to hold at the end of the week we define as Q^*_{cu}. Let us abstract from the possibility of individual investment in Z, so that it must be true that:

$$\text{(5)}\qquad \bar{X}_{cz}P_z + Q_{cu} \equiv X_{c1}P_1 + Q^*_{cu}$$

[35] O. Lange, (4).

For simplicity, we further assume that the consumer's demand for money to hold at the end of the week is a simple function of his purchases of consumer goods:

$$(6) \qquad Q^*_{cu} = k_c X_{c1} P_1$$

where k_c is given. Then (6) specifies the demand for money as a stock (at the end of the week). The demand for money as a flow is merely the money value of the consumer's supply of factor services:

$$(7) \qquad X'_{cu} \equiv \bar{X}_{cz} P_z$$

His supply of money as a flow is the value of consumer goods he buys:

$$(8) \qquad \bar{X}'_{cu} \equiv X_{c1} P_1$$

Then the net increase in demand for cash during the period may be defined in either of two ways:

$$(9) \qquad \begin{array}{ll} 1. & \Delta Q_{cu} \equiv Q^*_{cu} - Q_{cu} \\ 2. & \Delta Q_{cu} \equiv X'_{cu} - \bar{X}'_{cu} \end{array}$$

Or, for all individuals, we may sum to obtain

$$(10) \qquad \begin{array}{ll} 1. & \Delta Q_u \equiv Q^*_u - Q_u \\ 2. & \Delta Q_u \equiv X'_u - \bar{X}'_u \end{array}$$

where ΔQ_u is the desired increment in cash holdings by all persons for the week. Let us also aggregate over (6) to obtain

$$(11) \qquad Q^*_u = K X_1 P_1$$

where K is some average of the k_c. Then, from (10)

$$(12) \qquad Q_u + \Delta Q_u = K X_1 P_1$$

Now, Say's Identity states that $\Delta Q_{cu} \equiv 0$, i.e., the *desired* increment in cash holdings is identically zero. Therefore, in a regime where it holds,

$$(13) \qquad \Delta Q_u \equiv X'_u - \bar{X}'_u \equiv Q^*_u - Q_u \equiv 0$$

From (13) it follows that demand for money as a stock must be identically equal to its supply and that demand for money as a flow must be equal to its supply as a flow. From (12) therefore,

$$(14) \qquad Q_u \equiv K X_1 P_1$$

or, in the classical fashion, we may rewrite (14) to be

$$(15) \qquad M \equiv KPT$$

since Q_u is the supply of money stocks. Say's Identity implies that the demand for cash balances is always equal to the supply, regardless of the price level P. In some unspecified manner, K must adjust instantaneously to changes in P, and any level for P is consistent with the model. Therefore, when the neoclassicals tacked on to the model an equation of the form

$$M = KP^{\circ}T^{\circ} \tag{16}$$

which was meant to yield P° as an equilibrium quantity, they were involved in a contradiction. The relation (15), contained implicitly in a Say's Identity system, and that in (16), contained explicitly, cannot coexist: the demand for cash balances cannot be both independent of the price level P and a determinant of it at the same time.[36]

The implications of this Langean analysis may be brought out in a second manner. Since there are only two options—goods or money—in the simplified economy above, an excess demand for money equal to zero at all times must mean that the sum of the values of excess demand for goods and factor services must always be zero. Now, suppose P_z and P_1 were doubled by external action, or by the adjustment processes in the market: Say's Identity would assure that the excess demand for money remained at zero. Moreover, since the relative prices of the economy are unchanged, the amounts demanded and supplied of real goods and factor services are similarly unchanged. The model has been effectively dichotomized, to use Patinkin's terms: no interaction between the monetary sector and the goods sector can exist by virtue of Say's Identity.

Another way of stating this dichotomy is to say that the so-called "homogeneity postulate" rules in the real goods sector of the economy;[37] i.e., to assert that excess demand equations for real goods and services are homogeneous of degree zero in money prices alone, rather than money prices *and* the individual's stock of money. Only in a Say's Identity economy, where the stock of money can have no effect in the sense relevant here, can the "homogeneity postulate" be equated to the second (and more defensible) concept. For the homogeneity postulate implies that if we multiply a random set of positive money prices by a positive constant, individual goods' excess demands will remain unchanged at

[36] Mosak views (16) as a *definition* of P or K that specifies which of an infinite number of possible values for these terms must rule. See J. Mosak, (1), pp. 37–8. This is an acceptance of the dichotomy forced upon the system by the adoption of Say's Identity. If the community rigorously insists upon holding $\frac{1}{3}$ of the money value of its transactions in money form, then only one K and one P will ever emerge from (15), even though an infinity of pairs would satisfy this identity. The important thing is to see that this interpretation prevents (16) from being viewed as the outcome of a market equilibration in a general system. See also S. Valavanis, (1), p. 357.

[37] Compare the definition of Leontief in (2), p. 193. See also Patinkin, (4), pp. 107–9.

some positive, negative, or zero level, while the excess demand for money is unchanged at zero. If, when the prices were increased proportionately, individual goods' excess demands could change such that their value sum were zero, Say's Identity would not necessarily imply the homogeneity postulate. But this latter cannot occur when Say's Identity rules: for if, when prices rise to a multiple of their former values, two or more excess demands for goods change, these excess demands must be functions of money prices. Therefore, in the general case, excess demand for money—the obverse of excess demand for goods in value terms—must also be a function of the price level, which is a result in violation of Say's Identity.

Therefore, the validity of Lange's criticism of such systems as that contained in Model V-1 hinges upon whether or not it contains Say's Identity. Since Model V-1 is a modified Walrasian money economy, let us ask in what sense, if any, Lange's criticisms are relevant to Walras' analysis.

5. The Walrasian Monetary Analysis

Walras' definitive presentation of his monetary theory can be interpreted in several ways, each of which can find support from passages in the *Éléments*. The interpretation offered in the presentation of Model V-1 is, therefore, not presented with claims of exclusiveness: what is asserted is that the Walrasian system, taken as a whole, emerged from a "vision" of economic processes which its author employed with consistency when thinking in terms of equation systems. From this "vision" and its rigorous formulation emerges an internal logic which interpretations must not contradict. Of the several interpretations of monetary processes consistent with this internal logic, it is believed that the one presented above, and to be expanded now, is the working framework of reference of Walras himself.

We have already elucidated the basic facts of Walras' integration of money: it is conceived as a good yielding no utility in itself, but, by furnishing "services" of an inventory nature, its possession allows consumers and entrepreneurs to command goods in the absence of receipts from current flows. Consumers equate the marginal utility of these services divided by the price of a unit of the service in *numéraire* to a similar ratio for all other goods to determine their demand for cash balances. Excess supply is taken to a market where it is lent at a price, $P_{u'}$, to entrepreneurs (primarily), whose demands for real balances are determined rigorously as constant coefficients per unit of product (we have made them a function of output values). The price of money in *numéraire*, P_u, is obtained by capitalizing the price of its service, $P_{u'}$, at a common net rate of return on assets, $\frac{1}{P_e}$.

To breathe an economic soul into this mathematical frame is another matter. The primary tenet of our interpretation is that Walras was an economic primitive: i.e., his economic models began *ab ovo*[38] with consumers and entrepreneurs acting within a complex of interrelated markets, with the former *literally* supplying all services *in kind* to entrepreneurs (primarily). Walras' vision of his economy never left for long nor strayed far from that of the literal exchange economy which was the chyrsalis of the more complex mutations.

As we have interpreted the models in Chapters 2 through the present one, Walras perceived the consumer taking each of these types of capital assets—land, labor, capital goods, raw materials, finished or unfinished products, and money—to a *literal* market in which contracts were made at the end of the market day against (1) payments during the week for use of the goods, gross of depreciation charges, and (2) return of the depreciated assets in kind at the end of the period, either identical assets to those leased or an equivalent value of others. The word *literally* is stressed. Sometimes Walras attempts to clothe his analysis in borrowed finery by bringing these market processes more in line with reality, but he quickly reverts in these instances to his more primitive constructs. The evidence for these contentions will now be cited in detail.[39]

First, there exists throughout the work a stress on real markets.[40] For example, Walras writes, ". . . It should be recalled, moreover, that what we have in mind throughout this volume is not to pose and solve the problem in question as if it were a real problem in a given concrete situa-

[38] The term is not used here in the sense that Walras employed it. In his usage, it merely means that the markets open with any given set of data and random prices as original conditions, in order to illustrate the achievement of general equilibrium. See, for example, L. Walras, (3), pp. 242, 282, 308, and 331. Of course, no support for our interpretation is claimed on the basis of Walras' mere usage of this term.

[39] The potential confusion possible if this primitive interpretation is dropped is well illustrated by the treatment of capital in A. de Pietri-Tonelli, (1), pp. 309–12. He seems to create a separate set of "banking" entrepreneurs who lease capital goods, but they seem to be identical with entrepreneurs who manufacture these capital goods. Their relations to consumers who enjoy the receipts from the sales of the services of capital goods are also unclear.

This interpretation springs from Pareto's rendering of an essentially Walrasian system. He, too, has entrepreneurs hiring savings, producing new capital goods, and then, seemingly, leasing the capital goods to other entrepreneurs. In his presentation of the consumer's budget equations he includes savings as an entry on the purchase side, but says that if a person has savings and sells its services, the prices for these will be found in the sale of factor services, while if he consumes these services the prices will be found on the account of goods consumed. He seems here to be confusing a stock of previous saving with current saving; yet he says that each person has the revenue from "the rents of the capital goods he possesses and from the savings he has made" (1), p. 59. It is difficult to see exactly what interpretation he has in mind of the capital formation and capital good leasing process, given these three statements. See (1), pp. 49–62, 303–4.

[40] See J. Schumpeter's emphasis upon the importance of the stress on markets in Walras' analysis. J. Schumpeter, (5), pp. 1000–2. See also E. Antonelli, (1), pp. 44–5.

tion, but solely to formulate scientifically the nature of the problem which actually arises in the market where it is solved empirically. . . ."[41] At the beginning of the analysis of his investment model, he writes: "From our point of view, there can be no prices other than market prices. Consequently, just as we previously contemplated a products market and a services market to determine the prices of products and the prices of services, so now we must contemplate a market which we shall call a *capital goods market,* where capital goods are bought and sold. . . ."[42]

Other evidence of his thinking in terms of literal markets for all goods and services may be cited: the use of identifiable markets "to fix our ideas" in multiple exchange analysis without *numéraire* ((3), p. 158) and with *numéraire* ((3), p. 162), as well as in his production model ((3), pp. 222–3); his criticism of the English economists for obtaining prices of productive services without reference to markets for them ((3), p. 223); his criticism of Böhm-Bawerk's interest theory on grounds of its failure to specify markets for future goods ((3), pp. 45–6); and his introduction of specific markets to make "the following operations easier to grasp" ((3), p. 243).

Second, and more directly to the point, are those passages yielding direct evidence of capital goods, inventories, raw materials, and money being hired in kind in literal markets. In his introduction to the money model, Walras says explicitly: ". . . We shall . . . endow our landowners, workers and capitalists, viewed as consumers, with random quantities of circulating capital [inventories] and money, just as we endowed them before with random quantities of fixed assets in the form of landed capital, personal capital, and capital proper. Furthermore, we shall suppose our entrepreneurs to borrow the circulating capital goods and the money they need for production, just as we previously supposed them to borrow the fixed capital goods they required. . . ."[43] And a little later: "If the economy were liquidated at the end of the second phase [the fulfillment week], the *old capital goods, both fixed and circulating,* would be returned *in kind* by the entrepreneurs to the capitalists, and the circulating capital goods would be returned in the form of *similar* goods."[44] But, in his consideration of the economy with fixed capital, he writes: "It may perhaps be useful to point out that, under the conditions we have laid down, we are assuming for the time being that capital proper is lent in

[41] L. Walras, (3), p. 157. Quoted by permission of Richard D. Irwin, Inc., George Allen & Unwin, Ltd., and the American Economic Association.

[42] L. Walras, (3), p. 267. Quoted by permission of Richard D. Irwin, Inc., George Allen & Unwin, Ltd., and the American Economic Association.

[43] L. Walras, (3), p. 318, bracketed expression supplied. Quoted by permission of Richard D. Irwin, Inc., George Allen & Unwin, Ltd., and the American Economic Association.

[44] L. Walras, (3), p. 319. Quoted by permission of Richard D. Irwin, Inc., George Allen & Unwin, Ltd., and the American Economic Association.

kind. We have already explained in section 190, however, that actually, in the real world, capital is lent in cash, because the capitalist accumulates it in that form by saving. Later on we shall consider both the creation and the lending of capital in the form of money."[45]

The promised reference introduces money capital of necessity, since it deals with the double-entry bookkeeping of entrepreneurs. It occurs in section 235 in a one-paragraph explanation of why abstraction from the money capital market is possible. Walras explains that the "money capital market" is merely an annex to the service market and states later that it appears distinct from the capital goods market. This is a score against the contention of this book, since the only "money market" in which services are sold, in our interpretation, is the market where money balances are hired for their services, *not* to purchase capital goods. Only if this "money capital market" can be interpreted as our securities market can it fit our interpretation.[46]

Lastly, to support our hypothesis, in his preface to the definitive edition, Walras writes: "Thus, the current prices of these services [those of inventories and money] are determined exactly like the prices of all other

[45] L. Walras, (3), p. 243. Quoted by permission of Richard D. Irwin, Inc., George Allen & Unwin, Ltd., and the American Economic Association.

[46] This is the section that Schumpeter seized upon and by virtue of which he confuses the market for cash balances and the market for securities. He speaks of the demand side of the first as the demand by firms to buy capital goods, rather than as a demand for working balances [(5), pp. 1022–3]. He identifies, i, the interest rate, and i_k, the net rate of return on capital goods, arguing that changes in $P_{u'}$ change the value of capital goods directly, without specifying the path of reaction [(5), p. 1024]. In his search for an answer to Patinkin's charges of an indeterminate price level in Walras, Schumpeter used this (false, in the present interpretation) linkage to assert that money had peculiar properties, such that "money prices are not proportional to *numéraire* prices . . . ." [(5), p. 1024] As will be shown below, this mystical quality (however conceived) need not be assumed to obtain a non-zero price of money in the Walrasian economy.

Lange, after noting that the presentation in the later editions of the *Éléments* is "somewhat obscure," also identifies i and i_k, the latter as manifested in the market for real inventories. He goes on to translate "taux de revenue net" as "rate of interest," feeling it necessary " in this connotation," although Walras is discussing the demand for securities. In the interpretation we have used, i and i_k are determined in two different markets and are equal only in equilibrium. See O. Lange, (5), pp. 179-80.

M. Allais's money market is close to the Walrasian concept and separate from the financial market:

" The operations effected on the money market (discounting, advances on titles, extension of credit on open account, contango on the stock market, and so forth) all come down to a hiring of money for a short period. They are essentially pawnbroker loans . . . ." [(1), p. 268] Quoted by permission.

". . . [it] appears essentially as a market where the services of money are obtained . . . ." [(1), p. 268] Quoted by permission.

The interest rate is distinct from the rate of return found in the financial market, being set by the demand for and supply of cash balances, in Allais's scheme. The two are equal in equilibrium and arbitrage is explicitly involved in the process of equating them. [(1), pp. 268–72]

services. . . ."[47] This same assertion is repeated on p. 325, and the price of inventory services in being in the form of existing goods is referred to explicitly as determined by demand and supply equations on p. 329.

We do not wish to deny that there are sections of the analysis in which other hypotheses receive support. Capital is defined on p. 317 as "the sum total of fixed and circulating goods *hired*, not in kind, but *in money*, by means of *credit*."[48] Moreover, a discussion follows of the continuous receipt of repayments of capital in money, and its flow back to the capital market. But, one paragraph thereafter, where he begins to become more rigorous in presenting the preconditions of the model, Walras moves explicitly to the interpretation given here. That is, contracts are made by entrepreneurs for the delivery to them of capital goods and money at specified dates in the forthcoming week against payments for their use at designated dates and their return at the end of the week. The cash is not hired to purchase new capital goods: that is done in the securities market, not the promissory note market. The capital goods in existence are not held by firms which borrow money to pay consumers at the beginning of the fulfillment week; these are held in kind by consumers in the form of

[47] L. Walras, (3), p. 43. Quoted by permission of Richard D. Irwin, Inc., George Allen & Unwin, Ltd., and the American Economic Association.

[48] This might very well be the textual evidence on which Henry L. Moore based his interpretation of Walras' monetary theory in (1), Chapters V, VI, and VII. In it he defines a "supply of credit" function dependent upon all prices including "the rate of interest." The term "credit" is nowhere defined, but Moore states on p. 130 that the "new capital goods must be paid for eventually out of savings, but at a given time the cost may be expressed in terms of credit," and defines an equation making the value of new capital goods equal (identically?) to the supply of credit. Letting I denote the value of new capital goods and $\bar{X}_c$ the supply of credit, we obtain from Moore's system the condition that

$$I = \bar{X}_c \tag{1}$$

Next, he defines savings as income less consumption, *with interest earned on the supply of credit as an income source:*

$$\bar{X}_z P_z + \bar{X}_c i - X_j P_j = S \tag{2}$$

where $\bar{X}$ denotes supplies, X denotes demand, S symbolizes savings, and z denotes a factor service. In equilibrium

$$I^\circ = S^\circ \tag{3}$$

Therefore, in equilibrium, current additions to capital goods stocks yield an indirect income during the period of their construction as interest payments to suppliers of funds. But nowhere in Walras' equations will one find an income term consisting of the value of new investment times the interest rate. The analogous term in Walras' equations is the term $\bar{X}_u P_{u'}$, or the supply of money services times the price of these services, which can only be interpreted as the income earned from the lending of working capital. This is an error into which Patinkin fell, as we shall show below.

Moore's analysis is merely one example of attempts to discern the relationships between money, savings, and capital goods in the Walrasian theory. An interesting variant of Moore's interpretation springing from Paretian roots will be discussed below in dealing with Aupetit's work.

stocks, and delivered at specified times in the week, at which times payments are made with money.[49]

Nowhere is Walras more difficult to understand than in his infrequent attempts to indicate how money capital, or in his pre-money economy, *numéraire* capital, whatever that is, are visualized in terms of his model. Section 255 best exemplifies this confusion and incomprehensibility. Again and again one is forced back to the "primitive" interpretation of the models.

Given the validity of the present interpretation of the role of money and the function of money markets in the Walrasian vision, what are the consequences that flow from them in terms of the model's construction? It is asserted that this interpretation gives a model to economic theory which is new and valuable in interpreting the role of money. It is valuable in revealing the relationship between money as flow and money as stock. Say's Law can be made a more sophisticated concept than it is ordinarily presented to be. And a clearer understanding of the relationship of the rate of interest to the rate of return on capital can be gained.

As has been discussed above, in Walras' models all delivery dates and quantities are contract certain, and payments for all goods and services are made at the time of delivery. The two types of "synchronization media," i.e., money balances and real inventories, can be regarded as having delivery dates at the beginning of the fulfillment week. Since neither can be lent for shorter periods than a week, since they are in existence at the beginning of the week, and since the purchaser of their services gets maximum use from them only if allowed their immediate use, it seems a logical construction in accordance with the function they perform in the system. It is impossible to find these specific assumptions in Walras, however, and they are so valuable in pointing up the peculiar qualities of inventories and money in the theory that it is difficult to understand why he did not make them explicit.

In the Walrasian model, so interpreted, the demand to hold cash balances at the *start* of the fulfillment week, which is a demand for the

[49] An example of the confusion possible by a failure to keep these markets (for money services and for securities) in a Walrasian economy separate is found in M. Brodsky and P. Rocher (1), pp. 296–301. Throughout, Rocher identifies securities with promissory notes created to obtain cash balances, such notes being liquidated at the beginning of the next period in money. In his model, however, firms own capital goods, and therefore must issue securities to purchase these goods. These, of course, cannot be liquidated at the beginning of the next week, though the money for such goods is borrowed in the same manner as cash balances and in the same market.

Schumpeter disagrees with this "primitive" interpretation of capital goods services being sold by consumers to firms. He says that "it is only for perfect equilibrium in pure competition that the process is supposed to go on *as if* capitalists were owners of produced durable goods." This is unclear, since these two conditions are the only ones regnant in Walras. The stress which Schumpeter places upon his point that money capital is lent to entrepreneurs prevents us from claiming support from this passage for the present interpretation. J. Schumpeter, (5), pp. 1001, 1010. Quoted by permission.

services of money during the execution of contracts, becomes clearly different from the acquisition of money at the *end* of the week. Money, in the latter sense is an asset and must be demanded for its use as an asset in later periods; it becomes a source of salable services, and as such is desired as any physical capital good would be. It is, indeed, this symmetry of treatment of the monetary and physical asset, with entrepreneurs demanding services from an existing stock for use during the fulfillment week and consumers seeking individually to build up or reduce their stocks at the end of the period, that allows us to distinguish clearly between money services and money assets.[50] This structure also allows us to abstract from the short-term problems of building up or reducing cash balances to desired levels over a succession of weeks in the Marshallian tradition.[51] The consumer and the entrepreneur buy the cash balance services they desire, and therefore are capable of reaching an equilibrium for the long term quite quickly.

Further, the Say's Identity assumption in Walras' model becomes a more sophisticated one than that ordinarily associated with it: the demander of cash balances for use during the coming week cannot increase them by increasing his excess supplies of goods and services; he must obtain them by going to the money service market (promissory note market) to borrow them literally. Only if he is willing to accept the accretion of money at the *end* of the period, as he would any other new capital accretion, in the form of assets, not services during the current week, can he obtain cash by increasing his excess supplies of goods and services. Therefore, the mere assumption that persons do not seek to change their stocks of money held as assets at the end of the period does not imply that they do not change their holdings of money during the period by changing their purchases of its services from week to week.[52]

[50] That this symmetry did not exist for Walras' original model because of his adoption of Say's Identity will be developed below.

[51] See the discussion in G. Archibald, (1), pp. 2–9.

[52] The Keynesian and Walrasian outlooks are similar in that changes in the supply of money are reflected initially in financial market movements, not in goods markets. When Patinkin writes that this case was never advanced in the (neoclassical) literature, he neglects the fact that it is the Walrasian model. See D. Patinkin, (4), p. 109. A further similarity of treatment of money in the Keynesian and Walrasian models is that in the former, as in the latter, "liquidity preference" shifts were not primarily at the expense of current consumption, but were concerned with shifts in the holding of assets. Cf. J. Keynes, (1), p. 166, and F. Hahn, (1), p. 59. Indeed, this feature of Keynes's model is so pronounced that, as we shall develop below, it serves to dichotomize that model partially.

Also, Patinkin's interpretation of the supply of money in excess of consumers' demands as being used by them to purchase real capital goods cannot be a correct reading of the Walrasian system, since new capital goods do not begin to pay a return until the period after their construction, and no current income is earned on securities. The term that does represent the gross demand for new fixed and circulating capital in Walras' system, $X_e P_e$, does not introduce any interest payments into the budget equation. The term $\bar{X}_u P_{u'}$ must be seen as the amount earned in current income by

It will be recalled that the securities market is a mart where those who would purchase new capital goods (including, now, inventories of finished and unfinished goods) go to purchase perpetuities guaranteeing the riskless receipt of one unit of *numéraire* at a price P_e. These securities are redeemed at the end of the week in new fixed and circulating capital to an equivalent value, which goods are added to similar stocks already in the consumer's possession. Since all these redemptions are made at equilibrium prices, consumers will be indifferent as to the actual kinds of goods received. Lastly, while all new capital goods are delivered at the end of the period, deliveries of the securities occur throughout the period, and payments for them are made throughout the period.[53]

Securities and promissory notes are not substitutes on either side of the market. If an entrepreneur who desires working capital sells a security and "covers" his obligation by purchasing a new capital good for delivery at the end of the week, he will not be supplied with cash balances at the start of the week. For the consumer, purchase of a promissory note yields a current income, purchase of a security does not. For him, also, they serve separate functions.

In the securities market it seems clear that Walras throughout thought in terms of P_e as a magnitude actively determined by the interaction of buyers and sellers, rather than the prices of fixed and circulating capital goods being determined as would be true if securities were truly fictitious. That is, P_e and its reciprocal i_k, are determined, and this rate of return is transmitted in some unspecified way to the submarkets for individual types of fixed and circulating capital goods.[54]

---

purchasing promissory notes as a means of lending entrepreneurs (primarily) their working balances in a primitive economy of the type discussed above. See D. Patinkin, (4), pp. 399–400.

[53] We would therefore agree with Patinkin and disagree with Jaffé in believing that the good "securities" did actually exist in Walras' thinking, although our more general tendency is to move in the direction of primitivistic interpretation used by Jaffé in this instance.

Two reasons lead to this conclusion: (1) it provides an explanation for the *monnaie d'épargne* that Walras includes in the consumer's demand for money balances, since cash balances must be held against the delivery of securities which would not have to be held if consumers contracted for capital goods to be delivered at the end of the period; but, more importantly, (2) it allows the net rate of return, i_k, identically equal to $\frac{1}{P_e}$, to be the actively-determined variable on the capital market, rather than the prices of the several capital goods themselves. Markets for these do indeed exist, but the existence of a securities market yields a unification and a focus.

Also, our different interpretation of the circulating capital term in the budget equation from that of Jaffé will be apparent. See his discussion of these points in L. Walras, (3), pp. 542–3.

[54] This is most clearly seen in L. Walras, (3), p. 331, and also pp. 268, 282, and 329. It is therefore misleading to say, as Stigler does, that i_k is *defined* as the ratio of the net price of the service of a capital good to its price as an asset, if this be taken to imply that i_k follows passively from two actively-determined prices for each type of asset,

At this point there is an unwritten chapter in Walrasian theory: Walras never specifies the manner in which changes in i_k are transmitted to the separate fixed and circulating capital goods markets. He *defines* the selling prices of these goods as the capitalized value of the services of the goods, so that these selling prices can never depart from this value; yet he does not furnish the links to indicate how he arrives at this result or what mechanism exists to guarantee it.[55] All of his reasoning about the achievement of equilibrium by *tâtonnements* in the capital goods markets starts from the assumption that selling prices are rigorously determined when i_k is given. The equilibrium condition is that price must be brought into equality with the costs of production in each capital good market, and the sum of these prices times their respective quantities of new circulating and fixed capital goods produced must equal savings *ex ante*.[56]

While we may condemn Walras for a good deal of obscurity in his analysis of capital goods in these respects (and others), the basic elements of price and quantity determination are present in the mechanism. For example, if we create a class of arbitrageurs in the securities markets who

---

or that i_k can differ even momentarily for two or more goods. See G. Stigler, (1), p. 247.

[55] See R. Kuenne, (2), p. 331. Schumpeter discusses these markets briefly, but indicates that Walras abandons them for the stock market. He treats securities as fictitious but he is not clear as to whether P_e is determined by capital goods prices or *vice versa*. At one point he says:

". . . it is not the fall in the rate of interest [i_k in our terminology] which plays any direct causal role, but it is the rise in the value of capital goods which reduces (tautologically) the rate of interest. Of course, the rate of interest thereupon also assumes an active role so far as it enters the demand and supply functions of all products and services. Yet it is important to notice, *in this analysis*, it plays a passive role in the first instance because this puts a different complexion on its significance in the economic process and serves especially to put the capitalists' reactions in a different light: they are reactions to the increase in the price of a service he renders." J. Schumpeter, (5), p. 1019. Quoted by permission. See also p. 1017. Earlier in the same volume he speaks of the market that determines the price of the capitals, hence also the rate of new (net?) revenue (p. 1001).

Allais follows Walras in this construction:

"In fact, the price of a good, always equal to the present value of its present and future returns, is not determined by the cost of production, but the workings of the economic mechanism leads it to coincide with costs, when equilibrium is attained." M. Allais, (1), p. 70. Quoted by permission.

This, and the discussion preceding, implies that no equilibrium play-of-the-market is necessary to establish selling prices for an asset, say in the case where no production of it occurs. The price seems always to be equal to the discounted value of the good's services. But one is entitled to ask "why"?

[56] Compare Keynes:

". . . the equality between the stock of capital-goods offered and the stock demanded will be brought about by the prices of capital-goods, not by the rate of interest. It is equality between the demand and supply of loans of money, i.e., of debts, which is brought about by the rate of interest." J. Keynes, (1), p. 186n. Quoted by permission. Keynes is here criticizing Marshall for reasons similar to our criticism of Walras: Marshall's analysis assumed that in some mysterious manner the market for securities yielded a price which was immediately reflected in all capital goods markets.

seek to profit by selling securities at P_e and buying capital goods at prices reflecting higher rates of return, but who, like Walras' entrepreneurs, make no profits in the end, the mechanism can be provided. When this is done there is no need to assume that the selling prices of all types of capital goods are identically equal to their service prices capitalized at the rate of return i_k implicit in P_e.

But it is otherwise with the theory of money. In this analysis, $P_{u'}$ is actively determined in the promissory note market, but i, the rate of return on the asset money, or the rate of interest, and P_u, the *numéraire* price of money, remain to be determined.[57] Walras, as in the case of the circulating and fixed capital analysis, had a choice: given $P_{u'}$, how is either i or P_u determined? One other market process must be specified.

The whole weight of the logic of the model and its symmetry up to this point argues for one solution: *a market for money as an asset.* In principle, consumers who desire to increase their stock of wealth can "invest" in new fixed capital, new circulating capital, or "new" additions to their stocks of money. Yet nowhere does Walras indicate this alternative of buying money as an asset: Say's Law, in Lange's sense of a demand for increases in money *stocks* being identically zero for every consuming unit, is implicit.[58] This inability of Walras to shake loose the "neutral" money dictates of his contemporaries led him to sacrifice the major contribution in the monetary sphere of his method.

To us this contribution was not the bringing of money into a utility framework, for this had been implicit in the treatment of money by earlier economists; moreover, the extension of the marginal apparatus to it was inevitable and, as we have indicated above, a not very notable advance.

[57] Patinkin is correct in asserting that it is $P_{u'}$, not i, that is actively determined in the promissory note market in Walras' analysis. In the second edition—before the concept of $P_{u'}$ and a promissory note market had been developed—Walras speaks in terms of the direct relationship of the demand for money upon i:

"Suppose that one day the existing amount of money . . . diminishes or that the *encaisse desirée* . . . representing the utility of money, increases . . . . Equilibrium will be established the next day on the market at a new rate of interest higher than the old at which the *encaisse desirée* will be reduced." L. Walras, (1), p. 383. But the logic of the definitive model led to the determination of $P_{u'}$.

Patinkin, in (4), pp. 406–7, goes on to assert that Schumpeter believed it to be i that was determined by *tâtonnements* in this market. But on the page where Schumpeter discusses this ((5), p. 1024), he explicitly speaks of i instead of $P_{u'}$ only under the assumption that money is *numéraire* in which case they are identical. Patinkin then asserts that the present writer followed Schumpeter in viewing i as being determined in the money market in R. Kuenne, (2), and in proof cites a footnote in which we pointed out his error in believing in an earlier article that $P_{u'}$ was the price level P_u instead of what was loosely referred to by us as the rate of interest. The body of the article spoke consistently of $P_{u'}$ as the term determined in the money market.

[58] But we must change the specific sense in which Lange refers to the demand for money balances from that for money services to that for money as an asset. As shown above, in the Walrasian model, desires to change amounts of cash holdings for purposes of transacting are *not* identically zero.

A greater achievement was the establishment of money as an asset *in a stationary flow*, and, therefore, as a logical object of purchase alternative to real goods. No need for uncertainty about interest rate movements was required: merely the preconditions for the existence of money in a static, stationary flow.

To fully appreciate the innovatory character of this achievement one must see that the hoary catalog of functions of money—standard of account, medium of exchange, store of value—does not truly describe the nature of the asset market for money. The accretion of money stocks by individuals at the end of a week is no more a method of storing value than is the purchase of a fixed or circulating capital good. In every sense that is true of these latter types of goods, money is an asset in the Walrasian system: but only in logic.

Walras did not follow this path; rather he took an incorrect route. Although he recognized that i is determined in a different market from i_k, and is equal to i_k only in equilibrium, he nevertheless fell into the error of treating the two as identically equal.[59] Just as he obtained the price of capital goods by capitalizing the prices of their services at i_k, so he obtained the price of money, P_u, by capitalizing $P_{u'}$ at $i_k \equiv i$.[60] However, Walras indicts himself: earlier he had taken great pains to explain that assets would have no prices in conditions such as those of Model IV-1 where individuals were not seeking to invest or disinvest in holdings of real assets. In this case a capital identity, fully analogous to Say's Identity in the Walrasian sense, forbade the emergence of a price. But the same must hold for money: if some persons are not seeking to increase or decrease their holdings of cash as an asset as the market's equilibrating process progresses there can be no price of money, since all will borrow its services if they wish to increase their use of it. Economically, P_u is indeterminate, even if mathematically it is determinate.[61]

[59] See L. Walras, (3), pp. 289–90, 327, and 332, for his realization that i and i_k are equal only in equilibrium. On this point, compare P. Boninsegni, (1), p. 193.

[60] See D. Patinkin, (4), p. 405, for his belief that Walras failed to deal sufficiently with the market in which the absolute price level (in our case, P_u) is determined.

[61] Compare Walras' statement for fixed capital:

"... Up to this point we have assumed that the quantities of land, personal faculties and capital proper are given, and that landowners, workers, and capitalists exchange all the services of their capital goods for consumers' goods and services, except for that fraction of the services of their capital goods which they consume directly. Under such circumstances, there could be no purchase or sale of capital goods, for these goods could only be exchanged for one another in ratios proportional to their net incomes; and such transactions, being theoretically without rational motive, could not give rise to any prices of capital goods in terms of *numéraire*. If there is to be a demand for, a supply of, and prices of capital goods, we must suppose that there are landowners, workers and capitalists who purchase consumers' goods and services in amounts that either fall short of or exceed their incomes ...." L. Walras, (3), p. 269. Quoted by permission of Richard D. Irwin, Inc., George Allen & Unwin, Ltd., and the American Economic Association.

Applying this same reasoning to money, we find Say's Identity a bar to determining

Another difficulty arises because had Walras retained his explicit assumption that $i = i_k$ only in equilibrium, the demand for nominal balances in his model would have been correct only for that condition. The two rates of return must be identical to escape this criticism.[62]

The method by which the theory must be reconstructed is clear: consumers must be given the opportunity of alloting savings to the purchase of additional money *as an asset* for delivery at the end of the period, and i must be allowed to depart from i_k except in equilibrium.[63] The value of P_u is then determined by the necessity for the total demand for increased cash balances in the asset sense to be zero in equilibrium.[64] The rate of interest, i, then follows identically as the ratio of $P_{u'}$ to P_u. We shall indicate the formal changes in Model V-1 which are necessary to accommodate these new assumptions.

P_u in any asset market by capitalizing the value of its service. Since the nature of money's function requires that it be priced in a sense that capital goods need not be, and since by assumption its service has a utility, either we must create the ability for money as an asset to be acquired or money cannot exist in a stock-of-asset sense.

[62] See R. Kuenne, (6), pp. 246–7.

[63] A most interesting example of the grip which Say's Identity had upon the neoclassical thinker can be obtained from the work of Aupetit. We have sought diligently in the rather extensive literature built upon Walras' model for an interpretation similar to the present one. Most generally, they are of the type of Antonelli, (1), pp. 171–89, which merely repeats the Walrasian equations with no attempt to interpret them economically.

A notable exception is the work of A. Aupetit, (1). In his analysis, i is consistently distinguished from i_k, and $P_{u'}$ is determined in a clear-cut promissory note market. Having made these decisions, Aupetit could not escape the need to determine either P_u or i. Where would he get his needed relationships? Would he be forced to find a money asset "market" and overthrow Say's Identity?

It was not to be. There is another way out: he assumes that money is reproducible as a commodity under the gold standard and determines P_u by allowing new production until the cost of production and $P_{u'}$ have attained the common equilibrium rate of return on all other reproducible goods:

". . . Thus is determined for money, under the same conditions as for other capital goods, the quantity of money added to the existing stock and the interest rate." A. Aupetit, (1), p. 151. See also pp. 123–8, 148. This is, of course, an overthrow of Say's Identity, but, in context, not a very interesting one.

Aupetit, trying as others had, to find the link between money, savings, and capital formation in Walras' system, did so by seizing upon Pareto's "savings function" of money. Aupetit reasoned that entrepreneurs producing capital goods delivered them at the end of the period to their buyers. Since payments are made on delivery, such producers had to borrow in the promissory note market *all* of their costs of production in money form. Therefore, Aupetit said, money has a "savings function" as well as its medium-of-exchange function. But this result follows from the arbitrary assumptions about the model: the "savings function" would be true of any use of money to produce goods requiring the entire period to produce and is true of all goods to the extent that *some* balances will have to be borrowed. Therefore, as Aupetit recognized, the "savings" function of money is merely the medium-of-exchange function related to a specific set of goods.

[64] It is no solution to assert that money can be the *numéraire* and therefore that its price is "legally" unity, for if $P_{u'} < i_k$, demand for money would be zero and it would become a free good. Rocher falls into this error in P. Rocher, (1), p. 314.

For the individual, *c*, a new good, "money assets," is created, whose unit is the nominal amount of money necessary to obtain a unit of *numéraire* in perpetuity through the purchase of promissory notes. A stock of these assets is held at the start of the market day, Q_{cq}, and demand (positive or negative) for this good will be denoted X_{cq} at price P_q per unit. Desired gross savings are then

$$(17) \qquad X_{ce}P_e + X_{cq}P_q = X_{cs}$$

where S denotes savings. We may also define stocks of savings at the start of the week as

$$(18) \qquad Q_{ce} + Q_{cq} = Q_{cs}$$

In the maximization-of-satisfaction model for the consumer, where λ° is the equilibrium marginal preference for income, the equilibrium conditions for savings read

$$(19) \qquad \begin{aligned} &1. \quad \frac{M_c^s}{P_e} = \lambda^\circ, \text{ when } i_k \geqq i \\ &2. \quad \frac{M_c^s}{P_q} = \lambda^\circ, \text{ when } i_k < i \end{aligned}$$

From these and the other equilibrium conditions, we obtain as part of the nonspecific solution the savings equation

$$(20) \qquad X_{cs} = H_{cs}([P];[\bar{P}_c], [Q_c])$$

where $[Q_c]$ now includes the element Q_{cu}.

For the economy we may sum over all individuals to obtain:

$$(21) \qquad \begin{aligned} &1. \quad X_s \equiv \sum_c X_{cs} \equiv X_e + X_q \\ &2. \quad X_q \equiv \sum_c X_{cq} \end{aligned}$$

We may define the new price as

$$(22) \qquad P_q \equiv \frac{1}{i}$$

Instead of Walras' equilibrium condition that the price of money services divided by the price of money equal the common rate of return, we substitute the definition:

(23) $$i \equiv \frac{P_{u'}}{P_u}$$

and the equilibrium condition that

(24) $$i^{\circ} = i_k^{\circ}$$

where

(25) $$i_k \equiv \frac{1}{P_e}$$

Lastly, since in equilibrium the aggregate demand for money asset additions must be zero, we add the condition that desired gross savings be equal to the value of capital goods:

(26) $$X_e^{\circ} P_e^{\circ} = \sum_i X_{Z_i}^{\circ} P_{Z_i}^{\circ} + \sum_j X_j^{\prime\prime\circ} P_j^{\circ}$$

With this reconstruction Walras' monetary theory is determinate and completely integrated into the body of "real equations." In order to obtain this result, we have been forced to give an economic interpretation of the Walrasian analysis of savings, investment, and capital goods, as well as of money. Say's Identity, which had no logical place in the model, has been eliminated and Lange's criticism no longer applies.

Pigou has indicated an interesting possibility in such an economy where savings can be sought by the individual in the form of increased money asset holdings. Were assets to be acquired as in our model only for the utility of their future earnings, in equilibrium the last dollar spent on assets will reflect the marginal time preferences of the individual. If these are generally positive, the rate of interest will remain above zero and never drop below the minimum return which just keeps money in existence. But, if individuals derived from their stocks of assets a certain sense of security, they might even seek to save were the interest rate to fall below zero. In our schema, this would drive money out of existence, but if it did not, the ability to acquire money (when $P_{u'} = 0$) would prevent the interest rate from falling below zero. As individuals' money balances increased (velocity of money fell), prices would fall steadily, increasing the real wealth of the money assets, satisfying the sense of security, and reducing the saving on a net basis to zero once more. This is the famous "Pigou effect" which we will meet in shorter-run contexts below.[65]

A similar model has been constructed by de Scitovoszky for an economy in which all resources are assumed fixed in quantity or at least un-

[65] See A. Pigou, (2), (3), and (4), Chapter IX.

alterable for economic reasons. A desire to save for the economy as a whole can then only be reflected in a desire to hoard money. With flexible prices the price level would fall period after period; with rigid prices, income and employment would fall. The rise in the real value of all wealth would tend to decrease the desire to save over long periods.[66]

6. Model V-2: The Completed Money Model

We have reached the goal of Part II: the construction of a complete general equilibrium model with the theories of exchange, production, investment, and money included simultaneously. In it the full interdependence of decisionmaking and of economic variation has been captured, at least to the extent these phenomena are amenable to treatment by static intertemporal, spatially punctiform, models in stationary equilibrium.

Because this model is the culmination of our lengthy and detailed study of general models, we shall present it in its full complexity.

6.a. The Data of the Model

We are given the following information:

1. Q_{cZ_i}: consumer c's endowment of capital goods, Z_i, $c = 1, \ldots, s$, $i = 1, \ldots, m$.
2. Q_{cj}: consumer c's endowment of inventory holdings of goods Y_j, $j = 1, \ldots, n$.
3. Q_{cu}: consumer c's endowment of money.
4. $[\bar{P}_c]$: consumer c's price expectations.
5. Q_{Z_i}: aggregate consumer endowments of capital goods Z_i.
6. Q_j: aggregate consumer endowments of consumer goods inventories.
7. Q_u: the money supply of the economy.
8. $[\bar{P}]$: the set of all consumers' price expectations.
9. k_c: consumer c's fraction of expenditure desired in cash balance form.
10. $k_{vj'j}$: firm v's inventory service requirements of good $Y_{j'}$ for a unit of output of good j, $v = 1, \ldots, o$, $j' = 1, \ldots, n$.
11. $k_{vj'Z_i}$: firm v's inventory service requirement of good $Y_{j'}$ for a unit of output of good Z_i.
12. k_{vu}: firm v's fraction of value of output desired to be held in cash balances.
13. u_i: the proportion of the value of capital good Z_i lost through depreciation in one week.
14. $P_1 \equiv 1$: the definition of the *numéraire*.
15. $M_c = M_c(X_{cj}, X_{cs}, Q_{cj} - \bar{X}_{cj'}, Q_{ci} - \bar{X}_{ci})$: consumer c's preference function.

[66] T. de Scitovszky, (1).

16. $J_v(\bar{X}_{vj}, \bar{X}_{vZ_i}, X_{vi}, X_{vj}) = 0$: firm v's technological transformation function.
17. $[\bar{P}_v^*]$: firm v's price expectations.
18. $[\bar{P}^*]$: the set of all firms' price expectations.

6.b. The Variables to be Determined

The following are the values to be determined by the model:

1. X_{cj}: consumer c's consumption of good Y_j.
2. X_{cs}: consumer c's demand for increments of earning assets.
3. X_{cq}: consumer c's demand for increments of money assets.
4. X_{ce}: consumer c's demand for securities.
5. $\bar{X}_{ci}$: consumer c's supply of factor service z_i, $i = 1, \ldots, m$.
6. $\bar{X}_{cj'}$: consumer c's supply of inventory service $Y_{j'}$, $j = 1, \ldots, n$.
7. $\bar{X}_{cu}$: consumer c's supply of cash balance services.
8. X_j: aggregate consumer demand for goods Y_j, $j = 1, \ldots, n$.
9. X_s: aggregate consumer demand for increments of earning assets.
10. X_q: aggregate consumer demand for increments of money assets.
11. X_e: aggregate consumer demand for securities.
12. $\bar{X}_i$: aggregate supply of factor service z_i.
13. $\bar{X}_{j'}$: aggregate supply of inventory service $Y_{j'}$.
14. $\bar{X}_u$: aggregate supply of cash balances.
15. X_{Z_i}: aggregate demand for capital good Z_i, $i = 1, \ldots, m$.
16. X_j'': aggregate demand for gross inventory investment in good Y_j.
17. X_{vj}: firm v's demand for intermediate good Y_j.
18. X_{vi}: firm v's demand for factor service z_i.
19. $X_{vj'}$: firm v's demand for inventory services $Y_{j'}$.
20. X_{vu}: firm v's demand for cash balances.
21. $\bar{X}_{vj}$: firm v's output of good Y_j.
22. $\bar{X}_{vZ_i}$: firm v's output of good Z_i.
23. X_i: aggregate entrepreneurial demand for factor service z_i.
24. X_j^*: aggregate entrepreneurial demand for intermediate good Y_j.
25. $X_{j'}$: aggregate entrepreneurial demand for inventory service $Y_{j'}$.
26. X_u: aggregate entrepreneurial demand for cash balances.
27. $\bar{X}_j$: aggregate output of good Y_j.
28. $\bar{X}_{Z_i}$: aggregate output of good Z_i.
29. P_j: price of good Y_j, $j = 2, \ldots, n$.
30. P_i: price of factor service z_i.
31. P_e: price of securities.
32. P_q: price of an amount of money earning one unit of *numéraire* in perpetuity.
33. $P_{j'}$: price of a unit of inventory service $Y_{j'}$.
34. $P_{u'}$: price of a unit of cash balance service.
35. P_u: price of a unit of money.

36. P_{Z_i}: price of capital good Z_i.
37. i_k: the rate of return on capital goods and inventories.
38. i: the interest rate, or rate of return on money.

6.c. The Relationships of the Model

The equations and functions of the model may now be stated. First, in the individual consumer sector of the model:

(V-2-0)

$$
\begin{aligned}
&1. \quad X_{cj\neq 1} = H_{cj\neq 1}(P_{j\neq 1}, P_i, P_e, P_{u'}, P_u, P_{j'}; [\bar{P}_c], Q_{cZi}, Q_{cj}, Q_{cu}) \\
&\qquad\quad = H_{cj\neq 1}([P]; [\bar{P}_c], [Q_c]) \\
&2. \quad \bar{X}_{ci} = Q_{cZi} - H_{ci}([P]; [\bar{P}_c], [Q_c]) \\
&3. \quad X_{cs} = H_{cs}([P]; [\bar{P}_c], [Q_c]) \\
&4. \quad X_{cq} = X_{cs} \text{ when } i_k < i, \ X_{cq} = 0 \text{ when } i_k \geqq i \\
&5. \quad X_{cs} = X_{cq} + X_{ce} \\
&6. \quad \bar{X}_{cj'} = Q_{cj'} - H_{cj'}([P]; [\bar{P}_c], [Q_c]) \\
&7. \quad \bar{X}_{cu} = Q_{cu} - \frac{k_c\left(\sum_j X_{cj}P_j + X_{ce}P_e + X_{cq}P_q\right)}{P_u} \\
&8. \quad X_{c1} = \sum_i \bar{X}_{ci}P_i + \sum_j \bar{X}_{cj'}P_{j'} + \bar{X}_{cu}P_{u'} - \sum_{j\neq 1} X_{cj}P_j \\
&\qquad\quad - X_{ce}P_e - X_{cq}P_q
\end{aligned}
$$

The aggregate functions are:

(V-2-1)

$$
\begin{aligned}
&1. \quad X_{j\neq 1} = H_{j\neq 1}([P]; [\bar{P}], [Q]) \\
&2. \quad \bar{X}_i = Q_{Z_i} - H_i([P]; [\bar{P}], [Q]) \\
&3. \quad X_s = H_s([P]; [\bar{P}], [Q]) \\
&4. \quad X_q = \sum_c X_{cq} \\
&5. \quad X_e = \sum_c X_{ce} \\
&6. \quad \bar{X}_{j'} = Q_j - H_{j'}([P]; [\bar{P}], [Q]) \\
&7. \quad \bar{X}_u = \sum_c \bar{X}_{cu} \\
&8. \quad X_1 = \sum_c X_{c1}
\end{aligned}
$$

Aggregate entrepreneurial demand and supply functions may be defined:

$$\text{(V-2-2)}\quad \begin{aligned}
&1. \quad X_i = G_i(P_{j\neq 1}, P_i, P_{Z_i}, P_e, P_{j'}, P_{u'}, P_u; [\bar{P}^*]) \\
&\qquad\;\; = G_i([P^*]; [\bar{P}^*]) \\
&2. \quad X_j^* = G_j([P^*]; [\bar{P}^*]) \\
&3. \quad \bar{X}_j = G_J([P^*]; [\bar{P}^*]) \\
&4. \quad \bar{X}_{Z_i} = G_{Z_i}([P^*]; [\bar{P}^*]) \\
&5. \quad X_{j'} \equiv \sum_v X_{vj'} \\
&6. \quad X_u = \sum_v X_{vu}
\end{aligned}$$

Net profits for each firm are zero in equilibrium:

$$\text{(V-2-3)}\quad \sum_j \bar{X}_{vj}^{\circ} P_j^{\circ} + \sum_i \bar{X}_{vZ_i}^{\circ} P_{Z_i}^{\circ} - \sum_i X_{vi}^{\circ} P_i^{\circ} - \sum_j X_{vj}^{\circ} P_j^{\circ} - \sum_j X_{vj'}^{\circ} P_{j'}^{\circ} - X_{vu}^{\circ} P_{u'}^{\circ} = 0$$

All real goods markets must be cleared in equilibrium:

$$\text{(V-2-4)}\quad \begin{aligned}
&1. \quad X_i^{\circ} = \bar{X}_i^{\circ} \\
&2. \quad X_j^{\circ} + X_j^{*\circ} + X_j^{\prime\prime\circ} = \bar{X}_j^{\circ} \\
&3. \quad X_{Z_i}^{\circ} = \bar{X}_{Z_i}^{\circ} \\
&4. \quad X_{j'}^{\circ} = \bar{X}_{j'}^{\circ}
\end{aligned}$$

The firms' demand and supply functions are defined:

$$\text{(V-2-5)}\quad \begin{aligned}
&1. \quad X_{vi} = G_{vi}([P^*]; [\bar{P}_v^*]) \\
&2. \quad X_{vj} = G_{vj}([P^*]; [\bar{P}_v^*]) \\
&3. \quad \bar{X}_{vj} = G_{vJ}([P^*]; [\bar{P}_v^*]) \\
&4. \quad \bar{X}_{vZ_i} = G_{vI}([P^*]; [\bar{P}_v^*]) \\
&5. \quad X_{vj'} = \sum_j k_{vj'j} \bar{X}_{vj} + \sum_i k_{vj'Z_i} \bar{X}_{vZ_i} \\
&6. \quad X_{vu} = \frac{k_{vu}}{P_u} \left(\sum_j \bar{X}_{vj} P_j + \sum_i \bar{X}_{vZ_i} P_{Z_i} \right)
\end{aligned}$$

In the securities and promissory note markets, equilibrium must rule:

$$\text{(V-2-6)}\quad \begin{aligned}
&1. \quad X_e^{\circ} P_e^{\circ} = \sum_i X_{Z_i}^{\circ} P_{Z_i}^{\circ} + \sum_j X_j^{\prime\prime\circ} P_j^{\circ} \\
&2. \quad X_u^{\circ} = \bar{X}_u^{\circ}
\end{aligned}$$

Net rates of return must be equal on all assets:

$$(\text{V-2-7}) \quad \begin{aligned} &1. \quad P^{\circ}_{Z_i} = (P^{\circ}_i - u_i P^{\circ}_{Z_i})P^{\circ}_e \\ &2. \quad P^{\circ}_j = (P^{\circ}_{j'} - P^{\circ}_j)P^{\circ}_e \\ &3. \quad P^{\circ}_u = P^{\circ}_{u'}P^{\circ}_q \end{aligned}$$

And we include the definitions:

$$(\text{V-2-8}) \quad \begin{aligned} &1. \quad P_e = \frac{1}{i_k} \\ &2. \quad P_q = \frac{1}{i} \end{aligned}$$

As an equilibrium condition:

$$(\text{V-2-9}) \qquad i^{\circ} = i^{\circ}_k$$

We may eliminate one input or output equation for each firm from (V-2-5) as redundant, and we may eliminate one equation from (V-2-3) as redundant. If this is done, the number of equations equals the number of unknowns at $s(2n + m + 4) + o(3n + 2m + 2) + 8n + 6m + 10$.

7. The Invalid Dichotomy

The recent publication of Professor Patinkin's *Money, Interest, and Prices* may be regarded as the summary statement of the thought of its author as it has evolved over the last decade. Taken together with the criticism of Lange which we discussed in Section 4, Patinkin's challenge to the determinacy of neoclassical monetary theory in general[67] and the Walrasian model in particular is the most formidable attack ever made against it. As such we must examine it in detail.

The bibliography of this controversy is already an extensive one.[68] Further discussion is necessary, however, because of the marked evolution of views apparent between earlier articles and the book. Patinkin's present analysis makes the categories of "right" and "wrong," provable "existence" or "nonexistence" of the Invalid Dichotomy, in which terms much of the previous discussion took place, largely outmoded. As a result, future appraisal and discussion must turn much more than past around the detailed analysis of neoclassical systems in the book; in particular, Supplementary Notes B through H and L, as well as Chapters I-VIII.

Lange's analysis is the most convenient starting point for consideration of Patinkin's current criticisms. We have seen that the validity of

[67] Patinkin's definition of "neoclassical" monetary theory is that body of theory using the cash-balance or transactions-type of equation to validate the quantity theory of money. See (4), p. 96. His summary of charges against these theorists is contained in Chapter 8 of the book.

[68] Compare D. Patinkin, (4), pp. 477–8 and 488.

Lange's criticism of neoclassical theorists hinges upon the acceptance by the theorists of Say's Identity. But this is not true of Patinkin's criticism, or, rather, his criticism goes beyond Lange to include the Say's Identity case as a subcase. Patinkin explicitly sides "with those who deny that [Say's Identity] is a basic component of the classical and neoclassical position."[69] What, then, is the "Invalid Dichotomy" present in neo-classicism if it is not the rigorous segregation of money and real sectors (to the extinction of the first) which we have found to be implicit in Say's Identity?

For Patinkin, the problem arises because these theorists implicitly accepted the outlook that the homogeneity postulate was necessary to a rational economy and did not consistently relate it to their attitudes (explicit or implicit) toward Say's Identity. Therefore, they were led to assert that relative prices were determined in real goods markets and, independently, the price level was fixed in the "money market," thereby dichotomizing their models, without explicitly recognizing the inter-dependence necessary to avoid monetary indeterminacy. Or, less strongly, if they did not assert this dichotomy, they did not deny its possibility:

"This is the crucial point. The dynamic groping of the absolute price level toward its equilibrium value will—through the real-balance effect—react back on the commodity markets and hence on relative prices. And it is precisely the constant failure to find this point explicitly recognized—and, indeed, the constant sensation of being just on the verge of having it explicitly contradicted—that is the basis of our original contention that the roots of the invalid dichotomy are to be found in the neo-classical analyses of Walras, Fisher, Pigou, and Cassel."[70]

In its starkest form, Patinkin's thesis may be presented in the following manner. Assume that in a "typical" neoclassical system Say's Identity is rejected, so that we recognize the possibility that consumers may wish to end the week with larger or smaller balances than those with which they began it. With some real good as *numéraire*, if we desire to force the homogeneity postulate to hold it must be true for all real goods and services that demands and supplies will be unaffected by a change in P_u. In the consumer sector,

$$(27)\qquad \begin{aligned} &1. \quad \lambda^0 X_{cj} = H_{cj}(P_j, P_i, \lambda P_u),\ \lambda > 0 \\ &2. \quad \lambda^0 \bar{X}_{ci} = Q_{cZ_i} - H_{ci}(P_j, P_i, \lambda P_u) \end{aligned}$$

Of necessity, if Walras' Identity holds, then in this "typical" neoclassical system, the demand for money increments will be equal to the excess

[69] See D. Patinkin, (4), p. 119.

[70] D. Patinkin, (4), p. 112. Quoted by permission. The quoted paragraph draws mainly upon the analysis of pp. 107–19.

value of sales over purchases in money terms:

$$\Delta X_{cu}P_u = \sum_i \bar{X}_{ci}P_i - \sum_j X_{cj}P_j \tag{28}$$

Therefore, if P_u changes to λP_u, $\lambda > 0$, the *real* value of cash accretions desired by the consumer must remain unchanged if the homogeneity postulate is to rule. Then, Patinkin writes, we may follow two paths:

1. In the neoclassical systems, (28) was not written in the above residual form, but rather in the Cambridge-k form:

$$\Delta X_{cu}P_u = k_c \sum_j X_{cj}P_j - Q_{cu}P_u \tag{29}$$

Now it is readily seen that (29) does not meet the constancy-of-real-money accretions condition implied by the homogeneity postulate, if k_c and Q_{cu} are positive constants. Therefore, the "typical" neoclassical system contained an inconsistency, in that there were present in the model functional relationships which were contradictory.

2. If (29) is removed from the neoclassical system and (28) is retained, the inconsistency is removed, but only at the price of eliminating the determinacy of money prices. For if we solve the excess demand equations springing from individuals' equations of the type (27) for an exchange economy, then multiple solutions for real goods' excess demands will occur, since any value of P_u will satisfy them. Therefore P_u is indeterminate. We have $n + m - 1$ conditions that excess demands be zero to determine $n + m - 1$ prices, but we can solve $n + m - 2$ real excess demand equations by eliminating P_u from them to get the $n + m - 2$ real goods prices. This solution will fit the eliminated real good excess demand if the system is consistent but will not fit it if the system is not consistent. Say's Identity, by making ΔX_{cu} identically equal to zero, makes the price of the $n + m - 1$ good consistent with the solution of $n + m - 2$ equations, but, if Say's Identity does not hold, this need not be true. In any event, the economy has been dichotomized into a real and a money sector.

We assume, as Archibald and Lipsey do,[71] that the $(n + m - 1)$th real good excess demand equation is dependent upon the other $n + m - 2$ real goods equations. In an economy where every consumer is under the constraint of Walras' Identity, this must imply that Say's Identity holds for each consumer. For if the consumer's demand in a net sense for (say) good Y_1 is a mirror reflex of the excess net supply of all other real goods, obviously the net excess demand for money can never be anything but zero. And, of course, this will hold for the economy as a whole if it

[71] G. Archibald, (1), pp. 9–17.

holds for each individual; i.e.,

$$E_u \equiv 0 \tag{30}$$

where E_u is the aggregate excess demand for increments of cash.

Archibald and Lipsey, nevertheless, in their example, after solving for the $n + m - 2$ relative prices in the real sector, substitute absolute prices in the Cambridge-k equation

$$K\left[\sum_j X_j P_j\right] - Q_u = 0 \tag{31}$$

where money is taken as *numéraire*. If (31) were to be part of the *ex ante* system, it would have to be written in identity form, implying that the K is tautological. It cannot be given a value to reflect an *ex ante* desire to hold real balances, for the structure of the system forbids this. It must adjust to any level of prices, and any set of prices, whether it fits the $n - 1$ real equations or not, to keep (30) and (31) identically zero.

Let us argue by analogy. Suppose we had a Walras' Law economy where all investment was done by those who save, and the building of investment goods was the only alternative for savers. Then, *ex ante*, the desire to save must always equal the desire to invest. This is the equivalent of (30) above:

$$E_s \equiv S - I \equiv 0 \tag{32}$$

where E_s is the excess desire to save, S is desired saving, and I is desired investment. Now, we may write if we wish,

$$S = kY \tag{33}$$

where $0 < k \leqq 1$ and Y is income, and we may interpret k as an *ex ante* determinant of saving. But, obviously,

$$E_s \equiv kY - I \equiv 0 \tag{34}$$

can never be used to determine an interest rate since it holds independent of the level of the interest rate.

Now, however, let us assume the government arbitrarily tells each person he must buy specified amounts of investment goods, the total adding up to I. This is analogous to setting a value of Q_u in (31). Then, k can have no *ex ante* meaning in (34): it must adjust to the value needed to make saving equal to a given I. It is tautological and misleading if interpreted in its former *ex ante* sense. Archibald and Lipsey realize this, of course, but they alter the content of the neoclassical model. From a model which determines a solution by *ex ante* functions and without the homogeneity postulate, they obtain the whole set of stationary state solutions for varying quantities of money. Their model is that which would be obtained if Model V-2 were solved in nonspecific form; it stands in relation to Model V-2 as demand functions are related to a simple exchange model. Then, their "general equilibrium system" describes, for any given Q_u, the prices and quantities emerging in all markets in full stationarity. The real-balance effect need not enter into the real goods equations, of course, and the price level can be found from a Cambridge-k expression. However, this system presupposes the underlying "determining" system we have been dealing with: we may distinguish it as an "equilibrium descriptive" system as opposed to an "equilibrium-determining" system. It bears the onus of never giving information of consumers' actions for values of $P_u \neq P_u^\circ$.[72]

To return to Patinkin's analysis, we find his focus less upon the logical conditions of some such rigorous model as that of Model V-2—as Lange's is—and more upon the implications of these authors' discussions of how equilibrium is attained in real and money markets. Lange's analysis would lead us to ask the question, "Does the rigorous Walrasian model contain Say's Identity or not?" It also permits a second question: "Apart from Walras' specific assumptions, does the internal logical structure of his system lead to a contradiction of Say's Identity or not?" Although Lange did not ask these questions of Walras' analysis, they spring logically from his paper. We have answered both questions in the light of Lange's criticisms.

On the other hand, Patinkin's criticisms lead to some such question as the following: "Whatever the conclusion about Say's Identity, as posed in the two questions above, when Walras steps outside the equilibrium conditions of his model to discuss the *tâtonnement* process by which equilibrium is reached, does he tend to dichotomize these market processes into real and monetary?"

7.a. A Generalization of the Decomposability of the Money System Implied by the Invalid Dichotomy

Before we seek to answer this question for the specific case of Walras, it will be valuable to generalize the Lange-Patinkin line of criticism in order to gain greater insight into the nature of a general equilibrium system. We have seen that something of the same nature as Say's Identity existed in Model IV-1 for capital assets, and we shall now seek to exploit that similarity.

Assume that we are describing the general equilibrium of a system with $n - 1$ real goods plus money, in which all prices are measured in units of some *numéraire* outside the system. We shall begin, then, with n excess demand equations which are equated to zero (one of which is not independent by virtue of Walras' Identity). We shall say no more about

[72] Compare also S. Valavanis, (1).

the characteristics of the system, but we will assume that the price vector $[P^\circ]$ is found whose elements fit the model. Next, let us relax the conditions of the model sufficiently to permit the lifting of the variable P_k from the system and permit an arbitrary increase of its value to $P_k^\circ + dP_k$. If we temporarily abandon all of our preconceived notions of how well-behaved, rational, logically-constructed economies should react, three cases will hold an interest for us.

Case 1. No excess demand in the system departs from zero, and therefore, no other price in the system is affected. We shall term this the case of complete nonintegration, for when a price change has no impact upon a system, in the sense of failing to impose the need for a new *tâtonnement* process, the price in question is not truly a part of that system.

Case 2. The excess demand for the good whose price changes is affected, and departs from zero, but in such a way as to have no effect upon any other excess demand or price in the system. (Once more the reader is enjoined to suppress his Euclidean economic notions.) We shall term this the case of partial integration.

Case 3. At least one other excess demand besides that for the good whose price is disturbed departs from zero, in which case full integration of the price, P_k, in the model, is achieved.

Now, assume that we assert the general impossibility of Case 2 in a rational economic model: that is, that in a system containing all possible alternatives for expenditures, any one excess demand can change without effecting changes in at least one other, forcing a new *tâtonnement* process upon the system. If, in spite of this general restriction, we still assert that there is one good whose price does not have this otherwise necessary property, we are involved in a contradiction. Either the structure of the system does not in fact deny the possibility of Case 2 and we have a partially integrated variable, or, contrary to appearance, Case 2 must not exist and Case 1 or Case 3 must be operative. If we have structured the system specifically to prevent Case 3 from ruling for this good's price—taking care that the price of the good under discussion does not affect any other excess demand—then we must in fact have Case 1. That is, in spite of the appearance of affecting only its own excess demand, the logic of the system must dictate that it is completely nonintegrated.

What is it in the nature of the relationships among most goods which makes of their price changes Case 3 examples? We have seen in Chapter 3 that for a production economy, the substitution, income, and expansion effects are the paths of interdependence that give the system coherence. Since our concern is not with the stability of the system or gauging the strength or net direction of changes in variables, given the existence of a nonzero level for any or all three of these effects, even should they cancel out at the end of the *tâtonnement* phase, our condition for full integration will have been met.

The essence of Say's Identity is that the inability of changes in the price of money to lead to substitution, income, or expansion effects implies that the demand for and supply of it are independent of its price and identically equal in real terms.

Patinkin's Invalid Dichotomy asserts that the neoclassicals argued as if, when the price of money departed slightly from the equilibrium value, with no compensating changes in its quantity, the *excess* demand for real balances remained unchanged while other excess demands were undisturbed. Therefore, they implicitly treated money as a Case 1 good in real terms. As far as nominal balances are concerned, Patinkin argues, a change in the price of money was interpreted as affecting only the excess demand for nominal cash balances. But, since interdependence of the system denied this possibility in the general case, this implied that the price of money does not affect the excess demand for cash balances, so that any price level could rule. Again, money is shown to be a completely nonintegrated commodity.

Lastly, Patinkin's stress on the necessity for an effect which he rechristens the "real-balance effect" is the demand that the income-substitution-expansion effects for money be built into the system so that Case 3 integration can occur.

7.b. Patinkin's Criticism of Walras

We may now turn to Patinkin's criticism of Walras. He asserts that the Invalid Dichotomy's presence in the latter's analysis is "highly probable"[73] or, at least, if Walras did not adopt it he certainly did not oppose it.[74] With the modification of Model V-1 introduced in Model V-2 to eliminate Say's Identity, Patinkin seems to accept the integration of money as a Case 3 good in the latter model. For suppose P_u and $P_{u'}$ rise proportionately, so that i and all other prices are unchanged initially. Then the aggregate budget equation term, $\bar{X}_u P_{u'}$, will change and via this change in income at least one other excess demand will have to change. On the other hand, if only P_u were to change, direct substitution for or against goods and securities would occur in addition to the change in the budget equation term. Ergo, in the Walrasian system, whose essence is contained in Model V-1, reconstructed to eliminate Say's Identity in Model V-2, money is a Case 3, fully integrated, good.

Thus, in spite of Patinkin's assertion that the "real-balance effect" must enter at least one equation in order to yield a determinate price level, the Walrasian system obtains this result without linking the absorption of goods to the value of a stock of money wealth. Rather, the real value of an *income flow*—the earnings on money lent as a working capital fund—provides the nonhomogeneity required. Therefore,

[73] D. Patinkin, (4), p. 108.
[74] D. Patinkin, (4), pp. 455–6.

Patinkin's criticism of the absence of the real-balance effect is not relevant.[75]

But as we have stressed, the main burden of Patinkin's criticism has moved to Walras' discussion of the *tâtonnement* process. The primary basis for this criticism is the following passage from Walras which we must quote at some length:

"On referring back to the various terms that enter into the composition of [the value of inventories to be demanded in money form, as symbolized in Model V-1 above], we perceive that they are not absolutely independent of $P_{u'}$, since $P_{u'}$ figures in the term $[\bar{X}_{cu}P_{u'}]$ of the [budget constraint], which, together with the equations of maximum satisfaction, enables us to deduce the quantities [of inventory services, desired in money form] for any one party to the exchange and, consequently the aggregate quantities [of such services] for all parties together. We must admit, however, that the dependence of these items on $P_{u'}$ is very indirect and very weak. That being the case, the equation of monetary circulation, when money is not a commodity, comes very close, in reality, to falling outside the system of equations of economic equilibrium.

"If we first suppose economic equilibrium to be established, then the equation of monetary circulation would be solved almost without any *tâtonnements*, simply by raising or lowering $P_{u'}$ according [as the demand for money differed from the supply], at a price $P_{u'}$, which had been cried at random. If, however, this increase or decrease in $P_{u'}$ were to change [the value of inventory services desired in money form] ever so slightly, it would only be necessary to continue the general process of adjustment by *tâtonnements* in order to be sure of reaching equilibrium. This is what actually takes place in the money market."[76]

After quoting this passage at somewhat greater length, Patinkin asserts:

"This is the sum total of Walras's discussion of the *tâtonnement* by which the level of $P_{u'}$ and hence P_u is determined. It shows that Walras is quite willing to assume that, with $P_{u'}$ arbitrarily fixed at the level $P'_{u'}$, a *tâtonnement* in the commodity markets first achieves equilibrium there; that, once this is accomplished, a *tâtonnement* in the money market then determines the equilibrium level of $P_{u'}$; *and that this latter* tâtonnement *can be carried out without reacting back and disturbing the equilibrium initially achieved in the commodity markets.* It fails to indicate any realization on the part of Walras that such a dichotomization of the pricing

[75] D. Patinkin, (4), p. 411.

[76] L. Walras, (3), pp. 326–7. Quoted by permission of Richard D. Irwin, Inc., George Allen & Unwin, Ltd., and the American Economic Association. The phrases in brackets have been substituted for Walras' symbols, and the quotation has been broken into two paragraphs.

process contradicts the very conditions necessary for the existence of a monetary economy."[77]

Walras is deserving of a great deal of criticism for his ambiguities, carelessness, and sheer error in these areas, as our previous discussion makes clear. The exasperation of economists who have spent hours, as Patinkin clearly has, in the pondering of the meaning of passages, is understandable. If Patinkin is arguing that there are places in the work where Walras argues as he claims, no dispute arises; but if he argues that Walras consistently wrote as if money could be considered as a Class 2 good, then we must argue that Patinkin neglects important evidence to the contrary.

First, his argument that the discussion of the *tâtonnement* fails to reveal a recognition that cutting the link to $P_{u'}$ via the budget constraint contradicts the conditions for a monetary economy, clearly flies in the face of the statement by Walras quoted above to the effect that the lack of strength of the dependence comes close to excluding the monetary equation from the system. Incidentally, the strength of the effect is not important, as Patinkin himself points out in another connection: it is the existence of this income impact, as we have shown above, that yields determinacy of the price level.[78]

Second, the very passage quoted by Patinkin contains a statement by Walras that only if the demand for and supply of money balances were brought into equality, given the attainment of equilibrium in all markets but those for cash balances and the *numéraire*, could demand and supply for the latter be equated. This is explicit evidence of reasoning that included the required linkage of the promissory note market to the real sector.

Third, Patinkin's charge that Walras did not bother to trace out the reactions back upon the real sector's prices of the *tâtonnements* in $P_{u'}$ is true, but Patinkin makes too strong a case on the basis of this neglect. After all, Walras does recognize the "feedback" case as what actually occurs in the market in the quotation above; and, at this point, he had already illustrated this feedback effect for the multiple exchange economy, the production economy, and the capital goods economy, so that it could be quite reasonable to assume that he felt it to be unnecessary to repeat it. Lastly, in order to avail himself of the use of a well-known body of partial techniques in monetary theory, he had to make the simplification he did, as Schumpeter points out.[79]

This last point derives support from the evidence of a Marshallian urge in Walras. In his introduction to the discussion of the process of

[77] D. Patinkin, (4), pp. 402–3. Quoted by permission.
[78] D. Patinkin, (4), p. 22.
[79] J. Schumpeter, (5), p. 1025.

achieving equilibrium in the capital goods markets, he at once illustrates the futility of his system as an analytical device when a multitude of primary and secondary effects are considered, and his propensity to adopt partial methods when the occasion demands:

"Theoretically, all the unknowns of an economic problem depend on all the equations of economic equilibrium. Nevertheless, even from the viewpoint of static theory, it is permissible to consider some of these unknowns as especially dependent on the equations which were introduced at the same time as the unknowns when the problem of their determination was first raised. It is all the more legitimate to do this when we pass from the static to the dynamic point of view, or better still, when we pass from the realm of pure theory to that of applied theory or to actual practice, for then the variations in the unknown quantities will be the effects of either the first or the second order, that is to say, effects which need or need not be taken into consideration, according as they arise from variations in the special or the general data. Consequently, having already formulated the law of the establishment of the rate of net income from a consideration of the whole economic system, we can now construct purchase and sales curves of new capital goods against *numéraire* [and analyze on the assumption that the equality of investment and savings determines the rate of return on capital goods and the requirement that all capital goods have common rates of return determines the quantities of each produced]."[80]

In this quotation is an explicit attempt to justify the very thing Patinkin is criticizing. In the passage cited by Patinkin, Walras could very well have been expecting the reader to fill in the "feedback" process, and for this reason have moved into a partial analysis. For example, on page 329—in the midst of his treatment of money—he refers to the price of inventory services as being determined by one equation (excess demand for them equal to zero), yet it would be difficult to infer that he consistently envisions them as Case 2 goods.

Finally, Patinkin himself quotes Walras on tracing the impact of an increase of money (which is in this instance also a commodity such as gold) upon prices, in which the latter tries to show (imperfectly, as Patinkin justly points out) how reactions throughout the price system result in a neutral effect upon the interest rate.[81]

Therefore, there is evidence that tends to contradict the thesis that Walras believed that it was possible to dichotomize the economy into real and monetary sectors—a position which Patinkin presumably would find too strong to accept. We should meet Patinkin's charge that Walras

[80] L. Walras, (3), pp. 307–8. Quoted by permission of Richard D. Irwin, Ltd., George Allen & Unwin, Ltd., and the American Economic Association.

[81] D. Patinkin, (4), p. 406, and L. Walras, (3), p. 333.

occasionally speaks this way with the background evidence to indicate the implicit or explicit viewpoint which justified it analytically. Walrasian monetary theory, and, more generally, neoclassical monetary theory, is more subject to the Lange criticism than the broader challenge of Patinkin, although, as indicated above, even the former must be modified for Walras. At the same time, however, Patinkin's present attack is a more sophisticated one than Lange's, and, therefore, less susceptible to "proof" or "disproof" in some final sense. Indeed, it is not far from the truth to say that the Invalid Dichotomy is a state of the theorist's mind rather than of his model.

8. A Model of the Firm's Demand for Cash Balances with Minimal Uncertainty

The determination of the amounts demanded of inventories and cash balances in Models V-1 and V-2 by firms has been assumed to fall outside the traditional maximization techniques with which we have become familiar in this book. As a final step in the consideration of Model V-2 we shall ask how the determination of cash demands will be made if we assume that firms do seek optimal amounts in a maximization-of-profits analysis. Our feelings as to the need for such frameworks in a stationary flow with certainty have already been stated. Moreover, we have already seen one solution to the optimization-by-marginal-analysis for the consumer's demands for inventories and money balances. If we are willing to enter such services in the preference function of the consumer and/or the transformation function of the firm, we can bring such demands under the regime of familiar techniques. We shall rest with this possibility at the consumer level.

Let us consider maximization techniques for treating money in the entrepreneurial sector. We debar the inclusion of money in the transformation function, as well as the inclusion of inventories, since we feel that in a certain world synchronization inputs are of a fundamentally different nature from "productive" types of inputs. If we attempt to introduce maximization techniques into reasoning about synchronization media, we must deal with certain troublesome discontinuities and introduce new assumptions about the state of knowledge within which the entrepreneur is operating. The newer techniques of economic theory—linear programming, game theory, and Wald decision theory—offer means of coping with these complications which were nonexistent a few decades ago. We shall, therefore, seek the aid of these techniques to develop methods for determining a firm's demand for cash balances and inventories jointly at the start of the fulfillment week—all within the framework of Models I through V with which it is the purpose of Part II to deal.

Our model remains essentially static, with time continuing to exist explicitly. Rates of change and other dynamic forms of the variables play no part in any decisionmaking, expectations of the future continue to be given, and lack of certainty plays a limited role within the model. Moreover, in final adjustment the system is stationary, within the bounds of nonfixity allowed by such writers as Marshall.[82]

First, let us begin with the temporal assumptions of Model V-2. On the market day the firm must formulate a production plan which includes nonnegative levels of activities on each of the following five days. For simplicity, assume each firm produces only one output, and let that output on Day d, $d = 1, \ldots, 5$, be denoted by the symbol $\bar{X}_{vd}$, where we have dropped the subscript denoting the good produced. Since we shall deal throughout most of the analysis with only one firm, we may also drop the firm's subscript, so that the output on Day d becomes $\bar{X}_d$. Similarly, we denote the intraweek deliveries of the firm as X_d—the amounts of its product delivered on Day d.

Initially, let us assume that the percentage of weekly output desired daily by the firm's customers is treated as known for certain by the firm:

$$X_d = b_d \bar{X} \tag{35}$$

where

$$\bar{X} = \sum_d \bar{X}_d \tag{36}$$

and where

$$\text{(37)} \qquad \begin{aligned} &1. \quad b_d \geqq 0 \\ &2. \quad \sum_d b_d = 1 \end{aligned}$$

Now, let us make the conditions of production for the firm more explicit than for previous models:

1. The production of Day d is completed by the end of Day d and employs only the factor services and goods purchased on Day d.

2. Two capacity limitations operate on the firm. C_{d1} is the amount of productive capacity available on Day d, and C_{d2} the amount of storage capacity available for product from the end of Day $d - 1$ to the start of Day d. Therefore, C_{12} does not exist in the model, since all production is sold by the end of the week, and there exist 9 capacity limitations on the firm's intraweek pattern of output, given as data.

[82] See his description of the stationary state, with its motionless economy full of movement, in (2), pp. 366–7. Our own model of entrepreneurial demand for cash contains much less movement than Marshall's stationary state, and such as our model does contain is purely stochastic.

3. We revert to the transformation conditions of Model III-1 and assume constant coefficients of production per unit of output, defining a productive activity in the manner of (11) in Chapter 3. Inventory and cash balance requirements are not included in the vector of inputs and output defining a unit level of activity.

4. Only one productive process exists for any of the five days' output, but it is possible to substitute external inventory borrowings (the purchase of inventory services from the market) and storage of previous days' production for production on Day d. All substitutability within the system springs from the ability to substitute to varying extents among these three types of processes.

We shall term the inventories acquired from the inventory service market on the market day "external inventories" to distinguish them from the amounts of previous days' outputs held for sale in future, which stocks we shall term "internal inventories."

5. As in the previous models, all sales of factor services are for the full week, and factor price is quoted for that whole period of use. We shall assume, however, that regardless of the day of use, $\frac{1}{5}$ of the total factor cost is paid each day by the firm to the public. However, all profits are paid out to their claimants on Day 5.

These conditions deny the firm the possibility of acquiring intraweek inventories of its own raw materials; i.e., it must use materials delivered today for today's output. If it had some incentive, the firm might be thought to use any excess of receipts over payments on Day d to buy such inventories for use on subsequent days within the week, but, actually, the conditions of the model assure that firms will not seek to acquire them. Since the prices of raw materials do not vary within the week, the firm would acquire such inventories only if the storage costs of goods were less than the storage costs of money. If we assume the latter to be zero, the firm will choose to hold its excess receipts in money form.

But, of course, it may hold internal inventories of its own product: indeed, it is one of the functions of money to permit the firm to acquire them over the week. That is, in the face of the $[X_d]$ which may not have uniform components, or a level of productive capacity which varies from day to day, it may pay the firm to produce more on Day 2 than it sells on Day 2, and to hold the excess for sale on Day 3, and/or Day 4, and/or Day 5. Then,

$$\bar{X}_d = \Delta k_d + S_d \tag{38}$$

where Δk_d is the amount of Day d's production added to stocks and S_d is the sales from Day d's production. Of course,

$$\Delta k_d \geqq 0, \bar{X}_d \geqq 0, S_d \geqq 0 \tag{39}$$

The nonnegative additions to stock, Δk_d, are destined as follows:

$$\Delta k_d = S_{dk} + k_{d+1} - k_d, \qquad d = 1, 2, 3, 4 \tag{40}$$

where S_{dk} are the sales from stocks in Day d, and k_d are the initial levels of stocks at the beginning of the fulfillment week d. Of course,

$$S_{dk} \geqq 0; \; k_1 = 0; \; k_2, k_3, k_4 \geqq 0 \tag{41}$$

For Day 5 the condition is altered, since repayment of inventories leased from the inventory service market (external inventories) must be made from the stocks on the last day:

$$\Delta k_5 = \sum_{d=1}^{4} j_d + S_{5k} - k_5 \tag{42}$$

where j_d is defined as external inventories sold on Day d. Also,

$$j_d \geqq 0 \tag{43}$$

The equilibrium condition for sales is that

$$X_d^\circ = S_d^\circ + S_{dk}^\circ + j_d^\circ \tag{44}$$

Lastly, we place the production and warehousing capacity limits upon production and storage:

$$\begin{array}{lll} 1. & \bar{X}_d + w_{d1} = C_{d1} & \\ 2. & k_d + w_{d2} = C_{d2}, & d = 2, 3, 4, 5 \end{array} \tag{45}$$

where w_{d1} and w_{d2} are disposal activity levels, such disposals being costless. By definition, each unit of production requires a unit of productive capacity, and each unit of stock is defined as requiring one unit of warehousing.

Thus far we have included seven types of activities in the planning of the firm:

1. production activities with levels $\bar{X}_d$.
2. production-to-storage activities with levels Δk_d.
3. production-to-sales activities with levels S_d.
4. storage-to-sales activities at levels S_{dk}.
5. storage-to-storage activities with levels k_d, when $\Delta k_d = S_{dk} = 0$.
6. external inventories to sales with activity levels j_d.
7. disposal activities with levels w_{d1} and w_{d2}.

For the five-day production week we have been using for our models, this would yield a total of 36 different activities for combination by the firm into an optimal program.

We may proceed to derive the firm's objective function. First, we define the excess of payments over receipts on Day d as

$$e_d = .2\left[\sum_i a_i\bar{X}P_i + X_uP_{u'} + \sum_d j_dP_{j'}\right] + \sum_j a_j\bar{X}_dP_j - X_dP \tag{46}$$

where a_i is the unit requirement of factor service i, a_j the unit requirement of intermediate good Y_j, P_i and P_j the prices of these factor services and intermediate goods, $P_{j'}$ the price of inventory services, and P the price of a unit of product.

The gross demand for cash on Day d is quite simply e_d. However, net demands for money, which when positive must be met with borrowed cash balances, are computed by deducting from any day's positive gross demand any positive supply carryover from the previous day. Letting X_{du} denote net demand for cash on Day d, we obtain

$$X_{du} = e_d + \min\,[0,\ X_{d-1,u}] \tag{47}$$

Then the demand for money is the sum of the positive X_{du}:

$$X_u = \sum_d \max\,[0,\ X_{du}] \tag{48}$$

Lastly, we seek:

$$\max Z = -\sum_d e_d - F \tag{49}$$

where F is the value of fines levied against the firm for failure to cover its payments on any one date.

One of these equations may be omitted as redundant. If the equations of (44) are added together and substitutions made from (35), (36), and (37-2), the same sum is obtained as that from the sum of systems (40) and (42) substituted into the sum of (38). We may, therefore, eliminate one equation from any of these systems.

From the solution to the model there will emerge a demand for money and external inventories which reflect the given prices of all factor services and that of the product, the relative pattern of deliveries, and the production and storage constraints on the firm. If we allow the price vector to change, parametric programming techniques allow the computation of "demand functions" for cash balances and external inventories for the firm. Summation over all firms yields a total entrepreneurial demand for cash balances which can be used in place of (V-2-2-6) and for inventories which can replace (V-2-2-5), where each firm desires inventories only of its own product.

Now, into this certainty model we introduce risk: the vector of delivery ratios $[b_d]$ we shall henceforth assume to be unknown to the firm during the market day, revealing itself only as the week unfolds. We assume again that the firm must commit itself to a program of the kind just portrayed, unalterable until the following market day. Since it will contract to sell all the output it plans to produce (and will produce), the firm will never end the week with positive or negative excess output. Therefore, the impact of the uncertainty must fall upon profits by virtue of (1) production and/or storage capacity wasted through failure to phase production optimally through time, and (2) penalties levied for the delayed delivery of goods. As far as these latter are concerned, we shall simply assume that whenever desired purchases are greater than planned sales on any day, those consumers whose wants are not satisfied are paid given fines per unit of goods delayed in delivery, such fines being paid at the end of the week when profits are distributed. In the event these fines are greater than profits we shall assume that I.O.U.'s are issued for redemption from profits in future periods, but that the firm is liquidated if the number of such claims surpasses a given cumulative level.

Since there is an infinity of $[b_d]$ available to the firm from which to select the one on the basis of which its plans are formulated, we shall assume that when it is faced with the need to consider more than one $[b_d]$ the firm considers them in finite steps of (say) 5 ratio points, so that its planning takes place over a finite number of points in the five-dimensional vector space in which the $[b_d]$ are mapped.[83] The other "player" may be taken to be "the public," which has an identical set of strategies to play in the form of imposing a $[b_d]$ upon the firm, for the latter is entirely at the mercy of its customers. The game may be regarded as zero-sum, assuming negative, positive, and zero profits yield satisfactions linear with their values, when the firm is viewed as the maximizing player. Each cell's payoff is the result of the firm following an element in its strategy set A, say A_i, which is a given expected $[b_d]$, when in fact the public plays an element in its strategy set S, say S_j, which is the $[b_d]$ enforced upon the firm. The selection of an act from the firm's viewpoint is a choice of strategy to oppose "nature," or a second player who is not really a malevolent minimizing opponent. In other words, we find the firm confronted with a problem of choice under conditions of risk or uncertainty.

The case of decisionmaking in conditions of certainty presented above can be looked upon as the "majorant" of this game, i.e., the decision-making of the firm if it knew in advance which strategy its opponent had chosen. Obviously, since the main diagonal of the matrix contains the

[83] In the absence of this assumption we should have a game-theoretic structure with infinite strategy sets for both "players"—a type of game which offers some difficulties, although the set of strategies can be defined over the unit square to yield a case which has been solved for a finite approximation to infinite sets. Also, the payoff function in our model is continuous and allows us the use of these game-theoretic techniques for solution. If one of the sets of strategies could be made finite, we should be assured of the existence of an optimal solution for the firm and of "the value" of the game, but it is the nature of our problem that the payoff matrix is square, and if one set of strategies becomes finite, the other does as well. Cf. R. Luce, (1), pp. 450–1.

row maxima, foreknowledge of the public's strategy would lead the firm to choose the same strategy in order to obtain the diagonal payoff.[84]

In our treatment of consumer decisionmaking we have defined five states of ignorance: perfect risk, the game-theoretic, the risk-game-theoretic, the imperfectly uncertain, and the perfectly uncertain environments. Because of the static, stationary nature of our models, the pure risk and perfect uncertainty cases are of greatest interest for us: the second may be viewed as holding at the start of the move toward full stationary equilibrium, and, in that state, the first type of environment may rule for the firm. The imperfectly uncertain environment then becomes a transitional environment before full stationary equilibrium has been achieved, and for its analysis the Wald sequential decision process analysis seems ideally suited.

Let us turn, then, to the full equilibrium state—stationarity in a pure risk environment. We draw upon the discussion of the von Neumann-Morgenstern utility index and criteria for choice under conditions of risk contained in Sections 1.a.4.b. and 2.a. of Chapter 2. We postulate that the axiomatic basis for the von Neumann-Morgenstern index exists so that its values, u_{ij}, can be associated with outcomes in the payoff matrix such that strategy A_i is not preferred to A_j only if the expected utility of A_i is not higher than that of A_j. In the absence of an ability to obtain this set u_{ij} by observation, we shall make the further and objectionable assumption that money payoffs, π_{ij}, are linear with a von Neumann-Morgenstern utility index; i.e., that

$$\pi_{ij} = a + bu_{ij} \tag{50}$$

As discussed in Chapter 2, this is quite likely to be a poor assumption about the relationship of money and the firm's preferences under risk, but it yields operational theorems for testing and provides a starting point for such analyses as these. We shall hope to alter the assumption in conditions of absolute uncertainty in order to be more acceptable intuitively, perhaps through the use of a Wald-Savage "regret-function" of the type used in Chapter 3.

This theory of demand for cash balances properly integrated into the general equilibrium model, completes the latter as a model of behavior under static, stationary conditions with an element of risk, as defined above. For any given set of factor endowments and prices, consumer preferences, and product prices, there exist determinate supplies of factors and consumer good demands. From these there emerges a specific time pattern of income receipts and a desired pattern of consumption for each good, in the form $[b_d]$. The individual firm assumes a relative pattern of deliveries, again in the form $[b_d]$, and fills a square payoff matrix of the standard type in Chapter 2.

[84] J. von Neumann, (2), pp. 100–5.

Each row in this payoff matrix will represent a given level of output, in the general case, different from every other row. Realistically speaking, synchronization costs should not lead to a large range of outputs, and since the probabilities over the S-set will be generated from a sampling distribution, some given size of sample might be assumed throughout to prevent the probabilities from changing from row to row. This is not necessary, however, and we shall not assume it: rather, it must be kept in mind that the probabilities will change with the A_i.

Every firm then chooses that level of output which results from a strategy A_i with the maximum expected-value if the latter is zero or better, and a level of zero if the maximum expected-value is negative. The result provides the entrepreneurial contribution to the demand for factor services and intermediate goods. If market demand exceeds supply, product price rises, factor prices may change, distribution of income changes as does consumption, and a new desired $[b_d]$ emerges for the public as a whole. A whole new payoff matrix is determined for each firm, and the market process continues until excess demand equals zero in all markets at prices that equal average cost. Moreover, the expected value of each firm's strategy must be zero, since the firm controls no scarce resources the value of the game to it must be zero, and expected surpluses which might tempt in other firms must redound to other factors of differential efficiency. Implicitly, such reasoning introduces some concept such as "the representative firm" since we are dealing with such subjective manifestations as "expected values." Lastly, negative profits, which we assume are paid by I.O.U.'s, are redeemed with positive profits in future weeks, but over a succession of weeks the firm may expect to earn nothing.

We turn for a brief look at the case of absolute ignorance of the probability vector over the public's strategy set. The minimax-regret criterion of Wald and Savage seems a likely one to adopt in the present circumstances: it compares alternative strategies against available opportunities, it is a compromise between the extremely optimistic and extremely pessimistic outlooks of straightforward maximax and minimax procedures, and the range of positive and negative profits in the usual case should be small enough so that its symmetrical treatment of positive and negative "losses" will not be overly troublesome. These considerations are discussed at greater length in Chapter 3.

From this analysis the firm once more chooses a $[b_d]$ with which to plan its production, and once more its demands for synchronization media are forthcoming. Week after week, knowledge of consumer dispositions is acquired until the sampling distributions of which we spoke become known and absolute ignorance gives way to risk.

9. The Keynesian Model

As a last exercise, we shall compare the neoclassical Model V-2—our ultimate expression of general neoclassicism—with the general equilibrium model of John Maynard Keynes. What was the contribution of

Lord Keynes to the development of general equilibrium theory? It is becoming possible now, with the passage of a quarter-century, to view his *General Theory* as an (important) episode in the continuous development of the general neoclassical system we have been treating in Part II. From one vantage point, it is paradoxical that his work should have been accepted as the Grand Departure from its neoclassical progenitors—even though Keynes presented it in that light—since his interpretations of these systems are almost always kept visible for purposes of comparison in the *General Theory*. On the other hand, Keynes's impact on economic policy, on the methodology and analytics of quantitative economics, and on the working economist's vision of reality, may be seen even today to be of that order of power rightfully termed "revolutionary."

From the restricted viewpoint of the pure theory of general economic systems, however, Keynes's fundamental challenge to neoclassical theory is quite clear: it lies in his construction of a model from which flexibility of the money wage rate cannot eliminate an excess supply of labor. In the sense of pure general equilibrium theory this is the core of the Keynesian performance, and his alterations to general neoclassicism to achieve such a theory of employment are the most interesting aspects of "the Keynesian Revolution."[85]

In the main current of doctrinal development, the overthrow by Keynes of Say's Law (in the Identity sense of Becker and Baumol[86]), if in fact he did this, was a necessary but pedestrian clearing of ground for the major work.[87] We say this because, as discussed above at great length, even if it were shown that Say's Identity was a customary assumption of the neoclassical models of Keynes's day, it is now clear, by virtue of the work of Lange and Patinkin, that it is not a necessary projection of the logic of these systems. Not only does Say's Identity effectively remove money as a good from models which retain it as a postulate, but it violates the logical symmetry which a proper neoclassical model employs to integrate money with the body of real goods equations. This part of the "Revolution" may now be seen, twenty-five years later, to be only deceptively disturbing to the postulates of neoclassicism, if indeed it was necessary at all.[88]

[85] In this sense, Chapter 19 is the most important chapter of *The General Theory*, for it deals with the effects upon the Keynesian model of changes in the wage rate most explicitly (but unsatisfactorily).

[86] G. Becker, (1), pp. 356–7.

[87] Compare G. Haberler, (4), pp. 173–5. For a recent contrary view, see E. Edwards, (1), p. 420. Edwards asserts that Keynes's major contribution was to emphasize the aggregate demand curve, although, in retrospect, he neglected factors which would eliminate excess demand for money at full employment. But to say this is to imply that a distinctively Keynesian static theory does not exist, and that Keynesian unemployment was due to the slowness of adjustments in a neoclassical world. In short, something more than the possibility of an excess demand for money is needed: namely, a set of postulates providing for its perpetuation.

[88] To choose another illustration of our point: even though Patinkin's hypothesis that Keynes's speculative money holdings were not a function of the price level were

The essence of the Keynesian system is of quite different stuff. It consists in altering the neoclassical postulates to derive qualitatively different theorems about the employment of labor—a fundamentally new set of theorems derived from postulates not contained in the neoclassical model and violating its vision of economic reality.

It is the irony of the Keynesian Revolution that, while Keynes is viewed by his adherents as having laid the basis for his innovations by destroying Say's Law, it is necessary in rigorously depicting his own model to introduce into it an identity as intuitively objectionable as the one he rejects! Sketched out in the Marshallian vagueness of the *General Theory* is this rigidity which we shall call "Keynes's Identity," and it serves to "semi-dichotomize" his model into real and nonreal sectors in the same manner as the much maligned Say's Identity.

We shall approach Keynes's Identity by discussing first a simplified Model V-1 and its dichotomization by Say's Identity, drawing upon the analysis of Section 4. We shall then proceed to an economy where the assumption of Say's Identity is dropped but where the monetary effect of price changes is identically zero. Against this system we shall then derive and discuss Keynes's Identity and the partial dichotomization of the economy. Finally, we shall give a brief summary and conclusion of our analysis of Keynes's model.

A fundamental difficulty charged with great potential for misunderstanding must be faced at the outset: we must formalize "the Keynesian model." The *General Theory* is many theories, the analysis bears the sophistication of genius, the qualifications genuinely meant to confront a recalcitrant reality rather than carping critics. Any attempt to formalize such analysis is destined to be unfair to its subtlety and to be to some extent a distortion. Nonetheless, in gauging the theoretical contributions of Keynes, sooner or later one must seek the fundamental essence of his system. Not to do so is to deny him a major strength: the creation of a model coordinate with, but alternative to, the neoclassical equilibrium model.

9.a. A Simplified Model V-1 with Say's Identity

Let us simplify Model V-1 by assuming only two goods, Y_1 and Y_2; two factor services z_1 and z_2, the latter consisting of labor services; one type of security, E, with no promissory note market, individuals and firms adjusting their holdings of cash by either reducing their demand for goods they purchase or by increasing their supplies of the goods they sell, or both; and, lastly, we assume the existence of money, U.

---

proved, not only is such a postulate unnecessary for his system, but it violates the logic of the system. Its removal cannot but improve the model and may constitute an important preliminary, if indeed the postulate is present at all. But such removal cannot be a major disturbance to the Keynesian model. Cf. D. Patinkin, (4), pp. 173–4.

The conditions on excess demand equations for an equilibrium are then:

$$(51)\quad \begin{aligned} &1. \quad E_j(P_1, P_2, P_{z_1}, P_{z_2}, P_{Z_1}, P_e) = E_j([P]) = 0, \qquad j = 1, 2 \\ &2. \quad E_i([P]) = 0, \qquad i = 1, 2 \\ &3. \quad E_{Z_1}([P]) = 0 \\ &4. \quad E_e([P]) = 0 \end{aligned}$$

and, from Walras' Identity

$$(52)\qquad -E_u - E_eP_e \equiv \sum_j E_jP_j + \sum_i E_iP_i + E_{Z_1}P_{Z_1}$$

where money is chosen as *numéraire.*

For convenience we shall term the goods whose equations are found in (51) "included" goods, and the equations "included" equations, while good U (money) will be denoted the "excluded" good. The latter is merely the good whose value of excess demand is implied by Walras' Law from the value of excess demands for all other goods. We have shown that it may be selected quite arbitrarily and need not even be the *numéraire* good. We have chosen money as the excluded good in this model, however, since it is truly the obverse of other markets, reflecting their states of excess demand directly in a manner not true of other goods, given the peculiar role of money in the system.

We retain the interpretation given the securities and capital good markets in Model V-1 from our discussion of Walras' analysis: securities are supplied by middlemen who obtain money by their sale in order to purchase capital goods, and redeem their securities in the capital good at the end of the period. Consequently, at the beginning of the period, all wealth is held either as physical wealth (stocks of Z_1) or in paper money which is the debt of an external agency (the government). No stocks of securities exist, and, further, the value of excess demand for securities is not identical with the value of excess supply for the capital good.

From a position of general equilibrium we suppose the economy to be jarred by an increase in the excess demand for money to a positive level, and the consequent dislocation of all other markets. Prices in all included markets but that for labor (z_2) are adjusted to re-equilibrate those markets, leaving the excess demand for money (the excluded good) identically equal to the value of excess supply of labor.

If the model is to return to full equilibrium it will be necessary for price flexibility to exist in the labor market, for P_{z_2} to fall, and, having fallen, to induce a rise in E_{z_2} (excess demand for labor). We may depict the changes in the equilibrium values of all prices but P_{z_2} and the change in E_{z_2} after all markets but the markets for z_2 and money have been returned to equilibrium after a fall in the money wage rate, by the system below:

$$(53)\qquad \begin{bmatrix} E_1^1 & E_1^2 & E_1^{z_1} & 0 & E_1^Z & E_1^e \\ E_2^1 & E_2^2 & E_2^{z_1} & 0 & E_2^Z & E_2^e \\ E_{z_1}^1 & E_{z_1}^2 & E_{z_1}^{z_1} & 0 & E_{z_1}^Z & E_{z_1}^e \\ E_{z_2}^1 & E_{z_2}^2 & E_{z_2}^{z_1} & -1 & E_{z_2}^Z & E_{z_2}^e \\ E_Z^1 & E_Z^2 & E_Z^{z_1} & 0 & E_Z^Z & E_Z^e \\ E_e^1 & E_e^2 & E_e^{z_1} & 0 & E_e^Z & E_e^e \end{bmatrix} \begin{bmatrix} \frac{dP_1}{dP_{z_2}} \\ \frac{dP_2}{dP_{z_2}} \\ \frac{dP_{z_1}}{dP_{z_2}} \\ \frac{dE_{z_2}}{dP_{z_2}} \\ \frac{dP_Z}{dP_{z_2}} \\ \frac{dP_e}{dP_{z_2}} \end{bmatrix} = \begin{bmatrix} -E_1^{z_2} \\ -E_2^{z_2} \\ -E_{z_1}^{z_2} \\ -E_{z_2}^{z_2} \\ -E_Z^{z_2} \\ -E_e^{z_2} \end{bmatrix}$$

or

$$(54)\qquad [E_{44}][dV] = [E^{z_2}]$$

where $E_s^t = \dfrac{\partial E_s}{\partial P_t}$, the subscript has been dropped from Z_1 as unnecessary, and where, if we denote by $[E]$ the matrix obtained by substituting the column vector $[E^{z_2}]$ for the fourth column of $[E_{44}]$, the latter may be seen to be the matrix of the principal minor of $|E|$ formed by striking out the fourth row and fourth column of $[E]$.

From (52) we obtain

$$(55)\qquad \frac{-dE_u}{dP_{z_2}} \equiv E_{z_2} + P_{z_2}\left(\frac{dE_{z_2}}{dP_{z_2}}\right)$$

and, since we began from a position where (52) was reduced to

$$(56)\qquad -E_u \equiv E_{z_2}P_{z_2}$$

we may substitute for E_{z_2} in (55) to get

$$(57)\qquad P_{z_2}\frac{dE_{z_2}}{dP_{z_2}} \equiv \frac{E_u}{P_{z_2}}\left[1 - \frac{dE_u}{E_u}\frac{P_{z_2}}{dP_{z_2}}\right]$$

And we may solve (53) by Cramer's method for $\dfrac{dE_{z_2}}{dP_{z_2}}$:

$$(58)\qquad \frac{dE_{z_2}}{dP_{z_2}} = \frac{|E|}{|E_{44}|}$$

Now, it was assumed in neoclassical analysis that P_{z_2} was flexible and that $\dfrac{dE_{z_2}}{dP_{z_2}} < 0$. In the Hicksian "stability" analysis of neoclassical systems, for example, it is required only that the economy be imperfectly stable to ensure that the ratio of determinants in (58) will be negative, although, of course, perfect stability will guarantee it, *a fortiori*. If all individuals are "maximizing satisfactions" and all firms are maximizing profits, and aggregate income effects may be neglected, the necessary and sufficient conditions for perfect stability will hold, as we showed in Chapter 3.[89] Thus, whatever one's feelings about the shortcomings of Hicksian stability analysis, if one is willing to make rather unheroic assumptions one can obtain a negative $\frac{dE_{z_2}}{dP_{z_2}}$ as a theorem derivable from the postulate of maximizing behavior in the neoclassical model, or, failing that degree of boldness, merely assume it as Keynes does in his presentation of rival models.

It is obvious from (57) that a condition for effecting any shift downward in E_{z_2} is that E_u be flexible, that is, that it be possible to change the excess demand for money. But, as we have seen, Say's Identity states that $E_u \equiv 0$. Therefore, were that restriction to be postulated, $\frac{dE_{z_2}}{dP_{z_2}}$ would not be defined for our initial position since such a position could not exist. If we assert that all but one included market is in equilibrium, and the excluded good is money, we must be incorrect under a Say's Identity regime; the inability of the market for money to be in disequilibrium implies that the remaining included market must be in equilibrium.

Or suppose Y_1 is chosen as excluded good and *numéraire*, as we have assumed in our earlier models. Then when an excess supply of labor arises, it can have no effect upon E_u under the regime of Say's Identity, and neither can the price changes evoked throughout the system to re-equilibrate the relevant markets. Also if one remaining condition is met—that changes in P_u have no effect upon the excess demands for any other good in the system—money is a completely nonintegrated good. That is, to generalize, if one of the included equations is an identity, it cannot be used to define an equilibrium condition. Were that good's price to have an impact upon other included goods' prices, we should have one more price to determine than equations to do the determining. If it has no such impact, we may remove it bodily and retain a determinate system of prices in terms of the *numéraire*, Y_1. The economy is so effectively di-

[89] As we shall develop in Chapter 8, except for those cases where the conditions for Hicksian perfect stability are necessary and sufficient for true dynamic stability—when only two goods exist in the economy, when the matrix $[E]$ is negative definite or negative quasi-definite, when all goods are gross substitutes, and when the complicated Morishima conditions rule—we cannot derive the condition that the relevant principal minors of $|E|$ must be opposite in sign to $|E|$. Only the sign of $|E|$ is derivable in general from the Routhian conditions, which are the necessary and sufficient conditions for the real parts of the latent roots of the characteristic equation of a linear dynamic system to be negative.

chotomized into real and money sectors that money disappears and barter conditions prevail.

9.b. The Zero Monetary Effect and Lange's Relation

Let us now relax the assumption that $E_u \equiv 0$, so that the public may seek to adjust its nominal balances to fit its purposes with the money supply fixed. Then (57) begins to have some interest for us, since the excess demand for money may now depart from zero. It states that if P_{z_2} (the wage rate) falls k per cent and all other included markets are returned to equilibrium, the excess supply of labor will fall if, and only if, the relative change in the excess demand for nominal cash balances is (1) negative and (2) greater than k in absolute value.[90] Only in this case will the real value of excess demand for money decrease with a rise in the "price of money" (the reciprocal of the price level), which means that the real purchasing power spent on included goods must rise. This influx of new purchasing power spent on such goods cushions the induced fall of prices of goods other than labor, preventing at least one of them from falling the full k per cent. The result must be an increased excess demand for labor by virtue of the induced substitution of labor for other factors, or the expansion of outputs by virtue of marginal costs falling more than the prices of all outputs, or a combination of both effects.

We may trace through the effects of a k per cent fall in P_{z_2} by assuming that all other prices but P_e fall k per cent instantaneously, P_e remaining constant. Then i_k, the net rate of return on capital goods, remains the same, and the demand for and supply of securities will rise to keep real investment unchanged. The new set of prices will be an equilibrium set for all goods but z_2 and U, unless excess demand for the latter falls by more than k per cent. The case where the relative fall in excess demand for cash balances equals k per cent is one that Lange has called the "zero monetary effect."[91]

In this case we may measure the decline in the "price of goods" unambiguously as k per cent, so that we need not measure the real value of the decline in cash balances in wage units. Suppose, then, we had an economy which was characterized at all points by a zero monetary effect; that is, one where

$$(59) \qquad \frac{dE_u}{E_u} \equiv \frac{dP_{z_2}}{P_{z_2}}$$

[90] This result was derived explicitly by Lange, (6), pp. 5–20, but it was clearly stated by Keynes, (1), pp. 259–60. Lange develops his analysis for an economy in which all real excess demands are homogeneous of degree zero in all prices but P_e (the price of securities), the supply of money, and the supply of securities, which is the homogeneity postulate implicit in neoclassical systems not characterized by Say's Identity.

[91] O. Lange, (6), pp. 5–20.

We shall term such an unrealistic economy a "quasi-Say's Identity" economy. Such a system would be one in which wage flexibility would fail to eliminate unemployment, and prices would tumble toward zero as abortive efforts to reduce the real wage were made by laborers. If, instead, we began from a position of full employment equilibrium, and by relaxing our equilibrium conditions, effected arbitrarily a k per cent reduction in all prices but P_e, real-balance effects would be zero. We should have the special case of the zero monetary effect where $E_u \equiv 0$, and we should have a full-blown Say's Identity economy. Just as in the latter, a quasi-Say's Identity economy would be a dichotomized economy, if all prices were flexible, with an indeterminate price level.

But such a model would be an alteration of the neoclassical models in two important respects. First, the *excess* demand for money balances in neoclassical systems is not homogeneous of degree one in all prices but P_e, even if *demand* for such balances were assumed to be. At an initial position of positive excess demand for cash, the fixity of the money supply assured that a k per cent decline in all prices but P_e and (we assume for the moment) a k per cent decline in the demand for money balances would lead to a greater-than-k percentage decline in excess demand for money.[92] Under these conditions, then $\frac{dE_{z_2}}{dP_{z_2}} < 0$.

The neoclassical models implied, if they did not state explicitly, a second quality of the excess demand for nominal cash balances. The quantity theory of money assumed that a k per cent increase in the supply of money, ceteris paribus, with a fixed output and velocity of money, would lead to a k per cent increase in all prices but P_e. The mechanism which projected the economy to the new price level was the operation of the real-balance effect of an increase in the money supply. For the individual, demands for and supplies of the included goods were functions of real balances. Were this "real-balance effect" not to operate, so that the public swallowed increases in the money supply indefinitely, we should have a Say's Identity or quasi-Say's Identity economy, depending upon whether we began with an equilibrium or disequilibrium in the money market, and the economy would be effectively dichotomized.[93]

But a drop in all prices save P_e by k per cent, the supply of money being constant, is equivalent to a rise in the money supply by $100\left(\frac{k}{100 - k}\right)$ per cent. This enhancement of real purchasing power inherent in the public's stock of money wealth should lead to shifts in the demand for goods in the included sector. It may increase the demand for consumption

[92] O. Lange, (6), p. 14. With a fixed supply of money, Q_u, the demand for money, X_u, must fall by $k\left(1 - \frac{Q_u}{X_u}\right)$ if the excess demand for money is to fall by k per cent.

[93] This work is, of course, that of Patinkin. See (4), pp. 39–45.

goods, in which case the "Pigou effect" operates to prevent all prices from falling k per cent in equilibrium, thereby decreasing the excess supply of labor in the manner stated above.[94] Should it increase the demand for securities we have the "Keynes Effect."[95] Or, lastly, should it decrease the supply of labor (increase the demand for leisure) by virtue of the larger real balances held by laborers, we should have the "Tobin effect."[96] Any or all of these effects will lead to a fall in the excess supply of labor, or, identically, a decline in the nominal excess demand for money by more than k per cent. Continued declines in P_{z_2} under such conditions will lead the economy back to full equilibrium.

Therefore, with the real supply of money increasing and the real demand for it decreasing as its price rises, the neoclassical system should yield the desired result. But, if we wish to make the assumption that the demand for nominal cash balances falls exactly $k\left[1-\frac{Q_u}{X_u}\right]$ per cent with a k per cent decline in all prices but P_e, or the assumption that the monetary authorities reduce the money supply by k per cent while the demand for cash balances is homogeneous of degree one in all prices but P_e, we may have a quasi-Say's Identity economy, and thereby achieve Keynes's goal. Needless to say, it is difficult to find any virtue in such a *deus ex machina*.

9.c. Keynes's Identity

Of course, Keynes did not simply employ the above model with a zero monetary effect to obtain his results. He did state the problem as we have done:

[94] This effect was discussed by A. Pigou in (3); (2); and (4), pp. 123–34. Pigou's analysis originally was stated in terms of the long run and for the effect of a drop in prices on the supply of money wealth. Kalecki pointed out that the effect could operate only on that portion of the money supply which was not offset by private indebtedness to the banking system. See M. Kalecki, (1), pp. 131–2. Pigou changed his concept in his later work to one of the effect of a fall in prices on physical as well as money wealth, but concept remained a long-run concept.

This effect was stressed by Haberler in (2), pp. 242, 389, 403, and 491–503, in the context of the short-run. It was independently discovered by T. de Scitovszky, (1), but he felt it to be of such long-run quality that it held true only of generations, not of individuals (pp. 72–3) His wealth concept is one of money balances in the special conditions of his noncapitalistic model.

The effect of wealth enhancements upon consumption has received extensive consideration since these early formulations. Patinkin has refined Pigou's "wealth" concept to one of net indebtedness of government. See (2), and J. Tobin, (1), p. 112. The effect of an increase in physical wealth upon consumption was noted briefly by Keynes. Cf. G. Ackley, (1), and D. Patinkin, (4) p. 464.

[95] This will be discussed extensively below. The term is Haberler's used in (5), and is to be distinguished from Ackley's use of the same term for the long-run effect described in the previous footnote.

[96] J. Tobin, (1). Should this effect operate, as Tobin points out, the supply of labor becomes a function of the money wage, lending credence to the familiar Keynesian assumption. See p. 118.

"... For, whilst no one would wish to deny the proposition that a reduction in money-wages *accompanied by the same aggregate effective demand as before* will be associated with an increase in employment, the precise question at issue is whether the reduction in money-wages will or will not be accompanied by the same aggregate effective demand as before measured in money, or, at any rate, by an aggregate effective demand which is not reduced in full proportion to the reduction in money-wages. . . . ."[97]

And he was quite dogmatic in answering it for one set of postulated circumstances—his model in which changes in expectations and other shift-inducing factors were not allowed to occur, so that his functions did not shift in response to such factors:

"... Does a reduction in money-wages have a direct tendency, *ceteris paribus*, to increase employment, '*ceteris paribus*' being taken to mean that the propensity to consume, the schedule of the marginal efficiency of capital and the rate of interest are the same as before for the community as a whole? . . . we have already answered in the negative. . . . ."[98]

The one hedge on direct effects was that the interest rate be held constant, an assumption we shall discuss below.

In his discussion of a second model, where he allows shifts in the schedules to occur, Keynes concludes that the impact upon the propensity to consume will probably be downward because of the redistribution effects of wage changes, and that shifts in the liquidity preference and marginal efficiency schedules are likely to be unfavorable to a reduction in the excess supply of labor. These conclusions are much less dogmatic than those of the "first" model above.[99]

We shall return to this first model where distributional and expectational shifts are absent. How did Keynes obtain these results? One of the difficulties encountered in answering the question is that neither Keynes nor his critics possessed the Ricardian virtue so admired by Keynes in the following quotation:

"... Ricardo offers us the supreme intellectual achievement unattainable by weaker spirits, of adopting a hypothetical world remote from experience as though it were the world of experience and then living in it consistently. With most of his successors common sense cannot help breaking in—with injury to their logical consistency."[100]

Common sense obstructs logical consistency at crucial points. Keynes's

[97] J. Keynes, (1), pp. 259–60. Quoted by permission.
[98] J. Keynes, (1), p. 260. Quoted by permission.
[99] J. Keynes, (1), pp. 261–71.
[100] J. Keynes, (1), p. 192. Quoted by permission.

hedge concerning the constant rate of interest in his conclusion above is one such example. From the side of his critics the debate whether rigid money wages are or are not required in the Keynesian model to obtain an underemployment equilibrium is another example. Those who would argue that they are do so in this wise: if wages were not rigid downward, the decline in prices would lower the interest rate, the impact of which upon investment would decrease unemployment, or, failing that, would bring about real-balance effects which would ultimately restore full employment. Therefore, the Keynesian model must rely upon rigid wages for its underemployment.[101]

Let us follow the Ricardian high road, arguing (1) that Keynes did construct a system which yielded an excess supply of labor with no tendency towards self-correction, (2) that it was not merely the existing neoclassical subcase of rigid money wages, and (3) that it was not a naïve quasi-Say's Identity economy. We shall seek the conditions necessary to obtain the desired results within the Keynesian framework, taking care to guard against the intrusion of "common sense" modifications of the conclusions following from logical consistency.

We alter our assumption about expectations in only one respect: by assuming that there is given for expectations of any future P_e (the price of securities) a schedule relating it to current P_e, and that this schedule is stable and invariant throughout our analysis. We also make one alteration in our premises concerning securities, assuming now that a stock of them exists at the beginning of the period, all of which are held by and are debts of private individuals. This assumption assures us that, if individuals and firms are similar in their reactions to gains and losses in real wealth, no "real-indebtedness effect" will occur with price declines, since the gain in real wealth by creditors will be exactly matched by the rise in the burdens of debtors.[102] The only other non-money stock of existing wealth at the start of the period is holdings of Z_1, the nondepreciating capital good, whose value changes proportionately with P_{z_1}.

Now, let us start with a full general equilibrium and assume that the public suddenly desires increased real balances, obtaining them by reducing excess demands for consumption and investment goods. Let all markets but those for labor and money be reequilibrated, so that (56) holds at the initial disequilibrium position in this economy as in our neoclassical economy.

As before we assume that P_{z_2} (the wage rate) is bid down k per cent, and that all prices but P_e fall an equivalent percentage. This will not disturb the equilibrium of the markets for Y_1, Y_2, z_1, and Z_1, nor will it

[101] Compare F. Modigliani, (1), p. 211; A. Pigou, (3), pp. 241–51; D. Patinkin, (2), pp. 278–9; and G. Haberler, (4), p. 167.

[102] This result springs from Kalecki's exception to Pigou's early analysis and is explicitly applied to securities by Patinkin in (4), p. 205.

change the excess supply of z_2, if no real purchasing power enters this real sector from the paper (money and securities) sector.

If we denote by dE_u^* the differential of cash balances before the securities market is returned to equilibrium, then, when only the markets for U, e, and z_2 are out of equilibrium, it follows from (52) that

$$\text{(60)} \qquad \frac{-dE_u^*}{dP_{z_2}} - P_e \frac{dE_e}{dP_{z_2}} \equiv E_{z_2} + P_{z_2} \frac{dE_{z_2}}{dP_{z_2}}$$

and, substituting for E_{z_2} from (56)

$$\text{(61)} \qquad \frac{E_u}{P_{z_2}} \left[1 - \frac{dE_u^*}{E_u} \frac{P_{z_2}}{dP_{z_2}} - P_e \frac{dE_e}{E_u} \frac{P_{z_2}}{dP_{z_2}} \right] \equiv P_{z_2} \frac{dE_{z_2}}{dP_{z_2}}$$

Since we shall rule out negative real-balance effects, in order that $\frac{dE_{z_2}}{dP_{z_2}} = 0$ it is required that

$$\text{(62)} \qquad \frac{dE_u^*}{E_u} + P_e \frac{dE_e}{E_u} = \frac{dP_{z_2}}{P_{z_2}}$$

That is, the money value of the change in excess demand for paper assets as a percentage of the excess demand for money formerly existing in the initial state of disequilibrium must be equal to the percentage price change. But since we assume constant stocks of money and may assume negligible changes in the stock of securities by virtue of current investment demand, changes in the excess demand for money and for securities are equal to changes in the *demand* for these paper assets. Therefore, we may state condition (62) as follows: the value of the change in demand for paper assets must equal $-k$ times the excess demand for money in the initial disequilibrium position.

If this condition holds, the direct impact of the wage decline on the real sector, the rate of interest held constant, (which is equivalent to P_e being held constant) will be nonexistent, in line with Keynes's conclusion. But, of course, the real value of money holdings will have increased by virtue of the price decline. Since P_e is "the price which equilibrates the desire to hold wealth in the form of cash with the available quantity of cash,"[103] or, in Metzler's apt phrase, P_e is determined "largely by the decisions of asset-holders concerning the proportions in which they wish to hold money and securities,"[104] the ratio of real money wealth to real security wealth will have risen, and under Keynes's assumption that the desire to hold money rises as P_e rises, the latter must be allowed to restore equilibrium in the paper asset sector. Holding tenaciously to our goal of obtaining a model in which such adjustments do not affect the excess supply of labor, we must obtain this re-equilibration of the securi-

[103] J. Keynes, (1), p. 167.
[104] L. Metzler, (4), pp. 97–8.

ties market without disturbing E_{z_2}. Let

$$(63) \qquad k' = \frac{dE_u}{E_u}$$

where dE_u is the final change in the excess demand for nominal cash balances after all markets but that for labor have been reequilibrated, and E_u is the excess demand for cash in the initial disequilibrium position. Then Keynes's Identity states that

$$(64) \qquad dE_u^* - dE_u \equiv Q_e dP_e$$

or

$$(65) \qquad k' \equiv \frac{dE_u^* - Q_e dP_e}{E_u}$$

where Q_e is the initial stock of securities. That is, Keynes's Identity states: given a state of excess supply in the labor market and a fall in the money wage rate, this excess supply will never be affected if the monetary effect is confined to the securities market or is absent.[105]

If the demand for money is less-than-infinitely elastic with respect to P_e in this "Keynesian" model, P_e must rise and all potential effects of this rise (equals a fall in the rate of interest) on the real goods sector must be effectively nullified to preserve Keynes's Identity. The demand for consumption and investment goods must be completely interest-inelastic, or else net investment would occur to contradict Keynes's Identity. That is, we should be back to the neoclassical world where falling interest rates were changing investment (and savings?) to reduce the excess supply of labor.

This neoclassical model is a step toward the economy Keynes envisages: Keynes's Identity holds, but substitution, expansion, and income effects springing from the reduction in the interest rate act to reduce the excess supply of labor. In his constant interest rate hedge, above, and in the following quotation, it appears clear that we have not yet reached a distinctively Keynesian economy:

". . . in the extreme case where money-wages are assumed to fall without limit in face of involuntary unemployment through a futile competition for employment between the unemployed laborers, there will, it is true, be only two possible long-period positions—full employment and the level of employment corresponding to the rate of interest at which liquidity-preference becomes absolute (in the event of this being less than full employment). . . ."[106]

[105] Patinkin seems to have been the first to state this explicitly in (4) pp. 14, 163, and pp. 463–71. See also L. Metzler, (4), p. 95.

[106] J. Keynes, (1), p. 191.

We may now relax our Ricardian rigor to assume that E_{z_2} rises as the economy functions in a crippled neoclassical manner until the liquidity trap is reached. Keynes's Identity appears to be a peculiar encumbrance, keeping direct real-balance effects out of the real goods markets, but income, expansion, and substitution effects are operating in the familiar way to reduce unemployment.

But when we have reached the point where the demand for cash balances becomes infinitely elastic, say at P'_e, before E_{z_2} shrinks to zero, we have reached the distinctively Keynesian model.[107] Further declines in the interest rate are arrested and shifts in the savings, investment, and supply of labor schedules by virtue of the real-balance effect are prevented by Keynes's Identity: the economy effectively becomes a quasi-Say's Identity economy. Substitution and income effects ceased with cessation of rises in P_e at the ceiling P'_e, and now the real-balance effect, the only remaining effect which can reduce unemployment, disappears.

Common sense will out! Haberler simply refuses to accept this Keynesian equilibrium as a resting place. If P_{z_2} continues to fall, even in the liquidity trap the schedules must shift by virtue of the real-balance effect, he argues, and "the truth is that what would happen in this case cannot be told within the Keynesian framework."[108] A continuous rise in real wealth being wholly expended on money balances cannot continue, common sense argues. But it must if the contribution of Keynes to general equilibrium systems is to exist at all, and we shall retain the Ricardian virtue.

Going down the Keynesian road to its logical end, we are troubled by the effective appearance of Lange's zero monetary effect in a world without income, substitution, or expansion effects to anchor us. P_e is consistent with any level of money prices which does not lower it from the liquidity trap value P'_e. Therefore, the price level is indeterminate, and, if P_{z_2} remains flexible, it will fall toward zero and take all prices but P_e with it. We may determine a price level, of course, by arbitrarily setting a price floor on some one good, such as the money wage rate, as Keynes does. Thus, rigid money wages are necessary to determine a price level, not to obtain a less-than-full-employment equilibrium in the Keynesian model.

But note what has been done to the neoclassical general equilibrium model in constructing this Keynesian model. Initially, money and real goods are substitutes in the sense that the public will seek to increase its excess demand for money by reducing excess demand for real goods, or, presumably, *vice versa*. But once this initial substitution has taken place, the economy is suddenly dichotomized to a partial extent.[109] Even while

[107] Or at least what Metzler has called the Keynesian system at its simplest. L. Metzler, (4), pp. 95–6. See also D. Patinkin, (1), p. 257.

[108] G. Haberler, (4), p. 169, and also (5).

[109] Patinkin hints at this when, after discussing Keynes's limitation of the real-balance effect to securities, he says:

P_e rises it is the income, substitution, and expansion effects which are holding paper and real sectors together; no real-balance effect is operating to hold them together. When this tenuous reed breaks, the dichotomy is complete; the public swallows increased real balances limitlessly.

This is what we mean by "partial dichotomization." The real value of excess demand in the real goods sector remains constant as that of the paper sector swells without limit. The price level is indeterminate and P'_e (the ceiling price of securities) ceases to exercise any effect upon the excess demands for real goods. The initial ability of the public to increase excess demand for cash at the expense of excess supplies of real goods indicates that the dichotomy is not complete. Why it is that once crossed the bridge ceases to exist is not clear, even given the expectations of future movement in P_e. If the public always sought to change its real balances by adjusting only its holdings of securities, we should have a complete dichotomy between paper and real sectors in this sense, even though income, substitution, and expansion effects would hold both together. But, then, how Pyrrhic would be the Keynesian "victory" over Say's Identity!

9.d. A Summary

In an attempt to isolate the meaning of Keynesian economics for the body of general equilibrium theory, we have sought to find in it a rigorous model which achieves the results its author desired. Certainly we have been rigorous and simple, perhaps overly so for a fair presentation of the kernel of theoretical Keynesianism stripped of its *obiter dicta.* Once more we plead the inevitability of the vice given the choice of the task, and leave to the reader the decision of how great the distortion is.

We have attempted to show the differences of Keynes's model from those such as Model V-2 by bringing to the fore the Keynesian Identity—a statement of the exclusive nature of the real-balance effect permissible in the system. More importantly, we have pointed to the implications of this Identity, strictly adhered to in full Ricardian virtue, for the dichotomization of the economy into real and paper-asset sectors.

What remains of the Keynesian performance in this theoretical area if one's intuition leads one to view its theorems sceptically because of the presence of the Keynes Identity postulate? The writer believes that Patinkin's interpretation will grow to be more widely accepted in the future.[110] This is that involuntary unemployment is most readily, perhaps only, explainable in terms of the dynamics of adjustment of the market economy. To the extent that Keynes focussed attention upon the slow-

"Looking back on the nature of these errors, we cannot but be struck by the irony that they should have emanated from the man who did most to demonstrate the fundamental inseparability of the real and monetary sectors of the economy." (1), p. 270.

[110] D. Patinkin, (4), pp. 236–7.

ness, or weakness, of these adjustments, his analysis contributes fruitful insights. But in the field of static general equilibrium theory, where the existence of counteracting forces, however weak, is sufficient to yield full employment, his performance was essentially a failure.

10. A Recapitulation

The introduction of inventories and money as capital goods with synchronization functions—for the individual and society in the first case and for the individual in the second—has been the theme of this chapter. In the case of money, we have attempted to show that the symmetry of treatment of it with physical capital good assets allows the development of a theory of money which is most fruitful in bringing out the conditions for its existence, for the role it performs in the economy, and for the separability of price determination for its services and for itself as an asset.

The introduction of money and inventories led us to the development of our final and complete neoclassical general equilibrium model, Model V-2. We have constructed it in such wise as to eliminate Say's Identity and have shown that money is a fully integrated good in it. Further, in the entrepreneurial sector, we have developed a linear programming-game theoretic model for the firm's determination of money balances in a profit maximization schema, both for perfect certainty and for pure risk.

Finally, with this background, we have compared a more recent general equilibrium model—the Keynesian—with our own, and drawn the conclusion that it contains elements of dichotomization which are not present in Model V-2.

PART III

EXTENSIONS OF THE NEOCLASSICAL CONSTRUCTS

CHAPTER 6

STATIC LINEAR SYSTEMS

1. Introduction

It has been a consistent theme in Parts I and II of this book that the ability of general models to yield operational theorems is rapidly exhausted for any given level of abstraction from empirical data as the number of variables and equations increases. Indeed, we have not attempted an equilibrium displacement analysis for any full production, investment, or money model, but have restricted such treatment to submodels of them. The distressing complexity of Models III, IV, and V is ample evidence of the analytical impotence of general systems which was illustrated in Chapter 1.

Also indicated in Chapter 1, however, were paths of exit from such Minoan labyrinths as have been developed in Part II: partial analysis, aggregation, and simplification of the interrelationships to the point where some hope might exist of obtaining the matrices of slopes needed for the derivation of theorems. Of course, any method which is successful in yielding operational theorems, particularly of a quantitative nature, is likely to have used all three simplifying procedures to achieve analytical meaningfulness.

One significant direction of movement for modern economic theory is the increasing reliance upon the third method, not only for general but for partial systems as well. Two separate sources of impulsion have inspired this movement: the desire to fit general systems statistically and the development of computational techniques and equipment to solve extremum problems previously beyond practical handling. Game theory, statistical decision theory in large part, linear programming, and input-output analysis are current analytical frameworks applicable to linear economic systems—models incorporating linear relationships among variables to represent realistic functions accurately or approximately.

The potential richness of input-output analysis and linear programming for the analysis of general interdependence imposes the need to consider them extensively. Leontief's input-output technique is a frontal assault on the problem of retaining some of the complex interdependence of our models in Part II in the derivation of theorems with quantitative content. In this chapter we shall discuss the open static model at some length and describe the closed static model; we shall treat the dynamic model in Chapter 8. We have already developed the theory of linear programming in terms of vector spaces—a form which best serves the over-all purposes of this book—in Chapter 3, so that our treatment of it need be less extensive than that of input-output systems, and will be in the context of its use in general theoretical systems.

2. The Open Input-Output Model As an Equilibrium Model

It is most fruitful in judging the extent of retreat from our models of Part II along the routes indicated above to derive an input-output model from the neoclassical models. We shall return, therefore, to Model III-1 of Chapter 3, which depicts a production economy for conditions of fixed minimal coefficients of production. We shall be most interested in the simplified version of the model as presented in (7) of Chapter 3, where the symbol x has been substituted for equilibrium total demand and equilibrium total supply. We shall let $n = 3$ and $m = 2$, and reproduce that system for this case as follows:

$$
(1)\quad
\begin{aligned}
&1. && X_2^\circ - H_2(P_1, P_2, P_3, P_{z_1}, P_{z_2}; Q_{Z_1}, Q_{Z_2}) = 0\\
&2. && X_3^\circ - H_3(P_1, P_2, P_3, P_{z_1}, P_{z_2}; Q_{Z_1}, Q_{Z_2}) = 0\\
&3. && X_1^\circ P_1 - x_{z_1}P_{z_1} - x_{z_2}P_{z_2} + X_2^\circ P_2 + X_3^\circ P_3 = 0\\
&4. && x_{z_1} + H_{z_1}(P_1, P_2, P_3, P_{z_1}, P_{z_2}; Q_{Z_1}, Q_{Z_2}) - Q_{Z_1} = 0\\
&5. && x_{z_2} + H_{z_2}(P_1, P_2, P_3, P_{z_1}, P_{z_2}; Q_{Z_1}, Q_{Z_2}) - Q_{Z_2} = 0\\
&6. && x_1 - X_1^\circ - X_1^{*\circ} = 0\\
&7. && x_2 - X_2^\circ - X_2^{*\circ} = 0\\
&8. && x_3 - X_3^\circ - X_3^{*\circ} = 0\\
&9. && X_1^{*\circ} - a_{11}x_1 - a_{12}x_2 - a_{13}x_3 = 0\\
&10. && X_2^{*\circ} - a_{21}x_1 - a_{22}x_2 - a_{23}x_3 = 0\\
&11. && X_3^{*\circ} - a_{31}x_1 - a_{32}x_2 - a_{33}x_3 = 0\\
&12. && x_{z_1} - a_{z_1 1}x_1 - a_{z_1 2}x_2 - a_{z_1 3}x_3 = 0\\
&13. && x_{z_2} - a_{z_2 1}x_1 - a_{z_2 2}x_2 - a_{z_2 3}x_3 = 0\\
&14. && P_1^\circ - a_{11}P_1^\circ - a_{21}P_2^\circ - a_{31}P_3^\circ - a_{z_1 1}P_{z_1} - a_{z_2 1}P_{z_2} = 0\\
&15. && P_2^\circ - a_{12}P_1^\circ - a_{22}P_2^\circ - a_{32}P_3^\circ - a_{z_1 2}P_{z_1} - a_{z_2 2}P_{z_2} = 0\\
&16. && P_3^\circ - a_{13}P_1^\circ - a_{23}P_2^\circ - a_{33}P_3^\circ - a_{z_1 3}P_{z_1} - a_{z_2 3}P_{z_2} = 0
\end{aligned}
$$

Note that we are using an external *numéraire*. Henceforth, we shall eliminate the "degree" marks denoting equilibrium values, although we retain their meaning implicitly.

We shall now focus upon the problems of converting (1) into a model which can be fitted with realistic data and solved. To do so requires the recognition that certain of the functions are in all probability nonlinear in form and much too difficult to fit empirically. In particular, the functions H_j and H_i, and the variables whose values they determine "directly,"

X_1, X_2, X_3, x_{z_1}, and x_{z_2}, cannot be included in the operational model as variables. Therefore, (1) we convert X_1, X_2, and X_3 to data of the model, (2) we assume that at the current P_{z_1} and P_{z_2} supplies of z_1 and z_2 are perfectly elastic for all relevant ranges in which our solutions will occur, and, therefore, that (3) P_{z_1} and P_{z_2} are also data of the model. Thus, unemployment of any factor service will not result in downward pressures on its price, and excess demand for it will be ignored as a possibility; in both these respects we are to some degree in the land of Keynes.

These assumptions allow us to simplify the model in (1). We may remove equations (1-1) through (1-5)—the functions depicting non-specific solutions to simple exchange models—from the system since the phenomena they depict as variable are now taken as parameters. Equations (1-12 and -13) may be removed as merely statements of rather uninteresting identities *defining* the demands for and supplies of each factor service. If we substitute from (1-6, -7, and -8) for the X_j^*-terms, system (1) reduces to the following much simpler model:

(2)

$$
\begin{aligned}
&1. \quad (1 - a_{11})x_1 - a_{12}x_2 - a_{13}x_3 = X_1 \\
&2. \quad -a_{21}x_1 + (1 - a_{22})x_2 - a_{23}x_3 = X_2 \\
&3. \quad -a_{31}x_1 - a_{32}x_2 + (1 - a_{33})x_3 = X_3 \\
&4. \quad (1 - a_{11})P_1 - a_{21}P_2 - a_{31}P_3 = a_{z_11}P_{z_1} + a_{z_21}P_{z_2} \\
&5. \quad -a_{12}P_1 + (1 - a_{22})P_2 - a_{32}P_3 = a_{z_12}P_{z_1} + a_{z_22}P_{z_2} \\
&6. \quad -a_{13}P_1 - a_{23}P_2 + (1 - a_{33})P_3 = a_{z_13}P_{z_1} + a_{z_23}P_{z_2}
\end{aligned}
$$

These are six equations to solve for the x_j and P_j, with the a-coefficients, X_j, and P_i as data.

In matrix form, (2) would become:

(3)

$$
\begin{bmatrix}
1 - a_{11} & -a_{12} & -a_{13} & 0 & 0 & 0 \\
-a_{21} & 1 - a_{22} & -a_{23} & 0 & 0 & 0 \\
-a_{31} & -a_{32} & 1 - a_{33} & 0 & 0 & 0 \\
0 & 0 & 0 & 1 - a_{11} & -a_{21} & -a_{31} \\
0 & 0 & 0 & -a_{12} & 1 - a_{22} & -a_{32} \\
0 & 0 & 0 & -a_{13} & -a_{23} & 1 - a_{33}
\end{bmatrix}
\begin{bmatrix} x_1 \\ x_2 \\ x_3 \\ P_1 \\ P_2 \\ P_3 \end{bmatrix}
=
\begin{bmatrix} X_1 \\ X_2 \\ X_3 \\ a_{z_11}P_{z_1} + a_{z_21}P_{z_2} \\ a_{z_12}P_{z_1} + a_{z_22}P_{z_2} \\ a_{z_13}P_{z_1} + a_{z_23}P_{z_2} \end{bmatrix}
$$

or

(4)

$$[D][V] = [K]$$

Since this is a linear system $[D]$ remains unchanged if $[V]$ were to become $[dV]$ and $[K]$ were to become $[dK]$. It should be compared, therefore, with $[D]$ in (8) of Chapter 3, which was obtained from shocking the generating model of (2) in the present chapter. The present matrix is much smaller than (8) of Chapter 3, which was obtained from shocking the more complicated model, and it does not contain any price terms or slopes of demand functions, as the latter does. It is, therefore, a considerably simpler system, and, insofar as it involves only technological constants, it affords the hope that it can be fitted with empirical data.

A second, and noteworthy, feature of (3) above is that $[D]$ is decomposable:[1] given the vector of final demands $[X]$ it is possible to solve for the "equilibrium" gross outputs (i.e., entrepreneurial demand for intermediate account plus consumer demand on final account) without any need to specify the a_{z_ij} coefficients or the P_i. Similarly, it is possible by specifying these latter to solve for the P_j without specifying the level of final demand necessary for consumers. Gross outputs independent of factor prices and produced good prices independent of level of output indicate that our simplifying assumptions have allowed us to split Model III-1 down the middle.

Define

$$(5) \qquad [a^*] = \begin{bmatrix} a_{11} & a_{12} & a_{13} \\ a_{21} & a_{22} & a_{23} \\ a_{31} & a_{32} & a_{33} \end{bmatrix}$$

Then when all vectors are column vectors unless transposed:

$$(6) \qquad 1. \quad [\mathrm{I} - a^*]\begin{bmatrix} x_1 \\ x_2 \\ x_3 \end{bmatrix} = \begin{bmatrix} X_1 \\ X_2 \\ X_3 \end{bmatrix}$$

$$2. \quad [P_1, P_2, P_3]'[\mathrm{I} - a^*] = \begin{bmatrix} a_{z_11}P_{z_1} + a_{z_21}P_{z_2} \\ a_{z_12}P_{z_1} + a_{z_22}P_{z_2} \\ a_{z_13}P_{z_1} + a_{z_23}P_{z_2} \end{bmatrix}'$$

where $[I]$ is the identity matrix.

We may take advantage of this separability of outputs and prices in the following way. Given (1) the fixed nature of the a_{z_ij} coefficients and the P_i, (2) given the assumptions concerning prices of goods and costs of production, which in the model above exclude all profits, and (3) given $[a^*]$, the P_j cannot change. Since our policy uses of the model usually center upon outputs as variables, we may define a homogeneous unit to measure all inputs and outputs: the unit of *numéraire*'s worth, or, more realistically, the dollar's worth. As long as prices are constant, a dollar's worth of oranges is a physical unit for the measurement of quantities of oranges. Instead of dealing with dozens of oranges, we may deal with a

[1] See the discussion in Section 2 of Chapter 1. The development of the input-output model we are about to present occurred in W. Leontief, (3) and (4).

dollar's worth and never leave the domain of the physical unit. From the a-coefficients we derive a'-coefficients in the following manner:

$$a'_{st} = a_{st}\frac{P_s}{P_t}, \quad s = j = 1, 2, 3, \ t = j = 1, 2, 3 \tag{7}$$

and

$$\begin{aligned} &1. \quad x'_j = x_j P_j \\ &2. \quad X'_j = X_j P_j \end{aligned} \tag{8}$$

We define

$$[a] = \begin{bmatrix} a'_{11} & a'_{12} & a'_{13} \\ a'_{21} & a'_{22} & a'_{23} \\ a'_{31} & a'_{32} & a'_{33} \end{bmatrix} \tag{9}$$

and system (6-1) may be rewritten:

$$[I - a]\begin{bmatrix} x'_1 \\ x'_2 \\ x'_3 \end{bmatrix} = \begin{bmatrix} X'_1 \\ X'_2 \\ X'_3 \end{bmatrix} \tag{10}$$

which is the model with which we shall deal.

The model in (10) contains three equations in three unknowns. For a given vector of final demands (consumer absorptions of the product of each "sector") in dollar values, the model determines on the basis of the "technological structure" of the economy (i.e., $[a]$) the gross outputs required from each sector in dollar value to support the net levels required for final demand. The difference between gross and net output levels comprises entrepreneurial demands for the output of each sector. Thus, in the final analysis, the Leontief static input-output model for the determination of outputs is a schema which predicts the entrepreneurial demands for each sector's product for use as intermediate product from the desired bill of goods for final demand.

To fix our ideas, it will be convenient to identify each of the three sectors in our model with a realistic industry: let us say that sector 1, producing Y_1, is the agricultural sector; sector 2, producing Y_2, is the automotive industry; and sector 3, with product Y_3, is the paint industry, producing industrial and household finishes. Further, in order to work through several methods of solution to the model, let us assume specific values for the a'-coefficients:

$$[I - a] = \begin{bmatrix} 1 & 0 & 0 \\ 0 & 1 & 0 \\ 0 & 0 & 1 \end{bmatrix} - \begin{bmatrix} .05 & 0 & .40 \\ .01 & .08 & 0 \\ .03 & .30 & .05 \end{bmatrix} = \begin{bmatrix} .95 & 0 & -.40 \\ -.01 & .92 & 0 \\ -.03 & -.30 & .95 \end{bmatrix} \tag{11}$$

The diagonal element in each row of $[a]$ reveals the cents' worth of each dollar's worth of gross output which is used by the producing industry itself: for every \$1 of agricultural products produced by sector 1, \$.05 of agricultural product is used up, so that only \$.95 of agricultural product leaves the industry, and so forth. Off-diagonal elements in each row reveal the shipments to all other sectors per dollar of those sectors' outputs: the agricultural sector ships no product directly to the automotive industry and \$.40 of product for every \$1 of gross output of the paint industry, and so forth. Each column depicts, for the industry associated with that column, the cents' worth of each sector's goods, including its own, that enter into the production of one dollar's worth of its product: \$.05 of agricultural output enters into every dollar of agricultural output, \$.01 of automotive products and \$.03 of paint products also enter, and so forth. Since we derived this input-output model from Model III-1, where no investment occurs and all surpluses are eliminated in equilibrium, each column must sum to \$1 when the absorptions of factor services z_i, which are external to the model for reasons developed above, are added in. Let us make the further assumptions:

$$\begin{aligned} a'_{z_1 1} &= .60,\ a'_{z_2 1} = .31 \\ a'_{z_1 2} &= .50,\ a'_{z_2 2} = .12 \\ a'_{z_1 3} &= .30,\ a'_{z_2 3} = .25 \end{aligned} \tag{12}$$

In a period of limited war we assume that the nation's planners desire to increase automotive production for the military by \$10(billion), but that, because of the already existing strain upon the limiting resources in the agricultural sector, they fear that such an injection of new demand would be infeasible. The input-output system is constructed to yield an answer to such a feasibility problem: given the bill of goods

$$[\Delta X'] = [0,\ 10,\ 0]$$

what increases in gross outputs of all sectors would be necessary to sustain such an increment, with particular reference to the increase in output implied for sector 1, the agricultural sector?

In terms of our analysis of Chapter 1, we may solve this system to obtain a specific solution for the given data $[\Delta X']$, or to obtain a nonspecific solution. We shall obtain a specific solution in two ways: iteratively and directly.

2.a. The Specific Solution: Iterative Method

In a naïve approach to answering the question posed by the planners we might be tempted to multiply $[a]$ by $[\Delta X']$ to obtain the direct requirements of the bill of goods, and view the result as the answer sought. That is, with the column-vector convention of this book in force,

$$[a][0,\ 10,\ 0] = [0,\ .80,\ 3.00] \tag{13}$$

Thus, we might conclude that the desired bill of goods imposes no burden upon the agricultural sector, a cost of \$.80 (over and above the \$10 of final automotive product) of automotive product, and a burden of $3 in paint products. The bill might be termed feasible since agricultural products are not revealed as requisite.

But the vector of requirements derived in (13) is only the *direct* requirements of the bill of goods: those direct requirements have direct requirements of their own which have not been taken into account. Therefore, we should inject these direct requirements into the system exactly as we did the bill of goods:

$$(14) \qquad [a][0, .8, 3] = [1.20, .06, .39]$$

But these in turn have direct requirements to the following extent:

$$(15) \qquad [a][1.2, .06, .39] = [.22, .01, .08]$$

And these have direct requirements:

$$(16) \qquad [a][.22, .01, .08] = [.04, 0, .01]$$

and so forth indefinitely.

If the question is to be answered accurately—taking into account the interdependence of system (10)—*all* of these requirements must be added to obtain the *total* impact of the bill of goods upon the economy. That is,

$$(17) \qquad \begin{bmatrix} \Delta x_1' \\ \Delta x_2' \\ \Delta x_3' \end{bmatrix} = \begin{bmatrix} 0 \\ 10 \\ 0 \end{bmatrix} + \begin{bmatrix} 0 \\ .80 \\ 3.00 \end{bmatrix} + \begin{bmatrix} 1.20 \\ .06 \\ .39 \end{bmatrix} + \begin{bmatrix} .22 \\ .01 \\ .08 \end{bmatrix} + \begin{bmatrix} .04 \\ 0 \\ .01 \end{bmatrix} + \cdots \cong \begin{bmatrix} 1.46 \\ 10.87 \\ 3.48 \end{bmatrix}$$

Of course we may continue this process of obtaining iterative rounds indefinitely, but in practice after six or seven such rounds the requirements will have fallen to such small amounts as to allow extrapolation of the results rather accurately to obtain good approximations to the sums which would have been obtained had the rounds been infinitely numerous.

These iterative rounds are a computational technique which can be given economic meaning in the manner adopted above, but they must not be given a temporal meaning, i.e., that one succeeds the other in time. This would be giving a tempting but unwarranted dynamic interpretation to economic processes deriving from a wholly static model.

The iterative process is essentially one of expanding a geometric series and summing the results; symbolically,

$$(18) \qquad [\Delta x'] = ([I] + [a] + [a]^2 + [a]^3 + \cdots)[\Delta X'] = [I - a]^{-1}[\Delta X']$$

the last equation holding if the series converges to zero. Thus, if we assure ourselves that this convergence will occur, we may solve the system directly by inverting $[I - a]$. Before we do this, however, let us obtain the specific solution in a direct manner.

2.b. The Specific Solution: Cramer's Method

Obviously we may simply treat system (10) as a set of n linear, nonhomogeneous equations in n unknowns and solve in straightforward fashion. Indeed, this is the mathematical manner of obtaining the sum in (17) without the need for an infinite number of iterative multiplications. If we do solve in this manner, using Cramer's method, we obtain the vector of answers

$$(19) \qquad [\Delta x'] = [1.50, 10.90, 3.50]$$

which are quite close to our approximations of (17).

This method yields a solution specific to the data $[\Delta X']$ and therefore has the disadvantage that every time the bill of goods is changed it is necessary to recompute the solution. Therefore, particularly in situations where injections of bills of goods may be numerous, a nonspecific solution which can yield answers for any bill with small computational effort will be preferable.

Before we move to the derivation of this nonspecific solution, however, let us pause to note the policy implications of the results in (19). Obviously, the injection of this bill of goods into the economy *will* have an impact upon agricultural output to the extent of requiring \$1.50 of such product, even though there exists no direct requirement of agricultural goods to produce automobiles. All of this derives, therefore, from the indirect needs of the automotive industry: it requires paint which requires agricultural goods, agricultural goods require agricultural goods and paint, and so forth. Had the policy decision been based only upon the direct requirements of the automotive industry and indirect requirements neglected, the conclusion that the bill of goods was feasible would have been incorrect.

2.c. The Nonspecific Solution

To obtain the nonspecific solution let us interpret the Leontief model as the simplest form of linear production model, and, following the methods discussed in Chapter 3, interpret it in vector spaces. In this interpretation $[I - a]$'s n column vectors depict unit levels of operation of the n productive activities of the economy, and $[x']$ is the vector of activity levels which is mapped by $[I - a]$ onto bill-of-goods space (the equivalent of capacity space in our presentation of Chapter 3). The unit vectors of activity space, mapped onto bill-of-goods space by $[I - a]$, yield a basis of n vectors in this latter space, and the solution $[x']$ is that set of weights which, when applied to this basis, yields $[X']$. The distinctive feature of this model, when compared with the linear programming models of

Chapter 3, is the existence of only one potential basis for bill-of-goods space, instead of a large number of them, implying the existence of only one solution if any solution exists. That is, if any solution exists to a Leontief input-output analysis, it will be unique: only one combination of activities $[x']$ will support the production of any bill of goods, $[X'] \geq 0$.

But if we are interested in the nonspecific solution to the model we are interested in that matrix $[I - a]^{-1}$ which maps $[X']$ onto $[x']$; i.e., we are interested in the system:

$$[I - a]^{-1}[X'] = [x'] \tag{20}$$

In vector space terms, $[I - a]^{-1}$ maps the unit vectors in bill-of-goods space into activities space, showing what levels of each activity must be adopted to obtain successively the unit of each sector's output as final demand. This provides n vectors in activities space from which one basis may be formed, and $[X']$ then becomes the set of weights which carries this basis into the vector $[x']$. As our notation indicates the set of column vectors which maps the unit vectors of bill-of-goods space onto activities space will be the inverse of the $[I - a]$ matrix.

Therefore, the computation of the nonspecific solution to the Leontief model consists in the inversion of $[I - a]$. It is well known that the necessary and sufficient condition for a square matrix to have a unique inverse is that it not be singular, i.e., that the determinant formed by it not disappear. In addition to these mathematical requirements, we shall have to specify that the inverse possess certain characteristics which make it economically meaningful and which must also be reflected in constraints upon $[I - a]$. For the moment we assume both the mathematical and economic conditions to be met.

We may use the pivot method described in Chapter 3 to invert the matrix. Our initial tableau is

(21)

	v_1	v_2	v_3	K	u_1	u_2	u_3
u_1	.95	0	−.4	0	1	0	0
u_2	−.01	.92	0	10	0	1	0
u_3	−.03	−.3	.95	0	0	0	1

where u_1, u_2, and u_3 are the unit vectors in bill-of-goods space, v_1, v_2, and v_3 are the unit vectors in activity space, and K is the bill of goods vector. To get the *specific* solution we shift the basis of (21) to $[v_1, v_2, v_3]$ and get the tableau

(22)

	v_1	v_2	v_3	K	u_1	u_2	u_3
v_1	1	0	0	1.50	1.07	.15	.45
v_2	0	1	0	10.90	.01	1.09	0
v_3	0	0	1	3.50	.04	.32	1.07

The inverse is, then, the matrix formed by the u_j column vectors.

We may write this nonspecific solution for our problem as follows:

$$(23)\qquad \begin{bmatrix} A_{11} & A_{12} & A_{13} \\ A_{21} & A_{22} & A_{23} \\ A_{31} & A_{32} & A_{33} \end{bmatrix} \begin{bmatrix} X'_1 \\ X'_2 \\ X'_3 \end{bmatrix} = \begin{bmatrix} x'_1 \\ x'_2 \\ x'_3 \end{bmatrix}$$

and, substituting,

$$(24)\qquad \begin{bmatrix} 1.07 & .15 & .45 \\ .01 & 1.09 & 0 \\ .04 & .32 & 1.07 \end{bmatrix} \begin{bmatrix} X'_1 \\ X'_2 \\ X'_3 \end{bmatrix} = \begin{bmatrix} x'_1 \\ x'_2 \\ x'_3 \end{bmatrix}$$

Further, from our treatment of the dual linear programming problem we may interpret the u_j vectors in (22) as the absorptions directly and indirectly per unit of final product of the output of each activity. If, then, column by column of $[A]$ in (24) we multiply these activity levels by the respective cost per unit of the activity and sum we will obtain the price of the output, i.e., the P_j. The only costs of each activity in a linear programming sense are the inputs from the external sectors, or factor services, since ultimately all produced goods may be resolved into these factor services exclusively. From (12), and denoting by C_j the factor service cost of the jth sector,

$$(25)\qquad \begin{aligned} &1. \quad C_1 = a'_{z_1 1} + a'_{z_2 1} = .91 \\ &2. \quad C_2 = a'_{z_1 2} + a'_{z_2 2} = .62 \\ &3. \quad C_3 = a'_{z_1 3} + a'_{z_2 3} = .55 \end{aligned}$$

Then,

$$(26)\qquad [C_1, C_2, C_3]'[I - a]^{-1} = [P'_1, P'_2, P'_3]'$$

and

$$(27)\qquad P'_1 = P'_2 = P'_3 = 1$$

This is a correct result which follows from the conversion of the system to a value basis rather than retaining physical units, for such a procedure may be seen from (6), (7), and (8) to be equivalent to converting each product price to unity.

Let us now ask the question: given the existence of an inverse, what conditions on an indecomposable $[I - a]$ are necessary and sufficient to yield an economically meaningful $[I - a]^{-1}$? To be economically meaningful, $[x] \geqq 0$, which implies that $[I - a]^{-1} > 0$ if $[a]$ is indecomposable and, indeed, that $[x] > 0$. For $[x] > 0$ in an indecomposable system, it is necessary and sufficient that the second equation of (18) hold. One sufficiency condition for this convergence when $[a] \geqq 0$ and is indecomposable is due to Solow. If at least one column of $[a]$ sums to less than unity while all other column sums are at most equal to unity, a meaningful solution will exist.[2] Note that in our equilibrium system, where all profits are zero, this implies the requirement that nonproduced inputs enter into at least one activity in order that a "leakage" from the system will occur round by round. In Leontief systems in which the no-profit constraint is not binding, however, this sufficiency condition does not rule out negative profits, so that nonnegative profits for all sectors is not a necessary condition for a meaningful $[I - a]^{-1}$.

Metzler has proved the following sufficiency theorems for meaningfulness. If the $[I - a]$ matrix has (1) all nondiagonal elements nonpositive, (2) all principal diagonal elements positive, and (3) the sum of each row is positive, then the cofactors of all elements of $[I - a] > 0$ and $|I - a| > 0$. From these two qualities it follows that all elements of the inverse will be positive and finite—satisfying not only the requirements for the existence but for the meaningfulness of the inverse as well.[3] Still another interesting theorem for this case is that, in any row, the cofactor for any nondiagonal element will be less than the cofactor of the diagonal element. This implies that an increase of \$1 in X_j' will have a greater impact upon x_j' than upon any x_k', $j \neq k$, and thus that the diagonal element in each column of the inverse will be the maximum element.[4]

More profoundly, the crucial determinant of whether or not a solution exists and is meaningful is whether or not *every* sector can yield net product for final demand after the direct and indirect intermediate requirements for it are taken into consideration. For example, in the simplest case, suppose one or more of the diagonal elements in $[I - a]$ were nonpositive. Suppose $(1 - a_{11}')$ were negative: this implies that to produce \$1 gross output of agricultural products requires current inputs of more than \$1 in agricultural products. If no stocks of agricultural products exist to finance such an illogical operation, there is no possibility of obtaining agricultural output from the model. The agricultural sector is "self-consuming" or "autophagous." It can neither meet the needs of other industries nor of consumer net demand. Similarly, $(1 - a_{jj}')$ cannot equal zero if solutions to the indecomposable system are to exist. Conse-

[2] Compare H. Chenery, (1), pp. 31, 52, and R. Solow, (2). This convergence will occur if and only if the characteristic roots of $[a]$ are less than 1 in modulus. Since a matrix and its transpose have the same characteristic values, the restrictions are equally valid for sums of rows rather than columns. From this it follows that $[I - a]^{-1}$ may be obtained iteratively as $[I - a]^{-1} = [I] + [a] + [a]^2 + [a]^3 + \cdots$. Since all elements in $[I]$ and $[a]$ are nonnegative, it follows that no element of $[I - a]^{-1}$ can be negative, whether or not this series converges. Therefore, this type of economic nonmeaningfulness can be eliminated as a possibility.

[3] These follow from the method of inverting a matrix by use of the adjoint of the matrix. Positive cofactors insure that every term in the adjoint will be positive. Division of these elements by $|I - a|$ when the latter is positive insures positive and finite elements in the inverse.

[4] L. Metzler, (3), pp. 433–8.

quently, one necessary condition upon the $[I - a]$ matrix is that all diagonal terms be positive.

But autophagy can occur in other ways, not so straightforward, but equally effective in preventing the product of a sector from escaping subsystems of sectors. For example, consider the following variation of our input-output example:

$$[I - a] = \begin{bmatrix} .95 & 0 & -.475 \\ -.01 & .93 & 0 \\ -.50 & -.30 & .25 \end{bmatrix} \tag{28}$$

Taken separately each sector is capable of producing product for other sectors, but consider the subsystem formed by sectors 1 and 3. Suppose we desired to produce another unit of agricultural product (sector 1) for consumer demand. We should then have to increase gross output of agricultural products initially by about 1.052 units, given the need for such products to produce themselves. But to produce 1.052 units of agricultural products requires 1.052 $\times$ .5 of paint products (sector 3), or .526 worth of paint products. To produce .526 more of paint for agriculture requires, given the high demands for paint to produce paint, an increase in gross output of .526 $\times$ 4 or 2.104 increase in paint products. But to produce 2.104 new units of paint requires 2.104 $\times$ .475 of agricultural products, or 1 unit of agricultural product—the unit needed for the consumer sector. A similar inability of the paint industry to provide produce to any sector other than the agricultural is revealed in our example. Consequently, although taken separately each industry yields products for outside use, taken together they yield the same type of phenomenon as $(1 - a'_{jj}) = 0$. Therefore, such indirect autophagy must be guarded against.

The method of doing so is best seen with a graph used by Dorfman, Samuelson, and Solow.[5] Figure 6-1 depicts x'_1 on the horizontal axis and x'_3 on the vertical axis. For given desired final demands, X'_1 and X'_3, the following two equations are graphed:

$$\text{(29)} \qquad \begin{aligned} &1. \quad (1 - a'_{11})x'_1 - a'_{13}x'_3 = X'_1 \\ &2. \quad -a'_{31}x'_1 + (1 - a'_{33})x'_3 = X'_3 \end{aligned}$$

We have denoted equation (29-1) as L_1 on the figure and it has an intercept with the horizontal axis where x'_3 is 0 at $\frac{X'_1}{1 - a'_{11}}$, or the gross output necessary to produce only the net demand X'_1. Our requirement that the denominator be positive means that this intersection with the x'_1-axis will not occur at an infinite or a negative value, the latter implying mathematically that the process should be run at negative levels to generate the

[5] R. Dorfman, (1), p. 213. See also W. Evans, (1), p. 56.

net ouput needed. Analogous statements hold for L_2, or (29-2), with its intercept with the x_3'-axis.

The slope of L_1 is $\frac{1 - a_{11}'}{a_{13}'}$ which is positive or negative as a_{13}' is positive or negative. Similarly, the slope of L_2 is $\frac{a_{31}'}{1 - a_{33}'}$, whose sign depends upon the sign of a_{31}'. As a necessary condition to insure that any intersection of

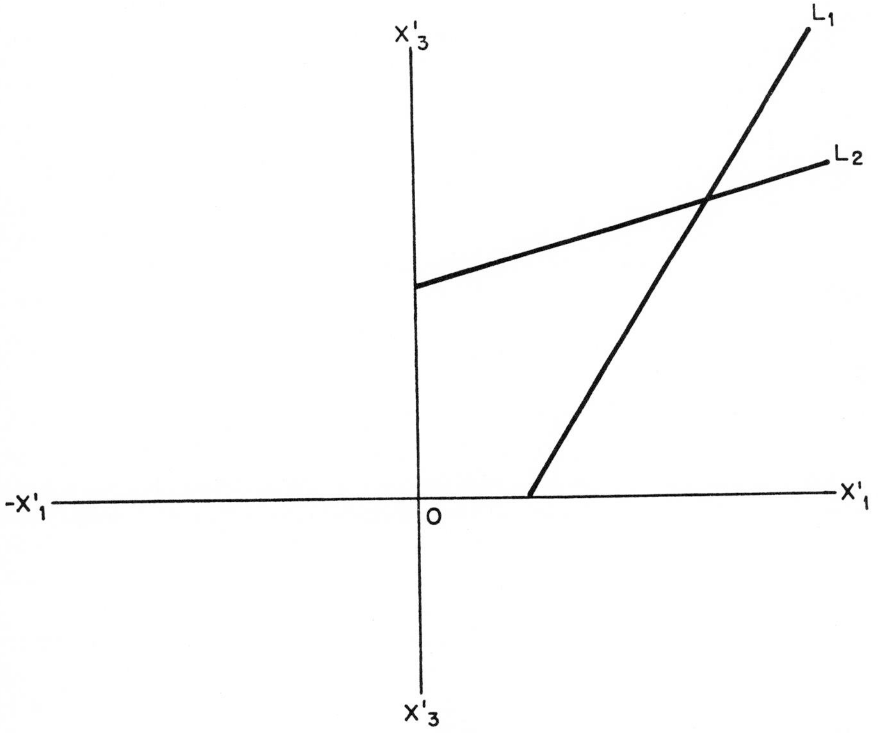

Figure 6-1. The Input-Output Solution

the two curves, if one exists, will occur in the first quadrant where both output levels are positive, we require that all off-diagonal elements in the $[a]$ matrix be nonnegative which will, with the constraints that $(1 - a_{jj}') > 0$ guarantee that L_1 and L_2 will lie in the positive quadrant.

Though this is a necessary condition for a meaningful solution it is not sufficient, since it is quite possible for the slopes of L_1 and L_2 to be such that the lines do not intersect in the positive quadrant. The intersection of the lines yields the values of gross outputs which will provide sufficient product to yield the desired final demands plus the supporting intermediate goods. But if, either the slope of L_1 is equal to the slope of L_2, or the slope of L_1 is less than the slope of L_2, no intersection in the first quadrant will occur, and no meaningful solution will exist.

But these two embarrassing cases will arise only if the two sectors taken together cannot generate product for use outside—the case we have been discussing. The equality of the two slopes, for example, implies that

$$\frac{(1 - a'_{11})}{a'_{13}} = \frac{a'_{31}}{(1 - a'_{33})} \tag{30}$$

But this is the description of the agricultural-paint sector impasse described in (28); if we substitute the values into (30) the trouble is immediately apparent:

$$\frac{.95}{.475} = \frac{.50}{.25} \tag{31}$$

The two lines depicted in Fig. 6-1 with these slopes would be parallel and never intersect. On the other hand, the slope of L_1 being less than the slope of L_2 implies

$$\frac{1 - a'_{11}}{a'_{13}} < \frac{a'_{31}}{1 - a'_{33}} \tag{32}$$

The interpretation of this in terms of our agricultural-paint sector example is the case where the circle of needs created by a desire to get an extra unit of agricultural goods for final demand leads not to a zero output of agricultural goods but to a negative output, and similarly for the case of attempting to increase net output of paint products. In Fig. 6-1, this is illustrated as an intersection of L_1 and L_2 in the third quadrant of the graph where both output levels are negative.

Therefore, the analogue conditions in two-sector interdependence to the $(1 - a'_{jj}) > 0$ conditions are that

$$\frac{(1 - a'_{jj})}{a'_{jk}} > \frac{a'_{kj}}{(1 - a'_{kk})}, \qquad j = 1, \ldots, n, \; k = 1, \ldots, n \quad j \neq k, \tag{33}$$

or, in determinantal form

$$\begin{vmatrix} 1 - a'_{jj} & -a'_{jk} \\ -a'_{kj} & 1 - a'_{kk} \end{vmatrix} > 0 \tag{34}$$

That is, for any Leontief matrix with n sectors, *every* pair of sectors must meet these conditions to assure that no pair forms an indirectly autophagous subsystem.

But in this n-sector system what of triads of sectors forming such subsystems; i.e., of the three-dimensional planes depicting the subsystems failing to intersect at a point in the positive orthant of the three dimensional space? To ward against this possibility, it is necessary that

$$(35) \qquad \begin{vmatrix} 1 - a'_{jj} & -a'_{jk} & -a'_{jr} \\ -a'_{kj} & 1 - a'_{kk} & -a'_{kr} \\ -a'_{rj} & -a'_{rk} & 1 - a'_{rr} \end{vmatrix} > 0$$

where $j = 1, \ldots, n$, $k = 1, \ldots, n$, and $r = 1, \ldots, n$. That is, for *all* subsystems of three sectors that can be formed this condition must hold.

Similarly, this must hold for subsystems of 4, 5, . . . sectors, and so forth, up to and including the one subsystem which has all n sectors in it. In this last system the necessity for the determinant $|I - a| > 0$ is seen to be a requirement that the system as a whole can generate net output for the external final demand sectors.

These conditions, which may be shown to be not only necessary but sufficient for a meaningful solution to a decomposable or indecomposable Leontief input-output system, i.e., for $[\mathrm{I} - a]^{-1}$ to exist with finite positive elements, are that all expressions of the following types be positive:

$$(36) \quad 1 - a'_{jj}, \quad \begin{vmatrix} 1 - a'_{jj} & -a'_{jk} \\ -a'_{kj} & 1 - a'_{kk} \end{vmatrix}, \ldots \quad \begin{vmatrix} 1 - a'_{jj} & \cdots & -a'_{jn} \\ -a'_{kj} & \cdots & -a'_{kn} \\ \cdot & \cdots & \cdot \\ -a'_{nj} & \cdots & 1 - a'_{nn} \end{vmatrix}$$

where all a-coefficients are nonnegative. They are termed the "Hawkins-Simon" conditions,[6] and they guarantee that the characteristic roots of $[a]$ will be less than 1 in absolute value, and, therefore, that the second equality of (18) will hold.

2.d. The Substitution Theorem

Even in Model III-1, from which we have derived the open input-output system, the "economic dimension"—purposive human choices among material ends in the face of limited means—in the entrepreneurial sector of the economy was minimized. Cost-minimization was a prior process performed in the definition of the production function; the choice of a transformation process was identical to the choice of a single-product output; the firm's output level was either zero or indeterminate without some further and arbitrary condition imposed upon it. The firm as an operational decisionmaking unit is an actor responding as an automaton in an unclear fashion to forces in a field in which its alternatives are few. But the economic dimension in the consumer sector is as complete as our theory of consumer choice (developed in Models I and II) could build in.

The Leontief system places all of the equations depicting human choice in Model III-1 outside the system, as we have seen. Further, factor

[6] D. Hawkins, (2), pp. 245–8.

service markets are not constrained in supply by explicit availabilities, so that this most important feature of the economic dimension disappears. We might also add positive profits in each industry as "equilibrium" payments at arbitrary levels for fictitious external factor services without disturbing the outputs of the sectors, cutting the ill-defined link between the existence of positive profits and firm outputs in Model III-1.

Samuelson has shown that under exceptional circumstances it is possible to interpret the Leontief matrix as the result of explicit cost minimization procedures, thereby injecting into the system some semblance of an economic dimension. In addition to the two assumptions which we have been making implicitly in treating the Leontief system as a linear programming system, i.e.,

1. each process produces one output;
2. processes are divisible, so that any finite quantity of scarce factor(s) can be used to produce some finite quantity of every product in the economy;

we add the following more special assumptions:

3. only one primary factor (say) labor exists in fixed quantity and enters into at least one production function;
4. all production functions are linear and homogeneous in all inputs;
5. the minimization procedures of the model yield interior solutions.

A first theorem which follows from such a system is that the a-coefficients in $[a^*]$ and the a_{z_1j}-terms will be constants, independent of the size and composition of the bill of goods and of the amount of scarce resource, Z_1. This may be seen intuitively if we set $P_{z_1} = 1$, so that all prices are indices of the physical amount of labor contained in the produced goods. Then prices will be unaffected by the amount of the resource available. Since all production conditions are linear and homogeneous, costs will not rise or fall with amounts of the bill of goods items desired. If the absolute price of labor should rise, since all goods are ultimately only labor, all input and output prices will rise proportionately and, under linear, homogeneous conditions, coefficients formerly optimal will remain optimal.

Let

(37) $$x_j = T_j(x_{zj}, x_{1j}, x_{2j}, \ldots, x_{nj})$$

where

(38)
$$1. \quad x_{zj} = a_{zj}x_j$$
$$2. \quad x_{1j} = a_{1j}x_j, \text{ etc.}$$

and where

(39) $$T_j(\lambda x_{zj}, \lambda x_{1j}, \lambda x_{2j}, \ldots, \lambda x_{nj}) = \lambda T_j(x_{zj}, x_{1j}, x_{2j}, \ldots, x_{nj})$$

when $\lambda > 0$.

We may define X_j, the final demand for good Y_j, as

$$X_j = T_j(x_{zj}, x_{1j}, x_{2j}, \ldots, x_{nj}) - \sum_{J=1}^{n} x_{jJ} \tag{40}$$

Then, let us set all final demands but one (say X_1) and (for $n = 3$) maximize it subject to given X_2, X_3, and Q_z:

(41)

1. $\max X_1 = T_1(x_{z1}, x_{11}, x_{21}, x_{31}) - \sum_{j=1}^{3} x_{1j}$
2. subject to:

   a. $X_2 = T_2(x_{z2}, x_{12}, x_{22}, x_{32}) - \sum_{j=1}^{3} x_{2j}$

   b. $X_3 = T_3(x_{z3}, x_{13}, x_{23}, x_{33}) - \sum_{j=1}^{3} x_{3j}$

   c. $\sum_{j=1}^{3} a_{zj}x_j = Q_Z$

Set up the Lagrangean expression, S:

$$\begin{aligned} S = {} & T_1(x_{z1}, x_{11}, x_{21}, x_{31}) - \sum_j x_{1j} \\ & + \lambda_2 \left[x_2 - T_2(x_{z2}, x_{12}, x_{22}, x_{32}) - \sum_j x_{2j} \right] \\ & + \lambda_3 \left[x_3 - T_3(x_{z3}, x_{13}, x_{23}, x_{33}) - \sum_j x_{3j} \right] \\ & + \lambda_z \left[Q_Z - \sum_j x_{zj} \right] \end{aligned} \tag{42}$$

and differentiate it with respect to each variable, setting such partial derivatives equal to zero:

(43)

1. $\frac{\partial S}{\partial x_{11}} = T_1^1 - 1 = 0$
2. $\frac{\partial S}{\partial x_{21}} = T_1^2 - \lambda_2 = 0$
3. $\frac{\partial S}{\partial x_{31}} = T_1^3 - \lambda_3 = 0$
4. $\frac{\partial S}{\partial x_{z1}} = T_1^z - \lambda_z = 0$
5. $\frac{\partial S}{\partial x_{12}} = \lambda_2 T_2^1 + 1 = 0$
6. $\frac{\partial S}{\partial x_{22}} = \lambda_2 T_2^2 + \lambda_2 = 0$
7. $\frac{\partial S}{\partial x_{32}} = \lambda_2 T_2^3 + \lambda_3 = 0$
8. $\frac{\partial S}{\partial x_{z2}} = \lambda_2 T_2^z + \lambda_z = 0$
9. $\frac{\partial S}{\partial x_{13}} = \lambda_3 T_3^1 + 1 = 0$
10. $\frac{\partial S}{\partial x_{23}} = \lambda_3 T_3^2 + \lambda_2 = 0$
11. $\frac{\partial S}{\partial x_{33}} = \lambda_3 T_3^3 + \lambda_3 = 0$
12. $\frac{\partial S}{\partial x_{z3}} = \lambda_3 T_3^z + \lambda_z = 0$

plus the three equations of (41-2). Also,

$$(44) \qquad d^2S < 0$$

Since the T_j functions are homogeneous of degree one, the T_j^k and T_j^z functions must be homogeneous of degree zero; therefore, the marginal productivities are functions of the *relative* amounts of inputs only:

$$(45) \quad \begin{aligned} &1. \quad T_j^k = G_{jk}\left(1, \frac{x_{1j}}{x_{zj}}, \frac{x_{2j}}{x_{zj}}, \ldots, \frac{x_{nj}}{x_{zj}}\right) \\ &2. \quad T_j^z = G_{jz}\left(1, \frac{x_{1j}}{x_{zj}}, \frac{x_{2j}}{x_{zj}}, \ldots, \frac{x_{nj}}{x_{zj}}\right) \end{aligned}$$

By substituting these functions into (43) and (41-2), remembering that they are homogeneous of degree zero, we see that the variables x_{jk} and x_{zk} are determined independently of Q_Z and X_j.

A second theorem is that relative prices will be independent of the bill of goods and of the amount of scarce resources. This is seen intuitively if the *numéraire* is labor: then, relative prices of all goods will be their direct and indirect labor content. Since input coefficients are not affected by the bill of goods or the quantity of labor available, neither will the direct and indirect labor content of any good be so affected. More rigorously, where all vectors are column vectors before transposition,

$$(46) \qquad [P_1, P_2, P_3]' \begin{bmatrix} 1 - a_{11} & -a_{12} & -a_{13} \\ -a_{21} & 1 - a_{22} & -a_{23} \\ -a_{31} & -a_{32} & 1 - a_{33} \end{bmatrix} = \begin{bmatrix} a_{z1} \\ a_{z2} \\ a_{z3} \end{bmatrix}'$$

whose solution, given the first theorem, is independent of X_j and Q_Z.

A last theorem proved by Samuelson is that the economy's "efficiency frontier"—all baskets of final goods which are optimal in the sense that given all quantities of X_j but one, the amount of that one is a maximum under given resource constraints—will be linear and the rates of substitution between final goods will depend only upon the a-coefficients.

This result is also intuitively clear, in that the rates of transformation between goods in the society must be the ratios of the total labor contained in the goods in direct and indirect form, since labor is the only scarce resource. Given the solution to the system:

$$(47) \qquad [x] = [I - a^*]^{-1}[X]$$

we may define A_{zj} as the total amount of labor, direct and indirect, contained in a unit of final demand X_j:

$$(48) \qquad [A_{z1}, A_{z2}, A_{z3}]' = [a_{z1}, a_{z2}, a_{z3}]'[I - a^*]^{-1}$$

From the resource constraint (41-2-c):

$$(49) \qquad A_{z1}X_1^\circ = Q_Z - A_{z2}X_2 - A_{z3}X_3$$

where X_1 is a maximum, given X_2 and X_3, determined from the model in (43) and (41-2). The expression in (49) is the society's efficiency frontier. By the reasoning of the first two theorems it is seen to be linear with A_{zj} and dependent only upon the *a*-coefficients.

Samuelson sketched a proof that these three theorems can also be derived when production possibilities are defined by a finite number of divisible, additive activities rather than continuous, differentiable production functions. Koopmans, for the case of $n = 3$, showed the validity of Samuelson's results for similar production conditions when (1) the Hawkins-Simon conditions are met, and (2) for a given amount of primary factor, the set of net output possibilities open to each sector form a closed and bounded set.[7] Arrow extended Koopman's proof to $n > 3$ with two minor changes in the technological assumptions.[8]

It is possible, therefore, to provide the conditions under which the Leontief model's solution emerges as an equilibrium solution with potential substitution among inputs, and possesses the properties of the purely competitive solution. It is, in short, possible to build into the Leontief model an economic dimension if one is willing to accept the classical postulates of the labor theory of value—a general model whose Marxist version reveals an inability to explain the set of prices and outputs emerging from a free market economy even in the long-run.

3. The Open Input-Output Model As a Nonequilibrium Model

We have discussed the basic qualifications to the view of the open input-output system as an equilibrium model in the sense defined in Chapter 1, and have indicated the limited "generalness" of its analysis by the substantial portions of Model III-1 which are lifted from the "variable" to the "data" category in its derivation. When the Leontief system is abstracted from some such model as Model V-2, in addition to the consumer sector with its demands for goods and supplies of services, we find the variables germane to the investment and the money sectors also excluded from the variable category. The interpretation of the open input-output model as an "operational general equilibrium" system, in the present senses of those words, is misleading therefore.

An alternative method of interpreting the Leontief model is that it is merely a manner of determining entrepreneurial amounts demanded for marginal final good changes small enough to warrant an assumption that (1) the requirements can be produced with roughly constant marginal materials cost and (2) the prices of primary factors will not be bid up materially by such changes, in such manner as to enforce substitution

[7] These conditions will be discussed in Chapter 9.

[8] P. Samuelson, (6), pp. 142–6; T. Koopmans, (2), pp. 147–54; and K. Arrow, (1), pp. 155–64.

among the factor services. In this view the solutions are identities *defining* gross outputs as approximative linear extrapolations:

$$[\Delta x'] \equiv [I - a]^{-1}[\Delta X'] \tag{50}$$

when $[\Delta X']$ consists of increments small enough to allow the simple linear projection of our current technological relationships. The stress is upon the smallness of the changes in the bill of goods in this interpretation since it is based upon projections which are made *in neglect of* equilibrating responses in the real economy not *as a result of* such processes.

4. The Closed Input-Output Model

We shall now assume that the "household" sector of the input-output model discussed in Section 2 is included within the matrix, so that $[a^*]$ becomes an $n + 1 \times n + 1$ square matrix. The $n + 1^{\text{th}}$ column of coefficients $a_{1n+1}, a_{2n+1}, \ldots, a_{n+1,n+1}$, contains the physical amounts of each product absorbed by households per unit of "household" product. We assume this latter may be compressed into one "product," whose inputs into each sector are found in the $n + 1^{\text{th}}$ row, defined in amounts per unit of each sector's product as $a_{n+1,1}, a_{n+1,2}, \ldots, a_{n+1,n+1}$. Thus, the household sector is viewed as selling units of a "factor service" to every sector and absorbing inputs from every sector in order to produce this factor service. The model has, therefore, been closed, in the sense that no product escapes from the model for use by any external sector.

It will be convenient to define the gross output of each sector as net of the amount of its own good absorbed in production. That is, a_{jj}, $j = 1, \ldots, n + 1$, are netted out of gross output and a unit of total product in the system below is equal to $1 - a_{jj}$ in the open system. Then,

$$\begin{bmatrix} 0 & a_{12} & a_{13} & \cdots & a_{1,n+1} \\ a_{21} & 0 & a_{23} & \cdots & a_{2,n+1} \\ \cdot & \cdot & \cdot & \cdots & \cdot \\ a_{n+1,1} & a_{n+1,2} & a_{n+1,3} & \cdots & 0 \end{bmatrix} = [a] \tag{51}$$

and

$$[I - a][x] = [0] \tag{52}$$

where, of course, $[x] \geqq 0$.

This set of homogeneous linear equations can be solved only for *relative* quantities; given one solution $[x]$, $[\lambda x]$, $\lambda > 0$, is also a solution. We obtain the solution $[v] = [x]$, through a suitable choice of units, so

$$[I - a^*][v] = [0] \tag{53}$$

where $[v]$ is a column matrix composed of $n + 1$ unity elements, or a unit column vector.

We shall use an external *numéraire* to define vectors of prices $[P] = [P_1, P_2, \ldots, P_{n+1}]$, and define a solution price vector as one for which every sector's value of ouput is no less than its value of inputs:

$$[P^\circ]'[I - a^*] \geqq [0] \tag{54}$$

where $[P^\circ] \geq 0$ and is the solution vector of prices.

We shall now prove that *if* there is a solution price vector the equality in (54) must hold, for if one sector makes positive profits at least one other must make negative profits which violates (54). To show this, *assume* a $[P^\circ]$ exists. From (54) if nonnegative profits exist in each sector, total profits must also be nonnegative:

$$[[P^\circ]'[I - a^*]][v] \geqq 0 \tag{55}$$

Since

$$[[P^\circ]'[I - a^*]][v] = [P^\circ]'[[I - a^*][v]] \tag{56}$$

it follows from (53) that the equality holds in (55), and from (54) that

$$[P^\circ]'[I - a^*] = [0] \tag{57}$$

We may now show the assumption that $[P^\circ]$ exists to be correct. By a theorem on linear homogeneous equations, it may be shown that *either*

$$[I - a^*][T] > [0] \tag{58}$$

has a solution for some $[T]$, or (57) has a solution for some $[P^\circ]$.[9] If therefore, it can be shown that no $[T]$ exists that can satisfy (58), the existence of $[P^\circ]$ will have been proved.

Economically, showing that no $[T]$ exists is to prove that even if we allow some sectors to operate at negative levels, it is impossible to find a set of activity levels $[x]$ which will yield a net product in *every* sector for external use. Suppose for the moment $[T]$ does exist: then,

$$[a^*][T] < [T] \tag{59}$$

and, from (53)

$$[a^*][v] = [v] \tag{60}$$

Now, let t_j be the minimum element in $[T]$, and assume j is (say) 1. We multiply (60) by t_1 to obtain

$$[a^*][t_1] = [t_1] \tag{61}$$

Subtract (61) from (59) to get

$$[a^*][T - t_1] < [T - t_1] \tag{62}$$

[9] For a proof of this theorem, see D. Gale, (1), p. 48.

For $j = 1$,

$$\sum_k a_{jk}(T_k - t_1) < 0 \tag{63}$$

Therefore, if (58) is true, (63) is implied.

But t_1 is the minimum element of $[T]$, and therefore $[T_k - t_1] \geqq 0$, and since all a-coefficients are nonnegative, the sum of cross-products of a-coefficients and $T_k - t_1$ elements must be nonnegative. Therefore, (63) cannot be true, and (58) must be rejected. It follows, therefore, that $[P°]$ exists, and, our former proof demonstrates that $[P°]$ will be that vector of nonnegative prices which reduces profits in each sector to zero. Further, this $[P°]$, for an indecomposable $[I - a^*]$, will be unique up to a multiplicative constant $\lambda > 0$, since only relative prices are determined in this model, and no free goods will exist; i.e., $[P°] > 0$. This last point follows from the fact of indecomposability. If any good in the model had a price of 0, it would follow that that good had in its production no inputs of nonfree goods, either directly or indirectly. If this were true, the matrix would be decomposable, and therefore it cannot be true.

We have shown that for a closed Leontief system, when that system is indecomposable, and where no subgroup of sectors is autophagous except that subsystem which is the whole system, it is possible to obtain *relative* outputs and *relative* prices with the properties listed above. We shall not be interested in this completely closed model, although we have already treated an allied system when we used Kaldor's model in Chapter 4, and we shall employ a similar structure in Chapter 8 when we use von Neumann's closed model of moving equilibrium.

5. The Generalized Linear Production Model

The Leontief open model discussed in Section 2 is the simplest type of linear production model. We shall proceed to complicate it somewhat and use this generalization as a bridge to other linear static production models.

In our three-good, two-factor example of Section 2, we assumed that the factor requirements of the bill of goods were forthcoming at constant prices; i.e., we interpreted the following system as identities:

$$\begin{bmatrix} a'_{z_11} & a'_{z_12} & a'_{z_13} \\ a'_{z_21} & a'_{z_22} & a'_{z_23} \end{bmatrix} \begin{bmatrix} x'_1 \\ x'_2 \\ x'_3 \end{bmatrix} = \begin{bmatrix} X'_{z_1} \\ X'_{z_2} \end{bmatrix} \tag{64}$$

where X'_{z_i} is defined as the demand for primary factors imposed by the solution values for gross outputs. Our assumption is that

$$Q'_{Z_i} \geqq X'_{Z_i}, \qquad i = 1, 2 \tag{65}$$

while

$$P_i = K_i \tag{66}$$

where K_i are constants.

Suppose, however, we now recognize the fact that resources are scarce, and that we impose the condition that not only must gross outputs be large enough to yield the given bill of goods, but that resources must be used up:

$$\begin{bmatrix} 1 - a'_{11} & -a'_{12} & -a'_{13} \\ -a'_{21} & 1 - a'_{22} & -a'_{23} \\ -a'_{31} & -a'_{32} & 1 - a'_{33} \\ a'_{z_1 1} & a'_{z_1 2} & a'_{z_1 3} \\ a'_{z_2 1} & a'_{z_2 2} & a'_{z_2 3} \end{bmatrix} \begin{bmatrix} x'_1 \\ x'_2 \\ x'_3 \end{bmatrix} = \begin{bmatrix} X'_1 \\ X'_2 \\ X'_3 \\ Q'_{Z_1} \\ Q'_{Z_2} \end{bmatrix} \tag{67}$$

Of course, the system is overdetermined: we have five equations to solve for three unknowns. In a five-dimensional requirements space (not only must the system generate the X'_j, but it must *absorb* the Q'_{Z_i} as well) we have only three vectors (the unit vectors of activity space mapped into requirements space) to form a basis. Generally speaking, it will be impossible to produce a given bill of goods *and* just exhaust the resources available.

Three paths out of this impasse are possible. First, we may take Leontief's route and simply eliminate the equations enforcing the using up of resources. Second, we can convert m of the n X'_j final goods requirements from data into variables, when $n > m$, and by specifying $n - m$ of these requirements solve for the unspecified net as well as all gross outputs. Third, we can create the m additional activities required to obtain the vectors necessary for a basis in the requirements space by introducing disposal processes.

We shall follow the second of these routes, converting (say) X'_1 and X'_2 to unknowns. We obtain from this system the following nonspecific solution:

$$\begin{bmatrix} x'_1 \\ x'_2 \\ x'_3 \\ X'_1 \\ X'_2 \end{bmatrix} = \begin{bmatrix} 0 & 0 & B_{13} & B_{14} & B_{15} \\ 0 & 0 & B_{23} & B_{24} & B_{25} \\ 0 & 0 & B_{33} & B_{34} & B_{35} \\ 1 & 0 & B_{43} & B_{44} & B_{45} \\ 0 & 1 & B_{53} & B_{54} & B_{55} \end{bmatrix} \begin{bmatrix} 0 \\ 0 \\ X'_3 \\ Q'_{z_1} \\ Q'_{z_2} \end{bmatrix} \tag{68}$$

and, more interestingly,

(69)

1. $X'_1 = B_{43}X'_3 + B_{44}Q'_{z_1} + B_{45}Q'_{z_2}$
2. $X'_2 = B_{53}X'_3 + B_{54}Q'_{z_1} + B_{55}Q'_{z_2}$

With fixed amounts of resources and a specified bill of final requirements for Y_3, these equations yield the levels of X'_1 and X'_2 which will just exhaust the remaining amounts of factor services.

This system, therefore, permits us to determine only one point in the bill-of-goods space: given $n - m$ coordinates, the other m are determined by technology and the exhaustion-of-resources constraint. But why should we desire to attain this point? There is no immediately apparent reason why a society should desire that structure of final goods which happens to prevent unemployment of any resource. The optimization of society's welfare may well require one or more resources to be used at less than full employment levels; agricultural land may lie idle as a *result* of the societal optimization process, not in contradiction to it. The above solution, therefore, is not one of compelling interest.

The third route allows us to investigate the problem just raised, however. It opens the possibility of solutions in which all resources are not used, but in which baskets of final goods more desirable in some sense may be feasible. We introduce this possibility by placing inequalities in the last two equations of (67), thereby enforcing the need that the solution require no more than Q'_{z_1} and Q'_{z_2} in factor services. To convert these to equalities, we introduce the costless disposal processes whose unit levels of operation dispose of one unit of z_i, and which operate at levels d_1 and d_2. The ability to "waste" resources makes it mathematically possible to obtain a solution for any bill of goods, but since we may not operate disposal processes at negative levels to "generate" resources, only the feasible subset of these solutions for bills of goods which lead to nonnegative disposal processes (as well as nonnegative gross outputs) is acceptable.

By a simple procedure, we can derive this subset of feasible solutions and thereby present the menu of possible bills of goods society may have from employment of its resources. Let us return to the nonspecific solution to a Leontief system in (23): we may derive the value of factor service z_1 used directly and indirectly in the production of a unit of X'_1 by the same manner of definition as employed in (48):

$$(70) \qquad A'_{z_1 1} = \sum_j a'_{z_1 j} A'_{j1}$$

In similar fashion we may derive $A'_{z_1 2}$, and so forth. Then, from the resource constraint:

$$(71) \qquad \begin{aligned} &1. \quad A'_{z_1 1}X'_1 + A'_{z_1 2}X'_2 + A'_{z_1 3}X'_3 = Q'_{z_1} \\ &2. \quad A'_{z_2 1}X'_1 + A'_{z_2 2}X'_2 + A'_{z_2 3}X'_3 = Q'_{z_2} \end{aligned}$$

In order to remain in two dimensions instead of three, let us arbitrarily impose the condition that $X'_3 = 0$. Then we may graph the resulting simplified equations in Fig. 6-2. The first shows all baskets of final goods X'_1 and X'_2 which may be obtained *taking into account only the constraints imposed by a fixed* Q'_{z_1}. Similarly, the second simplified equation shows all baskets of goods which might be had if Q'_{z_2} were fully employed and we need worry about no other scarcities.

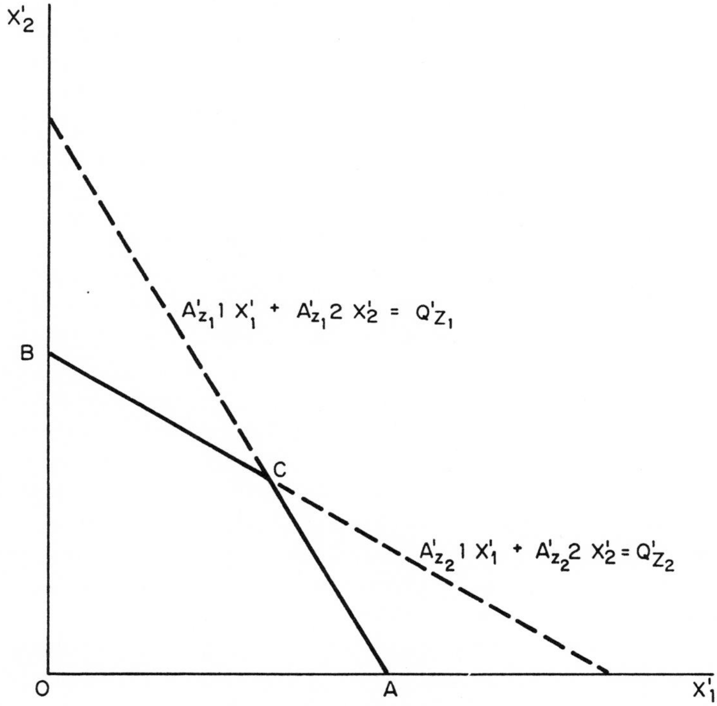

Figure 6-2. The Efficiency Frontier

Since the production of final goods requires both scarce resources, either factor is limitational and its exhaustion sets the upper limit to production. Therefore, for every value of X'_1, the lower of the two resource constraint equations sets the limit to the amount of X'_2 that can be produced. We have drawn those portions of the resource constraint lines which form effective boundaries or frontiers to final product as solid lines: it will be noted that from B to C the resource z_2 sets the limit to production, while z_1 is not fully employed, while from C to A the opposite is true. Only at C are both resources employed to the limit—the point determined by taking the second route in the introduction of resource constraints. Any basket of final goods in the polygon $OACB$, including the boundary lines, may be produced from existing resources, and our model with disposal processes would yield a feasible solution for any such basket. We have obtained that subset of baskets which are feasible.

The simplest type of maximization reasoning argues that the society will choose from those baskets that lie upon the frontier BCA, since it shows, for any feasible X_1', the maximum amount of X_2' which is obtainable. As long as the society is unsatiated with either good, for any point in the interior of the polygon there will be at least one point on the frontier which is preferable in that it will yield at least as much of one final good and more of the other. In the absence of any other criteria than these "Pareto optimality" bases, however, there is no manner of specifying any point on the frontier as preferable to all others; specifically, as discussed above, no reason exists why C is a self-evident optimum, merely because it happens to employ all resources.

6. The Koopmans Production Model

With this background we may approach the general production model of Koopmans.[10] We have, indeed, been exploiting his work, in showing how a Leontief model may be used to generate an efficiency frontier with explicit introduction of primary factor restrictions. In this wise, the Koopmans model specifies its "requirements" not as a specific Leontief bill of goods, but either as (1) all technologically feasible bills of goods which minimize the use of primary factor services when these factor services, *à la* Walras, have final uses; (2) all technologically feasible bills of goods which meet the Pareto optimality criteria when these primary factor services have no final uses and are limited in amount; or (3) a specific bill of goods which maximizes an objective function on the efficiency frontier generated by (2).

Throughout the analysis below, we assume that all goods with intermediate uses also possess a final use. It is then possible to eliminate intermediate goods from the activity vectors by characterizing all goods as final, primary, or final and primary, using $A_{z_i j} = \frac{A'_{z j}}{P_i}$ as the basis for the formation of the input coefficients in Koopmans' activities, when the special case of a Leontief technology occurs, with its assumption of a single activity for the production of each good and one output per activity. We assume the existence of k divisible and additive basic activities defined for arbitrary unit levels of activity as column vectors $[b_{1s}, \ldots, b_{ns}, -b_{z_1 s}, \ldots, -b_{z_m s}]$ where, as can be seen, joint production may occur. It is now possible that each good is produced by more than one activity. If any of the factor services have final uses, we create a b_{js} to depict its production by diverting a unit of it from production, in a process $[b_{js}, -b_{z_i s}]$, $j = n + 1, \ldots n + m$.

Koopmans rejects Walras' definition of different classes of capital

[10] T. Koopmans, (2), Ch. 3.

goods, with inputs of their services entering the activity vectors, for reasons which are not wholly clear. Therefore, those Z_i in our models which are capital goods are assumed in the Koopmans model to be free goods in all conceivable solutions, although depreciation and wastage coefficients may be introduced into the activities to account for the physical depletion of the goods.[11] We shall ignore the implications of these assumptions for the rate of interest in Koopmans' static and stationary system, except to say that the Schumpeterian circular flow would be approached.

The restrictions upon the current flows of primary factors are stated in the availability vector $[Q_i]$, $i = 1, \ldots, m$. Since we no longer have single-output activities we can no longer identify activities with the output produced by them. We denote by $[S]$ the vector of activity levels S_s, $s = 1, \ldots, k$.

6.a. The Technology

From these assumptions we define a matrix, $[B]$, whose columns are the productive activities of the economy defined for a unit level of operation. Lastly, we define a vector $[X^*]$ consisting of X_j and $-X_i$ elements, or final demands for goods and factor services. Then,

$$[B][S] = [X^*] \tag{72}$$

Consider the set of all points in the space containing the vectors $[X^*]$—let us call this W-space—which $[B]$ maps onto this space for all $[S] \geqq 0$. These will form an infinite number of vectors; that is, these points will lie along an infinite number of rays from the origin of W-space. Further, we know that a basis of W-space obtained from the mapping of unit activity levels for the processes will "span" all of the rays in the sense that every point on them may be described as the sum of positively weighted basis vectors. The set of points in W-space lying along the rays described above, and framed by the mappings of unit activity levels, is a "cone" with vertex at (and including) the origin, and we shall term it the set of *possible* points. That is, the set of goods and factor demands generated by all activities levels whose components are nonnegative are potentially capable of attainment *considering only technological constraints.*

Koopmans places the following restrictions upon the technology as revealed by its mapping onto the cone of possible points:

1. *The irreversibility postulate.* In the cone of possible points, no point lies on a vector which extends through the origin of W-space. This is equivalent to saying that it is impossible to find a vector of activity levels, $[S] \geqq 0$ which yields $[X^*] = 0$. In W, vectors will have positive and negative components. Imagine a basis for the space. Then if it is possible to obtain a set of positive weights which, when applied to

[11] T. Koopmans, (2), p. 42. See also footnote 7, Chapter 3 above.

the basis, yields a vector at 180° to another vector similarly attained, this postulate is violated. If such vectors exist it is possible to express the origin of W-space as the sum of two activity level vectors not all of whose components are zero and none of whose components is negative. If at least one of the primary factors cannot be produced and enters directly or indirectly into the production of every good, this condition will be met. It may be shown that for this postulate and Postulate 2 to hold it is necessary and sufficient that a vector, $[T] > 0$, exist, which forms an obtuse angle with every column vector in $[B]$; i.e.,

$$[T]'[B] < 0, \qquad [T] > 0 \tag{73}$$

2. *The impossibility of producing something from nothing.* This postulate asserts that no point in the cone of possible points lies wholly in the positive orthant of W; or, no point (except [0]) has only nonnegative coordinates; or, given a basis of vectors in W, it is impossible to weight them with a set of nonnegative weights not all of which are zero and sum to obtain a vector all of whose components are nonnegative.

It may be shown that a necessary and sufficient condition for this postulate is that there exist a column vector $[T] > 0$ which forms a non-acute angle with every column vector in $[B]$; i.e.,

$$[T]'[B] \leq 0 \qquad [T] > 0 \tag{74}$$

Thus, if (73) holds, (74) also holds, although the reverse may not be true.

A third postulate defining the possibility of commodity production is stated by Koopmans in a strong and weak form:

3.a. *The strong possibility postulate:* it is possible to find an activity level vector $[S] \geq 0$ which is within the primary factor availabilities of the economy (is feasible) and which yields $X_j > 0$ for all j. That is, with given factor availabilities, the economy *can*, if it so desires, produce positive amounts of *all* goods. There must be at least one point with positive coordinates for all X_j in W-space.

3.b. *The weak possibility postulate:* this postulate weakens the condition in 3.a. to the requirement that at least one point in the possibility cone be feasible and all $X_j \geqq 0$, with $X_j > 0$ for at least one j. In this case the economy may not be able to produce all goods with a given vector of available factor services.

6.a.1. The Efficiency Conditions with No Factor Availability Restraints

Suppose, first, that no resource limitations are placed upon the economy, but that factor services have final uses and are positively weighted in the objective function. It will follow, then, that the economy will, if it is optimizing, attempt to produce any given bill of goods, excluding factor services as final goods, at minimum resource cost.

A point $[X]$ in the cone of possible points is termed efficient if any of its coordinates can be increased only at the expense of decreasing one or more other coordinates; that is, it is efficient if it is Pareto-optimal, taking into account the final uses of factor services. Let $[X']$ be another point in the possibility cone: then if $[X' - X] \geq 0$, $[X]$ is not an efficient point. The set of all such efficient points in the possibility point set is the efficiency set. If $[X]$ is efficient, $[\lambda X]$, $\lambda > 0$, must also be efficient, which conditions imply that $[X]$ must be a boundary point of the cone of possible points. It is a necessary and sufficient condition for a boundary point at $[X]$ to be efficient that there exist a positive normal $[P]$ to the cone at $[X]$.

This vector $[P]$ may be interpreted as a vector of shadow prices for each of the goods and factor services which, since $[P] \cdot [X] = 0$, reduces the "profit" on all goods to zero. Since $[X]$ is the result of a positively weighted sum of some basis of activities, this restricts the profitability of these activities. Indeed, it may be shown that profits will be zero on all activities included in the basis and less than or equal to zero in all activities which are excluded from the basis.

6.a.2. The Efficiency Conditions with Given Factor Service Availabilities

Let us now assume that primary factors are not desired as final goods, and that a vector $[-Q_i]$ of factor service availabilities exists. Koopmans defines an *attainable* set of points as those points which are possible and feasible in terms of factor availabilities. An efficient point can be defined solely in terms of the Y_j, since by assumption factor services are not desired as final goods. In the efficient set there must exist no point $[X']$ whose elements are larger than or equal to the X_j elements in the efficient set $[X]$, for all j, and not all differences equal to zero.

It is necessary and sufficient for the attainable point $[X]$ to be an efficient point that a price vector $[P]$ with positive components for all Y_j, nonnegative components for all Z_i which are exhausted, and zero components for all Z_i which are not exhausted, be normal to the possible point cone at $[X]$. These conditions require that $[X]$ be a boundary point of the cone, and lead to a bounded efficiency set.

If there exists a set of positive weights, $[c]$, over the n final goods, and a function Z is formed

$$Z = \sum_j c_j X_j \tag{75}$$

and if this function reaches a maximum in the attainable set for a given $[c]$, then it is necessary and sufficient for the $[X]$ at which the maximum is reached to be efficient. By varying the $[c]$ appropriately the whole efficiency point set may be obtained. If postulate 2 holds—ruling out the possibility of producing something from nothing—for every $[c] > 0$ there will exist at least one efficient point among the attainable points.

Further, if postulate 3.b. holds, the origin will not be an efficient point, so that a nontrivial solution is guaranteed even if every [*c*] leads to the same efficient point.

7. A Recapitulation

In this chapter we have studied the application of modern linear systems techniques to the construction of general models of the static type. We began with the simplest of these constructions—the Leontief open input-output system. It was marked by the lack of explicit constraints upon the availability of primary factors, and was found to be difficult to interpret as an economic model. After pausing to consider the Leontief closed model, we have moved to the complication of the Leontief system by the introduction of factor constraints, binding as equalities and as equalities or inequalities. Lastly, the model with the latter characteristics was further complicated by the dropping of the assumptions of single output processes and unique processes for each good to obtain the Koopmans general linear production model.

CHAPTER 7

SPATIAL MODELS

1. Introduction

Economic stocks and flows are concepts germane to points in two dimensions: space and time. Realistic economic systems involve accumulations at points in both time and space and movements over intervals of both dimensions. Indeed, we may use Pareto's concept of economic activity as involving three transformations: material transformations or production, spatial transformations, and temporal transformations.[1]

Of course, when convenience or necessity requires, it is permissible to abstract from the existence or the effective consequences of the existence of these dimensions, at the sacrifice of a portion of the models' realistic relevance. Indeed, in Models I through IV-1, we have in fact abstracted from space and meaningful time. However, in Model IV-2, with the consideration of time preference in the consumer's tastes, through our final Model V-2, with the monetary implications of time, we have sought to cope with some of the simpler consequences of time within the constraints of static, stationary methodology. In Chapter 8 we shall step beyond these bounds to study other problems of a temporal economy which can be attacked only with dynamic frameworks.

We have not yet introduced space into the models, and some rather close parallels between temporal and spatial economic phenomena would seem to indicate gaps of coordinate importance in our analysis. As we may identify a time structure of productive processes defined in terms of kinds, amounts, and durabilities of capital goods used in them, so we may specify a spatial structure of such processes in terms of the amounts and directions of "transport inputs" entering them.[2] Corresponding to the consumer's time preference for goods, a space preference may be identified. As we seek the "price" of movement through time—the interest rate—so may we seek the "price" of movement through space—the transport rate. And, as we may expect, in equilibrium, the "discounting" of values from a terminal point in time to an origin point, we may also expect it to occur over space.

Moreover, as we may seek in an Austrian analysis to determine the time structure of a process or reactions of it to changes in the determining parameters, so may we seek the spatial structure or its responses by studying the forces determining the location of farms, industries, resources,

[1] V. Pareto, (2), pp. 175–6.

[2] The term is W. Isard's, signifying the movement of a unit of weight a unit distance. See (5), pp. 77–90.

and consumers. Or, given the time structure of a process, we may study the pattern of input flows through time, and, similarly, given the spatial structure of a process, we may seek to find the equilibrium flows over space and relevant market areas and supply areas, as well as exports and imports.[3]

Several explanations exist for the relative neglect of spatial phenomena when compared to the treatment of temporal problems in economic theory. First, the overwhelming importance of the phenomena, problems, and institutions which can be approached only within a temporal framework when compared with similar factors within a spatial framework, argues for the pre-eminence of the time dimension. Even within the static, stationary framework, the phenomena of capital, interest, and money must be grounded in a time matrix, as we have shown in Part II. The introduction of its real-life concomitants—risk and uncertainty—results in the further complications of speculation, risk-bearing, liquidity, hedging, hoarding, insurance, and so forth. And, at a higher analytical level, the lags in response to the emergence of stimuli throughout the market economy contribute to the problems of economic mechanisms that of possible instability of the pricing process. When laid against this catalogue of temporal phenomena, the theoretical implications of space seem secondary to say the least: its independent contribution to uncertainty, its requirements of specific resources for movement of goods, and the price of such services of movement with its implication of the economic non-homogeneity of spatial segments.[4]

Second, for many analyses only the *costs* of movement through space are required, and these are derivable from a standard pricing analysis. That is, frequently, spatial considerations may be summarized by a cost figure without any important conceptual differences from costs which are not spatially conditioned. When this is true, peculiarly spatial aspects may rightfully be neglected. In similar fashion, there are analyses in which the interest rate suffices as a summary measure of time—as for example in the study of the firm's production decisions—and for such we could rightfully treat capital as merely another factor of production insofar as its durability did not introduce complications. We merely assert that the occasions when the complications of time may be escaped so conveniently are much more infrequent than the occasions when spatial complications may be.[5]

Third, frequently the spatial and temporal dimensions are analytically intertwined, and what appear to be spatial aspects are more genuinely temporal aspects. For example, even were the transport rate proper to be

[3] See W. Isard, (5), pp. 81–6, for a further treatment of the similarities between economic time and space.

[4] Compare B. Ohlin, (1), pp. 3–6.

[5] For a contrary view, see W. Isard, (5), pp. 79–80, especially p. 80*n*.

zero, there would often be a "spatial" preference for goods in one spot over another by virtue of the time required to transport them; the desire to locate near customers may be enhanced by the need to supply them quickly, service equipment without delay, or reduce the inventories individual customers are required to carry; the perishability of goods may enforce spatial constraints; and so on. On the other hand, it is not so easy to find examples of the converse: temporal aspects which are more genuinely spatial economic aspects.

Merely to multiply the parallels between temporal and spatial phenomena, therefore, is not to show that economic theorists have misplaced their emphasis upon the time dimension and its problems. But a last reason we shall consider for the de-emphasis of spatial phenomena in economic theory has a different basis: the smooth and continuous functions which may be assumed for analysis of the temporal dimension or static economic problems, and the interior solutions they may be assumed to yield, are frequently not applicable in the spatial dimension. The analysis of time in economic theory has, in largest part, been a projection of marginal techniques of the neoclassical type with the implications of this for the functions involved, as our study in Chapter 4 revealed. The productivity curves for resources invested over different lengths of time, the exponential relationship between interest rates for shorter and longer periods, the discount factor for consumers' preferences over time, the value of a good if it is related to the mere passage of time, and so forth, may be represented as well-behaved differentiable functions of time. This allowed the assumption of interior maxima or minima to be made and straightforward, simple extremum techniques to be used. While we undoubtedly violate reality by the adoption of such smooth functions, they do not appear to contradict the nature of the phenomena under analysis.

But the same cannot be said of many relations in spatial analysis: it is not wholly accidental that linear programming was so closely linked in its origins to transportation problems, for example.[6] The very basis of existence of so much of spatial analysis is the explanation of discrete phenomena and the impacts of discontinuity upon economic variables. Although Isard speaks of the continuous substitution of transport inputs for other inputs or other transport inputs, he indicates that frequently marginal movements *toward* some point have no "marginal productivity": either a discrete jump is made (say to a consumption or resource site) or no movement at all is made.[7] To include transport inputs in a conventional transformation function and imply their ability to be handled in the marginal framework—as Isard does—is misleading as to the nature of spatial phenomena in many analyses. Similarly, as Lösch has emphasized,

[6] Compare P. Samuelson, (7).
[7] See W. Isard, (5), p. 86*n*.

finding a maximum profit location which is local under such conditions does not guarantee the nonexistence of a more profitable site beyond the neighborhood of the one in question.[8] This fundamental difference in spatial phenomena led Lösch to assert the nonexistence of a simultaneous-equation solution to locational problems and the need for a trial-and-error examination of a limited set of alternatives: "Hence Weber's and all the other attempts at a systematic and valid location theory for the individual firm were doomed to failure."[9]

Nodal points[10] and transshipment points in the transportation network, raw material or cheap labor sites, are, similarly, noncontinuous elements in the spatial structure. Indeed, the existence of transport routes to canalize movement along discrete lines is a most fundamental discontinuity. Frequently price relationships between points in space must be stated as inequalities: for example, if A does not import a good from B, the price of B's product plus transport cost must be no less than the price of A's locally produced good.

These difficulties in a real sense are part of the problem: they cannot be abstracted from without substantially altering the problem. They also mark off spatial theory from the body of neoclassical marginalism, while the analytical framework of capital theory fits into it. These considerations formed another set of reasons for the relative neglect of the spatial dimension by neoclassical theorists.

In spite of this judgment as to the relative importance of the two dimensions, we shall in this chapter construct models which will attempt to correct the deficiency in spatial depth. Exactly as was done in our treatment of time, we may divide spatial models into two basic types: those which take the spatial structure of the economy as given and which seek to determine the equilibrium patterns of prices and flows of goods over space, and those which add to these latter unknowns the spatial structure itself.[11]

In the first type of model, as it related to time, it was assumed that a given constellation of eternal capital goods existed with given mobility among uses. Its spatial analogue is one in which the spatial coordinates of all resources, entrepreneurial activity, and consumers are given and immutable, while transportation channels are similarly fixed with transportation technology defined along with that of all other productive activities in the economy. The weights of all goods and factors are fixed

[8] A. Lösch, (1), p. 24*n*.

[9] A. Lösch, (1), p. 29.

[10] A nodal point on a transportation network is a point at which a break in the type of transportation occurs; if, for example, ocean routes meet river routes, railroad routes meet truck routes, and so forth, a nodal point occurs.

[11] For a novel and interesting approach to the simple statistical model incorporating time and space simultaneously, using Stewart's "potential" concept, see W. Warntz, (1). In our models we shall treat space in the absence of time.

and given as data. As a limiting case, the spatial coordinates of all resources, entrepreneurs, and consumers may be taken as identical, in which case the spatial structure is punctiform—the implicit assumption we have made up to this point in our development. Or, as in classical international trade theory, several such punctiform economies may exist in the model, with infinite transport rates on resources and entrepreneurs between points and finite transport rates on at least some goods (frequently the transport rate on such goods was implicitly or explicitly treated as zero) assumed to exist.

In the second type of model, where time was involved, the possibility of altering the economy's structure was recognized. In the first step, the ability to recover and reinvest depreciation allowances in new forms was admitted as well as the possibility of net investment. Ultimately, the final structure was viewed as a steady state solution, contingent upon the fixity of the ruling data of the model. Where space is the relevant dimension, and where general models are concerned, the steady state solution is studied with little attention paid to momentary equilibrium points enforced by recovery-of-costs or net investment constraints. That is, the attendant investment needs and costs that are ordinarily involved in changing the spatial structure of an economy are customarily neglected. Of course, ideally, the interest in the stationary spatial structure centers in the ability to derive operational theorems about its solution movements when equilibrium is displaced.

The first type of model we shall term an "interregional trade" model and the second type a "locational" model. We shall treat each in turn.

2. Interregional Trade Models

As in our previous treatment, we shall distinguish between models of this type which are in the neoclassical tradition and those which are in the modern operational mould. The touchstone of the distinction is the operationalism of the model rather than its dependence upon nonlinear or linear techniques. In the first category we shall deal with a projection of Walras' model into the interregional problem, the Ohlin and Mosak models, Isard's general interregional equilibrium models, and Lefeber's construction. In the latter category we shall study the Isard-Kuenne regional model, Isard's interregional input-output model, the Leontief intranational input-output model, and the Chenery-Moses input-output model.

2.a. Interregional Models: Nonoperational Types

We begin our consideration of spatial models with a variant of Model V-2 and move into more complex forms as we discover the complications of space. After employing these models for the development of spatial problems, we shall approach the more empirically-oriented models.

2.a.1. A Walrasian Type of Interregional Model With Zero Effective Transport Costs

Let us return to Model V-2, the most complex of the neoclassical constructions in this book, and build into it a spatial dimension. For each firm and for each consumer with his associated resource stocks we assume a given location at one of z regional sites, r, $r = 1, \ldots, z$. These regions are punctiform in that no transport costs are involved in movement within any given region. In each region, all markets are assumed to be purely competitive. We shall observe the following conventions: (1) all spatial subscripts (with the exception of those relevant to transportation variables) will precede the symbols used for variables; (2) where it is necessary to indicate another region other than a first region, the subscript r' will be used; and (3) where two spatial subscripts are used, the first will indicate region of origin and the second region of destination.

We assume, also, that the consumer is immobile in terms of his purchases, so that although he will travel between regions within any given "week," all of his sales of factor services and purchases of goods (with the exception of purchases of those transport services not originating within his own region) are transacted in his own region's markets.[12]

A good, d, is introduced into the model, whose unit is defined as the movement of one weight unit (we shall use the average weight of a person as this arbitrary unit) one distance unit. The spatial distances $s_{rr'}$ are data, as are the weights of units of goods Y_j and Z_i, denoted w_j and w_i, while securities and money are assumed to move costlessly between regions ($w_u = w_e = 0$). Transport costs are taken to be proportionate to weight and distance alone. The transportation industry in each region is purely competitive (or forced to act as if it were) and is structured so that each region possesses a monopoly over at least one route, a route being defined as transportation from one region to another and return. There will exist $.5(z^2 - z)$ such routes, exclusive rights to which are distributed arbitrarily among the regions, subject to the route being controlled by a region located on it and to each region having control of at least one such route when $z > 2$. Such transportation industries are assumed to employ factor services from their region of control only.

To the consumer's preference function we add goods $d_{rr'}$. At the end of the week we insist upon all consumers being at their region of origin, but during the week they may travel freely in their leisure time among any and all regions.[13] We denote by P_{d_r} the price of a unit of transport service

[12] This includes the neoclassical factor immobility assumption discussed above. In our case it implies the unrealistic assumption that while newly produced capital goods Z_i and goods Y_j can flow between regions, stocks of existing Z_i and, more objectionably, inventory stocks of Y_j, cannot so move.

[13] At this point some of the complications of space are being ignored in the treatment of transport services as other forms of goods. First, the discontinuous nature of

originating in region r and by $P_{d_{rr'}}$, the price of a trip for a consumer from region r to r' and from region r' to r, obtained by multiplying P_{d_r} by the distance between the regions. The consumer is then viewed as adjusting his purchases to the point where the marginal preferences for each trip divided by its price equals the common marginal preference of income.

We assume that all regions use the same good as *numéraire*, say Y_1, so that ${}_rP_1 \equiv 1$, $r = 1, \ldots, z$, where ${}_rP$ in general denotes a price ruling in region r's markets. If we adopt the guide lines of Model V-2 for this first spatial model, Model VI-1, we need merely rewrite the former's equation system V-2-0:

$$\text{(VI-1-0)} \qquad 1. \quad {}_rX_{cj\neq 1} = {}_rH_{cj\neq 1}({}_rP_{j\neq 1}, {}_rP_i, {}_rP_e, {}_rP_{u'}, {}_rP_{j'}, P_{d_1}, \ldots, P_{d_z}; [{}_r\bar{P}_c], {}_rQ_{cZ_i}, {}_rQ_{cj}, {}_rQ_{cu}) = {}_rH_{cj\neq 1}([{}_rP]; [{}_r\bar{P}_c], [{}_rQ_c])$$

Each of the equations (V-2-0-2) through (V-2-0-6) is similarly rewritten with the subscripts r:

$$2. \quad {}_r\bar{X}_{ci} = {}_rQ_{ci} - {}_rH_{ci}([{}_rP]; [{}_r\bar{P}_c], [{}_rQ_c])$$

$$3. \quad {}_rX_{cq} = {}_rX_{cs} \text{ when } {}_ri_k < {}_ri, \; {}_rX_{cq} = 0 \text{ when } {}_ri_k \geqq {}_ri$$

$$4. \quad {}_rX_{cs} = {}_rH_{cs}([{}_rP]; [{}_r\bar{P}_c], [{}_rQ_c])$$

$$5. \quad {}_rX_{cs} = {}_rX_{cq} + {}_rX_{ce}$$

$$6. \quad {}_r\bar{X}_{cj'} = {}_rQ_{cj'} - {}_rH_{cj'}([{}_rP]; [{}_r\bar{P}_c], [{}_rQ_c])$$

$$7. \quad {}_r\bar{X}_{cu} = {}_rQ_{cu} - \left[\frac{{}_rk_c}{{}_rP_u}\left(\sum_j {}_rX_{cj}\, {}_rP_j + \sum_r \sum_{r'} X_{cd_{rr'}} P_{d_{rr'}} + {}_rX_{ce}\, {}_rP_e + {}_rX_{cq}\, {}_rP_q\right)\right]$$

$$8. \quad {}_rX_{cd_{rr'}} = {}_rH_{cd_{rr'}}([{}_rP]; [{}_r\bar{P}_c], [{}_rQ_c])$$

$$9. \quad {}_rX_{c1} = \sum_i {}_r\bar{X}_{ci}\, {}_rP_i + \sum_j \bar{X}_{cj'}\, {}_rP_{j'} + {}_r\bar{X}_{cu}\, {}_rP_{u'} - \sum_{j\neq 1} {}_rX_{cj\neq 1}\, {}_rP_j - \sum_r \sum_{r'} {}_rX_{cd_{rr'}} P_{d_{rr'}} - {}_rX_{ce}\, {}_rP_e - {}_rX_{cq}\, {}_rP_q$$

---

the consumer's demand for "trips," while not peculiar to such services, is so distinctive a feature of them as to warrant special comment. Second, the complementarity implied by the need for at least one complete circle is ignored. And, even more importantly, our continuous, smooth functions are assumed to yield an interior maximum, requiring that the consumer purchase some of each region's trips. To assume that the individual's optimal market basket will include purchases of such services from all regions is objectionable. Two alternatives suggest themselves: to deny consumers the ability to travel or to recognize the strong presumption of corner solutions and adopt a programming approach with some imagined cardinal preference concept.

The aggregate functions may be written:

(VI-1-1) 1. $_rX_{j\neq 1} = {}_rH_{j\neq 1}([_rP]; [_r\bar{P}], [_rQ])$

and so forth. Aggregate entrepreneurial functions are defined:

(VI-1-2) 1. $_rX_i = {}_rG_i({}_rP_{j\neq 1}, {}_rP_i, {}_rP_{Z_i}, {}_rP_e, {}_rP_{j'}, {}_rP_{u'}, {}_rP_u, {}_rP_{d_r}; [_r\bar{P}^*])$

and so forth, with like alterations of (V-2-2) for equations (VI-1-2-2) through (VI-1-2-6), and with the addition

7. $\bar{X}_{d_r} = {}_rG_r([_rP^*]; [_r\bar{P}^*])$

The zero profits constraint is imposed for each firm in each region:

$$\text{(VI-1-3)} \quad \sum_j {}_r\bar{X}^{\circ}_{vj}\, {}_rP^{\circ}_j + \sum_i {}_r\bar{X}^{\circ}_{vZ_i}\, {}_rP^{\circ}_{Z_i} + \bar{X}^{\circ}_{vd_r} P^{\circ}_{d_r} - \sum_i {}_rX^{\circ}_{vi}\, {}_rP^{\circ}_i - \sum {}_rX^{\circ}_{vj}\, {}_rP_j - \sum_j {}_rX^{\circ}_{vj'}\, {}_rP_{j'} - {}_rX^{\circ}_{vu}\, {}_rP^{\circ}_{u'} = 0$$

In each region, demands and supplies of immobile factor services must be equal in equilibrium, and a similar condition must rule for money which, being useful only in the region in which it circulates, will not be exported:

(VI-1-4)

1. $_rX^{\circ}_i = {}_r\bar{X}^{\circ}_i$
2. $_rX^{\circ}_{j'} = {}_r\bar{X}^{\circ}_{j'}$
3. $_rX^{\circ}_u = {}_r\bar{X}^{\circ}_u$

For exportable goods and services, however, our conditions are changed from Model V-2 in that domestic outputs plus imports ($_rI$) or minus exports ($-{}_rI$) must equal domestic demands:

4. $_rI^{\circ}_j = {}_rX^{\circ}_j + {}_rX^{*\circ}_j + {}_rX''^{\circ}_j - {}_r\bar{X}^{\circ}_j$
5. $_rI^{\circ}_{Z_i} = {}_rX^{\circ}_{Z_i} - {}_r\bar{X}^{\circ}_{Z_i}$
6. $\sum_R \sum_{R'} {}_RX^{\circ}_{d_rR'} + X^*_{d_r} = \bar{X}_{d_r}$

In the last equation, the capital R is used to denote the summation index. The first term is the demand from consumers in all regions for "trips" in which region r has a monopoly of routes, and the second term is importers' demands for the transportation services of region r and will be defined below.

Thus, besides the introduction of transport services into the model, another complication of the spatial dimension consists in the possibility that a region's excess demand for a good or service can be sustained at a nonzero equilibrium level. The determination of these equilibrium excess demand or import terms and the transportation service demands they imply are the major innovations in Model VI-1.

The firm's demands and supplies are described in the following system:

$$\text{(VI-1-5)} \qquad 1. \quad {}_rX_{vi} = {}_rG_{vi}([{}_rP^*]; [{}_r\bar{P}^*_v])$$

and so forth for the same equations in Model V-2 with the obvious modification of regional subscripts through (V-2-5-4). The demands for inventories and money balances are modified as follows:

$$5. \quad {}_rX_{vj'} = \sum_j {}_rk_{vj'j}\, {}_r\bar{X}_{vj} + \sum_i {}_rk_{vj'Z_i}\, {}_r\bar{X}_{vZ_i} + {}_rk_{vj'd_r}\, \bar{X}_{vd_r}$$

$$6. \quad {}_rX_{vu} = \frac{{}_rk_{vu}}{{}_rP_u}\left[\sum_j {}_r\bar{X}_{vj}\, {}_rP_j + \sum_i {}_r\bar{X}_{vZ_i}\, {}_rP_{Z_i} + \bar{X}_{vd_r}\, P_{d_r}\right]$$

And the supply equations for transportation services are added:

$$7. \quad {}_r\bar{X}_{vd_r} = {}_rG_{vd_r}([{}_rP^*]; [{}_r\bar{P}^*_v])$$

The following equalities must rule in each region's securities and money markets:

$$\text{(VI-1-6)} \qquad 1. \quad {}_rX^\circ_e\, {}_rP^\circ_e = \sum_i {}_rX^\circ_{Z_i}\, {}_rP^\circ_{Z_i} + \sum_j {}_rX''^\circ_j\, {}_rP^\circ_j$$

Within every region the rates of return on assets must be equal on a net basis:

$$\text{(VI-1-7)} \qquad 1. \quad {}_rP^\circ_{Z_i} = ({}_rP^\circ_i - u_iP^\circ_{Z_i})\, {}_rP^\circ_e$$

and so forth, as in (V-2-7) with regional subscript modifications.

The same identities are defined as in Model V-2:

$$\text{(VI-1-8)} \qquad 1. \quad {}_rP_e \equiv \frac{1}{{}_ri_k} \qquad 2. \quad {}_rP_q \equiv \frac{1}{{}_ri}$$

as is the equilibrium condition

$$\text{(VI-1-9)} \qquad {}_r\dot{i}^\circ_k = {}_r\dot{i}^\circ$$

A new requirement must rule in that the region must remain within the limits of its income, so that the value of imports and exports as a whole must cancel to zero:

$$\text{(VI-1-10)} \quad \sum_j {}_rI_j\, {}_rP_j + \sum_i {}_rI_{Z_i}\, {}_rP_{Z_i} - \left(\sum_R \sum_{R'} {}_RX_{d_rR'} + \sum_{r'} X_{d_{rr'}}\right) P_{d_r} + \sum_{r'} {}_rX_{d_{r'r'}}\, P_{d_{r'}} = 0$$

where the last three terms on the left-hand side define the net value of domestic purchases of transportation services.

So much for regional requirements. We now consider all regions taken together to obtain the demand for transportation services by importers. These latter are individuals in every market who purchase goods in the region where market cost plus transportation costs are the cheapest non-domestic source of the goods, when that cheapest cost is less than the domestic cost. Their existence is the crucial institutional innovation of this model, for by virtue of their activities their aggregate demand for transportation services may be defined as follows:

(VI-1-11)

$$1. \quad X^*_{d_r} = \sum_{r'} {}_{r'}X^*_{d_r}$$

$$2. \quad {}_{r'}X^*_{d_r} = \sum \max\,[0, {}_{rr'}I_j w_j s_{rr'}] + \sum_i \max\,[0, {}_{rr'}I_{Z_i} w_i s_{rr'}]$$

where rr' define routes whose transport services are produced in region r.

The region's total import terms are defined as the sum of its imports from and exports to every other region:

(V1-1-12)

$$1. \quad {}_rI_j = \sum_{r'} {}_{rr'}I_j$$

$$2. \quad {}_rI_{Z_i} = \sum_{r'} {}_{rr'}I_{Z_i}$$

The desire to import must be matched by the exporting region's equivalent desire to export in equilibrium:

(VI-1-13)

$$1. \quad {}_{rr'}I^\circ_j = -{}_{r'r}I^\circ_j, \qquad r < r'$$

$$2. \quad {}_{rr'}I^\circ_{Z_i} = -{}_{r'r}I^\circ_{Z_i}, \qquad r < r'$$

Also,

(VI-1-14)

$$1. \quad \sum_r {}_rI^\circ_j = 0$$

$$2. \quad \sum_r {}_rI^\circ_{Z_i} = 0$$

As a special case of the more general model we shall develop, let us suppose that space is effectively removed from the decisionmaking of importers by an external agency which provides transportation services to importers on demand at no charge, using resources derived from sources external to the model to provide these services. Effectively, then, for importers, $s_{rr'} = 0$, $r = 1, \ldots, z$, $r' = 1, \ldots, z$, for all goods which are mobile, although transport industries exist within our model to satisfy consumer demands. Under these simplified conditions relative prices of goods must be equal if they can move between regions:

$$\text{(VI-1-15)} \quad \begin{aligned} &1. \quad {}_rP^\circ_{j\neq 1} = {}_{r'}P^\circ_{j\neq 1} \\ &2. \quad {}_rP^\circ_{Z_i} = {}_{r'}P^\circ_{Z_i} \\ &3. \quad {}_rP^\circ_u = e_{rr'}\, {}_{r'}P^\circ_u \end{aligned}$$

The $e_{rr'}$ terms are $z - 1$ in number ($e_{rr} \equiv 1$) and express the number of units of money in region r which exchange for a unit of money of region r'; i.e., they are exchange rates. Our system is one of z paper currencies used only in their respective regions. Absolute price levels need not be equal among regions and therefore exchange rates will emerge in equilibrium. On the other hand, if exchange ratios are given—say by a rigorous gold standard which really unites all currencies into a single currency—then we should convert all currency demands into a demand in terms of region r's currency:

$$\text{(1)} \quad {}_rX^*_u = {}_rX_u + \sum_{r'} {}_{r'}X_u\, e_{rr'}$$

and all cash balance supplies into the equivalent in region r's currency:

$$\text{(2)} \quad {}_r\bar{X}^*_u = {}_r\bar{X}_u + \sum_{r'} {}_{r'}\bar{X}_u\, e_{rr'}$$

and require that

$$\text{(3)} \quad {}_rX^{*\circ}_u = {}_r\bar{X}^{*\circ}_u$$

This will determine ${}_rP_u$ and from the $e_{rr'}$ terms all ${}_{r'}P_u$. This latter treatment would require that money be mobile between regions, so that an import term for it is introduced into (VI-1-4):

$$\text{(VI-1-4-7)} \quad \begin{aligned} &1. \quad {}_rI_u = {}_rX_u - {}_r\bar{X}_u \\ &2. \quad e_{rr'}\, {}_{r'}I_u = e_{rr'}({}_{r'}X_u - {}_{r'}\bar{X}_u) \end{aligned}$$

where

$$\text{(VI-1-12-3)} \quad {}_rI_u = \sum_{r'} e_{rr'}\, {}_{rr'}I_u$$

$$\text{(VI-1-13-3)} \quad \sum_r {}_rI_u\, e_{rr'} = 0$$

Thus, if we wish to introduce known exchange rates we should introduce the three systems immediately above into our model.[14]

We may eliminate one equation per region (say one from system VI-1-4-1) because it is derivable from (VI-1-10), (VI-1-3), and (VI-1-4).

[14] For a similar treatment, see J. Mosak, (1), pp. 54–5.

Also, for the now familiar reasons we can eliminate one equation defining an input demand for each firm in each region. Lastly, we may eliminate $m + n - 1$ equations from (VI-1-13), since they will follow from the rest of the system.

For a readily discerned reason, Model VI-1 is not soluble. Under the spaceless conditions of importers' decisionmaking in the model, the regional import terms ${}_rI_j$ and ${}_rI_{Z_i}$ are determinate, but their distribution among regions—a distribution which if economically rational would be made on the basis of some concept of spatial costs—is not determined by the model since these costs do not exist in meaningful forms. For example, assume that the solution dictated that region 1 produce 5000 units of Z_1 in excess of its own requirements of 10000 units. No reason exists to prevent the export of 6000 units of region 1's production and the subsequent import from (say) region 10 of 1000 units, and such expensive (in external resources) cross-haulage is potential in many different patterns.

We may correct these indeterminacies by arbitrarily assuming a pattern of ${}_{rr'}X_j$ and ${}_{rr'}X_{Z_i}$. There are $z^2n - zn$ and $z^2m - zm$ respectively of such terms, but by the restrictions that they equal the regional export terms (see (VI-1-4)), that the reciprocity relationships hold among regions (see (VI-1-13)), and that the regional import terms sum to zero (see (VI-1-14)), the number of terms that can be specified arbitrarily as data is reduced to $.5z^2n - 1.5zn + n$ and $.5z^2m - 1.5zm + m$ respectively.

This may be seen in the following example. Suppose for good Y_1 in a four-region model we filled in (VI-1-12):

(4)

1. $${}_1I_1 = {}_{12}I_1 + {}_{13}I_1 + {}_{14}I_1$$
2. $${}_2I_1 = {}_{21}I_1 + {}_{23}I_1 + {}_{24}I_1$$
3. $${}_3I_1 = {}_{31}I_1 + {}_{32}I_1 + {}_{34}I_1$$
4. $${}_4I_1 = {}_{41}I_1 + {}_{42}I_1 + {}_{43}I_1$$

All but one of the reciprocity relationships are stated in (VI-1-13), since one was eliminated:

(5)

1. $${}_{12}I_1 = -{}_{21}I_1$$
2. $${}_{13}I_1 = -{}_{31}I_1$$
3. $${}_{14}I_1 = -{}_{41}I_1$$
4. $${}_{23}I_1 = -{}_{32}I_1$$
5. $${}_{24}I_1 = -{}_{42}I_1$$

And, lastly, from (VI-1-14),

(6) $${}_4I_1 = -{}_1I_1 - {}_2I_1 - {}_3I_1$$

If we substitute from (5) and (6) into (4) we obtain:

$$(7)\quad \begin{aligned} &1. && {}_1I_1 = {}_{12}I_1 + {}_{13}I_1 + {}_{14}I_1 \\ &2. && {}_2I_1 = -{}_{12}I_1 + {}_{23}I_1 + {}_{24}I_1 \\ &3. && {}_3I_1 = -{}_{13}I_1 - {}_{23}I_1 + {}_{34}I_1 \\ &4. && {}_4I_1 = -{}_{14}I_1 - {}_{24}I_1 - {}_{34}I_1 \end{aligned}$$

Now, given the ${}_rI_j$ terms, if we specify $z - 2$ terms in (7-1), the remaining term follows. If we specify $z - 3$ terms in (7-2), the other term follows. In general, the number of degrees of freedom is the sum of the degrees of freedom in each equation, or

$$(8)\quad [(z-1)-1] + [(z-1)-2] + \cdots [(z-1)-(z-1)]$$

which reduces to

$$(9)\quad (z-1)^2 - \sum_{y=1}^{z-1} y$$

where y denotes positive integers. The sum of the first $z - 1$ positive integers is $.5(z^2 - z)$, which may be substituted into (9) to obtain

$$(10)\quad (z-1)^2 - .5(z^2 - z) = .5z^2 - 1.5z + 1$$

For n goods Y_j, therefore, we must specify

$$(11)\quad .5nz^2 - 1.5nz + n$$

of the ${}_{rr'}I_j$ terms as data, leaving

$$(12)\quad nz^2 - zn - .5nz^2 + 1.5nz - z = .5nz^2 + .5nz - n$$

such terms as variables. Similarly, we have

$$(13)\quad .5mz^2 + .5mz - m$$

of the ${}_{rr'}I_{Z_i}$ terms as variables.

Let us now gauge the number of equations and unknowns in Model VI-1 to see that they remain in equality. We may multiply the unknowns and equations of Model V-2 by z, the number of regions, and count the additions to unknowns and equations added by Model VI-1 to this augmented number in Model V-2.

To the unknowns we have added: (a) ${}_rX_{cd_{rr'}}$, $.5(s)(z^3 - z^2)$ in number; (b) ${}_rX_{d_{rr'}}$, $.5(z^3 - z^2)$ in number; (c) P_{d_r}, z in number; (d) $\bar{X}_{vd_r}$, oz in number; (e) $\bar{X}_{d_r}$, z in number; (f) $X^*_{d_r}$, z in number; (g) ${}_{r'}X^*_{d_r}$, $z(z-1)$ in number; (h) ${}_rI_j$, nz in number; (i) ${}_rI_{Z_i}$, mz in number; (j) ${}_{rr'}I_j$, $z^2n - zn$ in number; (k) ${}_{rr'}I_{Z_i}$, $z^2m - zm$ in number; and (l) the $e_{rr'}$, $z - 1$ in number. However, by virtue of the conclusions in (12) and (13) we reduce the number of variables in (j) and (k) in the above specification to (j′) $.5nz^2 + .5nz - n$ and (k′) $.5mz^2 + .5mz - m$.

To the equations we have added: (a) (VI-1-0-8), $.5s(z^3 - z^2)$ in number; (b) (VI-1-1-8), $.5(z^3 - z^2)$; (c) (VI-1-2-7), z; (d) (VI-1-4-6), z; (e) (VI-1-5-7), oz; (f) (VI-1-10), z; (g) (VI-1-11), $z + z(z - 1)$; (h) (VI-1-12), $zn + zm$; (i) (VI-1-13), $.5z(zn + zm - n - m)$; (j) (VI-1-14), $m + n$; and (*k*) (VI-1-15), $zn + zm - n - m$. However, some of these equations are redundant. First, an equation may be dropped from (VI-1-10). If this system is added together, the sum is the same as the sum over all regions of (VI-1-4-6) multiplied by their respective prices and (VI-1-14) times their respective prices. Therefore, we substitute for (f): (f′) (VI-1-10), $z - 1$. Second, we may remove $m + n$ equations from (VI-1-13), since substitutions from it and (VI-1-14) into (VI-1-12) will yield one ${}_{rr'}I$ term for each good considered. Therefore, (VI-1-13) in (i′) has $.5z(zn + zm - n - m) - n - m$ equations.

The number of equations equals the number of unknowns and the system therefore meets the *prima facie* conditions of solubility.

Given the specified number of ${}_{rr'}I$ terms as data, the model ideally would allow us to trace the flow of interregional goods among the regions and the demand by the external agency for transport services *of the types* produced by each region but obtained externally. They may be determined by determining the ${}_{r'}X^{*o}_{d_r}$ and $X^{*o}_{d_r}$ from (VI-1-11), but, of course, these values are zero in all other systems of the model.

This model of effectively zero spatial frictions is of some interest. First, in static equilibrium before a stationary state is reached, real factor prices will be equalized among regions when newly produced units of such factors are mobile among regions. However, factor services, being immobile by assumption, need not be equalized in price among regions, and therefore, the equilibrium interest rates and net rates of return on capital, though equal within each region need not be equal among regions. However, as capital goods depreciate out of existence, yielding amortization allowances which may be sent abroad as new capital goods, interest rates and rates of return among regions must approach equality if the marginal productivity functions for labor and land in all processes are continuous. In full stationarity, the equality will have been achieved given such restrictions upon technology functions.

Second, another interesting aspect of the model is that in equilibrium every region is assumed, by virtue of the interior maximum achieved, to produce some of every good but those transport services over which it has no monopoly. This, of course, requires through the imposition of the second-order equilibrium conditions we have assumed, the assumption of rising marginal cost curves in the neighborhood of the firm's equilibrium. In equilibrium, every firm in every region will produce marginal units of output at the same cost, but intramarginal units may be produced at different costs reflecting the different factor service prices ruling in the region. If all regions were carbon copies in all relevant data no interregional trade need occur, but, under our effectively spaceless economy, no penalties would attach to movement of goods among regions in any pattern that kept net flows nil.

2.a.1.a. The Ohlin Interregional Model

Ohlin's famous interregional model[15] is a variation of Model VI-1 in which technology in each single-product industry in every region is identical with that of the same industry in every other region. Moreover, it is characterized by linear homogeneous production functions. These two assumptions would yield identical horizontal marginal (and average) cost functions for each industry in each region if factor service prices were to be equal among regions. In Ohlin's general solution, factor immobility among regions and the inability of money or securities to move interregionally lead to different factor prices and interregional trade.[16] His model—in the Casselian tradition and much simpler than Model VI-1—assumes for each of z regions ($z = 2$ in Ohlin's presentation) a set of demand functions for goods Y_j obtained by summing over underlying sets of individual demands given as data:[17]

(14)

$$1.\quad {}_rX_{j\neq 1} = {}_rH_{j\neq 1}([P_j^*], [{}_rP_i]; [{}_rQ_{ci}])$$

$$2.\quad {}_rX_1 = \sum_c \sum_i {}_rQ_{ci}\, {}_rP_i - \sum_{j\neq 1} {}_rX_{j\neq 1}\, P_j^*$$

[15] B. Ohlin, (1), pp. 553–62. We have substituted our own symbols and have generalized the model from 2 to z regions.

[16] For an Ohlin-type model, neglecting demand conditions, Samuelson has shown that relative factor prices will be equal in all countries (their values in a non-money *numéraire* will be equalized) under a broad range of conditions. When $n = m$, so that in every nation the number of primary resources just equals the number of goods produced, when goods and services taken singly and in groups are technologically distinctive, when technology is similar among the regions as well as linear and homogeneous, and no barriers to goods movement exist, this equalization must occur. Also, when $n > m$, and when all P_j adjust to the costs of production such that profits do not exist, under the same additional assumptions above, as long as no region's factor endowments are so different from another's as to lead it to produce fewer than m goods, factor service price equalization will also occur. When $n < m$, factor endowments must be given for a determination of factor service prices, and factor price equalization will not occur. See P. Samuelson, (8).

[17] Ohlin's model differs from the variant presented here in several respects:

a. He places individuals' incomes in the demand functions, but since he determines these and factor service prices, we may replace incomes with the factor service endowments (= supply of factor services in Ohlin);

b. Ohlin's model is essentially a barter model, although he mentions vaguely that financial conditions are implicit which determine the price of one regional money unit as unity and all other regional money units are related to it (presumably in some equilibrium relationship), so that exchange rates are determined outside the model.

As explained in Chapter 5, we find this dichotomized and implicit treatment of "money" unsatisfactory. Ohlin is merely using an external *numéraire* in which to define all prices, as, for example, discussed by J. Mosak, (1), pp. 9–10. We shall choose instead an internal *numéraire*, in an explicit barter economy. We let $P_1^* = 1$, by definition, i.e., the price of Y_1 ruling in all regions is unity, so that all of our prices are on the same basis.

c. We have made one of our demands dependent upon income and all other purchases, which Ohlin does not do explicitly but recognizes the need to do.

where the P_j^* denote the *ruling* prices in all regions, in or out of full interregional equilibrium.

The *virtual* prices of goods *if they were in fact produced* in region r—whether they are produced or not—would be equal to the average cost of production, given potential competition:

(15) $$_rP_j = \sum_i {_ra_{ij}}\,{_rP_i}$$

The $_ra_{ij}$ are *virtual* average (and marginal) production coefficients derived from linear homogeneous production functions linking *virtual* output to inputs:

(16)
1. $$_r\bar{X}_j = {_rT_j}({_ra_{ij}}\,{_r\bar{X}_j})$$
2. $$_ra_{ij} = {_rH'_{ij}}({_rP_i})$$

Factor services, which are perfectly mobile among uses within regions and perfectly immobile between regions, must achieve a local balance of supply and demand:

(17) $$\sum_j {_ra_{ij}}\,{_r\bar{X}_j} = \sum_c {_rQ_{ci}}$$

Net import terms are defined as

(18) $$_rI_j = {_rX_j} - {_r\bar{X}_j}$$

In full equilibrium, from virtual prices and virtual outputs there will emerge actual prices, P_j^*, which are defined as

(19) 1. $$P_j^* = \min_r\,[{_rP_j}]$$

For those virtual outputs whose virtual prices are above P_j^*, we require that actual values of zero rule, which we may write[18]

2. $$_rP_j\,{_r\bar{X}_j} = 0, \qquad {_rP_j} \neq P_j^*$$

For each good, total output over all regions must equal total demand:

(20) $$\sum_r {_rI_j} = 0$$

[18] We assume, with Ohlin, that only one region produces each good in equilibrium. We have seen in our linear programming models that if two or more processes are equally profitable we need operate only one of them, and it is assumed the assignment is made in some way to a specific region, say the region with the smallest symbol number.

Lastly, each region must import only the value of its exports:

$$\sum_j {}_rI_j P_j^* = 0 \tag{21}$$

We may eliminate three sets of equations from systems (14)—(21), which constitute the Ohlin model. First, for familiar reasons, if $m - 1$ markets for factor services are in equilibrium and the region is balancing its import-export account, the mth must be in balance, so that z equations in (17) may be dropped. Second, since production functions are linear and homogeneous, Euler's Theorem holds for each industry in each sector. From our analysis of Chapter 3, we know that this fact combined with the profit maximization conditions, allows us to drop one equation per industry per region from (16-2). Lastly, if all regions are in external balance, and net imports over all regions for $n - 1$ goods are zero, it must follow that the nth good also has zero net imports. Therefore, we may eliminate one equation from (20).

The equations, therefore, number: (a) system (14), $nz - z$; (b), system (15), zn; (c), system (16), znm; (d), system (17), $zm - z$; (e) system (18), zn; (f), system (19), zn; (g), system (20), $n - 1$; and (h), system (21), z. The unknowns are: (a) ${}_rX_j$, nz in number; (b) ${}_r\bar{X}_j$, nz in number; (c) ${}_rI_j$, nz in number; (d) ${}_rP_j$, nz in number; (e) P_j°, $n - 1$ in number; (f) ${}_rP_i$, mz in number; and (g) ${}_ra_{ij}$, nmz in number. The equations equal the unknowns in number.

The major differences between Model VI-1's solution and the Ohlin-type model's solution are the lack of all-region production of every good in the latter, although both reflect their essential spacelessness by uniform goods prices among regions.

Under what conditions need there be no interregional trade in the Ohlin model?[19] Ohlin deals with this problem at some length and shows, of course, that if tastes are similar in all regions, under the similar technology and linear homogeneity assumptions, equal relative factor endowments will result in equal relative prices for factor services. These will induce the same factor proportions for the production of the same good in every region, and lead to uniform relative prices in all regions for goods. Thus, one set of conditions which will lead to identical relative prices for all goods among regions and permit the possibility of no trade is met where every region is a scale model taste-wise, resource-wise, and technologically of every other. A second case of identical relative prices would result if regional demands just compensated for differing regional resource endowments, so that relative to consumer demand, resources were equally scarce among regions. For example, the nation with large land endowments would prefer agricultural goods to such an extent that the relative

[19] Even in conditions where all regions will not gain from interregional trade it still may occur without penalty because of zero transportation costs.

price of such goods before trade would equal the prices of such goods in industrial countries.

In either of these two cases, assume a paper currency exists in each region and is immobile between regions. When ${}_rP_j = P_j^\circ$ for all r and all j, let ${}_rP_u \neq {}_{r'}P_u$; i.e., the *numéraire* prices of money depart from equality. In the absence of money flows no tendencies to equality of money prices would exist, for while a unit of Y_1 might buy 2 units of region 2's currency and only 1 unit of region 1's, it would have to be repatriated to region 1 in goods which cost twice as many monetary units in region 2 as compared with region 1.[20]

As we have constructed our model—where the real costs of goods transport are no burden to the active decisionmaker—the ultimate decision as it bears upon interregional trade patterns could be a quite wasteful one in terms of the externally-derived resources used for transportation, as we have demonstrated by an example above. Presumably, however, the external agency which underwrites goods movement will desire to minimize its own costs and even feed them back into the solution to the model so as to place their burden upon importers. In the next section we shall consider such models, beginning with simple schemes for minimization of goods' movement costs and working toward a full recognition of the fictitious nature of our external agency by introducing a minimization-of-costs submodel into Model VI-1.

2.a.2. A Walrasian Type of Interregional Model With Nonzero Transport Costs

We shall assume the external decisionmaker—"the government"—desires initially merely to minimize the number of ton-miles involved in interregional movement of the gross outputs derived from Model VI-1 and now assumed as given from its solution. We shall then move into models which minimize the economic costs of movement. Finally, we shall introduce these "transport costs" as internal costs to the model in order to arrive at a full solution to the interregional trade economy.

2.a.2.a. The Minimization of Ton-Miles

Initially, then, the government, impressed by the need to introduce some constraint upon goods movement, assumes every ton-mile to be like every other in cost, or, identically equal in price to unity.

We may decompose the problem into separable analyses for each good, since there are no interdependences among them insofar as their transport costs are concerned. Therefore, if the number of ton-miles expended on each good is minimized, the total number of ton-miles will have been minimized: suboptimization procedures will have led to a grand optimum. Let us choose, then, any good, Y_j, and seek the minimum of transport

[20] Cf. B. Ohlin, (1), pp. 10–7, 560–2.

costs; i.e.,

$$\min Z_j = \sum_r \sum_{r'} w_j s_{rr'} \, (-_{rr'}I_j) \tag{22}$$

where

$$_{rr'}I_j \geqq 0 \tag{23}$$

subject to

$$\begin{aligned} &1. \quad _rI_j = \sum_{r'} - _{rr'}I_j \\ &2. \quad _{r'}I_j = \sum_r {_{rr'}I_j} \end{aligned} \tag{24}$$

where r denotes known exporting regions and r' denotes the known importing regions. Note that we include only the $.5(z^2 - z)$ importing terms $_{rr'}I_j$ as unknowns.

The formulation of systems (22) – (24) resembles a simple linear programming problem after the introduction of slack variables, or disposal processes. It is, in fact, a "canonical minimum" problem which seeks to minimize an objective function subject to a set of equalities, into which form, as we have seen in Chapters 3 and 6, a linear programming problem is cast for solution. Effectively, there are only $z - 1$ primary constraints. Given the exports of exporting regions and imports of the importing regions, if all but one region's $_{rr'}I_j$ are given, this remaining region's I_j-term must follow from the need of exports to equal imports of the good. It follows that the number of variables ($_{rr'}I_j$) will be greater than the number of *effective* constraints for all $z > 2$.

The government, then, might seek to introduce some concept of economy into goods movement by means of independent linear programming studies of this type. But it would be more sensible, of course, to take into account not only distance and weight but economic cost as well. We shall generalize the ton-mile minimization to a transport-cost minimization model.

2.a.2.b. The Minimization of Transport Costs: The "Classic" Transportation Model

When this is done we have a famous type of linear programming model with broader applications than to transportation problems alone. The problem was originally posed by F. Hitchcock, L. Kantorovich, and T. Koopmans in the 1940's.[21]

In our application we merely modify the objective function of (22)

[21] See T. Koopmans, (1), and (2), Chs. XIV, XXIII; R. Dorfman, (1), Ch. 5; and P. Samuelson, (7).

to include the given transport costs:

$$Z_j = \sum_{r} \sum_{r'} w_j s_{rr'} P_{d_r} (-_{rr'}I_j) \tag{25}$$

In our formulation, P_{d_r} must be understood to be the rate per ton-mile for direct shipment from r, whether or not the transport service is produced with the external resources.

As explained above, the problem is constrained by z equalities in (24) and the nonnegativity requirements of (23), only $z - 1$ of which equalities are independent. Therefore, the basic theorem of linear programming assures us that, at most, only $z - 1$ of the $.5(z^2 - z)$ import terms need to be nonzero in the optimal solution.

The structure of this type of linear programming model is so simple that the computational techniques for its solution are quite easy. To gain greater insight into the nature of this spatial model we shall deal with a five-region example. Suppose in the solution to the prior Model VI-1 relevant to the problem, regions 1 and 2 were net exporters of the product and regions 3, 4, and 5 were importers. Further, assume that ${}_1I_j^\circ = -40$, ${}_2I_j^\circ = -60$, ${}_3I_j^\circ = 20$, ${}_4I_j^\circ = 50$, and ${}_5I_j^\circ = 30$ in that larger model's solution, and that $P_{d_1} = 4$, $P_{d_2} = 5$, regions 1 and 2 having control over the transport routes originating from their territories to the importing regions and return. The table of $s_{rr'}$ is assumed to be that given in Table 7-1:

TABLE 7-1.
ASSUMED DISTANCES BETWEEN REGIONS

		Regions				
		1	2	3	4	5
	1	—	60	50	80	20
	2	—	—	15	90	40
Regions	3	—	—	—	60	10
	4	—	—	—	—	80
	5	—	—	—	—	—

If $w_j = 1$, the transport costs in *numéraire* per unit of Y_j for all possible routes in the solution are given in Table 7-2:

TABLE 7-2.
UNIT TRANSPORT COSTS BETWEEN REGIONS

	1	2	3	4	5
1	—	—	200	320	80
2	—	—	75	450	200
3	—	—	—	—	—
4	—	—	—	—	—
5	—	—	—	—	—

The costs in Table 7-2 are the direct costs of shipping a unit of product from each exporting region to each importing region.

The objective function may be written:

$$(26)\quad Z = 200(-{}_{13}I_j) + 320(-{}_{14}I_j) + 80(-{}_{15}I_j) + 75(-{}_{23}I_j) + 450(-{}_{24}I_j) + 200(-{}_{25}I_j)$$

and the $z - 1$ constraints

$$(27)\quad \begin{aligned} &1. \quad {}_{13}I_j + {}_{14}I_j + {}_{15}I_j = 40 \\ &2. \quad {}_{23}I_j + {}_{24}I_j + {}_{25}I_j = 60 \\ &3. \quad {}_{13}I_j + {}_{23}I_j = 20 \\ &4. \quad {}_{14}I_j + {}_{24}I_j = 50 \end{aligned}$$

where we have multiplied (27-1 and -2) by -1. We also require

$$(28)\quad -{}_{rr'}I_j \geqq 0$$

The first step to a solution is to find a basic feasible solution. We select region 2 and determine the cheapest transport costs to an importing region to be those to region 3. We assume all of region 3's imports come from region 2, leaving 40 units of capacity in region 2 undistributed. The second cheapest destination for region 2's goods is region 5, which we supply totally, after which 10 units of region 2's equilibrium production are left for shipment to region 4. Filling in for region 1's pattern of exports, we obtain the following basic feasible solution:

TABLE 7-3.
A BASIC FEASIBLE SOLUTION

		Importing Regions			
		3	4	5	
Exporting Regions	1	0	40	0	40
	2	20	10	30	60
		20	50	30	

This gives us as included routes 1-4, 2-3, 2-4, and 2-5, and as excluded routes 1-3 and 1-5.

The second step is to define the indirect cost of a shipment as the cost of moving a unit of Y_j along an excluded route by compensated adjustments along included routes. In linear programming terms this is nothing but the equivalent combination of an excluded activity. To get a unit of good from region 1 to region 3 (an excluded route) using only included routes, we should have to decrease goods moving along 1-4 by 1 unit, increase goods moving from 2 to 4 one unit to compensate for the loss, and reduce goods movement from 2 to 3 by a unit. That is, to get the pattern in Table 7-4, the increments must be as shown in Table 7-5.

TABLE 7-4.
INTRODUCTION OF A UNIT MOVEMENT ALONG ROUTE 1-3

		Importing Regions 3	4	5	
Exporting Regions	1	1	39	0	40
	2	19	11	30	60
		20	50	30	

TABLE 7-5.
INCREMENTS IMPLIED BY A COMPENSATED MOVEMENT ALONG ROUTE 1-3

		Importing Regions 3	4	5
Exporting Regions	1	+1	−1	0
	2	−1	+1	0

The net addition to transport costs ascribable to the unit movement along this first excluded route is the sum of the *direct* costs of the movement (found in Table 7-2), symbolized c_{13}, and the *indirect* costs which spring from the need to compensate for the movement, symbolized $\overline{c_{13}}$:

(29) $$\Delta Z = c_{13} + \overline{c_{13}}$$

where

(30) $$\overline{c_{13}} = c_{24} - c_{14} - c_{23}$$

If the combined increment to costs is negative, the introduction of the unit movement along the excluded route will be a profitable substitution; and, because of the linear nature of the model, it will pay for as many units as the model will allow to be so moved.

For route 1-3,

(31) $$\Delta Z = 200 + 55 = 255$$

(32) $$\overline{c_{13}} = 450 - 320 - 75 = 55$$

Therefore costs will rise with an introduction of route 1-3 into the basic feasible solution, and we reject it. For route 1-5,

(33) $$\Delta Z = c_{15} + \overline{c_{15}} = 80 - 70 = 10$$

(34) $$\overline{c_{15}} = c_{24} - c_{14} - c_{25} = 450 - 320 - 200 = -70$$

In this case, neither excluded route offers potential transportation cost savings over the included routes, and so we have happened to choose an optimal basic solution to the problem.

Had we begun with the nonoptimal solution of Table 7-6, we should have found a $\Delta Z < 0$.

TABLE 7-6.
A SECOND BASIC FEASIBLE SOLUTION

	3	4	5	
1	20	20	0	40
2	0	30	30	60
	20	50	30	

From our knowledge of the optimal solution it will prove to be true that excluded route 2-3 will lead to a profitable substitution:

$$\Delta Z = c_{23} + \overline{c_{23}} = 75 - 330 = -255 \tag{35}$$

$$\overline{c_{23}} = c_{14} - c_{24} - c_{13} = 320 - 200 - 450 = -330 \tag{36}$$

The net contribution to costs of route 1-5 has already been calculated in (33). The net result is that it will pay to introduce route 2-3 into the solution, and we would proceed to do so. In order to prevent shipments from falling to negative levels we replace that route in Table 7-6 which enters (36) as a negative number and whose shipments in the initial solution are a minimum. In our case, routes 1-3 and 2-4 enter (36) as negative in costs, and from Table 7-6 we find that 20 and 30 units of product move over them respectively. Therefore, we substitute route 2-3 for route 1-3, and from our knowledge of the solution we know that this modified basis will provide the optimal solution.

Lastly, we may assume that we have worked out similar solutions for all $-_{rr'}I_j$ and $-_{rr'}I_{Z_i}$ in the model. By substituting these into (VI-1-11) we may obtain the demand for transportation services for goods movement. As long as these are borne by external factor services our model is complete.

2.a.2.b.1. THE DUAL SOLUTION TO THE CLASSIC TRANSPORTATION PROBLEM. As we have seen in Chapter 3 every linear programming model has a dual problem which is frequently of more than formal interest to the economist. If we solve the dual for the "government's" problem in the transportation case, we can derive certain price relationships which must hold in temporary equilibrium (i.e., before feedbacks via the introduction of transport costs into Model VI-1).

To obtain the dual we must recast the original model into a different and more familiar mold, by rewriting the constraints to include the possibility of inequalities:

$$\text{(37)} \quad \begin{aligned} &1. \quad {}_rI_j \leqq \sum_{r'} {}_{rr'}I_j \\ &2. \quad -{}_{r'}I_j \leqq \sum_{r} - {}_{rr'}I_j \end{aligned}$$

The first set of constraints states that exporting regions must produce at least enough to cover shipments to importing regions, and the second set that imports received by importing regions must be no more than the sum of such shipments from exporting regions. As long as the postulates of the system include the condition that $-\Sigma_r\, {}_rI_j = \Sigma_{r'}\, {}_{r'}I_j$, as is true in (VI-1-14), the optimal solution will never allow the inequality signs to hold, so that the differences between this statement of constraints and that in (24) are wholly formal.

Following the rules defining the dual as developed in Chapter 3, we set up the following problem:

$$\text{(38)} \qquad \max Z^* = \sum_{r'} {}_{r'}I_j\, {}_{r'}P_j^* + \sum_{r} {}_rI_j\, {}_rP_j^*$$

subject to

$$\text{(39)} \qquad {}_{r'}P_j^* - {}_rP_j^* \leqq s_{rr'}P_{d_r}$$

when

$$\text{(40)} \qquad {}_{r'}P_j^* \geqq 0,\ {}_rP_j^* \geqq 0$$

We may interpret the ${}_rP_j^*$ variables as the shadow prices of regions' exports and the ${}_{r'}P_j^*$ variables as the shadow prices of regions' imports. For given exports, imports, and transport costs, we may look upon the "government" as minimizing transport costs by choosing a set of shadow prices which maximizes the total value of imports over exports when both are valued at shadow prices, such that no import price exceeds an export price by more than transport costs. That is, the government seeks a set of prices which would emerge from a purely competitive market system if it were allowed to function.

Our knowledge of linear programming techniques tells us that the inequality will hold for all ${}_{rr'}I_j$ which are not in the optimal solution, while the equality will hold for those ${}_{rr'}I_j$ included in that solution at positive levels. From our prior solution of the primal problem, we know that the following equalities will hold in our example:

$$\text{(41)} \quad \begin{aligned} &1. \quad {}_4P_j^* - {}_1P_j^* = 320 \\ &2. \quad {}_3P_j^* - {}_2P_j^* = 75 \\ &3. \quad {}_4P_j^* - {}_2P_j^* = 450 \\ &4. \quad {}_5P_j^* - {}_2P_j^* = 200 \end{aligned}$$

There are four price differences and four equations. We may get absolute prices by having the government substitute the known market price in one exporting region—say region 1—for the corresponding shadow price, ${}_1P_j^*$; then,

$$(42)\qquad \begin{aligned} &1. \quad {}_4P_j^* = {}_1P_j^\circ + 320 \\ &2. \quad {}_2P_j^* = {}_1P_j^\circ - 130 \\ &3. \quad {}_3P_j^* = {}_1P_j^\circ - 55 \\ &4. \quad {}_5P_j^* = {}_1P_j^\circ + 70 \end{aligned}$$

As in all such programming problems, the minimum $Z =$ the maximum Z^*, or 24,800 units of *numéraire*—the minimum transport bill as well as the maximum excess of delivered value at prices reflecting transport costs over f.o.b. values of the goods entering interregional trade—are equal.

The next step is to relax the twin assumptions which allow us to decompose Model VI-1 into two dependent but noninterdependent models: that external decisionmakers use external resources to move goods interregionally. Let us drop them in turn. First, assume the government continues to bear the costs of the $X_{d_r}^{*\circ}$, but that these services are produced by the regions in the model; i.e., our solution to the transportation model feeds back into the initial solution which was derived on the assumption that $X_{d_r}^* = 0$. The new solution to Model VI-1 will require a new optimal solution to the transportation problem, which would feed back into the larger model, and so forth. Ultimately, we should suspect, given the proper structural properties of the model, these iterative solutions would converge to a limiting solution.

Indeed, by dropping the fiction that the government is responsible for the transport decisionmaking, and internalizing it as part of the purely competitive process, it is possible to obtain the above solution directly as a solution to a complex programming problem which includes Model VI-1, less systems (VI-1-15-1) and (VI-1-15-2) as constraints. For these two systems we substitute the conditions derived from our linear programming dual:

$$(\text{VI-1-15}')\qquad \begin{aligned} &1. \quad ({}_{r'}P_j^\circ - {}_rP_j^\circ - w_j s_{rr'} P_{d_r})({}_{rr'}I_j) = 0 \\ &2. \quad ({}_{r'}P_{Z_i}^\circ - {}_rP_{Z_i}^\circ - w_i s_{rr'} P_{d_r})({}_{rr'}I_{Z_i}) = 0 \end{aligned}$$

These $zn - z - n + 1$ and $zm - m$ conditions substitute for an equal number in (VI-1-15-1) and (VI-1-15-2).[22]

[22] Pareto, facing the problem of deriving and stating these conditions for his two-region international trade model took a wrong turn. He states the conditions for equilibrium in both nations after the introduction of trade between them, and then says that if a good is not produced in a nation, one of the equations requiring the equality of prices of that good in both countries becomes an inequality. He states, however, that while one equation is lost so is one unknown—the quantity of good

As in the previous two variants of Model VI-1, we should have to solve such a model by iterative methods and we assume that, with properly behaved functions, such iterations would converge to the equilibrium values described by the model.

The derivation of equilibrium conditions from a maximization model when partial derivatives do not exist by virtue of transport cost functions was first done by P. Samuelson in a generalization of Enke's electric analogue model.[23] For the one-good, two-region case of Enke, and the more general one-good, z-region case, in both of which import-export terms may be viewed as functions of a single price, Samuelson derives a "net social payoff" function over all regions by adding the integrals of the regions' net import functions and subtracting the transport cost functions. By maximizing net social payoff Samuelson derives the analogue of conditions (VI-1-15′-1) and (VI-1-15′-2) and demonstrates, as we have done above, that when the terms ${}_rI_j$ are given, this maximization implies the Koopmans cost-minimization model. Although he makes no attempt to generalize the analysis to import functions of more than one price, he does in a footnote point the solution used here, which involves the dual of the transportation problem.

Isard attempted the generalization to a general equilibrium system of the Samuelson method, using an allied artificial concept, "surplex," maximization of which yielded the conditions (VI-1-15′-1 and VI-1-15′-2).[24] Although the functions he deals with are multidimensional in prices, Isard treats them as unidimensional in these variables, and, consequently, the nature of the analysis is not clear. In a later article with D. Ostroff,[25] he abandons the surplex generalization and adopts the method used above which is related to the dual of the Koopmans model. These authors adopted the convenient manner used in VI-1-15′ of stating the conditions for equilibrium.

2.b. Interregional Models: Operational Types

After the treatment in previous chapters, the reader need not be reminded that such models as Model VI-1 have little analytical use, other than as road maps to the spatial economic terrain. We turn our attention now to general spatial models with given space structures which do have potentialities for application to realistic problems.

It will not be surprising that these models are linear in structure:

---

produced in the nation in question—and determinateness is salvaged. This is a result that must flow from the solution to the model, not be assumed to be known in advance. V. Pareto, (1), Vol. I, pp. 181–2. He follows the same course when confronted with factor services becoming free goods—a problem which will concern us in Chapter 9. See (1), Vol. II, p. 212*n*.

[23] P. Samuelson, (7), and S. Enke, (1).

[24] W. Isard, (6).

[25] W. Isard, (8).

either extensions of the input-output analysis already presented in Chapter 6, or applications of linear programming to interregional flows, as our presentation of the transportation model above will illustrate. We shall present four well-known spatial input-output models: (1) the Isard-Kuenne regional model, (2) Leontief's intranational model, (3) Isard's interregional model, and (4) the Chenery-Moses interregional model. Lastly, we shall discuss the general interregional linear programming model, associated primarily with the names of Henderson and Stevens.

2.b.1. The Isard-Kuenne Regional Input-Output Model

The simplest input-output model involving spatial considerations is one which focusses upon a single region and abstracts from its relationships with all other regions in most important aspects. The "spatial" aspect of the model, therefore, inheres primarily in the definition on a spatial basis of a submodel of a complete spatial economic unit. If this model is derived *ab ovo*, it presents the same conceptual problems as the "national" model discussed in Chapter 6, with the added complications of constructing regional input coefficients from poorly defined data.

As a matter of practice, however, it may be derived from the national model by altering the elements in the $[a^*]$ matrix of that model to correspond to regional values.[26] The matrix $[_ra^*]$ is then the matrix of coefficients which show the amounts of region r's domestically-produced inputs into region r's outputs on a physical basis; it is obtained by adjusting the national coefficients to reflect regional peculiarities in technology and resource availability. Suppose a_{37} were the amount of coal used nationally per kilowatt hour of electric power output. If the region were one which used much more hydroelectric power than the nation as a whole, perhaps the regional electric power industry would use only one third the national coal input. We may then define a coefficient, $_rb_{37} = .33$, which, when applied to a_{37}, will yield the regional *requirement* of coal for a kilowatt hour of regional electric current. Further, we may define such $_rb$-values for every a_{ij} in the national table, and we may derive $[_ra'']$ as the matrix of products $a_{ij} \times {_rb_{ij}}$. Then

$$(43) \qquad [I - {_ra''}][_rx''] = [_rX]$$

yields the vector of regional *requirements* (*not outputs*) $[_rx'']$ for a given bill of regional outputs on final demand account $[_rX]$.

In the national model a similar distinction arises in treating competitive imports, or those which are similar in use to goods produced in the nation. Noncompetitive imports as inputs into the nation's sectors are found in the imports row—external to the matrix in the same manner as primary inputs are external. Suppose it requires \$.30 of natural rubber to

[26] See W. Isard, (3); F. Moore, (1); and R. Miller, (1).

produce \$1 of United States rubber products, and \$.20 of synthetic rubber inputs. If natural and synthetic rubber are treated as separate products, the latter being domestically produced, the natural rubber input would be external to the $[I - a]$ matrix and the synthetic rubber input internal to it. A bill of goods will not therefore yield an x'-term, or gross output term, for natural rubber. Effectively, this term for natural rubber *produced in the United States* is zero, and were all imports so treated the vector $[x']$ could be treated as we described it in Chapter 6 as gross outputs.

But suppose the classification of industries makes no distinction between synthetic and natural rubber. Then, in the Leontief table, imports of natural rubber are allocated in the import row to the synthetic rubber industry as an input, and this industry's output row reveals the distribution of its own output and natural rubber imports to all sectors in the table. A bill of goods will then yield a solution vector $[x']$ in which the value for the synthetic rubber industry represents the *requirements* for all rubber needed to support that bill of goods, not only domestically-produced rubber. The requirements figure will overstate the response of the domestic industry to the bill of goods by the induced import requirements for natural rubber. If we are interested in the output-impact of a bill of goods on domestic industry, we are interested in x' less import requirements for the synthetic rubber industry. If, however, the nation's imports are small relative to gross outputs, and/or most of them are noncompetitive, import requirements found in the table may be neglected with little distortion.

In regional analysis, however, the economy is not usually so closed nor the degree of noncompetitiveness so great. Moreover, frequently the desideratum of the analysis is to derive the impact of some change in the local bill of goods requirements upon local *outputs*, not local industrial requirements. Therefore, we define a set of coefficients, ${}_rc_i$, one for each row, which specify the proportion of the requirements for each sector which are derived from production within the region. If the region provides 10 per cent of all its coal requirements from domestic mines, then ${}_rc_3 = .1$, and we define[27]

$$(44) \qquad {}_ra_{37} = {}_rc_3 \times {}_ra''_{37}$$

or

$$(45) \qquad {}_ra_{37} = {}_rc_3 \times a_{37} \times {}_rb_{37}$$

[27] These adjustments can be made in an iterative solution by multiplying the round requirements by the ${}_rc_i$. Isard and Chenery have suggested this method to correct for the rigidities of supply areas imposed by the vector $[{}_rc_i]$. That is, if the requirements for some input fall slowly round by round, perhaps a larger percentage of it will be sought from outside the region, and the value of ${}_rc_i$ applied to the requirements of later rounds may be heightened appropriately.

This may be dangerous practice for two reasons. First, and less importantly, it might seem to endow the rounds of an iterative solution with a realistic significance

The matrix $[_ra^*]$ of the $_ra_{ij}$ coefficients depicts the input requirements of regionally produced goods and services into regionally produced goods. Then,

$$[I - {_ra^*}][_rx] = [_rc_i\, {_rX_i}] \tag{46}$$

yields regional outputs implied by regional bills of goods, and

$$[_rx'' - {_rx}] \tag{47}$$

yields the regional imports required to support the bill of goods.

The two sets of correction coefficients will remove all rows i from the regional matrix whose products are not produced regionally ($_rc_i = 0$) and the columns of such sectors will similarly disappear ($_rb_{ij} = 0$, $i = 1, \ldots, n$). All other elements in the matrix will be adjusted to regional magnitudes, and the solution will represent regional outputs induced by regional bills of goods. With the regional matrix we may attack those types of problems which were attacked on the national level, and the analogous criticisms and qualifications are applicable. We must consider in addition, however, the specific assumptions implied about the spatial structure of the interregional complex from which the region is abstracted.

First, just as we have frozen the technological structure of national industries, so we have frozen the spatial structure of the region. The region is assumed, even when we desire to increase or decrease the bill of goods, to supply the same given percentage of increments or decrements of all sectoral requirements. From two given supply areas—the domestic and rest-of-the-world—come unchanging proportional responses to the region's requirements. Of course, if all industries in the economy were characterized by linear homogeneous production functions, and primary factor and other capacity limitations could be abstracted from, in the absence of institutional interferences with trade flows all $_rc_i$ could be set at either 0 or 1. They could never exceed 1 because of the assumption that a region's intermediate goods production is a function solely of its own outputs; $_rc_i > 1$ would imply that the rest-of-the-world's input requirements were a function of our region's output—a realistic assumption which is not built into our regional model. Only if industries were characterized by rising marginal costs or if capacities were limited would the $_rc_i$ have intermediate values. In this sense, then, the use of $_rc_i$ with intermediate values

which, as we pointed out in Chapter 6, they do not have. They do not reflect the dynamics of an adjustment process occurring in the economy. But, second, it affords the researcher too much subjective control over the solution $[_rx]$, allowing him to shape his results consciously or subconsciously to conform to those he feels intuitively are proper. To avoid this, sector by sector studies of capacity limitations in every region specified in the analysis would have to be made and from them values of the $_rc_i$ should be made over ranges of requirement levels *before* injecting the bill of goods. Such procedures become speedily unmanageable. See W. Isard, (4), pp. 314–6, and H. Chenery, (2), pp. 343–5.

is a violation of the strict logic of the model in a way that the use of constant coefficients of production for the national model is not.

Accepting the necessary approximative character even of the "ideal" regional model, we must ask how realistic is the assumption of constant supply areas, especially for incremental bills of goods with more than marginal significance. Presumably these supply areas will be more stable the greater the degree of aggregation of extraregional supply areas; i.e., the flow of coal to the Middle Atlantic region from all other regions lumped together into a rest-of-the-world category is more stable than the flow from West Virginia. Therefore, our regional model, with its single outside supply area, should be reasonably safe from this point of view, the source of instability being domestically initiated changes in its own ${}_rc_i$ coefficients only.[28]

Second, this model neglects the feedbacks of its impact upon other regions to itself; i.e., it is *regional* rather than *interregional.* When our region increases its output of rubber products, it increases the demand for natural rubber from the rest-of-the-world; this stimulates requirements of (say) carbon black, some of which may come from the region under consideration. If this feedback were allowed to stimulate the region's outputs, our regional gross output solution would be larger.

The larger the region relative to the rest of the world, the greater the absolute amounts of output involved in this feedback effect, but the relative error may not increase greatly when comparing the gross output without feedbacks and the gross output with feedbacks. Nevertheless the "partial" nature of the framework, spatially, robs the analysis of the comprehensiveness of a more closed system in the spatial sense.

Third, and allied to the second criticism, is the inability of the model to yield impacts upon regional gross outputs of changes in the bills of goods of *other* regions. The implications for the region of a change in the rest of the world's output on final account is not answered by such a model. Once again the lack of an interregional dimension restricts the usefulness of the model.

We shall concentrate attention upon the last two of these criticisms in the remainder of the input-output analysis, since operational means for correcting the first rigidities must be found in linear and nonlinear programming techniques, if the more intuitive and cruder technique of altering the ${}_rc_i$ in the iterative solution (discussed in footnote 27) is rejected.

2.b.2. The Leontief Intranational Model

Leontief's spatial model makes a frontal attack upon the third of the above criticisms.[29] The keystone of the Leontief model is a *vertical*

[28] See the previous footnote.

[29] See W. Leontief, (4), Ch. 4. See also W. Isard, (2), and H. Chenery, (2), and (1), pp. 65–70.

definition of regions with the analytical lines of liaison running from larger to smaller. At any given level of region-size, interaction among all such regions is ignored in favor of studying the relations of such regions with larger and smaller regions. For this reason Leontief terms the model "intranational" to distinguish it from a true interregional model.

To derive the model, let us think of a national model which either has no export-import relations with the outside world, or has such terms given as data. Let us now define a set of mutually exclusive regions r, $r = 1, \ldots, z$, which exhaust the spatial extent of the nation. Then the n sectors of the national model can be partitioned into two sets: (1) those with output wholly consumed within the regions of production, or "regional" sectors and goods, say $l = 1, \ldots, h$; and (2) those with outputs which cross regional boundaries and whose supply-requirements balances are struck nationally, or "national" sectors and goods, say $w = h + 1, \ldots, n$.

Although we need not, let us neglect differences in regional techniques and assume the ${}_rb_{ij} = 1$. Then, given a bill of goods vector $[X']$ for the nation, we may start with the national level of output requirements for all n goods;

$$[I - a][x'] = [X'] \tag{48}$$

Next, we descend to the lower level of analysis to determine $[{}_rx']$, the vectors of gross outputs for the regions. This vector may be broken into two n-component vectors: $[{}_rx_1', \ldots, {}_rx_h', 0, \ldots, 0]$ and $[0, 0, \ldots, 0, {}_rx_{h+1}', \ldots, {}_rx_n']$—the regional output of regional goods and the regional output of national goods respectively. Leontief assumes the regional bill of goods for local goods to be given, $[{}_rX_1']$, and the regional output of national goods to be a fixed proportion of the national output of such goods:

$$[{}_rx_w'] = [{}_rk_w]\,[x_w'] \tag{49}$$

where $[{}_rk_w]$ is a diagonal matrix with ${}_rk_w$ along the diagonal, $w = h + 1, \ldots, n$. Then, the regional gross outputs of regional goods follow from the system

$$[I - a_{ll}][{}_rx_l'] - [a_{lw}][{}_rx_w'] = [{}_rX_l'] \tag{50}$$

where $[a_{ll}]$ is the matrix of requirements of local sectors for local sectors' inputs, $[a_{lw}]$ the matrix of local sectors' inputs into regional outputs of national goods, and $[{}_rX_l']$ the vector of region r's bill of goods requirements for local goods. Then,

$$[{}_rx_l'] = [I - a_{ll}]^{-1}[{}_rX_l'] + [I - a_{ll}]^{-1}[a_{lw}]([{}_rk_w][x_w']) \tag{51}$$

Since $[x'_w]$, the gross output vector of national goods for the nation, is a function of $[X']$, the national bill of goods, $[_rx'_l]$ is a function of (1) $[X']$, (2) $[_rk_w]$, and (3) $[_rX'_l]$.

If there were a second set of mutually exclusive regions, groups of which were wholly contained in the first set of regions and every subregion were contained in one and only one region, we could repeat the above analysis with the larger regions taking the place of the nation and the subregions the place of the regions in the above analysis. We should then have national goods, regional goods, and subregional goods, and the subregions would be assumed to provide fixed percentages of the regional goods production.

This model, therefore, does attempt to deal with the third criticism of the regional model: it does allow us to obtain a regional impact from an extraregional shock. An increased output of national goods resulting from a rise in another region's final demand for regional goods or from a rise in national final demand for national goods has the same impact upon regional outputs of these goods *no matter where* the regional destination for final use may be. The region of use for the final good is ignored in determining the impact upon national goods production in a given region. We therefore purchase the ability to obtain a limited extraregional impact by accepting rigid supply areas and ignoring areas of demand.

Finally, it should be pointed out that Leontief recommended, hesitantly, the inclusion of the household sector in the model for regional analyses, in order to capture the generation of income and its impact upon goods requirements. He is not clear as to the reasons why this procedure is more germane to regional analyses than to national analyses.[30] Chenery and Clark say, in general, that such a procedure is advisable because of the strong impact of local consumption upon local production; but this reasoning does not seem compelling in itself, since for a national model and analysis consumption impacts are "local" and most powerful.[31] We are not arguing that there are not times when excluding the household sector would result in greater distortions than putting it in the matrix even in the most naive fashion. But it is difficult to see why these occasions should be more numerous in regional analyses than in national input-output projections.

2.b.3. The Isard Interregional Model

Isard has constructed a true interregional system which seeks to meet the second criticism of the regional model (which Leontief's model does not) while at the same time it copes even more successfully with the third criticism than does the intranational model.[32] The model is structured

[30] W. Leontief, (3), pp. 100–1.
[31] H. Chenery, (1), pp. 68, 315.
[32] See W. Isard, (1).

horizontally through a set of z regions which constitutes a partition of the nation. Where, in Leontief's system, goods were homogeneous in the eyes of users when they crossed regional boundaries, Isard in effect makes every good produced in region r different from physically similar goods produced in all other regions r'. A given type of steel in Chicago is treated as a different good from the same type of steel in Pittsburgh. Consequently, for n sectors and z regions there are zn sectors over all regions. The balance equations for goods Y_j produced in region r are written:

$$(52) \qquad {}_{r}x'_{j} - \sum_{r'=1}^{z} \sum_{J=1}^{n} {}_{rr'}a_{jJ}\, {}_{r'}x'_{J} = {}_{r}X'_{j}, \qquad \begin{matrix} r = 1, \ldots, z \\ j = 1, \ldots, n \end{matrix}$$

When goods are 'regional' in Leontief's terminology, the corresponding ${}_{rr'}a_{ij}$ terms, $r \neq r'$, are zero, but when goods are "national," these coefficients may be positive. Although the spatial structure is frozen in Isard's model, in that constancy of the ${}_{rr'}a_{ij}$ imposes an absence of substitutability among physically similar but geographically differentiated goods, a greater refinement of the spatial structure is possible than that in the Leontief model since the bill of goods must be specified by regions for all goods, not for regional goods alone. A $1 billion increase in automobile final demand in the Isard model must be broken down into its regional components, with different spatial impacts depending upon the specific pattern chosen, whereas in Leontief's model, constant regional percentages will determine the pattern of national good production regardless of where the increase on final account is assumed to occur.

A distinctive feature of Isard's model is the variability of the sources of imports of the same good among regional users of the good. Let us deal with the good produced by sector 10 of region 2: it may constitute 10 per cent of the needs for sector 10's product in sector 15 of region 1 but only 3 per cent of such needs by sector 5 of region 1. This implies that the products of all regions' sector 10's are not (technologically) perfect substitutes, and/or the intraregional spatial structure is being implicitly taken into account, and/or other monopolistically competitive elements enter the model tacitly. Practically speaking, however, such assumptions multiply the statistical information needed to fill the model, and, consequently, a different model employing a simplifying assumption has been developed by workers in the empirical field.

2.b.4. The Chenery-Moses Interregional Model

Chenery, in his model of the Italian economy, and L. Moses in a model of the American economy, have assumed, essentially, that if a given region 1 imports 10 per cent of its needs for sector 10's product from region 2, every sector in region 1 using this product will take 10 per cent of its needs from sector 10 of region 2. That is, in Isard's model we assumed that there existed a set of ${}_{rr'}a_{ij}$ which were different technical requirements. Assume, now, that the outputs of sector j from any region are indeed technically homogeneous, so that there exists an ${}_{r'}a_{ij}$, or the requirement for input i in sector j in region r'. Then Isard's coefficient would be defined as

(53) $$ {}_{rr'}a_{ij} = {}_{r'}a_{ij} \times {}_{rr'}t_{ij} $$

where the ${}_{rr'}t_{ij}$ denote the proportions of region r''s sector j requirements of product i that come from region r. The Chenery-Moses model makes the simplifying assumption that

(54) $$ {}_{rr'}t_{ij} = {}_{rr'}t_{i} \text{ for all } j $$

The ${}_{rr'}t_{ij}$ terms are the "supply coefficients" of Chenery's model[33] and the "trade coefficients" of Moses's model.[34]

Thus as do their "national" precursors, the regional, intranational, and interregional input-output models achieve a degree of operationalism by rigidifying highly complex relationships. In the spatial models we have a choice of the kind of rigid spatial structures we desire to accept: Leontief's assumption that national outputs of interregional goods are supplied in a fixed relative pattern independent of the region of final use; those of the regional and Isard models with their assumptions of fixed sectoral supply areas; and those of the Chenery-Moses model with assumptions of fixed regional supply areas.

2.b.5. Interregional Linear Programming

The most straightforward application of programming techniques which suggests itself in the spatial problem is to incorporate capacity constraints for regional sectors and primary factors, define regional bills of goods as requirements, and seek to minimize the transport costs on the fulfillment of these bills. But to do so is to solve a suboptimization problem which may have little interest for us. If all sectors had the same technology and resources were in the same relative supply in all regions, only regional final demands and sector capacities would vary among regions, and the suboptimization problem which featured transportation costs would have real meaning. It would, however, minimize such costs on rigidly fixed deliveries which might imply that resources which could be used for production in excess of the bills of goods requirements remain unemployed.

But when we attempt to step beyond such a model, we encounter immediately the fundamental failure of linear programming for general system analysis: a present inability to cope with problems of demand. We are therefore forced to specify prices of final goods as data in such

[33] H. Chenery, (2), pp. 343–4, and (1), pp. 65–70, 314–8.
[34] L. Moses, (1).

models—prices which should emerge as part of the solution. If transportation is a final good, transport rates among regions for final uses must be given. Moreover, if the price of cotton textiles in region 1 is *assumed* to be greater than the price of such goods in region 2 by less than the assumed transport costs between the regions, we have again assumed a result which we sought as a solution in our discussion of the rigidities of supply areas in input-output models.[35]

Therefore, as in the Koopmans model, and unless we have some compelling reason to adopt one set of final good prices over all others, these techniques allow us to define the efficiency frontier of activity levels for all regions, given fundamental resource and capacity restrictions for all regions and any consistent set of final goods prices. Such a frontier, we have seen, "maximizes outputs" in the sense of Pareto, since Koopmans has shown that this procedure is equivalent to maximizing a value-of-final-goods objective function.[36] The solution to the dual problem will be a set of primary factor prices and capacity prices which would emerge in a purely competitive, profit-maximizing economy in the first case, and which would be the minimum values which could be imputed as accounting prices to units of capacity and would exhaust surpluses in the second case. This approach has been taken by Lefeber.[37] Still another modification of this approach has been taken by Isard and Stevens, who assume a set of final goods prices, but constrain the optimal activity levels to meet certain minimum final goods requirements of the regions. The set of optimal solutions defined by all consistent final goods price vectors constitutes a frontier of "semi-efficient" points in Stevens's terminology. We shall consider the Isard-Stevens approach first.

2.b.5.a. The Isard-Stevens Model

For each of z regions we define k activities which are divisible and additive and whose outputs and inputs for a unit level of operation form the columns of the matrix $[{}_rB]$, where output elements are nonnegative and input elements nonpositive. For every region r we may divide the k activities into the following categories:

1. *Productive Activities,* $s = 1, \ldots, d$. These activities absorb primary factor inputs and intermediate goods (except transport services) and yield outputs of intermediate goods (except transport services).

2. *Transport Service Activities,* $s = d + 1$. These activities absorb intermediate goods, except transport services, and primary factor services, to yield transport services, D, as an intermediate good output.[38]

[35] Cf. W. Isard, (7), pp. 45–50, and B. Stevens, (1), pp. 62–3.
[36] See Theorem 5.6 in T. Koopmans, (2), pp. 85–6.
[37] L. Lefeber, (1), pp. 1–97.
[38] Neither Isard nor Stevens includes transport services as a final good. We shall include them, however.

3. *Shipment Activities*, $s = d + 2, \ldots, h$. These activities absorb an intermediate good of region r and transport services from region r to region r' as inputs, and yield a unit of good shipped as an intermediate good to region r' and absorbed by one of its sectors. The shipped output is denoted by the symbol ${}_{rr'}a_{js}$, where s is the activity of region r' which absorbs it.

4. *Final Good Activities*, $s = h + 1, \ldots, k$. These activities absorb a unit of intermediate good in region r and yield a unit of final good. They are wholly formal activities—dummy activities—created for the convenience of the analyst. In the programming models of Chapter 6 intermediate goods were resolved into their primary factor service contents, but Isard and Stevens choose to retain them and consequently must distinguish final goods in this fashion. The inputs of such activities are ${}_ra_{js}$ and the outputs ${}_ra_{Js}$.

We define a vector of coefficients $[{}_rC_s]$ which is the value of each activity, obtained by multiplying the *final* outputs by their given prices and summing, activity by activity. Since final outputs are found only in activities $h + 1, \ldots, k$, only these will have a non-zero value.

Given ${}_rP_j$ and ${}_rP_d$, the latter the prices of transport services, the model seeks to maximize the value of all regions' final output:

$$\max Z = [{}_rC_s] \cdot [{}_rS_s] \tag{55}$$

where $[{}_rS_s]$ is an activity level vector, when this maximization is constrained by the following regional primary factor constraints:

$$\sum_s {}_ra_{is}\, {}_rS_s \leqq {}_rQ_i, \qquad r = 1, \ldots z \tag{56}$$

The ${}_rQ_i$ are the regional endowments of factors.

A second set of constraints requires that the production and net importation of intermediate outputs in region r equal intermediate inputs in region r:

(57)

$$1.\quad \sum_{s=1}^{d} {}_ra_{Js}\, {}_rS_s + \sum_{s=d+2}^{h} \sum_{r'} {}_{r'r}a_{Js}\, {}_{r'r}S_s - \sum_{s=d+2}^{h} \sum_{r'} {}_{rr'}a_{js}\, {}_{rr'}S_s - \sum_{s=h+1}^{k} {}_ra_{js}\, {}_rS_s - \sum_{s=1}^{d+1} {}_ra_{js}\, {}_rS_s = 0$$

$$j = 1, \ldots, n,\ r = 1, \ldots, z$$

$$2.\quad {}_ra_{D,d+1}\, {}_rS_{d+1} - \sum_{s=d+2}^{h} \sum_{r'} {}_{rr'}a_{Ds}\, {}_{rr'}S_s - \sum_{s=h+1}^{k} {}_ra_{Ds}\, {}_rS_s = 0$$

A third set of constraints is a set of "availability constraints," requiring that each region receive at least certain given minimal amounts of each good:

$$(58) \qquad -\sum_{s=h+1}^{k} {}_ra_{Js}\,{}_rS_s \leqq -{}_rR_J, \qquad j = 1, \ldots, n+1$$

where the ${}_rR_J$ terms depict these constraints, and where $d = n + 1$.

2.b.5.b. The Lefeber Model

Lefeber has developed two types of interregional trade model: the first with fixed locations of sectors and zero transport costs on final goods, and the second including positive transport costs on final goods. Moreover, he has designed both models for nonlinear or linear programming, but we shall confine our attention to the latter. Further, we shall deal exclusively with the second transport cost model which includes the first as a special case.

Let there be z points of production to which firms producing final goods Y_j are assigned immovably, and assume that consumption of these goods occurs at a given number of points which, for convenience, we shall assume coincide with production sites. There exist, at each region, given stocks of factor services, ${}_rQ_i$, which are fully mobile among regions. In Lefeber's model, the problem is to allocate the resources and finished goods among production sites in such a way as to maximize the value of final goods output, given a set of final goods prices for all regions. He derived the efficiency frontier for such allocations net of the transport costs of factor and goods movement and unconstrained by Isard's and Steven's availability constraints.

Although Lefeber indicates the ability of his model to include intermediate goods[39] his final model does not do so and we shall follow his practice. We therefore define the following activities:

1. *Production-Shipment Activities.* These activities absorb ${}_ra_{ij}$ of factor service z_i from the pool at region r as well as ${}_{rr'}a_{dj}$ of transportation services to deliver one unit of good Y_j to region r' as final good. We designate activity levels of these activities by ${}_{rr'}\bar{X}_j$.

2. *Transportation Activities.* It is assumed that factor services used for transportation services require no transportation. These activities absorb ${}_ra_{id}$ units of inputs from region r's pool and yield one unit of transport service as an output originating in region r. Activity levels are symbolized ${}_r\bar{X}_d$.

3. *Factor Shipment Activities.* These absorb ${}_ra_{is}$ of a single factor service as input, plus ${}_{rr'}a_{ds}$ of transport services, and yield one unit of

[39] L. Lefeber, (1), pp. 111–2.

delivered factor service a_i to region r'. We define ${}_{rr'}S$ to be activity levels of these activities.

Given ${}_rP_j$ as final good prices in region r, and given production-shipment activities which yield only one output each, the objective is to maximize the total value of final products over all regions:

$$\max Z = \sum_r \sum_j {}_r\bar{X}_j \, {}_rP_j \tag{59}$$

subject to resource constraints not being violated:

$$\sum_{r'=1}^{z} \sum_j {}_ra_{ij} \, {}_{rr'}\bar{X}_j + {}_ra_{id} \, {}_r\bar{X}_d + \sum_{r'} {}_{rr'}S \, {}_ra_{is} - \sum_{r'} {}_ra_{is} \, S_{r'r} \leqq {}_rQ_i \tag{60}$$

Also, we require that the output of transport services cover transport requirements:

$$\sum_r \sum_{r'} \sum_j {}_{rr'}a_{dj} \, {}_{rr'}\bar{X}_j + \sum_r \sum_{r'} \sum_i {}_{rr'}a_{ds} \, {}_{rr'}S - \sum_r {}_r\bar{X}_d \leqq 0 \tag{61}$$

We define:

$${}_r\bar{X}_j - \sum_{r'=1}^{z} {}_{rr'}\bar{X}_j = 0 \tag{62}$$

and require that

$${}_{rr'}\bar{X}_j \geqq 0, \; {}_r\bar{X}_d \geqq 0, \; {}_{rr'}S \geqq 0 \tag{63}$$

In this form we determine regional consumption of final output, regional production of transportation services, and interregional shipments of factors. By varying the ${}_rP_j$ we may define the efficiency frontier of regional consumption. However, given the price structure, the solution will require or allow all of each good to go to a single region—a result Isard and Stevens prevented with their availability constraints.

Neither of these interregional linear programming models helps us in attacking the problems whose existence we noted in the discussion of spatial input-output models. The Lefeber model, especially, with its unconstrained linear maximization yields wholly unrealistic market area results, since even if it were used by planning authorities they could not state their objectives in the straightforward maximization-of-gross national product manner contained in it. On the other hand, if minimal final goods consumption levels are set, and prices are found which meet these minima, no assurance exists that it is a better solution than some other set of final goods prices also meeting the constraints but yielding different supply patterns. In short, the absence of the ability to handle demand relationships in these programming models requires the injection of arbitrary price or other assumptions of necessity unsatisfying.

2.b.5.c. The Graham International Model

One such interregional programming model which does have demand relationships built into it is the international trade model of F. Graham.[40] Its inherent spatial characteristics are minimal, the essence of the model being capable of inscription in a wholly nonspatial framework without distortion. It is, considered most generally, a simplified Koopmans production model, with each activity yielding a single output and absorbing a single primary input, and with each activity divisible and additive. Only primary factor services appear in the activities, and these primary factors originate in the region of production. Therefore, we may look upon intermediate goods as either nonexistent, as having been reduced to primary factor service content, or upon every activity as being wholly integrated so that intermediate products appear as unfinished product within the activity. No intermediate products enter into interregional trade.[41]

In this Leontief-like construction we may identify activities and outputs, and demand curves may be introduced without complications. The problem is to produce a set of goods which is a solution to the demand functions and which is feasible from the point of view of a set of factor service endowments. The fact that the factor services are designated as "labor" in each of z regions is incidental to the basic structure of the model. Transport costs do not exist in it, and demands are not distinguished by regions but are dealt with in the aggregate. Were we given z different factor services in a punctiform economy, therefore, we should have a simple general production model without any spatial implications.

For each region r we define a set of activity vectors specifying for a unit input of its labor service, which is immobile, the output of each Y_j it can produce:

$$(64) \qquad [{}_rB] = \begin{bmatrix} {}_ra_1 & 0 & 0 & \cdots & 0 \\ 0 & {}_ra_2 & 0 & \cdots & 0 \\ \cdot & \cdot & \cdot & \cdots & \cdot \\ 0 & 0 & 0 & \cdots & {}_ra_n \\ -1 & -1 & -1 & \cdots & -1 \end{bmatrix}$$

where ${}_ra_j > 0$, $r = 1, \ldots, z$, $j = 1, \ldots n$, so that every region can

[40] Graham constructed the arithmetic examples which sketch out the model. See F. Graham, (1), Chs. 5 and 6. We are employing the analytical statement of it constructed by L. McKenzie in (2), pp. 148–50.

[41] See L. McKenzie, (2), p. 150.

produce every good. Then

(65) $[B] =$

$$\begin{bmatrix} {}_1a_1 & 0 & 0 & 0 & {}_2a_1 & 0 & 0 & \cdots & 0 & \cdots & {}_za_1 & 0 & \cdots & 0 \\ 0 & {}_1a_2 & 0 & 0 & 0 & {}_2a_2 & 0 & \cdots & 0 & \cdots & 0 & {}_za_2 & \cdots & 0 \\ \cdot & \cdot & \cdot & \cdot & \cdot & \cdot & \cdot & \cdots & \cdot & \cdots & \cdot & \cdot & \cdots & \cdot \\ 0 & 0 & \cdot & {}_1a_n & 0 & 0 & 0 & \cdots & {}_2a_n & \cdots & 0 & 0 & \cdots & {}_za_n \\ -1 & -1 & -1 & -1 & 0 & 0 & 0 & \cdots & 0 & \cdots & 0 & 0 & \cdots & 0 \\ 0 & 0 & 0 & 0 & -1 & -1 & -1 & \cdots & -1 & \cdots & 0 & 0 & \cdots & 0 \\ \cdot & \cdot & \cdot & \cdot & \cdot & \cdot & \cdot & \cdots & \cdot & \cdots & \cdot & \cdot & \cdots & \cdot \\ 0 & 0 & 0 & 0 & 0 & 0 & 0 & \cdots & 0 & \cdots & -1 & -1 & \cdots & -1 \end{bmatrix}$$

The column vector of activity levels is defined as

(66) $[x] = [{}_1x_1, {}_1x_2, \ldots, {}_1x_n, {}_2x_1, \ldots, {}_2x_n, \ldots, {}_zx_1, \ldots, {}_zx_n]$

and the requirements vector is defined as

(67)
1. $[\bar{X}] = [\bar{X}_1^*, \ldots, \bar{X}_n^*, {}_1X_i^*, {}_2X_i^*, \ldots, {}_zX_i^*]$
2. $[B][x] = [\bar{X}]$

where the $\bar{X}_j^*$ are the requirements of final outputs and the ${}_rX_i^*$ the requirements of each region's factor service implied by a pattern of production. It is further required that

(68) $$-{}_rX_i^* \leqq {}_rQ_i$$

where ${}_rQ_i$ is an element in $[Q_i]$, the given vector of capacities; also,

(69) $$[x] \geqq 0, \; [Q_i] > 0$$

Koopmans has shown that in such a model a set of final outputs is efficient if and only if the set of $\bar{X}_j^*$ is feasible and profits are zero on employed activities, negative or zero on unemployed activities, when $P_j > 0$. From the dual it follows that ${}_rP_i > 0$ when $-{}_rX_i^* = {}_rQ_i$ and that ${}_rP_i = 0$ when $-{}_rX_i^* > {}_rQ_i$. In our discussion of the Koopmans model in Chapter 6 it was also asserted that these conditions imply the existence of a vector $[P_j]$ normal to the set of feasible outputs at $[\bar{X}_j^*]$, since at this set of prices the objective function is a maximum.

But the distinctive feature of Graham's model is the specification of one $[\bar{X}_j^*]$ on the efficiency frontier as optimal by virtue of the requirement that this vector fulfill a set of demand and supply functions. That is, we require that

(70) $$-{}_r\bar{X}_i = {}_rQ_i \text{ when } {}_rP_i > 0$$

or that at all positive prices for regional primary factor services the desire to supply must equal the available quantity, while at ${}_rP_i = 0$ the desire to supply is undefined.

World income, Y, is defined as the value of world output:

$$Y \equiv \sum_j \bar{X}_j^* P_j \tag{71}$$

The demand curve for good Y_j is defined as follows:

$$X_j = \frac{b_j Y}{P_j}, \; b_j > 0, \sum_j b_j = 1 \tag{72}$$

The world demand for a good has unit price elasticity at all points, and a constant proportion of income is spent upon it; it is, therefore, of unit elasticity with respect to income as well, and is homogeneous of degree zero in all prices.

We require

$$P_j > 0, \; \Sigma P_j = 1 \tag{73}$$

and, in equilibrium,

$$X_j^\circ = \bar{X}_j^{*\circ} \tag{74}$$

It will be noted that for each good demand increases indefinitely as its price approaches zero, so that consumers' demands for all goods are insatiable. Therefore, prices of all goods must be positive, and with a single factor service per region (70) must hold for all r.

Finally, we impose the equilibrium profit conditions:

$$(75) \quad \begin{array}{lll} 1. & P_j\,{}_r a_j - {}_r P_i = 0, & \text{when } {}_r X_j > 0 \\ 2. & P_j\,{}_r a_j - {}_r P_i < 0, & \text{when } {}_r X_j = 0 \end{array}$$

Now conditions (67-2), (68), and (69) guarantee the feasibility of an output vector, and (75) gives the competitive profits conditions, which, taken together assure that the equilibrium set of X_j will lie on the efficiency frontier as long as $P_j > 0$ for all j. The positive prices we have seen are assured by the structure of the demand functions. Thus, the set of $[P_j]$ normal to the feasible cone at the equilibrium $[\bar{X}_j^*]$ must also satisfy the demand restrictions (70), (71), (72), and (74). In Chapter 9 we shall present McKenzie's proof that such an equilibrium does exist in Graham's model and, further, that it is unique.

3. Locational Models

Up to this point we have been speaking of spatial models in which z regional "points" exist at which consumption and production occur. Moreover, in the nonoperational, nonlinear general equilibrium models we constructed, it was assumed not only that each region could produce each nonlocal, mobile good, but that in the equilibrium each region did produce some of all such goods. The extents of interregional flows, therefore, not the location of discretely distributed production facilities, were the novel variables in these models.

The introduction of programming techniques to recognize the possibility that production of each commodity may not exist in each region is a bridge between interregional trade models and locational models. In this sense, the systems of Isard and Stevens above, and of the Lefeber model to be discussed presently, are models which mix both spatial components in elemental ways.

If we then cross over these bridges by assuming that the conditions of consumption are fixed in simple fashion while the locus or loci of production may vary in more complex manners, it is possible to focus upon the location of production or the origin(s) of a given flow rather than the extent of flow between fixed points. The two aspects of economic space are not distinguished in a clearcut fashion, of course, being abstractions from a completely general model which includes space, but the distinction is clear enough for our purposes.

We shall not attempt to deal with all aspects of location theory. We assume a set of points in two-dimensional Euclidean space which defines a plain over which production and consumption occur in prescribed manners. The set of points is compact, i.e., closed and bounded. We assume, unless otherwise noted, that within the set all inputs of firms are available on the same terms at any point (in the terminology of location theory, all inputs are "ubiquitous"). This assumption is sufficient to indicate that we will consider only a portion of Weberian location theory.[42] Technique will also be assumed identical at all points. Transport costs are equal to a rate per unit of weight times the straight-line distance between two points on the plain times the weight of the product.

The cases we shall consider will be composed of permutations of the following conditions:

1. production may occur only at a specified finite subset of points, and, optimally, *will* occur at only one of those points.
2. production *may* occur at any point of the set and, optimally, will occur at only one point.
3. consumption will occur only at a specified finite subset of points.
4. consumption will occur at all points of the set.
5. consumption at points where it may occur is given and fixed.
6. consumption at points where it may occur is variable and a given function of delivered price only.

We shall depart from these cases in one or two instances to treat existing models of some interest.

[42] A. Weber, (1).

3.a. Case 1: Finite Subset of Virtual Production Points, Finite Subset of Consumption Points, Fixed Rates of Consumption

One of the simplest Weberian location models is that involving the delivery of a fixed amount of good Y_j to a single consumption point from one of a set of alternative production sites all of whose production costs are linear and identical, while transport costs are proportional to weight and distance along straight-line routes. This is immediately seen to resolve into a standard linear programming model, with minimization of transport costs (miles) the objective and the constraints requiring at least as much production as the fixed requirements.

This may be complicated with capacity limitations at the virtual production points, so that the solution may yield more than one production point in the optimal pattern. We may similarly build in differing costs of the virtual production points' activities because of nonidentical costs in the assembling of nonubiquitous raw materials (termed "localized" materials) at the point of production, or in the production process itself. We may multiply the number of consumption points with fixed flows to any finite number. We may allow these consumption points to coincide with virtual production points. With any or all of these complications, a linear programming model remains appropriate with the objective of minimizing the cost in resources of the fixed flows of consumption goods.

An interesting problem arises in this type of model when (1) virtual production may occur at any one of a subset of points for every industry, (2) no two industries may colocate at the same production point, and (3) the profits of one industry are related to the locations of other industries, as, for example, when industries employ other industries' products as inputs, and differential transport costs must be paid depending upon the region of origin of the input. Koopmans and Beckmann[43] have shown that if n industries must be assigned to n regions, if a matrix of profits exists whose elements are the earnings of the industries at each location, and *if these are independent of the assignments of all other industries to other locations*, a linear programming model can be set up and solved *as if* fractional industrial and regional assignments obtained. It follows that there exists a dual problem in which rents may be assigned industries and locations whose sum will exhaust the profits of assignments in the optimal solution and exceed those not in the optimal assignment. Moreover, the existence of the dual assures us that a decentralized pricing system of the purely competitive type can sustain the optimal assignment once reached, since no industry will have an incentive to change location for higher profits.

Now, however, deduct from the profit matrix elements transport

[43] T. Koopmans, (3).

costs on intermediate product flows. This destroys the independence of profits of one assignment from all others and converts the problem from a linear to a quadratic assignment problem. If we relax the requirement that each location must contain all of an industry or none and allow fractional industrial locations, the problem may be kept linear, a solution obtained, and a dual derived from which the rents on location and industries as well as prices of intermediate goods at their production points follow. This latter yields the assurance that a decentralized price structure does exist to sustain the optimal assignment.

However, as long as any intermediate flow is positive, no basic feasible solution, including optimal basic feasible solutions, in which integral assignments are made can be sustained by the operation of the competitive market. That is, for any integral basic feasible solution, no prices are derivable for locations, industries, and products which will not yield an incentive to at least one industry to relocate. For the optimal solution, prices of the locations, industries' opportunities, and intermediate goods must be such that: a. for included assignments, intermediate goods must differ in price between locations only by transport costs; b. for excluded assignments, intermediate product prices between locations must differ by less than transport costs; c. for included assignments profits must be zero after payment of rents and intermediate good prices plus transport costs; d. for excluded assignments potential profits must be negative.

If these conditions hold, no industry will have an incentive to break away from an optimal integral solution. But they will not hold, for Koopmans and Beckmann demonstrate that no integral optimal solution can continue to exist. Therefore, if attained, the system of prices which would rule in a decentralized system would not preserve the optimal assignment. Again, however, we may escape these problems if we allow industries to fractionalize their production, as we have assumed above.

3.b. Case 2: Finite Subset of Virtual Production Points, Finite Subset of Consumption Points, Variable Rates of Consumption

Going still further, we may convert the conditions of production from those of a finite number of divisible and additive activities to an infinite number (i.e., assume linear and homogeneous conditions of production of all goods); introduce demand functions for all goods at all points; and, by enforcing the appropriate equalities and inequalities, fully generalize the model such that nonlinear programming techniques could be applied to its solution. Among the variables would be outputs of each good at each location, and, therefore, the location of production would emerge as a solution to a wholly generalized "Walrasian" model. Such, for example, is the full Lefeber model.[44]

[44] L. Lefeber, (1), pp. 135–47.

The construction of spatial models where production and consumption are distributed in finite subsets through space, and where demand is fixed or variable is the most simple extension of nonlocational models. Moreover, conceptually both aspects of space that we have stressed—the interregional model with fixed locations of production and the locational model—may be integrated into a full spatial model *à la* Lefeber.

3.c. Case 3: Finite Subset of Virtual Production Points, Continuous Consumption, Fixed Rates of Consumption

A classic locational model is that which assumes a continuous distribution of consumers over the plain, with fixed demand rates, and a fixed, finite number of alternative production sites. Usually it is assumed that economies of scale will dictate that either one or all of the virtual points will be optimal production sites in the solution. The problem is to find the market areas of each actual production site and the sales volume of such sites. This "market area" model is most closely associated with the names of Launhardt, Fetter, Palander, and Hoover.[45]

From the viewpoint of the consumer at any point in space, the problem is a trivial one: to choose that production site from which the delivered cost of his fixed consumption rate is a minimum. Let $z = 2$ and assume that we require two production sites to divide the total market. Let ${}_rS$ be that subset of points tributary to site $[R] = [x_r, y_r]$, the latter being the coordinates of point $[R]$. Let $[C] = [x_c, y_c]$ be a consumption point on the plain with the indicated coordinates. Then $[C]$ will belong to ${}_rS$ ("be an element of the set ${}_rS$") if the delivered price from $[R]$ of a unit of good is no more than the delivered price from region r'. We will write this:

$$(76) \qquad [C] \in {}_{r'}S \text{ if } {}_rP_j + w_js_{rc}P_{d_r} \leqq {}_{r'}P_j + w_js_{r'c}P_{d_{r'}}$$

where $\in$ stands for "element of". Thus, we may define ${}_rS$ as that part of the set of points, $[C]$, possessing the property described in (76):

$$(77) \quad {}_rS = \{[C] \mid {}_rP_j + w_js_{rc}P_{d_r} \leqq {}_{r'}P_j + w_js_{r'c}P_{d_{r'}}, [R] \neq [R'], \text{ for all } [R']\}$$

In our case for $z = 2$ we have arbitrarily included the boundary line of ${}_rS$ in ${}_rS$; in the more general case it would belong to a pair of such subsets at all points along it. For our simple case the boundary line may be rewritten from the definitions in (76) and (77):

$$(78) \qquad s_{rc} - \left(\frac{P_{d_{r'}}}{P_{d_r}}\right) s_{r'c} = \frac{{}_{r'}P_j - {}_rP_j}{P_{d_r}}$$

[45] W. Launhardt, (1); F. Fetter, (2); T. Palander, (1); E. Hoover, (1), Chs. 2, 3, and 5; and C. and W. Hyson, (1).

Now:

1. when ${}_rP_j = {}_{r'}P_j$, or the f.o.b. prices in both regions are equal, and when $P_{d_r} = P_{d_{r'}}$, so that transport rates from both points are equal, the boundary line is traced out by that set of points equidistant from both production points, and will be a straight line.

2. when ${}_rP_j \neq {}_{r'}P_j$, but $P_{d_r} = P_{d_{r'}}$, (78) reduces to

$$s_{rc} - s_{r'c} = {}_{r'}P_j - {}_rP_j, \text{ when } P_{d_r} = 1 \tag{79}$$

Every boundary point is fixed so that the differences of the distances always equals the differences in f.o.b. prices, when the transport rate is unity. These conditions define the market boundary as a hyperbola.[46]

3. when ${}_rP_j = {}_{r'}P_j$, but $P_{d_r} \neq P_{d_{r'}}$, (78) becomes

$$s_{rc} - \frac{P_{d_r}}{P_{d_{r'}}} s_{r'c} = 0 \tag{80}$$

This condition—that the ratio of the distances to the boundary line be rigidly proportional to transport rates—defines a circle.

4. when ${}_rP_j \neq {}_{r'}P_j$ and $P_{d_r} \neq P_{d_{r'}}$, we have the general case, in which boundary lines are part of the family of curves termed Descartes' ovals, which describe the conditions that

$$s_{rc} \pm \frac{P_{d_{r'}}}{P_{d_r}} s_{r'c} = \pm k \begin{cases} +k = \dfrac{{}_{r'}P_j - {}_rP_j}{P_{d_r}} > 0 \\ -k = \dfrac{{}_{r'}P_j - {}_rP_j}{P_{d_r}} < 0 \end{cases} \tag{81}$$

Since $\frac{P_{d_{r'}}}{P_{d_r}} > 0$, only that portion of the curve defined by

$$s_{rc} - \frac{P_{d_{r'}}}{P_{d_r}} s_{r'c} = \pm k \begin{cases} +k = \dfrac{{}_{r'}P_j - {}_rP_j}{P_{d_r}} > 0 \\ -k = \dfrac{{}_{r'}P_j - {}_rP_j}{P_{d_r}} < 0 \end{cases} \tag{82}$$

is relevant, or curves the Hysons have termed "hypercircles,"[47] which curves include the first three cases as special cases.

When $z > 2$, the total area of the plane will be covered by subareas whose boundaries will be segments of such curves as those just described, and sales will be proportionate to the area tributary to each production point. Let ${}_cX_j$ be taken as the demand for good Y_j for a unit area of S centered on point $[C]$ and very small in magnitude. Of course, population density is thus taken to be unity. Then,

$${}_cX_j \equiv K \tag{83}$$

where K is some given constant, over the unit area of region S. Given the

[46] Cf. F. Fetter, (2), p. 525.
[47] C. and W. Hyson, (1), p. 321.

boundary lines, ${}_rX_j$ is the total sales in the market area tributary to production site $[R]$, and is defined as

$$(84) \qquad {}_rX_j = KA$$

where A is the area in units described above.

3.d. Case 4: Finite Subset of Virtual Production Points, Continuous Consumption, Variable Rates of Consumption

In this situation, demand at each point in S (or, more accurately, in each tiny unit area centering on point $[C]$) is a continuous function of the delivered price of Y_j. The potential market areas of each production site will be equivalent to those of Case 3, given the same f.o.b. prices and transport rates as that case presented. That is, even if no sales are made in portions of the areas by virtue of delivered prices exceeding those prices at which positive demand occurs, if such demand curves were to shift and sales to occur, they would accrue to the designated production point.

Actual sales of the production point within its area become a more complex phenomenon to compute. Let ${}_rP_j$ be the f.o.b. price at point $[R]$ and s_{rc} the distance to $[C]$ from $[R]$, as before. Then we are given

$$(85) \qquad {}_cX_j = {}_cH_j({}_rP_j + w_js_{rc}P_{d_r})$$

Given ${}_rP_j$, the coordinates (x_r, y_r) and (x_c, y_c), then

$$(86) \qquad {}_cX_j = {}_cH_j({}_rP_j + w_jP_{d_r}\sqrt{(x_c - x_r)^2 + (y_c - y_r)^2})$$

Let $[C']$ with coordinates $(x_{c'}, y_{c'})$ be a point s_{rc} from $[R]$ where consumption becomes zero. Draw a circle with $[R]$ as center and $s_{rc'}$ as radius, denoting the set of points on and outside the circle ${}_rS'$:

$$(87) \qquad {}_rS' = \{[C'] \in {}_rS \mid {}_{c'}H_j({}_rP_j + w_js_{rc}P_{d_r}) = 0\}$$

Then, let $C_{rs'}$ be the complement of ${}_rS'$ in S, and it will be the area within which production point r makes positive sales:

$$(88) \qquad {}_rX_j = \iint_{C_{rs'}} {}_cH_j({}_rP_j + w_jP_{d_r}\sqrt{(x_c - x_r)^2 + (y_c - y_r)^2})\, dC_{rs'}$$

3.e. Case 5: Continuous Virtual Production, Finite Set of Consumption Points, Fixed Rates of Consumption

If we assume that actual production as well as virtual production is continuous, while consumption points are finite in number, we have the classic case of *supply areas* about fixed consumption points. We may describe these areas through a direct and obvious extension of Case 3. Such a result may occur if some indispensable resource has a spatial dimension, such as agricultural land, which prevents concentration of production at the market sites to reduce all transport costs to zero.

But suppose we remain with the assumption of a concentrated production site in the solution and assume $s > 2$, where s is the number of consumption sites in the economy. What point in S would yield a minimum bill of transport costs given the need to deliver the fixed consumption amounts ${}_cX_j$?

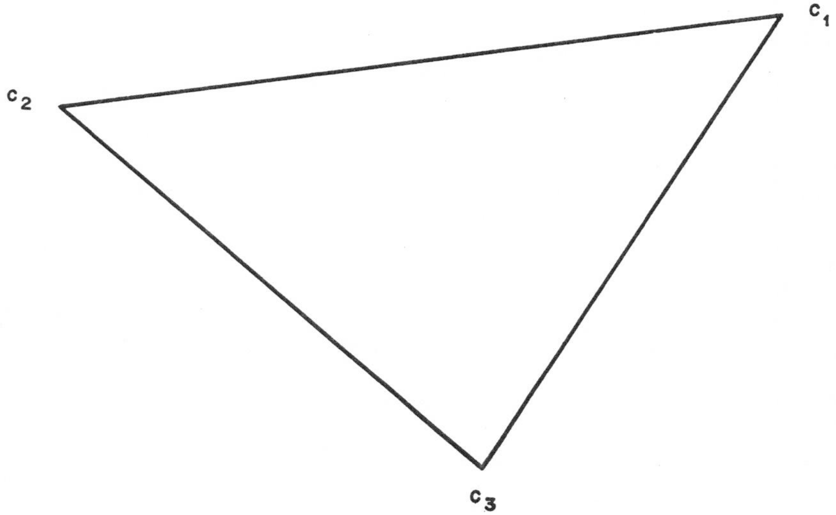

Figure 7-1. The Three Consumption-Point Problem

For the case where $z = 3$, and where (per our assumption at the beginning of this analysis) the ${}_cX_j$ are identical, while transport rates are the same per ton-mile over the whole plain, the question is identical with Steiner's Problem.[48] First, we may assert that a solution to the problem does exist by virtue of Weierstrass' theorem; since the plain will be a compact set, in effect shrinking to that subset bounded by the straight lines connecting the three consumption points, and since transport costs are a continuous function of the coordinates x_r and y_r of the production site, there will exist a maximum and minimum value for transport costs for this problem by virtue of this theorem.

The point $[R]$ is either on the triangle whose vertices are the consumption points or it is interior to the triangle. It cannot be outside the triangle, for if it were, it is possible to move toward the triangle in such a way as to be closer to all consumption points $[C]$ or no farther from some points and closer to others. Similarly, if the optimum production point is

[48] See, for example, R. Courant, (1), pp. 354–61.

on the perimeter, it must lie at a vertex. If at a vertex it must be at that vertex which corresponds to the largest angle of the triangle, since only this solution will yield s_{rc}-values coinciding with sides of the triangle which are the shortest.

Figure 7-1 depicts three consumption sites, $[C_1]$, $[C_2]$, and $[C_3]$, and the triangle which they form in the plain S. Now, assume we knew the opti-

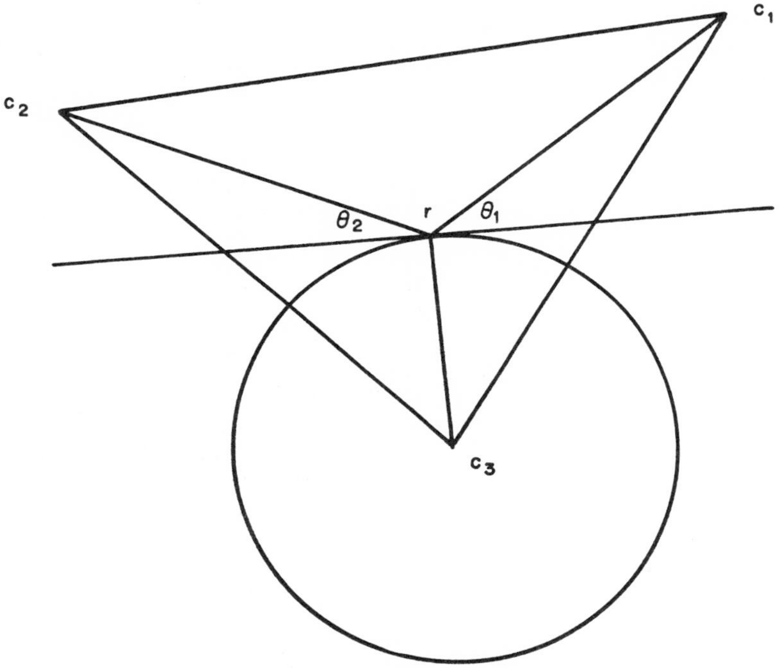

Figure 7-2. Steiner's Problem

mum production point, $[R]$, when the rate of consumption at each consumption point is identical. We then draw the circle about any consumption point, say $[C_3]$, whose radius is the optimal distance, s_{rc_3}, as depicted in Fig. 7-2. If $[C_1]$ and $[C_2]$ are exterior to the circle, as they are in Figure 7-2, we may employ an extension of Heron's theorem which states that s_{rc_1} and s_{rc_2} will be minimized when the routes' lines make equal angles with the tangent to the circle at r; i.e., when $\theta_1 = \theta_2$. Since we chose $[C_3]$ arbitrarily as the center of the circle, it follows that the same construction must hold for s_{rc_2} and s_{rc_3} when the circle is drawn around $[C_1]$, and for s_{rc_1} and s_{rc_3} when it is drawn about $[C_2]$. It follows, therefore, that $[R]$ must lie at the point where the routes s_{rc_1}, s_{rc_2}, and s_{rc_3}, make equal angles, i.e., angles of 120°.

We shall now demonstrate that if an interior point is optimal neither

$[C_1]$ nor $[C_2]$ can be interior to the circle drawn about $[C_3]$. Suppose the optimal solution were as depicted in Fig. 7-3, where $[C_1]$ is interior to the circle. Then,

(89) $$s_{rc_1} + s_{rc_2} \geqq s_{c_1c_2}$$

and, since $[C_1]$ is interior to the circle,

(90) $$s_{rc_3} \geqq s_{c_1c_3}$$

Adding (89) and (90), we obtain

(91) $$s_{rc_1} + s_{rc_2} + s_{rc_3} \geqq s_{c_1c_2} + s_{c_1c_3}$$

Since we are assuming $[R]$ is not a vertex, and since the equality in (91) can hold only if $[R]$ is a vertex, the inequality must hold in (91), which is

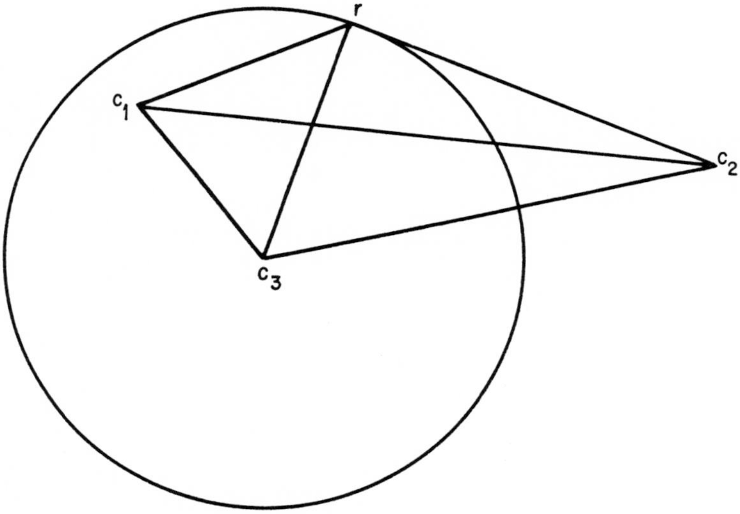

Figure 7-3. A Consumption Point Interior to the Circle

to say that distances from $[R]$ can be reduced by moving from $[R]$ to a vertex. Therefore, $[R]$ is not the minimum, and the optimum $[R]$, when it is not a vertex, must be such that in the construction of Fig. 7-3, $[C_1]$ and $[C_2]$ are exterior to the circle. And, since the selection of $[C_3]$ as the center was arbitrary, similar statements must hold for nonvertex optimal production points for $[C_2]$ and $[C_3]$ when the circle is drawn about $[C_1]$ and for $[C_1]$ and $[C_3]$ when it is drawn about $[C_2]$.

When the minimal production point falls at a vertex, of course, one or two consumption points may lie on a circle, but none can be interior to it.

The case of the vertex solution occurs when any angle of the triangle equals or exceeds 120°; in this case [R] will coincide with the vertex of that angle. In all other cases the nonvertex solution will hold.

We have proved that when the nonvertex case holds the optimal nonvertex production point occurs at the point where the sides of the triangle subtend 120° angles, but we have not proved it to be better than a vertex solution. However, it may be easily proved that the sum of the s_{rc} is less than the sum of any two sides of the triangle, and, therefore, the nonvertex solution is indeed minimal, considering all points in and on the triangle. The proof of this proposition we leave to the reader.

When the number of consumption points is 4, and ${}_cX_j$ are equal for all four points, it may be shown that the optimal solution always lies at the intersection of the diagonals of the polygon of which the consumption points are the vertices.

3.e.1. The Weberian Locational Model

For the cases where the number of consumption points is greater than two and where ${}_cX_j$ are not identical the solution is more complicated and formerly could be obtained only by using geometrical constructions or physical analogue models. These cases include as a subcase the classic location model of Alfred Weber: to ship given weights from and to an unknown production point—from localized raw material sites and to a market or markets—when transport costs are proportional to weight and the straight-line distances, in such a way as to minimize the transport costs involved. For convenience, let $w_j = 1$ and $P_{d_r} = 1$. In the Weberian subcases, shipments *to and from r* will occur, but obviously this will make no difference to the solution, being merely a reversal of direction when compared with the previous models. We shall, therefore, continue to designate all points, even those from which raw materials originate, as [C] points. We desire to find a unique [R] which minimizes transport costs.

We shall deal with the consumption case in this section, where n consumption points with nonidentical ${}_cX_j$ are involved. Then the objective is to minimize

$$Z = \sum_c {}_cX_j s_{rc} \tag{92}$$

Weierstrass' theorem merely guarantees us the existence of a minimum. It does not guarantee that it will be interior to the polygon formed by connecting the consumption points by straight lines so that all points [C] lie on the polygon. Therefore, two types of solution may exist: (1) an interior solution or (2) a boundary solution.

1. The interior solution. If we know a boundary solution does not exist, we may adopt the coordinates of the optimal production point [R] as the unknowns, differentiate Z partially with respect to these variables, and set them equal to zero, to obtain the conditions which must hold at the equilibrium [R]:

$$(93)\qquad \begin{aligned} &1.\quad \frac{\partial Z}{\partial x_r} = \sum_c {}_cX_j \frac{\partial s_{rc}}{\partial x_r} = 0 \\ &2.\quad \frac{\partial Z}{\partial y_r} = \sum_c {}_cX_j \frac{\partial s_{rc}}{\partial y_r} = 0 \end{aligned}$$

where

$$(94)\qquad s_{rc} = \sqrt{(x_c - x_r)^2 + (y_c - y_r)^2}$$

and where

$$(95)\qquad d^2Z > 0$$

These conditions imply that if we hold constant all distances but two (force x_r and y_r to vary such that the sum of all distances but two are constant), we should have at the equilibrium

$$(96)\qquad {}_{c_i}X_j \frac{\partial s_{rc_i}}{\partial x_r} = - {}_{c_j}X_j \frac{\partial s_{rc_j}}{\partial x_r} \Bigg|\sum_{k \neq i,j} {}_{c_k}X_j \frac{\partial s_{rc_k}}{\partial x_r} = K$$

and

$$(97)\qquad {}_{c_i}X_j \frac{\partial s_{rc_i}}{\partial y_r} = - {}_{c_j}X_j \frac{\partial s_{rc_j}}{\partial y_r} \Bigg|\sum_{k \neq i,j} {}_{c_k}X_j \frac{\partial s_{rc_k}}{\partial y_r} = K$$

and

$$(98)\qquad \frac{{}_{c_i}X_j}{{}_{c_j}X_j} = - \frac{ds_{rc_j}}{ds_{rc_i}} \Bigg|\sum_{k \neq i,j} {}_kX_j\, ds_{rc_k} = K$$

That is, for any given sum of distances for $s - 2$ of the consumption points, transport costs will be minimized when differentials in distances from the remaining two points are inversely proportional to the weights to be moved to the two points, or, more generally, to the transport costs on the products to be moved.

If any two equations hold for (96) and the respective two hold for (97), or if any two equations hold for (98), the minimum will have been reached, since they will imply the others.

2. The vertex solution. Let Fig. 7-4 depict $s > 2$ consumption points and let the points form a polygon in the manner illustrated. At each corner of the polygon (we illustrate with the vertex c_1) draw an arbitrary straight line, LL', and let θ_{1c} be the angles cut off by lines from c_1 to the other vertices. Then, if

$$(99)\quad ({}_{c_1}X_j)^2 < [{}_{c_2}X_j \cos \theta_{12} + {}_{c_3}X_j \cos \theta_{13} + \cdots {}_{c_z}X_j \cos \theta_{1z}]^2 + [{}_{c_2}X_j \sin \theta_{12} + {}_{c_3}X_j \sin \theta_{13} + \cdots {}_{c_z}X_j \sin \theta_{1z}]^2$$

and if the like conditions hold for $({}_{c_2}X_j)^2$, $({}_{c_3}X_j)^2$, . . . $({}_{c_z}X_j)^2$, an interior minimum will occur. If one does not meet the conditions of the inequality, a solution will occur at that corner, since the resultant of forces acting on that corner is greater than the sum of all other resultants at the $s - 1$ other corners.[49]

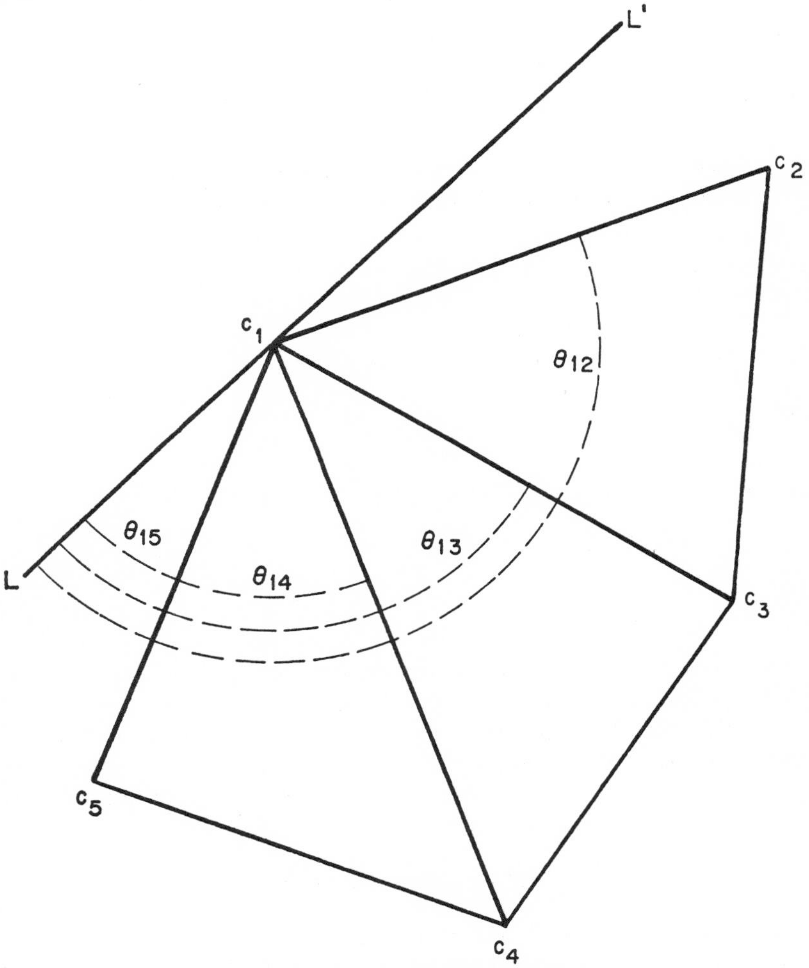

Figure 7-4. The Vertex Solution

[49] W. Isard, (5), pp. 222–30. It is now relatively easy to solve equations (93) algebraically for a solution to the generalized Weber problem by use of the Kuhn-Kuenne algorithm. See H. Kuhn, (2).

3.f. Case 6: Continuous Virtual Production, Finite Set of Consumption Points, Variable Rates of Consumption

Let

$$ {}_cX_j = {}_cH_j({}_rP_j + s_{rc}) \tag{100} $$

Then, if an interior minimum point rules in equilibrium, from (92)

$$ \begin{aligned} &1. \quad \frac{\partial Z}{\partial x_r} = \sum_c {}_cX_j \frac{\partial s_{rc}}{\partial x_r} + \sum_c s_{rc} \frac{\partial_c X_j}{\partial x_r} = 0 \\ &2. \quad \frac{\partial Z}{\partial y_r} = \sum_c {}_cX_j \frac{\partial s_{rc}}{\partial y_r} + \sum_c s_{rc} \frac{\partial_c X_j}{\partial y_r} = 0 \end{aligned} \tag{101} $$

3.g. Case 7: Continuous Virtual Production, Continuous Consumption, Fixed Rates of Consumption

The most famous examples of this case are (1) the case where S shrinks to a line segment and (2) the case where S shrinks to the perimeter of a circle.[50] We shall treat the more general problem.

Let ${}_cX_j$ again be defined as consumption in the small unit area of S, so that total consumption may be depicted as

$$ X_j = {}_cX_j \iint_A dA \tag{102} $$

We may define sales from a given point $[R]$ to point $[C]$ as

$$ \begin{aligned} {}_cX_j &= {}_cH_j({}_rP_j + w_jP_{d_r}\sqrt{(x_c - x_r)^2 + (y_c - y_r)^2}) \\ &= {}_cH_j(x_c, y_c; {}_rP_j, w_j, P_{d_r}, x_r, y_r) \\ &= {}_cH_j(x_c, y_c) \end{aligned} \tag{103} $$

or, more accurately, sales to the tiny area centering upon point $[C]$ are so defined. Then, the domain of ${}_cH_j$ will be $C_{rs'}$ as defined in Section 3.d. Now, within this domain and holding x_c constant, allow y_c to vary and to attain its maximum and minimum values at y_1 and y_2 respectively, then allow x_c to vary and attain x_a and x_b as a maximum and minimum respectively. Then (102) may be written

$$ X_j = \int_b^a \int_{y_2}^{y_1} {}_cH_j(x_c, y_c)dy_c dx_c = {}_cX_j \int_b^a \int_{y_2}^{y_1} dy_c dx_c \tag{104} $$

when ${}_cX_j$ is constant, as is our present assumption.

The subset $C_{rs'}$ is a homogeneous lamina. Let $[c]$ be the center of mass (centroid) of dA when $dA \to 0$. Then transport costs over the whole

[50] For the first case see H. Hotelling, (1); A. Smithies, (1). For the second case see E. Chamberlin, (1), Appendix C.

lamina from a variable point [R] will be

$$(105)\quad Z = {}_cX_j \int_b^a \int_{y_2}^{y_1} \int_b^a \int_{y_2}^{y_1} \sqrt{(x_c - x_r)^2 + (y_c - y_r)^2}\, dy_c dx_c dy_r dx_r$$

If Z is differentiated partially with respect to x_r and y_r and set equal to zero, we obtain

$$(106)\quad \begin{aligned} &1. \quad \frac{\partial Z}{\partial x_r} = {}_cX_j \int_b^a \int_{y_2}^{y_1} \frac{x_c - x_r}{s_{rc}}\, dy_c dx_c = 0 \\ &2. \quad \frac{\partial Z}{\partial y_r} = {}_cX_j \int_b^a \int_{y_2}^{y_1} \frac{y_c - y_r}{s_{rc}}\, dy_c dx_c = 0 \end{aligned}$$

That a minimum exists is guaranteed by Weierstrass' theorem and the assumption that it is an interior minimum is safe when ${}_cX_j$ is constant.

3.h. Case 8: Continuous Virtual Production, Continuous Consumption, Variable Rates of Consumption

Assume that (99) held for every unit area with centroid [c] in S. We may illustrate the "demand curve" in Fig. 7-5, where O_rP_j is the f.o.b.

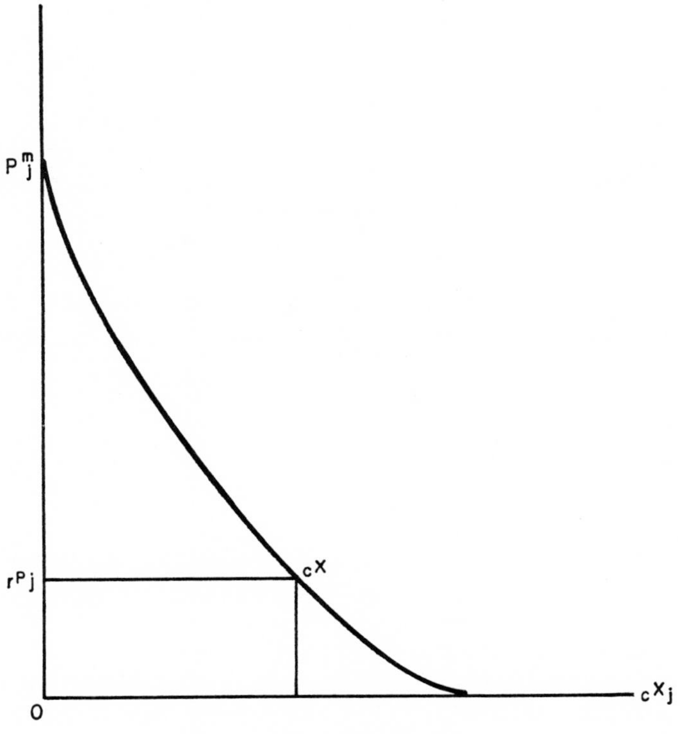

Figure 7-5. The Demand Curve

price at production point r and OP_j^m the delivered price at which sales become zero. The amount $OP_j^m - O_rP_j$ then becomes the maximum transportation costs, $\bar{s}_{rc}$, sustainable from point $[R]$, so that ${}_rP_j + \bar{s}_{rc} = P_j^m$ sets the boundary of region r's sales area in all directions.

If we turn the triangular area ${}_rP_j\,{}_cX\,P_j^m$ in Fig. 7-5 so that it rests upon ${}_rP_jP_j^m$ as a base, and place ${}_rP_j$ on the xy-plane at $[R]$, we may create a

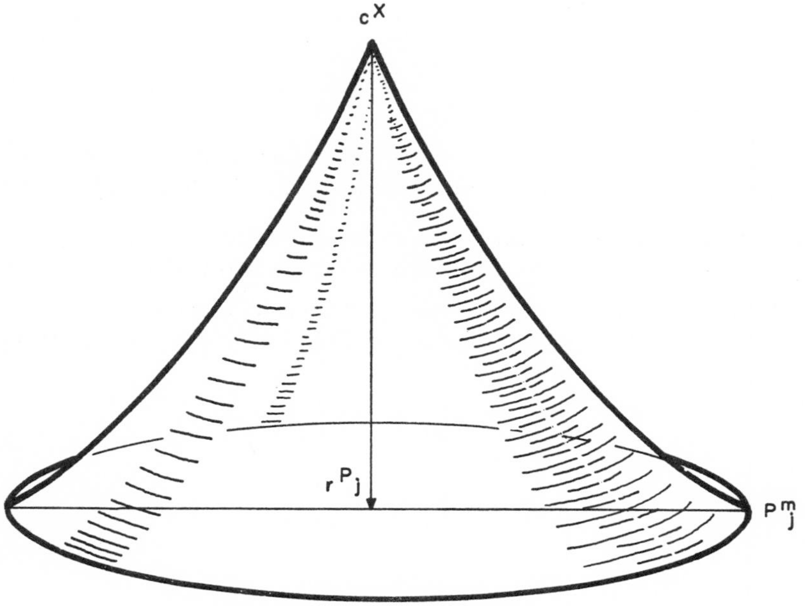

Figure 7-6. The Cone of Demand

solid of revolution by moving the point P_j^m in a complete circle. The "cone of demand" may then be represented as in Fig. 7-6, or as

(107) $${}_rX_j = \pi \int_0^{{}_cX} s_{rc}^2 d_cX$$

since, from (103) with given ${}_rP_j$,

(108) $$s_{rc} = {}_cJ_j({}_cX_j)$$

The subset of points under the cone, $C_{rs'}$ including the boundary of its intersection with S, is wholly contained within S. The point $[R]$ will be chosen to maximize ${}_rX_j$ and is not necessarily unique.

Thus far we have assumed that all production must occur at one point. Were we to assume at the other extreme that no penalties to the industry exist when it is fractionalized even in the limit, then, of course, the production points would be spread continuously over the plain S such that transport costs were reduced to zero and sales at each point were maximized. Between these two extremes of discrete and continuous production it is possible to constrain the number of production points to any level desired and solve for the sales maximization configurations.

3.h.1. The Lösch Model

A further step is to construct a model in which the number of production points is a variable rather than a datum. The model of August Lösch is an attempt at this type of generalization.[51] A convenient starting point is the extreme model of decentralization discussed above in which production occurs at the site of consumption. Then, assume that technology alters to yield traditional U-shaped cost curves for the production of Y_j in lieu of constant average cost curves. There then arise certain economies of scale to compensate for the transport costs concentration entails, and the pattern of completely fractionalized production disappears.

Lösch assumes the following as data:

1. ${}_cX_j = {}_cH_j({}_cP_j)$, where ${}_cP_j$ is the minimum delivered price to [C]. When technology is constant over the plain, all input prices identical, and transport rates ($=1$ for $w_j = 1$) equal everywhere in the plain, ${}_cP_j$ is the delivered price from the nearest production point r.
2. ${}_rP_j = {}_rG_j({}_rX_j)$, where ${}_rX_j$ is the total demand for the output of site r.
3. ${}_rC_j = {}_rC_j({}_rX_j)$, where ${}_rC_j$ is the average cost of production as a function of total sales at point r.
4. ${}_rX_j = {}_rH_j({}_cX_j, x_r, y_r, {}_r\sigma_{1j}, {}_r\sigma_{2j}, {}_r\sigma_{3j}, \ldots, {}_r\sigma_{qj}, D, {}_rD)$, the undefined terms to be explained below.
5. D is the density of population per unit of area outside production sites.
6. ${}_rD$ is the density of population at site r.
7. P_{d_r} is the freight rate.
8. S is the set of points in the plain.
9. ${}_r\pi_j$ are profits at site r on the production of good Y_j, defined as ${}_r\pi_j = {}_rX_j({}_rP_j - {}_rC_j)$.

The variables of the model include:

1. ${}_rP_j$, the f.o.b. price of good Y_j at site r.
2. ${}_rA_j$, the sales area of site r in the production of good Y_j.
3. z_j, the number of sites producing good Y_j.
4. $[x_r, y_r] = [R]$, the coordinates of site r.
5. ${}_r\sigma_{1j}, {}_r\sigma_{2j}, \ldots, {}_r\sigma_{qj}$, the abbreviations for the boundary lines of region r's sales area for good Y_j.

Let us now assume for simplicity that $n = 1$. In Lösch's general model the locational pattern of the producers of every good is independent of that of the producers of every other good, so that the complete model

[51] A. Lösch, (1), pp. 103–37, 94–100.

involving n goods is a superimposed pattern of n decomposable systems. Therefore, there is no interdependence to be sacrificed in this assumption or to involve us in the Koopmans-Beckmann difficulties.

The sets of equations setting forth the equilibrium conditions are as follows. First, the location of each firm is such that small movements about it will not increase profits:

$$\frac{\partial_r \pi^\circ}{\partial x_r^\circ} = 0, \qquad \frac{\partial_r \pi^\circ}{\partial y_r^\circ} = 0 \tag{109}$$

All consumers must be served, which implies that the sales areas of all points in equilibrium must sum to the total area of the plain:

$$\sum_r {}_rA = S \tag{110}$$

Profits of every firm must be zero:

$${}_r\pi = 0 \tag{111}$$

Now, the condition in (109) assures that for a given sales volume in equilibrium the firm is located in such a way as to derive maximum profit. It is also necessary to assure that the level of sales which is held given in (109) be held given for that level of output which is optimal for the firm in the conditions of Chamberlin's "monopolistic competition" or "large-group" case.[52] That is, it must be assured that the equality of average cost and average f.o.b. revenue (f.o.b. price) occurs at a tangency of the demand function and average cost curves, not at an intersection. Therefore, sales volume must be optimal, given the necessity of (111):

$$\frac{\partial_r \pi}{\partial_r A} = 0 \tag{112}$$

Lastly, the boundary lines are defined:

$$\begin{aligned} {}_r\sigma_1 &= {}_rP + P_{d_r}\sqrt{(x_c - x_r)^2 + (y_c - y_r)^2} \\ &= {}_{r'}P + P_{d_r}\sqrt{(x_c - x_{r'})^2 + (y_c - y_{r'})^2}, \text{ etc.} \end{aligned} \tag{113}$$

From the analysis of 3.c. above we know that when ${}_rP = {}_{r'}P$ and the transport rates from both regions are equal, these boundaries will be straight lines. Lösch indicates that these straight lines will form regular hexagonal market areas, since this shape among the possible configurations which can form networks which cover S without interstices (see (110)) most nearly conforms to the ideal circular form, in which the ratio of sales to area is a maximum and, therefore, the amount of sales per unit of expenditure on transport costs a maximum.

[52] E. Chamberlin, (1), pp. 81–94.

4. The Synthesis of Interregional Trade and Locational Models

As was pointed out above, only in the programming systems and especially in those of Graham and Lefeber, do we possess models which combine both spatial aspects—interregional flows and locations of production facilities—in simultaneously-determined, mutually-conditioned, indecomposable ways. But in these models "location" is taken in its simplest case—Case 1 in 3.a. above—where point production for point consumption either does or does not occur in the linear case. The more complicated forms of locational configurations are not dealt with in such general systems, the primary emphasis remaining with the interregional trade aspects of space.

At the other extreme, Lösch's model neglects entirely the general interrelations among economic activities to concentrate upon partial analyses (albeit these analyses are superimposed in further analysis to obtain transportation networks). Demand functions for good Y_j are functions of its price alone, for example, and no troublesome relationships among production sites of the Koopmans-Beckmann type exist on the supply side.

The ideal spatial model would be one that recognized a politically, geographically, and so forth, differentiated set of z regions, with given amounts or kinds of tastes, resources, and technologies, distributed in a given fashion over space. Such geographic opportunities as nodal points on natural transport routes would be included in the expanded list of resources. Within each region the spatial configuration of production and consumption would be related to that in every other such region. Specifically, included both within and among regions would be transport cost, the spatial friction. The interdependence of intraregional activities would include spatial interdependences, not only among different production activities but between production and consumption activities as well. It would be, in short, a true organic synthesis of the interregional trade and the locational models. This implies not only the in-building of the locational model, but the prior generalization of an area in economics which is marked by the abundance of partial analyses and the paucity of general analysis.

5. A Recapitulation

In this chapter we have dealt with the problems of building a spatial dimension into our previously spaceless models. This introduction was recognized to be required at two levels: space conceived as a friction to the flow of goods between fixed points and space conceived as a matrix for the placement of economic activities. Although both complications of space are not independent, it is simpler to deal in a general analysis with the frictional concept, and we have done so by building a general interregional trade model, considering others in the field, and studying operational types of interregional flow systems. The second type of spatial system is more difficult to generalize and to build into the first type. We have merely discussed eight cases considered to be most germane to the problems in the area, but we have not taken these cases out of their partial contexts into a general analysis. Lastly, we have attempted to define the type of synthesis that a complete spatial theory would require of these two types of models, but we have restricted the effort to a mere statement of *desiderata*.

CHAPTER 8

DYNAMIC MODELS

1. Introduction

It was made clear in Chapter 1 that the major emphasis of this book was on static rather than dynamic general systems, and a distinction between statics and dynamics was drawn with the nature of derivable theorems as the touchstone. We have now reached the point where the systems of Part II must for several reasons be related to dynamic models.

First, one of the most important advances in modern economic theory has been the increasing integration of static and dynamic analysis, with the former being demonstrated to be a particular case of the latter. The proper understanding of reality, and the uses of statics in interpreting it, require that dynamic microeconomic theory be developed and related to static theory and the same elusive reality. In this task, the names of Samuelson, Frisch, Hicks, Lange, Metzler, Mosak, and Arrow are notable for their accomplishments.[1]

Second, we have consistently stressed the basic goal of any economic model as that of yielding insights into, or operational theorems constraining, variation in phenomena from one equilibrium state to another. We have seen how, for the single market and for all markets, important properties of demand and supply curves, deduced from certain second-order conditions of equilibrium or merely postulated, were useful in deriving such theorems. Indeed, for the model of multiple exchange and for the production system, we presented Hicks's generalization of the single-market case to the n-market case, employing these same "stability conditions," grounded in certain properties of demand and supply curves which may be viewed as contingent upon maximization reasoning.

But these "stability conditions" seem in fundamental contradiction to our statement in Chapter 1 that an explicit dynamic analysis is necessary to establish the properties of an equilibrium system's movement when it is not in a position of rest. We saw how Walrasian equilibrium stability conditions were stated in terms of the slopes of static functions and how these conditions derived from implicitly assumed relationships of the form $\frac{dP}{dt} = G(E)$, where E denotes excess demand.[2] Since no such

[1] This chapter owes much to P. Samuelson, (4), Chs. 9–11, and (2); O. Lange, (6), Mathematical Appendix; R. Frisch, (1); and L. Metzler, (1).

[2] Marschak suggests a different viewpoint in asserting that Walrasian stability conditions are composed of two statements, the first dynamic in nature, the second static. The first is that at prices where $E > 0$, $\frac{dP}{dt} > 0$. The second, and static, state-

explicit dynamic analysis was introduced to demonstrate the justification for the Hicksian stability conditions, we should feel hesitant to employ them when arguing in stability terms. A proper study of stability conditions in a general equilibrium system is of necessity dynamic, and so an interest in stability *qua* stability or in getting information with which to evaluate comparative statics positions of rest, requires a study of dynamic models. This latter point, of course, is the essence of Samuelson's "Correspondence Principle."[3]

Third, even when the stability properties of market equilibrium states cannot be in point, as, for example, in the consideration of dynamic models which merely trace out paths of market equilibrium and yield no information on movements of the model in market disequilibrium, such dynamic models may be interesting in themselves for both purely theoretical and applied economic reasons. Such systems as Cassel's progressive economy, H. L. Moore's moving equilibrium system, Dantzig's dynamic programming model, and von Neumann's system—the first two of which are static and the second pair of which are dynamic "moving equilibrium systems"—possess an interest for us and will be discussed below.

For all these reasons: to discover the relationships of static systems to dynamic systems for a better understanding of the former; to develop a

ment, is that, given the restrictions on $\frac{dP}{dt}$, when it is positive, excess demand must fall, and when negative, excess demand must rise. Marschak then asks that if the first conditions yield the equilibrium resting place, would not the second conditions do so also? "Granted that Mr. Hicks has not succeeded in deducing the stability conditions in the market from the principle of maximum satisfaction, simultaneous for all the individuals, yet it has not been proved that the task is impossible." (P. 72).

However, Marschak is linking the static conditions to a dynamic form of the variable, which is to say once more that a dynamic model must be implicit or explicit in discussions of stability analysis, even those which seem to employ only static models. That is, Marschak is assuming that $\frac{dP}{dt} > 0$ when $E > 0$ and that $\frac{dP}{dt} < 0$ when $E < 0$. That these are not the only possible assumptions can be illustrated in this way. Suppose P were to rise to P': our static conditions, derived from a maximization-of-preference model, assuming a negative income effect, tell us that excess demand must fall if all individuals adjust instantaneously to the new positions desired by each as a final resting place. But a rise in price might set off expectations of further rises, if the rate of rise is large, and lead individuals to seek to buy more, not less. See J. Marschak, (1), and also M. Reder, (1).

Lange, also, in discussing the Hicksian conditions, says that $\frac{dP}{dt} > 0$ when $E > 0$ is implied. But is it implied or merely assumed? To say that an equilibrium point lies above or below another equilibrium or disequilibrium point is not to say that given a change in the data the next movement will be toward the equilibrium. One cannot interpret this comparative statics analysis as an analysis where rates of adjustment approach the infinite and are of given sign unless one *assumes* these rate-of-change signs and magnitudes. See O. Lange, (6), p. 94.

[3] P. Samuelson, (4), pp. 258, 262–3, 284, 350.

true dynamic stability analysis in order to seek methods to evaluate comparative statics equilibrium displacements; and to study a group of dynamic models for the interest they have on dynamic grounds alone, we shall proceed to analyze the role of time and its implications more deeply than we did in Chapters 4 and 5. We shall begin with a further development of the distinction between static and dynamic systems, study the group of moving equilibrium models mentioned above, and then consider a group of dynamic "potential disequilibrium" systems with an emphasis upon the stability of equilibrium within them.

2. Statics and Dynamics Reconsidered

In Chapter 1 we defined a dynamic potential disequilibrium system as one from which it was methodologically legitimate to seek operational theorems about the state of a model between two points of rest. On the other hand, a static system was defined as one in which operational theorems could be sought only for economies in states of rest. For the purposes at hand, this distinction was sufficient, but now as we seek to build dynamic models whose markets are never considered except in states of rest, it will be necessary to broaden our definition of dynamics and to inquire more deeply into the nature of such systems.

A "static" or "dynamic" model is distinguished by the *structure of the relationships* which define the model. A static model is one whose structural relationships do not contain time in any analytically meaningful way. By contrast, dynamic systems are those which do contain time-relationships among the relations of the variables in meaningful ways, i.e., in ways which could not be eliminated without affecting the solution to the system or eliminating the possibility of the solution. Ordinarily time enters such relationships in one or more of three ways:

1. The values of the variables for any point (or period) of time are related in the functional interrelationships of the model to the values of these variables at previous points (or during previous periods) in a direct manner. That is to say, the stationary state of Model V-2 is not dynamic even though we can relate the solution in week 0 to that of week 1 by virtue of our knowledge of the constancy of the data, i.e., $[U, T, R, \bar{P}]^0 = [U, T, R, \bar{P}]^{-1}$, and so forth. Such a relationship is indirect and dependent upon additional knowledge not contained within the equations of the static model.

2. As a special case of (1), rates of change in the variables with respect to time are related to the values of the variables at a point of time and relate them to other points of time. Thus, relationships which contain such rates in meaningful context do in fact contain variables related at different points in time.

3. Sums or integrals of the values of variables over past or future periods or points of time may enter into the relationships.

Following Frisch, we may distinguish between the *instantaneous* forms of the variables, say X_t, P_t, in the model, and the *dynamic* forms, $\frac{dX_t}{dt}$, $\frac{d^2X_t}{dt^2}$, $\int X_t dt$, X_{t-1}, and so forth.[4] These dynamic forms must be meaningful in an analytical sense: for example, into an otherwise static system we could introduce the production of a product from the beginning of time to the present (a sum or integral) and define current output as the time rate of change of this analytically meaningless construct. When meaningful dynamic forms are present with instantaneous forms of the variables, the relationships are "dynamic." In contradistinction, a "static" system is one whose relationships contain no dynamic forms of the variables which are meaningful. The dependence of present states of the system on past and of future states on present—as introduced by time derivatives, time lags, and/or sums or integrals in dynamic systems—does not exist.

The concept of "dating the variables" in a dynamic system and of not doing so in a static analysis does not capture the essence of these distinctions, for the mere dating of the variables can be done not only to include them as dynamic forms in structural relationships, but also to study mere sequences through time.[5]

Reder's definition also has some troublesome aspects. He defines static systems as those "in which the value taken by any variable of the system (at any moment of time) is determined (given the parameters and functional form of the system) solely by the values taken by the other variables of the system at that moment." On the other hand, dynamic systems are those "in which the value taken at any given moment of time by any variable of the system is determined partly or wholly by the values taken by that variable and/or other variables (given the parameters and the functional form of the system) at some moment or moments of time in the past."[6]

But we have seen in the static models of Part II that given the data and structure of a model, the variables' values are determined simultaneously. "The values taken by the other variables" at a moment of time emerge simultaneously with the present value of the variable in question. It is the parameters and functional forms of the model that are the determinants of the solution values. Does this outlook change in a dynamic system, or must we continue to regard data and function forms

[4] R. Frisch, (1). See also J. Tinbergen, (1), p. 27.
[5] This distinction is the one used by Hicks in (5), p. 115.
[6] M. Reder, (1), pp. 103–4. Quoted by permission.

as leading to the solution of the model? For an answer we may turn to Frisch's formulation: given a set of n variables and n equations with the instantaneous forms of each of the n variables in at least one equation, and containing dynamic forms also, in general, when certain initial conditions are specified, a "solution" will be forthcoming. The solution, however, is not a set of values invariant to time, but an "evolution" or path through time: "The essential character of a set of equations that is dynamic in the above sense is, indeed, that it does not 'lock' the system (does not stop motion) although it is determinate, (i.e., although it contains the same number of equations as unknowns). In this respect it differs from a set of static equations."[7]

Now, if, following Reder, we stop this "evolution" solution at point t, we should have determinate values which were obtained from the data and functional form of the system, where the former are taken to include the initial conditions of the model. The values of the variables in t are not directly related to their values in $t - 1$ in some sense independent of the data and functional forms of the system. In this sense it resembles the static system. The difference lies in the functional form of the system, i.e., the structure of that system, and the definition we have adopted focusses upon this, while Reder's concentrates upon a distinction which vanishes upon closer inspection. Reder is really expressing our point above that in dynamic systems the functional relations relate states of the system at different points of time, while in static systems they do not.

Following Frisch's discussion of the solution to static and dynamic systems, and the distinction between them by virtue of the nature of the solutions, we saw that the static solution was "locked" in time and the dynamic solution was a path through time. To the extent that the static solutions have a time pattern they must be related by structural relationships without dynamic forms to sets of data ruling at points t. As long as $[U, T, R, \bar{P}]$ is invariant, the solutions will be invariant over time, and we should have a stationary set of solutions, one for each time period. On the other hand, if $[U, T, R, \bar{P}]$ varies from period to period, the set of solutions will vary, and we should have a nonstationary set. As pointed out below, Model V-2, looked upon as yielding the same solution week after week, gave us the first type of static solution set through time; i.e., our stationary state was obtained by the repetition of unchanged data in a static framework. Had we varied our data in some pattern, as we shall do below in Cassel's and Moore's models, we would have obtained a progressive, retrogressive, or other state. In short, we may have a set of solutions which is static and stationary or static and nonstationary.

The solution to a dynamic system—with the "evolutionary" nature of which Frisch speaks—may also be stationary or nonstationary, but note that we speak of only one solution (if the model yields a unique solution),

[7] R. Frisch, (1), pp. 101–2. Quoted by permission.

not of a set of same from repetitive or nonrepetitive data sets in a plurality of static systems. If a dynamic model is left undisturbed, and if as $t \to \infty$ the variables $[X_t, P_t]$ approach the values $[X^\circ, P^\circ]$, which values satisfy the relationships of the model identically, the solution approaches a stationary state in the longer run. On the other hand, the solution may show no such tendency: it may be characterized by periodic movements of constant or increasing amplitude or by exponential growth. If a stationary solution does exist, reached after transient states have yielded to the long-term solution,[8] all motion must have ceased: $\frac{dX}{dt}, \frac{d^2X}{dt^2}$, and so forth, must be zero.

Let us assume an n-equation system in n variables X_j, where each variable enters at least one equation, where dynamic forms of at least one variable enter at least one equation, and where we define $\dot{X}_j = \frac{dX_j}{dt}$. The system is then:

$$(1) \quad F_j(X_{1t}, X_{2t}, \ldots, X_{nt}, \dot{X}_1, \dot{X}_2, \ldots, \dot{X}_n) = 0, \qquad j = 1, \ldots, n$$

The concept of stationarity or equilibrium in a dynamic system is concerned with the approach of the evolutionary pattern through time to the limiting values, X_j°, if the system is left undisturbed. By substituting a presumed stationary solution into (1) we may ask: is this dynamic system capable of accepting one or more solutions where movement has ceased?

If the answer is in the negative, we may term the solution "nonstationary." We shall be particularly interested in this characteristic of a solution for certain types of dynamic economic systems we have called "potential market disequilibrium systems." By this term we mean systems whose structural equations allow us to trace the evolution of market variables out of their equilibrium states.

Assume that we have a dynamic model with a stationary solution. If at a point t' where the variables have ceased motion we break the equilibrium by changing the initial position of the model, the system will embark on a new path which may be stationary or nonstationary. If it is stationary at the same set of solution values for the variables as those which ruled before the disturbance, we term the equilibrium which was disturbed a "stable" equilibrium. If this convergence to the stationary values previously ruling occurs only for disturbances in a neighborhood of the initial equilibrium, the equilibrium is said to be stable "in the small" or "locally stable." If this result occurs for every possible set of initial conditions and for every solution path to the equilibrium if multiple solutions occur, the equilibrium is said to be stable "in the large," or "globally" stable.[9] If such a disturbance leads the model to attain *another*

[8] D. Hawkins, (1), pp. 313–5.

[9] P. Samuelson, (4), pp. 260–3; R. Frisch, (1), pp. 101–3; and K. Arrow, (6), p. 524. It is interesting that, in his earlier work, Pareto defined the concept of an equi-

position of stationarity, different from the original equilibrium, we may term the original equilibrium "neutrally" stable. Alternatively, we may lump this possibility with that in which no new equilibrium is attained and term an equilibrium displaying either "unstable," globally or locally.

Up to this point, we have spoken only of the stability of an equilibrium position. We may extend this definition to cover the possibility of more than one position of rest satisfying a dynamic model with given initial data. If, for all paths or solutions, every set of initial conditions leads to a position of rest, the *model* may be said to be stable. A stable system, with a unique equilibrium, is globally stable, while an equilibrium point which is globally stable must be unique.

We shall treat these concepts more extensively in our discussion of stability, but we should like to emphasize these points at this stage of our discussion:

1. Stability is a dynamic property, first and foremost, of an equilibrium position.
2. It is relevant only to dynamic systems which conceivably get out of equilibrium, i.e., depart from positions of rest, if only temporarily.
3. The "stationary state" may be either a series of static solutions serially related by repetitive values of the data, or a truly dynamic stationary solution. Samuelson terms Schumpeter's model of the circular flow an example of the latter,[10] while our Model V-2 provides an example of the former. The term "stationary" refers merely to the behavior over time of a set of variables.

Having drawn the distinction between static and dynamic models at some length, we may now show how, under explicit assumptions, the former may be looked upon as a limiting case of the latter. Since a dynamic system contains dynamic as well as instantaneous forms of the variables, and a static system contains only instantaneous forms, we may consider a static system as one where meaningful dynamic forms do not occur, or, where they occur, can be neglected. We may adopt Reder's outlook: past values of the variables do not enter directly into the functional forms of the static system, and all time rates of change approach infinity and therefore can be ignored. Therefore, we may assume explicitly that all time rates of change have a specific sign and all adjustments take place instantaneously. This latter term means that no matter how small

---

librium in dynamic terms: a state of the system such that if the conditions were relaxed, exactly equal and opposite conditions will be forthcoming to return the system to rest. He went further to distinguish between local and global stability which he interpreted as unstable and stable equilibrium respectively. See (1), Vol. I, p. 18.

Wicksell echoed this inseparability of the concept of equilibrium and stability, arguing that if Walrasian stability conditions do not rule at an intersection of demand and supply functions no real equilibrium exists but only a temporary equality of supply and demand. See (1), p. 87.

[10] P. Samuelson, (2), p. 61.

the duration of t is taken to be, the time necessary for a new adjustment to occur is so much smaller that it can be neglected.[11] But these assumptions are required, not implied by the static method.

For example, suppose the time rate of price change in a given market were defined as a linear function of excess demand:

$$(2) \qquad \frac{dP}{dt} = KE, \qquad \frac{dP}{dt} = 0 \text{ when } E = 0$$

where K is a constant greater than zero. Providing we assume these characteristics, then, if $\frac{dP}{dt} \to \infty$, when $E \neq 0$ the least departure of P from its equilibrium level will be corrected with infinite speed. Actual price will always be equilibrium price, given the sign and magnitude of K and the arrest of motion at $E = 0$. Indeed, we are most justified in using a comparative statics approach when we can make just these assumptions: that an equilibrium is stable, the approach to it rapid, the path strongly damped.[12]

3. Equilibrium Models

We shall deal in this section with five models which trace out the path of general equilibria through time. Two of them—Cassel's model and Moore's system—are not true dynamic models by the definitions of Section 2: they contain no dynamic forms of the variables in the structural relationships of the model, although the laws of change of the data (in Cassel's model) or of the equilibria resulting from externally determined data changes (Moore's model) are explicit functions of time. We deal with these two static systems here because they do yield moving static equilibria and they form a link between the static stationary state and the truly dynamic model's path through time.

The three remaining models are truly dynamic by our definition. Those of Dantzig and von Neumann are similar in structure, the latter focussing upon the solution only in the very long-run when the influence upon the equilibrium path of "transient" solutions has become negligible and the assumed position of rest dictated by the dominant root may be isolated. However, the Leontief dynamic models do concern themselves with the short-run path of the system as well as with the long-run path enforced by the dominant root. Nevertheless, they are placed in this section because (1) they are linear and akin in this respect to the other two dynamic systems, (2) like all other models in this section, the Leontief models are marked by equilibrated markets at all times, and (3) the major interest of Leontief is in the long-run, steady-state solution.

All five models possess in common the feature of being incapable of

[11] M. Reder, (1), pp. 107–12.
[12] P. Samuelson, (4), p. 331.

describing economic reactions in markets which are not equilibrated. There is no potential for this particular form of disequilibrium, and in these respects these models are essentially static. Therefore, to speak of the "stability" of *market* equilibria in these models is to exceed their proper limits, although, of course, it is legitimate to be concerned with the stability of their proper solutions and to analyze it when (1) one of the three dynamic models is the subject of the inquiry, and (2) sufficient structural information is given to allow the analysis to be made.

3.a. Cassel's Progressive Economy

Just as the stationary state is the simplest introduction of time flow into the static general system, so the smoothly progressive state is the simplest introduction of variation through time into time-flow states. But, in contrast to other neoclassical theorists like Walras and Pareto, Cassel consistently viewed the analysis of general equilibrium systems against the backdrop of time process. He was interested in general equilibrium as a step toward the understanding of the movement of an economy through time, and, consequently, his "evenly progressive economy" is of some interest to us as a bridge between stationary, static models and truly dynamic systems, even though its relations contain no truly dynamic forms of the variables and may be depicted in wholly static terms.

Walras, as we have seen, viewed dynamic analysis *of the system as a whole* as a series of rapidly imposed changes in the data of the model interpreted statically within a time context. When he examined the time process it was to study the Ricardian implications of nonaugmentable land resources; indeed, he introduced his marginal productivity analysis in the setting of expanding labor and capital resources and constant land resource endowments, with the consequent need to substitute against the latter.[13]

Wicksell points the way to the progressive state in balanced growth when he writes (in discussing changes in the parameters of stationary states):

> "If in all these relationships a certain *rate* of progression may be assumed to be given, then it is clear that equations of production and exchange can be laid down. We have then, so to speak, a problem of dynamic equilibrium, instead of a problem of static equilibrium with which to deal.
>
> "It would be quite a different matter to try to lay down laws for determining the rate of progression itself. I personally make no attempt in this direction . . . ."[14]

[13] L. Walras, (2), Lesson 36.

[14] K. Wicksell, (1), p. 165. Quoted by permission of George Allen & Unwin, Ltd.

Cassel's construction is quite simple.[15] As we have seen, his static model is an adaptation of Walras' simplest production model—Model III-1—with (1) entrepreneurial demand for intermediate production eliminated and (2) factor service supplies equal to resource endowments. To it we shall add the savings-investment phenomena which he discusses in his literary presentation of the progressive state. We depict the model in the symbols used throughout this book. First, the consumer's sector in the aggregate sense is presented:

$$(3)\quad \begin{aligned} &1. \quad X_{j\neq 1} = H_{j\neq 1}(P_{j\neq 1}, P_i, P_e; [Q]) = H_{j\neq 1}([P]; [Q]) \\ &2. \quad X_e = H_e([P]; [Q]) \\ &3. \quad \bar{X}_i = Q_i \\ &4. \quad X_1 = \sum_i Q_i P_i - \sum_{j\neq 1} X_{j\neq 1} P_{j\neq 1} - X_e P_e \end{aligned}$$

Demands and supplies of goods and factor services must be equal in equilibrium:

$$(4)\quad \begin{aligned} &1. \quad X_j^\circ = \bar{X}_j^\circ \\ &2. \quad \sum_j a_{ij}\bar{X}_j^\circ + \sum_{Z_i} a_{iZ_i}\bar{X}_{Z_i}^\circ = Q_i \end{aligned}$$

Prices must equal average costs in equilibrium:

$$(5)\quad \begin{aligned} &1. \quad P_{j\neq 1}^\circ = \sum_i a_{ij} P_i^\circ \\ &2. \quad P_{Z_i}^\circ = \sum_i a_{iZ_I} P_i^\circ \end{aligned}$$

And, in the investment-savings sector, the two familiar conditions must hold:

$$(6)\quad \begin{aligned} &1. \quad \sum_{Z_i} \bar{X}_{Z_i}^\circ P_{Z_i}^\circ = X_e^\circ P_e^\circ \\ &2. \quad P_{Z_i}^\circ = (P_i^\circ - u_i P_{Z_i}^\circ) P_e^\circ \end{aligned}$$

Let $x = X^\circ = \bar{X}^\circ$, and we may simplify this system to:

$$(7)\quad \begin{aligned} &1. \quad x_{j\neq 1} = H_{j\neq 1}([P]; [Q]) \\ &2. \quad x_e = H_e([P]; [Q]) \\ &3. \quad x_1 = \sum_i Q_{Z_i} P_i^\circ - \sum_{j\neq 1} x_{j\neq 1} P_{j\neq 1}^\circ - x_e P_e^\circ \\ &4. \quad \sum_j a_{ij} x_j + \sum_{Z_i} a_{iZ_i} x_{Z_i} = Q_i \end{aligned}$$

[15] G. Cassel, (1), pp. 34–42, 148–52.

$$(7)\quad \begin{aligned} &5. \quad P^{\circ}_{j\neq 1} = \sum_{i} a_{ij\neq 1}P^{\circ}_{i} \\ &6. \quad P^{\circ}_{Z_i} = \sum_{i} a_{iZ_I}P^{\circ}_{i} \\ &7. \quad \sum_{Z_i} x_{Z_i}P^{\circ}_{Z_i} = x_e P^{\circ}_{e} \\ &8. \quad P^{\circ}_{Z_i} = (P^{\circ}_{i} - u_i P^{\circ}_{Z_i})P^{\circ}_{e} \end{aligned}$$

This system may be viewed as depicting the equilibrium at week t_0. If we shrink the weeks to points in time we may define derivatives of the functions with respect to time, and denote these by placing dots above the variables involved. Assume that the instantaneous rate of population growth is $r \times 100$ per cent, and that demand and supply curves therefore shift by $r \times 100$ per cent at equilibrium quantities (it will be recalled that demand curves are data in the Casselian system). That is,

$$(8)\quad \begin{aligned} &1. \quad \dot{x}_j = rx_j \\ &2. \quad \dot{x}_e = rx_e \end{aligned}$$

Moreover, we assume that all resources expand at the same rate:

$$(9)\quad \dot{Q}_i = rQ_i$$

Therefore, the solutions to (8) and (9) may be written

$$(10)\quad \begin{aligned} &1. \quad x_{jt} = x_{j0}e^{rt} \\ &2. \quad Q_{it} = Q_{i0}e^{rt} \\ &3. \quad x_{et} = x_{e0}e^{rt} \end{aligned}$$

If these are substituted in (7) it will be seen that the exponential terms do not appear in expressions involving prices unless they may be washed out. Therefore,

$$(11)\quad \begin{aligned} &1. \quad P_{jt} = P^{\circ}_{j} \\ &2. \quad P_{it} = P^{\circ}_{i} \\ &3. \quad P_{et} = P^{\circ}_{e} \\ &4. \quad P_{Z_it} = P^{\circ}_{Z_i} \end{aligned}$$

As the economy progresses smoothly prices remain constant, while resources and outputs expand at $r \times 100$ per cent per instant of time. The stationary state is the special case where $r = 0$, and if $r < 0$ the economy is retrograde and approaches extinction in a balanced way.

This model, as mentioned before, is dynamic only in the sense that three sets of data, Q_{Z_i}, X_j, and X_e, are following an autonomous law of change which imposes a succession of comparative statics equilibria upon a linear structure. Dynamic forms appear only among the parameters, not the variables of the model. The result is a static "balanced growth" model, a balanced growth which is optimal as long as no excess capacity is allowed in the system. But if, on the other hand, the period-to-period increment in producible resources were part of the solution as in Kaldor's model in Chapter 4, and the model traced out a path of balanced growth, we should obtain a truly dynamic model. Such models we shall deal with in Leontief's closed dynamic system, which retains Cassel's full employment of resources, and von Neumann's closed dynamic system, the solution to which need not be so characterized.

3.b. Moore's Moving General Equilibrium Model

Another model of the market clearing type without the smoothly progressive features of Cassel's system necessarily implied is that of Henry Moore.[16] This model was designed in pioneering enthusiasm for the statistical fitting of a Walrasian investment model. We shall, however, subordinate in our consideration of it the econometric features to the wholly theoretical.

In his most ambitious model Moore adopts the Walrasian system depicted in (3)–(6), except that he (1) introduces the ambiguous concept of "credit" into his savings treatment, a concept we discussed in Chapter 5 and will dispense with here for the reasons given in that discussion, and (2) assumes the production functions to be linear and homogeneous, thereby converting the a-coefficients to variables. Their definition is given below and must be added to (3)–(6) to complete the system:

$$(12)\qquad \begin{aligned} &1. \quad a_{ij} = \frac{X_{ij}}{\bar{X}_j} \\ &2. \quad a_{iZ_i} = \frac{X_{iZ_i}}{\bar{X}_{Z_i}} \end{aligned}$$

where X_{ij} and X_{iZ_i} are the demands for resource services to produce goods. The production functions are constrained to be linear and homogeneous:

$$(13)\qquad \begin{aligned} &1. \quad \bar{X}_j = T_j(X_{1j}, X_{2j}, \ldots, X_{mj}) \\ &2. \quad \bar{X}_{Z_i} = T_{Z_i}(X_{1Z_i}, X_{2Z_i}, \ldots, X_{mZ_i}) \end{aligned}$$

Therefore, maximum profits conditions are given by the minimum cost conditions:

$$(14)\qquad \frac{\dfrac{\partial \bar{X}_j}{\partial X_{z_1 j}}}{P_{z_1}} = \frac{\dfrac{\partial \bar{X}_j}{\partial X_{z_2 j}}}{P_{z_2}} = \cdots \frac{\dfrac{\partial \bar{X}_j}{\partial X_{z_m j}}}{P_{z_m}}$$

and so forth.

[16] H. Moore, (1), pp. 92–145.

Now Moore simply assumes, *ex post facto*, a period of T weeks, $t = 1, \ldots, T$, in which successive general equilibria of the system *have been* achieved, and that the loci of points of equilibrium may be depicted as simple functions of time:

$$
(15)\quad
\begin{array}{llll}
1. & x_{jt} = L_j(t) & 6. & x_{Z_it} = L_{Z_i}(t) \\
2.^{17} & x_{it} = L_i(t) & 7. & P^{\circ}_{j\neq 1,t} = P_{j\neq 1}(t) \\
3. & x_{et} = L_e(t) & 8. & P^{\circ}_{it} = P_i(t) \\
4. & x_{ijt} = L_{ij}(t) & 9. & P^{\circ}_{Z_it} = P_{Z_i}(t) \\
5. & x_{iZ_it} = L_{iZ_i}(t) & &
\end{array}
$$

He proposed to obtain these in concrete terms by fitting trend lines of the type

$$(16)\qquad L^{\circ}(t) \text{ or } P^{\circ}(t) = a_1 + a_2t + a_3t^2 + \cdots a_{T+1}t^T$$

to the raw data. Having obtained them in the concrete, Moore proposed to obtain trend relatives of the observed data, of the form:

$$(17)\qquad \frac{X}{x}, \frac{P}{P^{\circ}}$$

where X and P are observed data and x and P° the "equilibrium" trend values. There are three basic sets of functions needed in the system to be derived from these data—demand, supply, and production functions—and Moore derives them from the trend relatives on the basis of assumed characteristics of the curves. For example, assume that the price elasticities of demand curves will be constant:

$$(18)\qquad e_{jk} = \frac{\partial X_j}{\partial P_k}\frac{P_k}{X_j} = B_{jk}$$

This would lead to a set of demand functions with logarithmically-additive terms:

$$(19)\qquad \frac{X_j}{x_{jt}} = \left[\left(\frac{P_{j\neq 1}}{P^{\circ}_{j\neq 1}}\right)^{B_{jj}}\left(\frac{P_i}{P^{\circ}_i}\right)^{B_{ij}}\left(\frac{P_e}{P^{\circ}_e}\right)^{B_{ej}}\right]$$

Or, more realistically, assume one of the following relationships to hold true:

$$
(20)\quad
\begin{array}{ll}
1. & e_{jk} = B_{jk} + B'_{jk}P_k \\
2. & e_{jk} = B_{jk} + B'_{jk}P_k + B''_{jk}P_k^2
\end{array}
$$

where the B_{jk}, B'_{jk}, and B''_{jk} are parameters derived from fitting the data with the relevant types of functions. In similar fashion, supply functions may be obtained, and the a-coefficients estimated for an assumed linear

[17] Moore substitutes the Walrasian $\bar{X}_i = Q_i - H_i([P]; [Q])$ for $\bar{X}_i = Q_i$.

homogeneous production function. Moore did not deal with the problems of identification involved in such ambitious undertakings or with any of the more modern econometric qualifications which would arise in such fittings. But one must be impressed by the dramatic grandeur of his design, which was nothing less than the depiction of a general equilibrium system in motion, and by the imagination displayed in his pioneering statistical framework.

3.c. Dantzig's Linear Programming Model

In what has now become a familiar linear programming approach, Dantzig describes a set of linear processes which defines a technology and objective function based upon the following postulates:

1. There exists a set of possible activities, A;
2. There exists a finite set of goods, Y_j, $j = 1, \ldots, n$;
3. With each activity and for each good there can be associated a (cumulative) flow function of time, t, $-\infty < t < \infty$, written $T_j(t; A)$, $j = 1, \ldots, n$;
4. These flow functions for different activities and the same good are additive and can be multiplied by any nonnegative scalar by virtue of the assumption that every activity is infinitely divisible;
5. There exists a finite basis in A such that any activity in A can be expressed as some positive linear combination of activities in this basis;
6. There exists a linear objective function over the elements of A.

Assume that we stop a production process at point t, start it up again, and stop it at point $t + 1$. Let the goods Y_j include unfinished goods and capital goods as well as all current inputs and outputs. Then, under the assumption of linear processes in (4), we may depict process k by the following vector:

$$(21) \quad [A_{1kt}, \ldots, A_{nkt}; a_{1k}, \ldots, a_{nk}; \bar{a}_{1k}, \ldots, \bar{a}_{nk}; A_{1k,t+1} \ldots, A_{nk,t+1}]$$

where the A_{jkt} are initial stocks, $A_{jk,t+1}$ are terminal stocks, the a-terms are constant rates of flow per time unit of the inputs, and the $\bar{a}$-terms constant rates of flow per time unit of the outputs. Instead of dealing with the full generality of production we may single out only certain of these possibilities:

1. In static models we may abstract from stocks at different points of time and study only the flows $[a, \bar{a}]$. When only one $\bar{a}$ is defined for each process, we have the special case of the Leontief closed static model, where the time unit for which the a and $\bar{a}$ coefficients are defined is one period in duration. This kind of system keeps changes in stocks in the data category, as we have seen in Chapter 6.

2. In the above stated conditions when the positive $\bar{a}$-terms are greater than one in number, alternative 1 depicts the Koopmans model if we deal with $[\bar{a} - a]$, or net flows of goods.

3. If no flows occur, or we choose a time period so small that we may arbitrarily add all a terms to the corresponding A_{jt} and all $\bar{a}$ coefficients to the corresponding A_{jt+1} terms, the result is a definition of the activities of the von Neumann model.

4. If we retain full generality, but define a and $\bar{a}$ terms for the period $(t + 1 - t)$, we have the Leontief dynamic model.

5. If we retain full generality but define a and $\bar{a}$ terms as uniform flows over the time interval we have the earlier Dantzig model.[18]

Now let us adopt an interval of time $(t + 1 - t)$, say the week, and assume that we analyze the economy in successive unit time periods of this length, $t = 0, 1, \ldots, T$. All inputs enter the productive or other activities k at the start of week t and all outputs emerge from the activities at the end of the week. Since such current "flows" occur at points of time, we may treat them as flows or stocks. Dantzig chooses the former method, and we shall follow his usage. Inputs in week t are employed in the k internal activities of the model or are used in external applications to the extent of $Y_{j,t}$. Outputs in week $t - 1$ are derived from the internal activities in that week or from external sources to the extent $Y_{j,t-1}$.

Each week, inputs into internal and external activities are derived from the previous week's outputs of internal and external activities. Given the inclusion of all activities in the model, including disposal activities, we require that:

$$(22) \qquad \sum_k A_{jk,t-1}S_{k,t-1} = \sum_k A_{jk,t}S_{k,t} + Y_{j,t} - Y_{j,t-1} \qquad \begin{matrix} j = 1, \ldots, n \\ t = 1, \ldots, T \end{matrix}$$

All $Y_{j,t}$ and $Y_{j,t-1}$ terms, positive or negative, are among the data of the model and all $A_{jk,0} = 0$, while the $S_{k,t}$ terms are unknown activity levels.

Relations (22), along with the constraints

$$(23) \qquad S_{k,t} \geqq 0$$

define a set of all programs which are feasible, period by period, and for the whole horizon, $t = 1, \ldots, T$. From this convex set we may obtain an efficiency frontier, and select the optimal activity-level set over time by maximizing the objective function:

$$(24) \qquad Z = \sum_t \sum_k K_{k,t}S_{k,t} \qquad t = 1, 2, \ldots, T$$

where the K_{kt} are the community preference constants of some type.

Before leaving the Dantzig model, however, we note two things: first,

[18] This is the model defined in M. Wood, (1), and G. Dantzig, (2). The revised model we shall present is that in G. Dantzig, (3).

it is truly dynamic in our sense, since it includes in its structural equations dynamic forms of the variables $S_{k,t}$. An explicit dependence of one period's inputs upon the previous period's outputs is a constraint operating via the difference equations of (22). Second, a single (in general) equilibrium point is derived from an efficiency frontier by virtue of an explicit objective function to be maximized.

3.d. Von Neumann's Model

This model was presented first at Princeton in 1932 and holds an interest for us in several respects.[19] Not the least of these is that it presents a general equilibrium model of a purely competitive economy, if one modification is made in the postulates, as a kind of two-person, zero-sum game between a mythical maximizing "planner" and an equally noncorporeal minimizing fiction termed "competition."

Let us assume a purely competitive, closed economy with goods Y_j, $j = 1, \dots, n$. These emerge from a set of multiproduct linear processes A_k, $k = 1, \dots, s$, excluding disposal activities, with inputs consisting also of the goods Y_j. The processes may be defined for an arbitrary unit level as vectors of inputs, a_{jk}, and outputs, b_{jk}:

$$[b_{1k}, \dots, b_{nk}; a_{1k}, \dots, a_{nk}] \tag{25}$$

In order to assure an indecomposable system and a unique growth rate and rate of return on capital, von Neumann assumes that every good enters every process as input and/or output:[20]

$$a_{jk} + b_{jk} > 0 \tag{26}$$

Of course, the usual restrictions of linear activities are implied: fixed coefficients, constant returns to scale, and the inability to substitute one good for another within the process.

The economy is explicitly dynamic in the same manner as Dantzig's: a stock of inputs existent at the beginning of a discrete week t, which is the *net* output of week $t - 1$, is used to produce a net output in week t, which net output is withdrawn as a stock at the end of week t. As we pointed out in our discussion of Dantzig's model, von Neumann's "weeks" may be taken as so short that all flows may be added to the stock of inputs needed at the beginning of the week or to its stocks of outputs at the end. Processes may be included which require more than one period for completion by creating new goods which represent semi-finished articles at the end of the week, and capital goods which endure beyond

[19] See J. von Neumann, (1).

[20] This restriction is weakened in the generalization of the von Neumann model by J. Kemeny, O. Morgenstern, and G. Thompson, in J. Kemeny, (1), p. 122. It will be described below.

one period may similarly be treated as products in different states of depreciation.

All primary factors, if they exist, must be considered free goods, so that all goods in the model are producible and, of course, are viewed as absorbing inputs; if labor is included in the model it is viewed as receiving a "subsistence" input. This input vector may vary if we create more than one process for the "production" of labor services. However, the model assumes that all output above subsistence and other intermediate production requirements is reinvested in the following period, with the exception of those goods produced in excess amounts, which become free and require costless disposal to the extent of their surplus. If labor is one of these free goods, of course, it is sloughed off in Malthusian agonies. These heroic assumptions allow demand considerations to be reduced to a minimum and the technological to become all-important, providing interesting if primitive insights into growth and interest as they are affected by the conditions of production.[21]

The model may now be reproduced. First, von Neumann ignores the transient states of the model in which input stocks are being adjusted to that composition which will support the long-term state. That is, he goes immediately to the assumed dynamic equilibrium. If we let r be the rate of growth of all economic (i.e., nonfree) outputs, and let $\Delta = 1 + r$, then we may state that in the long-run equilibrium

$$\frac{\sum_k b_{jk}S_k}{\sum_k a_{jk}S_k} \geqq \Delta, \qquad j = 1, \ldots, n \tag{27}$$

and

$$\left(\sum_k b_{jk}S_k - \Delta \sum_k a_{jk}S_k\right) P_j = 0, \qquad j = 1, \ldots, n \tag{28}$$

Together these conditions state that the rate of growth for each good, taken separately, in equilibrium, cannot be less than the equilibrium rate of growth contained in Δ, and, where it is greater (where the inequality holds in equilibrium) the price of that good must be zero.

The system (27) is completely analogous to (22)—suitably adjusted for flows—for, if we eliminated disposal processes from Dantzig's model, reduced the Y_j terms to zero, and revised symbols accordingly we should have

$$\frac{\sum_k b_{jk}S_{k,t}}{\sum_k a_{jk}S_{k,t+1}} \geqq 1 \tag{29}$$

[21] Compare D. Champernowne, (1).

which is merely to say that the inputs of one period cannot exceed the outputs of the previous period. This is a constraint upon the system which can be converted into (27) by tacitly defining

$$\sum_k b_{jk}S_{k,t+1} = \Delta \sum_k b_{jk}S_{k,t} \tag{30}$$

in equilibrium and after multiplying both sides of (29) through by Δ.

Prices remain to be determined. In the long-run equilibrium with which we are concerned, the cost of any process at equilibrium prices must be equal to or greater than the value of its outputs if zero profits are to characterize the equilibrium. Costs of production must be defined to be the equilibrium value of inputs plus the equilibrium rate of return on capital. If i_k equals this rate of return, and $\varepsilon = 1 + i_k$, then

$$\frac{\sum_j b_{jk}P_j}{\sum_j a_{jk}P_j} \leqq \varepsilon, \qquad k = 1, \ldots, s \tag{31}$$

but when the inequality holds, the process cannot be used in equilibrium:

$$\Big(\sum_j b_{jk}P_j - \varepsilon \sum_j a_{jk}P_j\Big) S_k = 0, \qquad k = 1, \ldots, s \tag{32}$$

This closed system will allow the derivation only of relative prices and relative process levels. Let us therefore normalize both sets of variables. In the case of process levels this requires at least one process to be used at a positive level.[22] Further, we require nonnegative prices and process levels:

$$S_k \geqq 0,\ \Sigma S_k = 1,\ P_j \geqq 0,\ \Sigma P_j = 1 \tag{33}$$

Our unknowns are S_k, P_j, Δ, and ε. Note that we place no nonnegativity restrictions upon r and i_k, except, of course, that if negative, r would lead the economy to extinction.

In von Neumann's construction, free goods and unused processes can occur, unlike the Leontief and Hawkins dynamic closed models. In equilibrium, if one exists, it will be true that:

1. All economic (non-free) goods will be expanding at a common rate of growth, r;

[22] This leads to the result that $\sum_j \sum_k b_{jk}S_kP_j > 0$, or that the value of the outputs of the system will not be zero. Von Neumann assumes this in his proof of existence of a solution but did not include it in the model proper. Without it, and using only (26), the proof of existence of an equilibrium does not guarantee a positive value of output. See J. Kemeny, (1), p. 122.

2. Some goods may be expanding at a rate larger than r and will be in continuous excess supply, and therefore will be free;

3. All processes used in equilibrium will imply costs exactly equal to the value of output, so that they will earn i_k as a rate of return and no more;

4. Some processes may be unable to earn the common rate of return and will not be used;

5. At least one good will not be free;

6. At least one process will be used at a positive level.

Von Neumann uses a generalization of Brouwer's fixed-point theorem to prove that an equilibrium always exists for such a model. System (27) states that with a given set of S_k satisfying (33), every good must be growing at least as fast as some common rate r'. This can be only if Δ' is chosen as the minimum rate of growth for individual goods' productions. That is, the slowest growing good must set the pace for balanced growth. If, for every possible vector $[S_k]$ we choose the minimum of the expressions in (27), we have a function $\Psi([S_k])$. We should seek to maximize this function: select that value of Ψ which maximizes the minimum expansion factor for each $[S_k]$. That is,

$$\Delta = \max_{k} \min_{j} \left(\frac{\sum_k b_{jk} S_k}{\sum_k a_{jk} S_k} \right) \tag{34}$$

where the k over which maximization occurs is taken to include combinations or mixtures of processes. From (33) it follows that the $[S_k^\circ]$ which yields Δ will not be null and, with (26), assures that $\Delta > 0$.

In similar fashion, (31) says that in equilibrium all processes in use must be earning no more than the equilibrium rate of return. Also, at any vector of prices $[P_j]$ satisfying (33), all processes must be earning no less than a common return. This implies the common return must be the maximum process return for that $[P_j]$. If, for every possible set $[P_j]$, we choose the maximum return, a function $\theta[(P_j])$ is defined. If the economy seeks to economize on payments to the owners of stocks of capital, as competition will lead it to do, the equilibrium ε should be the minimum of $\theta([P_j])$,

$$\varepsilon = \min_{[P_j]} \max_{k} \left(\frac{\sum_j b_{jk} P_j}{\sum_j a_{jk} P_j} \right) \tag{35}$$

From (33) it follows that the equilibrium $[P_j^\circ]$ which yields ε will not be null and from (26) it follows that $\varepsilon > 0$.

Now, if the condition of footnote 22 holds, as it must in the system, it follows from (28) that when $[S_k^\circ]$, $[P_j^\circ]$, Δ, and ε are solutions to the system

$$\sum_j \sum_k b_{jk} P_j S_k = \sum_j \sum_k \Delta a_{jk} P_j S_k > 0 \tag{36}$$

and from (32)

$$\sum_k \sum_j b_{jk} P_j S_k = \sum_k \sum_j \varepsilon\, a_{jk} P_j S_k > 0 \tag{37}$$

from which it follows that

$$\Delta = \varepsilon > 0 \tag{38}$$

That is, given that a solution always exists, as von Neumann proves, the solution is such as to make the rate of expansion of the economy positive and equal to the rate of return on capital.

We may demonstrate this equality in yet another way. Let $[S_k']$ and $[P_j']$ be feasible activity and price vectors, and define a function of them which is the value of output divided by the value of input:[23]

$$\Phi([S_k'], [P_j']) = \frac{\sum_k \sum_j b_{jk} P_j' S_k'}{\sum_k \sum_j a_{jk} P_j' S_k'} \tag{39}$$

Von Neumann shows that at least one solution ($[S_k^\circ]$, $[P_j^\circ]$) exists, that $\Phi([S_k^\circ], [P_j'])$ reaches a minimum when $[P_j'] = [P_j^\circ]$, and that $\Phi([S_k'], [P_j^\circ])$ reaches a maximum when $[S_k'] = [S_k^\circ]$; that is, there exists a saddle point at which the solution occurs. But, in equilibrium, all nonfree goods expand at the rate r per period, so

$$\Delta = \frac{\sum_j \sum_k b_{jk} P_j^\circ S_k^\circ}{\sum_k \sum_j a_{jk} P_j^\circ S_k^\circ} = \Phi([S_k^\circ], [P_j^\circ]) \tag{40}$$

Therefore, Δ' and ε' are the same function and (38) holds. Moreover, von Neumann shows that while $[S_k^\circ]$ and $[P_j^\circ]$ may not necessarily be unique, Δ and ε are unique if (26) holds. To show this uniqueness let us assume two solutions $[S_k', P_j']$ and $[S_k'', P_j'']$. From the fact that the equilibrium is a saddle point, it follows:

$$\text{(41)} \quad \begin{aligned} &1. \quad \Delta' = \Phi([S_k'], [P_j']) \leqq \Phi([S_k'], [P_j'']) \\ &2. \quad \Delta'' = \Phi([S_k''], [P_j'']) \geqq \Phi([S_k'], [P_j'']) \end{aligned}$$

[23] The Φ-function has been called "the return to the dollar" by Georgescu-Roegen, this return being made up of interest and profit. See N. Georgescu-Roegen, (1), p. 103.

and, therefore,

$$\Delta' \leqq \Delta'' \tag{42}$$

But, in similar fashion,

$$\begin{aligned} &1. \quad \Delta' \geqq \Phi([S_k''], [P_j']) \\ &2. \quad \Delta'' \leqq \Phi([S_k''], [P_j']) \end{aligned} \tag{43}$$

and

$$\Delta' \geqq \Delta'' \tag{44}$$

Therefore, from (42) and (44),

$$\Delta' = \Delta'' \tag{45}$$

and, by (38),

$$\varepsilon' = \varepsilon'' \tag{46}$$

Moreover, Δ and ε will provide the fastest possible balanced expansion rate and lowest possible rate of return on capital in a profitless economy. The von Neumann economy is one which conserves all of its growth energy, subject to some nonproducible resource limiting $\Delta = \varepsilon$ to 1—the Ricardian stationary state solution.

A last aspect of this model with substantial interest to us is that it can be shown to be a form of two-person, zero-sum game.[24] The ability to bring to bear upon the model the powerful analytical tools of game theory can be useful in proving the existence of a solution (von Neumann did so outside the game theory framework, merely commenting upon the similarity of the proof to that of the minimax theorem of game theory), in describing the characteristics of the equilibrium, and in solving the system. Moreover, the mere achievement of depicting a purely competitive economy—however abstractly—as a game with a minimax solution is an achievement of the highest theoretical order, yielding new insights into the constraining forces guiding the invisible hand in the capitalistic system. The extension of the method by Arrow and Debreu, which we shall study in Chapter 9, has yielded the most general proof of the existence of equilibrium in a general system that we possess.

The minimizing player we shall term Competition, and his pure strategy set is the conferral of all of society's largesse upon the producers of any one good Y_j. Were he to play strategy Y_7, a price $P_7 = 1$ is implied which leaves all other prices $P_{j \neq 7} = 0$. But, of course, he need not distribute largesse in such exclusive ways; he can distribute it as the vector $[P_j] \geq 0$, $\Sigma P_j = 1$, which has certain formal similarities with a mixed strategy in game theory. The term "optimal" has the following definition when applied to Competition's strategy: since waiting is the only cost

[24] Compare J. Kemeny, (1).

in von Neumann's model, Competition will seek to minimize it and with it the social cost of production by selection of a suitable price vector. That is, Competition desires a set of prices and hence, from (31) the smallest possible ε, such that for every process that is used no profits occur. Therefore, that set of prices implied by the minimax ε is sought against the pure strategies of the opponent.

This latter—the maximizing player—we shall call the Producer. His set of strategies is the set of processes A, with s elements each of which is one of the Producer's pure strategies. He seeks a vector $[S_k]$, $S_k \geqq 0$, $\Sigma S_k = 1$, which yields him the maximum of the minimum profits afforded by his options.

In the payoff matrix in Table 8-1, we reverse the conventional arrangement by placing the maximizing player's strategies in the columns and the minimizing player's strategies in the rows. The payoffs are still recorded from the standpoint of the maximizing player's welfare:

TABLE 8-1. THE PAY-OFF MATRIX

		Producer			
		A_1	A_2	$\cdots$	A_s
Competition	I_1	M_{11}	M_{12}	$\cdots$	M_{1s}
	I_2	M_{21}	M_{22}	$\cdots$	M_{2s}
	$\vdots$	$\vdots$	$\vdots$	$\cdots$	$\vdots$
	I_n	M_{n1}	M_{n2}	$\cdots$	M_{ns}

where we define $M_{jk} = b_{jk} - \varepsilon\, a_{jk}$, or the net outputs of the product singled out for a nonzero price in the activity in question. Now, from (27) and (38),

(47)
$$\sum_k S_k M_{jk} \geqq 0$$

and, from (31)

(48)
$$\Sigma P_j M_{jk} \leqq 0$$

If we multiply M_{jk} by P_j before summing and (48) by S_k before summing, we see that in equilibrium:

(49)
$$\sum_j \sum_k S_k P_j M_{jk} = 0$$

But, interpreting the M_{jk} as payoffs in a game matrix, and S_k and P_j as the normalized elements in vectors of mixed strategies, (49) may be seen as a constraint that the value of the game in equilibrium must be zero. That is, we must choose that ε which yields a value of zero. We have the unusual game situation where the values of the payoffs depend upon the strategy of the minimizing player.

That is, the value of the Producer's strategies, given a strategy of Competition, is

$$(50)\quad L_k = P_1 M_{1k} + \cdots P_n M_{nk} = P_1(b_{1k} - \varepsilon\, a_{1k}) + \cdots P_n(b_{nk} - \varepsilon\, a_{nk})$$

For every possible price vector, the Producer chooses that value, L'_k, which is a maximum; let V' be the set of these maxima:

$$(51)\qquad V' = \{L'_k\}$$

Then, Competition can hold the Producer to the minimum element of $V' = V$ by choosing the optimal (not necessarily unique) $[P_j]$. Below this Competition cannot reduce the producer, but at the same time the Producer cannot get above it. The problem is to choose

$$(52)\qquad V = \min V'$$

subject to

$$(53)\quad \begin{array}{rl} 1. & P_1M_{11} + P_2M_{21} + \cdots P_nM_{n1} - V \geqq 0 \\ 2. & P_1M_{12} + P_2M_{22} + \cdots P_nM_{n2} - V \geqq 0 \\ \cdot & \cdot \quad \cdot \quad \cdots \quad \cdot \quad \cdot \quad \cdot \\ s. & P_1M_{1s} + P_2M_{2s} + \cdots P_nM_{ns} - V \geqq 0 \\ s+1. & P_1 + P_2 + \cdots P_n = 1 \end{array}$$

and, of course,

$$(54)\qquad P_j \geqq 0$$

But (49) tells us that $V = 0$. Therefore, we may set ε at various levels in (53), solve for $[P_j]$, and choose that ε which yields a $[P_j]$ that makes $V = 0$. Having obtained this ε, we substitute it into the M_{jk}, using this new payoff matrix to calculate $[S_k]$. To illustrate, we shall work out a numerical example. Suppose $n = 2$ and $s = 3$, while

$$(55)\quad \begin{array}{llll} 1. & M_{11} = 5 - 3\varepsilon & 4. & M_{22} = 3 - 2\varepsilon \\ 2. & M_{21} = 3 - 1\varepsilon & 5. & M_{13} = 2 - 1\varepsilon \\ 3. & M_{12} = 4 - 1\varepsilon & 6. & M_{23} = 6 - 1\varepsilon \end{array}$$

We may substitute these values into (53), and we obtain for various assumptions of ε optimal vectors designated $[P_1, P_2, V]_{\varepsilon=c}$:

$$(56)\qquad \begin{aligned} &1. \quad [.67, .33, 2.32]_{\varepsilon=1} \\ &2. \quad [.68, .32, 2.09]_{\varepsilon=1.2} \\ &3. \quad [.71, .29, 1.14]_{\varepsilon=2} \\ &4. \quad [.75, .25, 0]_{\varepsilon=3} \end{aligned}$$

Therefore, equilibrium $\varepsilon^\circ = 1 + i_k = 3$, the optimal rate of return of 2 being implied by Competition's price strategy [.75, .25]. The payoff matrix to the Producer is therefore:

$$(57)\qquad \begin{bmatrix} -4 & 1 & -1 \\ 0 & -3 & 3 \end{bmatrix}$$

which will hold only when Competition plays the optimal strategy given above.

From the Producer's viewpoint, the task is to select an optimal process mix, $[S_1, S_2, S_3]$, such that the value of profits will be the maximum of the minimum values to which Competition can hold him. That is, let $[S_1', S_2', S_3']$ be a feasible level of activities, and let

$$(58)\qquad L_j^* = S_1'M_{j1} + S_2'M_{j2} + S_3'M_{j3}$$

be the value of the product mix when $P_j = 1$. Let V'^* be the minimum value of L_j^* for each $[S']$. Then the Producer seeks to attain the maximum element in V'^*:

$$(59)\qquad V^* = \max V'^*:$$

subject to

$$(60)\qquad \begin{aligned} &1. \quad -4S_1 + 1S_2 - 1S_3 - V^* \leqq 0 \\ &2. \quad 0S_1 - 3S_2 + 3S_3 - V^* \leqq 0 \\ &3. \quad S_1 + S_2 + S_3 = 1 \end{aligned}$$

where

$$(61)\qquad S_k \geqq 0$$

This yields $[S_1^\circ, S_2^\circ, S_3^\circ, V^*] = [0, .5, .5, 0]$. From (34),

$$(62)\qquad \Delta = \min_j \left(\frac{3}{1}, \frac{4.5}{1.5}\right) = 3 = \varepsilon^\circ$$

The workings of the purely competitive economy can be analyzed as a kind of modified game between two purposive opponents.

Kemeny, Thompson, and Morgenstern have softened the von Neumann assumption in (26) to the following two assumptions:

1. every process uses at least one good as an input; i.e., $[a_{jk}] \geq 0$ for all k;

2. every good is capable of being produced, i.e., every good enters into at least one process as an output.

This generalization removes the uniqueness properties of Δ (and ε) which obtains in von Neumann's solution. If all those ε which yield a $V = 0$ are termed "allowable," then when more than one allowable solution exists, and where the two assumptions above hold, there will always exist at least one and no more than a finite number of ε's which yield meaningful economic solutions (i.e., with positive values of output).

3.e. The Leontief Dynamic Input-Output Model

In Chapter 6 we dealt with a Leontief model which included, within the body of variation to be determined, only the flows of output for a period of time, and which was constructed from relationships defining only the interdependence among flows. In this sense it was the antithesis of von Neumann's model which defined relationships among stocks at different points of time, although we have seen how the von Neumann model may be interpreted with periods so short that flows and stocks may be merged.

In his dynamic system, Leontief has sought to build these stock-flow relationships into his structural equations.[25] We shall consider his models in both closed and open forms. Under the first heading we must consider the completely reversible system, the completely irreversible system, and the system with incomplete reversibility.

3.e.1. The Closed Leontief System

We return to a Leontief economy where there are n endogeneous sectors and one primary factor of production not produced under the regime of economic motivation. Then, the static model in physical terms is depicted, where all vectors are column vectors before transposition,

$$[I - a^*][x] = [X] \tag{63}$$

where the symbols have been explained in Chapter 6, and, if prices are defined as equal to average cost

$$[P]'[I - a^*] = [a_{zj}]'P_z \tag{64}$$

If we add the "household sector" (producing factor service z) to the matrix and close the system, we get, finally,

$$[I - \bar{a}^*][x] = [0] \tag{65}$$

[25] See W. Leontief, (4), pp. 53–90, and D. Hawkins, (1), as amended in (2).

where the barred term in the first matrix indicates that the system is closed. From this system we may derive the relative outputs, as demonstrated in Chapter 6.

We now introduce dynamic relationships into the model by assuming that the production of each sector's output requires a stock of Y_j as well as a current input of such goods on flow account. For example, as in Chapter 6, to produce a unit of good Y_1 requires a_{21} of good Y_2 (in physical quantities), which includes any depreciation occurring in any stock of Y_2 needed to produce Y_1. We may now include that stock, however, where previously we omitted it. Let us fix it per unit of output Y_1 in the coefficient b_{21}, or, more generally, b_{jk}. The stock of Y_j required to produce x_κ is then defined as:

(66) $$\overline{C_{jk}} = b_{jk}x_k$$

and, letting $\dot{C}_{jk}$ and $\dot{x}_k$ denote time derivatives, we have

(67) $$\dot{C}_{jk} = b_{jk}\dot{x}_k$$

These definitions assume that the stock-flow relationships are linear and homogeneous in the same manner as the flow-flow relations of the static models. When outputs change, stock requirements change, according to (66): that is, investment or disinvestment (when and to the extent possible) occurs as a response to internal states of the model. Previously, in the static model, these changes in stock levels were found in the data sector, where their generated flow requirements could be derived from the model as the flow requirements of any other bill of goods item were derivable.

Period by period, Leontief writes the economy balance equations in the following manner:

(68) $$x_j - \sum_{k=1}^{n+1} a_{jk}x_k - \sum_{k=1}^{n+1} b_{jk}\dot{x}_k = 0$$

The b-terms may be defined as capital coefficients (average and marginal) and the ratio $\frac{b_{jk}}{a_{jk}}$ the period of turnover of good Y_j in the production of Y_k, or, to revert to the terminology of Chapter 4, the average period of investment of good Y_k in the production of Y_j. The whole system may be depicted as:

(69)
$$\begin{bmatrix} 1 - a_{11} & -a_{12} & \cdots & -a_{1z} \\ -a_{21} & 1 - a_{22} & \cdots & -a_{2z} \\ \cdot & \cdot & \cdots & \cdot \\ -a_{z1} & -a_{z2} & \cdots & 1 - a_{zz} \end{bmatrix} \begin{bmatrix} x_1 \\ x_2 \\ \cdot \\ x_z \end{bmatrix} - \begin{bmatrix} b_{11} & b_{12} & \cdots & b_{1z} \\ b_{21} & b_{22} & \cdots & b_{2z} \\ \cdot & \cdot & \cdots & \cdot \\ b_{z1} & b_{z2} & \cdots & b_{zz} \end{bmatrix} \begin{bmatrix} \dot{x}_1 \\ \dot{x}_2 \\ \cdot \\ \dot{x}_z \end{bmatrix} = \begin{bmatrix} 0 \\ 0 \\ \\ 0 \end{bmatrix}$$

or

$$(70) \qquad [I - \bar{a}^*][x] - [b][\dot{x}] = [0]$$

As we have noted at several points in the discussion, the von Neumann model is analogous to this closed system if we treat flows in the former on the point-input, point-output basis discussed above. When that is done, the distinctive characteristic of Leontief's system becomes apparent immediately: equalities rule throughout. In this reconstructed system actual stocks of goods must always equal desired stocks. No excess capacity in any sector can exist. In the long-run solution, this is equivalent for the von Neumann model to converting (27) to equalities for $n + 1$ equations and (31) to equalities for $n + 1$ equations. These $2n + 2$ equations are sufficient to determine the n relative quantities and n relative prices plus the Δ and ε roots of the system.[26] This implies that no goods are free at any time and, in the very long-run, when the dominant root is dictating the time path, *all* processes (again capable of being identified with single products) are advancing at the same rate of growth.

The Leontief formulation has its advantages of permitting (70) to be solved as a system of differential equations yielding the x_{jt} for every point (or, more loosely, period) of time, rather than abstracting from transient states to concentrate upon the very long term as von Neumann's model does. Dantzig's model is not constructed to yield only long-term solutions but certainly its solution is much more difficult than Leontief's system. The difficulty with the Leontief-Hawkins assumption is that the system may require at some points that $\dot{x}_{jt} < 0$, which implies, if the equalities of the balance equations are to be maintained, that disinvestment in stocks should be unimpeded. Further, in extreme cases, it may require disinvestment to go so far that stocks are reduced to negative levels—an economically meaningless result.

In response to these difficulties we shall discuss the solution to the Leontief model under these assumptions: (1) the complete reversibility of investment; (2) the complete irreversibility of investment; and (3) the partial reversibility of investment. In the first case, incremental stock requirements are positive when the $\dot{x}_j$ are positive and negative when the $\dot{x}_j$ are negative; in the second case incremental stock requirements are positive when the $\dot{x}_j$ are positive and zero when the $\dot{x}_j$ are negative; and, in the third case, incremental stock requirements are positive when the $\dot{x}_j$ are positive, and negative to certain limits when the $\dot{x}_j$ are negative, zero beyond these points.

3.e.1.a. The Complete Reversibility Case

Both Leontief and Hawkins solve their models initially on the assumption of complete reversibility, although Leontief moves on to the difficul-

[26] This is also done in Hawkins' system, (1). Cf. also R. Dorfman, (1), Ch. 11.

ties of the assumption, while Hawkins does not. Under these assumptions, when $\dot{C}_{jk} \gtreqless 0$, before the initial conditions are introduced, the solutions to system (70) will be of the form

$$x_{jt} = \sum_{k=1}^{n+1} K_{jk} e^{\lambda_k t}, \qquad j = 1, \ldots, n+1 \tag{71}$$

where λ_k are the roots of the characteristic equation of the system and where the K_{jk} are constants. If we introduce a set of initial outputs into the model so that absolute values can be obtained, a set of constants, c_j, $j = 1, \ldots, n + 1$, is introduced into the equations:[27]

$$x_{jt} = \sum_{k} c_k K_{jk} e^{\lambda_k t}, \qquad j = 1, \ldots, n+1 \tag{72}$$

To fix our ideas let us present (70) with two industrial sectors and the household sector:

$$\begin{bmatrix} 1 - a_{11} & -a_{12} & -a_{1z} \\ -a_{21} & 1 - a_{22} & -a_{2z} \\ -a_{z1} & -a_{z2} & 1 - a_{zz} \end{bmatrix} \begin{bmatrix} x_1 \\ x_2 \\ x_z \end{bmatrix} - \begin{bmatrix} b_{11} & b_{12} & b_{1z} \\ b_{21} & b_{22} & b_{2z} \\ b_{z1} & b_{z2} & b_{zz} \end{bmatrix} \begin{bmatrix} \dot{x}_1 \\ \dot{x}_2 \\ \dot{x}_z \end{bmatrix} = \begin{bmatrix} 0 \\ 0 \\ 0 \end{bmatrix} \tag{73}$$

for which, with given initial conditions, the solution will be:

$$\begin{aligned} x_{1t} &= c_1 K_{11} e^{\lambda_1 t} + c_2 K_{12} e^{\lambda_2 t} + c_z K_{1z} e^{\lambda_3 t} \\ x_{2t} &= c_1 K_{21} e^{\lambda_1 t} + c_2 K_{22} e^{\lambda_2 t} + c_z K_{2z} e^{\lambda_3 t} \\ x_{zt} &= c_1 K_{z1} e^{\lambda_1 t} + c_2 K_{z2} e^{\lambda_2 t} + c_z K_{zz} e^{\lambda_3 t} \end{aligned} \tag{74}$$

If complex roots occur they will do so in conjugate pairs; for example, if λ_2 and λ_3 are complex, we could write them as a sum and difference of real and imaginary parts:

$$\begin{aligned} &1. \quad \lambda_2 = \alpha + \beta i \\ &2. \quad \lambda_3 = \alpha - \beta i \end{aligned} \tag{75}$$

and (74) would read

$$x_{1t} = c_1 K_{11} e^{\lambda_1 t} + c_2 K_{12} e^{\alpha t} \cos(\beta t + c'_{12} + k'_1) \tag{76}$$

and so forth, where the term $\cos(\beta t + c'_{jk} + k'_j)$ fluctuates between -1 and $+1$ in periodic fashion as $t \to \infty$.

Now, if λ_1, λ_2, and λ_3 are all positive, or when complex, if the real parts α are positive, x_j, $j = 1, 2, z$, will grow as t grows; if the λ_j are all negative, or when complex, if the real parts α are negative, x_j, $j = 1, 2, z$, will

[27] We shall deal at great length with the solution of dynamic linear equations in the discussion of potential market disequlibrium systems, but the reader is referred to any book on elementary differential equations.

approach zero as $t \to \infty$. If λ_1, λ_2, and λ_3 are zero, the x_j, $j = 1, 2, z$, will remain constant; if one root is zero and the other two are complex with $\alpha = 0$, x_j will fluctuate over time.

Let us now select that root, λ_j^*, which is dominant in size, and assume it is λ_1. If λ_2 and λ_3 are less than zero but $\lambda_1 > 0$, x_j will approach the values given by the $c_1 K_{j1} e^{\lambda_1 t}$ as $t \to \infty$. Even if λ_2 and λ_3 are greater than zero, as time approaches infinity, the above terms will be closer and closer approximations to the x_{jt} values. That is, for t sufficiently large $x_{1t} \cong c_1 K_{11} e^{\lambda_1 t}$, and so forth. If these values are substituted into (73), we obtain:

$$(77)\quad \begin{bmatrix} 1 - a_{11} - b_{11}\lambda_1 & - a_{12} - b_{12}\lambda_1 & - a_{1z} - b_{1z}\lambda_1 \\ - a_{21} - b_{21}\lambda_1 & 1 - a_{22} - b_{22}\lambda_1 & - a_{2z} - b_{2z}\lambda_1 \\ - a_{z1} - b_{z1}\lambda_1 & - a_{z2} - b_{z2}\lambda_1 & 1 - a_{zz} - b_{zz}\lambda_1 \end{bmatrix} \begin{bmatrix} K_{11} \\ K_{21} \\ K_{31} \end{bmatrix} = \begin{bmatrix} 0 \\ 0 \\ 0 \end{bmatrix}$$

or

$$(78)\qquad [D][K] = [0]$$

Relative outputs, $\frac{x_{kt}}{x_{jt}}$, will approach the ratios $\frac{K_{k1}}{K_{j1}}$, for which (78) may be solved. If these ratios are to be economically meaningful, then the Hawkins-Simon conditions require that all principal minors of $|D|$ be positive. These conditions are analogous to those of the static model in that they guarantee net outflows from all sectors and subsystems of sectors except that subsystem containing all $n + 1$ sectors.

Let us now convert the physical units into value units when the system has attained the long-term equilibrium. Assume that the value of a unit of output in any sector is equal to the value of its inputs on current account plus the value of its capital coefficients times the percentage rate of growth of the products involved. Then, for Y_j, say Y_1,

$$(79)\quad P_1 = a_{11}P_1 + a_{21}P_2 + \cdots a_{z1}P_z + b_{11}\left(\frac{\dot{x}_1}{x_1}\right)P_1 + \cdots b_{z1}\left(\frac{\dot{x}_z}{x_z}\right)P_z$$

for each point of time, t. If we go to our long-run state of growth,

$$(80)\qquad \frac{\dot{x}_1}{x_1} = \frac{\lambda_1 c_1 K_{11} e^{\lambda_1 t}}{c_1 K_{11} e^{\lambda_1 t}} = \lambda_1$$

The percentage rate of growth for every sector will be the same—just as in the von Neumann model where $\Delta = 1 + \lambda_1$, for those goods which were not in excess supply; of course, the difference in results springs from Leontief's rejection of inequalities in his structural relations. This rate of growth is independent of initial conditions and depends solely upon $[I - \bar{a}^*]$ and $[b]$. The farther the actual rate of growth is from this long-term rate, the greater is the influence of transient roots.

Then (79) becomes by substitution from (80):

$$P_k = \sum_j a_{jk}P_j + \lambda_1 \sum_j b_{jk}P_j \tag{81}$$

The price of every commodity must equal the value of current inputs plus the value of average investment times the dominant root. Intuition tells us that λ_1 must be the interest rate but let us derive it rigorously. We define $a'_{jk} = a_{jk}\left(\frac{P_j}{P_k}\right)$ and $b'_{jk} = b_{jk}\left(\frac{P_j}{P_k}\right)$. From (81),

$$1 = \sum_j a'_{jk} + \lambda_1 \sum_j b'_{jk} \tag{82}$$

Let $a'_k = \sum_j a'_{jk}$ be the current input cost of a unit of Y_j and $b'_k = \sum_j b'_{jk}$ be the value of stocks per unit of Y_j in *numéraire*. Then,

$$\lambda_1 = \frac{1 - a'_k}{b'_k} \tag{83}$$

In the long run, the excess of price over current input cost as a proportion of capital value per unit of output must be equal for each good and equal to the dominant root. This is the rate of interest and it is equal to the rate of growth in the long run—another von Neumann result for the model with inequalities.

It must be recalled, however, that this result follows only from the competitive assumption that the output of each sector must be sold at a price which includes current cost and a common rate of return on investment only.

3.e.1.b. The Complete Irreversibility Case

One fundamental difficulty with this model is that it assumes that if $\dot{x}_j < 0$, previously accumulated stocks may be drawn upon as sources of Y_j alternative to current production. That is to say (70) requires that an industry's output balance with the amounts absorbed by all sectors on current or capital account. If, therefore, $\dot{x}_j$ becomes negative, in the reversible model stocks are freed in this sector and, implicitly, transferred to other sectors. While this may hold true for stocks of Y_j held as inventories or circulating capital, it will not be true generally of durable capital goods whose life extends beyond the period. As a first approximation to this problem of irreversibility—the asymmetry between stock build-up and depletion—let us assume that (1) no transfer of stocks occurs between sectors, and (2) within the sector complete irreversibility holds.[28]

In the case of complete reversibility, the possibility for oscillation of the economy hinges upon the occurrence of one or more pairs of complex roots. If the real part of a complex root is positive and dominant, such oscillation will characterize the long-run solution; otherwise it will merely add an oscillatory component to the transient states of the model's solution. But the present model allows us to admit a second type of oscillation in our model: relaxation oscillation.[29] It results from the abrupt switching of a process from one phase or regime to another as a result, in our present case, of a fall in $\dot{x}_j$ rather than a rise or constancy.

If the path of the economy toward its long-run steady state contains reversals of directions in any or all sectors' outputs (and theoretically, in a system with $n + 1$ real roots, each of the sectors could reverse its direction as many as n times in the approach even where no periodic fluctuations can occur), an abrupt switch from Phase 1 to Phase 2 occurs for a sector at the point(s) where $\dot{x}_j$ becomes negative. Whenever this occurs, the appropriate b_{jk} become zero.

We must specify the set of rules under which the switching from Phase 1 to Phase 2 or vice versa is done. Let $\overline{C_{jk}}$ be the desired stock of Y_j in the production of Y_k. Then, excess capacity, C_{jk}^*, is defined

$$C_{jk}^* = C_{jk} - \overline{C_{jk}} \tag{84}$$

where C_{jk} is actual stock and $\overline{C_{jk}}$ is defined as:

$$\overline{C_{jk}} = b_{jk}x_k \tag{85}$$

Phase 1 exists while $C_{jk}^* = 0$ and lasts until the period when

$$C_{jk}^* = 0, \ \dot{x}_k = 0, \ \ddot{x}_k < 0 \tag{86}$$

where $\ddot{x}_k = \dfrac{d^2x_k}{dt^2}$. That is, Phase 2 begins in the period when excess stocks of all goods in a given sector are zero, but growth of the sector's output has ceased and will start to decline the next time period. We then break the model in (70) using the relative outputs this period as initial values, and substitute $b_{jk} = 0$.

Phase 2 for Y_k ends when, after $C_{jk}^* > 0$ in Phase 2, the following conditions occur (if they ever do):

$$C_{jk}^* = 0, \ \dot{x}_k > 0 \tag{87}$$

At this point a switch is made once more into the Phase 1 regime, the relative output values at the point of switching being initial values.

[28] For the case where such mobility of excess stocks among sectors is allowed to occur, see R. Dorfman, (1), pp. 286–300.

[29] P. Le Corbeiller, (1), and N. Georgescu-Roegen, (2).

Given $n + 1$ sectors the number of possible combinations of phases is 2^{n+1}, since every good can either be in Phase 1 or Phase 2. The number of splicings, given the theoretical ability of the sectors to reverse their directions n times could therefore become quite large.

3.e.1.c. The Partial Reversibility Case

Let us now introduce into all or some of the sectors an ability to move stocks in a negative direction to a partial extent, not by a transfer of a given good from one sector to another when stocks of it are in excess supply but (1) by using undesired inventories as current inputs, or (2) by failing to replace worn out stocks by current absorption of inputs to the extent r_{jk}, the latter term being the proportion of a_{jk} going to such uses each period.

Let t° be the time period at which the sector enters the $\dot{x}_k = 0$, $\ddot{x}_k < 0$ phase. Then the actual stock in period t of the downward phase will be

$$C_{jkt} = C_{jkt^\circ} - b_{jk} \int_{t^\circ}^{t} \dot{x}_{kt} dt \tag{88}$$

and, for the replacement depletion,

$$C_{jkt} = C_{jkt^\circ} - r_{jk} \int_{t^\circ}^{t} \dot{x}_{kt} dt \tag{89}$$

The switching will occur when $\dot{x}_k < 0$, $\ddot{x}_k < 0$, but where $C_{jk}^* = 0$. At this point both b_{jk} and r_{jk} are equated to zero, so a_{jk} becomes $a_{jk} - r_{jk}$. The switching point to Phase 1 (if it comes) is the same as previously given.

3.e.1.d. A Criticism of the Closed Model

A major difference between the static input-output model and the dynamic models just presented must be pointed out. In the former, as we should interpret it, the analysis may be carried out in total ignorance of resource or sectoral capacity limitations on gross outputs. These may indeed be included to define efficiency frontiers for final bills of goods, but we have chosen to view the model as a method of determining the amounts demanded of entrepreneurial inputs. In the dynamic model, however, one group of inputs—the services rendered by stocks—has an explicit past, generated by the model, whose impact upon today's production must be taken into account. A stock built yesterday and existing today may, by today's decisionmaking, become partially redundant, and in so doing, affect the current production of the product forming the stock. The sectoral stocks must, therefore, enter into the workings of the model in a way which was not true of the static model.

The balance conditions of (70) require that rates of change $\dot{x}_j$ be such that outputs, after reduction for entrepreneurial and household demands on current account, exactly equal the sum of *desired* investment in the product over the whole economy. In a reversible system, of course, or even a partially reversible system to a bounded degree, these desired investments, sector by sector, in Y_j, may be negative if existing stocks permit, depending upon the signs of the rates of change of x_j. But, as cited above, generally speaking, the only conditions under which it will be true that desired investment, positive or negative, can be approximated by multiplying a fixed coefficient by a rate of change in output is when stocks are fully utilized. For given a set of initial x_{k0}, no sector's C_{jk0} can be less than desired levels set by $b_{jk}x_{k0}$, since, if it were, these outputs would be infeasible. If, in a sector, some actual stocks were greater than desired stocks, desired investment could not be represented by $b_{jk}x_{k0}$, for were $\dot{x}_k > 0$, desired investment would be less than this figure by the amount of excess capacity; were $\dot{x}_k = 0$, desired investment would be negative, not zero; and if $\dot{x}_k < 0$, desired investment at $t = 0$ equal to the given production implies that no excess capacity exists. Moreover, the same conditions must hold for every t, and no excess capacity can characterize any of the successive equilibrium points traced out by the model's evolution. In this respect it differs from a Dantzig or von Neumann equilibrium.

As we have seen, from any equilibrium initial position, each sector will approach a long-run steady state where

$$\frac{x_{jt}}{x_{kt}} \rightarrow \frac{K_{j1}}{K_{k1}} \text{ as } t \rightarrow \infty \tag{90}$$

where λ_1 is taken to be the dominant root of the system. Therefore the equilibrium structure of capital stocks of good Y_j will be

$$\frac{C_{jkt}}{C_{jit}} \rightarrow \frac{b_{jk}x_{kt}}{b_{ji}x_{it}} \rightarrow \frac{b_{jk}K_{kj}}{b_{ji}K_{ij}} \text{ as } t \rightarrow \infty \tag{91}$$

The ratios of outputs and stocks would have to be adjusted to the structure indicated by (91), this readjustment to be accomplished without bringing about excess capacity in any sector at any time. This may require disinvestment for long periods of time or, if some roots are complex, on a cyclical basis. If or when this degree of disinvestment becomes impossible, the model enters Phase 2, as we discussed above. Leontief's switching rules are meant to be a relaxation of the rigidities which yield nonmeaningful degrees of disinvestment.

Dorfman, Samuelson, and Solow demonstrate that movement along "Leontief trajectories" may not be the most efficient path of approach to optimal balanced growth. It may, under the production conditions of the model, be inefficient to use all of society's resources at all times, for reasons we have demonstrated in our discussions of linear programming. Some other path which allows some goods to become free, *à la* von Neumann and Dantzig, may yield more of all goods or as much of some and more of all others for all periods in the future after optimal growth is achieved. Leontief gets a determinate path by virtue of his equations, but were a planned economy to seek to optimize an objective function and allow excess capacity, it might very well find a better path.[30]

3.e.2. The Open Leontief Dynamic Model

Finally, we shall open the model of (70) to obtain data upon which policy measures may operate. As in the static case, the model becomes interesting in a policy sense only when we may specify certain parameters and see what adjustments in the variables are required to sustain these data. For our purposes, we shall treat the $n + 1^{\text{th}}$ sector as households and once more as external to the system. The reconstructed model (wholly or partially reversible, or irreversible), will then be

$$(92) \qquad [I - a^*][x_j] - [b][\dot{x}_j] = [X_j], \qquad j = 1, \ldots, n$$

where $[X_j]$ is the vector of final demand by households, at a given point in time. It may be possible to approximate the given path of final demand over time by such a function as

$$(93) \qquad X_{jt} = m_{j1}e^{u_1t} + m_{j2}e^{u_2t} + \cdots m_{jr}e^{u_rt}$$

or perhaps

$$(94) \qquad X_{jt} = m_{j1} + m_{j2}t + m_{j3}t^2 + \cdots m_{jr+1}t^r$$

The solution to (92) will be of the form

$$(95) \qquad x_{jt} = c_1K_{j1}e^{\lambda_1t} + c_2K_{j2}e^{\lambda_2t} + \cdots c_nK_{jn}e^{\lambda_nt} + L_j(t)$$

where the $L_j(t)$ term is the particular solution springing from the bill of good items. For example, if the exponential forms of (93) are used to represent the bill of goods, then $L_j(t)$ becomes

$$(96) \qquad L_j(t) = w_{j1}e^{u_1t} + w_{j2}e^{u_2t} + \cdots w_{jn}e^{u_rt}$$

where the w_{jk} depend upon the m_{ji}, $[a^*]$, and $[b]$. If the bill of goods items are depicted by the polynomial forms of (94), then

$$(97) \qquad L_j(t) = w_{j1} + w_{j2}t + w_{j3}t^2 + \cdots w_{jr+1}t^r$$

where the w-terms depend upon the m-terms of (94), $[a^*]$, and $[b]$.

We may then specify the bill of goods required for each point (period) of time and the gross outputs for $t = 0$, and solve for the gross outputs at

[30] R. Dorfman, (1), pp. 335–45.

all points in time over the given interval. All of the criticisms of the closed dynamic model may be applied to the open model.

4. Potential Market Disequilibrium Models

We now approach the second type of dynamic economic system: that kind which yields as a solution the path of the variables through time when markets are out of equilibrium as well as when they are in equilibrium. As we have defined the term, stability is primarily a characteristic of an equilibrium, although it can be extended to a system. Our concern with potential market disequilibrium systems will be all but exclusively to study the stability properties of the market equilibria to which they (are assumed to) give rise. Therefore, we turn to the analysis of stability immediately.

4.a. The Stability of Economic Equilibrium

The selection of the dynamic forms to be included in the structural relationships of an economic model and the manner in which they are linked to the data and instantaneous forms of the variables is inherently a behavioral question. How do economic units react in the trial and error search for an equilibrium to changes in the parameters they face, and how are these individual decisions linked to the movement of the model's variables in the market? Which of the variables may be viewed as adaptive and which as initiating? To seek answers in specific cases let us construct models of the types presented in Part II, proceeding from the simplest to the more complex.

4.a.1. The Model of Consumer Choice: Simple Exchange

We shall return to the simple exchange Model I-3 as a start for our stability analysis. To obtain a prediction of consumer choice we assumed prices and income as given and enforced the equality of prices and marginal rates of substitution, within the budget constraint. But we also enforced a second-order equilibrium condition, to insure that the preference function depicting the consumer's tastes be strictly quasi-concave locally at the equilibrium point. This second-order condition is frequently termed a stability condition, in the sense that it is asserted that if a choice is made and the function is strictly quasi-concave, the position defined by the first-order conditions will be reattained in the event of perturbations in the values of the variables in the neighborhood of the equilibrium.

But this is a first instance of a confusing choice of terminology in the treatment of stability. Conceptually, the second-order equilibrium condition is of a fundamentally different character from the true stability conditions of an equilibrium position. The former merely yield more information about the equilibrium position itself, or, rather, they specify that a point which has the appearance of an extremum position is indeed one. Even though defined in terms of a neighborhood of the critical point, the second-order equilibrium conditions do not have an explicit dynamic meaning. They do not tell us, for example, that a slight movement away from the critical point will result in a return to it or a departure from it to a greater extent; such a theorem can be derived only from an explicit dynamic model. We have seen that in the case of the partial demand-supply model the conditions for dynamic stability can be stated in terms of the slopes of the static curves and the same may hold true for general models. That is to say, given quasi-concavity of the consumer's preference function, it may indeed be true that some dynamic model will make this property a necessary and sufficient condition for dynamic stability. But the point we stress is that the property of the function is of interest quite independently of stability considerations as a necessary element in the definition of a concept with quite definite static meaning, viz., equilibrium.

What, then, is the explicit dynamic model from which we may derive the stability conditions for the individual consumer's equilibrium?[31] First, we reproduce the primary equilibrium conditions:

(I-3-2)
$$
\begin{aligned}
&1. \quad G^j - \lambda^{*\circ} P_j = 0 \\
&2. \quad \sum_j X_j^\circ P_j - Z = 0
\end{aligned}
$$

To fix our ideas, assume $n = 3$ and that Y_1 is the *numéraire*. The consumer can only adapt his purchases of goods to fixed prices within a fixed income: therefore, the dynamic adjustment process must be stated in terms of quantities varying from their equilibrium values, and the "marginal preference of income" measure, λ^*, also varying in this manner.

We shall define the reactions of the consumer to a departure from these equilibrium conditions in the following way. Let $\dot{X}_j = \frac{dX_j}{dt}$ and $\dot{\lambda}_i^* = \frac{d\lambda^*}{dt}$, where the latter term correlates negatively with the correctional movements of the time rate of change of excess spending. We hypothesize that these time derivatives are related to the departure of the actual values of marginal preference index values from the corresponding equilibrium values as follows:

(98)
$$
\begin{aligned}
&1. \quad \dot{X}_1 = F_1(G^1 - \lambda^{*\circ}),\ F_1' > 0,\ F_1(0) = 0 \\
&2. \quad \dot{X}_2 = F_2(G^2 - \lambda^{*\circ} P_2),\ F_2' > 0,\ F_2(0) = 0 \\
&3. \quad \dot{X}_3 = F_3(G^3 - \lambda^{*\circ} P_3),\ F_3' > 0,\ F_3(0) = 0 \\
&4. \quad \dot{\lambda}^* = F_\lambda(X_1 + X_2 P_2 + X_3 P_3 - Z),\ F_\lambda' > 0,\ F_\lambda(0) = 0
\end{aligned}
$$

[31] Pareto discusses very briefly an adjustment over time of the consumer's purchases which implicitly assumes the dynamic stability of the consumer model. See V. Pareto, (2), pp. 145–6.

That is, the time rates of change in our variables are related to the size of the departure of marginal preference index values or spending from equilibrium values. But we may think of $S_j = G^j - \lambda^{*\circ}P_j$ as an "excess marginal preference function" related to the degree of disequilibrium in the variables of the system. We define excess demands, $E_j = X_j - X_j^\circ$, and $E_\lambda = \lambda^* - \lambda^{*\circ}$, and we obtain:

$$(99)\quad \begin{aligned} &1.\quad S_j = S_j(E_j, E_\lambda) = G^j(E_j) - E_\lambda P_j \\ &2.\quad S_\lambda = E_1 + E_2P_2 + E_3P_3 \end{aligned}$$

Substituting these into (98) and, at the same time, putting the excess spending function in terms of the E_j and E_λ, we get:

$$(100)\quad \begin{aligned} &1.\quad \dot{X}_1 = F_1'[S_1(E_1, E_2, E_3, E_\lambda)] \\ &2.\quad \dot{X}_2 = F_2'[S_2(E_1, E_2, E_3, E_\lambda)] \\ &3.\quad \dot{X}_3 = F_3'[S_3(E_1, E_2, E_3, E_\lambda)] \\ &4.\quad \dot{\lambda}^* = F_\lambda'[E_1 + E_2P_2 + E_3P_3] \end{aligned}$$

For positions close to but distinct from equilibrium points we may use Maclaurin's theorem to expand the S_j, retaining only the linear part of the expansions and neglecting derivatives higher than the first order:

$$(101)\quad \begin{aligned} &1.\quad \dot{X}_1 = F_1'[G^{11}E_1 + G^{12}E_2 + G^{13}E_3 + S_1^\lambda E_\lambda] \\ &2.\quad \dot{X}_2 = F_2'[G^{12}E_1 + G^{22}E_2 + G^{23}E_3 + S_2^\lambda E_\lambda] \\ &3.\quad \dot{X}_3 = F_3'[G^{13}E_1 + G^{23}E_2 + G^{33}E_3 + S_3^\lambda E_\lambda] \\ &4.\quad \dot{\lambda}^* = F_\lambda'[E_1 + P_2E_2 + P_3E_3] \end{aligned}$$

where the F' and G^{ij} are taken as constants. In matrix form:

$$(102)\quad \begin{bmatrix} F_1'G^{11} & F_1'G^{12} & F_1'G^{13} & -F_1' \\ F_2'G^{12} & F_2'G^{22} & F_2'G^{23} & -F_2'P_2 \\ F_3'G^{13} & F_3'G^{23} & F'G^{33} & -F_3'P_3 \\ F_\lambda' & F_\lambda'P_2 & F_\lambda'P_3 & 0 \end{bmatrix} \begin{bmatrix} E_1 \\ E_2 \\ E_3 \\ E_\lambda \end{bmatrix} = \begin{bmatrix} \dot{X}_1 \\ \dot{X}_2 \\ \dot{X}_3 \\ \dot{\lambda}^* \end{bmatrix}$$

where the substitutions $S_1^\lambda = -1$, $S_2^\lambda = -P_2$, and $S_3^\lambda = -P_3$ have been made from (I-3-2).[32]

Letting $a_{ij} = F_i'G^{ij}$, and substituting $X_j - X_j^\circ$ for E_j, we obtain:

$$(103)\quad a_{11}X_1 + a_{12}X_2 + a_{13}X_3 + a_{1\lambda}\lambda^* - \dot{X}_1 = a_{11}X_1^\circ + a_{12}X_2^\circ + a_{13}X_3^\circ + a_{1\lambda}\lambda^{*\circ}$$

[32] Throughout our discussion of dynamic stability, we shall deal only with such linear differential systems of the first order. For the derivation of necessary and sufficient conditions for the stability of equilibrium in mixed differential-difference equations, for example, see E. Burger, (1).

and so forth. We shall symbolize the terms on the right-hand side of the equations containing the equilibrium values of the variables, K_s, and reduce the system to

$$(104)\qquad \begin{aligned} &1. \quad a_{11}X_1 - \dot{X}_1 + a_{12}X_2 + a_{13}X_3 + a_{1\lambda}\lambda^* = K_1 \\ &2. \quad a_{21}X_1 + a_{22}X_2 - \dot{X}_2 + a_{23}X_3 + a_{2\lambda}\lambda^* = K_2 \\ &3. \quad a_{31}X_1 + a_{32}X_2 + a_{33}X_3 - \dot{X}_3 + a_{3\lambda}\lambda^* = K_3 \\ &4. \quad a_{\lambda 1}X_1 + a_{\lambda 2}X_2 + a_{\lambda 3}X_3 + 0\lambda^* - \dot{\lambda}^* = K_4 \end{aligned}$$

We may proceed to the solution of this first-order linear differential equation system by using the operator D and neglecting the K-constants:

$$(105)\qquad \begin{bmatrix} a_{11} - D & a_{12} & a_{13} & a_{1\lambda} \\ a_{21} & a_{22} - D & a_{23} & a_{2\lambda} \\ a_{31} & a_{32} & a_{33} - D & a_{3\lambda} \\ a_{\lambda 1} & a_{\lambda 2} & a_{\lambda 3} & -D \end{bmatrix} \begin{bmatrix} X_1 \\ X_2 \\ X_3 \\ \lambda \end{bmatrix} = \begin{bmatrix} 0 \\ 0 \\ 0 \\ 0 \end{bmatrix}$$

The determinantal equation is

$$(106)\qquad \begin{vmatrix} a_{11} - y & a_{12} & a_{13} & a_{1\lambda} \\ a_{21} & a_{22} - y & a_{23} & a_{2\lambda} \\ a_{31} & a_{32} & a_{33} - y & a_{3\lambda} \\ a_{\lambda 1} & a_{\lambda 2} & a_{\lambda 3} & -y \end{vmatrix} = 0$$

whose general form for the four-equation case above is

$$(107)\qquad A_0y^4 + A_1y^3 + A_2y^2 + A_3y + A_4 = 0$$

where

$$(108)\qquad \begin{aligned} A_0 &= 1 \\ A_1 &= -(a_{11} + a_{22} + a_{33}) \\ A_2 &= a_{11}a_{22} + a_{11}a_{33} + a_{22}a_{33} - a_{13}a_{31} - a_{2\lambda}a_{\lambda 2} \\ A_3 &= -a_{11}a_{22}a_{33} + a_{11}a_{2\lambda}a_{\lambda 2} + a_{13}a_{22}a_{31} + a_{2\lambda}a_{33}a_{\lambda 2} \\ A_4 &= (-1)^4 \begin{vmatrix} a_{11} & a_{12} & a_{13} & a_{1\lambda} \\ a_{21} & a_{22} & a_{23} & a_{2\lambda} \\ a_{31} & a_{32} & a_{33} & a_{3\lambda} \\ a_{\lambda 1} & a_{\lambda 2} & a_{\lambda 3} & 0 \end{vmatrix} \end{aligned}$$

The solution to our system (104) will be of the form

$$(109)\qquad \begin{aligned} &1. \quad X_{1t} = X_1^\circ + c_{11}e^{y_1t} + c_{12}e^{y_2t} + c_{13}e^{y_3t} + c_{1\lambda}e^{y_4t} \\ &2. \quad X_{2t} = X_2^\circ + c_{21}e^{y_1t} + c_{22}e^{y_2t} + c_{23}e^{y_3t} + c_{2\lambda}e^{y_4t} \\ &3. \quad X_{3t} = X_3^\circ + c_{31}e^{y_1t} + c_{32}e^{y_2t} + c_{33}e^{y_3t} + c_{3\lambda}e^{y_4t} \\ &4. \quad \lambda_t^* = \lambda^{*\circ} + c_{\lambda 1}e^{y_1t} + c_{\lambda 2}e^{y_2t} + c_{\lambda 3}e^{y_3t} + c_{\lambda\lambda}e^{y_4t} \end{aligned}$$

where the y_j are roots of the characteristic equation (106) and (107), and in which the c terms are coefficients determined by the matrix of a coefficients as well as the K_s terms of (104).

It is not necessary to solve (106) for the roots y_j to see if their real parts are all negative and therefore if (101) is dynamically stable in the neighborhood of the equilibrium. The Routhian conditions—necessary and sufficient for negative real parts of all roots in the characteristic equation—on the A coefficients in the polynomial (107) will simplify the analysis. The degree of this polynomial will equal the number of equations—$n + 1$ in the above case. To state the conditions we construct the Routhian matrix as follows: in the first row we write the odd-numbered A coefficients from left to right, filling out the remainder of the row with zeroes until the number of elements in this row vector equals the degree of the polynomial. In the second row, the same process is repeated with the even-numbered A terms, counting A_0 as an even-numbered coefficient. The third row is obtained by displacing the A terms of the first row one column to the right, as illustrated in (110). The fourth column is obtained from the second by displacing the A terms one column to the right, and so forth until the number of rows also equals the degree of the polynomial. For our four-equation case the Routhian matrix is

$$(110) \qquad \begin{bmatrix} A_1 & A_3 & 0 & 0 \\ A_0 & A_2 & A_4 & 0 \\ 0 & A_1 & A_3 & 0 \\ 0 & A_0 & A_2 & A_4 \end{bmatrix}$$

where $A_0 > 0$. The Routhian conditions are simply that the principal minors of this matrix be positive; that is, that the following be positive:

$$(111) \qquad A_1, \begin{vmatrix} A_1 & A_3 \\ A_0 & A_2 \end{vmatrix}, \begin{vmatrix} A_1 & A_3 & 0 \\ A_0 & A_2 & A_4 \\ 0 & A_1 & A_3 \end{vmatrix}, A_4 \begin{vmatrix} A_1 & A_3 & 0 \\ A_0 & A_2 & A_4 \\ 0 & A_1 & A_3 \end{vmatrix}$$

It is therefore implied that $A_4 > 0$, or, from (108):

$$(112) \qquad A_4 = (-1)^s F_1' F_2' F_3' F_\lambda' \begin{vmatrix} G^{11} & G^{12} & G^{13} & -1 \\ G^{12} & G^{22} & G^{23} & -P_2 \\ G^{13} & G^{23} & G^{33} & -P_3 \\ 1 & P_2 & P_3 & 0 \end{vmatrix} > 0$$

where s is the number of rows (or columns). In our case $n = 3$, and since the F' terms are positive (see (98)) the determinant in (112) must be positive. But this determinant is nothing else but $|H|$ in (120) and (134) of Chapter 2; there, by virtue of the second-order equilibrium conditions, it was shown that $|H|$ would be positive, and now, on the basis of the Routhian conditions for the stability of the system, we derive the same result.

We may revert to an old theme: it was seen in the derivation of operational theorems from Model I-3 that the second-order equilibrium conditions were of use analytically only in yielding the sign of $|H|$ and the subdeterminants formed by striking out the row and column of any diagonal element or elements, excepting the border diagonal term and providing the number of rows in such principal minors was greater than 2. We have now shown that if we construct a dynamic system explicitly in the form (98), simplify it by linearizing it, and solve, in order for it to be dynamically stable the sign of $|H|$ must correspond to that yielded by the second-order equilibrium conditions. Since the sign of $|H|$ forms part of the necessary and sufficient conditions for the existence of a maximum and its stability, it follows that when $|H| \ngtr 0$ a true maximum position cannot have been achieved and the equilibrium cannot be stable.

But it is possible to go farther in associating these two concepts of existence of an extremum and stability for the case in hand. In this case, we know that $[H]$ is symmetric. It can be shown that all the roots of the characteristic equation will be real when symmetry holds. Moreover, it may be shown that if the matrix is negative definite—if second-order equilibrium conditions are met—$[H]$ will be Routhian. Therefore, under the conditions of the symmetry of $[H]$ and negative definiteness, the necessary and sufficient conditions for a maximum and for dynamic stability are identical. Thus, if the integrability conditions are met in the definition of the consumer's preference function, dynamic stability is in fact implied by the second-order equilibrium conditions.

The relative speeds of adjustment, F', may be arbitrarily converted to unity by changing the physical unit in which goods are measured. As long as these speeds are positive, they cannot interfere with the reattainment of a disturbed equilibrium. This is true because the speed of adjustment in the quantities desired of any one good does not affect the speed of adjustment of any other. Since complex roots cannot occur the solution cannot oscillate. Thus, if the consumer moves toward the equilibrium value of marginal preferences and these lie at a true constrained maximum, he will reattain the equilibrium.

It follows, then, that in this rather uninteresting dynamic stability analysis, three possible causes of instability exist:

1. the equilibrium point is not a constrained maximum.

2. one or more of the variables are incapable of adjustment by the consumer, for whatever reason. That is, some $F' = 0$, and for obvious reasons the consumer will not be able to attain the static equilibrium point if he begins from a point in its neighborhood.

3. one or more of the variables are adjusted in perverse directions.

That is, one or more $F' < 0$. Again, it is obvious that an equilibrium point will be unattainable.

4.a.2. The Model of Entrepreneurial Choice

We may deal speedily with the dynamic model in the entrepreneurial sector which is analogous to that for the consumer. We may use Model III-4's firm as an example, and assume the entrepreneur adjusts his inputs, outputs, and common marginal cost level for all outputs (λ) to fixed prices. The equilibrium conditions are stated in (125) of Chapter 3, and we depict our dynamic system below:

$$
(113)\quad
\begin{aligned}
&1.\quad \dot{X}_i = S_i(\lambda^\circ V^i - P_i),\ S_i' > 0,\ S_i(0) = 0\\
&2.\quad \dot{X}_j = S_j(\lambda^\circ V^j - P_j),\ S_j' > 0,\ S_j(0) = 0\\
&3.\quad \dot{\bar{X}}_1 = \bar{S}_1(\lambda^\circ - P_1),\ \bar{S}_1' < 0,\ \bar{S}_1(0) = 0\\
&4.\quad \dot{\bar{X}}_{j\neq 1} = \bar{S}_J(-\lambda^\circ V^J - P_J),\ \bar{S}_J' > 0,\ \bar{S}_J(0) = 0\\
&5.\quad \dot{\lambda} = S_\lambda(\bar{X}_1 - V(X_1, \ldots, X_n, X_{z_1}, \ldots, X_{z_m}, \bar{X}_2,\\
&\qquad\qquad \ldots, \bar{X}_n)),\ S_\lambda' < 0,\ S_\lambda(0) = 0
\end{aligned}
$$

For positions close to but distinct from equilibrium points, when $E_i = X_i - X_i^\circ$, and so forth, the functions of (113) may be approximated by

$$
(114)\quad
\begin{aligned}
&1.\quad \dot{X}_i = S_i'\Big[\sum_i \lambda^\circ V^{ii}E_i + \sum_j \lambda^\circ V^{ij}E_j + 0E_{\bar{1}}\\
&\qquad\qquad + \sum_{J\neq 1} \lambda^\circ V^{iJ}E_J + V^iE_\lambda\Big]\\
&2.\quad \dot{X}_j = S_j'\Big[\sum_i \lambda^\circ V^{ij}E_i + \sum_j \lambda^\circ V^{jj}E_j + 0E_{\bar{1}}\\
&\qquad\qquad + \sum_{J\neq 1} \lambda^\circ V^{jJ}E_J + V^jE_\lambda\Big]\\
&3.\quad \dot{\bar{X}}_1 = \bar{S}_i'\Big[\sum_i 0E_i + \sum_j 0E_j + 0E_{\bar{1}} + \sum_{J\neq 1} 0E_J + 1E_\lambda\Big]\\
&4.\quad \dot{\bar{X}}_{J\neq 1} = \bar{S}_J'\Big[\sum_i - \lambda^\circ V^{iJ}E_i + \sum_j - \lambda^\circ V^{jJ}E_j + 0E_{\bar{1}}\\
&\qquad\qquad + \sum_{J\neq 1} - \lambda^\circ V^{JJ}E_J - V^JE_\lambda\Big]\\
&5.\quad \dot{\lambda} = S_\lambda'\Big[\sum_i - V^iE_i + \sum_j - V^jE_j + 1E_{\bar{1}}\\
&\qquad\qquad + \sum_{J\neq 1} - V^JE_J + 0E_\lambda\Big]
\end{aligned}
$$

where the S' terms are taken to be constant and where the V terms are elements in the matrix of the system (128) in Chapter 3. We let $a_{st} =$

$S'_s V^{st}$, and so forth, and letting $K_s = \Sigma_i a_{is} X_i^\circ + \Sigma_j a_{js} X_j^\circ - \Sigma_J a_{Js} \bar{x}_j^\circ + a_{s\lambda}\lambda^\circ$, and so forth, using the operator D we may depict the system for $i = 1$, $j = 2$, as follows, when Y_1 is taken as *numéraire:*

$$
(115) \quad \begin{bmatrix} a_{zz} - D & a_{z1} & a_{z2} & 0 & -a_{z\bar{2}} & a_{z\lambda} \\ a_{1z} & a_{11} - D & a_{12} & 0 & -a_{1\bar{2}} & a_{1\lambda} \\ a_{2z} & a_{21} & a_{22} - D & 0 & -a_{2\bar{2}} & a_{2\lambda} \\ 0 & 0 & 0 & -D & 0 & 1 \\ -a_{\bar{2}z} & -a_{\bar{2}1} & -a_{\bar{2}2} & 0 & -a_{\bar{2}\bar{2}} - D & -a_{\bar{2}\lambda} \\ -a_{\lambda z} & -a_{\lambda 1} & -a_{\lambda 2} & 1 & -a_{\lambda\bar{2}} & -D \end{bmatrix} \begin{bmatrix} X_z \\ X_1 \\ X_2 \\ \bar{X}_1 \\ \bar{X}_2 \\ \lambda \end{bmatrix} = \begin{bmatrix} K_z \\ K_1 \\ K_2 \\ K_{\bar{1}} \\ K_{\bar{2}} \\ K_\lambda \end{bmatrix}
$$

The solution to this system will be of the form

$$
(116) \quad X_{it} = X_i^\circ + c_{11}e^{f_1 t} + c_{12}e^{f_2 t} + c_{13}e^{f_3 t} + c_{14}e^{f_4 t} + c_{15}e^{f_5 t} + c_{16}e^{f_6 t}
$$

and so forth, where the f are the roots of the characteristic equation:

$$
(117) \quad A_0 f^6 + A_1 f^5 + A_2 f^4 + A_3 f^3 + A_4 f^2 + A_5 f + A_6 = 0
$$

where $A_0 > 0$. We form the Routhian matrix:

$$
(118) \quad \begin{bmatrix} A_1 & A_3 & A_5 & 0 & 0 & 0 \\ A_0 & A_2 & A_4 & A_6 & 0 & 0 \\ 0 & A_1 & A_3 & A_5 & 0 & 0 \\ 0 & A_0 & A_2 & A_4 & A_6 & 0 \\ 0 & 0 & A_1 & A_3 & A_5 & 0 \\ 0 & 0 & A_0 & A_2 & A_4 & A_6 \end{bmatrix}
$$

and require as a necessary and sufficient condition for the real parts of all roots to be negative that the principal minors be positive.

Now, we may write A_6 as

$$
(119) \quad A_6 = B \begin{vmatrix} \lambda^\circ V^{zz} & \lambda^\circ V^{z1} & \lambda^\circ V^{z2} & 0 & \lambda^\circ \bar{V}^{z2} & V^z \\ \lambda^\circ V^{z1} & \lambda^\circ V^{11} & \lambda^\circ V^{12} & 0 & \lambda^\circ \bar{V}^{12} & V^1 \\ \lambda^\circ V^{z2} & \lambda^\circ V^{12} & \lambda^\circ V^{11} & 0 & \lambda^\circ \bar{V}^{22} & V^2 \\ 0 & 0 & 0 & 0 & 0 & -1 \\ -\lambda^\circ \bar{V}^{z2} & -\lambda^\circ \bar{V}^{11} & -\lambda^\circ V^{12} & 0 & -\lambda^\circ \bar{\bar{V}}^{22} & -\bar{V}^2 \\ -V^z & -V_1 & -V^2 & 1 & -\bar{V}^2 & 0 \end{vmatrix} > 0
$$

where $B = (-1)^{m+2n+1}(S'_z S'_1 S'_2 \bar{S}'_1 \bar{S}'_2 S'_\lambda)$. By a sequence of obvious operations, we may obtain

$$
(120) \quad B(\lambda^\circ)^3 \begin{vmatrix} V^{zz} & V^{z1} & V^{z2} & 0 & \bar{V}^{z2} & V^z \\ V^{z1} & V^{11} & V^{12} & 0 & \bar{V}^{12} & V^1 \\ V^{z2} & V^{12} & V^{11} & 0 & \bar{V}^{22} & V^2 \\ 0 & 0 & 0 & 0 & 0 & -1 \\ \bar{V}^{z2} & \bar{V}^{11} & \bar{V}^{12} & 0 & \bar{\bar{V}}^{22} & \bar{V}^2 \\ V^z & V^1 & V^2 & -1 & \bar{V}^2 & 0 \end{vmatrix} > 0
$$

where the determinant may be seen to be $|V|$ in (129) of Chapter 3.

By virtue of the second-order equilibrium conditions imposed there for $m = 1$ and $n = 2$, it was shown that $|V| > 0$. Since in the same conditions the exponent of (-1), in (119) will be even and since all S' terms are positive except S'_λ and $\bar{S}'_1$, which are negative, it follows that if the Routhian condition holds $|V| > 0$. Further, this will generalize for n and m in such fashion as to yield the same sign for $|V|$ as those holding from imposition of the second-order equilibrium conditions.

Discussion of the nature of the relationships between the static second-order equilibrium conditions and dynamic stability conditions need not be repeated, since it follows precisely that of their nature in the simple exchange model. Once more the symmetry of the $[V]$ implies dynamic stability as well as a maximum profit position if it is negative definite, seeming to make the dynamic analysis unnecessary. We take a purist viewpoint again, however; the conditions happen to coincide, they are not dealing with the same problems. To have shown the nature of the assumptions that lie behind the imposition of second-order equilibrium conditions and the ability to imply dynamic stability conditions from them is an important demonstration.

4.a.3. The Model of Multiple Exchange

We have seen that in the decisionmaking of individual economic units, where the process may be cast into a maximizing-minimizing mold, the analysis of dynamic stability properties added no new information usable in the derivation of operational theorems. But stability analysis takes on more interest for us, both as a tool for the gaining of information useful for evaluating determinants, and for itself, when no extremum framework is present in the analysis. We turn, therefore, to a multiple exchange economy where we possess only the market functions for the goods exchanged. We return to Model II-2 to develop the simplest analysis, extending it to the case of nonstatic expectations investigated by Arrow, Enthoven, McManus, and Nerlove. Let us deal with the case where $n = 3$. First, our excess demand equations may be written as $E_j \equiv X_j - Q_j$. We shall exclude the excess demand for Y_1 from consideration, since it is derivable from knowledge of the state of excess demand in the markets for Y_2 and Y_3. We postulate that price rates of change are functions of excess demand in the market for the good itself:

$$(121)\quad \begin{aligned} &1. \quad \dot{P}_2 = G_2(E_2), \qquad G'_2 > 0,\ G_2(0) = 0 \\ &2. \quad \dot{P}_3 = G_3(E_3), \qquad G'_3 > 0,\ G_3(0) = 0 \end{aligned}$$

where expectations of future prices are nonexistent.[33]

[33] It was Lange's suggestion that the rates of adjustment, G'_j, may differ among markets for arbitrary selections of units in which to measure goods. Cf. (3), pp. 176–7, and (6), p. 96. Samuelson suggested the further complication that the rate of

By Maclaurin's theorem, in the neighborhood of an equilibrium, neglecting higher derivatives of the second order or greater, we obtain

$$(122)\qquad \begin{aligned} &1.\quad \dot{P}_2 = G_2'[H_2^2(P_2 - P_2^\circ) + H_2^3(P_3 - P_3^\circ)] \\ &2.\quad \dot{P}_3 = G_3'[H_3^2(P_2 - P_2^\circ) + H_3^3(P_3 - P_3^\circ)] \end{aligned}$$

where

$$(123)\qquad X_j = H_j(P_2, P_3; Q_1, Q_2, Q_3)$$

The G_j' are taken to be constants, and, it will be noted, the H_j^k are *not* elements in a *symmetric* matrix—a departure from the dynamic models of the consumer and the firm—unless the aggregate income effects are zero in each term, making $H_j^k = S_{jk}$, or unless for any other special reason the matrix of these H_j^k terms is symmetric.

Let $G_j'H_j^k = a_{jk}$, and $a_{jj}P_j^\circ + a_{jk}P_k^\circ = K_j$. Then, from (122), and using the operator D,

$$(124)\qquad \begin{bmatrix} a_{22} - D & a_{23} \\ a_{32} & a_{33} - D \end{bmatrix} \begin{bmatrix} P_2 \\ P_3 \end{bmatrix} = \begin{bmatrix} K_2 \\ K_3 \end{bmatrix}$$

The determinantal form of the equation will be

$$(125)\qquad \begin{vmatrix} a_{22} - y & a_{23} \\ a_{32} & a_{33} - y \end{vmatrix} = 0$$

whose polynomial form may be written

$$(126)\qquad A_0y^2 + A_1y + A_2 = 0$$

The solution to (124) will be of the form

$$(127)\qquad \begin{aligned} &1.\quad P_{2t} = P_2^\circ + c_{11}e^{y_1t} + c_{12}e^{y_2t} \\ &2.\quad P_{3t} = P_3^\circ + c_{21}e^{y_1t} + c_{22}e^{y_2t} \end{aligned}$$

The roots of (126) will be of the form y_1 and y_2 and must be negative if P_j is to approach P_j°, $j = 2, 3$, as $t \to \infty$. To assert the necessary and sufficient conditions for stability, we form the Routhian matrix

$$(128)\qquad \begin{bmatrix} A_1 & 0 \\ A_0 & A_2 \end{bmatrix},$$

---

adjustment of one market varies with the excess demands in other markets as well as the "own" market.

These G_j' coefficients play a large role in Metzler's analysis of stability in multiple exchange, and he shows that for a system to be dynamically stable for every possible set of $G_j' > 0$, it is necessary that Hicksian perfect stability characterize the system. Further, as a projection of the analysis of gross substitution, if all off-diagonal elements of a Hicksian matrix are nonnegative, the Hicksian perfect stability conditions become sufficient as well as necessary for Routhian stability.

Metzler and Lange were also interested in the subcase where a subset of the $G_j' = 0$, in which case stability is dependent upon Hicksian perfect stability. See L. Metzler, (1), and O. Lange, (6), pp. 96–7.

where $A_0 > 0$, and we require that

$$A_1 > 0, \; A_1A_2 > 0 \tag{129}$$

Since

$$A_2 = (-1)^s \begin{vmatrix} a_{22} & a_{23} \\ a_{32} & a_{33} \end{vmatrix} \tag{130}$$

and since the a_{jk} can be broken down,

$$A_2 = (-1)^{n-1} G_2' G_3' \begin{vmatrix} \dfrac{\partial X_2}{\partial P_2} & \dfrac{\partial X_2}{\partial P_3} \\ \dfrac{\partial X_3}{\partial P_2} & \dfrac{\partial X_3}{\partial P_3} \end{vmatrix} \tag{131}$$

and, under the assumption that the $G_j' > 0$, the Jacobian will be positive when $n = 3$. More generally, for n goods where Y_1 is *numéraire:*

$$A_{n-1} = (-1)^{n-1} \prod_j G_j' \begin{vmatrix} \dfrac{\partial X_2}{\partial P_2} & \cdots & \dfrac{\partial X_2}{\partial P_n} \\ \cdot & \cdots & \cdot \\ \dfrac{\partial X_n}{\partial P_2} & \cdots & \dfrac{\partial X_n}{\partial P_n} \end{vmatrix} > 0 \tag{132}$$

so the Jacobian will have the sign $(-1)^{n-1}$.[34]

A glance at the Hicksian stability conditions will recall that imperfect stability in Hicks's sense requires that for every good $j = 2, \ldots, n$ the ratio

$$\frac{|J|}{|J_{jj}|} < 0 \tag{133}$$

where $|J|$ is the Jacobian of (132) and $|J_{jj}|$ a principal minor formed by striking out the relevant diagonal term's row and column. We shall show that the Routhian conditions (129) in the general case do not guarantee that all $|J_{jj}|$ will have the sign $(-1)^n$, and therefore that Hick's imperfect stability conditions are not necessary for true dynamic stability.

From the expansion of (126) and conditions of (132):

(134)

1. $A_0 = 1$
2. $A_1 = -[a_{22} + a_{33}] > 0$
3. $A_2 = (-1)^2 \begin{vmatrix} a_{22} & a_{23} \\ a_{32} & a_{33} \end{vmatrix} > 0$
4. $A_1A_2 = -a_{22}^2 a_{33} + a_{22}a_{23}a_{32} - a_{22}a_{33}^2 + a_{23}a_{32}a_{33} > 0$

[34] Lange treats the case where only $m < n - 1$ prices are allowed to change, so $G'_{m+1} = G'_{m+2} = \cdots G'_n = 0$, and $P_{m+1} = P^{\circ}_{m+1}, P_{m+2} = P^{\circ}_{m+2}, \cdots P_n = P^{\circ}_n$. The characteristic equation (124) then becomes one of order m and the determinant a principal minor of the Jacobian in (132). His static analogue is his "partial stability of rank m." See (6), pp. 96–7.

We substitute into (134-2) and (134-4):

(135)

1. $-G_2'H_2^2 - G_3'H_3^3 > 0$

2. $-G_2'^2(H_2^2)^2G_3'H_3^3 + G_2'H_2^2G_2'H_2^3G_3'H_3^2 - G_2'H_2^2G_3'^2(H_3^3)^2 + G_2'H_2^3G_3'H_3^2G_3'H_3^3 > 0$

For the first of these conditions to be met it is necessary that only one of the partial derivatives be negative. Suppose $H_3^3 > 0$ but that (135-1) is met. Then

(136)

1. $-G_2'^2(H_2^2)^2G_3'H_3^3 < 0$

2. $-G_3'^2(H_3^3)^2G_2'H_2^2 > 0$

If H_2^3 and H_3^2 are of opposite sign

(137)

1. $G_2'H_2^3G_3'H_3^2G_3'H_3^3 < 0$

2. $G_2'H_2^3G_3'H_3^2G_2'H_2^2 > 0$

And these can violate Hicksian imperfect stability.

For example, assume $G_2' = 1$, $G_3' = 1$, $H_2^2 = -4$, $H_2^3 = 9$, $H_3^2 = -1$, and $H_3^3 = 2$. Then

138)

$$[J] = \begin{bmatrix} -4 & 9 \\ -1 & 2 \end{bmatrix}$$

Also, $A_1 = 2$, $A_2 = 1$, and $A_1A_2 = 2$, meeting the requirements of (129). However, the Hicksian determinants are

(139)

1. $\dfrac{|J|}{|J_{22}|} = .5$

2. $\dfrac{|J|}{|J_{33}|} = -.25$

Thus, from (139-2) it is clear that Hicksian perfect or imperfect stability are not necessary conditions for true dynamic stability.

Hicksian perfect stability requires that the conditions in (233) of Chapter 2 hold. Much of the modern work in the stability of general systems has been devoted to studying the conditions under which Hicksian perfect stability conditions and the Routhian conditions do or do not coincide.

When only two goods exist in the economy the Routhian and Hicksian conditions for perfect stability are the same; when three goods exist, the Hicksian perfect stability conditions are sufficient but not necessary for Routhian stability. Also, as an extension of our treatment of consumer and entrepreneurial stability, if $[J]$ is negative definite (which implies its symmetry) necessary and sufficient conditions for which are stated by the Hicksian perfect stability conditions when such symmetry exists, it will also be Routhian.[35]

A third case of the equivalence of Hicksian and Routhian conditions was developed by Metzler. When all goods are gross substitutes, i.e., $\frac{\partial X_j}{\partial P_k} > 0, j = 1, \ldots, n, k = 2, \ldots, n, j \neq k$,[36] so that all off-diagonal elements of [*J*] are positive and all diagonal elements are negative, the Hicksian and Routhian conditions coincide.[37] If [*J*] is negative quasi-definite[38] (a Hicksian perfect stability matrix is not necessarily negative quasi-definite) the equilibrium will be dynamically as well as Hicksian stable in the perfect sense. But Hahn, Negishi, and Arrow-Bloch-Hurwicz have shown that when gross substitution is complete, [*J*] *will be* Hicksian.[39] Therefore, when gross substitution characterizes [*J*] this matrix will be perfectly stable in the sense of Hicks and dynamically stable.

Fourth, Morishima has proved the theorem that if [*J*] has elements such that the signs $\frac{\partial X_j}{\partial P_j}$ equals the sign $\frac{\partial X_j}{\partial P_i}$ and the sign $\frac{\partial X_i}{\partial P_j}$ equals the sign $\left(\frac{\partial X_i}{\partial P_k} \times \frac{\partial X_k}{\partial P_j}\right)$, the Hicksian and Routhian conditions will be identical.[40]

In the general case, however, the Hicksian perfect stability conditions are neither necessary nor sufficient for true dynamic stability. We have shown with a counterexample the nonnecessity of the former for the latter to exist. Samuelson has shown that in some cases the Hicksian conditions are not sufficient for the Routhian conditions to hold.[41]

Further, the conditions under which Hicks derives his "stability conditions" for multiple exchange are strained, to say the least. He assumes that, when one market is out of equilibrium, all other prices either remain constant or adjust instantaneously to reequilibrate their markets. The failure to relate these results to a dynamic model springs from a simple projection of reasoning from the static stability conditions of the single market; it is a false step to argue that if excess demand falls with a rise in price in the single market, stability exists, and therefore, the same conditions will guarantee stability in multiple market systems. The single market result may be deduced from an explicit dynamic model of the type with which we are dealing, while we have seen above that

[35] See P. Samuelson, (4), pp. 271–2; O. Lange, (6), p. 97; H. Hotelling, (2); and K. Arrow, (6), pp. 534–6.

[36] Given these conditions the homogeneity of degree zero in all normalized prices of the excess demand functions and Euler's Theorem will guarantee that $\frac{\partial X_j}{\partial P_j} < 0$, $j = 2, \ldots, n$. See footnote 62, Chapter 2.

[37] L. Metzler, (1), pp. 273–92.

[38] For a definition of this property, see P. Samuelson, (4), pp. 140–1.

[39] See Section 2.b.2, Chapter 2.

[40] See Section 2.b.2, Chapter 2.

[41] P. Samuelson, (3), pp. 256–7.

Hicks's conditions cannot in the general case. In Metzler's phrase, Hicks has generalized the conclusions of the single market case rather than the dynamic model which underlies it.[42] Happily, to date, the one major contribution to the derivation of operational theorems from such general systems as we are treating made by Hicks's stability analysis is also derivable from true dynamic stability analysis. This is, of course, the sign of $|J|$. The Hicksian conditions are primarily of interest in yielding us additional knowledge about the signs of its principal minors in those special cases where these conditions coincide with true dynamic stability conditions, but to date they have been of limited use in deriving operational theorems.[43]

It is, of course, in these terms that Samuelson's "correspondence principle" has its major interest.[44] When confronted with a static general exchange system whose changes following an equilibrium displacement are of interest to us, by *assuming* the new equilibrium position is the steady state of a stable equilibrium, we may derive as a theorem the sign of $|J|$; but, since the information about the determinant does not involve the signs of principal minors, except in the special cases when Hicksian conditions are also met, it has proved to be of limited applicability in the derivation of theorems.[45]

4.a.3.a. Multiple Exchange With Extrapolated Expectations

The simplest manner of introducing expectations of prices into the dynamic model of (121) is that developed by A. Enthoven and K. Arrow.[46] They assume that in each market the price expectations of all participants can be represented by one value, that only the events in that market affect the price expectations of the good traded, and that we deal only with that part of expectations induced by the model, neglecting any autonomous effect. Then, system (123) is altered to read:

$$(140) \qquad X_j = H_j(P_2, P_3; Q_1, Q_2, Q_3, \bar{P}_j)$$

where $[\bar{P}]$ is the vector of market price expectations for all future periods.

[42] In this Hicks followed the lead of Bowley, although in less naïve fashion:

". . . Whether the position is stable can be judged from the intersection of the pairs of demand and supply curves for each factor and commodity as discussed in the following chapter. There is stability if the supply curve crosses the demand curve from below or the left to above or the right." A Bowley, (1), p. 53. The discussion in the following chapter concerns the case of the single market.

[43] Two exceptions are those theorems derived by Hicks for the case of gross substitutes and perfect stability, and Morishima's case with perfect stability. See the discussion of these in Section 2.b.2. In both cases, however, true dynamic stability conditions coincide with perfect stability conditions.

[44] P. Samuelson, (4), pp. 5, 258, 263, 284, 350–1.

[45] Cf. D. Patinkin, (3).

[46] A. Enthoven, (1). Also, K. Arrow, (5).

Further, in equilibrium,

$$[\bar{P}] = [P^\circ] \tag{141}$$

or expected and equilibrium prices coincide.

Then, the dynamic model is designed as follows:

$$\begin{aligned} &1. \quad \dot{P}_j = G_j(E_j),\ G_j' > 0,\ G_j(0) = 0, && j = 2, 3 \\ &2. \quad \bar{P}_j = P_j + \pi_j \dot{P}_j, && j = 2, 3 \end{aligned} \tag{142}$$

where π_j are constant expected price factors.

By Maclaurin's theorem, neglecting higher-order derivatives,

$$E_j = \sum_k H_j^k(P_k - P_k^\circ) + \bar{H}_j^j(\bar{P}_j - P_j^\circ), \qquad j = 2, \ldots, n,\ k = 2, \ldots, n \tag{143}$$

where $\bar{H}_j^j$ is the partial derivative of demand for Y_j with respect to the expected price of Y_j. Further application of the theorem to the functions in (142) yields

$$\dot{P}_j = G_j'\left[\sum_k H_j^k(P_k - P_k^\circ) + \bar{H}_j^j(P_j - P_j^\circ) + \bar{H}_j^j \pi_j \dot{P}_j\right], \qquad k = 2, 3 \tag{144}$$

when substitutions are made from (142-2) into (143). For an n-good system, we should have

$$\begin{bmatrix} 1 - G_2'\bar{H}_2^2\pi_2 & 0 & \cdots & 0 \\ 0 & 1 - G_3'\bar{H}_3^3\pi_3 & \cdots & 0 \\ \cdots & \cdots & \cdots & \cdots \\ 0 & 0 & \cdots & 1 - G_n'\bar{H}_n^n\pi_n \end{bmatrix} \begin{bmatrix} \dot{P}_2 \\ \dot{P}_3 \\ \cdot \\ \dot{P}_n \end{bmatrix} \tag{145}$$

$$= \begin{bmatrix} G_2' & 0 & \cdots & 0 \\ 0 & G_3' & \cdots & 0 \\ \cdots & \cdots & \cdots & \cdots \\ 0 & 0 & \cdots & G_n' \end{bmatrix} \begin{bmatrix} H_2^2 + \bar{H}_2^2 & H_2^3 & \cdots & H_2^n \\ H_3^2 & H_3^3 + \bar{H}_3^3 & \cdots & H_3^n \\ \cdots & \cdots & \cdots & \cdots \\ H_n^2 & H_n^3 & \cdots & H_n^n + \bar{H}_n^n \end{bmatrix} \begin{bmatrix} P_2 - P_2^\circ \\ P_3 - P_3^\circ \\ \cdot \\ P_n - P_n^\circ \end{bmatrix}$$

or

$$[I - G'\bar{H}\pi][\dot{P}] = [G'][H + \bar{H}][P - P^\circ] \tag{146}$$

and

$$[\dot{P}] = [I - G'\bar{H}\pi]^{-1}([G'][H + \bar{H}][P - P^\circ]) \tag{147}$$

It can be seen that in the case of static expectations, i.e., $\pi_j = 0$, this system reduces to (122). The determinantal equation of this static expectational system may be written:

$$\begin{vmatrix} G_2'(H_2^2 + \bar{H}_2^2) - y & G_2'H_2^3 & \cdots & G_2'H_2^n \\ G_3'H_3^2 & G_3'(H_3^3 + \bar{H}_3^3) - y & \cdots & G_3'H_3^n \\ \cdots & \cdots & \cdots & \cdots \\ G_n'H_n^2 & G_n'H_n^3 & \cdots & G_n'(H_n^n + \bar{H}_n^n) - y \end{vmatrix} = |B| = 0 \tag{148}$$

Suppose $[B]$ is Metzlerian. Then we know that if it meets the Hicksian perfect stability conditions it will also meet the Routhian conditions: the case of static expectations will be dynamically stable. But now suppose all $\pi_j > 0$, so that expectations are no longer static. The left-hand side of the determinantal equation now becomes $|B|$ with each diagonal term multiplied by the corresponding term in $[I - G'\bar{H}\pi]^{-1}$, which inverse matrix will be a diagonal matrix whose elements are the reciprocals of the elements in $[I - G'\bar{H}\pi]$. If and only if the terms of this inverse are all positive will the new matrix remain Metzlerian and will it continue to be Routhian (and Hicksian).[47] But $[I - G'\bar{H}\pi]$ is a diagonal matrix and therefore will meet these conditions if and only if each term along its diagonal is positive. Consequently, if

$$(149) \qquad 1 = G'_j\bar{H}^j_j\pi_j > 0, \qquad j = 2, \ldots, n$$

$$(150) \qquad \frac{1}{G'_j} > \bar{H}^j_j\pi_j, \qquad j = 2, \ldots, n$$

the equilibrium will be Routhian. That is, let $[C] = [I - G'\bar{H}\pi]^{-1}([G][H + \bar{H}])$ and let $|C| = 0$ be the corresponding determinantal equation. Then, $|C|$ will have negative roots when $[G'][H + \bar{H}]$ is Metzlerian if and only if the elements of $[I - G'\bar{H}\pi]^{-1}$ are positive.

Now $\frac{1}{G'_j}$ is the measure of insensitivity of a price to excess demand levels. As $G'_j \to \infty$, $\frac{1}{G'_j} \to 0$, and it is necessary for $\pi \leqq 0$ to retain stability. On the other hand, the greater the friction and inertia of markets, the more sensitive in the positive direction expectations can be to current price changes.

But what of the case where $[G'][H + \bar{H}]$ is Routhian but not Metzlerian? Arrow and McManus have extended the analysis to such cases.[48] First we define a matrix as negative quasi-definite when, for every real, non-null column vector, $[T]$, it is true that

$$(151) \qquad [T]'[B][T] < 0$$

It has been shown that $[B]$ will be Routhian under these conditions.[49] When $[B]$ is symmetrical and (151) holds, the matrix is said to be negative definite, so that the symmetry case is a subcase of the more general category. Arrow and McManus show that if the matrix of (148) is negative quasi-definite, and if some matrix $[S]$ is a symmetrical matrix, then $[S][B]$ will be Routhian if and only if $[S]$ is positive definite; that is, if $|S|$ and all of its principal minors are positive. Since $[I - G'\bar{H}\pi]^{-1}$ is diagonal

[47] The sufficiency of this condition is self-evident. Proof of the necessity of it is more complicated and the reader is referred to A. Enthoven, (1), pp. 291–2.

[48] K. Arrow, (4).

[49] P. Samuelson, (4), p. 438.

it is symmetrical, and so $[B]$ need not be Metzlerian but merely negative quasi-definite for the Enthoven-Arrow theorem to hold.[50]

Further, Arrow and McManus show that if $[E]$ is any diagonal matrix which is not null, including those whose nonzero elements are unity, and if

$$[E][B][E]^{-1} \tag{152}$$

is (a) negative definite, (b) negative quasi-definite, or (c) Metzlerian, $[I - G'\bar{H}\pi]^{-1}[B]$ will be Routhian if, and only if, $[I - G'\bar{H}\pi]^{-1}$ is positive definite. Note that this will not hold for all Routhian $[B]$.

4.a.3.b. Multiple Exchange with Adaptive Expectations

Arrow and Nerlove improve the palatability of the Enthoven-Arrow assumption that the $\bar{P}_j$ are the expected prices for all periods in the future by assuming them to be average levels about which future prices fluctuate.[51] Then, $\bar{P}_j$ is the "expected normal price." As a further generalization, they assume that the current demand for one good is a function of the expected prices of all goods. Then (140) is altered to

$$X_j = H_j(P_2, \ldots, P_n; Q_1, \ldots, Q_n, [\bar{P}]) \tag{153}$$

The dynamic equations now include time rates of change in the expected prices:

$$\dot{\bar{P}} = \varepsilon_j(P_j - \bar{P}_j), \qquad \varepsilon_j \geqq 0 \tag{154}$$

The rate of change of expected prices depends upon the difference between them and current prices. As $\varepsilon_j \rightarrow \infty$ the case of static expectations is approached, or instantaneous change to keep current and expected normal prices equal.

We use Maclaurin's theorem once more to approximate E_j, noting this time the dependence of each E_j upon *every* expected price:

$$E_j = \sum_k H_j^k(P_k - P_k^\circ) + \sum_k \bar{H}_j^k(\bar{P}_k - P_k^\circ), \quad j = 2, \ldots, n \tag{155}$$

and, assuming (142–1),

$$\dot{P}_j = \sum_k G_j'H_j^k(P_k - P_k^\circ) + \sum_k G_j'\bar{H}_j^k(P_k - P_k^\circ) \tag{156}$$

while we rewrite from (154), by adding and subtracting P_j° on the right-hand side

$$\dot{\bar{P}}_j = \varepsilon_j(P_j - P_j^\circ) - \varepsilon_j(\bar{P}_j - P_j^\circ) \tag{157}$$

[50] Every negative quasi-definite matrix is Hicksian, or meets the Hicksian perfect stability conditions, but not every Hicksian matrix is negative quasi-definite.

[51] K. Arrow, (5).

Then, in matrix form, using the operator D, the system may be written:

(158)

$$\begin{bmatrix} G_2'H_2^2 - D & \cdots & G_2'H_2^n & G_2'\bar{H}_2^2 & \cdots & G_2'\bar{H}_2^n \\ \cdot & \cdots & \cdot & \cdot & \cdots & \cdot \\ G_n'H_n^2 & \cdots & G_n'H_n^n - D & G_n'\bar{H}_n^2 & \cdots & G_n'\bar{H}_n^n \\ \varepsilon_2 & \cdots & 0 & -\varepsilon_2 - D & \cdots & 0 \\ \cdot & \cdots & \cdot & \cdot & \cdots & \cdot \\ 0 & \cdots & \varepsilon_n & 0 & \cdots & -\varepsilon_n - D \end{bmatrix} \begin{bmatrix} P_2 \\ \cdot \\ P_n \\ \bar{P}_2 \\ \cdot \\ \bar{P}_n \end{bmatrix} = \begin{bmatrix} \sum_k G_2'H_2^kP_k^\circ + \sum_k G_2'\bar{H}_2^kP_k^\circ \\ \cdot \\ \sum_k G_n'H_n^kP_k^\circ + \sum_k G_n'\bar{H}_n^kP_k^\circ \\ 0 \\ \cdot \\ 0 \end{bmatrix}$$

or

$$[C - D][P] = [K] \tag{159}$$

where

$$[C] = \begin{bmatrix} G'H & G'\bar{H} \\ \varepsilon & -\varepsilon \end{bmatrix} \tag{160}$$

For a system without expectations, $[C]$ reduces to $[G'H]$. Where expectations are static, $\varepsilon_j \to \infty$, and $[C]$ becomes $[G'H + G'\bar{H}]$ in a dynamic system of the form in (124). Now, assume that $[C]$ is Metzlerian: under these conditions, Arrow and Nerlove show that $[C]$ is Routhian if, and only if, $[G'H + G'\bar{H}]$ is Routhian for the system with static expectations. That is, if the matrix under static expectations is stable, adaptive expectation with $\varepsilon_j \geqq 0$ cannot destabilize it— regardless of the inertia in the system. Since, as we shall see, Arrow and Hurwicz demonstrate that the stability of a system under static expectations is highly plausible, so should be such a system when adaptive expectations of this sort are introduced.

4.a.3.c. A Summary of Stability Theorems for Multiple Exchange

Before we continue with our discussion of stability, let us pause to gather all those theorems we have discussed concerning the conditions under which an equilibrium meets the Routhian conditions. We discuss dynamic systems of the form $[\dot{P}] = [a][P - P^\circ]$. We shall call $[a]$ Routhian if the equilibrium in whose neighborhood the system is defined is dynamically stable, and, unless otherwise noted, stability will be local (in the small). The names in parentheses denote the investigators from whose work the theorems derive:

1. if the economy contains only two goods, and [*a*] is Hicksian, it is also Routhian (Walras, Arrow-Hurwicz).

2. if [*a*] is negative quasi-definite, or, where [*a*] is symmetrical, negative definite, it is Routhian (Samuelson). Since every negative quasi-definite matrix is Hicksian, Hicksian perfect stability conditions will be met.

3. if gross substitutability prevails throughout the economy, so that all diagonal elements of [*a*] are negative and all off-diagonal terms positive, and similar restrictions apply to the *numéraire*, [*a*] is Routhian if and only if it is Hicksian (Metzler), which it will in fact be (Hahn, Negishi, Arrow-Block-Hurwicz). Moreover, under suitable assumptions, it will be globally stable (Arrow-Block-Hurwicz).

4. if [*a*] has elements such that the signs of a_{ij} and a_{ji} are the same, and the signs of a_{ik} equal the sign of the product a_{ij} and a_{jk}, [*a*] is Routhian if and only if it is Hicksian (Morishima).

5. if [*a*] is Metzlerian and Routhian, and [*D*] is a diagonal matrix, then [*D*][*a*] is Routhian if, and only if, [*D*] is positive definite, i.e., meets the Hawkins-Simon conditions (Arrow-Enthoven).

6. if [*a*] is negative quasi-definite, and thereby Routhian, and [*S*] is symmetric, [*S*][*a*] will be Routhian if, and only if [*S*] is positive definite (Arrow-McManus). Thus, (5) is a subcase of (6), since a diagonal matrix is symmetric.

7. if [*E*] is any diagonal matrix which is nonnull, and if $[E][a][E]^{-1}$ is (a) negative definite, (b) negative quasi-definite, or (c) Metzlerian, [*D*][*a*] will be Routhian if, and only if, [*D*] is positive definite (Arrow-McManus).

8. if [*a*] is derived from a system with adaptive expectations, and is of the form of the matrix in (160), and is Metzlerian, then [*a*] will be Routhian if, and only if, the submatrix $[G'H + G'\bar{H}]$ is Routhian for a static system (Arrow-Nerlove).

4.a.3.d. Conditions Under Which Stability Conditions Will Occur

In all of the above analysis of the multiple exchange equilibrium, dealing as we have been with questions of Routhian conditions, their relation to Hicksian conditions, and characteristics of matrices which will yield Routhian conditions, we have ignored a further problem: *when, in fact, will these conditions rule in general models*? Are they plausible in terms of their implications for the structure of general models, so that we should expect such systems to have stable equilibria, or are they implausible? In short, what kinds of models have equilibria which are characterized by true dynamic stability?

Arrow and Hurwicz address themselves to this question. They derive theorems for a number of special cases, confess the nonuniversality of their results, but also assert that in no case did they find the purely competitive system unstable.[52] However, Scarf has constructed counterexamples, at least one of which implies that departures from global stability of purely competitive systems may occur relatively often, even with the usual assumptions of quasi-concave preference functions and concave production functions.[53] However, a possible route out of such potential system instability is to overthrow the assumption that market equilibrium is attained in a recontracting *tâtonnement* process and to substitute for it an equilibrating process which permits nonequilibrium transactions to occur. *Nontâtonnement* equilibration may prove to be the answer.

In a pure exchange economy, assume that every household's excess demand functions are continuous and single-valued, and assume also that after its income is spent the household's satisfaction at the margin for at least one good is positive. In the special case where no exchange occurs at full equilibrium, where initial endowments Q_{cj} for all j and all c correspond to desired amounts, the system will be stable at an existent equilibrium point, providing the weak axiom of revealed preference holds for each household. This special case would rule if all households were alike in their preferences and their endowments of goods, or if they were different in preferences but their goods endowments were Pareto optimal, since such a pattern implies and is implied by a purely competitive equilibrium. Further, if we abstract from individual excess demand curves and assume the market curves are single-valued and continuous, and meet the weak axiom of revealed preference, the same results will hold for the no-trade case.

Arrow and Hurwicz also show that the Morishima conditions cannot hold for all price vectors without violating the requirement that excess demands be homogeneous of degree zero in all (non-normalized) prices.

These results are meager and quite restricted in generality, and further progress must be made in investigating the conditions under which theorems such as those in the preceding section will be applicable. However, as Arrow and Hurwicz stress, the results thus far are optimistic as far as the general purely competitive case is concerned, or, at least, not pessimistic.

5. Stability of Equilibrium in the Production Model

Lastly, we may dynamize Model V-2 of Chapter 5. The excess demand functions for each market may be written, with E_u the excluded equation and the demand for money as an asset written as a residual. Money will be taken as *numéraire*. Then, postulating that time rates of change in prices are functions of the excess demands, good by good, we obtain the

[52] K. Arrow, (6), pp. 529–30.

[53] H. Scarf, *International Economic Review*, I (1960), pp. 157–172.

dynamic model:

$$(161)\quad \begin{aligned}
&1. \quad \dot{P}_j = L_j(E_j),\ L_j' > 0,\ L_j(0) = 0, && j = 1, \ldots, n\\
&2. \quad \dot{P}_i = L_i(E_i),\ L_i' > 0,\ L_i(0) = 0, && i = 1, \ldots, m\\
&3. \quad \dot{P}_{Z_i} = L_{Z_i}(E_{Z_i}),\ L_{Z_i}' > 0,\ L_{Z_i}(0) = 0, && i = 1, \ldots, m\\
&4. \quad \dot{P}_{j'} = L_{j'}(E_{j'}),\ L_{j'}' > 0,\ L_{j'}(0) = 0, && j = 1, \ldots, n\\
&5. \quad \dot{P}_{u'} = L_{u'}(E_{u'}),\ L_{u'}' > 0,\ L_{u'}(0) = 0\\
&6. \quad \dot{P}_e = L_e(E_e),\ L_e' > 0,\ L_e(0) = 0
\end{aligned}$$

To fix our ideas, let $n = 2$, $m = 1$. Also, let us assume the existence of aggregate $K_{j'j}$ and K_{uj} coefficients, abstracted from the analogous individual firm coefficients somehow, and a K value in the determination of household demand for cash balances, abstracted from individual consumer k_c values. We may then use Maclaurin's theorem to expand the equations of (161), and, letting $S_{st} = L_s' \dfrac{\partial E_s}{\partial P_t} = L_s'E_s^t$, and $K_s = \sum_t S_{st}P_t^\circ$ we obtain the following linear equation system:

$$(162)\quad \begin{bmatrix}
S_{11}-D & S_{12} & S_{1z} & S_{1Z} & S_{11'} & S_{12'} & S_{1u'} & S_{1e}\\
S_{21} & S_{22}-D & S_{2z} & S_{2Z} & S_{21'} & S_{22'} & S_{2u'} & S_{2e}\\
S_{z1} & S_{z2} & S_{zz}-D & S_{zZ} & S_{z1'} & S_{z2'} & S_{zu'} & S_{ze}\\
S_{Z1} & S_{Z2} & S_{Zz} & S_{ZZ}-D & S_{Z1'} & S_{Z2'} & S_{Zu'} & S_{Ze}\\
S_{1'1} & S_{1'2} & S_{1'z} & S_{1'Z} & S_{1'1'}-D & S_{1'2'} & S_{1'u'} & S_{1'e}\\
S_{2'1} & S_{2'2} & S_{2'z} & S_{2'Z} & S_{2'1'} & S_{2'2'}-D & S_{2'u'} & S_{2'e}\\
S_{u'1} & S_{u'2} & S_{u'z} & S_{u'Z} & S_{u'1'} & S_{u'2'} & S_{u'u'}-D & S_{u'e}\\
S_{e1} & S_{e2} & S_{ez} & S_{eZ} & S_{e1'} & S_{e2'} & S_{eu'} & S_{ee}-D
\end{bmatrix}
\begin{bmatrix} P_1\\ P_2\\ P_z\\ P_Z\\ P_{1'}\\ P_{2'}\\ P_{u'}\\ P_e \end{bmatrix}
=
\begin{bmatrix} K_1\\ K_2\\ K_z\\ K_Z\\ K_{1'}\\ K_{2'}\\ K_{u'}\\ K_e \end{bmatrix}$$

or

$$(163)\qquad [S][P] = [K]$$

The determinantal equation with y substituted for D may be represented:

$$(164)\qquad |S| = 0$$

and it will yield a polynomial of the form

$$(165)\quad A_0y^8 + A_1y^7 + A_2y^6 + A_3y^5 + A_4y^4 + A_5y^3 + A_6y^2 + A_7y + A_8 = 0$$

The solution to (161) will be of the form

$$P_{kt} = P_k^{\circ} + c_{k1}e^{y_1t} + c_{k2}e^{y_2t} + \cdots c_{k8}e^{y_8t} \tag{166}$$

and equilibrium will be stable if and only if the roots $y_1, \ldots, y_8$ are all negative in real parts. This requires that the Routhian matrix below and its principal minors be positive:

$$\begin{bmatrix} A_1 & A_3 & A_5 & A_7 & 0 & 0 & 0 & 0 \\ A_0 & A_2 & A_4 & A_6 & A_8 & 0 & 0 & 0 \\ 0 & A_1 & A_3 & A_5 & A_7 & 0 & 0 & 0 \\ 0 & A_0 & A_2 & A_4 & A_6 & A_8 & 0 & 0 \\ 0 & 0 & A_1 & A_3 & A_5 & A_7 & 0 & 0 \\ 0 & 0 & A_0 & A_2 & A_4 & A_6 & A_8 & 0 \\ 0 & 0 & 0 & A_1 & A_3 & A_5 & A_7 & 0 \\ 0 & 0 & 0 & A_0 & A_2 & A_4 & A_6 & A_8 \end{bmatrix} = [A] \tag{167}$$

Therefore $|A| = A_8|A_{88}| > 0$. But

$$A_8 = (-1)^{2m+2n+2} \prod L' \begin{vmatrix} E_1^1 E_1^2 E_1^z E_1^Z E_1^{1'} E_1^{2'} E_1^{u'} E_1^e \\ \cdots\cdots\cdots\cdots \\ \cdots\cdots\cdots\cdots \\ E_e^1 E_e^2 E_e^z E_e^Z E_e^{1'} E_e^{2'} E_e^{u'} E_e^e \end{vmatrix} > 0 \tag{168}$$

Since all $L' > 0$, $|E|$ must have the sign of (-1) raised to the exponent given above, as in the exchange model. Once more the Hicksian perfect and imperfect stability conditions yield the same limited result as the dynamic stability analysis.

6. A Recapitulation

In this chapter we applied the tools of dynamic analysis to our heretofore static systems. Perhaps the most striking result of their application to obtain additional information for the evaluation of operational theorems is the realization of how little dynamic analysis adds to this capability. Secondly, it turns out, that the dynamic models for the individual consumer and firm are of limited interest for these purposes, in that the symmetry of the relevant matrices assures that if second-order maximum conditions are met and the decisionmaker reacts to disequilibrium by movements in the obvious direction, the dynamic systems will be stable. Thirdly, in that area where symmetry of the relevant matrices does not exist, dynamic stability conditions may be different from Hicksian conditions, and are disappointingly niggardly in yielding useful information. Further, the evidence would seem to point to the fact that in general systems, if second-order equilibrium conditions are fulfilled, the equilibria attained will be dynamically stable. Thus, the introduction of time into potential market disequilibrium models, in the form of linear differential equation approximations to general functions, does not take us much farther in our ability to derive operational theorems than we attained in Part II. On the other hand, the dynamic analysis which was implicit in Part II has now been made explicit, so that derivations are clearer—a gain of some significance.

We have also analyzed a group of moving market-clearing models, with some interesting qualities of their own. Each of these allows us to introduce investment into linear models, but, unfortunately, only in a linear disaggregated "accelerator" fashion whose rigidities are patent.

CHAPTER 9

THE EXISTENCE AND UNIQUENESS OF EQUILIBRIUM

1. Introduction

Up to this point in our discussion, we have been assuming the existence of a meaningful economic solution to most of our models.[1] Although we have not naïvely postulated that an equality between the number of equations and unknowns was either necessary or sufficient for a meaningful solution to exist, we have referred to such a condition as a *prima facie* presumption of the strong plausibility of such existence. On the other hand, except in the two cases mentioned in footnote 1, we have not insisted upon the existence or economic exigency of a unique solution; rather, implicitly, we have accepted the viewpoint that the models could be expected to yield a sufficiently restricted number of meaningful solutions as guides to realistic variation (which may not itself exhibit unique solutions) to be useful to us.[2]

Because ultimately the data of our models have determined the solution values of the variables, and the equations and functions are reflections of the constraining nature of our postulates, the question of existence and uniqueness of a solution must be addressed to the nature of these data and postulates. Specifically, the question is whether the data and postulates give rise to functions and conditions whose nature assures the existence of a vector of values for the variables which is a solution, and, if so, whether more than one such vector can exist.

In Chapter 1 we took a rather pragmatic initial position on these questions: we assumed that if the data of the model and its postulates did not give rise to a solution, these data and postulates could be altered in economically secondary ways to attain one. Although this was an article of faith, it was essentially involved with economic faith as well as mathematical; our vision of economic process led us to believe that nothing of a technological, psychological, or resource nature, and no aspect springing from behavioristic assumptions, would interfere with the

[1] Important exceptions are the Leontief static open input-output system, for which the Hawkins-Simon conditions have been presented, and the von Neumann model, in Chapters 6 and 8 respectively.

[2] Such a viewpoint is not universal. Compare P. Rocher's assertion:

"From the point of view of logic, this theory [of multiple exchange] presents a serious gap. The 'definition' which it gives to the equilibrium price would be correct only if the conditions imposed on this equilibrium price were logically compatible and logically sufficient to determine one and only one price." P. Rocher, (1), p. 258. Quoted by permission.

existence of meaningful prices and quantities in a purely competitive world. We did not assert, of course, the idealness of such an attitude: merely that it seemed no more intuitively objectionable an assumption than others we employ. It may be compared in this respect, for example, with the rather tentative conclusions concerning the existence of stability as a characteristic of purely competitive equilibria which were derived from the Arrow-Hurwicz analysis in Chapter 8.

However, it makes little sense to continue to include as a postulate of a system a proposition which can be derived as a theorem. As Wald writes in direct contradiction to our article of faith, "Nor should we be content to argue that a solution must exist on the basis of the economic meaning of the equations, for something may be overlooked all too easily."[3] The question of the existence of a solution concerns the self-sufficiency and mutual consistency of the economic relationships we envision; not to be able to prove the existence of a meaningful solution to them is to be unable to prove that our economic vision is complete or consistent. Moreover, however unlikely, it is possible that to assume the existence of a solution when in fact it does not exist, and to state theorems concerning the nature of such a nonexistent state, may be not only futile but positively misleading. For example, to use an analogy, we might assert that the largest natural number is 1, on the basis that if x is the largest positive integer it must meet the condition that $x^2 \leqq x$. Since only the natural number 1 meets this condition, we might conclude that 1 is the largest possible integer. Of course, the fallacy of our "theorem" springs from the nonexistence of the solution we seek: there is no maximum positive integer, and to set up the conditions which must exist for this nonexistent solution is to mislead. The proposition, "If there exists a maximum positive integer, it must be 1" must not be perverted by a neglect of the conditional part. While possible, it is doubtful that our analogous assumption of Chapter 1 would lead to such grossly fallacious propositions, but the example does serve to illustrate in an extreme way the difficulties potential in our pragmatic approach.

For these reasons we must conclude our consideration of general systems with the complicated mathematical analyses concerning these questions of existence and uniqueness of solutions.

2. Walras' Analysis

It is greatly to Walras' credit that he recognized the desirability of demonstrating the solubility of his equation systems. Actually his attempts to cope with the problem of existence of equilibrium are amalgams of stability analysis and existence analysis, and it is not clear that the two questions were entirely separable in his thought. In the model of complex exchange, Walras began his existence "proof" from a state in

[3] A. Wald, (1), p. 403.

which a price vector $[P] = [P_2, \ldots, P_n]$ rules with nonzero excess demands in each market. He then selects a P_2' which eliminates excess demand in the market for Y_2, so that the set $[P_2', \ldots, P_n]$ rules. Next, holding all other prices constant, P_3 is adjusted to P_3' to equilibrate the market of Y_3, the price vector $[P_2', P_3', P_4, \ldots, P_n]$ rules, and the market for Y_2 is once more thrown into disequilibrium. This adjustment process is continued until $[P_2', P_3', P_4', \ldots, P_n']$ is obtained in which, generally, only the market for Y_n is in equilibrium. Walras asserts that the system will be "closer" to full equilibrium at $[P']$ than at $[P]$, and that if the process is continued in the same way in order to obtain $[P'']$, $[P''']$, and so forth, the full equilibrium will be approached.[4]

As Wald points out,[5] one immediately faces the problem of defining the concept of "closer" for the values of excess demand to universal zero values. In the final analysis it must mean that successive price vectors will yield excess demands for every good which are closer in absolute value to zero (or at least as close for some goods and closer for at least one) than those of the previous price vectors with the exception of Y_n, excess demand for which will always be zero. Walras' reason for believing this to be true (he never proved it for it is not a provable proposition) was that as P_j was changed to P_j', the equilibrium of the market for Y_k was disturbed, but via effects on the demand and supply functions of Y_k which were indirect and could be counted upon to be compensating to some degree. The net indirect effects could be expected to be of a different order of magnitude than the direct effect of the adjustment of P_k to $P_{k'}$ on the market for Y_k.[6] Effectively, therefore, Walras sought to prove the existence of a path of approach to equilibrium by a neglect of the interdependence of the system—an extremely un-Walrasian tack, but additional evidence of his willingness to become Marshallian when the occasion demanded it. He relied upon the same chain of reasoning to "show" the existence of an equilibrium in his production model, his investment model, and his money model.[7]

Wald shows that simply by starting with a vector $[P]$ which makes excess demand in the market for one good zero, and moving to a vector $[P']$, we will move the market away from zero excess demand and thus will violate the definition of "closer" which Walras seems to have had in the back of his mind, even if all other excess demands move closer to zero. In any event, Walras' consideration is not a proof of anything, but is akin to the rough-and-tumble plausibility argument we have employed in previous chapters.

Lastly, it will be noted that his "proof" is really an assertion of the

[4] L. Walras, (2), pp. 132–3.
[5] A. Wald, (1), pp. 384–5.
[6] L. Walras, (2), p. 133.
[7] L. Walras, (2), pp. 228–30, 272–3, and 310–1.

existence of an equilibrium with a primitive stability analysis of the system; an assertion that the structure of the market mechanism would allow the system to move toward a solution if an external agency moved the price vectors in the stated way. Although this is different from the proposition that the unplanned *"tâtonnement"* process would move the model to an equilibrium, it is akin to it.

3. Wald's Analysis

The first attack upon the problems of existence and uniqueness of a general equilibrium with the complicated mathematical apparatus the task requires was made by A. Wald in a classic article published in German in 1936 and translated into English in the article quoted above. The model which Wald investigated is close to that of Model III-1 in Chapter 3, but differs in omitting intermediate goods and supply functions of factor services, while it makes the Casselian assumption of given demand curves. It is stated below:

$$\text{(1)} \qquad \begin{aligned} &1. \quad P_j = F_j(X_1, \ldots, X_n), && j = 1, \ldots, n \\ &2. \quad P_j = \sum_i a_{ij} P_i, && i = 1, \ldots, m \\ &3. \quad \sum_j a_{ij} X_j = Q_i \end{aligned}$$

Several characteristics of this model distinguish it. First, the demand functions are written with market baskets of goods rather than prices as arguments. Secondly, they do not contain the prices of factor services, so that as stated demand prices are unrelated to the wherewithal of consumers. Thirdly, all equations are treated as independent and all prices as determinate in absolute value.

Dorfman, Samuelson, and Solow have objected to use of the "inverted" demand functions on the basis that they are not economically correct.[8] Written in the usual way, $X_j = H_j([P])$, and interpreted as "functions," demand relations imply that for any constellation of prices there exists a unique basket of goods demanded $[X]$. However, for two price vectors $[P]$ and $[P']$ it may be true that $[X] = [X']$. Now, if we invert the function in the form of (1-1) and continue to hold the view that a vector of quantities demanded implies a single price vector we are obviously in contradiction, if we interpret "function" to mean single-valued relationships. Even if the usual demand functions are single-valued, the inverted versions need not be. They must, therefore, be interpreted properly, and, where treated as data, the restrictions upon them must be viewed in the light of the characteristics of the curves.

[8] R. Dorfman, (1), p. 352*n*.

The second characteristic is even more objectionable, since it makes demand seem to be independent not only of the distribution of income but of total income as well. Wald deals with this second point by showing that these equations may be viewed as homogeneous of degree zero in product prices and total income.[9] Income is defined as $\Sigma_j X_j P_j = Y$. Now, if we "reinvert" the demand functions we should have

$$X_j = H_j([P], Y) = H_j([P], \Sigma X_j P_j) \tag{2}$$

Then if

$$X_j = H_j([\lambda P], \Sigma X_j \lambda P_j), \quad \lambda > 0, j = 1, \ldots, n \tag{3}$$

as would be true if the X_j were homogeneous of degree zero in prices of products and income, amounts demanded are a function of relative income only. We may arbitrarily set $Y = 1$, measure all prices in income units, and get

$$X_j = H_j([P]) \tag{4}$$

where the elements of $[P]$ are now the proportions of total income absorbed by purchase of a unit of each good. Therefore, (1-1) may be thought of as containing income implicitly and as *numéraire*. However, demands are functions of total real income alone, distribution among individuals being ignored. In this respect and in another important regard to be discussed below, society's demands are treated as if they were relevant to a single individual.

3.a. Earlier Treatments of Aspects of Determinateness of Equilibrium in the Production Economy: Neisser, Stackelberg, and Zeuthen

Among the first to treat aspects of the problem of existence of equilibrium in the Walrasian-Casselian systems were (1) Neisser, who stressed the possibility of solutions which were not meaningful—specifically, the possibility of negative prices or quantities, and (2) Zeuthen, who pointed out the implications inherent in (1-3).[10] These implications are now familiar to us: "Here one does not know at the outset which goods are free goods, so one should insert into the equality the possibility of an unused residual and, at the same time, stipulate among the conditions, that either this residual or the price of the resource equals zero."[11]

[9] A. Wald, (1), pp. 378–9.
[10] H. Neisser, (1), pp. 422–5, and F. Zeuthen, (1), especially pp. 5–12.
[11] F. Zeuthen, (1), pp. 2–3.

That is, in this linear production system as in previous models we have studied, under certain conditions some productive resources may, in the solution, be free goods; therefore, Zeuthen argues, anticipating the inequalities of linear programming, a disposal or slack variable must be added. We denote it R_i:

$$\sum_j a_{ij}X_j + R_i = Q_i \tag{5}$$

Wald formalized Zeuthen's further condition as follows:

$$R_i P_i = 0 \tag{6}$$

Zeuthen treated at length a simple system of this type where $n = m = 2$, correctly concluded that both R_i could not be zero in a solution if demands were insatiable and, in effect, also specified the conditions that the R_i be positive or zero for the equilibrium to be meaningful.

Stackelberg pointed out for this case where $n = m$ that systems of the type in (1) were decomposable into three separate independent subsystems.[12] When $n = m$, he did not point to the possibility of one or more factors becoming free goods, as he did when $m > n$. Assuming implicitly that all equalities held in system (1-3) in equilibrium, however, he did indicate that it was possible to solve the n equations for the n unknown X_j.

Samuelson also has studied the model where $n = m$ at great length for the case of linear homogeneous production functions rather than fixed coefficients. His presentation, modified for the case of Cassel's model, focusses upon equations (1-2). With a given price vector $[P_j]$ one may expect a determinate set of prices $[P_i]$ if only the number of equations and unknowns is taken into account. Samuelson shows that if there exists a solution to (1-2) when $n = m$, it will be unique if there exists a numbering of the goods and factors such that

$$a_{z_1 1} \neq 0, \quad \begin{vmatrix} a_{z_1 1} & a_{z_2 1} \\ a_{z_1 2} & a_{z_2 2} \end{vmatrix} \neq 0, \quad \begin{vmatrix} a_{z_1 1} & a_{z_2 1} & \cdots & a_{z_m 1} \\ \cdot & \cdot & \cdots & \cdot \\ a_{z_1 n} & a_{z_2 n} & \cdots & a_{z_m n} \end{vmatrix} \neq 0 \tag{7}$$

These conditions rule out the technological similarity of goods and factor services.[13]

As a result of giving most of his attention to system (1-3), Stackelberg was troubled by the case where $n > m$. In terms of system (1-2), however, given an arbitrary price vector $[P_j]$, an overdetermined system results

[12] H. von Stackelberg, (1), pp. 463–72. Stackelberg's system differs slightly and unimportantly from that of Wald and Zeuthen in that the first set of equations in his model requires the equality of the demand and supply variables. In Wald and Zeuthen this is obtained by substituting demand terms for supply terms in (1-3).

[13] P. Samuelson, (8).

when we seek to determine $[P_i]$. This is the classical case of comparative advantage, understandable from linear programming analysis as the case of n activities and $m < n$ constraints. By the basic theorem of linear programming, production of no more than m of the goods will occur (or, rather, need occur) under a regime of profit maximization, the excluded $n - m$ goods being incapable of enhancing profits. If, however, the prices of these excluded goods are allowed to adjust to average cost it is possible at no decrease in profits to produce some or all goods, when the same no-profit condition is ruling for included goods. When the P_j remained inflexible, the optimal set of goods could be used to place zeros in (1-3) for all X_j not produced, which cleared up the underdeterminateness of that set.

It was Zeuthen's contribution to point out that even when $n = m$, it could not be assumed that in the solution all of the equalities of (1-3) would hold, and when (5) was substituted for (1-3) and (6) was added, the independence of the relations between demand and supply of factors from the remainder of the system disappeared.

However, Stackelberg's distinctive contribution was to emphasize the strong presumption of free factor services when $m > n$, and consequently the general inability of all equalities of (1-3) to rule in the solution. At present, we find the Stackelberg criticisms of Cassel easy to understand by virtue of our conditioning with linear programming techniques. System (1-3) is a set of m constraints in n activity levels. When $m > n$ and where we attempt to make all the equalities of (1-3) rule, we are in the position of attempting to make m ($> n$) hyperplanes in n dimensions meet at a single point. For example, if $m = 3$ and $n = 2$, we should have three straight lines defined in two-dimensional space which would not in general intersect at a single point $[\bar{X}_1, \bar{X}_2]$. Any pair of lines would yield such a point—a basket of goods which exhausted the amounts of the two relevant resources available—but this combination will not in general satisfy the equality of demand and supply for the third factor service represented by the omitted curve. There exists in general no solution which exhausts all resources for system (1-3) and if no solution exists for this subsystem no solution of this type can exist for the whole system (1).

The Walrasian "solution" to this problem of factor redundancy was to include factor services among the directly consumable goods in the individual's budget, so that their quantities supplied are not fixed but functions of factor service prices as well as all other prices.[14] Stackelberg objects that such dependence of factor service supplies is questionable in realistic terms, especially in the case of land. Also, in the cases of capital and land services, he believed there was a lower limit to any such function below which price of the factor service could not fall, in much the same manner as the Keynesian liquidity trap set a floor on the interest rate in

[14] Compare Section 1.a., Chapter 3.

Keynes's system. He felt that therefore the Walrasian "solution" would be inoperative when one of these limits was reached.[15] However, Stackelberg need not have been so restrictive in requiring "traps" to exist in the consumers' demand functions for factor services: if at near-zero prices the values of such functions were finite, the possibility exists for one or more to become free goods.[16] Walras was incorrect in thinking (if, in fact, he did so believe) that the assumption of supply variability annulled the contradiction inherent in the equalities; an additional assumption that such services are incapable of satiating consumer desires is also necessary.[17]

The other path out of the difficulty which Stackelberg saw was to make the production coefficients of the Casselian system variable rather than constant. Such relations enhance the probability that all resources would be economic goods in the equilibrium—indeed, just as Walras' factor service supply assumptions do—but they could not guarantee the existence of such a solution. Generally speaking, if it is possible for marginal products of factor services to become zero when their use is increased, a factor price can fall to zero.[18] Therefore, while the departures from the rigidities imposed by the linearities of system (1) discussed here do lessen the chances of free resources in equilibrium, they do not eliminate them.

The economically-justified path out of such difficulties is the one suggested by Zeuthen, Neisser, Schlesinger, von Neumann, and Wald: to accept the possibility of redundancy of one or more factor services and, in such a case, to require the prices of such factor services to be zero. The existence of such solutions no longer appears as frightening as it did in periods before the present ability was developed to cope with maxima which are corner extremum points.

3.b. Wald's Existence Proof

Wald begins from this point with a system containing (1-1), (1-2), (5), and (6), with $2m + 2n$ equations and an equal number of unknowns: X_j, P_j, P_i, and R_i. Given are the inverted demand functions, the technological coefficients, and the quantities of factor services available. The question: *what restrictions must be placed upon the data to insure the existence of a meaningful and unique solution to this simplest of general production systems?*

To guarantee the existence of unique, nonnegative values for X_j, P_j, and R_i, and the existence of at least one nonnegative set of solutions for P_i, Wald specified six necessary and sufficient conditions:

[15] H. von Stackelberg, (1), p. 466.
[16] R. Dorfman, (1), p. 365.
[17] Compare K. Arrow, (2), p. 281.
[18] R. Dorfman, (1), pp. 365–6.

1. $Q_i > 0, i = 1, \ldots, m$.

2. $a_{ij} \geqq 0, i = 1, \ldots, m, j = 1, \ldots, n$. This guarantees that all input coefficients are nonnegative.

3. for each Y_j, $[a_{ij}] \geq 0$, so that at least one input enters each good's production.

4. consider the demand functions $P_j = F_j([X])$. For any $[X]$ in which all elements are positive or zero and $X_j > 0$, it is required that $P_j \geqq 0$ and F_j be continuous. This condition guarantees nonnegative prices and requires that the demand functions not possess any discontinuities which could lead to indeterminate prices.

5. consider once more $P_j = F_j([X])$. Let $[X^k]$, $k = 1, 2, \ldots$ be a sequence of vectors in which the element $X_j^k > 0$ for all k, and which sequence converges to a $[X]$ in which $X_j = 0$. It is required that as k grows larger without limit, $P_j \rightarrow \infty$. This must hold for all demand functions. This requirement states that for any finite price P_j demand for the good Y_j must be positive. Wald himself realized that this was a stronger requirement than he needed, quoting Menger's proof that P_j need only approach a determinable finite number calculated from the a_{ij} coefficients in the limiting process. Nevertheless, he felt the stronger conditions were not overly restrictive, since the requirement is merely that X_j depart ever so slightly from zero for high prices—so slightly that for all practicable purposes it could be regarded as zero. This condition is needed only to guarantee that $X_j > 0, j = 1, \ldots, n$.

Given these five conditions, there will exist at least one meaningful solution for the economy's unknowns, and, moreover, $X_j > 0$ for all j. Wald, however, adds a sixth condition which is sufficient for the uniqueness of the solution for X_j, P_j, and R_i, and is necessary for the uniqueness of P_i as well as the existence of an equilibrium. It is the following:

6. the weak axiom of revealed preference characterizes the demand functions.[19] Be it noted that Wald is imposing these conditions upon *aggregate* demand functions, not necessarily upon all individuals', for which the requirement is intuitively rational. Wald shows that if we require the condition to hold for each consumer, if the consumer's preferences reveal independence of the utilities, and if the marginal utilities decrease monotonically in function of each good's consumption, the weak axiom of revealed preference will hold for all aggregate demand functions. Further, even if independence of the utilities is abandoned as an assumption, as long as the rate of marginal utility of a good is larger in an absolute sense than the rate at which the utility of that good changes for any other good's variation, his aggregate demand functions will be characterized by the axiom of revealed preference if the individual functions are so characterized.

[19] See footnote 39, Chapter 2.

However, even if the condition holds for all persons' demand curves, Wald recognizes that it may not characterize market demands by virtue of changes in the distribution of income which may occur between two equilibria. Wald's assumption that the demands in the market are independent of the distribution of income helps in this respect, but only at the cost of making society in effect one single-minded consumer.[20] That is, this assumption assures that the society will choose among baskets of goods as if it were following a single set of preferences. However, Hicks's counterexample, quoted in footnote 20, reveals that even this assumption is not sufficient to allow the consistency of the aggregate demand functions with the weak axiom to be deduced from the similar consistency of all individuals' demand functions.

Finally, Wald adds a last assumption necessary to guarantee the uniqueness of $[P_i^\circ]$:

7. consider the matrix of coefficients of production:

$$[a] = \begin{bmatrix} a_{z_1 1} & a_{z_1 2} & \cdots & a_{z_1 n} \\ \cdot & \cdot & \cdots & \cdot \\ a_{z_m 1} & a_{z_m 2} & \cdots & a_{z_m n} \end{bmatrix} \tag{8}$$

There must be m columns of $[a]$ which will form a submatrix whose determinant will not vanish. That is, there must be at least one set of m processes which are linearly independent of one another. The first six conditions guarantee a solution vector $[P_i^\circ]$; this condition guarantees that it will be unique. Suppose every set of m process vectors formed a determinant that vanished, for example, because in every such subset there existed two rows which were identical, or proportional, element by element. This implies that in every use included in those submatrices two factor services entered in the same proportions into the production of every good. Then, mathematically, these two factor services would be one, whose joint price is determinate, but for which any two separate prices adding to the joint price would be acceptable. This condition assures that such joint-factors are not formed.

4. The Arrow-Debreu Existence Theorems

In a classic article, Arrow and Debreu narrowed the scope of Wald's analysis by ignoring the quality of uniqueness or nonuniqueness of

[20] A. Wald, (1), pp. 373–6, and R. Dorfman, (1), p. 368. See also K. Arrow, (2), p. 289, and L. McKenzie, (2), p. 147. Hicks demonstrates a case where no income redistribution occurs (although the absolute incomes of individuals may change) between two solutions but where the group choices are inconsistent with the weak axiom even though the individuals' choices are consistent with it. The example reveals that differences in taste alone, without redistribution effects, can lead to such aggregate inconsistency. J. Hicks, (6), pp. 55–7.

equilibrium, but generalized the existence analysis.[21] This generalization was made in several directions:

(1) consumer preference functions are included as data in the production and exchange models in lieu of aggregate demand functions, which allows Arrow and Debreu to escape the Wald conditions upon the latter. (It will be recalled that the most objectionable of these Wald conditions concerned the application of the weak axiom of revealed preference to aggregate demand functions. This was needed in part to guarantee uniqueness, a quality with which Arrow and Debreu do not concern themselves.)

(2) Arrow-Debreu Model 1 is not necessarily characterized by fixed coefficients of production, but merely by nonincreasing returns to scale of output, while in Arrow-Debreu Model 2, fixed coefficients of production are possible universally if labor always has positive direct utility.

(3) Arrow-Debreu economies may retain the Walrasian assumption of consumer absorption of factor services, so that the supply of them need not be perfectly inelastic.

(4) the Arrow-Debreu equilibrium may include nonnegative profits, and does not require them to be zero.

(5) firms in the Arrow-Debreu economies need not be single product firms.

(6) individual consumer demands are dependent upon wealth and income, and therefore aggregate demands are functions of the distribution of wealth and income.

The core of the Arrow-Debreu performance is the proof of the existence of an equilibrium for two types of economies by an imaginative application of n-person game theory. In such theory, the mere definition of the conditions of equilibrium has been a bone of contention, several having been suggested. One of these definitions is that of J. F. Nash, who, in addition, derived the necessary and sufficient conditions for an n-person game to possess an equilibrium point of this type.[22] Arrow and Debreu show that their economies can be made to fit the description of a variant of an n-person, noncooperative game, prove the equivalence of equilib-

[21] K. Arrow, (2). Nikaidô has used essentially the same technique to prove the existence of equilibrium for a multiple exchange economy. This proof is similar to the Arrow-Debreu proof of Model 1's equilibrium in that (1) it assumes that each person has positive quantities of *all* goods at the start of the market day, and (2) it uses the fiction of a "market participant" who seeks to maximize the value of excess demand by choice of a price strategy.

The most important departure from the Arrow-Debreu proof, however, is the guarantee of nonzero prices by virtue of an assumption of strictly increasing total utility functions, so that the consumer always prefers more of every good to less, with the condition that excess demand for every good in equilibrium be zero. See H. Nikaidô, (1). He relaxed the condition that every consumer have some of every good for the condition that he have a positive quantity of some goods, when for the economy as a whole positive quantities of all goods exist. See (2).

[22] J. Nash, (1), and also, R. Luce, (1), pp. 170–7.

rium points in the n-person game and their economies, and demonstrate the conformity of the relevant sets and functions or correspondences of their economies to the conditions for existence of equilibrium determined by Nash. We shall now proceed to (1) define each of the Arrow-Debreu economies in turn, (2) state the definition of equilibrium in an n-person game and Nash's existence theorem, (3) establish the conformity of the economies to the game, and (4) prove the equivalence of the definition of equilibrium and the conformity of the data, functions, and correspondences to the requirements of the Nash theorem.

4.a. The Arrow-Debreu Model 1

The distinctive feature of the first model is that *every* consumer is assumed to possess stocks of *every* good and factor service large enough that for any permissible set of prices it will be *possible* for the consumer to supply some of *every* good Y_j as well as *every* factor service z_i to the market. The reason for this assumption will be made clear in due time.

4.a.1. The Assumptions in the Production Sector

The following postulates are asserted:

Assumption 1. There exists a finite number of distinct goods and factor services (in the Arrow-Debreu presentation all factor services are various types of labor services), denoted $Y_j, j = 1, \ldots, n$, and $z_i, i = 1, \ldots, m$, respectively. This formulation allows such goods and services to include goods and services at different points in time or space, so that either or both of these dimensions may be viewed as present in these limited senses.

Assumption 2. There exists a finite number of existing or potential firms, $v = 1, \ldots, o$, which produce the goods Y_j.

Assumption 3. For each firm v there exists a set of production vectors' T_v, whose elements are $[\bar{X}_v] = [\bar{X}_{v1}, \ldots, \bar{X}_{vn}, -X_{vz_1}, \ldots, -X_{vz_m},$ $-X_{v1}, \ldots -X_{vn}]$. We shall employ the net output basis, subtracting intermediate goods inputs from outputs, to obtain $[\bar{X}_v] = [\bar{X}_{v1}, \ldots, \bar{X}_{vn}, -X_{vz_1}, \ldots, -X_{vz_m}]$, where the $\bar{X}_{vj}$ can be positive, negative, or zero.

Assumption 4. Let R^{m+n} be the $m + n$-fold cartesian product of the real numbers R. It is, then, the set of all vectors with $m + n$ real components.[23] It is therefore assumed that the $[\bar{X}_v] \in R^{m+n}$.

[23] We define a Euclidean s-dimensional vector space, R^s, more precisely as follows. If two vectors are assumed, $[a] = [a_1, \ldots, a_s]$ and $[b] = [b_1, \ldots, b_s]$, and if:
1. $[a] = [b]$ is defined to mean $a_1 = b_1, a_2 = b_2, \ldots, a_s = b_s$;
2. $[a] + [b]$ is defined to mean $[a_1 + b_1, a_2 + b_2, \ldots, a_s + b_s]$;
3. when k is real, $k[a]$ is defined to mean $[ka_1, ka_2, \ldots, ka_s]$;
4. $-[a]$ is defined to mean $(-1)[a] = [-a_1, -a_2, \ldots, -a_s]$;

Assumption 5. It is assumed that T_v, $v = 1, \ldots, o$, is a closed convex subset of R^{m+n}, containing the null vector [0]. The last assumption implies that each firm has the option of not producing and of earning zero profits. Convexity means that a straight line connecting any two points in T_v will be wholly contained within T_v. For example, consider the points [0] and $[\bar{X}_v']$ in T_v. If $0 \leqq \lambda \leqq 1$, then the straight line defined by $\lambda[\bar{X}_v'] + (1 - \lambda)[0]$ must lie in T_v, i.e., $\lambda[\bar{X}_v'] + (1 - \lambda)[0] \in T_v$.

The economic importance of the convexity restriction is that, with the assumption that $[0] \in T_v$, it implies nonincreasing returns to the scale of production. Thus, if a given $[\bar{X}_v] \in T_v$ has all its inputs boosted 10 per cent, we require that outputs rise no more than 10 per cent. If, as we have seen in Chapter 6, in addition to convexity and the assumption that T_v owns the null vector we add the third assumption (which Arrow and Debreu do not) of additivity of the vectors $[\bar{X}_v]$, we should have the Koopmans production conditions of constant returns to scale. To forestall this assumption, Arrow and Debreu assume the existence of certain factor services which do not appear among the explicitly considered m; therefore, we do not have the three assumptions which lead to T_v being a convex cone in R^{m+n} with vertex at [0].[24]

Lastly, we define the concept of openness and closedness of a set in this fashion. Assume a three-dimensional Euclidean space and define a set therein. At point $[P]$ in that set define a *neighborhood* of that point as all points lying within the sphere centering on $[P]$ with radius λ, a fixed arbitrary distance. If some such neighborhood of $[P]$ lies wholly within the set, $[P]$ is an *interior* point of the set. If all points $[P]$ of the set are interior points, the set is open. Or, a closed set may be defined as a set which contains all points zero distances from it. This implies that a closed set must contain its boundary, even though a closed set can be indefinitely large. Indeed, the set T_v fits this description.

Assumption 6. The whole technology, or the set T, is the sum of all T_v; i.e., the set of all vectors formed by adding one vector from each T_v. Any vector or point in T, therefore, is obtained by the summation of vectors in the T_v. T is *not* assumed to be closed, but this quality of T can be deduced from Assumptions 5 (that the T_v are closed and convex) and 8 (that irreversibility holds).[25]

---

5. [0] is defined as the null vector, [0, 0, . . . , 0];

6. the length of $[a]$ is defined as $\sqrt{a_1^2 + a_2^2 + \cdots a_s^2}$; then these vectors are defined for a Euclidean space.

These rules assure, among other things, that the addition and subtraction properties of vectors will be those of real numbers.

[24] We may also show the following: (a) if constant returns and additivity were assumed, it is implied that T_v is a convex cone with vertex [0], and (b) if convexity of T_v and constant returns to scale are assumed, additivity is implied.

[25] Compare L. McKenzie, (1), p. 67.

Assumption 7. Let Ω be the set of all points in R^{m+n} whose components are all nonnegative. Then, the only point T has in common with Ω must be [0], which is owned by both sets (Assumption 5 and the definition of Ω). We have already encountered this restriction that $T \cap \Omega$ ("the intersection of sets T and Ω") $\subset$ ("is contained in") 0, where 0 is the set containing only [0], in Koopman's assumption that at least one input is required to produce an output. This assumption must be distinguished from another which is not violated by it: $T \supset -\Omega$ ("the set T contains the set $-\Omega$"). This assumption states that taking all technology as a whole, it is possible for firms to absorb inputs and produce zero net outputs. In this case "free disposal" of factor services rules, since all produced goods are used on intermediate account.[26] Free disposal with Assumption 8 below implies Assumption 7, for since $T \supset -\Omega$ it follows that $-T \supset \Omega$. Since the intersection of T and $-T$ is 0, it follows that Ω and T, if they intersect, must do so in the set containing only [0]. Since Ω and T both own [0], it follows that they do intersect and only in that point.

Assumption 8. Consider the set $-T$, consisting of T with the sign of every component of every vector reversed. It is required that $T \cap -T \subset 0$. This is familiar again as a Koopmans assumption—that of irreversibility. Nowhere in the production sector, either within a firm or between firms, does there exist a pair of $[\bar{X}_v] \neq 0$ which are mirror images of one another, such that net outputs of goods and factor services cancel to zero when they are added, nor is there any other linear combination of such activities which will yield [0]. This condition is automatically met if the z_i are assumed to be nonproducible, and to enter the $[\bar{X}_v]$ only as negative components, when at least one such primary factor service enters each $[\bar{X}_v]$ for all v.

None of these restrictions is particularly stringent or intuitively objectionable in the light of the analysis of the preceding eight chapters.[27]

[26] G. Debreu, (2), p. 42.

[27] Debreu has generalized these assumptions in the production sector to require Assumptions 1–4, 6, 8, and that part of Assumption 5 which requires that $[0] \epsilon T_v$, for all v. For the remainder of Assumption 5 he substitutes

Assumption 5′. T is closed and convex.
For Assumption 7, he substitutes the free disposal postulate:

Assumption 7′. $T \supset -\Omega$.
This last assumption assures that all price vectors will be nonnegative, since no one need accept a negative price for disposing of factor services.

But Assumption 7′ and Assumption 8 imply Assumption 7, as shown above, so that the Land of Cockaigne is excluded from his system as well as the Arrow-Debreu system. The inclusion of Assumption 7′, which insures that no equilibrium price vector will contain a negative component, allows this condition to be deduced from the assumptions, rather than to be imposed by the conditions of equilibrium as it is in the Arrow-Debreu systems (see Condition 3, Condition 4, and the definition of equilibrium); they infer that prices are nonnegative and, when zero, excess supplies are positive. See G. Debreu, (2), pp. 74–89, and L. McKenzie, (1), p. 54.

4.a.2. The Assumptions in the Consumption Sector

The following postulates restrict the data of the consumer sector of the model:

Assumption 9. There exists a group of consuming units, $c = 1, \ldots, s$, which supply all (explicitly included) factor services and consume Y_j and z_i.

Assumption 10. For each consuming unit there exists a set, C_c, of vectors $[X_c] = [X_{c1}, \ldots, X_{cn}, X_{cz_1}, \ldots, X_{cz_m}]$, whose components are demands for consumer goods and factor services.[28]

Assumption 11. The set C_c, $c = 1, \ldots, s$, is assumed to be contained in R^{m+n}, closed, convex, and bounded from below by the vector $[L_c] \leqq [X_c]$ for all $[X_c] \in C_c$. The first three of these restrictions are similar to those imposed upon T_v. The boundedness restriction, however, is novel.

Boundedness of a set, S, is defined as follows. A vector $[m]$ is a lower bound of S if, for all $[X] \in S$, $[X] \geqq [m]$. A vector $[M]$ is an upper bound of S if, for all $[X] \in S$, $[X] \leqq [M]$. Consider, further, the set m containing all $[m]$. If $[m^*] \in m$ such that $[m] \leqq [m^*]$ for all $[m] \in m$, then $[m^*]$ is the greatest lower bound, or infimum, of S. Similarly, let M be the set containing all upper bounds; i.e., $[M] \in M$. If $[M^*] \in M$ such that $[M] \geqq [M^*]$ for all $[M] \in M$, then $[M^*]$ is the least upper bound, or supremum, of S. For the case at hand, only a lower bound to C_c is assumed to exist. Since consumption of the Y_j and z_i can fall only to 0, the infimum of C_c, $[m^*]$, will be $[0]$.

Assumption 12. For each $c = 1, \ldots, s$, there exists on C_c an ordinal preference function $M_c([X_c])$, such that $M_c([X_c]) \geqq M_c([X'_c])$ if and only if $[X_c]$ is preferred or is indifferent to $[X'_c]$ by consumer c. This is familiar to us from the analysis of Chapter 2, except that no assumptions are made concerning the differentiability of M_c.

Assumption 13. The function $M_c([X_c])$ is continuous on C_c.

Assumption 14. For every consuming unit, c, and for every vector, $[X_c] \in C_c$, there is at least one other vector which is preferred; i.e., there exists an $[X'_c] \in C_c$ for which $M_c([X'_c]) > M_c([X_c])$. Therefore, no consuming unit could ever become satiated in all goods and services, since no one point or set of points in C_c is preferred to all others.

Assumption 15. The preference function possesses the quality of convexity. This somewhat misleading terminology means the following. Let $[X_c]$ and $[X'_c]$ be two elements of C_c (which is a convex set) such that

[28] Arrow and Debreu assume that factor services are nonconsumable and include quantities of factor services supplied as negative demands in these vectors. We shall retain the Walrasian assumption of consumable factor services.

$M_c([X_c]) > M_c([X'_c])$. Then, convexity requires that the line segment connecting these two points contain baskets of goods which are preferred to $[X'_c]$ except at the end points; i.e., when $0 < \lambda < 1$, $M_c(\lambda[X_c] + (1 - \lambda)[X'_c]) > M_c([X'_c])$.

Suppose the same condition held when $M_c([X_c]) \geqq M_c([X'_c])$. Then, since C_c is convex and M_c is continuous, M_c may be represented by a strictly quasi-concave function, and the conditions would imply the strict quasi-concavity of the preference function. That is, for any value $M_c([X'_c])$, C_c is partitioned into a subset C'_c such that $M_c([X_c] \epsilon C'_c) < M_c([X'_c])$, and a subset C''_c such that $M_c([X_c] \epsilon C'_c) \geqq M_c([X'_c])$. Strict quasi-concavity requires that C''_c be convex and that the line segment joining any two points on the boundary of C''_c lie in the interior of C''_c except at the end points. This is the usual implicit assumption in the typical depiction of two-dimensional indifference curves: the chord joining any two points on the curve lies wholly above the curve except at the end points. The Arrow-Debreu assumption is weaker than that of strict quasi-concavity and, to use the two-dimensional analogy, would allow straight-line segments in the indifference curves to exist, since the Arrow-Debreu conditions are defined only for points which are not indifferent to one another.[29]

On the other hand, suppose we softened the condition to require that when $M_c([X_c]) \geqq M_c([X'_c])$, $M_c(\lambda[X_c] + (1 - \lambda)[X'_c]) \geqq M_c([X'_c])$, $0 < \lambda < 1$: this is the condition of "weak-convexity" which, given the convexity of C_c and continuity of M_c, implies quasi-concavity of the preference function. This restriction allows a subset of points in C_c to exist to which the consumer is indifferent, some points of which may represent baskets of goods with more of all or some goods and no less of others than in baskets of goods also in the indifference class. This is a weaker restriction than the Arrow-Debreu restriction. Thus, this latter assumption of convexity—lying between the conditions of strict quasi-concavity and quasi-concavity of the preference function—allows linear segments to exist in the indifference varieties but rules out "thick" varieties. The Arrow-Debreu condition is necessary but not sufficient for strict quasi-concavity, while quasi-concavity is necessary but not sufficient for the Arrow-Debreu condition.

Assumption 16. For each consuming unit c there exists a vector of endowments $[Q_c] = [Q_{c1}, \ldots, Q_{cn}, Q_{cz_1}, \ldots, Q_{cz_m}] > 0$ and $[Q_c] \epsilon R^{m+n}$. In Arrow-Debreu the Q_{cz_i} components are zero (except when loans in

[29] This less restrictive assumption allows the possibility of nonunique solutions to occur in the model (picture a two dimensional budget constraint "tangent" to an indifference curve along a linear segment). As Debreu points out, strong convexity (strict quasi-concavity of M_c) is difficult to justify intuitively, therefore it need not characterize reality, and, as we argued at the beginning of this chapter, uniqueness of solutions need not be considered a desideratum of general systems. G. Debreu, (2), p. 66.

kind of these services are collectible by or payable to the consumer at the start of the week) and are found in the $[X_c]$ as $-Q_{cz_i}$ components. Also, the Q_{cj} components of $[Q_c]$ in Arrow and Debreu are taken to include loans collectible by the consumer or payable by him in kind.

Assumption 17. For each consuming unit c there exists a vector, $[\pi_c] = [\pi_{c1}, \ldots, \pi_{co}]$, whose elements are the proportions of the total profits of each firm received by it, where $\pi_{cv} \geqq 0$ for all c and all v, and $\Sigma_c \pi_{cv} = 1$, for all v.

Assumption 18. For each consuming unit c there exists in C_c at least one $[X_c] \in C_c$ for which $[X_c] < [Q_c]$. This assures that each consuming unit has the possibility of choosing an $[X_c]$ which would allow him to be a net supplier of *every* good and factor service in the economy. This unrealistic assumption is made to assure that the consumer will be able to supply at least one good or service with a positive price. Since at least one good in the economy will in fact have a positive price, as will be shown, the condition will be met. It may be pointed out that this postulate plays the same role in the Arrow-Debreu analysis as von Neumann's assumption that every good is an input or an output or both in each activity: it prevents the occurrence of an empty set and the nonexistence therefore of an equilibrium.

In the consumption sector, therefore, the only assumption which departs from those of our earlier presentation in the direction of greater restrictiveness is the requirement that all consumers begin the period with positive amounts of each good and service. Indeed, the restrictions upon the Arrow-Debreu preference function are much less binding than those of strict quasi-concavity which we imposed.

4.a.3. The Conditions for an Equilibrium in a Competitive Economy

An equilibrium for Model 1 is defined to hold when four conditions are met:

Condition 1. Each firm v must maximize its profits; i.e., $[\bar{X}_v^\circ]$ must maximize $[\bar{X}_v] \cdot [P^\circ]$ over T_v for all v.

Condition 2. The consumer's wherewithal consists of the value of his endowments of goods and services and his receipt of profits. At equilibrium prices, $[X_c^\circ]$ must maximize $M_c([X_c])$ over that subset of C_c for which $[X_c] \cdot [P^\circ] \leqq [Q_c] \cdot [P^\circ] + \Sigma_v \pi_{cv}[\bar{X}_v^\circ] \cdot [P^\circ]$.[30]

[30] It is easily seen that in equilibrium the equality sign must in fact hold. Suppose the inequality did hold for $[X_c^\circ]$ and $[P^\circ]$. By Assumption 14 there exists a preferred vector $[X_c']$ and by Assumption 15 it is possible to get a preferred vector arbitrarily close to $[X_c^\circ]$. Therefore, it is possible to get a vector in the neighborhood of $[X_c^\circ]$ for which the inequality holds and which is preferred to $[X_c^\circ]$—a contradiction of Condition 2. Therefore, the equality must hold, for only if it does are preferred vectors unattainable.

Condition 3. Let P be the set of all possible price vectors $[P]$. Instead of choosing one good as *numéraire*, the degree of freedom we possess because only relative prices are determinate is used to insure that for every $[P] \epsilon P$, $[P] \cdot [u] = 1$, where $[u]$ is a column vector of $m + n$ unity elements and where $[P] \geq 0$. We require in equilibrium that $[P^\circ] \epsilon P$.

Condition 4. Let $[X] = \Sigma_c[X_c]$, $[\bar{X}] = \Sigma_v [\bar{X}_v]$, and $[Q] = \Sigma_c[Q_c]$. Then $[E]$, the market excess demand vector, is defined as $[E] = [X] - [\bar{X}] - [Q]$. We then require that $[E^\circ] \leqq 0$, when $[E^\circ] \cdot [P^\circ] = 0$. These are the Zeuthen-Wald-Schlesinger conditions that excess demand be nonpositive and where negative that price equal zero. This last condition can hold only if every term in the inner product is zero; i.e., if $P_s^\circ E_s^\circ = 0$ for all s, where $s = i, j$.

4.a.4. Nash's Theorem on the N-Person Noncooperative Game

Let us construct a modified game in which the Arrow-Debreu economy will be depicted perfectly. As a first approximation, we shall imagine a group of $s + o + 1$ players in the game: all consumers, all potential and existing firms, and a "market participant." The latter player is a personification of market forces whose adjustment of prices acts to influence the strategy sets and/or payoffs of firms and consumers. Consider a single strategy for each type of player. It will be a vector in R^{m+n}. For the consumer, a strategy is a vector $[X_c]$,[31] for a firm a vector $[\bar{X}_v]$, and for the market participant a vector $[P]$. The initial strategy sets are then, respectively, C_c, T_v, and P. Any single play of the game involves a single vector drawn from each set.

There remain to be defined the payoff functions over the outcomes. These are straightforward: for the consumer there exists the preference function $M_c([X_c])$ defining his payoff for any point of his action space; for the firm we have a profit function $[P] \cdot [\bar{X}_v]$; and for the market participant we have the value of excess demands, $[P] \cdot [E]$. Given a pattern of excess demands resulting from the play of consumer and firm strategies, it will pay the market participant (who reacts in a purely competitive fashion) to choose on the next play a strategy which raises the price of those goods and factor services with positive excess demands and lowers prices on those with negative excess demands for goods whose price is not zero.

Nash's definition of an equilibrium point in such a game is a straightforward extension of the maximin notion of two-person, zero-sum game theory. A given strategy set is an equilibrium set if for each player it is simultaneously true that no alternative strategy available to him would increase his payoffs, given the strategies of every other player. That is, if,

[31] Given a consumption vector $[X_c]$ it follows from footnote (30) that the consumer will supply all $Q_{cs} - X_{cs}$ for which $P_s > 0$; therefore, the consumer's supplies are determined with the choice of $[X_c]$.

for consumer 1 it holds that

$$(9) \quad M_1([X_1]; [X_2], \ldots, [X_s], [\bar{X}_1], \ldots [\bar{X}_o], [P]) \geqq M_1([X'_1]; [X_2], \ldots, [X_s], [\bar{X}_1], \ldots, [\bar{X}_o], [P])$$

where $[X'_1]$ is any other element in C_c except $[X_1]$, and similar conditions hold for all other consumers, all firms, and the market participant, the strategy set $[X_1^\circ, \ldots, X_s^\circ, \bar{X}_1^\circ, \ldots, \bar{X}_o^\circ, P^\circ]$ is an equilibrium set. More specifically, and in terms of concepts presently to be developed, an equilibrium $[X_c^\circ]$ is one which is an element of $A_c([\bar{a}_c^\circ])$ and maximizes $M_c([X_c] \epsilon A_c([\bar{a}_c^\circ]))$; an equilibrium $[\bar{X}_v^\circ]$ is an element of T_v which maximizes $[P^\circ] \cdot [\bar{X}_v]$; and an equilibrium $[P^\circ]$ is an element of P which maximizes $[P] \cdot [E^\circ]$.

Assume for the moment that we attach an identifying number to every strategy available to a player, so that each such strategy is a point in one-dimensional space. The set of all available strategies to player t we denote A_t. Then $A = A_1 \times A_2 \times \cdots A_{s+o+1}$ is the set of ordered $s + o + 1$-tuples $[a_1, a_2, \ldots a_{s+o+1}]$; that is, a point in the set A depicts a choice of a strategy for each player, and all possible combinations of such strategies exhaust the set A. Also, we may define the subset $\bar{A}_t = A_1 \times A_2 \times \cdots A_{t-1} \times A_{t+1} \times A_{t+2} \times \cdots A_{s+o+1}$ with elements $[\bar{a}_t]$ as the set of all strategy combinations available to the players excluding player t.

Now, suppose that the strategy set of player t was not independent of the strategies of the other players: then for every point $[\bar{a}_t]$ there exists a set $A_t([\bar{a}_t])$, which is a subset of A_t, from which player t may choose his strategy. If his action space is independent of other players' strategy choices, then $A_t([\bar{a}_t]) = A_t$ for all $[\bar{a}_t]$. This assumption is true of the strategy sets of players in standard game theory, and it holds for firms and the market participant in our economy. However, it is not true of the consumer, constrained to choose a strategy from that subset of C_c which is within his budget constraint by Condition 2. Since this budget constraint is set by prices and profits, the subset of effectively available strategies is fixed by the strategy choices of firms and the market participant. Consequently, $A_c([\bar{a}_c]) \neq C_c$, although $A_v([\bar{a}_v]) = T_v$ and $A_{s+o+1}([\bar{a}_{s+o+1}]) = P$. This is the basic difference between Arrow and Debreu's "abstract economy" and the n-person game.

Consumer c's action space is the set $A_c([\bar{a}_c])$, or the action space relevant to a set of strategies selected by all players but consumer c, and is defined as

$$(10) \quad A_c([\bar{a}_c]) = \left\{ [X_c] | [X_c] \epsilon C_c, [P] \cdot [X_c] \leqq [P] \cdot [Q_c] + \sum_v \max \left[0, \pi_{cv}[P] \cdot [\bar{X}_v] \right] \right\}$$

This definition of the budget constraint differs from that stated in Condition 2 for the competitive economy in that it rules out negative profits. Were this change not made, randomly selected $[P]$ and $[\bar{X}_v]$ could lead to the empty set for $A_c([\bar{a}_c])$ and thereby violate a requirement in the proof of equilibrium to come. It may be readily seen that in equilibrium Condition 1 and the present method of ruling out negative profits must coincide, since $[0] \epsilon T_v$ for all v and firms would cease production before suffering negative profits.

Nash's Theorem as applied to such an "abstract economy" states that such an equilibrium set as $[X_1^\circ, \ldots, X_s^\circ, \bar{X}_1^\circ, \ldots, \bar{X}_o^\circ, P^\circ]$ will exist if the following conditions are met:

1. every strategy set A_t is nonempty, compact, and convex, where a compact set is defined as one which is closed and bounded. Thus, each of the convex action spaces must be bounded and must own its own boundary. Note that this is a restriction upon the complete action sets—in our case upon C_c, T_v and P—even if these differ from $A_t([\bar{a}_t])$.

2. the payoff functions for the three types of players are defined as $F_t([\bar{a}_t], [a_t])$, or, more specifically for our case:

$$\text{a. } M_c = M_c([a_c] \epsilon A_t([\bar{a}_c]))$$

$$\text{b. } [P] \cdot [\bar{X}_v]$$

$$\text{c. } [P] \cdot [E]$$

It is required that these $F_t([\bar{a}_t], [a_t])$ be continuous on the set A and quasi-concave in $[a_t]$ for every value of $[\bar{a}_t]$. Therefore, it is required that for each consumer and for every possible set of strategy choices of the other $s + o$ players, the preference function over $A_c([\bar{a}_c])$ be continuous, that every value F_c^* over this domain partition $A_c([\bar{a}_c])$ into two subsets, $F_c(A_c([\bar{a}_c])) < F_c^*$ and $F_c(A_c([\bar{a}_c])) \geqq F_c^*$, and that the latter be a convex set. Similarly, $[P] \cdot [\bar{X}_v]$ and $[P] \cdot [E]$ must be continuous over T_v and P respectively; every value of profits and aggregate excess demand, π^* and V^* respectively, must partition T_v and P; and the subsets of T_v and P for which $[P] \cdot [\bar{X}_v] \geqq \pi_v^*$, $[P] \cdot [E] \geqq V^*$, must be convex sets.

3. the sets $A_c([\bar{a}_c])$ may be viewed as the mappings of the set $\bar{A}_c$. We have, then, a "function," or, since mathematicians usually reserve that term for mappings of a point into a single point rather than a set of points, a "correspondence." For every point $[\bar{a}_c]$ in $\bar{A}_c$, there exists a subset of C_c containing elements $[X_c]$ which are feasible in terms of budget constraints. For reasons made clear in 2, the mappings $A_v([\bar{a}_v])$ and $A_{s+o+1}([\bar{a}_{s+o+1}])$ are the analogues in terms of correspondences to constants in functional terms.

It is required that $A_t([\bar{a}_t])$, or $A_c([\bar{a}_c])$, T_v, and P, be continuous, and, for all $[\bar{a}_t]$, the set $A_t([\bar{a}_t])$ be nonempty and convex, or that $A_c([\bar{a}_c])$

possess such qualities for all $[\bar{a}_c]$, and that T_v and P be nonempty and convex. Here, by abuse of notation, T_v denotes the correspondence mapping each point $[\bar{a}_v]$ to the entire set T_v, and similarly, P denotes the correspondence mapping each point $[\bar{a}_{s+o+1}]$ to the set P.

The continuity of a correspondence is akin to the continuity of a function. *When the image-set is a subset of a compact set,* upper semicontinuity of a correspondence at $[\bar{a}_t^*]$ is defined in terms of sequences: if as $[\bar{a}_t^q]$ approaches $[\bar{a}_t^*]$, a sequence $[X_t^q] \in A_t([\bar{a}_t^q])$ approaches $[X_t^*]$ as a limit, upper semicontinuity exists if $[X_t^*] \in A_t([\bar{a}_t^*])$. More crudely, this characteristic of a correspondence starts with the assumption of a point in a set and a sequence, together with a corresponding sequence approaching a limit in the image sets, and *asks* if this latter limit is in the image set of $[\bar{a}_t^*]$. In the figures below, Fig. 9-1-a shows a correspondence with upper semicontinuity at $[\bar{a}_t^*]$, and Fig. 9-1-b shows a correspondence not so characterized. In both illustrations, the image set of $[\bar{a}_t^*]$ is taken to be the boundary between points a and b. In Fig. 9-1-b, the sequence in the image-sets approaches a limit but this limit is not in $A_t([\bar{a}_t^*])$.

Lower semicontinuity at point $[\bar{a}_t^*]$ exists if a sequence $[\bar{a}_t^q]$ approaches $[\bar{a}_t^*]$ as a limit and if a point $[X_t^*] \in A_t([\bar{a}_t^*]$ is given, and it is shown that a sequence $[X_t^q] \in A_t([\bar{a}_t^q])$ exists which approaches $[X_t^*]$ as a limit. Again, crudely, this type of continuity assumes a sequence approaching a point in the set $\bar{A}_t$ and a point in the image of $A_t([\bar{a}_t^*])$, and *asks* if a sequence can be found in the image sets to get to $[X^*]$ in the limit. In Fig. 9-1-a, the point $[X_t^{**}]$ is in the image set of $[\bar{a}_t^*]$, but no sequence in the image sets of other points in $\bar{A}_t$ converges on it; therefore, the correspondence is not lower semicontinuous at $[\bar{a}_t^*]$. On the other hand, $[X_t^{**}]$in Fig. 9-1-b meets both conditions and is lower semicontinuous.

Upper and lower semicontinuity on the set $\bar{A}_t$ exist if the conditions for them are met at every point in $\bar{A}_t$. Continuity of the correspondence at $[\bar{a}_t^*]$ exists if both upper and lower semicontinuity exist at that point, and exists on the set if both characteristics hold at every point of $\bar{A}_t$. Note that $A_t([\bar{a}_t])$ is upper semicontinuous if and only if the graph of $A_t([\bar{a}_t])$ is a closed subset of the cartesian product $\bar{A}_t \times A_t$. Here ($[\bar{a}_t]$, $[a_t]$) is in the graph if and only if $[a_t] \in A_t[\bar{a}_t]$).

4.a.5. Kakutani's Fixed-Point Theorem

It will be convenient to study the basis for deriving these restrictions upon the action spaces and the payoff functions, since they are derived from a theorem for which we will have further use in this chapter. The basis of Nash's proof of the existence of an equilibrium point is the establishment of a "fixed point" in a correspondence by the use of Kakutani's fixed-point theorem.

Suppose we have a correspondence relating points $[X]$ in S to subsets of S itself; i.e., $\Phi([X])$, $[X] \in S$, carries $[X]$ into subsets Y of S. If a fixed point exists in the correspondence there will be a point $[X'] \in S$ which will be mapped into Y' by $\Phi([X'])$, where Y' is a subset of S and contains $[X']$ itself. The point $[X']$ maps into a subset which contains itself.

Kakutani's theorem states: (1) if S is a nonempty, convex subset of R^m; (2) if S is compact; (3) if Φ is an upper semicontinuous correspond-

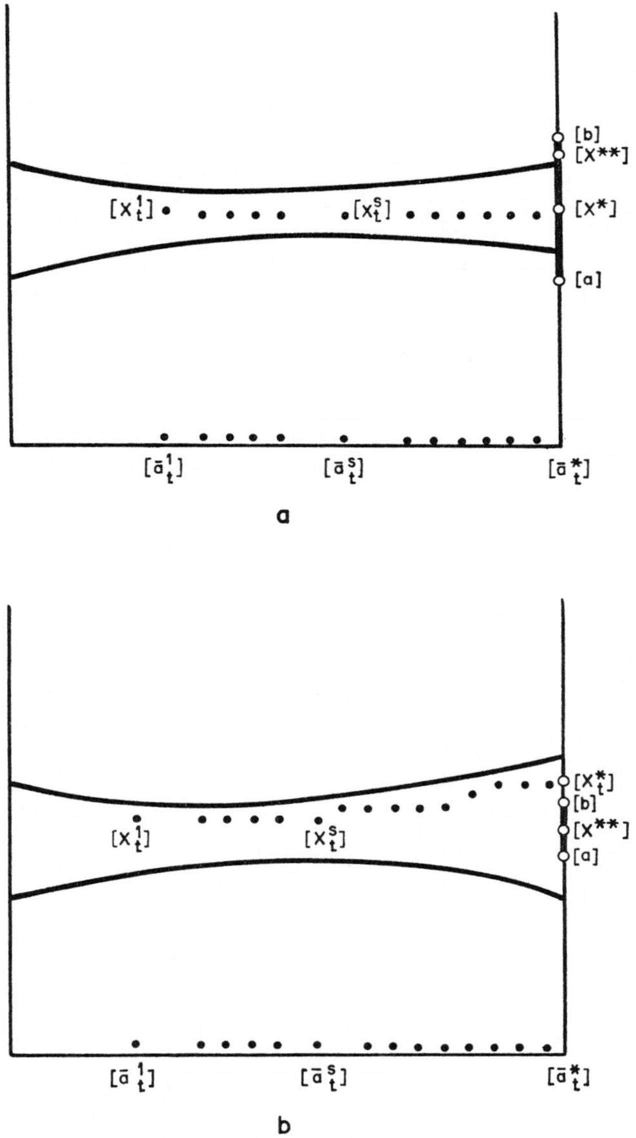

Figure 9-1. Illustrations of Semi-Continuity

ence from S to S; and (4) if for all $[X] \epsilon S$ the set $\Phi([X])$ is convex and nonempty, then $\Phi([X])$ has a fixed point.

We shall now apply the theorem to the economy of Arrow-Debreu Model 1. In the next section we shall define $[\hat{E}]$ as a subset of $[E]$, $\hat{C}_c$ as a subset of C_c, and $\hat{T}_v$ as a subset of T_v. We shall use these subsets in the present discussion, reserving until the next section an explanation of the reasons for their use. Then,

$$[\hat{E}] = \sum_c [\hat{X}_c] - \sum_v [\hat{\bar{X}}_v] - \sum_c [Q_c], \tag{11}$$

where $[\hat{E}] \epsilon \hat{E}$, $[\hat{X}_c] \epsilon \hat{C}_c$, and $[\hat{\bar{X}}_v] \epsilon \hat{T}_v$. We define the set P as we did in Condition 3 above. In the set $\hat{E} \times P$[32] we have the set of all elements $[\hat{E}, P]$, or of excess demands and allowable prices. Let this be the set corresponding to S in the discussion. The set $\hat{E}$ is nonempty even for those $[P]$ which would make $[\bar{X}_v] = [0]$ for all v by virtue of Assumption 18 and the above nonnegativity-of-profits constraint. The set $\hat{E}$ is also convex, because the sum or difference of convex sets is convex. P is nonempty by definition and is convex. Since the product of convex sets is convex, $\hat{E} \times P$ is convex, and is nonempty, so that condition 1 above is met. Since $\hat{E}$ will be shown to be the sum of compact sets, since the sum of compact sets is compact, since P is compact, and since the product of compact sets is compact, condition 2 is likewise met.

The correspondence from $\hat{E} \times P$ to itself, $\Phi([\hat{E}, P])$, we define as the product of two constituent correspondences:

$$\Phi([\hat{E}, P]) = \Phi_1([\hat{E}]) \times \Phi_2([P]) \tag{12}$$

Φ_1 is that set of prices which makes $[P] \cdot [\hat{E}]$ a minimum. Φ_2 is the set of $[\hat{E}]$ which is formed by subtracting the sum of all firms' optimal $[\hat{\bar{X}}_v]$ given $[P]$ and the sum of the $[Q_c]$ from the sum of consumers' optimal demands $[\hat{X}_c]$ given $[P]$. That is, Φ_2 is the set of optimal excess demands for $[P]$. The correspondence Φ then translates any point in $\hat{E} \times P$ into a set $\Phi([\hat{E}, P])$ contained in $\hat{E} \times P$.

It may be shown that both Φ_1 and Φ_2 are upper semicontinuous, and, therefore, that Φ is upper semicontinuous; similarly, it may be shown that $\Phi([\hat{E}, P])$ is nonempty and convex for each $[\hat{E}, P] \epsilon \hat{E} \times P$, since the constituent correspondences possess these qualities. Therefore, conditions 3 and 4 are met, and a fixed point exists, $[\hat{E}^\circ, P^\circ]$, such that $[\hat{E}^\circ, P^\circ] \epsilon \Phi([\hat{E}^\circ, P^\circ])$, or $[P^\circ] \epsilon \Phi_1([\hat{E}^\circ])$ and $[\hat{E}^\circ] \epsilon \Phi_2([P^\circ])$.

So: with excess demand and prices defined as indicated for the modified economy with $\hat{C}_c$, $\hat{T}_v$, $\hat{E}$, and P as relevant sets, there will exist at least

[32] If A and B are sets with elements $[A]$ and $[B]$ respectively, the cartesian product $A \times B$ yields the set of all ordered pairs $([A], [B])$.

one point $[\hat{E}^\circ, P^\circ]$ which will (1) meet the definitions and (2) achieve the optimum payoff for each consuming unit, firm, and the market participant.

4.a.6. The Equivalence of Equilibria in Arrow-Debreu Model 1 and the Abstract Economy

We must now show that the equilibrium defined in 4.a.4. will also meet the conditions for equilibrium in 4.a.3. An equilibrium point in the one model will be an equilibrium in the other, and conversely: the alteration of the consumers' action spaces does not affect the solution.

Assume that an equilibrium for the abstract economy exists; then we may study each condition for equilibrium in Arrow-Debreu Model 1 to see that it will be fulfilled in the equilibrium of the abstract economy.

Condition 1. Profits for each firm will be maximized, by the definition of equilibrium in the modified economy and the profits payoff function specified.

Condition 2. The difference in the definition of the consumer's receipts from profits has been discussed. There, also, an appeal was made to the intuition to demonstrate that the nonnegativity of profits would rule in the equilibrium of Arrow-Debreu Model 1 as well and therefore that the constrained maximum attained by each consumer would be the same in both models, given the definition of equilibrium in the abstract economy and the payoff function specified.

Condition 3. The requirement that equilibrium prices in the abstract economy be components in a vector which is an element of P derives from the definition of the market participant's action space. The conditions that $[P^\circ]$ be nonnegative and contain at least one positive component derives from the same characteristics of the abstract economy as those in the competitive economy: nonsatiation of consumer desires and the possibility of free disposal of factor services and goods.

Condition 4. Condition 2 implies that the consumer will spend all of his wherewithal, as we pointed out in footnote 30, and Condition 2 holds for the abstract economy. Summing over all consumers and recalling that $\Sigma_c \pi_{cv} = 1$, it follows, then, from (11) that

$$[P^\circ] \cdot [E^\circ] = 0 \tag{13}$$

It remains to be shown that an equilibrium in the altered model implies that $[E^\circ] \leqq 0$. Since the vector of prices which has all zero components except for the kth which is a unity component is an element of P, we may multiply $[E^\circ]$ by such a vector. By the definition of a maximum this inner product must be no higher than that of (13); that is,

$$E_k \leqq [P^\circ] \cdot [E^\circ] = 0 \tag{14}$$

which, of course, must hold for all excess demands taken singly. The only way in which the value of excess demands summed for all goods and services can exceed or equal the value of every component of $[E°]$ is if

$$[E°] \leqq 0 \tag{15}$$

Therefore (13) and (15) hold in the abstract economy and they express Condition 4.[33] It follows, therefore, that if the described equilibrium does exist in the abstract economy it will be an equilibrium for Arrow-Debreu Model 1, and conversely. Therefore those conditions which are necessary and sufficient for the existence of an equilibrium in the abstract economy are necessary and sufficient for the existence of equilibrium in Arrow-Debreu Model 1.

4.a.7. An Existence Theorem for a Modified Abstract Economy

Let us summarize the restrictions on our sets and functions of the abstract economy which must hold in order that an equilibrium will exist in the abstract economy:

1. T_v is convex, compact, and nonempty for all v.
2. C_c is convex, compact, and nonempty for all c.
3. P is convex, compact, and nonempty.
4. $M_c([X_c] \epsilon A_c([\bar{a}_c]); [\bar{a}_c])$ is continuous on the set $C_c \times T_v \times P$ and quasi-concave in $[a_c]$ for all c.
5. $[P] \cdot [\bar{X}_v]$ is continuous on the set $C_c \times T_v \times P$ and quasi-concave for all v.
6. $[P] \cdot [E]$ is continuous on the set $C_c \times T_v \times P$ and quasi-concave.
7. $A_c([\bar{a}_c])$ is continuous for all c.
8. $A_c([\bar{a}_c])$ defines a closed set for all c.
9. $A_c([\bar{a}_c])$ for every $[\bar{a}_c]$ is convex for all c.
10. $A_c([\bar{a}_c])$ is nonempty for all c.

We shall now take up each of these requirements in turn and show how Assumptions 1 through 18 will lead to their satisfaction for a modified abstract economy.

1. By Assumption 5, T_v for all v are convex and closed, and obviously nonempty, but no statement of their boundedness has been made. Since the T_v are defined by technological features alone, no inherent reason exists to expect them to be bounded.

But resource limitations on the primary factors do exist, and therefore there must be subsets of the T_v which are bounded in the sense that available resources will prevent higher input and output levels. If this

[33] Condition (15) implies that the "equilibrium space" in R^{m+n} will be confined to that subset of values of $[X_c]$ and $[\bar{X}_v]$ for which, over the economy as a whole $[E] \leqq 0$. Thus, we approach the definitions of $[\hat{X}_c]$ and $[\hat{\bar{X}}_v]$ used in 4.a.5. and not yet derived.

subset, $\hat{T}_v$, is substituted for T_v, it is intuitively clear that no change will be wrought in the equilibrium of the abstract model (and therefore in Model 1), since any equilibrium in the abstract and Model 1 economies will clearly occur in $\hat{T}_v$.

Let us define $\hat{T}_v$ formally as follows:

$$(16) \quad \hat{T}_v = \{[\bar{X}_v] | [\bar{X}_v] \in T_v, \text{ there exist } [\bar{X}_{v'}] \in T_{v'} \text{ and } [X_c] \in C_c \text{ for } v' \neq v \text{ and all } c, \text{ such that } [E] \leqq 0\}$$

That is, for a given firm v, $[\bar{X}_v] \in \hat{T}_v$ if and only if it is possible to find $[\bar{X}_{v'}]$ for all other firms and $[X_c]$ for all consumers which, with $[\bar{X}_v]$ and $[Q]$, will yield nonnegative excess supplies for all goods and factor services. Failing this ability $[\bar{X}_v]$ will be infeasible (if positive excess demand results in one or more factor service markets) or inside the efficiency frontier (if positive excess demand results in one or more goods markets) and therefore not Pareto optimal. For example, suppose firm v controlled the economy. It could then dictate that all v' be assigned $[\bar{X}_{v'}] = [0]$; its own production would be limited only by the available factor services; and it would not stop production if goods could be produced from any non-exhausted resources as long as excess demand existed for such goods (assuming it neglects its monopolistic impacts upon prices).

The meaning of $\hat{T}_v$ may also be developed in this way. In the space $C_1 \times C_2 \times \cdots C_s \times T_1 \times T_2 \times \cdots T_o$, and given $[Q]$, obtain the subset E' of points $[E']$ for which $\Sigma_c[X_c] - [Q] - \Sigma_v[\bar{X}_v] = [0]$. For a given Q_j the total consumption of Y_j may be allocated arbitrarily over all consumers in an infinite number of patterns, and outputs could be allocated among all firms in an infinite number of patterns, to obtain $X_j - \bar{X}_j = Q_j$. With two firms in the economy and two consumers, the hyperplane in R^4 defined by $X_{1j} + X_{2j} - \bar{X}_{1j} - \bar{X}_{2j} = Q_j$ will contain all of the possible patterns, and for s consumers and o firms a hyperplane in R^{s+o} will contain them. Taking into account all goods and services in the economy, we should have $m + n$ such hyperplanes in $R^{(s+o)(m+n)}$. These hyperplanes intersect to form a "linear manifold"[34], M, containing in it the set of all possible consumption vectors among individuals and of production vectors for all firms consistent with net demands for all goods and factor services equalling stocks. However, some of the points on the linear manifold may not be contained in $C_1 \times C_2 \times \cdots C_s \times T_1 \times T_2 \times \cdots T_o$, therefore, only the intersection of this space with M yields the set of possible points we seek.

Lastly, we relax the requirement that $[E] = 0$ to $[E] \leqq 0$. Then the hyperplanes bound half-spaces in $R^{(s+o)(m+n)}$ and the intersection of

[34] A linear manifold is the intersection of hyperplanes.

these half-spaces we denote M'. Then

$$(17)\quad F = \hat{C}_1 \times \hat{C}_2 \times \cdots \hat{C}_s \times \hat{T}_1 \times \hat{T}_2 \times \cdots \hat{T}_o$$
$$= M' \cap C_1 \times C_2 \times \cdots C_s \times T_1 \times T_2 \times \cdots T_o$$

and $\hat{T}_v$ is the projection of F on R^{m+n} containing T_v.[35]

We may now turn to the formal proof that $\hat{T}_v$ is indeed bounded. Suppose $\hat{T}_1$ were not bounded. By definition, we could find sequences k for $[\bar{X}_v]$ and $[X_c]$ such that

$$(18)\qquad \lim_{k\to\infty} |[\bar{X}_1^k]| = \infty,\ [\bar{X}^k] \geqq [X^k] - [Q],\ [\bar{X}_v^k] \in T_v,\ [X_c^k] \in C_c$$

That is, choosing a sequence of vectors for all firms and consumers from their sets T_v and C_c, we could if $\hat{T}_1$ is unbounded, push one or more components of firm 1's vector toward infinity, and stay indefinitely within the condition that excess supplies for all goods and services be nonnegative.

From Assumption 11 it will be recalled that $[L_c]$ was the vector which bounded consumer c's consumption set from below. It must, therefore, follow from (18) that under the conditions postulated,

$$(19)\qquad [\bar{X}^k] \geqq [L] - [Q],$$

where $[L] = \Sigma_c[L_c]$. Since in our presentation (though not in Arrow-Debreu's) $[L] = [0]$ while $[Q] > [0]$, the important implication of this statement is that the sum of firm demands for factor services will be less than the quantities available to the society as $k \to \infty$; this is obviously impossible for finite $[Q_{z_i}]$.

Let u^k be the maximum modulus over the $[\bar{X}_v^k]$,[36] and as k grows large enough $u^k \geqq 1$. Then, since all T_v are convex and contain [0] it follows that

$$(20)\qquad \left(\frac{1}{u^k}\right)[\bar{X}_v^k] + \left(1 - \frac{1}{u^k}\right)[0] \in T_v$$

From (18) and (19),

$$(21)\quad \sum_v \left(\frac{[\bar{X}_v^k]}{u^k}\right) \geqq \frac{[L - Q]}{u^k} \geqq \frac{[-Q]}{u^k},\ \frac{[\bar{X}_v^k]}{u^k} \in T_v \text{ for } k \text{ sufficiently large}$$

and

$$(22)\qquad \lim_{k\to\infty} u^k = \infty, \qquad \left|\frac{[\bar{X}_v^k]}{u^k}\right| \leqq 1 \text{ for all } v \text{ and each } k$$

[35] The set F contains $s + o$ coordinate sets, and a point in it possesses one coordinate in each coordinate set. The function, L, which carries each such point into the kth coordinate (say $\hat{C}_1$) is the projection into the kth coordinate set, and the image of a point by the function L is called the projection of that point.

[36] The modulus or absolute value of a vector, denoted $|[A]|$, is the distance of the point $[A]$ from the origin; i.e., $|[A]| = \sqrt{a_1^2 + a_2^2 + a_3^2 + \cdots}$.

Thus, the u^k will grow without limit as k does, while at each step of the sequence the moduli of $[\bar{X}_v^k]$ divided by u^k will form a compact set with boundaries 0 and 1. That is,

$$0 \leqq \left| \frac{[\bar{X}_v^k]}{u^k} \right| \leqq 1, \qquad \text{for all } v \text{ and each } k \tag{23}$$

Therefore $\left| \frac{[\bar{X}_v^k]}{u^k} \right|$ for each v is an element in an infinite sequence which may not approach a limit. However, a theorem on sequences states that from such an infinite sequence in a compact set it is always possible to extract a subsequence, k_q, which will converge to a limit within the set. Therefore, for each firm, there exists a limit to $\frac{[\bar{X}_v^{k_q}]}{u^{k_q}}$:

$$\lim_{q \to \infty} \frac{[\bar{X}_v^{k_q}]}{u^{k_q}} = [\bar{X}_v^*], \qquad \text{for all } v. \tag{24}$$

From (21) and (22) as well as the closedness of T_v,

$$\sum_v [\bar{X}_v^*] \geqq [0], \text{ where } [\bar{X}_v^*] \in T_v \text{ for all } v \tag{25}$$

since the $[-Q]$ divided by u^{k_q} will tend to [0] as a limit. Also,

$$\sum_v [\bar{X}_v^*] \in T \tag{26}$$

But from Assumption 7, which rules out the Land of Cockaigne, (25) cannot be true when the inequality holds, and, therefore,

$$\sum_v [\bar{X}_v^*] = [0] \tag{27}$$

or, from any firm v':

$$\sum_{v \neq v'} [\bar{X}_v^*] = -[\bar{X}_{v'}^*] \tag{28}$$

Because [0] is contained in every T_v, specifically in $T_{v'}$, the left-hand side of (28) is an element in T, as is $[\bar{X}_{v'}^*]$. Then the right-hand side must belong to both T and $-T$, which by Assumption 8 can only be if $[\bar{X}_{v'}^*] =$ [0], and, since v' can be any firm

$$[\bar{X}_v^*] = [0] \qquad \text{for all } v \tag{29}$$

Therefore, if $\hat{T}_1$ is unbounded and an infinite sequence is formed, it is possible to obtain for every firm a subsequence of vectors in T_v which will converge to [0]; i.e.,

$$\lim_{q \to \infty} \frac{[\bar{X}_v^{k_q}]}{u^{k_q}} = [0], \qquad \text{for all } v \tag{30}$$

But this violates the definition of u^{k_q} which must be the modulus of a vector for at least one v for every one of a number of values of q which approaches infinity; since q is indefinitely large, at least one v would appear in the list of u^{k_q} a number of times which would approach infinity as $q \to \infty$. But since (24) and (30) hold for every v, $u^{k_q} = \|[\bar{X}_v]\|$ can include any one v only a finite number of times. Hence, $\hat{T}_1$ and all $\hat{T}_v$ must be bounded.

Therefore, we substitute $\hat{T}_v$ and T_v and $\hat{T}$ for T in the abstract economy to allow the first restriction to be met without altering relevant spaces in the model.

2. The sets C_c are closed, convex, and obviously nonempty, possessing the first two qualities by Assumption 11. No boundedness in the upper direction is assumed to exist, however. Once more, as in the case of the T_v, we may define the attainable subset $\hat{C}_c$ and show that it is bounded. We define $\hat{C}_c$

$$(31) \quad \hat{C}_c = \{[X_c] | [X_c] \in C_c, \text{ there exist } [X_{c'}] \in C_{c'}, \text{ for all } c' \neq c \text{ and } [\bar{X}_v] \in T_v \text{ for all } v \text{ such that } [E] \leqq [0]\}$$

We have already indicated that $\hat{C}_c$ may be interpreted in the same manner as we interpreted $\hat{T}_v$ from the analogous definition in (16). $\hat{C}_c$ is also the projection of F on R^{m+n} containing C_c.

Let $[X_c] \in \hat{C}_c$. Then from (31) and the definition of $[L_c]$,

$$(32) \qquad [L_c] \leqq [X_c] \leqq [\bar{X}] - \sum_{c' \neq c} [X_{c'}] + [Q], \ [X_{c'}] \in C_{c'}, \ [\bar{X}] \in T$$

But $[X_{c'}] \geqq [L_{c'}]$ by Assumption 11, and $[\bar{X}_v] \in \hat{T}_v$ for all v since (31) and (16) so define $\hat{T}_v$. So

$$(33) \quad [L_c] \leqq [X_c] \leqq \sum_v [\bar{X}_v] - \sum_{c' \neq c} [L_{c'}] + [Q], \ [\bar{X}_v] \in \hat{T}_v \text{ for all } v.$$

Since the right-hand side of (33) is bounded it follows immediately that the set $\hat{C}_c \supset [X_c]$ is bounded. Therefore, we must have a subset of C_c, in which all $[X_c^\circ]$ must be contained, which is compact and the restrictions on C_c are met by proxy.

Paranthetically, it would now be possible to soften Assumption 14 to *Assumption 14'*: for every consuming unit and for every vector in $\hat{C}_c$ there is at least one preferred vector. Thus, even though we may accept the possibility of consumer satiation for all good and services somewhere in C_c, we need only the guarantee that resource limitations will never allow it to be reached for any consumer under the relevant resource restrictions.

Further, there exists some positive real number K greater than or equal to the absolute values of all components of all vectors in $\hat{C}_c$ and $\hat{T}_v$

which will define a cube in R^{m+n} containing all $\hat{C}_c$ and all $\hat{T}_v$ in its interior. We define $\tilde{C}_c$ as the intersection of $\hat{C}_c$ and this cube, and $\tilde{T}_v$ as the intersection of $\hat{T}_v$ and this cube. A new abstract economy—the modified abstract economy—is now created with $\tilde{C}_c$ substituted for C_c and $\tilde{T}_v$ substituted for T_v. All $\tilde{C}_c$ and $\tilde{T}_v$ will be convex, compact, and nonempty.

3. P is a linear set which includes its end points and so is convex and compact, and is obviously nonempty. Therefore the restriction upon it is met.

4. By Assumptions 13 and 15 the functions $M_c([\bar{a}_c]; [a_c])$ are continuous and quasi-concavity is implied by the latter assumption.

5. The function $[P] \cdot [\bar{X}_v]$ is linear and continuous. Since all linear functions are quasi-concave, this condition is met.

6. The function $[P] \cdot [E]$ is linear and continuous, and therefore quasi-concave.

7. Let $\tilde{A}_c([\bar{a}_c])$ correspond to $A_c([\bar{a}_c])$ in the modified abstract economy. We show that this correspondence is continuous, where continuity is defined in this wise: $\tilde{A}_c([\bar{a}_c])$ is said to be continuous at $[\bar{a}_c^*]$ if for every $[X_c^*] \in \tilde{A}_c([\bar{a}_c^*])$ and every sequence $\{\bar{a}_c^q\}$ converging to $[\bar{a}_c^*]$ there is a sequence $\{X_c^q\}$ converging to $[X_c^*]$ such that $[X_c^q] \in \tilde{A}_c([\bar{a}_c^q])$ for all q. This definition will be recognized as a requirement that both upper and lower semicontinuity hold at $[\bar{a}_c^*]$ when $F \times P$ is a compact set.

$\tilde{A}_c([\bar{a}_c])$ is a subset of $F \times P$ which, being the product of compact spaces, is compact. It is bounded from above by the linear inequality $[P] \cdot [X_c] \leqq [P] \cdot [Q_c] + \Sigma_v \max{[0, \pi_{cv}[P] \cdot [\bar{X}_v]]}$, which it obviously owns. Therefore, $\tilde{A}_c([\bar{a}_c])$ is closed on $F \times P$ and meets all the necessary and sufficient conditions for upper semicontinuity on $\bar{F}_c \times P$, where $\bar{F}_c$ is

$$\prod_{c \neq c'} \hat{C}_{c'} \times \prod_{v} \hat{T}_v .$$

The proof of lower semi-continuity is more complicated. It will be recalled that for a point in $\bar{F}_c \times P$, $[\bar{a}_c^*]$, a point in its image-set $[X_c^*] \in A_c([\bar{a}_c^*])$, and a sequence $\{\bar{a}_c^q\} \rightarrow [\bar{a}_c^*]$, it is necessary to prove there exists a sequence $\{X_c^q\} \in \tilde{A}_c([\bar{a}_c^q]) \rightarrow [X_c^*]$.

First, assume that $[X_c^*]$ is an interior point of $\tilde{A}_c([\bar{a}_c^*])$, so that, if $r_c = [P] \cdot [Q_c] + \Sigma_v \max{[0, \pi_{cv}[P] \cdot [\bar{X}_v]]}$, then $[P^*] \cdot [X_c^*] > r_c^*$. Then, because of the convexity of $\hat{C}_c$, for a q sufficiently large, say q' or larger, $[P^q] \cdot [X_c^*] < r_c^q$; that is, as $[\bar{a}_c^q]$ approaches arbitrarily close to $[\bar{a}_c^*]$, the value of consumption at $[\bar{a}_c^*]$ chosen as a terminal point at prices relevant to $[\bar{a}_c^q]$ must be less than r_c^*. Then, for all $q \leqq q'$, we may choose for the sequence $[X_c^q]$ arbitrary values such that $[X_c^q] \in \tilde{A}_c([\bar{a}_c^q])$, and, for all $q > q'$ the same value $[X_c^*]$ may be chosen. This yields a sequence $[X_c^q] \in \tilde{A}_c([\bar{a}_c^q]) \rightarrow [X_c^*]$.

Second, assume that $[X_c^*]$ is a boundary point of $\tilde{A}_c([\bar{a}_c^*])$, so that $[P^*] \cdot [X_c^*] = r_c^*$. Now, choose an arbitrary point $[X_c'] \in \tilde{A}_c([\bar{a}_c])$ such that $[P^*] \cdot [X_c'] < r_c^*$, so that $[X_c']$ is an interior point of $\tilde{A}_c([\bar{a}_c^*])$. Then for sufficiently large $q > q'$ it will be interior to $\tilde{A}_c([\bar{a}_c^q])$, $[P^q] \cdot [X_c'] < r_c^q$, while, at the same time, $[P^q] \cdot [X_c'] < [P^q] \cdot [X_c^*]$. Visualize a "budget line" relevant to $[P^q]$: then, "beneath" it lies the point $[X_c^*]$ and "beneath" $[X_c^*]$ lies $[X_c']$.

Now, along the budget line $[P^q] \cdot [B_c^q] = r_c^q$ is the set B_c^q which just exhausts the consumer's wherewithal at $[P^q]$. Also, let L be the straight line going through $[X_c']$ and $[X_c^*]$, and let $[L_q]$ be its intersection with $[P^q] \cdot [B_c^q] = r_c^q$. Then, as q grows larger, the budget line moves "downward" and $[L_q] \rightarrow [X_q^*]$. Therefore, the sequence can be formed as follows. For $q \leqq q'$, any $[X_c^q] \in \tilde{A}_c([\bar{a}_c^q])$ may be chosen; if $q > q'$ and $[B_c^q] \in \hat{C}_c$, then $[X_c^q]$ is taken to be $[B_c^q]$; if $q > q'$ but $[B_c^q] \notin \hat{C}_c$, then $[X_c^q]$ is taken to be $[X_c^*]$. This sequence $[X_c^q] \in \tilde{A}_c([\bar{a}_c^q]) \rightarrow [X_c^*]$ and meets the conditions required.

The correspondence is therefore continuous at $[\bar{a}_c^*]$. This point has an element of arbitrariness about it: implicitly it was assumed that $\tilde{A}_c([\bar{a}_c^*])$ was not empty. Since $\hat{C}_c$ is not empty, this set can be empty only if at $[P^*]$ the consumer's wherewithal is too small to purchase any $[X_c] \in \hat{C}_c$. Now, by Assumption 16 and Condition 3 we assure that $r_c^* > 0$, and by Assumption 18 that there will be at least one $[X_c] \in \tilde{A}_c([\bar{a}_c])$ for all $[\bar{a}_c] \in \bar{F}_c \times P$. Therefore, we may choose $[\bar{a}_c^*]$ arbitrarily and $\tilde{A}_c([\bar{a}_c])$ will be continuous on $\bar{F}_c \times P$.

Therefore, one critical point in the proof of existence of equilibrium is the guarantee of the continuity of the demand and supply functions of the consumer; more particularly, it is necessary to assure that (1) he will always be capable of obtaining wherewithal whatever the prices he faces, and (2) given this wherewithal that he will be able to buy some basket of goods with it. These requisites are the *raison d'être* of Assumptions 16 (insofar as it requires positive stocks of all goods and factors for all consumers) and 18.

8. We have shown $\tilde{A}_c([\bar{a}_c])$ to be compact in $F \times P$, which establishes it as closed by definition.

9. We must show that $\tilde{A}_c([\bar{a}_c])$ is convex; but since it is defined by a linear inequality in $[X_c]$, it is convex.

10. We may prove formally that no set $\tilde{A}_c([\bar{a}_c])$ is empty. By Assumption 18 there exits $[X_c']$, such that $[X_c'] \leqq [Q_c]$; we may set all $[\bar{X}_v] = [0]$ to get from (11)

$$\sum_c [X_c'] - [Q] \leqq [0]$$

which implies that $[X_c'] \in \hat{C}_c$ and of the cube whose interior contains $\hat{C}_c$. Given Assumption 18 and the discussion of Condition 2 in Section 4.a.6. $[X_c'] \in A_c([\bar{a}_c])$, they must be contained in the intersection of the cube and the $A_c([\bar{a}_c])$, or $\tilde{A}_c([\bar{a}_c])$.

Since $[X_c']$ for all c are vectors which can be enjoyed by each consumer, their presence guarantees that $\tilde{A}_c([\bar{a}_c])$ will not be empty.

Having satisfied all the conditions for an equilibrium, we may assert that an equilibrium will always exist in the *modified abstract economy*. If we can show that any equilibrium in the *modified* abstract economy will also be an equilibrium in the *abstract* economy, since we have already shown an equilibrium in the abstract economy to be an equilibrium in the Arrow-Debreu Model 1, we will have proved what we set out to prove.

4.a.8. The Establishment of Equilibrium in the Modified Abstract Economy as Equilibrium in the Abstract Economy

The existence of the equilibrium vector $[X_c^\circ, \bar{X}_v^\circ, P^\circ]$ for the modified abstract economy has been proved. If we may show that this point will meet Conditions 1 through 4 it will follow that the equilibrium of the modified abstract economy is also an equilibrium for the abstract economy.

Condition 1. $[\bar{X}_v^\circ]$ is an interior point in the cube. Suppose for some $[\bar{X}_v'] \in T_v$ that $[P^\circ] \cdot [\bar{X}_v'] > [P^\circ] \cdot [\bar{X}_v^\circ]$, $[\bar{X}_v^\circ] \in \tilde{T}_v$. Then, for $0 < \lambda < 1$, $[P^\circ] \cdot [\lambda \bar{X}_v' + (1 - \lambda)\bar{X}_v^\circ] > [P^\circ] \cdot [\bar{X}_v^\circ]$. But if λ is small enough the convex combination belongs to $\tilde{T}_v$ and therefore contradicts the definition of $[\bar{X}_v^\circ]$ for $\tilde{T}_v$. Therefore, $[\bar{X}_v^\circ] \in \tilde{T}_v$ must maximize $[P^\circ] \cdot [\bar{X}_v]$ for all $[\bar{X}_v] \in T_v$.

Condition 2. In similar fashion $[X_c^\circ]$ is an interior point of the cube, and $[X_c^\circ] \in \tilde{C}_c$ must maximize $M_c([X_c])$ for all $[X_c] \in A_c([\bar{a}_c])$. For suppose there existed $[X_c'] \in A_c([\bar{a}_c])$ such that $M_c([X_c']) > M_c([X_c^\circ])$. Then, for $0 < t < 1$, $M_c([\lambda X_c' + (1 - \lambda)X_c^\circ]) > M_c([X_c^\circ])$. But since it is possible to get arbitrarily close to $[X_c']$, the combination belongs to the cube containing $\tilde{C}_c$ in its interior and to $A_c([\bar{a}_c^\circ])$, it must belong to their intersection $\tilde{A}_c([\bar{a}_c])$, which contradicts the definition of $[X_c^\circ]$. Therefore, $[X_c^\circ]$ must maximize $M_c([X_c])$ over $A_c([\bar{a}_c])$ as well as $\tilde{A}_c([\bar{a}_c])$.

Condition 3. Since the domain of $[P]$ is unchanged in the modified abstract economy from the abstract economy or the original economy, $[P^\circ]$ for the modified abstract economy is an element of P.

Condition 4. $[0] \in \tilde{T}_v$ by the definition of the cube for all v so that

$$(34) \qquad \sum_v \max\,[0, \pi_{cv}[P^\circ] \cdot [\bar{X}_v^\circ]] = \sum_v \pi_{cv}[P^\circ] \cdot [\bar{X}_v^\circ]$$

and from the definition of $\tilde{A}_c([\bar{a}_c])$,

$$(35) \qquad [P^\circ] \cdot [X^\circ] \leqq [P^\circ] \cdot [Q_c] + \sum_v \pi_{cv}[P^\circ] \cdot [\bar{X}_v^\circ]$$

For all c

$$(36) \qquad [P^\circ] \cdot [X^\circ] \leqq [P^\circ] \cdot [Q] + [P^\circ] \cdot [\bar{X}^\circ]$$

or

(37) $$[P°] \cdot [E°] \leqq 0$$

This leads to the conclusion, as in Section 4.a.6., that

(38) $$[E°] \leqq [0]$$

when

(39) $$[P°] \cdot [E°] = 0$$

Thus our proof that the equilibrium in the modified abstract economy is in the interior of the cube establishes that equilibrium in this economy is an equilibrium in the abstract economy; and from Section 4.a.6 we assert as proved:

THEOREM 1: *for any economic system satisfying Assumptions 1 through 18, an equilibrium of the type defined by Conditions 1 through 4 will always exist.*

4.b. The Arrow-Debreu Model 2

Arrow and Debreu have succeeded in softening one of the most objectionable of their assumptions in Model 1: Assumption 18 which requires each consuming unit to be able to supply some of every good and factor service. As pointed out above this was done to assure some positive potential wherewithal which, with the explicit assumption of sufficiently small consumption vectors, would obviate the possibility of null sets in $\tilde{A}_c([\bar{a}_c])$ for some $[P]$ and $[\bar{X}_v]$. The innovations of Model 2 are two in number: (1) the assumption that each consumer has endowments of one or more primary resources whose services always have a positive marginal product in (2) the production of goods for which no consumer reaches the point of satiation. These assumptions assure the payment of a potential wherewithal which is positive to each household and, with the assumption that sufficiently small consumption vectors exist, the avoidance of the possibility of null sets in $\tilde{A}_c([\bar{a}_c])$.

4.b.1. Changes in and Additions to the Assumptions of Model 1

The formal introduction of these assumptions follows. For Assumption 18 we substitute:

Assumption 18′. For each consuming unit c there exists a vector of endowments $[Q_c] \geqq 0$: be it noted that in this model and in Model 3 to follow the consumer is no longer assumed to hold positive amounts of all goods and services. A related change in postulational basis of the model occurs in no longer requiring the existence of at least one vector in which the consumer is a net supplier of *all* goods and factor services: we require that vectors $[X_c]$ exist for which $[Q_c] - [X_c] \geqq 0$, and that, for at least one of this set of vectors, the component X_{ci} for at least one i be less than the corresponding Q_{ci}. The consumer, therefore, is capable of supplying at least one factor service to the market—no longer need he have this capability for all z_i and Y_j. This relaxation of Assumption 18 is a necessary but not a sufficient condition for the ability of the consumer to obtain wherewithal from the market for all allowable price vectors, since it is still possible that the price (or prices) of the factor service (or services) he owns may be zero in equilibrium.

Assumption 19. There exist $[X_c]$ and $[\bar{X}_v]$ such that it is possible that $[X] < [\bar{X}] + [Q]$. That is, it is possible, given only the technology, consumer endowments, and the psychologies of consumers, to obtain excess supplies for all goods and services. Paradoxically, this assumption is used to assure a positive price for productive factor services in the neighborhood of equilibrium and, thereby, continuity of demand functions at equilibrium, just as $\Sigma_c[X_c'] < [Q]$ was used in discussing requirement 10 in Section 4.a.7.

Assumption 20. From the set of goods Y_j, there exists a subset D (desired) of goods in the enjoyment of which no consumer is ever satiated. That is, for every consumer let $[X_c] \in C_c$, and let $[V^k]$ be a vector with zeros as components except the kth which equals unity. Then $[X_c] + \lambda[V^k]$, $\lambda > 0$, is a vector equivalent to $[X_c]$ plus λ more of good $Y_k \in D$. We require that

$$(40) \qquad M_c([X_c] + \lambda[V^k]) > M_c([X_c]) \qquad \text{for all } Y_k \in D$$

by way of definition of the set D which is further assumed to be nonempty.

Assumption 21. For the set of factor services, z_i, we require that where they appear in the vectors of T_v they appear as inputs, so that they are nonproducible. Also, for T, it must be possible to increase the output of one good or more from set D without reducing any other output or increasing any input but that of a single z_i. That is, for the case of continuous production functions which are differentiable for the society as a whole, if we had them, the marginal productivity of each factor service must be positive regardless of the amount of it used in the production of a desired good of set D. Note that if factor services are defined as consumable goods in Walrasian fashion, and if they are included in D, these requirements are met. We may see even more clearly now, however, why Walras' inclusion of them in the consumer preference functions was not sufficient to guarantee that their prices would be positive in equilibrium. This would not interfere with the existence of equilibrium, however, if the excess supply of factor services at an arbitrarily small positive price remained nonnegative at a zero price. Only if at a zero price supply fell below demand (say, consumers desired to supply none) would the market situation contradict the need for nonnegative excess supplies in equilibrium. The Walrasian demand for leisure, capital services, and land services, if included in D, will prevent this.

We assume the set z_i is nonempty. We have assumed it includes all factor services—an assumption which is not necessary.

4.b.2. The Conditions for an Equilibrium and Manner of Procedure

The conditions for an equilibrium in Model 2 are Conditions 1 through 4 of Section 4.a.3. If an equilibrium for Model 2 does exist, however, it is intuitively clear that Condition 3 will hold in a more restricted form. Under present assumptions, each consumer has some of a subset of goods, z_i, which are always productive, taken singly, in nonsatiating goods; therefore, all elements in P which contain zeros for any or all of these factor services are not allowable in equilibrium. The set P of Model 1 is therefore contracted in Model 2 to the subset P^e, defined as follows. Let e be a value

$$0 < e \leqq \frac{1}{2m} \tag{41}$$

where m is the number of factors services meeting the definition of Assumption 21 (all factor services in the present formulation). For any specified value of e in (41), we define

$$P^e = \{[P] | [P] \in P,\ P_i \geqq e \text{ for all } i\} \tag{42}$$

Then, from Assumption 18′, it will always be possible to select a vector $[X'_c]$ for each consuming unit such that components $X_{cj} \leqq Q_{cj}$ and $X_{ci} \leqq Q_{ci}$, while $X_{ci} < Q_{ci}$ for at least one i. Then, for any $[P] \in P^e$

$$[P] \cdot [Q_c - X'_c] \geqq \sum_i P_i(Q_{ci} - X'_{ci}) > 0 \tag{43}$$

and, thus, positive wherewithal will always be available. By an analysis similar to 7 of 4.a.7. above, it is possible to show that the correspondence $\tilde{A}'([\bar{a}_c])$ (defined below) is continuous on the relevant set.

The procedure of proving the existence of an equilibrium solution is similar to that used for the same purpose in Model 1:

1. The definition of the equilibrium of a competitive economy is accepted in Conditions 1 through 4, the same abstract economy defined in Section 4.a.4. is derived, and the equivalence of it to the competitive economy demonstrated in Section 4.a.6. is retained in the proof.

2. The abstract is replaced by a contracted abstract economy, which differs from the abstract economy of Model 1 in that the market participant must restrict his choices of strategy to the subset P^e of P.

3. For all e meeting condition (41) it is shown that the contracted abstract economy has at least one equilibrium by modifying that economy

to bound consumers' and firms' action spaces, in the manner of Section 4.a.7., and demonstrating the equivalence of equilibrium solutions for each e in this modification and for the contracted abstract economy.

4. Lastly, it is shown that for at least one value of e the equilibrium solution of the contracted abstract economy satisfies the abstract economy.

4.b.3. Restrictions Upon Equilibrium Values Inherent in the Conditions of Equilibrium

In the proof of the first theorem it was possible to state that if an equilibrium did exist for the abstract economy, then

$$[X_c^\circ] \in C_c,\ [\bar{X}_v^\circ] \in T_v,\ [P^\circ] \in P,\ [E^\circ] \leqq [0] \tag{44}$$

The last result hinged upon our ability to assert that the unit vectors $[P] = [0, 0, 0, \ldots 0, 1, 0, \ldots 0]$ were elements of the market participant's action spaces P. However, these $[P] \notin P^e$, since all P_i in all $[P] \in P^e$ must be positive. The definition of the space within which $[E^\circ]$ must lie for the contracted abstract economy, and therefore the hypercube which will contain all effective action spaces, becomes a more complex operation. The equivalents of the unit vectors in the new model will be, for goods Y_j, vectors in which all factor services are priced at e, all other goods at 0, and Y_j at $1 - \Sigma_i P_i$; and, the equivalents of the unit vectors for goods z_i will be vectors in which all $P_j = 0$, all other $P_i = e$, and the price of the factor service in question is $1 - \Sigma_{i'} P'_i,\ i \neq i'$.

We must perform the same types of preliminary operations upon the contracted abstract economy to obtain compact effective action spaces for consumers and firms. If an equilibrium exists, then $[X_v^\circ] \in A_c([\bar{a}_c^\circ])$, so

$$[P^\circ] \cdot [X_c^\circ] \leqq [P^\circ] \cdot [Q_c] + \sum_v \pi_{cv}[P^\circ] \cdot [\bar{X}_v^\circ] \tag{45}$$

and by previous reasoning

$$[P^\circ] \cdot [E^\circ] \leqq 0 \tag{46}$$

Since (46) is a maximum for all $[P] \in P^e$, it follows that

$$[P] \cdot [E^\circ] \leqq [P^\circ] \cdot [E^\circ] \leqq 0, \qquad \text{for all } [P] \in P^e \tag{47}$$

Now, select one good or factor service k'. Then, from (47),

$$P_{k'}E_{k'}^\circ \leqq \sum_{k \neq k'} -P_k E_k^\circ \qquad \text{for any } k' \tag{48}$$

when k equals all i and j not k'.

Whenever k' denotes a factor service z_i, by Assumption 21 it follows (since $\Sigma_v \bar{X}_{vi} \leqq 0$)

$$(49) \qquad \sum_c X^\circ_{ci} - \sum_v \bar{X}^\circ_{vi} \geqq \sum_c X^\circ_{ci} \geqq \sum_c L_{ci}, \qquad i = 1, \ldots, m$$

For a given k', define

(50)
1. $P_i = e,\ i = 1, \ldots, m$, when $k' \neq i$
2. $P_j = 0$, when $k' \neq j$
3. when k' is an i, $P_{k'} = 1 - \sum_{k \neq k'} P_k = 1 - (m-1)e$
4. when k' is a Y_j, $P_k = 1 - \sum_{k \neq k'} P_k = 1 - me$

Then, from (48) and (49),

(51)
1. if $k' \in z_i$, $[1 - (m-1)e]\, E^\circ_k \leqq e \sum_{i \neq k'} (Q_i - L_i)$
2. if $k' \in Y_j$, $[1 - me] E^\circ_k \leqq e \sum_i (Q_i - L_i)$

Since $(1 - me) > 0$ and $[1 - (m-1)e] > 0$, by the definition of e, and

$$(52) \qquad \frac{e}{1 - (m-1)e} < \frac{e}{1 - me}$$

For any $k' \in z_i$ or $k' \in Y_j$, from Assumption 18′

$$(53) \qquad Q_{k'} - L_{k'} \geqq 0$$

Dividing (72-1) by $[1 - (m-1)e]$, we obtain

$$(54) \qquad E^\circ_k \leqq \frac{e}{[1 - (m-1)e]} \sum_{i = k'} (Q_i - L_i), \qquad k' \in z_i$$

and from (52), since $(Q_{k'} - L_{k'}) \geqq 0$,

$$(55) \quad E^\circ_{k'} \leqq \frac{e}{1 - (m-1)e} \sum_{i \neq k'} (Q_i - L_i) < \frac{e}{1 - me} \sum_i (Q_i - L_i),\ k' \in z_i$$

A similar result holds if (51-2) is divided through by $(1 - me)$, i.e.,

$$(56) \quad E^\circ_{k'} \leqq \frac{e}{1 - (m-1)e} \sum_i (Q_i - L_i) < \frac{e}{1 - me} \sum_i (Q_i - L_i), \qquad k' \in Y_j$$

By the definition of e

(57) $$\frac{e}{1 - me} \leqq \frac{1}{m}$$

So

(58) $$E^{\circ}_{k'} \leqq \frac{1}{m} \sum_i (Q_i - L_i) \qquad k' \in Y_j \text{ or } z_i$$

That is, in equilibrium, the excess demand for any good or service can be no more than $\frac{1}{m}$th of the sum of the excesses of factor service endowments over the lower bounds on such services.

Define

(59) $$[Q'] = \left[Q + \frac{1}{m} \sum_i (Q_i - L_i) \right]$$

Then

(60) $$[X^{\circ}] - [\bar{X}^{\circ}] - [Q'] \leqq [0]$$

or

(61) $$[X^{\circ}] - [\bar{X}^{\circ}] \leqq [Q']$$

Therefore, we may assert that if an equilibrium exists for the contracted abstract economy it will lie within the region defined by

(62) $$[X^{\circ}] \in C_c,\ [\bar{X}^{\circ}] \in T_v,\ [P^{\circ}] \in P^e,\ [X^{\circ} - \bar{X}^{\circ}] \leqq [Q']$$

which should be compared with (44). No significance should be attached to the region in which $[X^{\circ} - \bar{X}^{\circ}]$ is found: these results are merely directed at obtaining the hypercube which will contain the compact action spaces.

4.b.4. Modifying the Economy to Obtain Compact Action Spaces

Define

1. $\hat{C}'_c = \{[X_c] | [X_c] \in C_c$, and there exist $[X_{c^*}] \in C_{c^*}$ for all $c^* \neq c$, $[\bar{X}_v] \in T_v$ for all v such that $[X - \bar{X}] \leqq [Q']\}$
2. $\hat{T}'_v = \{[\bar{X}_v] | [\bar{X}_v] \in T_v$, and there exist $[X_c] \in C_c$ for all c and $[\bar{X}_{v^*}] \in T_{v^*}$ for all $v^* \neq v$ such that $[X - \bar{X}] \leqq [Q']\}$

A cube is obtained to contain all $\hat{C}'_c$ and $\hat{T}'_v$ in its interior, and $\tilde{C}'_c$ and $\tilde{T}'_v$ are the intersections of the cube with $\hat{C}'_c$ and $\hat{T}'_v$.

It may then be proved by the method used in Model 1's treatment that the 10 requirements of Section 4.a.7. are fulfilled and, therefore, that the modified contracted abstract economy has an equilibrium $[X_c^\circ, \bar{X}_v^\circ, P^\circ]$ for each e.

4.b.5. Establishing that an Equilibrium in the Modified Contracted Abstract Economy is an Equilibrium for the Contracted Abstract Economy

The proof follows step-by-step that of 4.a.8.

4.b.6. Establishing the Conditions on e to Make an Equilibrium in the Contracted Abstract Economy Also an Equilibrium for Model 2

We may show that $[X_c^\circ, \bar{X}_v^\circ, P^\circ]$ is an equilibrium for Model 2 if, for the moment, we assume that

$$P_i^\circ > e, \qquad i = 1, \ldots, m \tag{63}$$

for some e meeting the conditions of (41). For let $[P] \epsilon P$, and $0 < \lambda \leqq 1$, and suppose $[P] \cdot [E^\circ] > [P^\circ] \cdot [E^\circ]$. Then, if $[P'] = \lambda[P] + (1 - \lambda)[P^\circ]$, it must also hold that $[P'] \cdot [E^\circ] > [P^\circ] \cdot [E^\circ]$. But, by the definition of P^e and its convexity, λ may be chosen arbitrarily small such that $[P'] \epsilon P^e$, and a contradiction of the definition of $[P^\circ]$ exists. Therefore, if (63) exists for some e, it follows that $[P^\circ]$ maximizes $[P] \cdot [E^\circ]$ for all $[P] \epsilon P$, not only the subset P^e. When this is added to Section 4.a.5., a proof exists that an equilibrium in the contracted abstract economy is also an equilibrium in the abstract economy—if, in fact, (63) holds for an e.

But will $[X_c^\circ, \bar{X}_v^\circ, P^\circ]$ yield P_i values uniformly greater than some e, as *assumed*? To prove that it will, we assume initially that the contrary is true, and that for any and every value of $e > 0$

$$P_i^\circ = e \quad \text{for at least one } i = 1, \ldots, m \tag{64}$$

For all e, $[P^\circ] \epsilon P$, $[X_c^\circ]$ and $[\bar{X}_v^\circ]$ are in the interior of the hypercube, and all of these sets are compact. Therefore, we may choose a converging sequence $\{e^q\}$ for e, for which $[X_c^{\circ q}, \bar{X}_v^{\circ q}, P^{\circ q}]$ is the corresponding equilibrium for the relevant abstract economy. The limits will be

$$\lim_{q \to \infty} e^q = 0, \quad \lim_{q \to \infty} [X_c^\circ] = [X_c^*], \quad \lim_{q \to \infty} [\bar{X}_v^{\circ q}] = [\bar{X}_v^*], \quad \lim_{q \to \infty} [P^{\circ q}] = [P^*] \tag{65}$$

These limits, by virtue of the closed nature of the sets, will meet the conditions

$$[X_c^*] \epsilon C_c, \; [\bar{X}_v^*] \epsilon T_v, \; [P^*] \epsilon P \tag{66}$$

For every value of an infinitely great q, by (64) at least one $P_i^q = e^q$. Since at least one i will appear an infinite number of times in this infinite number of equalities (say that $i = 1$), it follows that $P_{z_1}^* = 0$. Intuitively, by virtue of Assumptions 18′ through 21, it is clear that this cannot hold in equilibrium, but let us prove the point formally.

Condition 2 implies, at every equilibrium corresponding to q, that

$$[P^{\circ q}] \cdot [E^{\circ q}] = 0 \tag{67}$$

so, in the limit

$$[P^*] \cdot [E^*] = 0 \tag{68}$$

Also, the equilibrium conditions imply, for any given $[\bar{X}_v]$, that

$$[P^{\circ q}] \cdot [\bar{X}_v^{\circ}] \geqq [P^{\circ q}] \cdot [\bar{X}_v], \qquad [\bar{X}_v] \in T_v \tag{69}$$

and, in the limit,

$$[P^*] \cdot [\bar{X}_v^*] \geqq [P^*] \cdot [\bar{X}_v] \tag{70}$$

Choose any vector of C_c such that the individual involved prefers that vector to the limiting equilibrium consumption vector of the sequence:

$$M_c([X_c]) > M_c([X^*]), \qquad [X_c] \in C_c \tag{71}$$

For q sufficiently large

$$M_c([X_c]) > M_c([X_c^{\circ q}]) \tag{72}$$

Therefore

$$[X_c] \notin A_c([\bar{a}_c^q]) \tag{73}$$

and

$$[P^{\circ q}] \cdot [X_c] > [P^{\circ q}] \cdot [X_c^{\circ q}] \tag{74}$$

In the limit

$$[P^*] \cdot [X_c] > [P^*] \cdot [X_c^*] \tag{75}$$

By the definition of the set z_i, there exists a vector in T, $[\bar{X}']$, such that

$$\bar{X}'_i \geqq \bar{X}^*_i,\ i \neq 1,\ \bar{X}'_j \geqq \bar{X}^*_j, \quad \text{and } \bar{X}'_j > \bar{X}^*_j \text{ for some } j \in D \tag{76}$$

Taking the economy's technology as a whole, there exists by definition a set of output vectors such that absorptions of all factor services but one (which meets the condition of (64)) are no more than such absorptions by the vector which is limiting in the sequence, while the outputs of at least one *desired* good is greater than in the latter.

From (70) it must be true that

$$[P^*] \cdot [\bar{X}'] \leqq [P^*] \cdot [\bar{X}^*] \tag{77}$$

since this holds for each firm's vectors taken separately. Then,

(78) $$[P^*] \cdot [\bar{X}' - \bar{X}^*] = \sum_h P_h^*(\bar{X}_h' - \bar{X}_h^*), \qquad h = i, j$$

But since $P_{z_1}^* = 0$,

(79) $$\sum_h P_h^*(\bar{X}_h' - \bar{X}_h^*) = \sum_{h \neq z_1} P_h^*(\bar{X}_h' - \bar{X}_h^*)$$

Also

(80) $$\sum_{h = z_1} P_h^*(\bar{X}_h' - \bar{X}_h^*) \geqq P_{h'}^*(\bar{X}_{h'}' - \bar{X}_{h'}^*), \qquad h' \epsilon D$$

By the definition of D

(81) $$\bar{X}_{h'}' - \bar{X}_{h'}^* > 0$$

and so it follows that

(82) $$P_{h'}^* = 0 \text{ for at least one } h' \epsilon D$$

Thus, a $P_i^* = 0$ implies at least one desired good will be priced at zero.

We are therefore involved in an inconsistency. It should be impossible for a good to bear a zero price if consumers' desires for it are never satiated and if it absorbs at least one resource service whose marginal product in producing it is always positive. Let us proceed to prove the inconsistency formally.

For any consumer, let $[X_c] \epsilon C_c$, and $[X_c'] = \lambda[X_c] + (1 - \lambda)[X_c^*]$, $0 < \lambda \leqq 1$. From Assumption 20 there exists

(83) $$\lambda' > 0, M_c([X_c^*] + \lambda'[V^{h'}]) > M_c([X_c^*]), \qquad h' \epsilon D$$

Since $[X_c'] + \lambda'[V^{h'}] \rightarrow [X_c^*] + \lambda'[V^{h'}]$ as $\lambda \rightarrow 0$, for λ sufficiently small

(84) $$M_c([X_c'] + \lambda'[V^{h'}]) > M_c([X_c^*])$$

Then by (75),

(85) $$[P^*] \cdot [X_c' + \lambda' V^{h'}] \geqq [P^*] \cdot [X_c^*]$$

But, from (82) there is at least one good for which

(86) $$[P^*] \cdot [V^{h'}]\lambda' = \lambda' P_{h'}^* = 0 \qquad h' \epsilon D$$

Since

(87) $$[P^*] \cdot [X_c' + \lambda' V^{h'}] = \lambda[P^*] \cdot [X_c] + (1 - \lambda)[P^*] \cdot [X_c^*] + [P^*] \cdot [V^{h'}]\lambda'$$

it follows that

(88) $$[P^*] \cdot [X_c] \geqq [P^*] \cdot [X_c^*]$$

or

(89) $$[X_c^*] \text{ minimizes } [P^*] \cdot [X_c] \text{ over } C_c$$

And, for all consumers,

(90) $$[X^*] \text{ minimizes } [P^*] \cdot [X] \text{ over } C$$

Lastly, choose $[X]$ from C and $[\bar{X}]$ from T such that, by Assumption 19,

(91) $$[X] < [\bar{X}] + [Q]$$

By (90),

(92) $$[P^*] \cdot [\bar{X} + Q] > [P^*] \cdot [X] \geqq [P^*] \cdot [X^*]$$

or

(93) $$[P^*] \cdot [\bar{X}] > [P^*] \cdot [X^* - Q]$$

From (68),

(94) $$[P^*] \cdot [X^* - \bar{X}^* - Q] = 0$$

From (93) and (94)

(95) $$[P^*] \cdot [\bar{X}] > [P^*] \cdot [\bar{X}^*]$$

That is, for some firms, $[P^*] \cdot [\bar{X}_v] > [P^*] \cdot [\bar{X}_v^*]$, $[\bar{X}_v] \epsilon T_v$, which contradicts (70). Thus, the contradiction is demonstrated: if a desired good has a zero price, some firm or firms are not maximizing profits. Therefore, if one or more P_i are zero, some firm or firms are not maximizing profits. Therefore, the assumption that $P_i^* = e$ for at least one i must be false. It follows that (63) is true, and therefore that the following must hold:

THEOREM 2: *for any economic system satisfying Assumptions 1 through 17, 18′, and 19 through 21, an equilibrium of the type defined by Conditions 1 through 4 will exist.*

4.b.7. McKenzie's Contributions to the Proof of Existence of Equilibrium in the Arrow-Debreu Model 2

L. McKenzie has made several contributions to the simplification and generalization of the Arrow-Debreu Model 2, and we shall treat them briefly below.[37]

[37] L. McKenzie, (1).

4.b.7.a. The Arrow-Debreu Model 2 With the Production Set T a Convex Polyhedral Cone

McKenzie first deals with the model for an economy whose production set T can be treated as a closed, convex cone, as for example, when the $[\bar{X}_v]$ in all firms' T_v are additive and divisible, or when firms are small relative to the group, each may be assumed to operate at the minimum point of its U-shaped average cost curve, and no technological external economies or diseconomies are present at any scale. This effectively removes the firms from consideration as well as the possibility of positive profits in equilibrium. Consequently, the following assumptions of Model 2 are not relevant

(96) *Delete: Assumptions 2, 3, 6, 17*

The following assumptions are implicit or explicit in McKenzie's treatment:

(97) *Retain: Assumptions 1, 4, 9, 10, 16*

In McKenzie's model, $[X_c]$ equals the Arrow-Debreu $[X_c] - [Q_c]$ when $Q_{cj} \geqq 0$ for all j and all c. That is, consumers are assumed to hold non-negative stocks of goods Y_j and factor services enter $[X_c]$ as net supplies with negative values.

The following assumptions of Model 2 are explicitly contained in McKenzie's own assumptions, which we denote M-Assumptions:

(98) Explicit:

1. M-Assumption 1: Assumption 11 (excluding the lower boundedness restriction)
2. M-Assumption 2: Assumptions 11 (only that portion concerning the lower boundedness restriction), 12, 13, 15
3. M-Assumption 3: Assumption 5 (modified to refer to T and to yield T as a closed, convex cone)
4. M-Assumption 4: Assumption 7

The McKenzie assumptions are explained as follows:

M-Assumption 1. C_c is convex, and closed.

M-Assumption 2. C_c is bounded from below and is completely ordered by a convex, closed preference relation.

M-Assumption 3. T is a closed, convex cone.

M-Assumption 4. $T \cap \Omega = [0]$. This axiom rules out the Land of Cockaigne.

In this fashion we may narrow down the assumptions which are altered by McKenzie. Those Arrow-Debreu assumptions which have not yet appeared in (96), (97), and (98) are the following:

(99) *Unaccounted for: Assumptions 8, 14, 18′, 19, 20, 21*

McKenzie excludes Assumption 8, which is the irreversibility-of-production assumption. Arrow and Debreu require this to assure, with the assumed closure of T_v, the closure of T, as well as to obtain $\hat{T}_v$. M-Assumption 3 assumes the closure of T, and McKenzie's proofs do not require the effective bounds on T_v when the existence of firms is recognized in another of his treatments.

There remain, therefore, the following assumptions unaccounted for (we recall each with a brief indication of its nature):

Assumption 14. No consumer is satiated anywhere in C_c.

Assumption 18′. Every consumer can supply at least one productive factor service to the market.

Assumption 19. It is possible to achieve excess supplies for all goods and services simultaneously in the market.

Assumption 20. A set of always-desired goods for all consumers exists.

Assumption 21. A set of always-productive factor services exists.

Loosely speaking, we have seen that the greatest complications in the proof of Theorem 2 arose in guaranteeing that the sets $A_c([\bar{a}_c])$ possessed certain subsets which were not empty at certain $[P] \epsilon P$, in order to avoid the introduction of discontinuities into the demand or supply functions. The above conditions guarantee, therefore, that each consumer will command an income (it will be recalled that Assumption 19 helps to guarantee positive prices for the productive services) which will be used to demand goods.

For this group of assumptions McKenzie substitutes two groups:

M-Assumption 5a. $C_c \cap T$ is not empty. That is, taking into account only the state of the arts and feasible consumption vectors, every consumer can select at least one set of goods producible with a set of resources he is capable of supplying. For example, no consumer is foreclosed from markets or from producing because he possesses no factor services of any kind to supply.

M-Assumption 5b. Let $[X''] \epsilon C$. Then there is a point $[X'']$ in the relative interiors of C and T. This assures that it is possible technically, psychologically, and in terms of resource endowments, for excess supplies of all goods and excess demands for all services to exist. This assures in turn that at least one consumer will always have income.

This is shown as follows. In equilibrium, one of our conditions must be that $[P^\circ] \cdot [\bar{X}] \leqq 0$ for all $[\bar{X}] \epsilon T$. Therefore, we confine our attention to vectors $[P] \epsilon P$ where $P = \{[P] | [P] \cdot [\bar{X}] \leqq 0, [\bar{X}] \epsilon T\}$. Now let $[\bar{X}] \epsilon T$ be chosen such that $[P]$ is normal to the hyperplane defining the half-space $[P] \cdot [\bar{X}] \leqq 0$. This hyperplane will be bounding for C (i.e., $[P] \cdot [X] \geqq 0$ for all $[X] \epsilon C$) if and only if $[\bar{X}]$ is not interior to C. This assumption assures that for any $[P] \epsilon P$, there will exist an $[X] \epsilon C$ for which $[P] \cdot [X] < 0$. No $[P]$ exists to make $[P] \cdot [X] \geqq 0$ for all $[X] \epsilon C$ and $[P] \cdot [\bar{X}] \leqq 0$ for all $[\bar{X}] \epsilon T$.

These assumptions (given that of free disposal of goods implicit in Conditions 3 and 4) are analogous to Assumptions 18′ and 19. But, as in the Arrow-Debreu analysis, proof of equilibrium requires that every consumer have positive income in the neighborhood of equilibrium. Therefore, M-Assumption 6 is added to assure that some positive income is realized by each consumer. It is an implicit replacement of Assumptions 20 and 21.

M-Assumption 6. Let the set of consumers be partitioned into two subsets with C^1 and C^2 being the sum of the consumption sets for two groups of consumers. Now, for every possible partition of C into C^1 and C^2, if $[X^1] \epsilon T - C^2$, and if $[W] \epsilon T - C^2$, it is possible to distribute goods and services from $[W]$ in such a way that no one is worse off in the first group and at least one person is better off. This implies immediately that at least one member of the first group is not satiated, and since the first group may contain any one of the consumers alone, it is immediately implied that no consumer can be satiated with an $[X] \epsilon C \cap T$. Therefore, Assumption 14 is satisfied for attainable outputs.

This is the condition of irreducibility, a concept of Gale's.[38] It assures that when even one consumer has income by virtue of M-Assumption 5*b*, all must have such incomes.

McKenzie then defines equilibrium in this model as follows:

Condition M-1. $[\bar{X}^\circ] \epsilon T, [P^\circ] \cdot [\bar{X}^\circ] = 0$, where $[\bar{X}] \epsilon T, [P^\circ] \cdot [\bar{X}] \leqq 0$.

Condition M-2. $[X^\circ_c] \epsilon C_c([P^\circ]) \cap H_c([P^\circ])$ for all c. $C_c([P^\circ])$ is the set of all vectors within the budget constraint at $[P^\circ]$, while $H_c([P^\circ])$ is the set of all vectors to which no $[X_c] \epsilon C_c([P^\circ])$ is preferred. This condition states that the equilibrium market basket for each consumer will be feasible and will maximize preferences.

Condition M-3. $[X^\circ] = [\bar{X}^\circ]$

These conditions differ in three important respects from those of Arrow and Debreu:

1. prices are not required to be nonnegative. This is an overthrow of Arrow-Debreu's implicit assumption of free disposal of goods, recognizing

[38] D. Gale, (1), pp. 266–71.

that some goods may have negative prices if it requires scarce resources to dispose of them.

2. by virtue of (1), equality of demand and supply is enforced, even at negative prices. No possibility of excess supply at a zero price is admitted.

3. no profits can exist in equilibrium.

Lastly, McKenzie's alterations allow a simplification of the proof of equilibrium, employing Brouwer's fixed point theorem rather than Kakutani's, the latter being a generalization of the former. Brouwer's theorem deals with the mapping of functions into themselves rather than correspondences.

4.b.7.b. The Arrow-Debreu Model 2 in Full Generality

McKenzie's generalization of the Arrow-Debreu model without the assumption that T is a convex polyhedral cone is straightforward. The Arrow-Debreu assumptions relevant to an economy with well-defined firms are Assumptions 2, 3, 6, and 17, or those in (96) which were deleted from McKenzie's simplified model. The first and last—Assumptions 2 and 17—are now introduced explicitly, and the remaining two are introduced in a modified M-Assumption 3:

M-Assumption 3′. T_v is closed and convex, $[0] \epsilon T_v$. Also, to M-Assumption 4 we add the requirement that T is closed:

M-Assumption 4′. $T \cap \Omega = [0]$, T is closed. That is, the intersection of T and Ω must be that set which contains the one element, [0]. In the Arrow-Debreu model this was implied by irreversibility and implicit free disposal, so it does not appear in Assumption 7, as we have already noted. Since McKenzie has eliminated irreversibility, he must now introduce the closure of T explicitly.

With M-Assumptions 1, 2, 3′, 4′, 5a, 5b, and 6 we have a modified Arrow-Debreu economy in full generality, with profits interpreted as payments to a factor service z_i. In the definition of equilibrium we must now introduce the possibility of positive profits:

Condition M-1′. $[P°] \cdot [\bar{X}_v^°] \geqq [P°] \cdot [\bar{X}_v]$, for $[\bar{X}_v] \epsilon T_v$ and for all v. McKenzie's proof of the existence of an equilibrium for this model is a simpler variation of the Arrow-Debreu proof.

4.c. The Arrow-Debreu Model 3

Suppose each consumer held positive stocks of and is capable of supplying at least one z_i or at least one good $Y_j \epsilon D$. Formally:

Assumption 18″. For each consumer c, for some vectors $[X_c]$, the components X_{ch} are related to Q_{ch}, the components of $[Q_c] \epsilon R^{m+n}$, such that $X_{ch} \leqq Q_{ch}$, and for at least one $h \in D \cup z_i$ ("the union of sets D and z_i") $X_{ch} < Q_{ch}$.

The extension is a clear one and we shall not display the proof. If Assumption 18″ is substituted for Assumption 18′ we obtain Arrow-Debreu Model 3 and Theorem 3 which states that an equilibrium defined in the same manner as those of Models 1 and 2 will exist.

This case is especially applicable to the exchange economy, for the set z_i may be taken as the null set, and the goods in D bear the burden of the required restrictions. Thus, the equilibrium of a multiple exchange economy is established.

5. Wald's Pure Exchange Model

The Arrow-Debreu extension of the analysis to the pure exchange economy may be compared with the earlier theorems of Wald on a similar multiple exchange economy. Given such a system with s individuals and n goods Y_j, given the vector of goods endowments $[Q_c] \geq 0$ for all c, so that each consumer holds at least one good, and given pure competition, Wald altered Model II-2 to include the possibility of a maximum which does not include positive amounts of all goods in the individuals' equilibrium consumptions. Consumer preference functions, $M_c([Q_{cj} + X_{cj}])$, are given, and the marginal conditions may be written:

$$(100)\quad \begin{aligned} &1. \quad \frac{M_c^j}{P_j} = \frac{M_c^{j'}}{P_{j'}} \quad \text{when} \quad Q_{cj} + X_{cj} \neq 0,\ Q_{cj'} + X_{cj'} \neq 0 \\ &2. \quad \frac{M_c^j}{P_j} \leqq \frac{M_c^{j'}}{P_{j'}} \quad \text{when} \quad Q_{cj} + X_{cj} = 0,\ Q_{cj'} + X_{cj'} \neq 0 \end{aligned}$$

The budget constraints are met; no provision for satiation is made:

$$(101)\quad [P] \cdot [X_c] = 0, \qquad \text{for all } c$$

And excess demands for the market must be zero:

$$(102)\quad [E] = [0]$$

One equation may be eliminated from (102) and P_1 set equal to unity.

Wald proved that a solution to this model exists with $[P] > 0$, $[Q_c + X_c] \geqq 0$, if

1. $[Q_c] \geq 0$
2. $[Q] > 0$. Some of every good must exist in the economy.
3. The marginal preference functions, M_c^j, are of the form

$$(103)\quad M_c^j = H_c^j(X_{cj}) \cdot M_c([Q_c + X_c])$$

where M_c is any nonvanishing function (including a constant) and H_c^j is continuous, nonnegative, and a strictly monotonically decreasing function. These are integrability conditions and allow the indifference varieties $U_c([Q_c + X_c]) = k$ to be obtained. From them

$$\frac{\partial U_c}{\partial X_{ck}} = H_c^k \tag{104}$$

where U_c is a cardinal utility measure, H_c^k is marginal utility, and from (103) is assumed independent of all goods held but the quantity of that good for which it is defined. In this case it is the assumption of cardinally measurable utility functions with independence of the utilities.

As a strictly decreasing, nonnegative function, H_c^j implies the convexity of the indifference map and nonsatiation of every person for every good.[39] Thus, the restrictions on preference functions are a special case of those in Arrow-Debreu Model 3, when $Y_j \epsilon D$ for all j, $z_i \epsilon 0$. Wald's condition that the consumer hold at least one good in positive amount is met by Arrow-Debreu's Assumption 18″, the first condition eliminating negative holdings is a special case of Assumption 16, and the second condition is met by Assumption 18″. Therefore, the theorem asserting existence is subsumed in the Arrow-Debreu Model 3. Also, the special Walrasian case of complex exchange with independent cardinal utilities is proved to have an existence in that model.

Wald goes one step farther to show that if one more condition is met the equilibrium will be a unique one:

4. The functions H_c^j for all c and all j tend to ∞ as $X_{cj} \rightarrow 0$, and if an arbitrary coefficient $\lambda > 0$ is applied to X_{cj} it is true that

$$\frac{H_c^j(\lambda X_{cj})}{H_c^j(X_{cj})} > \frac{1}{\lambda} \tag{105}$$

This last condition is equivalent to the requirement that the relative changes in marginal utility divided by the relative change in X_{cj} at every point be less than unity, or that the elasticity of marginal utility with respect to quantity be less than unity.

6. Equilibrium and Uniqueness in Other Linear Models

We have already dealt in this chapter with Wald's linear production model and McKenzie's linearization of the Arrow-Debreu Model 2; in Chapter 6 we have treated the Hawkins-Simon conditions for an equilibrium in the Leontief static input-output model; and in Chapter 8 we mentioned the proof of equilibrium in von Neumann's model. We shall end this chapter by considering McKenzie's proof of equilibrium in the Graham model[40] and the Dorfman, Samuelson, and Solow proof for the linear model.

[39] A. Wald, (1), pp. 379–91.
[40] See Chapter 7.

6.a. The Existence of Equilibrium in Graham's Model

It is to McKenzie that we owe the first direct application of Kakutani's fixed-point theorem to the proof of existence of equilibrium in an economic model.[41] His proof was one of existence in Graham's model, but he generalized the proof. Also, he showed the uniqueness of the equilibrium in Graham's model. Although we may bring the Graham model under the assumptions of Arrow-Debreu Model 2, treating the consumption sector as made up of one consumer holding stocks of resources whose marginal productivities are always positive in products which are always positively valued, we shall deal briefly with McKenzie's proof because of the essential simplicity of the analysis.

As pointed out in Section 2.b.5.c. of Chapter 7, an equilibrium in the model exists if and only if (1) the output vector $[Y^\circ]$ is feasible, (2) $[P^\circ] > 0$ and maximizes $[P_j] \cdot [Y^\circ]$, and (3) $[P_j^\circ]$ and $[Y^\circ]$ satisfy the demand functions, while $[X_j^\circ] = [Y^\circ]$.

First, if $[P^\circ]$ maximizes the value of output, G, when the output vector $[Y]$ is given, then $[\lambda P^\circ]$, $\lambda > 0$, will also maximize G for $[Y]$. Moreover, if at $[P^\circ]$ the point $[X_j]$ is optimal for "the consumer," it will remain optimal for $[\lambda P^\circ]$. Therefore, since both production and consumption are homogeneous of degree zero in all prices, we may restrict prices in the model to the set $\{[P] | [P] \epsilon P, [P] \geq 0, [P] \cdot [v] = 1\}$ where $[v]$ is a vector of unity components.

Second, consider the set Y' defined as $\Phi_1([X_j'])$ such that when $[X_j']$ lies on the boundary of feasible production, $[Y'] = [X']$. A $[Y']$ must exist for every $[X']$, since a ray from the origin through any point in Y must intersect Y's boundary if extended far enough. Further, every value $[X']$ will correspond to a unique $[Y']$, so that we have a function Φ_1, and it may be shown to be continuous.

Third, consider the points $[Y'] \epsilon Y'$. We define a correspondence Φ_2 which maps the vectors $[Y']$ into sets of $P' = \{[P'] | [P'] \cdot [Y'] = \max [P] \cdot [Y']\}$; i.e., in terms of our linear programming analysis, the vectors $[P']$ are normal to the feasible production set at $[Y']$. We have, then, $\Phi_2([Y'])$ which maps into the set P' which is convex (if $[P'^1]$ and $[P'^2]$ are normal at $[Y']$, the straight line connecting them will form a set of points that also are normal at $[Y']$) and closed (since the income function $[P] \cdot [Y]$ is continuous).

Fourth, consider the demand functions: if we igmore all points in the set C but those $[X'] \epsilon C'$ which are on the boundary of Y, they may be written

$$\Phi_3([P]) = \frac{b_j G}{P_j}, \qquad P_j > 0 \tag{106}$$

[41] L. McKenzie, (2).

where

$$G = \max([P] \cdot [Y]) \tag{107}$$

Since these functions are not defined for $P_j = 0$, McKenzie modifies them so that they are continuous at zero. Obtain the vector $[L_j]$ by successively devoting all resources in each region to the production of the same good, and select a value L_j *larger* than the maximum output. These, then, are upper bounds to attainable amounts of each good, and any $[P]$ which yields a $\Phi_{3j}([P]) > L_j$ cannot be an equilibrium value. We define

$$\begin{aligned} \Phi^*_{3j}([P]) &= \Phi_{3j}([P]) \text{ if } \Phi_{3j}([P]) \leqq L_j \\ &= L_j \text{ if } \Phi_{3j}([P]) > L_j \text{ or } P_j = 0 \quad \text{for } [P] \in P \end{aligned} \tag{108}$$

Thus we may bound the consumer demand functions by considering attainable demands due to resource constraints, and obviously an equilibrium demand must lie within the attainable set.

Finally, it can be shown that Φ^*_{3j} is continuous as long as $G > 0$, which will be true since all prices cannot be zero, and for any price greater than zero there will be a set in Y with positive amounts of that good. Since G is the maximum value of output for a given price, it cannot be zero. We therefore define the set $\Phi^*_3([P])$ which is the set of $[X]$ at incomes generated by extreme points of the production set which fit the demand relations (are optimal from the consumer's viewpoint). It will therefore define points in C', will be a function, and will be continuous since the Φ^*_{3j} are continuous.

We have defined three mappings, two of which are functions (Φ_1 and Φ^*_3) and one of which is a correspondence (Φ_2):

(109) $\Phi_1([X'])$ maps points in the rays of consumption into points $[Y']$ in boundary production equal to $[X']$

(110) $\Phi_2([Y'])$ maps points in boundary production into price vectors, $[P']$, which are normal at $[Y']$ to the production surface; i.e., price sets which maximize $[P] \cdot [Y']$

(111) $\Phi^*_3([P])$ maps points in the price set into points of C'

Now consider

$$\Phi([X'], [Y'], [P]) = \Phi_1([X']) \times \Phi_2([Y']) \times \Phi^*_3([P]) \tag{112}$$

Φ can be seen to map the set $C' \times Y' \times P$ into itself. If it can be shown that there exists a point $[X'^\circ, Y'^\circ, P^\circ]$ which is in the mapping of $\Phi([X'^\circ, Y'^\circ, P^\circ])$, a fixed point exists, and an equilibrium is revealed. Now, from section 4.a.5., if:

1. $C' \times Y' \times P$ is nonempty, convex, and compact;

2. Φ is an upper semicontinuous correspondence;
3. for each point $[X', Y', P]$ the set $\Phi([X', Y', P])$ is nonempty and convex,

then Kakutani's fixed point theorem will apply. Since these conditions do in fact hold, there is an equilibrium point in the model.[42]

We may now check the characteristics of the equilibrium against the definition of a competitive equilibrium in a Graham model. The output vector $[Y'^{\circ}]$ is feasible by the definition of Φ_1. $[P^{\circ}]$ is normal to $[X'^{\circ}]$ by the definition of Φ_2, so $[P^{\circ}] \cdot [Y'^{\circ}]$ is the maximum of $[P] \cdot [Y'^{\circ}]$ and equals G.

It must be shown, however, that $P_j > 0$ for all j, which can be proved if the vector $[X'^{\circ}]$ fits the original demand functions $\Phi_{3j}([P])$ as well as the modified functions $\Phi^*_{3j}([P])$, since the former are not defined for zero prices. Then

(113) $$[P^{\circ}] \cdot [X'^{\circ}] = \sum_j P_j^{\circ} \Phi^*_{3j}([P^{\circ}])$$

where

(114) $$\Phi^*_{3j}([P]) \leqq \Phi_{3j}([P]), \text{ except when } P_j = 0$$

so

(115) $$[P^{\circ}] \cdot [X'^{\circ}] \leqq \sum_j P_j^{\circ} \Phi_{3j}([P^{\circ}]) = G$$

From Φ_1 we have the relation that if $[X]$ lies outside the interior of Y, then $Y = \theta X$, $\theta \leqq 1$. That is, there will exist a vector on the ray $(0, X)$ which lies on Y', the boundary of Y. Therefore,

(116) $$[P^{\circ}] \cdot [Y'^{\circ}] = [P^{\circ}] \cdot \theta[X] \geqq [P^{\circ}] \cdot [X'^{\circ}], \qquad \theta \leqq 1$$

This requires $\theta = 1$, so

(117) $$[Y'^{\circ}] = [X'^{\circ}], \text{ and therefore } [X'^{\circ}] \in Y$$

Now, unless $P_j > 0$

(118) $$\Phi^*_{3j}([P]) = L_j$$

and the vector $[L_j]$ lies outside Y by the definition of $[L_j]$. If $[X'^{\circ}]$ is contained in Y it cannot lie outside it, so $P_j > 0$ and

(119) $$\Phi_{3j}([P]) = \Phi^*_{3j}([P])$$

[42] To emphasize the continuity with our previous presentation, we have presented the problem in a different form from McKenzie. He forms the correspondence

(1) $$F[P] = \Phi_2(\Phi_1(\Phi^*_3([P])))$$

which maps $[P]$ into itself. He then applies Kakutani's theorem to this mapping.

Therefore, all the conditions for a competitive equilibrium are met and it has been proved that a competitive equilibrium always exists in the Graham model.

6.a.1. *The Uniqueness of Equilibrium in Graham's Model*

McKenzie also demonstrates that since Graham's demand functions satisfy the weak axiom of revealed preference, since Y is closed and convex, and since equilibrium output is on the boundary of Y with a price vector normal to Y at the equilibrium point, the equilibrium will be unique.

We start with an equilibrium $[Y°] = [X°]$. By the definition of a normal

$$[P°] \cdot [Y°] \geqq [P°] \cdot [Y'] \tag{120}$$

where $[Y'] \neq [Y°]$ is another point on the boundary of Y. By the same token, if $[P'] \cdot [Y'] \geqq [P'] \cdot [Y°]$ when $[P']$ is normal to $[Y']$, or if $[P'] = [P° + \Delta P]$ and $[Y'] = [Y° + \Delta Y]$, $[\Delta Y] \neq [0]$,

$$[P°] \cdot [\Delta Y] \leqq 0 \tag{121}$$

and

$$[P° + \Delta P][\Delta Y] \geqq 0 \tag{122}$$

But the weak axiom of revealed preference says that if

$$[X°] \cdot [P°] \geqq [X'] \cdot [P'] \tag{123}$$

or if

$$[P°] \cdot [\Delta X] \leqq 0 \tag{124}$$

then

$$[P° + \Delta P] \cdot [\Delta X] < 0 \tag{125}$$

Now, if $[P°, Y° = X°]$ is an equilibrium, and $[P', Y' = X']$ were also an equilibrium, it would be necessary for (122) and (125) to hold simultaneously, which is a contradiction. Therefore, no other point on the efficiency frontier can satisfy the demand equations when $[P°, Y°, X°]$ does.

6.a.2. *McKenzie's Generalization of the Graham Model*

McKenzie has also indicated some of the directions in which the restrictions of Graham's model can be relaxed without disturbing the proof of existence or uniqueness or the design of the proofs.

It is possible to drop the assumption that a boundary point exists for every set of relative amounts of final goods since insatiability in all goods is implicit in the demand functions, so that even if excess supply is introduced as a potential into the model, it will not characterize equilibrium. With the assumption can go the supporting assumption that all regions produce (potentially) all goods, if we allow final goods to be disposed of costlessly; i.e., if we introduce disposal processes absorbing no resources. By the same line of reasoning, joint production can be allowed to enter into the model.

The insatiability-of-demand assumption can be dropped (if joint production is admitted free disposal assumptions are necessary) if demand curves, at zero prices, are continuous; i.e., if the amounts demanded do not jump discontinuously to large amounts. This implies a normal $[P^\circ] \geq 0$ at $[Y^\circ]$ on the efficiency frontier and a solution to the demand equations. This proof is a special case of the Arrow-Debreu proof applied to an economy with a continuous demand function obeying Walras' Law.

Variable supplies of resources may be admitted under suitable assumptions as the assumption that z_i is a set with more than one element, if the continuity of demand functions is preserved, as in the Arrow-Debreu assumption that consumers will always be able to supply some positively priced good to the market.

6.b. The Dorfman-Samuelson-Solow Proof for a Linear Model

Dorfman, Samuelson, and Solow[43] have modified McKenzie's proof somewhat to take explicit account of the dual problem inherent in the linear model. By virtue of the definition of Graham's demand functions as including only income and the P_j, and the implicit dualistic definition of income as the maximum value of output, McKenzie was able to deal only with product prices P_j, and to abstract from the ${}_rP_i$.

Let us generalize and modify the Walras-Cassel model of (1-1), (1-2), (5), and (6), as follows:

(126)

1. $$X_{j\neq 1} = H_{j\neq 1}(P_1, \ldots, P_n, P_{z_1}, \ldots, P_{z_m})$$
2. $$\bar{X}_i = Q_i - H_i(P_1, \ldots, P_n, P_{z_1}, \ldots, P_{z_m})$$
3. $$X_1 = \frac{\sum_i \bar{X}_i P_i - \sum_{j\neq 1} X_j P_j}{P_1}$$

(127)

1. $$\sum_j a_{ij}\bar{X}_j^\circ + R_i^\circ = \bar{X}_i^\circ$$
2. $$\bar{X}_j^\circ = X_j^\circ$$

(128) $$R_i^\circ P_i^\circ = 0$$

(129) $$\sum_i a_{ij}P_i^\circ - R_j^\circ = P_j^\circ$$

[43] R. Dorfman, (1), pp. 366–75.

(130) $$R_j^\circ P_j^\circ = 0$$

(131) $$\sum_j P_j + \sum_i P_i \equiv 1$$

(132) $$X_j \geqq 0,\ \bar{X}_j \geqq 0,\ \bar{X}_i \geqq 0,\ P_j \geqq 0,\ P_i \geqq 0,\ R_i \geqq 0,\ R_j \geqq 0$$

This model assumes that intermediate goods either do not exist or have been reduced to their primary factor equivalents. It differs from the Wald-Schlesinger-Zeuthen modification of the Walras-Cassel model in that it permits certain goods not to be produced at all whenever R_j°, the excess cost, is positive.[44] Also, the supply of factor services is elastic and the prices of these services enter into demand functions. The following assumptions are made:

1. Demand and supply functions are continuous.
2. Demand and supply functions are defined for all price vectors $[P] \geq 0$.
3. Some of each resource is available to the economy.
4. $a_{ij} \geqq 0$ for all i and all j.
5. For each j, at least one $a_{ij} > 0$.

An interesting duality exists in the model. By the reasoning of the Koopmans model, for a given set of feasible prices of final goods, (127) through (132) define a competitive solution for which the value of output will equal the value of inputs. This follows from the duality theorem of linear programming. But the consumption sector is also constrained to meet this condition: since all output is for consumers, all inputs are sold by consumers, and no profits are earned, the value of output must equal the value of inputs, since consumers are constrained to spend all their income and no more. Therefore, given (1) a price vector which yields a production sector solution which is a competitive solution, (2) a consumer sector solution which is optimal (fits the functions of (126)), and (3) the equality of the two solutions, the model will have a solution.

Let us define the coordinate subspace in R^{m+n}. The set C then consists of the $m + n$-tuples $[X_1, \ldots, X_n, X_{z_1}, \ldots, X_{z_m}]$; the set T of the vectors $[\bar{X}_1, \ldots, \bar{X}_n, X_{z_1}, \ldots X_{z_m}]$; and the set P of $[P_1, \ldots, P_n, P_{z_1}, \ldots, P_{z_m}]$, where $[P] \cdot [v] = 1$. All the constraints of (132) also must be met. Now, for each $[P] \epsilon P$ there will be defined from (126) a point $[X] \epsilon C$, and we define this mapping

(133) $$[X'] = \Phi_3([P])$$

which is a function mapping the set P into the intersection of rays from the origin and the efficiency frontier of the convex polyhedral cone T. The function Φ_3 will be continuous since the demand curves and supply

[44] Wald's assumption 5 restricts the demand curves such that all goods will be produced.

curves are continuous, P is a closed set, and the efficiency frontier will be closed.

Next, we map $[X'] \epsilon C'$, the latter the subset of $C \cap T'$, where T' is the efficiency frontier, into those boundary points of production:

$$(134) \qquad [\bar{X}'] = \Phi_1([X'])$$

which is a continuous function.

Lastly, we map boundary points in T' into points $[P_j]$ which imply $[P_i]$, and so into points $[P] \epsilon P$, which are normal to T' at $[\bar{X}]$. This will be an upper semicontinuous correspondence, and we need not bound the demand functions since they are defined and continuous for all nonnegative prices:

$$(135) \qquad [P] = \Phi_2([\bar{X}'])$$

Once more we have met the conditions of Kakutani's theorem and an equilibrium set $[P^\circ, \bar{X}^\circ, X^\circ]$ must exist which will correspond to the definition of equilibrium of a competitive economy defined in the model.

6.b.1. The Uniqueness of Equilibrium in the Linear Model

If the additional assumption is met of satisfaction by all demand curves and supply functions of the weak axiom of revealed preference, equilibrium will be unique.

7. A Recapitulation

Judged not against the corresponding relations of economic reality, but wholly against the characteristics of our abstract economic models of Parts II and III, the pragmatic assertion of a faith that our data would need to be constrained in wholly acceptable ways to guarantee a solution under all allowable conditions of their initial values seems to be well justified on the whole. The linear models, in particular, seem to afford no restrictions that are intuitively objectionable in our idealized abstractions of reality. Even in the case of the most general models dealt with—the Arrow-Debreu models of production and exchange—the objectionable restrictions revolve about the problem of preventing the arising of a null set in the consumer's effective choice field, with its threat to the continuity of demand and supply functions in the event of most improbable conditions—the property of continuity being recognized as an outright idealization of reality.

The two gaps in the proofs presented—proof of existence for an investment model and for a money model, where money services enter the preference domain in Walrasian fashion—may be filled by simple introduction of capital goods, securities, money services, and money in the Arrow-Debreu models. However, no proof exists for the money model such as presented in Model V-2, where money services do not enter the preference function.

The proofs of uniqueness—a quality which we have recognized to be a nonnecessary and even undesirable quality of our models—on the other hand, require restrictions which, while acceptable for the individual demand and supply functions, are not intuitively acceptable for aggregate functions, given differing consumer tastes and the redistribution of income brought about under varying price vectors.

To judge the complex economic functions of reality, of course, is a wholly different operation. The question we propounded at the start of this chapter concerned, not reality, but highly idealized depictions of it. The restrictions of this chapter seem fanciful indeed judged against this troublesome backdrop: continuity, as one example, might be extremely difficult to establish in many functions, and the implied existence of null sets might seem not only possible but even likely.

BIBLIOGRAPHY

BIBLIOGRAPHY

Ackley, Gardner, (1). "The Wealth-Saving Relationship," *Journal of Political Economy*, LIX (1951), pp. 154–61.

Åkerman, Johan, (1). "Annual Survey of Economic Theory: The Setting of the Central Problem," *Econometrica*, 4 (1936), pp. 97–122.

Alchian, Armen, (1). "The Meaning of Utility Measurement," *American Economic Review*, XLIII (1953), pp. 26–50.

Allais, Maurice, (1). *Économie et Intérêt*, Librairie des Publications Officielles, Paris, 1947.

Allen, R. G. D., (1), (with J. Hicks). "A Reconsideration of the Theory of Value, II," *Economica*, NS I (1934), pp. 196–219.

Antonelli, Étienne, (1). *Principes d'Économie Pure*, Riviere, Paris, 1914.

Archibald, G., (1), (with R. Lipsey). "Monetary and Value Theory: A Critique of Lange and Patinkin," *Review of Economic Studies*, XXVI (1958), pp. 1–22.

Arrow, Kenneth, (1). "Alternative Proof of the Substitution Theorem for Leontief Models in the General Case," in T. Koopmans, (2), pp. 155–64.

———, (2), (with G. Debreu). "Existence of an Equilibrium for a Competitive Economy," *Econometrica*, 22 (1954), pp. 265–90.

———, (3), (with A. Enthoven). "A Theorem on Expectations and the Stability of Equilibrium," *Econometrica*, 24 (1956), pp. 288–93.

———, (4), (with M. McManus). "A Note on Dynamic Stability," *Econometrica*, 26 (1958), pp. 448–54.

———, (5), (with M. Nerlove). "A Note on Expectations and Stability," *Econometrica*, 26 (1958), pp. 297–305.

———, (6), (with L. Hurwicz). "On the Stability of the Competitive Equilibrium, I," *Econometrica*, 26 (1958), pp. 522–52.

———, (7), (with A. Enthoven). *Quasi-Concave Programming*, RAND Corporation, P-1847, December 16, 1959.

Aupetit, Albert, (1). *Essai sur la Théorie Générale de la Monnaie*, Guillaumin et Cie., Paris, 1901.

Barna, Tibor, (1). *The Structural Interdependence of the Economy*, Wiley & Sons, New York, 1955.

Baumol, William, (1). "The von Neumann-Morgenstern Utility Index—An Ordinalist's View," *Journal of Political Economy*, LIX (1951), pp. 61–6.

———, (2), (with G. Becker). "The Classical Monetary Theory: The Outcome of the Discussion," *Economica*, NS XIX (1952), pp. 355–76.

———, (3). "The Transactions Demand for Cash: An Inventory Theoretic Approach," *Quarterly Journal of Economics*, LXVI (1952), pp. 545–56.

Becker, Gary, (1), (with W. Baumol). "The Classical Monetary Theory: The Outcome of the Discussion," *Economica*, NS XIX (1952), pp. 355–76.

Beckmann, Martin, (1), (with T. Koopmans). "Assignment Problems and the Location of Economic Activities," *Econometrica*, 25 (1957), pp. 53–76.

Boninsegni, Pascal, (1). *Manuel Élémentaire d'Économie Politique*, Rouge, Lausanne, 1930.

Boulding, Kenneth, (1). "Time and Investment," *Economica*, NS III (1936), pp. 196–220.

———, (2), (with G. Stigler), ed. *Readings in Price Theory*, Irwin, Chicago, 1952.

———, (3). "Professor Knight's Capital Theory: A Note in Reply," *Quarterly Journal of Economics*, L (1935), pp. 524–31.

Bowley, Arthur, (1). *The Mathematical Groundwork of Economics*, Oxford University Press, Oxford, 1924.

Bresciani-Turroni, Constantino, (1). "Theory of Saving," *Economica*, NS III (1936), pp. 1–23.

Bridgman, Percy, (1). *The Logic of Modern Physics*, Macmillan, New York, 1927.

Brodsky, Michel, (1), (with P. Rocher). *L'Économie Politique Mathématique*, R. Pichon et R. Durand-Auzias, Paris, 1949.

Brown, E. H. Phelps, (1). *The Framework of the Pricing System*, Student Union Book Store, Lawrenceville, Kansas, 1949.

Brown, Harry Gunnison, (1). "The Marginal Productivity versus the Impatience Theory of Interest," *Quarterly Journal of Economics*, XXVII (1913), pp. 630–50.

Burger, E., (1). "On the Stability of Certain Economic Systems," *Econometrica*, 24 (1954), pp. 488–93.

Burnside, William, (1), (with A. Panton). *The Theory of Equations*, Dover, New York, 1960.

Carver, Thomas N., (1). "The Place of Abstinence in the Theory of Interest," *Quarterly Journal of Economics*, VIII (1893), pp. 40–61.

———, (2). "The Relation of Abstinence to Interest," *Quarterly Journal of Economics*, XVIII (1903), pp. 142–5.

Cassel, Gustav, (1). *Theory of Social Economy*, Harcourt, Brace, and Co., New York, 1924.

———, (2). *Fundamental Thoughts in Economics*, T. F. Unwin, London, 1925.

Chamberlin, Edward H., (1). *The Theory of Monopolistic Competition*, Sixth Edition, Harvard University Press, Cambridge, Mass., 1948.

Chambers, S., (1). "Fluctuations in Capital and the Demand for Money," *Review of Economic Studies*, II (1934).

Champernowne, D. G., (1). "A Note on J. von Neumann's Article on 'A Model of Economic Equilibrium'," *Review of Economic Studies*, XIII (1945–6), pp. 10–8.

Chenery, Hollis, (1), (with P. Clark). *Interindustry Economics*, Wiley & Sons, New York, 1959.

———, (2). "Interregional and International Input-Output Analysis," in T. Barna, (1).

Clark, John Bates, (1). "The Origin of Interest," *Quarterly Journal of Economics*, IX (1895), pp. 257–78.

Clark, Paul, (1), (with H. Chenery). *Interindustry Economics*, Wiley & Sons, New York, 1959.

Coombs, C., (1), (with R. Thrall and R. Davis), ed. *Decision Processes*, Wiley & Sons, New York, 1954.

Courant, Richard, (1), (with H. Robbins). *What is Mathematics?*, Oxford University Press, New York, 1941.

Cournot, Antoine, (1). *Researches into the Mathematical Principles of the Theory of Wealth*, (trans. by N. Bacon), Macmillan, New York, 1927.

Dantzig, George, (1), (with M. Wood). "Programming of Interdependent Activities, I: General Discussion," *Econometrica*, 17 (1949), pp. 193–9.

———, (2). "Programming of Interdependent Activities, II: Mathematical Models," *Econometrica*, 17 (1949), pp. 200–11.

———, (3). "The Programming of Interdependent Activities: Mathematical Model," in T. Koopmans, (2).

Davis, R., (1), (with R. Thrall and C. Coombs), ed. *Decision Processes*, Wiley & Sons New York, 1954.

Debreu, Gerard, (1), (with K. Arrow). "Existence of an Equilibrium for a Competitive Economy," *Econometrica*, 22 (1954), pp. 265–90.

———, (2). *Theory of Value*, Wiley & Sons, New York, 1959.

de Pietri-Tonelli, Alfonso, (1). *Traité d'Économie Rationnelle*, M. Giard, Paris, 1927.

de Scitovszky, Tibor, (1). "Capital Accumulation, Employment, and Price Rigidity," *Review of Economic Studies*, VIII (1941), pp. 69–88.

Divisia, François, (1). *Économique Rationnelle*, G. Doin et Cie., Paris, 1928.

Dorfman, Robert, (1), (with P. Samuelson and R. Solow). *Linear Programming and Economic Analysis*, McGraw-Hill, New York, 1958.

———, (2). "A Graphical Exposition of Böhm-Bawerk's Interest Theory," *Review of Economic Studies*, XXVI (1959), pp. 153–8.

———, (3). "Waiting and the Period of Production," *Quarterly Journal of Economics*, LXXIII (1959), pp. 351–72.

Edgeworth, Francis Y., (1). *Mathematical Psychics*, Paul, London, 1881.

———, (2). "The Theory of Distribution," *Quarterly Journal of Economics*, XVIII (1904), pp. 159–219.

Edwards, Edgar, (1). "Classical and Keynesian Employment Theories: A Reconciliation," *Quarterly Journal of Economics*, LXXIII (1959), pp. 407–28.

Einaudi, Luigi, (1). "Fifty Years of Italian Economic Thought: 1896–1946 Reminiscences," *International Economic Papers*, No. 5, Macmillan, New York, 1955.
Enke, Stephen, (1). "Equilibrium Among Spatially Separated Markets: Solution by Electric Analogue," *Econometrica*, 19 (1951), pp. 40–7.
Enthoven, Alain, (1), (with K. Arrow). "A Theorem on Expectations and the Stability of Equilibrium," *Econometrica*, 24 (1956), pp. 288–93.
———, (2), (with K. Arrow). *Quasi-Concave Programming*, RAND Corporation P-1847, 1959.
Evans, Wilmoth, (1). "Input-Output Computations," in T. Barna, (1).
Fetter, Frank, (1). "Interest Theories, Old and New," *American Economic Review*, IV (1914), pp. 68–92.
———, (2). "The Economic Law of Market Areas," *Quarterly Journal of Economics*, XXXVII (1924), pp. 520–9.
Fisher, Irving, (1). *Mathematical Investigations in the Theory of Value and Prices*, New Haven, 1926.
———, (2). "What is Capital?," *Economic Journal*, VI (1896), pp. 509–34.
———, (3). "The Role of Capital in Economic Theory," *Economic Journal*, VII (1897), pp. 511–37.
———, (4). *The Nature of Capital and Income*, Macmillan, New York, 1906.
———, (5). *The Rate of Interest*, Macmillan, New York, 1907.
———, (6). "The Impatience Theory of Interest," *American Economic Review*, III (1913), pp. 610–8.
———, (7). *The Theory of Interest*, Macmillan, New York, 1930.
Fossati, Eraldo, (1). "Vilfredo Pareto and John Maynard Keynes: One or Two Economic Systems," *Metroeconomica*, I (1949), pp. 126–30.
———, (2). *Essays in Dynamics and Econometrics*, University of North Carolina, Chapel Hill, 1955.
———, (3). *The Theory of General Static Equilibrium*, Blackwell, Oxford, 1957.
Friedman, Milton, (1), (with L. Savage). "The Utility Analysis of Choices Involving Risk," *Journal of Political Economy*, LVI (1948), pp. 279–304, reprinted in G. Stigler, (4), pp. 57–96.
———, (2), (with L. Savage). "The Expected-Utility Hypothesis and the Measurement of Utility," *Journal of Political Economy*, LX (1952), pp. 463–74.
———, (3). "Leon Walras and His Economic System," *American Economic Review*, XLV (1955), pp. 900–9.
Frisch, Ragnar, (1). "On the Notion of Equilibrium and Disequilibrium," *Review of Economic Studies*, III (1936), pp. 100–5.
Gale, David, (1). *The Theory of Linear Economic Models*, McGraw-Hill, New York, 1960.
Georgescu-Roegen, Nicholas, (1). "The Aggregate Linear Production Function and the Application to von Neumann's Economic Model," in T. Koopmans, (2).
———, (2). "Relaxation Phenomena in Linear Dynamic Models," in T. Koopmans, (2).
Gifford, C., (1). "The Concept of the Period of Production," *Economic Journal*, XLIII (1933), pp. 611–8.
Gilbert, J., (1). "The Demand for Money: The Development of an Economic Concept," *Journal of Political Economy*, LXI (1953), pp. 144–59.
Goodwin, Richard, (1). "Iteration, Automatic Computers, and Economic Dynamics," *Metroeconomica*, III (1951), pp. 1–7.
Graham, Frank, (1). *The Theory of International Values*, Princeton University Press, Princeton, 1948.
Haberler, Gottfried, (1). "Irving Fisher's 'Theory of Interest'," *Quarterly Journal of Economics*, XLV (1931), pp. 499–516.
———, (2). *Prosperity and Depression*, Third Edition, United Nations, Lake Success, New York, 1946.
———, (3), ed. *Readings in Business Cycle Theory*, Blakiston, Philadelphia, 1944.
———, (4). "The General Theory," in S. Harris, (1).
———, (5). "The Pigou Effect Once More," *Journal of Political Economy*, LX (1952), pp. 240–6.

Hahn, Frank, (1). "The Rate of Interest and General Equilibrium Analysis," *Economic Journal*, LXV (1955), pp. 52–66.

———, (2). "Gross Substitutes and the Dynamic Stability of General Equilibrium," *Econometrica*, 26 (1958), pp. 169–70.

Hancock, Harris, (1). *Theory of Maxima and Minima*, Dover, New York, 1960.

Hansen, Alvin, (1). "The Pigouvian Effect," *Journal of Political Economy*, LIX (1951), pp. 535–6.

Harris, Seymour, (1), ed. *The New Economics*, Knopf, New York, 1948.

Hausner, M., (1). "Multidimensional Utilities," in R. Thrall, (1).

Hawkins, David, (1). "Some Conditions of Macroeconomic Stability," *Econometrica*, 16 (1948), pp. 309–22.

———, (2), (with H. Simon). "Note: Some Conditions of Macroeconomic Stability," *Econometrica*, 17 (1949), pp. 245–8.

Hayek, Friedrich, (1). "Utility Analysis and Interest," *Economic Journal*, XLVI (1936), pp. 44–60.

———, (2). *The Pure Theory of Capital*, University of Chicago Press, 1941.

Henderson, James, (1), (with R. Quandt). "Walras, Leontief, and the Interdependence of Economic Activities: A Comment," *Quarterly Journal of Economics*, LXIX (1955), pp. 626–31.

———, (2). "Discussion: Interregional Equilibrium and Linear Programming," *Papers and Proceedings, Regional Science Association*, IV (1958), pp. 87–9.

Herstein, I., (1), (with J. Milnor). "An Axiomatic Approach to Measurable Utility," *Econometrica*, 21 (1953), pp. 291–7.

Hicks, John, (1). "Gleichgewicht und Konjunktur," *Zeitschrift für Nationalökonomie*, IV (1933), pp. 441–55.

———, (2). "Leon Walras," *Econometrica*, 2 (1934), pp. 338–48.

———, (3), (with R. G. D. Allen). "A Reconsideration of the Theory of Value, II," *Economica*, NS I (1934) pp. 196–219.

———, (4). "A Suggestion for Simplifying the Theory of Money," *Economica*, NS II (1935), pp. 1–9.

———, (5). "Wages and Interest: The Dynamic Problem," *Economic Journal*, XLV (1935).

———, (6). *Value and Capital*, Second Edition, Clarendon Press, Oxford, 1946.

———, (7). *A Revision of Demand Theory*, Oxford University Press, London, 1956.

Hoover, Edgar, (1). *Location Theory and the Shoe and Leather Industries*, Harvard University Press, Cambridge, Mass., 1937.

Hotelling, Harold, (1). "Stability in Competition," *Economic Journal*, XXXI (1929), pp. 41–57, reprinted in G. Stigler, (4).

———, (2). "Edgeworth's Taxation Paradox and the Nature of Demand and Supply Functions," *Journal of Political Economy*, XL (1932), pp. 571–616.

———, (3). "Demand Functions With Limited Budgets," *Econometrica*, 3 (1935), pp. 66–78.

Houthakker, Hendrik, (1). "Revealed Preference and the Utility Function," *Economica*, NS XVII (1950), pp. 159–74.

Hurwicz, Leonid, (1), (with K. Arrow). "On the Stability of the Competitive Equilibrium, I," *Econometrica*, 26 (1958), pp. 522–52.

Hyson, Charles, (1), (with W. Hyson). "The Economic Law of Market Areas," *Quarterly Journal of Economics*, LXIV (1950), pp. 319–27.

Isard, Walter, (1). "Interregional and Regional Input-Output Analysis," *Review of Economics and Statistics*, XXXIII (1951), pp. 318–28.

———, (2). "Some Empirical Results and Problems of Regional Input-Output Analysis," in W. Leontief, (4).

———, (3), (with R. Kuenne). "The Impact of Steel Upon the Greater New York-Philadelphia Industrial Region," *Review of Economics and Statistics*, XXXV (1953), pp. 289–301.

———, (4). "Location Theory and Trade Theory: Short-Run Analysis," *Quarterly Journal of Economics*, LXVIII (1954), pp. 305–20.

———, (5). *Location and Space-Economy*, Technology Press-Wiley & Sons, New York, 1956.

———, (6). "General Interregional Equilibrium," *Papers and Proceedings of the Regional Science Association*, III (1957), pp. 35–60.
———, (7). "Interregional Linear Programming: An Elementary Presentation and a General Model," *Journal of Regional Science*, I (1958), pp. 1–59.
———, (8), (with D. Ostroff). "General Interregional Equilibrium," *Journal of Regional Science*, II (1960), pp. 67–74.
Kaldor, Nicholas, (1). "Annual Survey of Economic Theory: The Recent Controversy on the Theory of Capital," *Econometrica*, 5 (1937), pp. 201–33.
———, (2). "On the Theory of Capital: A Rejoinder to Professor Knight," *Econometrica*, 6 (1938), pp. 163–76.
———, (3). *Essays on Value and Distribution*, Free Press, Glencoe, 1960.
Kalecki, M., (1). "Professor Pigou on the 'Classical Stationary State'—A Comment," *Economic Journal*, LIV (1944), pp. 131–2.
Kemeny, John, (1), (with O. Morgenstern and G. Thompson). "A Generalization of the von Neumann Model," *Econometrica*, 24 (1956), pp. 115–35.
Keynes, John M., (1). *The General Theory of Employment, Interest, and Money*, Harcourt, Brace, New York, 1936.
Knight, Frank, (1). "Professor Fisher's Interest Theory: A Case in Point," *Journal of Political Economy*, XXXIX (1931), pp. 211–2.
———, (2). *Risk, Uncertainty and Profit*, London School of Economics, London, 1933.
———, (3). "Capitalistic Production, Time, and the Rate of Return," in *Economic Essays in Honor of Gustav Cassel*, George Allen & Unwin, London, 1933, pp. 327–42.
———, (4). *Ethics of Competition*, Harper, New York, 1935.
———, (5). "Professor Hayek and the Theory of Investment," *Economic Journal*, XLV (1935), pp. 77–94.
———, (6). "Some Issues in the Economics of Stationary States," *American Economic Review*, XXVI (1936), pp. 393–411.
———, (7). "The Quantity of Capital and the Rate of Interest. I," *Journal of Political Economy*, XLIV (1936), pp. 433–63.
———, (8). "The Quantity of Capital and the Rate of Interest. II," *Journal of Political Economy*, XLIV (1936), pp. 612–42.
———, (9). "The Theory of Investment Once More: Mr. Boulding and the Austrians," *Quarterly Journal of Economics*, L (1935), pp. 36–67.
———, (10). "Note on Dr. Lange's Interest Theory," *Review of Economic Studies*, IV (1937), pp. 223–30.
———, (11). "On the Theory of Capital: In Reply to Mr. Kaldor," *Econometrica*, 6 (1938), pp. 63–82.
———, (12). "Professor Mises and the Theory of Capital," *Economica*, NS VIII (1941), pp. 409–27.
———, (13). "Diminishing Returns from Investment," *Journal of Political Economy*, LII (1944), pp. 26–47.
Koopmans, Tjalling, (1). "Optimum Utilization of the Transportation System," *Econometrica*, (Supplement), 17 (1949).
———, (2), ed. *Activity Analysis of Production and Allocation*, Wiley & Sons, New York, 1951.
———, (3), (with M. Beckmann). "Assignment Problems and the Location of Economic Activities," *Econometrica*, 25 (1957), pp. 53–76.
Kuenne, Robert, (1), (with W. Isard). "The Impact of Steel Upon the Greater New York-Philadelphia Industrial Region," *Review of Economics and Statistics*, XXXV (1953), pp. 289–301.
———, (2). "Walras, Leontief, and the Interdependence of Economic Activities," *Quarterly Journal of Economics*, LXVIII (1954), pp. 323–54.
———, (3). "Walras, Leontief, and the Interdependence of Economic Activities: Rejoinder," *Quarterly Journal of Economics*, LXIX (1955), pp. 631–6.
———, (4). "The Interregional Input-Output Model as a Derivative of a Walrasian Multiple-Point System," *Econometrica*, 22 (1954).
———, (5). "Location Theory, Input-Output, and Economic Development: An Appraisal: Rejoinder," *Review of Economics and Statistics*, XXXVII (1955), pp. 312–4.

———, (6). "The Architectonics of Leon Walras," *Kyklos*, Fasc. 2, 1956, pp. 241–9.

———, (7). "On the Existence and Role of Money in a Stationary State," *Southern Economic Journal*, XXV (1958), pp. 1–10.

———, (8). "On Hicks's Concept of Perfect Stability in Multiple Exchange," *Quarterly Journal of Economics*, LXXIII (1959), pp. 309–15.

———, (9). "Patinkin on Neoclassical Monetary Theory: A Critique in Walrasian Specifics," *Southern Economic Journal*, XXVI (1959), pp. 119–24.

———, (10). "Keynes's Identity, Ricardian Virtue, and the Partial Dichotomy," *Canadian Journal of Economics and Political Science*, XXVII (1961), pp. 323–36.

———, (11). "The Walrasian Theory of Money: An Interpretation and A Reconstruction," *Metroeconomica*, XIII (1961), pp. 94–105.

———, (12), (with H. Kuhn). "An Efficient Algorithm for the Numerical Solution to the Generalized Weber Problem," *Journal of Regional Science*, 4 (1962), pp. 21–33.

———, (13). "The Stationary State and the Technological Superiority of Present Goods," *Quarterly Journal of Economics*, LXXVI (1962), pp. 648–52.

———, (14). "The Technological Superiority of Present Goods," *Zeitschrift für Nationalökonomie*, XXII (1962).

Kuhn, Harold, (1), (with A. Tucker). "Nonlinear Programming," in J. Neyman, (1).

———, (2), (with R. Kuenne). "An Efficient Algorithm for the Numerical Solution to the Generalized Weber Problem," *Journal of Regional Science*, 4 (1962).

Landry, Adolphe, (1). *L'Intérêt du Capital*, V. Giard et E. Brière, Paris, 1904.

Lange, Oskar, (1). "The Determinateness of the Utility Function," *Review of Economic Studies*, I (1934), pp. 218–25.

———, (2). "A Note on the Determinateness of the Utility Function," *Review of Economic Studies*, II (1934–5), pp. 75–7.

———, (3). "The Stability of Economic Equilibrium," *Econometrica*, 10, (1942).

———, (4). "Say's Law: A Restatement and Criticism," in *Studies in Mathematical Economics and Econometrics*, University of Chicago Press, Chicago, 1942.

———, (5). "The Rate of Interest and the Optimum Propensity to Consume," in G. Haberler, (3).

———, (6). *Price Flexibility and Employment*, Principia, Bloomington, Indiana, 1944.

———, (7). "The Scope and Method of Economics," *Review of Economic Studies*, XIII (1945–6), pp. 19–32.

Launhardt, Wilhelm, (1). *Mathematische Begrundung der Volkswirtslehre*, Leipzig, 1885.

Le Corbeiller, P., (1). "Les Systèmes Autoentretenues et Les Oscillations de Relaxation," *Econometrica*, 1 (1933), pp. 328–32.

Lefeber, Louis, (1). *Allocation in Space*, North-Holland, Amsterdam, 1958.

Leontief, Wassily, (1). "Interest on Capital and Distribution: A Problem in the Theory of Marginal Productivity," *Quarterly Journal of Economics*, XLIX (1934), pp. 147–61.

———, (2). "The Fundamental Assumptions of Mr. Keynes's Monetary Theory of Unemployment," in S. Harris, (1).

———, (3). *The Structure of American Economy, 1919–1939*, Oxford University Press, New York, 1951.

———, (4). *Studies in the Structure of the American Economy*, Oxford University Press, New York, 1953.

———, (5). "Input-Output Analysis and the General Equilibrium," in T. Barna, (1), pp. 41–9.

Lerner, Abba, (1). "On the Marginal Product of Capital and the Marginal Efficiency of Investment," *Journal of Political Economy*, LXI (1953), pp. 1–14.

Lindahl, Erik, (1). *Studies in the Theory of Money and Capital*, George Allen & Unwin, Ltd., London, 1939.

Lipsey, R., (1), (with G. Archibald). "Monetary and Value Theory: A Critique of Lange and Patinkin," *Review of Economic Studies*, XXVI (1958), pp. 1–22.

Lösch, August, (1). *The Economics of Location*, Yale University Press, New Haven, 1954.

Luce, R., (1), (with H. Raiffa). *Games and Decisions*, Wiley & Sons, New York, 1957.

Lutz, Friedrich, (1), (with L. Mints), ed. *Readings in Monetary Theory*, Blakiston, Philadelphia, 1951.

Mackenroth, G., (1). "Period of Production, Durability, and the Rate of Interest in the Economic Equilibrium," *Journal of Political Economy,* XXXVIII (1930), pp. 629–59.

McKenzie, Lionel, (1). "On the Existence of General Equilibrium in a Competitive Market," *Econometrica,* 27 (1959), pp. 54–71.

———, (2). "On Equilibrium in Graham's Model of World Trade and Other Competitive Systems," *Econometrica,* 22 (1954), pp. 147–61.

McManus, Maurice, (1), (with K. Arrow). "A Note on Dynamic Stability," *Econometrica,* 26 (1958), pp. 448–54.

Marget, A., (1). "The Monetary Aspects of the Walrasian Theory," *Journal of Political Economy,* XLIII (1935), pp. 145–86.

Marschak, Jacob, (1). "Identity and Stability in Economics: A Survey," *Econometrica,* 10 (1942).

———, (2). "The Rationale of the Demand for Money and of 'Money Illusion," *Metroeconomica,* II (1950), pp. 71–100.

Marshall, Alfred, (1). *Industry and Trade,* Macmillan, London, 1919.

———, (2). *Principles of Economics,* Eighth Edition, Macmillan, New York, 1948.

Metzler, Lloyd, (1). "Stability of Multiple Markets: The Hicks Conditions," *Econometrica,* 13 (1945), pp. 272–92.

———, (2). "The Rate of Interest and the Marginal Product of Capital," *Journal of Political Economy,* LVIII (1950), pp. 289–306.

———, (3). "Taxes and Subsidies in Leontief's Input-Output Model," *Quarterly Journal of Economics,* LXV (1951), pp. 433–8.

———, (4). "Wealth, Saving, and the Rate of Interest," *Journal of Political Economy,* LIX (1951), pp. 93–116.

Mill, John S., (1). *Principles of Political Economy,* D. Appleton, New York, 1901.

Miller, Ronald, (1). "The Impact of the Aluminum Industry on the Pacific Northwest: A Regional Input-Output Analysis," *Review of Economics and Statistics,* XXXIX (1957), pp. 200–9.

Milnor, J., (1), (with I. Herstein). "An Axiomatic Approach to Measurable Utility," *Econometrica,* 21, (1953), pp. 291–7.

Modigliani, F., (1). "Liquidity Preference and the Theory of Interest and Money," *Econometrica,* 12 (1944), pp. 45–88.

Moore, F., (1), (with J. Peterson). "Regional Analysis: An Interindustry Model of Utah," *Review of Economics and Statistics,* XXXVII (1955), pp. 368–83.

Moore, Henry, (1). *Synthetic Economics,* Macmillan, New York, 1929.

Morgenstern, Oskar, (1). "Perfect Foresight and Economic Equilibrium," English translation, mimeographed, of original article in *Zeitschrift für Nationalökonomie,* VI (1935), pp. 337–57.

———, (2), (with J. von Neumann). *Theory of Games and Economic Behavior,* Princeton University Press, Princeton, 1953.

———, (3), (with J. Kemeny and G. Thompson). "A Generalization of the von Neumann Model," *Econometrica,* 24 (1956), pp. 115–35.

Morishima, M., (1). "On the Laws of Change of the Price System in An Economy which Contains Complementary Commodities," *Osaka Economic Papers,* X (1952), pp. 101–13.

Mosak, Jacob, (1). *General Equilibrium Theory in International Trade,* Principia, Bloomington, Indiana, 1944.

Moses, Leon, (1). "The Stability of Interregional Trading Patterns and Input-Output Analysis," *American Economic Review,* XLV (1955), pp. 803–32.

Mosteller, Frederick, (1), (with P. Nogee). "An Experimental Measurement of Utility," *Journal of Political Economy,* LIX (1951), pp. 371–404.

Nash, J., (1). "Equilibrium Points in *N*-Person Games," *Proceedings of the National Academy of Sciences,* 36 (1950), pp. 48–9.

Negishi, T., (1). "A Note on the Stability of an Economy Where All Goods are Gross Substitutes," *Econometrica,* 26 (1958), pp. 445–7.

Neisser, Hans, (1). "Lohnhöhe und Beschaftigungsgrad ins Marktgleichgewicht," *Weltwirtschaftliches Archiv,* 36 (1932), pp. 415–55.

———, (2). "A Note on Pareto's Theory of Production," *Econometrica,* 8 (1940), pp. 253–62.

Nerlove, Marc, (1), (with K. Arrow). "A Note on Expectations and Stability," *Econometrica,* 26 (1958), pp. 297–305.

Neyman, J., (1), ed. *Proceedings of the Second Berkeley Symposium on Mathematical Statistics and Probability,* University of California Press, Berkeley, 1951.

Nikaidô, H., (1). "On the Classical Multilateral Exchange Problem," *Metroeconomica,* VIII (1956), pp. 135–45.

———, (2). "A Supplementary Note to 'On the Classical Multilateral Exchange Problem'," *Metroeconomica,* IX (1957), pp. 209–10.

Nogaro, Bertrand, (1). *Principes de Théorie Économique,* Librairie Générale de droit et de jurisprudence, Paris, 1943.

Nogee, Philip, (1), (with F. Mosteller). "An Experimental Measurement of Utility," *Journal of Political Economy,* LIX (1951), pp. 317–404.

Ohlin, Bertil, (1). *Interregional and International Trade,* Harvard University Press, Cambridge, Mass., 1933.

Osorio, Antonio, (1). *Théorie Mathématique de l'Échange,* Giard, Paris, 1913.

Ostroff, David, (1), (with W. Isard). "General Interregional Equilibrium," *Journal of Regional Science,* II (1960), pp. 67–74.

Oulès, F., (1). "Les Insuffisances Théoriques de la Doctrine Économique de la Première École de Lausanne," *Metroeconomica,* II (1950), pp. 20–43, pp. 134–71.

Palander, Tord, (1). *Beiträge zur Standortstheorie,* Almqvist, Uppsala, Sweden, 1935.

Pantaleoni, Maffeo, (1). *Pure Economics,* Macmillan, London, 1898.

Panton, Arthur, (1), (with A. Burnside). *The Theory of Equations,* Dover, New York, 1960.

Pareto, Vilfredo, (1). *Cours d'Économie Politique,* Rouge, Lausanne, 1897.

———, (2). *Manuel d'Économie Politique,* V. Giard et E. Brière, Paris, 1909.

———, (3). "Mathematical Economics," in *International Economic Papers,* No. 5, Macmillan, New York, 1955.

Patinkin, Don, (1). "Relative Prices, Say's Law, and the Demand for Money," *Econometrica,* 16 (1948), pp. 135–54.

———, (2). "Price Flexibility and Full Employment," in F. Lutz (1).

———, (3). "The Limitations of Samuelson's 'Correspondence Principle'," *Metroeconomica,* IV (1952), pp. 37–43.

———, (4). *Money, Interest, and Prices,* Row, Peterson, Evanston, Illinois, 1956.

Peterson, J., (1), (with F. Moore). "Regional Analysis: An Interindustry Model of Utah," *Review of Economics and Statistics,* XXXVII (1955), pp. 368–83.

Phipps, C., (1). "Pareto and Walras on Production," *Metroeconomica,* VI (1954), pp. 31–8.

Pigou, A. C., (1). *The Economics of Stationary States,* Macmillan, London, 1935.

———, (2). "The Classical Stationary State," *Economic Journal,* LIII (1943), pp. 343–51.

———, (3). "Economic Progress in a Stable Environment," *Economica,* XIV (1947), reprinted in F. Lutz (1).

———, (4). *Employment and Equilibrium,* Macmillan, Second Edition, London, 1949.

Poincaré, Henri, (1). *La Science et l'Hypothèse,* Plon-Nourrit, Paris, 1926.

Quandt, Richard, (1), (with J. Henderson). "Walras, Leontief, and the Interdependence of Economic Activities: A Comment," *Quarterly Journal of Economics,* LXIX (1955), pp. 626–31.

Raiffa, Howard, (1), (with R. Luce). *Games and Decisions,* Wiley & Sons, New York, 1957.

Reder, Melvin, (1). *Studies in the Theory of Welfare Economics,* Columbia University Press, New York, 1947.

Ricci, Umberto, (1). "Pareto and Pure Economics," *Review of Economic Studies,* I (1933–4), pp. 3–21.

———, (2). *Éléments d'Économie Politique Pure, Théorie de la Valeur,* Malfasi, Milan, 1951.

Robbins, Herbert, (1), (with R. Courant). *What is Mathematics?,* Oxford University Press, New York, 1941.

Rocher, Pierre, (1), (with M. Brodsky). *L'Economie Politique Mathématique,* R. Pichon et R. Durand-Auzias, Paris, 1949.

Rosenstein-Rodan, P., (1). "The Coordination of the General Theories of Money and Price," *Economica*, NS III (1936), pp. 257–80.
Samuelson, Paul, (1). "Some Aspects of the Pure Theory of Capital," *Quarterly Journal of Economics*, LI (1937), pp. 469–96.
———, (2). "Dynamics, Statics, and the Stationary State," *Review of Economics and Statistics*, XXV (1943), pp. 58–68.
———, (3). "The Relation Between Hicksian Stability and True Dynamic Stability," *Econometrica*, 12 (1944), pp. 256–7.
———, (4). *Foundations of Economic Analysis*, Harvard University Press, Cambridge, Mass., 1948.
———, (5). "The Problem of Integrability in Utility Theory," *Economica*, NS XVII (1950), pp. 355–85.
———, (6). "Abstract of A Theorem Concerning Substitutability in Open Leontief Models," in T. Koopmans, (2).
———, (7). "Spatial Price Equilibrium and Linear Programming," *American Economic Review*, XLII (1952), pp. 283–303.
———, (8). "Prices of Factors and Goods in General Equilibrium," *Review of Economic Studies*, XXI (1953–4), pp. 1–20.
———, (9), (with R. Dorfman and R. Solow). *Linear Programming and Economic Analysis*, McGraw-Hill, New York, 1958.
Sargan, J., (1). "The Instability of the Leontief Dynamic Model," *Econometrica*, 26 (1958), pp. 381–92.
Savage, L., (1), (with M. Friedman). "The Utility Analysis of Choices Involving Risk," *Journal of Political Economy*, LVI (1948), reprinted G. Stigler, (4).
———, (2). "The Theory of Statistical Decision," *Journal of the American Statistical Association*, 46 (1951), pp. 55–67.
———, (3), (with M. Friedman). "The Expected-Utility Hypothesis and the Measurement of Utility," *Journal of Political Economy*, LX (1952), pp. 463–74.
———, (4). *The Foundations of Statistics*, Wiley & Sons, New York, 1954.
Schneider, Erich, (1). *Pricing and Equilibrium* (trans. by T. W. Hutchison), George Allen & Unwin, London, 1952.
Schultz, Henry, (1). "Marginal Productivity and the General Pricing Process," *Journal of Political Economy*, XXXVII (1929).
———, (2). *The Theory and Measurement of Demand*, University of Chicago Press, Chicago, 1938.
Schumpeter, Joseph, (1). *Business Cycles*, McGraw-Hill, New York, 1939.
———, (2). *Theory of Economic Development*, Harvard University Press, Cambridge, Mass., 1949.
———, (3). "Vilfredo Pareto (1848–1923)," *Quarterly Journal of Economics*, LXIII (1949), pp. 147–73.
———, (4). "Science and Idealogy," *American Economic Review*, XXXIX (1949), pp. 345–59.
———, (5). *History of Economic Analysis*, Oxford University Press, New York, 1954.
Senior, Nassau, (1). *Political Economy*, Richard Griffin, Third Edition, London, 1854.
Simon, H., (1), (with D. Hawkins). "Note: Some Conditions of Macroeconomic Stability," *Econometrica*, 17 (1949), pp. 245–8.
Slutsky, E., (1). "On the Theory of the Budget of the Consumer," in K. Boulding, (2).
Smithies, Arthur, (1). "Optimum Location in Spatial Competition," *Journal of Political Economy*, XLIX (1941), pp. 423–39.
Solow, Robert, (1), (with R. Dorfman and P. Samuelson). *Linear Programming and Economic Analysis*, McGraw-Hill, New York, 1958.
———, (2). "On the Structure of Linear Models," *Econometrica*, 20 (1952), pp. 29–46.
Stevens, Benjamin, (1). "An Interregional Linear Programming Model," *Journal of Regional Science*, I (1958), pp. 60–98.
Stigler, George, (1). *Production and Distribution Theories*, Macmillan, New York, 1941.
———, (2). "The Development of Utility Theory I," *Journal of Political Economy*, LVIII (1950), pp. 307–27.
———, (3). "The Development of Utility Theory II," *Journal of Political Economy*, LVIII (1950), pp. 373–96.

———, (4), (with K. Boulding), ed. *Readings in Price Theory,* Irwin, Chicago, 1952.

Taussig, Frank, (1). "Capital, Interest, and Diminishing Returns," *Quarterly Journal of Economics,* XXII (1908), pp. 333–63.

Theiss, E., (1). "Time and Capitalistic Production," *Journal of Political Economy,* XL (1932), pp. 513–31.

Thompson, Gerald, (1), (with J. Kemeny and O. Morgenstern). "A Generalization of the von Neumann Model," *Econometrica,* 24 (1956), pp. 115–35.

Thrall, Robert, (1), (with C. Coombs and R. Davis), ed. *Decision Processes,* Wiley & Sons, New York, 1954.

Tinbergen, Jan, (1). "Annual Survey of Significant Developments in General Economic Theory," *Econometrica,* 2 (1934), pp. 13–36.

Tobin, James, (1). "Asset Holdings and Spending Decisions," *American Economic Review, Papers and Proceedings,* XLIII (1952), pp. 109–23.

Triffin, Robert, (1). *Monopolistic Competition and General Equilibrium Theory,* Harvard University Press, Cambridge, Mass., 1940.

Tucker, A., (1), (with H. Kuhn). "Nonlinear Programming," in J. Neyman, (1).

Valavanis, Stefan, (1). "A Denial of Patinkin's Contradiction," *Kyklos,* VIII (1955) pp. 351–68.

Viner, Jacob, (1). "Cost Curves and Supply Curves," *Zeitschrift für Nationalökonomie,* III (1931), pp. 23–46.

Von Böhm-Bawerk, Eugen, (1). *The Positive Theory of Capital,* G. Stechert, New York, 1891.

———, (2). "*The Positive Theory of Capital* and Its Critics, I," *Quarterly Journal of Economics,* IX (1894), pp. 113–31.

———, (3). "*The Positive Theory of Capital* and Its Critics, II," *Quarterly Journal of Economics,* IX (1894), pp. 235–56.

———, (4). "*The Positive Theory of Capital* and Its Critics, III," *Quarterly Journal of Economics,* X (1895), pp. 121–55.

———, (5). *Capital and Interest,* Libertarian Press, South Holland, Illinois, 1959.

Von Bortkiewicz, L., (1). "Der Kardinalfehler der Böhm-Bawerkischen Zinstheorie," *Jahrbuch für Gesetzgebung, Verwaltung, und Volkswirthschaft,* 1906.

Von Neumann, John, (1). "A Model of General Economic Equilibrium," *Review of Economic Studies,* XIII (1944–5), pp. 1–9.

———, (2), (with O. Morgenstern). *Theory of Games and Economic Behavior,* Princeton University Press, Princeton, 1953.

Von Stackelberg, H., (1). "Zwei kritische Bemerkungen zur Preistheorie Gustav Cassels," *Zeitschrift für Nationalökonomie,* IV (1932–3), pp. 456–72.

Wald, Abraham, (1). "On Some Systems of Equations of Mathematical Economics," *Econometrica,* 19 (1951), pp. 368–403.

Walras, Leon, (1). *Éléments d'Économie Politique Pure,* F. Rouge, Second Edition, Lausanne, 1889.

———, (2). *Éléments d'Économie Politique Pure,* R. Pichon et R. Durant-Auzias, Édition Definitive, Paris, 1926.

———, (3). *Elements of Pure Economics,* Jaffé translation, George Allen and Unwin, London, 1954.

Warntz, William, (1). *Toward a Geography of Price,* University of Pennsylvania Press Philadelphia, 1959.

Weber, Alfred, (1). *Theory of the Location of Industries,* University of Chicago, Chicago, 1928.

Weston, J. F., (1). "Some Perspectives on Capital Theory," *American Economic Review, Papers and Proceedings,* XLI (1951), pp. 129–44.

Wicksell, Knut, (1). *Value, Capital, and Rent,* Rinehart, New York, 1954.

———, (2). *Interest and Prices,* Macmillan, London, 1936.

———, (3). *Lectures on Political Economy,* Routledge, London, 1935.

Wood, M., (1), (with G. Dantzig). "Programming of Interdependent Activities, I: General Discussion," *Econometrica,* 17 (1949), pp. 193–9.

Zawadzki, Wladyslaw, (1). *Les Mathématiques Appliquées à l'Économie Politique,* Librairie des sciences politiques et sociales, Paris, 1914.

Zeuthen, Frederick, (1). "Das Prinzip der Knappheit, technische Kombination, und Ökonomische Qualität," *Zeitschrift für Nationalökonomie,* IV (1932–3), pp. 1–24.

INDEX